Criminal Courts for the 21st Century

Criminal Courts for the 21st Century

Lisa Stolzenberg
Stewart J. D'Alessio

School of Policy and Management
Florida International University

Prentice Hall's Contemporary Justice Series

Prentice Hall
Upper Saddle River, New Jersey, 07458

Library of Congress Cataloging-in-Publication Data

Criminal courts in the 21st century / [compiled by] Lisa Stolzenberg, Stewart J. D'Alessio.
p. cm. —(Prentice Hall's contemporary justice series)
ISBN 0-13-080549-1
1. Criminal justice, Administration of—United States. 2. Criminal courts—United States. 3. Criminal procedure—United States. I. Stolzenberg, Lisa. II. D'Alessio, Stewart J. III. Title: Criminal courts in the twenty-first century. IV. Series: Contemporary justice series.
KF9223.C745 1998
345.73'01—dc21 98-40736
CIP

Acquisitions editor: *Neil Marquardt*
Assistant editor: *Cheryl Adam*
Production editor: *Holly Henjum*
Production liason: *Barbara Marttine Cappuccio*
Director of manufacturing and production: *Bruce Johnson*
Managing editor: *Mary Carnis*
Manufacturing buyer: *Ed O'Dougherty*
Editorial assistant: *Jean Auman*
Creative director: *Marianne Frasco*
Cover design: *Kiwi Design*
Formatting / page make-up: *Clarinda Company*
Printer/Binder: *R. R. Donnelly*

Simon & Schuster / A Viacom Company
Upper Saddle River, New Jersey 07458

Printed in the United States of America
10 9 8 7 6 5 4 3 2 1

ISBN 0-13-080549-1

Prentice-Hall International (UK) Limited, *London*
Prentice-Hall of Australia Pty, Limited, *Sydney*
Prentice-Hall Canada Inc., *Toronto*
Prentice-Hall Hispanoamericana, S.A., *Mexico*
Prentice-Hall of India Privated Limited, *New Delhi*
Prentice-Hall of Japan, Inc., *Tokyo*
Simon & Schuster Asia Pte. Ltd., *Singapore*
Editora Prentice-Hall do Brasil, Ltda., *Rio de Janeiro*

CONTENTS

PREFACE

Americans are enamored with the criminal courts. This fascination is most likely the direct consequence of exciting and highly publicized criminal trials, such as those involving O. J. Simpson, Erik and Lyle Menendez, and William Kennedy Smith. However, despite the public's interest, most scholarly books published on criminal courts give only cursory attention to the most important and controversial issues confronting America's criminal court system. *Criminal Courts for the 21st Century* is the exception. This comprehensive book of readings consists of 20 articles published in scholarly journals during the 1990s. Only interesting and well-written articles, which provide a reader with the most up-to-date information on the most important and contentious issues relating to criminal courts, were selected for inclusion in the book. Articles furnishing broad coverage of a topic, for the most part, were selected over statistical pieces that analyzed specific hypotheses or questions. It was our intention to gear this reader to students with an interest in the criminal courts, including those with a limited background in statistics.

Criminal Courts for the 21st Century is intended for criminal justice students enrolled in undergraduate and graduate college courses on criminal courts, judicial process, and judicial decision-making. Because of its extensive coverage of the most contemporary issues confronting the criminal courts, this book is appropriate as a stand-alone text or as a supplement to introductory textbooks in this area. It is also suitable for personal reference by college professors and instructors, librarians, judges, lawyers, policymakers, and others with an interest in the criminal court process.

Criminal Courts for the 21st Century is divided into four parts: (1) courts, prosecution and the defense; (2) pretrial procedures and evidentiary issues; (3) the criminal trial; and (4) punishment and sentencing. Each section contains a collection of five contemporary articles on a variety of salient topics. Part One, "Courts, Prosecution and the Defense," delves into the structure and operation of lower court (de novo) systems, drug diversion courts, and juvenile courts. The recent and highly controversial prosecutions of pregnant women who use illicit drugs, as well as the day-to-day practices of criminal defense attorneys, are also examined in this section. Part Two, "Pretrial Procedures and Evidentiary Issues," explores several key factors that influence the processing of criminal defendants, including bail guidelines, pretrial drug testing programs, and plea bargaining. A number of the issues pertaining to eyewitness identification, lineups, and the use of DNA evidence in the prosecution of criminal defendants are also examined. Part Three, "The Criminal Trial," focuses on the trial process, such as the role of jury science, nonevidentiary social influences on the jury, and judicial misconduct during jury deliberations. The use of cameras in the courtroom, and whether jury deliberations should be recorded, are also addressed in the readings. Part Four, "Punishment and Sentencing," presents several salient issues regarding the sanctioning of criminal offenders. Issues such as racial discrimination in sentencing, victim rights, three-strike laws, capital punishment for juvenile offenders, and corporal punishment are discussed in this section.

REVIEWERS

Karen McElrath, *Queens University, Belfast*
Steven W. Atchley, *Delaware Tech*
Patty O'Donnell Brummett, *California State University, Northridge*
W. Clinton Terry, *Florida International University*

Lisa Stolzenberg
Stewart J. D'Alessio

Criminal Courts for the 21st Century

PART ONE

Courts, Prosecution and the Defense

"Too often, when our citizens seek a dignified place of deliberation in which to resolve their controversies, they find instead aesthetic revulsion. They bear witness—not to dignity, but to deterioration, not to actual justice delivered, but to the perception of justice denied or, worse, justice degraded."

—Sol Wachtler, former chief judge,
New York State, 1995

INTRODUCTION

Should a defendant charged with a crime be released on bail prior to his or her trial? Should a prosecutor recommend a less severe sentence in exchange for a defendant's guilty plea? Should a rape victim be afforded the opportunity to testify at her assailant's sentencing hearing? Should a convicted felony offender be sent to prison and, if so, for how long? These important and controversial questions, as well as many others, are dealt with on a day-to-day basis by our criminal courts.

As articulated in the quote at the beginning of this section, many citizens have the impression that the criminal courts are places where "justice is done." However, such a belief is often unfounded. A major problem relates to how people conceptualize the abstract concept of justice. For example, defendants expect the criminal courts to be impartial and just in the handling of their cases. Crime victims seek satisfaction for the harm done to them and for the injuries they have suffered. Agents of the court pursue fair solutions that benefit all parties involved, including the defendant, victim, and society. The criminal court process is structured in such a way as to provide an open and impartial forum to discern the truth regarding a particular case and to reach a resolution that satisfies the rule of law. In many urban court systems, however, the backlog of criminal cases is so large that these objectives are rarely actualized. Instead, many of America's criminal courts are operating on the basis of accommodation rather than on an adversarial process in which an aggressive prosecution is pitted against a zealous criminal defense. Judicial decision-making occurs not only in formal court proceedings, but in situations much less visible to public scrutiny. In fact, the use of plea bargains and other discretionary alternatives, such as diversion, are far more common today than are formal criminal trials.

In this section, we examine the structure and operation of three different types of court systems: lower court (de novo) systems, drug diversion courts, and juvenile courts. The recent and highly controversial prosecutions of pregnant women who use illicit drugs is also considered, as well as the day-to-day practices of criminal defense attorneys.

In the first article in this section, "Justice Rationed in the Pursuit of Efficiency: De Novo Trials in the Criminal Courts," David A. Harris argues that while de novo systems increase efficiency and savings for the state, they have a number of shortcomings that hinder their current usage. First, the structure of these systems discourage defendants from requesting new trials. Second, de novo systems afford lower court judges a great deal of discretionary latitude in resolving criminal cases. Finally, because de novo systems handle a substantive number of criminal cases, they are the only contact that many people have with the criminal justice system. As a consequence, de novo systems provide an excellent opportunity to keep first-time misdemeanor defendants from recidivating. However, according to Harris, this opportunity is often squandered in the pursuit of efficiency. He concludes his article by urging policymakers to reform de novo systems so that they can at least function with the minimal degree of fairness that Americans would expect from their criminal courts.

In the second article, "Drug Diversion Courts: Are They Needed and Will They Succeed in Breaking the Cycle of Drug-Related Crime?," James R. Brown proffers that treatment-based drug diversion courts are effective in severing the cycle of drug dependency. There are several reasons for their effectiveness. First, these courts come into contact with illicit drug users at a time when they are most likely to enter a treatment program—at the point of arrest when the probability of incarceration is high. Second, drug treatment programs are court-supervised and clients are individually monitored. Additionally, the constant threat of punitive sanctions provides a powerful mechanism to induce clients to remain active in the program. Finally, compared to incarceration, drug-diversion courts are remarkably cost-effective. However, as Brown points out, not all drug-diversion courts are created equal. Successful drug-diversion courts must have an innovative and dedicated judiciary and broad-based community support for their goals. The author believes that the drug-diversion court located in Boston, Massachusetts has all the necessary ingredients to act as a model system for the rest of the country.

In the third article, "Pregnancy, Drugs, and the Perils of Prosecution," Wendy K. Mariner, Leonard H. Glantz, and George J. Annas discuss the assumptions underlying recent prosecutions of pregnant women who use illicit drugs. Specifically, they argue that the purported goals underlying these prosecutions are difficult to achieve with current criminal statutes, because the criminal offense that pregnant women are thought to commit cannot be defined in terms of any intelligible duty enforceable by criminal law. Additionally, the authors point out that prosecuting pregnant women for illicit drug use will have relatively little impact on curtailing the spread of illegal drugs or on improving the health prospects of children. Instead, the authors maintain that these prosecutions are likely to threaten the rights of women as autonomous individuals and, ultimately, adversely affect the future well-being of their children.

In his seminal work published in 1967, Abraham Blumberg challenged the traditional view of the defense lawyer as a zealous advocate for his or her client. Blumberg argued that in practice, defense lawyers were "double agents" functioning as manipulative con artists in the non-adversarial, plea-bargaining system of criminal justice. In the fourth article of this section, Rodney J. Uphoff assesses the validity of Blomberg's perspective. Specifically, he examines the day-to-day practices of criminal defense attorneys in three counties. His exploration leads to the discovery of a variety of systemic factors such as time, money, and risk that influence the behavior of defense attorneys. He concludes that the "beleaguered dealer" rather than the "double agent" best describes the modus operandi of most defense lawyers. To better enhance the devotion and quality of representation by defense attorneys, Uphoff recommends that jurisdictions make a concerted effort to improve the delivery of indigent defense services.

In the final article, "Juvenile (In)Justice and the Criminal Court Alternative," Barry C. Feld advances the argument that the juvenile court has evolved from an informal welfare agency into a scaled-down, second-class criminal court. This transformation is the direct result of a series of institutional reforms. These reforms have not only diverted less serious defendants from the juvenile court, but they have also shifted more serious juvenile defendants to adult criminal courts for prosecution. Feld recommends a number of policy initiatives to remedy this situation. First, he suggests that juvenile courts should be restructured so as to capture their original goal of rehabilitation. Second, he argues that if the meting out of punishment is to be the primary aim of delinquency proceedings, then criminal procedural safeguards must be instituted to protect the constitutional rights of defendants. Lastly, Feld maintains that serious consideration should be given to the possibility of abolishing juvenile courts. He believes that such an action would enable young criminal defendants, with certain substantive and procedural modifications, to be prosecuted in adult courts.

1

Justice Rationed in the Pursuit of Efficiency: De Novo Trials in the Criminal Courts

David A. Harris*

For the last three decades, the ever-expanding caseload of the nation's courts has attracted the attention of judges and scholars. All have sought ways—some old, some new—for courts to cope with the growing number of cases. The Supreme Court entered this debate on the criminal side in 1971,[1] by formally sanctioning plea bargaining as an essential and a highly desirable tool for disposing of most criminal cases.[2] Most commentators claimed that plea bargaining was inevitable; it was, and would always remain, the major method for disposing of criminal cases.[3] In the civil arena, numerous efforts have been made in the last ten to fifteen years intended to cut the backlog of civil cases by using alternative dispute resolution and other mechanisms.[4] Proponents of these techniques have hailed them as cost-effective methods of case disposition that benefit litigants at little cost.[5]

During the 1980s, however, scholars challenged these almost universally accepted propositions. Notwithstanding its wide use, they argued, plea bargaining is not a desirable way to dispose of cases. On the contrary, plea bargaining taints the criminal justice process, damages the defendant, and offends the Constitution.[6] Further, plea bargaining is not inevitable; a large court system can exist without reliance on it.[7] Opponents of plea bargaining have also recommended the use of procedures from other nations as alternatives.[8] In civil cases, critics have argued that the alternative dispute resolution movement's single-minded striving for case disposition ignores and exacerbates the imbalance of power inherent in much litigation, and thereby disadvantages litigants who are least powerful.[9]

With their emphasis on novel devices, these debates have ignored one traditional vehicle for expediting criminal litigation—the two-tiered de novo trial system. For many years, about half of the states have used this court structure to obtain rapid, efficient disposition of criminal cases. Misdemeanors and less serious felonies make up ninety percent[10] of the nation's criminal caseload. De novo systems handle misdemeanors and less serious felonies; de novo systems therefore affect overall case disposition profoundly.

In de novo court systems, defendants initially are tried in a lower court. These lower courts lack many of the basic protections associated with due process. If the lower court finds a defendant guilty, and the defendant is dissatisfied with the lower

Reprinted by permission of the *Connecticut Law Review* from vol. 24 (1992), pp. 382-431.

court's verdict or sentence, the defendant cannot appeal to a traditional appellate court for review of the trial record. Rather, the dissatisfied defendant may request, and is entitled to receive, a brand new trial—a trial de novo—in the court of general criminal jurisdiction. In the new trial, the full spectrum of constitutional safeguards apply, and all issues—legal and factual—are determined afresh. The Supreme Court says the defendant loses nothing in the de novo process because the second, full-dress trial is available to her simply for the asking;[11] indeed, she gains a second opportunity for an acquittal.[12] For its part, the state gains efficiency, as it realizes savings of time and resources for every case permanently disposed of[13] in the lower court without the full range of costly due process protections.[14]

Closer examination, however, shows that de novo systems do not perform as promised. This Article demonstrates that de novo systems do indeed yield efficiency and savings for the state, but for the wrong reason: New trials are *not*, in fact, freely available. On the contrary, the structure of de novo systems discourages defendants from requesting new trials. De novo systems operate invisibly but forcefully to deter the exercise of the express right to a new trial. De novo systems also leave lower court judges free to resolve cases on whatever basis they find desirable—personal proclivities, whim, or gut feeling—with virtually no enforceable requirement that the law govern their decisions. Further, like alternative dispute resolution, de novo systems shift power away from those who are already least advantaged. The fate of these individuals is easily disregarded by advocates of efficiency, who focus exclusively on decreasing the size of the caseload. Moreover, de novo systems handle a large portion of the criminal cases. Consequently, they represent the only contact many people have with the criminal justice system, and perhaps the system's only chance to keep first offenders from becoming repeat and felony offenders. These opportunities are squandered, however, in the pursuit of efficiency. Thus, examination of de novo systems engenders skepticism regarding mechanisms that are claimed to handle cases more efficiently than at present, at no cost to the defendant and with few implications for substantive change.

For these and other reasons, de novo systems should be abolished outright. Abolition, however, is unlikely. The combination of tradition and the siren song of efficiency ensures their survival. Accordingly, the goal of this Article is to urge the reform of de novo systems so that they can at least function with the minimal degree of fairness expected from American courts. After Part I describes de novo systems, Part II analyzes the Supreme Court's three decisions that examine the constitutionality of de novo systems. Part III demonstrates the falsity of the premise underlying all three decisions—that a new trial in the court of general jurisdiction is readily available. Part III also shows that de novo systems pose other, substantial problems for both the criminal justice system and society in general. Part IV proposes eight ways to improve these courts.

I. CHARACTERISTICS OF DE NOVO COURT SYSTEMS

A. De Novo Appeal

The signal characteristic of de novo courts is the right to request and receive a new trial in the superior court after a verdict of guilty in a lower court.[15] In a typical de novo system, the lower court has jurisdiction over a specified group of offenses.[16] At trial in the lower court, the defendant may plead not guilty and litigate the case, or plead guilty, with or without an agreement with the prosecutor.[17] If the defendant is found guilty, the court sentences the defendant. After sentencing, if the defendant wants a new trial—based on the judge's legal rulings before or during the course of the trial, the severity of the sentence, the mere possibility that the defendant will "do better" in the superior court, or any other reason—the defendant can request and receive a new trial in the superior court. This new trial will take place without reference to the prior trial or its outcome. Traditional review of legal issues by an appellate court is not available.[18]

Twenty-four states[19] utilize de novo systems. At least eight of these twenty-four states[20] have more than one lower court. Five other states[21] have de novo systems that allow new trials only when the lower court does not generate any record of the trial proceedings.

B. Unavailability of Juries

In half of the de novo systems,[22] a judge or some other judicial officer[23] hears the case in the lower court. If the defendant wants a jury trial, she may either make a pretrial request that the lower court transfer the case to the superior court, or have a trial in the lower court and then request a trial in the superior court. Some states allow the defendant to choose either option.[24] Other states require that the defendant go through the lower court proceeding.[25]

In the other states with de novo court systems, the defendant may elect to have a jury in the lower court determine her guilt or innocence.[26] If dissatisfied in any way with the lower court proceeding, the defendant may request,and receive a new trial in the superior court.

C. Streamlined Procedures

In approximately one-third of all de novo systems, certain basic procedures are either streamlined or eliminated in the lower court.[27] Those procedures often include discovery rules,[28] procedures requiring written briefing and separate hearings on legal issues,[29] and the availability of bills of particulars.[30] Presumably, the elimination or abbreviation of these procedures make the lower courts more efficient.[31]

D. Judges Without Legal Training

In approximately two thirds of the de novo court systems,[32] judges need not be members of the bar. While statutes may require these lay judges to attend a basic training course or successfully complete an examination,[33] they will nevertheless preside without the basic legal background required of the least experienced practitioner. Some systems require only a high school diploma for a person to be eligible for the bench.[34] Thus, many lower court judges are marginally qualified to rule on complex legal issues, decide guilt and innocence, and pass sentence.[35]

E. Limited Jurisdiction

All states using de novo systems limit the jurisdiction of their courts. Some limit jurisdiction to less serious felonies, misdemeanors, violations of local ordinances, or some combination of the three.[36] Other de novo systems limit jurisdiction according to the severity of the penalty authorized for an offense.[37] Still others have jurisdictional limitations which combine these and other criteria.[38] Notwithstanding these jurisdictional limitations, courts in many de novo systems still have substantial power over the persons they convict.[39]

F. Suspension or Vacation of Sentence Pending Appeal

In most de novo systems,[40] the sentence of the lower court remains in effect pending a new trial unless the defendant meets bail conditions set by the lower court sets.[41] In a few de novo systems,[42] a request for a new trial automatically vacates or suspends the sentence imposed by the lower court.

II. SUPREME COURT TREATMENT OF DE NOVO SYSTEMS

The Supreme Court has ruled twice on the constitutionality of de novo systems. In *Colten v. Kentucky*,[43] the Supreme Court rejected challenges to Kentucky's de novo system based on the due process and double jeopardy clauses. In *Ludwig v. Massachusetts*,[44] the Court decided that Massachusetts' de novo system did not violate either the constitutional right to trial by jury or the double jeopardy clause. Additionally, in a third case, *North v. Russell*,[45] the Court rejected a challenge to the use of lay judges in de novo and other types of lower criminal courts. As the following analysis of these cases shows, the Court's conclusions concerning the structure, premises and purposes of the de novo system are, at best, questionable.

A. Colten v. Kentucky

In *Colten*, police charged the defendant with disorderly conduct[46] in the lower court of Kentucky's de novo system.[47] He was tried, convicted, and fined ten dollars.[48] The defendant requested and received a new trial in the superior court, and was again found guilty.[49] The Kentucky Court of Appeals affirmed.[50]

In its opinion, the Supreme Court followed a brief recitation of the facts[51] with a general description of de novo systems.[52] The Court acknowledged that many of these courts operated without safeguards such as juries, judges with legal training, and a record of court proceedings.[53]

The Court then expressed its view of de novo systems. The defendant may accept or reject the lower court sentence, because it is "no more than an offer in settlement of his case" by which he is not bound.[54] The Court reasoned that "as long as [new full-dress trials] in the superior court are always available," it is irrelevant that defendants must go through less than constitutionally adequate lower court trials.[55] Trial in the lower court presents the defendant with numerous advantages, including speedy dispositions, ample discovery, and simpler procedures; the defendant need not reveal her own case to obtain these advantages because she can stand silent or plead guilty without putting on a defense.[56] The defendant's argument would be more tenable, the Supreme Court stated, if superior court judges wished to discourage new trials. However, these judges are actually likely to think a defendant entitled to a new trial because of the low quality of adjudication in the lower courts.[57] In its most telling passage, the Supreme Court quoted with approval from the opinion of the Kentucky Court of Appeals in Colten's case: "[T]he inferior courts are not designed or equipped to conduct error-free trials, or to insure full recognition of constitutional freedoms. They are courts of convenience, to provide speedy and inexpensive means of disposition of charges of minor offenses."[58] Despite the acknowledged deficiencies of de novo systems, the Court found them constitutional.

B. Ludwig v. Massachusetts

In *Ludwig*, the defendant was charged with reckless driving.[59] In the lower court, his motion for a "speedy trial by jury"[60] was denied, he was found guilty and fined.[61] At his superior court trial, the defendant moved to dismiss based on a deprivation of the right to a speedy jury trial in the lower court and protection against double jeopardy.[62] The court denied these motions, found him guilty and fined him.[63] The Supreme Judicial Court of Massachusetts affirmed.[64]

On appeal, the defendant argued that the de novo system deprived him of his right to be tried by a jury in the lower court. On the first issue, the Court acknowledged the importance of the jury as "'an inestimable safeguard against the corrupt or overzealous prosecutor and against the compliant, biased, or eccentric judge.'"[65] The de novo system in Massachusetts provides these safeguards to the accused, the Court reasoned, through a new trial in the superior court.[66] The Court conceded that the superior court trial, in which the protection of the jury was available, did not come without some costs.[67] These costs, the Court stated, include the expense of a second trial, the possibility of harsher sentence than the lower court's, and the additional psychological and physical hardship of a second trial.[68] The Court did not hold, however, that these costs amounted to an unconstitutional burden on the right to trial by jury. First, the Court minimized the financial costs of having to undergo two trials; the defendant could avoid the first trial altogether by standing silent or admitting facts sufficient to sustain a finding of guilt.[69] The state would provide an indigent defendant with counsel at trial,[70] and the defendant could use the first trial as an opportunity for discovery.[71] Second, the possibility of a harsher sentence after the trial de novo presented no new concern, because the Court already had decided that issue in *Colten*.[72] Third, the Court declared itself "not oblivious to the adverse psychological and physical effects that delay in obtaining final adjudication of one's guilt or innocence may engender."[73] The Court avoided this issue, however, by stating that the defendant had not shown that the delay would be any greater in the absence of the de novo system.[74] Indeed, a de novo system that increased delay would be "perverse," the Court said, when the "very purpose [of the de novo court system] is to increase efficiency."[75]

C. North v. Russell

In *North*, the defendant was charged in a Kentucky lower court[76] with driving while intoxicated.[77] Because the defendant was a first offender, the maximum possible penalty was a fine of $500; had he been a subsequent offender, he also could have been incarcerated for up to six months.[78] A lay judge presided over the trial[79] and heard the defendant's request for a jury trial,[80] to which Kentucky's Constitution[81] and statutes[82] absolutely entitled him. The judge denied the request,[83] convicted the defendant, sentenced him to thirty days in jail, a fine, and revoked his driver's license.[84] The defendant challenged the constitutionality of his trial before a lay judge.[85] Both the superior court[86] and the Kentucky Court of Appeals[87] denied relief.

Before the Supreme Court, the defendant argued that the due process clause required that in any case in which incarceration could be imposed, the presiding judge must have legal training.[88] The defendant claimed that without a requirement that a judge have legal training, the right to counsel becomes meaningless; counsel has diminished value to a defendant appearing before a judge who cannot comprehend counsel's arguments.[89] However, the Supreme Court found it unnecessary to resolve the issue, reasoning that pitfalls inherent in such a system do not rise to the level of constitutional infirmity because a new trial before a law-trained judge in the superior court is always available.[90] A request for a new trial in Kentucky would vacate the conviction in the lower court, and a defendant is entitled to bail pending the new trial.[91] The Court noted that even defendants without counsel would not suffer in a lay judge's court because these judges would no doubt fully advise defendants of their right to a new trial in the superior court before a fully trained judge.[92] That trial, of course, was freely available just for the asking.[93] Using much of the same language it used in *Colten*, the Court accepted and justified the existence of de novo court systems: With an ever-increasing number of criminal cases requiring more and more resources, lower courts in de novo systems provide faster and less costly adjudication than courts of general jurisdiction, because the latter are constitutionally bound to afford defendants the full spectrum of due process guarantees.[94] De novo systems offer the defendant advantages as well, and at little cost.[95] The defendant may avoid trial completely by not contesting the facts of the government's case; alternatively, the defendant may vacate the conviction completely by requesting a new trial and thus escape its consequences.[96] Any concern evidenced in past opinions with lay judges, the Court stated, was "directed at the need for independent, neutral, and detached judgment, not at legal training."[97]

D. *Colten, Ludwig* and *North* Analyzed

Colten, *Ludwig*, and *North* provide rich material from which to glean the Supreme Court's views of the purposes of de novo systems, and the premises underlying the Court's conclusion that these court systems are constitutional. Consistent references in these three opinions to the same underlying concepts reveal the presence of the same blind spots in each of these cases.

Colten sets the pattern. Lower courts provide benefits to the defendant, such as two chances for an acquittal and the opportunity for discovery. More importantly, de novo systems provide benefits to the state—rapid and efficient disposition of a large load of unimportant cases. The Court showed no concern that lower courts in de novo systems suffer from inadequacies that would be intolerable in a superior court. A trial that fully comports with due process always is available, and that fact saves de novo court systems from constitutional infirmity.

The similarities between *Colten* and *Ludwig* are striking. As in *Colten*, the Court in *Ludwig* conceded that de novo systems present defendants with certain costs; there are, indeed, defects in the lower courts.[98] Even conceding that these flaws could be problematic, a concession the Court does not make, they are tolerable because of the ready availability of a new trial in the superior court. The second trial costs the defendant little, and may give the defendant advantages.[99] The state also gains; lower courts in de novo systems dispose of less important criminal cases, which make up ninety percent of all criminal cases,[100] more quickly and less expensively—to use the Supreme Court's terminology, more efficiently—than if these same cases were handled in a superior court. Indeed, the Court explicitly acknowledged efficiency as the very purpose of de novo systems.[101]

North completes the circle. Again, the Court grants that de novo systems may not be "error-free" and certainly do not "insure full recognition of constitutional freedoms."[102] They do, however, increase the efficiency of a state's criminal justice system by disposing of many cases rapidly and inexpensively.[103] Any concerns arising from these arrangements do not rise to a constitutional level, the Court reasoned, because the defendant upon request receives a new trial, complete with all of the rights associated with due process of law.[104] Additionally, as the Court also pointed out in both *Colten* and *Ludwig*,[105] defendants obtain and exercise these rights at little or no cost;[106] indeed, advantages accrue to defendants in de novo systems.

III. PURPOSES AND PREMISES EXAMINED

In *Colten*, *Ludwig*, and *North*, the Supreme Court made numerous assumptions about the way de novo systems operate. As the next section of this Article demonstrates, these assumptions are questionable. Moreover, other problems inherent in the structure of de novo systems, not hinted at in the Supreme Court's cases, also present major difficulties.

A. How Can De Novo Systems Be Efficient?

The common thread that runs through *Colten*, *Ludwig*, and *North* is that de novo systems efficiently handle criminal cases. For a variety of reasons, however, de novo systems are not structured to be efficient; if they are efficient, it is for exactly the wrong reasons.

1. Two Trials for the Convicted

In the view of the Supreme Court, a defendant loses nothing by proceeding through the lower court before her case comes before a superior court. If conviction and sentence in a lower court dissatisfies the defendant for any reason, she simply requests and receives a new trial. Surely, if the lower court incarcerates her,[107] the request for a new trial will quickly restore the status quo. In other words, defendants have noth-

lower court? The answer must be that defendants are not as free to request new trials as the Supreme Court claims. In fact, defendants are discouraged from exercising their right to a new trial.[128] Justice Stevens neatly captured this point in his dissent in *Ludwig*, when he discussed the requirement that the defendant had to endure the lower court proceeding before he could obtain a full-dress trial in front of a jury:

> A defendant who can afford the financial and psychological burden of one trial may not be able to withstand the strain of a second. Thus, as a practical matter, a finding of guilt in the first-tier proceeding will actually end some cases . . . . [W]hy does [Massachusetts] insist on the *requirement* that the defendant must submit to the first trial? Only, I suggest, because it believes the number of jury trials that would be avoided by the required practice exceeds the number that would take place in an optional system. In short, *the very purpose of the requirement is to discourage jury trials by placing a burden on the exercise of the constitutional right.*[129]

As the next section of this Article will show, requiring that defendants go through a lower court before they can get to a superior court is only one of many ways that de novo systems discourage requests for new trials in the superior court.

B. Discouraging Requests for New Trials: Direct Process Barriers

Defendants who wish to receive a new trial in the superior court after a trial in the lower court face numerous obstacles. The Court acknowledged and minimized some of them; others went unrecognized.[130] These obstacles take the form of direct process barriers that are part of, or generated by, the dual-level de novo system itself.[131]

1. Monetary and Nonmonetary Costs

Costs that discourage new trials come in both monetary and nonmonetary forms. For defendants who are not indigent,[132] retaining counsel will carry a definite, dollars-and-cents price tag. While some defendants may find the cost of counsel for one trial manageable, the cost for a second appearance may be prohibitive.[133] Similarly, most de novo court systems require a defendant appealing for a new trial to pay a fee.[134] If the defendant is indigent, she may ask that the court waive the fee.[135] A waiver, however, does little for a person who, while impoverished, does not meet the applicable criteria for indigence. Further, courts might also pass on to the defendant the cost of summoning defense witnesses to trial. Because the Constitution explicitly protects the right to compulsory process,[136] an indigent defendant should be able to attain a waiver of this cost. "Court costs" represent another toll imposed on those who wish a second trial.[137] Add to this the costs of any out of the ordinary expenses, such as retaining an expert for two trials instead of one,[138] and it becomes clear that the defendant must run a financial obstacle course to obtain a second trial.

Nonmonetary costs also discourage defendants from taking appeals. These costs reach indigent as well as nonindigent defendants. For example, inasmuch as a request for a new trial in a de novo system starts the cycle of appearances, motions, and trial dates again, defendants face a new series of dates upon which they must choose to go to court rather than to engage in some other activity. For many defendants, the other activity will be employment. To the extent that defendants charged with misdemeanors as a group have limited discretion to take days off, this can become costly not only in terms of lost wages but also in terms of lost employment.[139] A second trial may also entail further meetings and preparation with counsel, especially if the second trial will be before a jury, or will require separate hearings preceding the second trial on matters such as motions to suppress and dismiss.[140]

Another type of nonmonetary cost comes in the form of atrophy or damage to the defendant's case.[141] In the same way that de novo systems may cause prosecution witnesses to lose interest,[142] defense witnesses may also disengage. Like the defendant, defense witnesses may have only limited flexibility in employment schedules. Subpoenae notwithstanding, witnesses also have much less at stake in the outcome of a trial than the accused. As a consequence, defense witnesses may fail to attend a second trial. Witnesses and evidence will also become harder to locate and gather the more time passes.[143] Having testified once in a trial in the lower court, defense witnesses will be vulnerable to impeachment in a second trial in a superior court.[144] Both witness discouragement and impeachment may cause the defendant to feel additional pressure either not to pursue a second trial, or to plead guilty in the superior court.[145] All of these costs deter the assertion of the right to a new trial in the superior court.[146]

2. *Psychological Burdens*

Having to proceed through the lower court before gaining access to a superior court represents a significant psychological burden. Unresolved charges carry a stigma, regardless of the court in which the charges are to be tried.[147] Because the Supreme Court recommends that the defendant admit guilt in the lower court in order to avoid the expense of two trials,[148] the defendant must also live with a lower court conviction until the superior court trial.[149] Moreover, obligating the defendant to defend herself in a de novo court system increases the amount of time it takes for the defendant to obtain a full-dress trial by jury.[150]

3. *The Risk of a Greater Sentence*

Whenever a defendant requests a new trial, she runs the risk that she will receive a more severe sentence at the hands of the superior court than she did in the lower court. If anything is a direct deterrent to exercise of the right to a new trial, it is this risk. Nevertheless, the Supreme Court stated in *Colten* that the possibility that the superior court might impose a greater sentence than the lower court did not violate the Constitution because the higher sentence would not result from vindictiveness.[151] Few would disagree, however, that the risk exists and may actually deter;[152] the gamble the defendant must take is intuitively obvious. Further, some have advanced strong arguments that the threat of a harsher sentence would indeed rise to the level of a constitutional violation.[153] While scholars debate these constitutional arguments, a lay person—a person incarcerated after one trial who successfully petitioned for another—puts the point more forcefully:

> I know it is usuelly [sic] the courts prosedure [sic] to give a larger sentence when a new trile [sic] is granted. I guess this is to discourage petitioners. Your Honor, I don't want a new trile [sic] I am afraid of more time . . . . Your Honor, I know you have tried to help me and God knows I apreceate [sic] this but please sir don't let the state re-try me if there is any way you can prevent it.[154]

4. *Incarceration Pending New Trial*

In any criminal trial system, a court may incarcerate defendants pending trial by setting bail conditions defendants cannot meet. Defendants in de novo systems face this prospect not once, but twice. The mere filing of a request for a new trial is insufficient to vacate or suspend the lower court verdict and sentence in most courts.[155] This incarceration is ironic in light of the Supreme Court's characterization of the lower court verdict as an offer the defendant may freely accept or reject.[156] Defendants who are too poor to meet even minimal bail conditions prior to trial are likely to remain incarcerated until the resolution of the case, or until a bail reduction, in the superior court. The amount of bail may have less to do with the likelihood that the defendant will appear for trial than with a preset "schedule" of bail amounts based solely on the offense charged.[157]

Incarceration between a lower court verdict and trial in the superior court has profound implications. First, defendants serve more time in jail prior to a superior court trial than as a result of any superior court sentence.[158] Second, a positive correlation exists between commitment to incarceration before trial and findings of guilt after trial,[159] between commitment to incarceration before trial and the likelihood of a jail sentence,[160] and between being Caucasian and receiving a bond that does not require the deposit of money with the court.[161] Thus, persons incarcerated pending a new trial in superior court are more likely to remain there after trial, and non-whites are at higher risk for this treatment. It would be surprising indeed to find defendants eager to appeal under these circumstances.

5. *Failure to Inform Defendant Adequately of Rights*

In all de novo systems, defendants have an unconditional right to a new trial in the superior court. This right supposedly saves de novo court systems from constitutional infirmity.[162] Ability to exercise this right presupposes knowledge of the right's existence and of the method of its exercise. Courts are duty bound to inform defendants of these critical facts; indeed, the Supreme Court explicitly assumed that lower court judges inform defendants that they have the right to a new trial in a superior court.[163]

Unfortunately, courts do not always inform defendants of their constitutional rights. In fact, the available evidence suggests that defendants usually do not receive full and effective advice of rights in misdemeanor courts.[164] Courts treat the obligation to inform defendants of their rights as a mere clerical function they must perform repeatedly, if they perform it at all.[165] Many courts advise defendants of their constitutional rights in large groups, or even address advice of rights to the courtroom as a whole.[166] That this phenomenon has persisted over a long period of time,[167] surviving even the requirement that most misdemeanor defendants receive appointed counsel,[168] is disheartening. More importantly, these practices weaken the argument that the availability of a new trial in the superior court serves as an adequate constitutional savior for de novo systems. Mileski sums up the likely effects of these practices well:

> If a defendant happens to be talking to his neighbor, if he is for some other reason inattentive, or if he arrives in court later than the scheduled ten o'clock, he is not formally informed of his rights unless the judge later informs him in a face-to-face encounter, as he sometimes does. Inattention or tardiness, then, may carry with it whatever are the consequences of ignorance of constitutional rights. Moreover, there is the matter of the defendant's inability to comprehend various rights—something that is inaccessible to an observer. The degree of comprehension may vary according to the form of apprising.[169]

Thus, failure to inform defendants properly—or at all—of their rights effectively hides the right to a new trial from the defendant's view.

C. Collateral Costs and Lack of Benefit to Defendant

In *Colten*, *Ludwig*, and *North*, the Supreme Court concluded that the efficiencies that de novo systems provide to the states come at little or no cost to defendants.[170] The Court even assumed that defendants in de novo systems have opportunities to improve their cases that defendants whose cases begin in superior courts do not.[171] In reaching these conclusions, however, the Court ignored a host of realities that defendants face. These realities render absurd the idea that defendants suffer no hardship by virtue of the workings of de novo systems. The previous section of this Article highlighted problems that are generated by, and take place in, the adjudicative process in the lower court itself. The following section focuses on hardships that are generated by the adjudicative process in the lower court but which find expression elsewhere. This latter group of problems will therefore be referred to as collateral costs.

1. Revocation of Probation

Courts often make use of probation as a form of punishment and supervision in lieu of incarceration. Probation usually takes the form of an agreement: the court refrains from executing all or part of a sentence if the defendant agrees to abide by rules for probation. These obligations, which could include reporting to a probation officer, maintaining steady employment and a place of residence, and participating in special programs, always include the obligation to obey all federal, state, and local laws.[172] If a defendant in a new case in a lower court is already on probation in a previous case, a conviction in the new case violates the terms of the probation in the previous case. This violation of probation occurs unless, under state law, a request for a new trial in the superior court vacates the lower court conviction. State law, however, usually does not vacate the prior conviction.[173] This poses potentially devastating problems for the defendant. Because the new lower court conviction violates the terms of the probation imposed upon the defendant in the earlier case, the judge assigned to the earlier case is free to revoke the probation immediately and impose any suspended sentence. Thus, even if the defendant has a right to a new trial in the superior court, the new lower court conviction may force her to await the superior court trial in jail. This belies the Supreme Court's benign characterization of lower court verdicts.[174]

2. *Sentencing Problems in Pending Cases*

Defendants often encounter more than one set of criminal charges at one time. If one set of charges results in a conviction in the lower court, and if this conviction stands pending a new trial in a superior court, this conviction carries consequences into other cases. For example, a number of states and the federal government use sentencing guidelines that typically give courts a range within which to sentence a defendant, based on facts about both the offense and the defendant.[175] Among the most important facts about the defendant these guidelines consider is the defendant's record of prior convictions.[176] If a lower court conviction stands pending a new trial in a superior court, guidelines applied to the defendant in another case might not distinguish this conviction from others, regardless of the fact that the superior court trial could arrive at a different outcome.[177] Even without guidelines, sentencing judges might well count lower court convictions from cases in which a new trial in superior court is pending against the defendant's record until the final resolution of any new trial in the superior court.[178]

3. *Damage to Reputation*

A lower court conviction that stands pending a new trial in the superior court may also damage the reputation of the person convicted.[179] The conviction is a clear, dry fact that few people have trouble understanding; the fact that there will be a new trial, with every issue open to redetermination is complex enough that few people will take the time and effort to understand. Therefore, unless the appeal to the superior court automatically vacates the lower court conviction, the damage to reputation may remain. The final resolution of the case in the superior court comes too long afterward to make a difference.

4. *Deportation*

Under the laws governing immigration, a noncitizen convicted of a crime may be deported in a variety of circumstances.[180] This power is not confined to large-scale or felony crimes. The government may deport persons convicted of misdemeanor-type offenses.[181] Lower court convictions for any of these crimes serve as bases for deportation, regardless of the possibility or likelihood of exoneration in a new trial in the superior court. Indeed, the government might deport a noncitizen on these grounds even before the opportunity arrives for the superior court trial.

5. *Loss of Licenses*

Another category of hardships the Supreme Court ignored is the loss of licenses. For example, states have made the loss of driver's license a statutorily required result of convictions for driving under the influence of alcohol and other misdemeanors.[182] Given that many people cannot work without transportation to and from their jobs, a lower court conviction that results in a suspension of a driver's license before the opportunity for a new trial in a superior court damages the defendant's ability to earn a living.

Newer statutes have a more direct impact on employment. These statutes can result in the revocation of state licenses necessary to engage in a variety of occupations and trades upon convictions for misdemeanors such as the possession of controlled substances.[183] Unlike the revocation of a driver's license, these statutes may not just make it more difficult to work; depending on the defendant's occupation, they may make employment impossible.

6. *Negative Impact on Defendant's Superior Court Trial*

A lower court trial can have a negative impact on the superior court trial. Witnesses become discouraged and unavailable through simple disinterest, and loss of income due to lost work.[184] Witnesses also become vulnerable to impeachment with prior testimony.[185] The lower court trial will likely polarize and harden witnesses' positions, and gives the state a chance to polish its case, curing defects that arose in the lower court.[186] The state's witnesses may even become more prosecution oriented.[187]

The greatest negative impact, however, may involve an even larger, overarching issue: the shadow that the lower court trial casts upon the presumption of innocence. No one questions the central place of this presumption to due process of law.[188] Even so, convictions from lower courts burden the all-important presumption of innocence during any trial in the superior court. For example, potential jurors, especially in a small-town setting, will likely know that the defendant appears in superior court because she failed to win an acquittal in the lower court.[189] Certainly, the judge in the superior court trial knows this even if the jurors do not. This knowledge may infiltrate the proceedings—through the judge's rulings, attitude, or even through the judge's direct statements to the jury.[190]

7. *Loss of Job*

The two-stage de novo system presents numerous difficulties for the employed defendant. Some of these were discussed earlier—for example, a doubling of the number of court appearances if the defendant wishes to have a trial in the superior court,[191] the lack of transportation due to the revocation of a driver's license,[192] and incarceration pending a new trial.[193] The lower court need not incarcerate the defendant, however, to cause problems with employment prior to a new trial in a superior court. Sentences that include reporting to a probation officer or attendance at special programs restrict freedom, albeit in a less direct way than incarceration. Being under the continuing control of the criminal justice system can cause defendants to miss work, to be unable to work necessary overtime, and to fail to perform other tasks for the employer. At best, these may make the defendant a less valued employee; at worst, the defendant may lose a job.

8. *Lack of Benefits to Defendants*

Beyond the collateral costs to the defendant that de novo systems carry, another assumption of the Supreme Court should be questioned. If, as the Court claims, defendants receive unique opportunities in de novo systems to improve their cases,[194] collateral costs should be viewed less harshly. At least, an intelligent assessment of collateral costs would require that they be balanced against these benefits. According to the Court, these benefits are the potential for discovery of the state's evidence during the lower court trial, and the fact that the de novo court system provides two opportunities for acquittal.[195] Careful thought, however, reveals little in the way of any real benefits to balance against collateral costs.

Use of the lower court trial for discovery presupposes the presence of an attorney. This type of discovery requires more than simply listening to the state's evidence. The right questions must be asked in the right form. Questions inartfully phrased might, at best, elicit answers indicating the general direction of the state's case, but have little value in establishing the specifics of the evidence through the possibility of later impeachment of witnesses.[196] Having an attorney to conduct discovery during the lower court trial requires that the defendant invest resources, in the form of money to employ private counsel or time to meet with counsel (whether privately paid or court appointed).[197] This drains resources available for the trial in superior court.

Further, many de novo systems do not generate any record of their proceedings.[198] To the extent that the defendant seeks a general idea of the direction of the state's case and its evidence, she may find the lower court trial of some value. Without a record, however, even if the defendant has an attorney who knows how to ask the right questions in the right manner, there is little hope of holding the state's witnesses to their lower court testimony during the superior court trial through impeachment.[199] Apart from the issue of impeachment, nothing requires that the prosecution use the same witnesses, evidence, or theory in the superior court that it used in the lower court. While an entirely new direction in the superior court might be uncommon, a second trial affords the state the opportunity to gather evidence and witnesses not available for the first trial, to prepare for defense motions, arguments and general strategy, and to repair any holes in its case illuminated by the defense in the lower court.[200]

Moreover, one cannot assume, as the Supreme Court does,[201] that the defendant will receive these benefits without having to expose her own case. In order to take advantage of the opportunity to use the lower court trial for discovery, the defense must at least cross-examine; standing silent will yield little not disclosed by the charging papers. For the court to allow the questioning, the questions must be relevant. Thus, even without offering defense evidence, the defendant may expose strategy or weaknesses in her case.[202]

D. Judicial Accountability

The de novo feature of the courts studied in this article has an important corollary: the actions of lower court judges seldom receive any scrutiny or review from higher courts.[203] As de novo systems are structured, traditional review of lower court actions by appellate courts simply has no place. In the event of an erroneous legal decision or interpretation, the defendant has the same remedy that she may use in the event of a determination of the facts she finds unfavorable: a new trial in the superior court. This runs contrary to traditional, well-established conceptions of appellate review.[204] In the most basic sense, the de novo feature means that these courts never receive guidance concerning the decisions and interpretations of the law that they render on a daily basis. Cases never return to these judges after review by a higher court and there are no opinions assessing the lower court judge's actions. In sum, lower court judges have no ongoing accountability for their decisions.[205] This means that several important functions of traditional appellate review go unserved in de novo court systems.

1. *Correction of Mistakes in Individual Cases*

In traditional types of appellate review, the appellate court reviews the record of the trial court for errors by the trial judge.[206] If the appellate court finds reversible error, and even when it does not, the trial judge receives guidance, usually in the form of a written opinion. The opinion tells the trial judge how she erred and how to correct the mistake—for example, hold a new trial or grant a particular kind of hearing. Appellate review may also inform the trial court that it acted correctly, indicating that a similar response to similar situations will be acceptable in the future. Thus, a traditional appeal not only corrects mistakes in individual cases, it also allows the monitoring of the general practices of the trial court by reviewing a particular case.[207] By acting in this fashion, the appellate court insures that all individuals before the trial court receive fair treatment.[208]

2. *Systemic Correction: "Quality Control"*

The review of trial court actions by appellate courts also serves to guide trial courts other than the one in which the particular case under review occurred. Written opinions by appellate courts allow all courts to take advantage of the experience of the trial court in question and learn from its successes and failures. The process educates both the particular trial judge and all other participants in the system—judges, prosecutors, defense attorneys, and other court personnel—concerning the correct interpretation of rules, statutes, and precedent. The possibility of appellate review, therefore, tends to control judicial misconduct in all reviewable cases, not just those particular cases that reach appellate courts.[209] Thus, the criminal process is "guided, in large part, from the top down."[210] Traditional appellate review of trial court actions in criminal cases form the ultimate guarantee of fairness of the process;[211] review on appeal explained in written opinions is the "quality control mechanism" for the system as a whole.[212]

3. *Uniformity*

Traditional appellate review also serves the function of assuring uniform interpretation and application of the law throughout judicial institutions.[213] Uniformity was a chief preoccupation of American courts in the eighteenth and nineteenth centuries.[214] Throughout the history of the American judicial system, some form of review of trial court decisions, including those of early petty offense courts, has always been available to ensure that the law was applied evenly.[215] Lack of uniformity creates disparities between courts, placing a premium on local knowledge rather than general principles,[216] and disadvantages outsiders to any community. Thus, the law becomes more a matter of experience than general rules by which persons may measure and formulate conduct. Further, the lack of appellate review manifests itself by destroying any incentive to develop a system of uniform court rules.[217] Without any recorded set of collective experiences, such as appellate court opinions reviewing the actions of trial judges, a rule maker will find little experiential grist for the mill and little reason to think any particular rule necessary. All of this tends to tolerate and promote sloppy, nonstandard procedures.[218]

4. *Lower Court Judges Need not Follow the Law*

Without the possibility of review by an appellate court, the actions of lower court judges need have nothing to do with the law. In fact, lower court judges' actions may be based on the judges' own proclivities rather than on the law.[219] Judges who are not reviewed may make decisions based on a personal world view, gut feeling of rough justice, local knowledge, or personal feelings about discipline and punishment,[220] rather than on general legal principles. The law, with its logical application of technical rules, need be paid little heed, because no one will scrutinize the actions of lower court judges to see how they meet legal standards. This ultimately leaves the lower court judge's power unchecked,[221] an especially worrisome result in a system in which many judges need not have legal training.[222]

Unchecked judicial power undermines the legitimacy of these courts in the eyes of those who move through them. Courts derive their authority to decide disputes—be they disputes between individuals in civil cases or between the state and individuals in criminal cases—from the law itself.[223] The law empowers courts to decide cases according to general principles and rules. If judges in de novo systems do not operate and decide cases according to law, the legitimacy and authority of courts as institutions and of government in general is undermined. Review of trial court decisions by appellate courts comprises one of the chief devices for ensuring that trial courts follow the law and are not governed by personal whim or caprice. Lack of appellate review unshackles the judge to roam the decisional landscape at will, with little regard for criteria and conclusions the law deems proper.

5. *Discipline Provided by the Jury*

Juries impose discipline on a judge. The presence of the jury obligates the judge to follow the law more closely than she might otherwise. The judge must handle the jury carefully, scrupulously assuring that the jury is correctly selected, that the lawyers respect the jury and its functions vis-a-vis the evidence during the trial, and that the jury is instructed correctly. Without traditional appellate review, none of the necessary scrutiny of the judge's handling of the jury function can take place. The presence of a jury also causes the judge to invest the process with more attention to the law and a greater degree of overall seriousness and dignity.[224] Juries are also more likely to acquit than judges presiding alone;[225] this shows the judge a conception of reasonable doubt different from her own,[226] and breeds necessary judicial skepticism of the government and its actors.[227] At the very least, use of juries puts citizens in courtrooms who are not part of the usual courtroom working group of judge, prosecutor, defense attorney, and staff. The mere presence of outsiders, especially as decision-makers, causes the judge to modify behaviors and methods of proceeding inappropriate for public observation. The Supreme Court has acknowledged this tendency as part of the function of the jury: The jury guards against government oppression, in the form of "the corrupt or overzealous prosecutor and against the compliant, biased, or eccentric judge."[228]

6. *The Only Accountability: Court Administrative Systems*

To the extent that any accountability exists for judges in de novo systems, it takes the form of regulations for court administration. These regulations, often implemented by chief judges, clerks of the court, professional court administrators, or other members of the court bureaucracy, emphasize the orderly, rapid disposition of cases and the efficient functioning of the bureaucracy above all else. Each of the states with a de novo system has a web of statutes, regulations, and administrative personnel[229] to move cases through the criminal justice system as quickly and inexpensively as possible.

When combined with the lack of any accountability for legal decisions through traditional appellate processes, these administrative imperatives move judges away from the time- and resource-consuming requirements of due process of law toward the goal of efficiently clearing the docket, regardless of the effect on defendants. When all that matters to the "superiors" of a lower court judge are caseload disposition figures, what happens in any one case becomes largely irrelevant.[230] No higher authority scrutinizes the judge's actions in any one case. Considerations such as fairness and the accuracy of determinations of guilt recede; interest in the caseload and its affects on the rest of the system becomes paramount.[231]

E. Courts as Teachers

Courts, especially criminal courts, do more than simply adjudicate disputes. They also educate the members of the public that pass through them about the real meaning of concepts central to our society—the rule of law, fairness, the importance of the individual, the needs of society, and the proper accommodation of each of these to the other. The structure of de novo court systems undermines the ability of the lower courts to play this role.

Despite the fact that serious crimes more often capture public attention, courts that handle less serious cases, such as the lower courts in de novo systems, remain vitally important.[232] To the extent that most citizens have just a few contacts in their lifetimes with the judicial system, such contacts are likely to be with the lower courts.[233] Therefore, these courts are largely responsible for forming citizens' impressions of the judiciary. The experiences citizens have in these courts will either build or undermine confidence in and respect for law.[234] Lower courts also represent one of the few points at which the judicial system might intervene before young offenders become repeat offenders.[235]

The nature of proceedings in misdemeanor courts is well documented.[236] Suffice it to say that lower courts' lack of respect for individuals and lack of awareness of the critical effects their actions can have on an individual's life are well known. The implications of these attitudes and the practices they foster loom large when combined with the lack of accountability of lower court judges, the lack of requirements of legal training for these judges, and other features of the lower courts in de novo systems. For all those that pass through the lower courts, whether as a complainant, witness, defendant in a traffic case, or defendant in a criminal case, the treatment they receive and the practices they observe hold a lesson. Lower courts may teach that the judge, not the law, is what matters, that there is little thought given to individuals in the lower courts, and that not even the appearance of justice is important.[237] Courts may also teach that the law is a set of abiding principles worth respecting, a source of moral authority deserving of deference, and that due process is not just a burden but a "valuable privilege worth claiming."[238] Lessons of the former nature seem likely to engender disrespect for the law,[239] to alienate people and to influence "the quality and extent of order found in society."[240] Only one point is certain: Citizens will learn whatever lessons the lower courts teach them.

IV. RECOMMENDATIONS

Thus far, this Article has described the characteristics of lower courts and demonstrated that the Supreme Court's analysis in *Colten*, *Ludwig*, and *North* is unsatisfactory. For a variety of reasons, de novo systems are not structured to produce efficiency; they invite waste, encourage duplicative actions by defendants, and require a redundant court bureaucracy. States retain de novo court systems, however, because by discouraging requests for new trials de novo systems dispose of criminal cases more quickly and less expensively than a system consisting only of superior courts. Lower courts also impose many costs on defendants, and the benefits the Court says defendants receive in the lower courts are illusory.

Viewed as a whole, the situation tempts the reformer to decry de novo systems as structurally defective and inherently unjust, and to call for their outright abolition.[241] Certainly, abolishing de novo court systems could help to ensure that all defendants receive the consideration and fair treatment due process dictates, regardless of the court in which they are tried.

Yet the weight of tradition is considerable; outright abolition of de novo systems is unlikely.[242] In lieu of abolition, this section of this Article contains recommendations.[243] They are aimed at enabling de novo systems to continue to benefit states by handling the large number of less serious criminal cases more rapidly and efficiently than a single, unified court system could, while providing some assurance that those whose cases move through the lower courts receive their due.

A. New Trial Request as Stay of Conviction and Consequences

A request for a new trial in the superior court should operate to stay or vacate any lower court conviction and its consequences. Statutes should make this process automatic upon the request for a new trial. Several state systems already operate this way.[244] This would give the Supreme Court's characterization of the verdict of lower courts as "an offer in settlement"[245] some substance. Currently, defendants convicted in the lower courts in most states must bear their convictions, and the consequences of these convictions, unless and until the superior court acts to the contrary. Some states allow a stay of incarceration upon the posting of a bond with the court.[246] Because most bonds contain some financial condition, the availability of a stay only with the posting of a bond assures that only those without money are incarcerated pending appeal; those with money go free.[247] If we intend that the defendant be free to accept or reject the lower court verdict or sentence, an automatic stay ensures real choice and equal treatment.

If a stay of lower court conviction and its consequences is not made automatic, legislatures should trim the power of lower courts to incarcerate defendants prior to trial in superior courts. Given the positive correlation between incarceration prior to trial, the probability of both being found guilty and further incarceration,[248] and given the fact that a white person has a better chance of staying free pending trial than does a black person,[249] courts should hesitate to use incarceration prior to trial in any case. A court should be especially cautious in choosing to incarcerate a defendant if the defendant has an unfettered right to a new trial, as in de novo systems. Unfortunately, courts in de novo systems lack any such caution. For example, in Feeley's study, ten percent of those arrested were detained until disposition, twice as many as were incarcerated after disposition.[250] As Feeley notes, this pretrial incarceration may exact a penalty heavy enough by itself that many defendants prefer to opt out of the system through an early guilty plea.[251] At the very least, therefore, when defendants seek release pending a new trial in the superior court, there should be a rebuttable presumption that no conditions of release more severe than those set prior to the lower court trial should be set after the lower court trial in the absence of evidence that those conditions will not secure the defendant's appearance at the new trial.[252] The lower court conviction alone should not be sufficient to rebut this presumption.

B. Optional Traditional Appellate Review

Instead of a new trial, de novo systems should allow the defendant to opt for a traditional appeal, in which a higher court reviews the record[253] for erroneous legal decisions by the trial court. Currently, one jurisdiction makes this option available.[254] Making a stay of conviction and any adverse consequences automatic[255] will encourage defendants to take this route. The option of filing a traditional appeal would put lower court trial judges on notice that appellate courts will be looking over their shoulders, and will therefore encourage judges to improve the caliber of lower court proceedings above their normally abysmal state.[256] To the extent that the appellate process teaches judges the law, the entire criminal justice system will benefit.[257] Mistakes in individual cases can be corrected, and the law will be more uniformly applied.[258]

C. A Record for All Lower Court Proceedings

The option of traditional appellate review requires that lower courts generate a record. This record might take forms other than traditional stenographic recordings, such as audio or video tape. A lower court record allows the use of lower court testimony in the superior court for purposes of impeachment[259] and discovery.[260] These records lend themselves to the documenting of abusive practices in the lower courts, whether by individual judges or by the lower court system in general. Records could also be important tools in any effort to see that defendants are properly advised of their rights and the possibility and consequences of waivers of those rights.[261]

D. Full Legal Education for All Judges

The irony in *North v. Russell* cannot have gone unnoticed by the members of the Supreme Court. In the very case in which the Court found the use of lay judges in de novo and other criminal court systems constitutionally defensible, a lower court lay judge sentenced to jail a defendant who was not, in fact, legally eligible to be incarcerated.[262] One could hardly imagine a more serious type of mistake than jailing a person who should remain free. While a judge with a full legal education could make the same mistake, this seems less likely. Beyond mistakes, lack of legal training influences the way a judge views the proceedings and parties before the court. Lack of legal training causes decisions to be based on judges' personal proclivities instead of law and principle, and shifts the balance in favor of the government.[263]

E. Limit the Authority of Lower Courts to Impose Penalties

The Supreme Court's opinions repeatedly refer to the limited powers of lower courts, especially the limited powers of these courts to incarcerate defendants.[264] Unfortunately, this is not the case. Many states give these courts a wide range of sentences to impose, including lengthy incarceration.[265] In courts in which the power of the judge is unchecked by judicial review, and in which the only remedy for a mistake or an injustice—a new trial—is actively discouraged, and where the judge may not have legal training, such broad power is indefensible. Even sentences of thirty days' incarceration could cause damage to careers and lives.[266] The power of lower courts to impose sentences should be limited so that they can do only small amounts of damage.[267]

F. Individualized Advice of Rights

States should address the failure to advise defendants of their rights to a new trial, and to other rights as well, by requiring that lower court judges advise defendants individually.[268] The court should also supply defendants with a written version of the court's advice,[269] a copy of which the defendant could initial to indicate that she had received the information. While this would not make absolutely certain that all who heard or saw their rights explained actually understood them,[270] such a procedure could provide some assurance that defendants leave court knowing they had a right to a new trial, and with some understanding of the basic mechanics of the process.

G. Sentencing Guidelines

A number of states[271] and the federal government[272] use sentencing guidelines in their criminal justice systems. While the particular purposes of these systems vary,[273] all utilize the same basic mechanism: use of a formula to calculate "scores" for the defendant, the offense, and other relevant factors, all of which are combined on a numerical matrix to calculate a particular range of punishment that the court may impose. Under some guidelines, the range of punishment binds the court; the court may depart from the prescribed range only under extraordinary circumstances or not at all. Under other systems, the guidelines are advisory, requiring only that the reason for the departure appear on the record.[274]

States with de novo systems should require lower court judges to follow binding sentencing guidelines that would prohibit lower court judges from exceeding the punishment that the defendant would receive in the same case in superior court.[275] This would address the problem of superior court trials that are generated by the disparity between the more severe sentences of lower court judges and the less severe sentences of superior court judges. By keeping lower court sentences in line with superior court sentences, sentencing guidelines remove a major incentive for new superior court proceedings in cases in which the defendant is not dissatisfied with either the trial process or the court's finding of guilt. Guidelines would also promote institutional uniformity; persons charged with the same crime in the same jurisdiction could expect the same outcome, regardless of the fact that the cases come before different courts.[276] Use of such guidelines would also forestall the use of adaptive strategies by superior court judges to discourage new trials, such as presumptively concluding that the sentence of the lower court is appropriate in every appealed case.[277] Though the guidelines should be binding,[278] they need not be inflexible. The circumstances under which departure from the guidelines is allowed should be carefully specified;[279] in the event of a departure, the lower court should be required to write an opinion demonstrating that the departure from the sentencing ranges met the specified criteria. This opinion should be made subject to traditional appellate review by a higher court. The point is that guidelines help prevent unnecessary appeals from overwhelming the superior court and turning efficiency into a cruel joke.

H. Optional Use of Juries

Use of juries in lower courts tempers the vast power of the judge in these courts, if for no other reason than that it is the jury that ultimately decides the case. Using juries in these courts also obligates judges to exercise more self-discipline and care in following procedures and applying the law.[280] If juries are available in lower courts in the first instance, defendants need not bear the costs of a lower court trial before having a jury trial in the superior court.[281]

I. Opting Out of the Lower Court

States should allow defendants to choose to avoid the lower court and proceed to superior court without the necessity of a lower court trial or guilty plea by making a simple request for a superior court trial. Like the use of juries in the lower court, this allows the defendant to obtain the advantages she perceives as important to her case, including the presence of a jury, the use of superior court procedures, or a legally trained judge, without the costs associated with a first trial. Some states already allow the defendant this choice.[282] To ensure that this procedure is not abused,[283] defendants should be required to make this request within a sufficient number of days before trial to allow sufficient notification of witnesses and court personnel. If the defendant violates this requirement and makes the request for a superior court trial on the day of his lower court trial, the request would be honored immediately—that is, the case would be put before a jury on the day of the request, eliminating the use of requests for superior court trials as de facto continuances.

J. Availability of Full Discovery

Few commodities are as important to the making of an intelligent decision as complete and accurate information.[284] The need for complete information is particularly strong in the criminal justice system because a journey through the system is replete with serious implications. More complete and accurate information will lead all actors in the process, including defense counsel and defendants, to make better decisions, whether these decisions concern trial strategy, the wisdom of accepting an offer to plead guilty, the length of a sentence, or even the guilt or innocence of the defendant. Better decisions mean fewer requests for superior court trials because fewer defendants will be dissatisfied. Further, with more information, decisions of lower courts will resemble the decisions of superior courts more closely, making a gamble on an improved decision in the superior court less likely to pay off.

V. CONCLUSION

This Article has examined a set of courts that are both vitally important and largely invisible. Lower courts in de novo systems hear misdemeanor and less serious felony cases in criminal courts in approximately half the states. Given the proportion of all criminal cases these courts handle, the significance of these courts looms large. Because they receive virtually no oversight in the form of traditional appellate review, and because they serve generally poor and noninfluential constituencies, lower courts attract little attention. Careful scrutiny shows that, notwithstanding the speculation of the Supreme Court, de novo systems do not benefit defendants. On the contrary, de novo systems increase the pressure on defendants to resolve cases as quickly as possible by making the exercise of constitutional rights, such as the right to trial by jury, more costly than in single-level systems that operate without the trial de novo feature. The availability of a new trial, which supposedly saves de novo systems from numerous constitutional maladies, is worse than an empty promise; it actually causes the defendant further damage. As with alternative dispute resolution, however, the goal of de novo court systems is efficiency and conservation of resources in the disposition of cases. Other concerns are secondary. Thus, de novo systems teach us to proceed with caution when asked to embrace new, more efficient methods of case disposition that supposedly benefit all concerned.

Perhaps the best course is the elimination of de novo systems and the processing of all cases through single level systems, regardless of the seriousness of the offense. Given the historic resistance to such proposals, the changes proposed here may serve as a useful middle ground. If our lower court systems cannot be uprooted, perhaps they can be reconstructed to work better and to preserve some of their advantages. At least these proposals might make for better decisions by the lower courts and for better trials for defendants in them; perhaps they will also help teach citizens who have contact with lower courts the lessons about our government that we would all prefer.

NOTES

*I would like to thank Roger Andersen, Bruce Campbell, William Richman, Daniel Steinbock, Benjamin Uchitelle, Elliot Uchitelle, and Allen Wolf for their insightful comments and suggestions. I also received valuable help from research assistants Matthew Harper and David Peltan, and from Marcia Minnick. Special thanks are due to the Honorable Stanley Klavan, Judge of the District Court of Montgomery County, Maryland, who encouraged me to think about the problems discussed in this Article, and to Rebecca Harris, for her unwavering support. The author gratefully acknowledges support by the University of Toledo Faculty Summer Research Grant Program.

1. Santobello v. New York, 404 U.S. 257 (1971).

2. *Id.* at 261. Commentary that finds plea bargaining a desirable way to handle criminal cases includes Arnold Enker, *Perspectives on Plea Bargaining*, *in* President's Comm'n on Law Enforcement and Admin. of Justice, Task Force Report: The Courts 108, 112 (1967) [hereinafter Task Force Report], and Thomas W. Church, Jr., *In Defense of "Bargain Justice"*, 13 Law & Soc'y Rev. 509 (1979); *see also* Warren E. Burger, *The State of the Judiciary—1970*, 56 A.B.A. J. 929, 931 (1970).

3. *E.g.*, Milton Heumann, Plea Bargaining 162, 170 (1978).

4. *E.g.*, Richard L. Abel, *A Comparative Theory of Dispute Institutions in Society*, 8 Law & Soc'y Rev. 217 (1973); Warren E. Burger, *Isn't There a Better Way?*, 68 A.B.A. J. 274 (1982); Melvin A. Eisenberg, *Private Ordering Through Negotiation: Dispute-Settlement and Rulemaking*, 89 Harv. L. Rev. 637 (1976); Warren E. Burger, Annotation, *Agenda for 2000 A.D.—A Need for Systematic Anticipation*, 70 F.R.D. 83, 93-96 (1976).

Calls for the institutionalization of alternative dispute resolution techniques and other methods of discouraging litigation continue. *See* Saundra Torry, *Quayle to Seek Trial Revisions Including Punitive Award Cap*, Wash. Post, Aug. 6, 1991, at A6 (outlining Bush Administration's proposal to cut litigation costs through, among other things, greater use of alternative dispute resolution methods).

5. A critic of the alternative dispute resolution movement has accurately summarized these arguments:

> The [alternative dispute resolution] movement promises to reduce the amount of litigation initiated, and accordingly the bulk of its proposals are devoted to negotiation and mediation prior to suit. . . . It extends to ongoing litigation as well, and the advocates of ADR have sought new ways to facilitate and perhaps even pressure parties into settling pending cases. . . . [I]t seems preferable to judgment because it rests on the consent of both parties and avoids the cost of a lengthy trial.

Owen Fiss, *Against Settlement*, 93 Yale L.J. 1073, 1075 (1984).

6. *See, e.g.*, Albert W. Alschuler, *Implementing the Criminal Defendant's Right to Trial: Alternatives to the Plea Bargaining System*, 50 U. Chi. L. Rev. 931, 932-35 (1983), and the many pieces of Alschuler's work on these alternatives cited therein.

7. At least one urban court system—Philadelphia—has handled large numbers of criminal cases for years without reliance on plea bargaining. Its primary tool is the bench trial. Stephen J. Schulhofer, *Is Plea Bargaining Inevitable?*, 97 Harv. L. Rev. 1037, 1050-87 (1984). The Philadelphia system performs well for both the state and the defendant. *Id.*

8. *E.g.*, Alschuler, *supra* note 6, at 957-95 (advocating, *inter alia*, use of procedure akin to type used in West Germany); Richard S. Frase, *Comparative Criminal Justice as a Guide to American Law Reform: How Do the French Do It, How Can We Find Out, and Why Should We Care?*, 78 Cal. L. Rev. 542, 641, 645-46 (1990) (recommending sentencing reforms, the charging of costs to the defendants, and the use of penal orders, based on use of these techniques in the French criminal justice system).

9. Fiss, *supra* note 5, at 1076; *see also* Eric K. Yamamoto, *Efficiency's Threat to the Value of Accessible Courts for Minorities*, 25 Harv. C.R.-C.L. L. Rev. 341 (1990).

10. Malcolm M. Feeley. The Process Is the Punishment xv, 5 (1979); *see also* John Robertson. Rough Justice: Perspectives on Lower Criminal Courts xxiii (1974) ("in terms of the sheer quantity of cases, as well as contact with citizens and impact on their lives, the courts that handle misdemeanor and other less serious cases are social institutions of major importance"); Task Force Report, *supra* note 2, at 2 (ninety percent of all convictions obtained by guilty pleas): Allan Ashman, *Help for our Nation's Busiest Courts*, 60 Judicature 415 (1977).

11. Colten v. Kentucky, 407 U.S. 104, 118-19 (1972).

12. *Id.*

13. In this context, "permanently disposed of" means cases in which the defendant accepts the lower court verdict and sentence and does not request a new trial in the court of general criminal jurisdiction.

14. Ludwig v. Massachusetts, 427 U.S. 618, 629 (1976) (system's "very purpose is to increase efficiency").

15. For purposes of this Article, the court hearing the case in the first instance will be referred to as the lower court; the court of general jurisdiction, in which the new trial is held, will be referred to as the superior court. In certain instances, the de novo systems of particular states will be described. When this is so, the names given to these courts by the particular state may be used. Instances of this usage will be specified.

16. *See infra* notes 36-39 and accompanying text.

17. In some lower courts in de novo court systems, the defendant has one other option: she may request the immediate removal of her case to the superior court. *E.g.*, *Ludwig*, 427 U.S. at 620-21.

18. *But see infra* notes 203-31 and accompanying text.

19. Ala. Code § 12-12-71 (1986) (appeal from District to Circuit Court), §§ 12-11-30, 12-14-70(a) (Supp. 1990) (appeal from Municipal to Circuit Court). Ark. Code Ann. § 16-17-703 (Michie Supp. 1989) (de novo appeals in general), § 16-19-1105 (Michie 1987) (appeals from Municipal to Circuit Court) (note that while § 16-19-1105, by its terms, applies to the Justice of the Peace courts, it has been held applicable to the Arkansas Municipal Courts, Casoli v. State, 763 S.W.2d 650 (Ark. 1989)); § 16-18-107 (Michie 1987) (appeals from Police to Circuit Court). Del. Code Ann. tit. 11, § 5719 (1987) (appeal from Municipal to Superior Court); Del. Code Ann. tit. 11, § 5917(b) (1987) (appeal from Justice of the Peace to Superior Court); Del. Code Ann. tit. 11, § 4503 (1987) (appeals from Alderman's or Mayor's court to Superior Court) (note that appeal from the Court of Common Pleas to the Superior Court takes the form of traditional appellate review on the law rather than trial de novo); Del. Code Ann. tit. 11, § 5301 (1987); *but see* State v. Cloud, 159 A.2d 588 (Del. 1960) (interpreting Del. Const. Art. of 1897, art. IV, § 28 to require de novo appeals in all cases in which the sentence could exceed one month of imprisonment or a fine of $100); Ind. Code Ann. § 33-10.1-5-9 (Burns 1985) (appeals from City to Circuit or Superior Courts); Kan. Stat. Ann. § 20-302b(c) (1988) (appeal from an order of a district magistrate judge to a judge in a full District Court); Kan. Stat. Ann. § 12-4602 (1982), §§ 22-3609 to -3611 (1988) (appeal from Municipal Court to District Court); La. Rev. Stat. Ann. § 13:1896(A)(1) (West Supp. 1991) (appeals from Justice of the Peace and Mayor's Courts to District Court); Md. Cts. & Jud. Proc. Code Ann. § 12-401 (1989) (appeals from District to Circuit Court); Mich. Comp. Laws Ann. § 774.34 (West 1982) (Mich. Stat. Ann. 28.1226 (Callaghan 1986)) (appeals from Municipal to Circuit Court); Miss. Code Ann. § 99-35-1 (Supp. 1990) (appeals from

Municipal and Justice of the Peace Courts to Circuit or County Courts); Mont. Code Ann. § 46-17-311 (1991) (appeals from Justice's Municipal and City Courts to District Court); Nev. Rev. Stat. Ann. § 266.565(1) (Michie 1986) (appeal from Municipal to District Court); N.H. Rev. Stat. Ann. § 599:1 (Supp. 1990); N.H. Sup. Ct. R. 92 (1991) (appeals from District or Municipal Court to Superior Court); N.M. Stat. Ann. § 35-13-2(A) (Michie 1988) (appeals from Magistrate to District Court), N.M. Mun. Ct. R. 8-703(1) (appeals from Municipal to District Court), and N.M. Metr. Ct. R. 7-703(1) (1988) (appeal from Metropolitan to District Courts); N.C. Gen. Stat. § 7A-290 (1989) (appeal from District to Superior Court and from judgment of District Court Magistrate to full District Court judge); Ohio Rev. Code Ann. § 1905.25 (Baldwin 1987) (appeals from Mayor's Court to Municipal or County Court); Okla. Stat. Ann. tit. 11, § 27-129(a) (1978) (appeals from Municipal to District Court); Or. Rev. Stat. § 221.390 (1989) (appeal from Municipal to District or Circuit Court); 42 Pa. Cons. Stat. Ann. § 1123 (Supp. 1991) (appeals from Philadelphia Municipal Court to Court of Common Pleas); R.I. Gen. Laws § 12-17-1 (1981) and Dist. Ct. R. Crim. P. 23 (appeals from District to Superior Court); Tenn. Code Ann. § 27-5-108 (1980) (appeal from court of General Sessions to Circuit Court); Utah Code Ann. § 78-4-7.5 (Supp 1990) (appeals from Justice to Circuit Court); Va. Code Ann. § 16.1-132-136 (Michie 1988) (appeals from District to Circuit Court); Wash. Rev. Code Ann. § 10.10.010 (West 1990), Wash. C.R.L.J. 9.1, 9.2, 9.3 (appeals from District to Superior Court); W. Va. Code § 50-5-13 (1986) (appeals from Magistrate to Circuit Court), W. Va. Code § 8-34-1 (1990) (appeals from Mayor or Police or Municipal Court to Circuit Court).

20. Alabama, Arkansas, Delaware, Kansas, Mississippi, Montana, New Mexico, and West Virginia have more than one court that allows a defendant convicted in a lower court to request a new trial in a superior court. *See supra* note 19.

21. Ariz. Rev. Stat. Ann. § 22-374 (1990); Colo. Rev. Stat. § 13-10-116 (1987), and Rainwater v. County Ct., 604 P.2d 1195 (Colo. Ct. App. 1979); N.J. Stat. Ann. § 2A:3-6 (West 1987), and R. Gov. Crim. Prac. 3:23-8; S.D. Codified Laws Ann. § 16-12A-26 (1987); Tex. Crim. Proc. Code Ann. §§ 44.17, .10 (West Supp. 1991). Similarly, Missouri allows requests for a new trial when the judge in the lower court is not licensed to practice law. Mo. Ann. Stat. § 479.200 (Vernon 1987). At least two other states that allow de novo trials upon appeal from a lower court are different enough in at least one fundamental respect that they are not necessarily susceptible to the same difficulties as the de novo systems discussed in this Article. In these courts, an appeal for a trial de novo is allowed only in the discretion of the court. Alaska Stat. § 22.10.020(d) (1988); Idaho Code § 1-2213 (1990). Because many of the difficulties that de novo systems share arise from the fact that an appeal from a lower court results in a new trial, making the lower court actions invisible, *see infra* notes 198-218 and accompanying text, these two states in which the de novo appeal feature is discretionary will not be considered in the discussion that follows.

22. Ariz. Rev. Stat. Ann. §§ 12-123, -142 (1990); Ark. Code Ann. § 16-17-703 (Michie Supp. 1989); Del. Code Ann. tit. 11, § 5701 (1985); Kan. Stat. Ann. § 12-4502 (1988); Md. Cts. & Jud. Proc. Code Ann. § 4-302(e) (1989 Repl.); Mich. Comp. Laws Ann. § 774.34 (West 1982); (Mich. Stat. Ann. § 28.1226 (Callaghan 1986); Nev. Rev. Stat. Ann. § 266.550 (Michie 1986); N.H. Rev. Stat. Ann. § 599.1 (Supp. 1990); N.C. Gen. Stat. § 15A-1114 (1988); Ohio Rev. Code Ann. § 1905.25 (Baldwin 1987); 42 Pa. Const. Stat. Ann. § 1123 (Supp. 1991); Tenn. Code Ann. § 27-5-108 (1980); Del. J.P. Crim. R. 15(a); R.I. Dist. Ct. R. Crim. P. 23; Utah R. Crim. Proc. 17.

23. Some states use judicial officers that are not judges in either title or the extent of powers granted them. *See, e.g.*, Kan. Stat. Ann. §§ 20-338, -302b(a) (1988) (establishing the office of district magistrate judge, and limiting powers of district magistrate judges to adjudicating traffic infractions, misdemeanor charges, and determinations of probable cause in preliminary hearings in felony cases); N.C. Gen. Stat. §§ 7A-3, 4, 171.2 (1989) (establishing the office of magistrate for District Court).

24. *See, e.g.*, Md. Cts. & Jud. Proc. Code Ann. §§ 4-302(e), 12-401(d), (e) (Repl. 1989). The former statute allows the defendant to elect a trial by a jury in the Circuit (superior) Court without

going through any proceeding in the District (lower) Court; the latter statute provides for trial by jury in any case in which the defendant has appealed from the verdict of the District Court.

25. *See, e.g.*, the Massachusetts de novo court system as described in Ludwig v. Massachusetts, 427 U.S. 618, 620-21 (1976). Essentially, the defendant in *Ludwig* could not avoid a proceeding in the lower court by simply demanding that his case be transferred to the jury court.

26. *E.g.*, Ind. Code Ann. § 33-10.1-5-5 (Burns 1985); Miss. Code Ann. § 99-33-9 (Supp. 1990); Mont. Code Ann. §§ 46-17-201, -403 (1991); Va. Code Ann. §§ 19.2-257, -258, -262 (Michie 1988); Wash. Rev. Code Ann. § 10.04.050 (West 1990); W. Va. Code § 50-5-8 (1986).

27. *See, e.g.*, Ark. R. Crim. P. 28.1 (speedy trial rule applies only in Circuit Court). The Arkansas statute has been held not to apply until case arrives there for new trial. Shaw v. State, 712 S.W.2d 338 (Ark. App. 1986); *see also* Del. J.P. Crim. R. 12 (defendant requesting discovery must show materiality and reasonableness, which is not necessary under Del. Sup. Ct. Crim. R. 16); Md. R. Crim. Causes 4-241, -252, -253, -262, -263; N.H. Dist. & Mun. Cts. R. 2.10 (discovery limited to listed items; Sup. Ct. R. 98-99-A also allows turning unlisted item over under court order); N.M. R. Crim. Pro. Mag. Ct. 6-504 (magistrate may order production of materials in possession of state); R. Crim. Pro. Dist. Ct. 5-501 (much broader); Va. Gen. Dist. Cts.-Crim. & Traffic 7C:5 (abbreviated version of Superior Court discovery rule); W. Va. R. Crim. Pro. Mag. 15 (limited discovery rule).

28. *Compare, e.g.*, Md. R. Crim. Causes 4-263 (discovery in Circuit (superior) Court), *with* Md. R. Crim. Causes 4-262 (discovery in District (lower) Court).

29. *Compare, e.g.*, Md. R. Crim. Causes 4-252 (motions in Circuit Court) *with* Md. R. Crim. Causes 4-251 (motions in District Court).

30. *See* Md. R. Crim. Causes 4-241 (rule regarding bills of particulars applies only in Circuit Court, leaving question of use in District Court open).

31. *See, e.g.*, Ludwig v. Massachusetts, 427 U.S. 618, 629 (de novo court systems' "very purpose is to increase efficiency").

32. *See, e.g.*, Del. Const. art. IV, § 30 (justices of the peace appointed by the governor with majority consent of the Senate; but no qualifications are specified); Miss. Const. art. VI, § 171 and Miss. Code Ann. § 9-11-3 (Supp. 1990) (no justice of the peace can commence the judicial functions of the office unless he has completed a training course at the judicial college of the University of Mississippi Law Center within six months of the start of each elected term); Ark. Code Ann. § 16-18-112 (Michie 1987) (city court judge must be either an attorney or a "qualified elector"); Ind. Code Ann. § 33-10.1-3-1.1 (West Supp. 1991) (judge of a city or town court shall be elected by the voters of the city or town; but no qualifications are specified); N.M. Stat. Ann. §§ 35-2-1 (1988) (magistrates in districts having a population of less than 200,000 must have attained the equivalent of a high school degree) and 35-14-3 (1988) (qualifications of municipal court judges are subject to city ordinance); N.C. Gen. Stat. §§ 7A-140, -171.2 (1989) (elected); Ohio Rev. Code Ann. 1905.05A (Anderson 1983); Tenn. Code Ann. § 17-1-106 (1980) (whether judges are required to be lawyers depends on the size of the county); W. Va. Code § 8-10-2 (1990) (no formal legal training required; *see* Hubby v. Carpenter, 350 S.E.2d 706 (W. Va. 1986)).

33. Kan. Stat. Ann. § 20-334 (1988) (district magistrate and municipal court judges must either have been admitted to practice for five years or be certified by the Kansas Supreme Court; certification requires the successful completion of an examination); Mont. Code Ann. §§ 3-10-202, -11-202 (1991) (judge on the city courts or a justice of the peace must be an attorney, a former judge, or have completed the Montana Supreme Court's orientation program); Nev. Rev. Stat. Ann. § 5.025 (Michie 1986) (supreme court may require training for municipal court judges from time to time, but judges need not be attorneys); Wash. Rev. Code Ann. § 3.34.060 (West 1988) (district court judge must be admitted to practice in Washington, a former judge, or have passed a qualifying examination); W. Va. Code § 50-1-4 (1986) (magistrates must attend a basic course in law and procedure and take continuing education courses).

34. *See infra* note 36 and statutes cited therein.

35. Note that the United States Supreme Court has held that the use of untrained judges in misdemeanor criminal cases does not violate due process. North v. Russell, 427 U.S. 328 (1976). For further discussion of *North*, *see infra* notes 76-97 and accompanying text.

36. *See, e.g.*, Ark. Code Ann. §§ 16-17-704, -18-101, -18-110 (Michie Supp. 1991) (misdemeanors and ordinances); Ind. Code Ann. § 33-10.1-2-2 (West 1983) (jurisdiction of city court limited to misdemeanors and ordinances); Kan. Stat. Ann. § 20-302b(a) (1988) (jurisdiction of magistrate courts limited to misdemeanors, traffic infractions and preliminary examinations in felony cases); Kan. Stat. Ann. § 12-4104 (1982) (municipal court jurisdiction limited to violations of city ordinances); Mont. Code Ann. § 3-11-103 (1991) (city courts' jurisdiction limited to violations of municipal ordinances and actions to collect five thousand dollars or more in back taxes); N.M. Stat. Ann. § 35-3-4 (Michie 1978) (jurisdiction of magistrate court limited to misdemeanors, petty misdemeanors, and ordinance violations); N.M. Stat. Ann. § 35-14-2 (1988) (jurisdiction of municipal court limited to ordinances); N.C. Gen. Stat. § 7A-272 (1989) (all criminal offenses below felony); Ohio Rev. Code Ann. § 1905.01 (Anderson 1983) (ordinances); R.I. Gen. Laws § 8-8-3(5) (1985) (ordinances); Va. Code Ann. § 16.1-123.1 (Michie 1988) (misdemeanors, traffic infractions, and ordinances); Wash. Rev. Code Ann. § 3.66.060 (West 1990) (misdemeanors, gross misdemeanors, and ordinances); W. Va. Code § 50-2-3 (1986) (misdemeanors).

37. *See, e.g.*, Miss. Const. art. VI, § 171 (jurisdiction of lower court limited to crimes in which punishment does not exceed a fine or one year imprisonment in county jail (county jail sentences limited to two years per offense, Miss. Code Ann. § 47-1-1(1981)); N.H. Rev. Stat. Ann. §§ 502-A:11, 502:18 (1983) (fine not exceeding $1000 and/or imprisonment not exceeding one year); Pa. Stat. Ann. tit. 42 § 1123 (1981) (imprisonment not exceeding five years).

38. *See, e.g.*, Md. Cts. & Jud. Proc. Code Ann. § 4-301 (Supp. 1991) (jurisdiction over all misdemeanors, specified felonies, and several specified offenses which require the accused to have attained a 18 years of age); Mont. Code Ann. § 3-10-303 (1991) (misdemeanors punishable by fine not exceeding $500, imprisonment not exceeding six months, or both).

39. *See, e.g.*, Md. Cts. & Jud. Proc. Code Ann. § 4-301(b)(1) (1989) (giving lower court jurisdiction of, *inter alia*, common law misdemeanors, including simple assault, an offense which carries a penalty of up to twenty years of imprisonment). *See* Md. Cts. & Jud. Proc. Code Ann. § 4-301(b)(2) (1989) (giving lower court jurisdiction of felony theft cases, which carry a penalty of up to fifteen years of imprisonment, Md. Ann. Code of 1957 art. 27 § 342(f) (1987)); Brown v. State, 379 A.2d 1231 (Md. App. 1977).

40. *See, e.g.*, Del. Code Ann. tit. 11, § 5917(b) (1987) (no conviction or sentence stayed pending appeal unless a bond is given within five days of conviction); Ind. Code Ann. § 33-10.1-5-9 (c) (West 1983) (appeal does not stay further proceedings on the judgment unless defendant enters into a recognizance); Miss. Code Ann. § 99-35-3 (Supp. 1990) (sentence is stayed if defendant files an appearance bond); Nev. Rev. Stat. §§ 177.105, .115, .125 (1986) (imprisonment and probation may be stayed, and fines must be stayed, if defendant is admitted to bail).

41. States vary regarding the conditions courts must examine in setting bond pending appeal. As with pretrial bail, conditions range from a written promise to appear, to requirements that money or property be posted with the court, to promises by third parties that they will guarantee the defendant's appearance or even take custody of the defendant pending trial. *See, e.g.*, 18 U.S.C. § 3142(b), (c) (1984), and Md. R. Proc. 4-216(d) (1991) (both allowing pretrial release under various conditions).

42. Kan. Stat. Ann. §§ 22-3609, -3609a (1988); La. Code Crim. Proc. Ann. art. 913 (West Supp. 1991) (an appeal suspends execution of a sentence if the defendant is admitted to post-conviction bail); Mont. Code Ann. § 46-20-204 (1989) (same as Louisiana); N.C. Gen. Stat. § 15A-143(f) (1988); Ohio Rev. Code Ann. § 1905.23 (Anderson 1983); W. Va. Code § 50-5-13 (1986); N.M. Crim. Proc. Mag. Ct. R. 6-703(C) and N.M. Mun. Ct. R. 8-703(D) (1990); Pa. R. Crim. Proc. 6011 (Purdon 1989).

43. 407 U.S. 104 (1972).

44. 427 U.S. 618 (1976).
45. 427 U.S. 328 (1976).
46. 407 U.S. at 107.
47. *Id.* at 108.
48. *Id.*
49. *Id.*
50. Colten v. Commonwealth, 467 S.W.2d 374 (Ky. 1971).
51. 407 U.S. at 106-08.
52. *Id.* at 112-14.
53. *Id.* at 114. The Court rejected challenges that the statute was unconstitutional both facially, as vague and overbroad, and as applied. *Id.* at 108-12.

The defendant also argued that the double jeopardy clause prohibited imposition of an enhanced penalty because the de novo system required the defendant to put himself in jeopardy a second time for the same offense as the price for receiving a trial that fully complied with the due process clause. *Id.* at 119. The Court brushed this contention aside, stating that the same argument had been made and rejected in North Carolina v. Pearce, 395 U.S. 711, 719-20 (1969). 407 U.S. at 119. Further, the Court said, the defendant can avoid having two trials "simply by pleading guilty and erasing immediately thereafter any consequence that would otherwise follow from tendering the plea." *Id.* at 119-20. The Court apparently believed that the consequences following conviction in a lower court, which may or may not be "erasable" while the defendant's appeal is pending, are of little consequence. *See infra* notes 170-90 and accompanying text.

The defendant also argued that Kentucky's de novo system violated the due process clause. *Id.* at 114 and 119. The de novo system in Kentucky allowed the superior court to sentence the defendant to a harsher penalty than had been received in the lower court. This possibility, according to the defendant, would inevitably chill the exercise of the right to appeal. *Id.* at 115-19. In *Pearce*, the Supreme Court had forbidden enhanced sentences following new trials that resulted from successful appeals because of the possibility that the resentencing court might be acting vindictively. The de novo system, the defendant argued, presented the same possibility of vindictiveness at sentencing, and thus violated the due process clause. 407 U.S. at 119.

The Supreme Court did not agree. *Pearce*, the Court said, rested on the possibility that a trial judge might act vindictively when, after a second trial, the judge sentences the same defendant who complained about the court's action in the first trial. *Id.* at 115-16. The possibility that the judge would give the defendant a harsher penalty as purposeful punishment for appealing moved the Supreme Court to forbid a harsher sentence after the second trial, absent special circumstances. *Id.* at 116. By contrast, the Court found no reason to assume that the superior court would deal more strictly with a defendant that utilized the de novo system than it would with those tried in the superior court originally. *Id.* at 117. The superior court would not know anything about the record below, and need not even know the sentence pronounced in the lower court. *Id.* at 117-18. Facts cited in *Ludwig* belie this assertion. 427 U.S. at 627 n.4. The idea that the superior court would simply ignore the fact that the defendant had been found guilty and sentenced already in the lower court disregards an understandable tendency that superior court judges would have to discourage an increase in their workload. *See supra* note 4 and accompanying text.

54. 407 U.S. at 119.
55. *Id.* at 118.
56. *Id.* at 118-19.
57. *Id.* at 117. The Court did not reveal the basis of its assumption that a superior court is more likely to view the defendant's appeal sympathetically rather than critically. In reality, the superior court's concern about its workload—and the additional burden of every appealed case—would cause the court to view appeals as a burden. Thus, the superior court, most likely, would adopt the understandable view that the defendant should be satisfied with the lower court proceeding. This is

speculation, of course, but no more so than the Court's own unsupported assumptions, and seems more grounded in human nature.

58. *Id.* (citing 467 S.W.2d at 379).

59. 427 U.S. 618 (1976). The full charge against the defendant was that he operated a motor vehicle "negligently . . . so that the lives and safety of the public might be endangered," in violation of Mass. Gen. Laws Ann. ch. 90, § 24(2)(a) (West 1989). The maximum possible penalty for the offense is a fine of $200, two years imprisonment, or both. 427 U.S. at 622-23.

60. 427 U.S. at 623.

61. *Id.*

62. *Id.*

63. *Id.*

64. 330 N.E.2d 467 (Mass. 1975).

65. 427 U.S. at 625 (quoting Williams v. Florida, 399 U.S. 78, 100 (1970) (quoting Duncan v. Louisiana, 391 U.S. 145, 156 (1968))).

66. 427 U.S. at 625-26.

67. *Id.* at 626.

68. *Id.*

69. The degree to which the Court seems unaware of the consequences of a finding of guilt in the lower court is striking. *See supra* notes 54-55 and accompanying text.

70. While indigent defendants charged with misdemeanors are eligible for appointed counsel under Argersinger v. Hamlin, 407 U.S. 25 (1972), this covers only those defendants deemed indigent by applicable financial guidelines. 427 U.S. at 627. Persons with financial resources too limited to afford counsel, but too great to qualify as indigent, are left without counsel.

71. 427 U.S. at 626-27.

72. *Id.* at 627.

73. *Id.* at 628.

74. *Id.* at 629.

75. *Id.* The Court concluded its opinion by finding that the requirement inherent in the de novo system that the defendant undergo two trials in order to obtain a trial that fully comports with due process does not violate the double jeopardy clause. *Id.* at 630-32. According to the Court, the defendant who goes through a second trial in a de novo court system does so of her own volition. As such, she is in the same position as a person who successfully appeals on the basis of the trial record and receives a new trial. *Id.* at 631. Accordingly, the Court said, there is no doubt that prosecution of the defendant in this situation is allowed. *Id.* at 631-32.

76. 427 U.S. 328 (1976).

77. *Id.* 329.

78. *Id.; see also* Ky. Rev. Stat. Ann. § 189.990(10) (Michie/Bobbs-Merrill 1987).

79. 427 U.S. at 330.

80. *Id.*

81. Ky. Const. § 11.

82. Ky. Rev. Stat. Ann. §§ 25.014, 26.400 (Baldwin 1971) (repealed 1978) (current version at Ky. Rev. Stat. Ann. § 29A.270 (Michie/Bobbs-Merrill 1991)); Ky. Rev. Stat. Ann. § 26.400 (Baldwin 1971) (repealed 1978).

83. North v. Russell, 427 U.S. 328, 330 (1976).

84. *Id.*

85. *Id.* at 331-32.

86. *Id.* at 332.

87. 516 S.W.2d 103 (Ky. 1974).

88. *North*, 427 U.S. at 333.

89. *Id.* at 334.

90. *Id.*
91. *Id.* at 334-35. The first of these propositions usually is not true. *See supra* notes 40-42 and accompanying text. The second proposition, even if true, means that those without resources remain in jail pending a new trial. *See infra* notes 155-61 and accompanying text.
92. *Id.* at 335. The Court's assumption is flatly contradicted by the available data on misdemeanor courts. *See infra* notes 162-69 and accompanying text.
93. *Id.* at 335.
94. *Id.* at 336.
95. *Id.*
96. *Id.* at 336-37. As in *Colten*, the Court ignored the full range of consequences of a conviction, even if an appeal vacates the lower court conviction, which it does not do in every state. *See infra* notes 130-90 and accompanying text.
97. *Id.* at 337. The Court concluded by dismissing the defendant's equal protection argument. *Id.* at 338-39.
98. Ludwig v. Massachusetts, 427 U.S. 618, 622, 626-29 (1976).
99. *Id.* at 626-29.
100. *See supra* note 10.
101. *Id.* at 629.
102. North v. Russell, 427 U.S. 328, 336 n.5 (1976) (quoting *Colten*, 407 U.S. at 117 (quoting Colten v. Commonwealth, 467 S.W.2d at 379)).
103. *North*, 427 U.S. at 336 (quoting *Colten*, 407 U.S. at 114).
104. *Id.* at 339.
105. *Ludwig*, 427 U.S. at 626-27; *Colten*, 407 U.S. at 118-19.
106. *North*, 427 U.S. at 336 (quoting *Colten*, 407 U.S. at 118-19).
107. *See supra* notes 88-93 and accompanying text.
108. *See supra* note 107 and accompanying text. *See infra* notes 109-16 and accompanying text.
109. Contrary to expectations, only a small number of cases are appealed to superior court. For example, in one study of a de novo system, out of 1,640 cases, the author observed not a single request for a new trial. Feeley, *supra* note 10, at 9.
110. *Colten*, 407 U.S. at 118. The defendant in *North*, no doubt, would disagree. He received a sentence of incarceration for one month, when the maximum sentence under law was a fine. *North*, 427 U.S. at 329-30.
111. *See supra* note 37 and accompanying text.
112. *See supra* note 39.
113. *See supra* note 37 (regarding jurisdictional limits for de novo courts in Mississippi, New Hampshire and Pennsylvania).
114. *Id.* Pennsylvania's limit is five years.
115. The fact that, in at least one study, few requests for new trials were filed indicates that something else is happening. *See* Feeley, *supra* note 10, at 9. New trials may be heavily discouraged, deterring de novo review despite harsh sentences. *See infra* notes 127-202 and accompanying text. Lenient sentences may be the rule, or the punishment may be inconsequential next to the various costs of going through the process. Feeley, *supra* note 10, at 199-243. One study of the de novo court system formerly in place in Massachusetts indicates that the perseverance of the defense in de novo systems is often rewarded—records of new trials in the superior court show that defendants in these cases "either receive lighter sentences than they did in [the lower] court or are found not guilty." Stephen R. Bing & S. Stephen Rosenfeld. The Quality of Justice in the Lower Criminal Courts of Metropolitan Boston 108 (1970).
116. *See* Scott Rodgers. *Binding Sentencing Guidelines: A Means of Controlling Utah's Prison Population*, 1990 Utah L. Rev. 309, 338 (without sentencing guidelines that bind the court, sentencing disparities will remain). For further discussion, see *infra* notes 271-79 and accompanying text.

117. Of course, depending on the adequacy of case tracking systems, computer notification, and the quality and speed of the court bureaucracy in general, the number of appearances could more than double.
118. *See* Laura Banfield & C. David Anderson, *Continuances in the Cook County Criminal Courts*, 35 U. Chi. L. Rev. 259, 280-87 (1968).
119. Defendants often receive one continuance of the trial date to retain counsel or otherwise make preparation. The prosecution, of course, might need a continuance as well, due to the unavailability of one or more witnesses, failure to complete necessary scientific tests of evidence, or similar prosecutorial responsibilities.
120. The President's Commission on Law Enforcement and Administration of Criminal Justice, *The Lower Courts*, from The Challenge of Crime in a Free Society 128-30 (1967), *excerpted in* Rough Justice: Perspectives on Lower Criminal Courts 57 (John A. Robertson ed. 1974).
121. Bing & Rosenfeld, *supra* note 115, at 108; Karen M. Knab & Brent Lindberg, *Misdemeanor Justice: Is Due Process the Problem*?, 60 Judicature 416, 418 (1977) (defendants in all courts frequently use delay to "wait out" prosecution witnesses). *But see* Ellen L. Bane, Note, *The De Novo Procedure—Assessment of its Constitutionality Under the Sixth Amendment Right to Trial by Jury and the Due Process Clause of the Fourteenth Amendment*, 55 B.U. L. Rev. 25, 40-41, 53 (1975) (suggesting that witnesses who come to the superior court for a new trial after a trial in the lower court are likely to be better, more polished witnesses in the second trial than they were in the first trial, because of the opportunity the first trial provides to practice testifying).
122. *See* John P. Ryan, *Adjudication and Sentencing in a Misdemeanor Court: The Outcome Is the Punishment*, *in* U.S. Dep't of Justice, National Institute of Justice, Misdemeanor Courts: Policy Concerns and Research Perspectives 93 (James J. Alfini ed. 1981) [hereinafter Policy Concerns and Research Perspectives] (while the number of *demands* for jury trials in some misdemeanor courts may be high, the number of actual jury trials is rare). This suggests that appeals in de novo court systems "may affect negotiation and adjudication strategies" and present an opportunity for tactical advantage that defendants and defense counsel can ill afford to ignore. James J. Alfini, *Understanding Misdemeanor Courts: A Review of the Literature and Recent Case Law*, in Policy Concerns and Research Perspectives, *supra*, at 1, 21.
123. *See supra* note 10.
124. *See supra* notes 117-22 and accompanying text.
125. The justifications for de novo systems based on efficiency bring another, perhaps more basic question to mind. Is there any deficiency in a lower court for which the ready availability of a new trial in the superior court would not atone? Put a different way, the efficiency justification proves too much. Would it justify, perhaps, trials without counsel? Would it justify lower court trials occurring so soon after the events in question that counsel would have no chance to prepare and become effective? Could evidence obtained in violation of the various exclusionary rules be used in the lower court, as long as it was not used in the superior court? One searches for a line demarcating the permissible from the forbidden, but the efficiency analysis does not provide one.
126. In the 19 years since the Supreme Court examined de novo systems in *Colten*, a few of the states that had de novo court systems have abolished them; an almost equal number of states have introduced de novo systems. *Compare* Colten v. Kentucky, 407 U.S. 104, 112 n.4 (1972) (listing the states that had adopted a two tier system as of 1972), *with* note 19 *supra* (listing the states that currently use a two tier system). A review of the legislation and legislative history making these changes in the various states reveals no clear pattern or overall set of rationales, either for abolishing or adding de novo systems.
127. *Colten*, 407 U.S. at 199.
128. This is so in either of two senses: defendants are actively discouraged from appealing, or the lower court's "offer" is so good that defendants do not want to reject it. As to the former idea,

discouragement of new trials in de novo court systems has been noted briefly elsewhere, *e.g.*, Feeley, *supra* note 10, at 291-92; Bane *supra* note 121, at 51 (low number of requests for new trials shows de novo system operates to burden exercise of right to jury trial); Howard I. Kalodner, Note, *Metropolitan Criminal Courts of First Instance*, 70 Harv. L. Rev. 320, 349 (1956) (requests for new trials occur in a low percentage of cases "because of the expense and the infrequency with which defendants are informed of their rights . . . ."), and has also been noted in similar contexts, such as the general discouragement of the exercise of due process rights by other kinds of courts. *E.g.*, Ryan, *supra* note 122, at 129-30; *but see* Alschuler, *supra* note 6, at 951-52 (1983) (acknowledging that the costs of going through the criminal process might induce persons to plead guilty, but asserting that this is fair as long as "the adjudicative balance is fair and the procedures seem worthwhile").

The latter idea—that courts that specialize in the rapid disposition of cases whether or not as part of de novo systems use lenient sentencing practices to clear cases out of the system—surfaces in Schulhofer, *supra* note 7, at 1050 n.54 (asserting that so few defendants file appeals in the de novo court system in Philadelphia because "[o]nly 14% of the defendants convicted . . . received any term of incarceration . . . .").

129. Ludwig v. Massachusetts, 427 U.S. 618, 634-35 (1976) (Stevens, J., dissenting) (latter emphasis added).

130. *See, e.g., supra* notes 56, 68-69 and accompanying text.

131. In addition to direct process barriers, de novo systems also generate collateral costs, that is, extra-process difficulties that have their genesis within the adjudicative process but find expression outside it. *See infra* notes 170-193 and accompanying text (discussing collateral costs).

132. Today defendants who meet the criteria for indigence can usually receive representation by counsel at no charge. Leaving aside the question of the appropriateness of any particular state's criteria for indigence, it is no longer the case everywhere that this free representation is, in fact, free. In Maryland, the public defender may recoup the reasonable value of services rendered to the defendant once the defendant becomes able to pay. *See* Md. Code. Ann. art. 27A, § 7(d)-(g) (1990). This arrangement is, at best, a logical absurdity; at worst, it is likely to prove highly corrosive to the always-fragile relationship between indigent client and publicly-provided attorney. This relationship always faces difficulties because of the perception on the part of defendants that these attorneys are co-opted, because they are on the state's payroll. Feeley, *supra* note 10, at 220-22. *But see* Fuller v. Oregon, 417 U.S. 40 (1974) (rejecting equal protection claim against state's recoupment statute).

133. Ludwig v. Massachusetts, 427 U.S. 618, 634-35 (Stevens, J., dissenting).

134. *See. e.g.*, Md. R. 1311(c) (1990).

135. *See, e.g.*, Md. R. 1-325, 1311(c)(3).

136. U.S. Const. amend. VI.

137. *E.g.*, Md. R. 4-353.

138. While defendants in most misdemeanor or less serious felony cases would not find it necessary to retain experts, expert witnesses are useful for a whole variety of issues faced in these cases. For example, experts in accident reconstruction are quite useful in a variety of cases involving vehicle collisions. Even more common might be cases in which defendants suffer from some mental illness. In such cases, while the impairment suffered by the defendant may not rise to the level of insanity that excuses criminal behavior, expert testimony is still extremely useful at sentencing and may provide the crucial information that makes the difference between the defendant receiving treatment or incarceration.

139. *See* Feeley, *supra* note 10, at 201 (missing work for a court appearance may be the only way an employer would find out about a defendant's legal difficulties; in fact, missing work may be the only thing about which the employer cares).

140. *Id.* at 238-40.

141. Ludwig v. Massachusetts, 427 U.S. 618, 635-36 (1976) (Stevens, J., dissenting) (noting various ways in which defendant's jury trial in a superior court may be "significantly different" for a defendant whose case begins in a lower court than when a jury trial begins in the superior court).
142. *See supra* notes 117-22 and accompanying text.
143. Public Defender Service of the District of Columbia, 1 Criminal Practice Institute Trial Manual § 2.3 (1987).
144. This assumes, of course, that the lower court generates and keeps a record of its proceedings which the state's counsel could then use to impeach a defense witness. *See supra* note 21 and accompanying text; *see also infra* notes 259-61 and accompanying text. Because the defense might also impeach the witnesses of the state, the impeachment argument cuts both ways.
145. In *Ludwig*, the Supreme Court acknowledged that financial burdens generated by the structure of the de novo court system exist, but it minimized them, admitting only that "they may, in an individual case, impose a hardship . . . ." 427 U.S. at 626. Certainly, however, this hardship did not as a general matter rise to the level of a constitutional violation in the form of an outsized burden on the right to a jury trial. *Id.* This was particularly true, the Court reasoned, because the accused could avoid the expense of a trial in the lower court by admitting facts sufficient to sustain a finding of guilt without mounting any real defense, and then request a new trial. *Id.* The Court seemed totally oblivious to the stigma or other difficulties the defendant who takes this route may encounter as a result of the suggested admission of facts. *See infra* notes 172-93 and accompanying text.
146. Pierce B. Hasler, *De Novo Juries, Misdemeanor Counsel and Other Problems: Changes Ahead for the Maine District Courts*?, 23 Me. L. Rev. 63, 81 (1971) ("that factors such as time, expense, and inconvenience deter is obvious; they are intended to.").
147. *Ludwig*, 427 U.S. at 637 (Stevens, J., dissenting); *but see* Feeley, *supra* note 10, at 201 (stigma of conviction has little meaning for most defendants). Presumably, Feeley would make the same argument for whatever stigma unresolved charges might carry.
148. *Ludwig*, 427 U.S. at 626. In *North*, Justice Stewart found unacceptable that "as a prerequisite to a constitutionally fair trial, a defendant must stand up in open court and inform a judge that he is guilty when in fact he believes that he is not." North v. Russell, 427 U.S. 328, 346 (1976) (Stewart, J., dissenting).
149. *See supra* notes 40-42 and accompanying text. On the burdens created by even a "temporary" conviction, see *infra* notes 172-93 and accompanying text. *But see* Feeley, *supra* note 10, at 201 (doubting that most defendants would concern themselves with the stigma of a conviction).
150. In a tangle of logic and references to the Speedy Trial Clause, the Court in *Ludwig* minimized the psychological burdens imposed by de novo systems. 427 U.S. at 628-29. The Court stated that the defendant had not presented any evidence to support the rather obvious proposition "that there is a greater delay in obtaining a jury in Massachusetts than there would be if the Commonwealth abandoned its two-tier system. We are reluctant to attribute to Massachusetts a perverse determination to maintain an inefficient system whose very purpose is to increase efficiency." *Id.* at 629. The Court thus closed its eyes to the central purpose of the lower court in de novo systems: they increase efficiency only by increasing the burdens on defendants enough to deter requests for new trials. *Id.* at 635 (Stevens, J., dissenting) ("In short, the very purpose of the requirement is to discourage jury trials by placing a burden on the exercise of the constitutional right."); Hasler, *supra* note 146, at 82-83 (calling criminal trial "an ordeal" that is "physically and mentally gruelling" because of its costs in monetary expense, time and embarrassment, any one of which could deter the defendant from demanding a second trial); Edward Soto, North v. Russell *and* Ludwig v. Massachusetts: *Unhappy Solutions to the Problems of Two-Tier Court Systems*, 8 Colum. Hum. Rts. L. Rev. 285, 302 (1977) (noting the double burden of having to endure the physically and mentally taxing ordeal of trial twice); *see also* Feeley, *supra* note 10, at 15.
151. Colten v. Kentucky, 407 U.S. 104, 114-19 (1972).

152. *E.g.*, Hasler, *supra* note 146, at 85 (there is no better example of a burden chilling the assertion of constitutional right than having to run the risk of heavier sentence in second trial); Stephen J. Schulhofer, *No Job Too Small: Justice Without Bargaining in the Lower Criminal Courts*, 1985 Am. B. Found. Res. J. 519, 525 n.37; Bane, *supra* note 121, at 52 n.202; *see also* Feeley, *supra* note 10, at 154-98 (few trials because judges penalize defendants for the exercise of the right to trial).
153. *See, e.g.*, George E. Dix, *Waiver in Criminal Procedure: A Brief for More Careful Analysis*, 55 Tex. L. Rev. 193, 255 n.223 (1977) (suggesting North Carolina v. Pearce, 395 U.S. 711 (1969), *overruled by* Alabama v. Smith, 490 U.S. 794 (1989), went beyond mere vindictiveness by sentencing authority; the decision's real concern is the potential discouraging effect of the possibility of a more severe sentence on retrial). By way of analogy, see also Bing & Rosenfeld, *supra* note 115, at 91 (use of heavier sentences by judges in lower court for defendants who wish to appeal); Thomas R. McCoy & Michael J. Mirra, *Plea Bargaining as Due Process in Determining Guilt*, 32 Stan. L. Rev. 887 (1980) (arguing for the application of the unconstitutional conditions doctrine in the analogous situation of waiving right to trial and right against self-incrimination for purposes of pleading guilty); Note, *Prosecutorial Vindictiveness in the Criminal Appellate Process: Due Process Protection After* United States v. Goodwin, 81 Mich. L. Rev. 194, 209 (1982) (due process requires a presumption of vindictiveness in the posttrial setting).
154. Patton v. North Carolina, 256 F. Supp. 225, 231 n.7 (W.D.N.C. 1966), *aff'd*, 381 F.2d 636 (4th Cir. 1967) (emphasis omitted) (quoting a letter from a successful petitioner in an earlier case, Perkins v. North Carolina, 234 F. Supp. 333 (W.D.N.C. 1964)), *cert. denied*, 390 U.S. 905 (1968). Neither *Patton* nor *Perkins* involved a de novo court system.
155. *See supra* notes 40-42 and accompanying text. There is some historical support for the argument that the filing of an appeal should suspend the judgment of the court below. Even early in the nation's history, statutes often operated to suspend the judgment of the court below pending resolution of an appeal based on a writ of error if the writ itself did not suspend the judgment. David Rossman, *'Were There No Appeal': The History of Review in American Criminal Courts*, 81 J. Crim. L. & Criminology 518, 544 & n.123 (1990).
156. Colten v. Kentucky, 407 U.S. 104, 119 (1972). Courts may even use incarceration pending appeal to the superior court for the express purpose of deterring requests for new trials. Bing & Rosenfeld, *supra* note 115, at 93-94.
157. Feeley, *supra* note 10, at 10; Kalodner, *supra* note 128, at 329.
158. *See* Feeley, *supra* note 10, at 10 (noting that percentage of persons incarcerated prior to lower court trial was more than twice the percentage incarcerated after trial). The same would be true of the superior court, especially because a de novo system would allow *two* periods of pretrial incarceration.
159. Bing & Rosenfeld, *supra* note 115, at 63.
160. *Id.* at 68-69.
161. *Id.* at 69.
162. *See, e.g., supra* notes 89-94 and accompanying text.
163. North v. Russell, 427 U.S. 328, 335 (1976).
164. In one study of a lower court, more than twenty-five percent of all defendants received no information whatsoever concerning their constitutional rights. In only twenty-two percent of the cases did the court advise defendants individually before the bench. In the remaining cases, defendants received information about constitutional rights in various kinds of group settings. Maureen Mileski, *Courtroom Encounters: An Observation Study of a Lower Criminal Court*, 5 L. & Soc'y Rev. 473, 484-85 (1971); *see also* Sheldon Krantz et al., Right to Counsel in Criminal Cases: The Mandate of Argersinger v. Hamlin 410 (1976) (about one-third of the judges in the Cleveland Municipal "tell the defendant absolutely nothing about right to counsel," with another third making only "half-hearted efforts"); John L. Barkai, *Lower Criminal Courts: The Perils of Procedure*, 69 J. Crim. L. & Criminology 270, 280 (1978).

165. Mileski, *supra* note 164, at 482. Mileski observed that the

> [a]ppraisings of rights in the lower court generally are like so many clerical details performed and reperformed, . . . if [the judge] informs [defendants] at all. He may inform a group in the audience, a smaller group assembled before the bench, a group before the bench with an individual follow-up, or an individual before the bench.

166. *Id.* at 482-85. As Feeley notes,

> [a]rrestees were arraigned in groups and informed of their rights *en masse.* At times the arrestees were not even aware that they are [sic] being addressed. Judges did not always look at them, and even if a judge made an effort to be heard, he could not always be understood over the constant din of the courtroom.

Feeley, *supra* note 10, at 10. *See also* Barkai, *supra* note 164, at 280 (judge's introductory remarks expected to serve as mass notification of various rights for all of those present in the courtroom); Lewis R. Katz, *Municipal Courts—Another Urban Ill*, 20 Case W. Res. L. Rev. 87, 95-96 (1968) (defendants often informed of rights in groups, information given to these groups often inadequate, and all information not repeated for all groups).

167. *See, e.g.*, Schulhofer, *supra* note 152, at 520-21.

168. Argersinger v. Hamlin, 407 U.S. 25 (1972). The findings of Krantz, *supra* note 164, at 410-11, came after *Argersinger*, yet they parallel the pre-*Argersinger* findings of Mileski, *supra* note 164, at 484-85.

169. Mileski, *supra* note 164, at 482-83.

170. *See, e.g.*, *supra* notes 104-06 and accompanying text.

171. *See, e.g.*, *supra* note 56 and accompanying text.

172. The probation forms used by Maryland Department of Parole and Probation, for example, include all of these conditions. Participation in programs is considered a special condition utilized on a case-by-case basis; the other conditions mentioned are standard. *See* Md. Ann. Code art. 27, § 641A (Supp. 1991). The court's authority to impose conditions of all kinds is broad. *Id.*

173. *See supra* notes 40-42 and accompanying text.

174. Colten v. Kentucky, 407 U.S. 104, 118-19 (1972).

175. *See infra* notes 271-74 and accompanying text.

176. *See, e.g.*, Administrative Office of the Courts, Maryland Sentencing Guidelines B-1 (Rev. 1987) [hereinafter Maryland Sentencing Guidelines].

177. In fact, Maryland's guidelines explicitly state that lower court convictions should be counted for purposes of analyzing the defendant's record even before a new superior court trial produces a final resolution. *Id.*

178. Even Feeley, who regards the stigma of a criminal conviction for a petty offense as insignificant to most lower court defendants, concedes that, even if "creating a record of petty criminal offenses may not significantly affect the future of most people who find themselves before the bench, it can have a long-lasting and unpredictable impact on some." Feeley, *supra* note 10, at 242. As the text accompanying note 10 demonstrates, sometimes the defendant need not wait very long to experience these effects.

179. Among authorities recognizing this basic truth are Ludwig v. Massachusetts, 427 U.S. 618, 637 (1976); Mitchell v. W.T. Grant Co., 416 U.S. 600, 606 n.8 (1974); Brown v. Walker, 161 U.S. 591, 605-06 (1896); Hasler, *supra* note 146, at 84; Soto, *supra* note 150, at 302; Bane, *supra* note 121, at 39; Ian O'Connor, *A Young Basketball Star Puts Ordeal Behind Him*, N.Y. Times, Sept. 4, 1991, at B11.

180. *See* 8 U.S.C. § 1251(a)(2) (Supp. II 1990).

181. *See* 8 U.S.C.A. § 1251 (a)(2)(A)(i).

182. *E.g.*, Md. Transp. Code Ann. § 16-205 (1990); N.C. Gen. Stat. §§ 20-17, -17.3, -17.4 (1989); Ohio Rev. Code Ann. § 4511.19 (Baldwin 1987); 75 Pa. Cons. Stat. Ann. §§ 1532, 1542 (1977 & Supp. 1990); Tenn. Code Ann. § 55-50-501 (1988).

183. *See, e.g.*, Drug Enforcement Act of 1990, ch. 410, 1990 Md. Laws 1666 (effective Jan. 1, 1991). For further discussion of the Act, see *Survey: Developments in Maryland Law, 1989–90*, 50 Md. L. Rev. 1029, 1240-51 (1991).
184. *See supra* notes 117-22 and accompanying text.
185. *See supra* note 144 and accompanying text.
186. Hasler, *supra* note 146, at 92-93.
187. For example, in Ashe v. Swensen, 397 U.S. 436 (1970), a charge of armed robbery was resolved in an acquittal; in a second trial, based on the identical conduct of the defendant but with a different victim, the witnesses had become more prosecution oriented, and a conviction resulted.
188. *See, e.g.*, Sandstrom v. Montana, 442 U.S. 510, 521 (1979) (presumption of fact critical to conviction "had the effect of relieving the State of the burden . . . on the critical question of petitioner's state of mind"); *In re* Winship, 397 U.S. 358, 364 (1970) (prosecution must prove every fact necessary beyond a reasonable doubt).
189. Soto, *supra* note 150, at 303; Bane, *supra* note 121, at 41-42. The phrasing of the sentence to which this footnote is appended gives one a clue as to how this might affect a superior court trial; jurors will notice that the defendant has failed to prove her innocence, rather than the other way around.
190. *See* Bane, *supra* note 121, at 41.
191. *See supra* note 139 and accompanying text.
192. *See supra* note 182 and accompanying text.
193. *See supra* notes 155-61 and accompanying text.
194. Ludwig v. Massachusetts, 427 U.S. 618, 626-27 (1976); Colten v. Kentucky, 407 U.S. 104, 118-19 (1972).
195. *Ludwig*, 427 U.S. at 626-27; *Colten*, 407 U.S. at 118-19.
196. *See, e.g.*, Thomas A. Mauet, Fundamentals of Trial Techniques 242 (2d ed. 1988) (impeachment requires that a statement by witness be used in a particular way to be effective).
197. *See supra* notes 132-40 and accompanying text.
198. *See supra* note 21; Katz, *supra* note 166, at 117.
199. Mauet, *supra* note 196, at 242-47.
200. Indeed, rules of criminal procedure may obligate the defense to point out these holes with specificity. *See, e.g.*, Md. R. 4-324, which requires that when the defense makes a motion for judgment of acquittal, "[t]he defendant shall state with particularity all the reasons why the motion should be granted." With this information, the state is well positioned to present a stronger case in the superior court than it did in the lower court.
201. Ludwig v. Massachusetts, 427 U.S. 618, 626 (1976); Colten v. Kentucky, 407 U.S. at 118 (1972).
202. *See* Bane, *supra* note 121, at 53.
203. There is at least one exception. *See* Ala. Code § 12-12-72 (1986 & Supp. 1991) (allowing a defendant the option of a traditional appeal instead of a trial de novo).
204. De novo systems may have *some* claim to legitimacy. In fact, de novo court systems have their origins in the historical development of the American judicial system. *See, e.g.*, Bing & Rosenfeld, *supra* note 115, at 37-40; Roscoe Pound, Criminal Justice in America 119, 153 (1930); Felix Frankfurter & Thomas G. Corcoran, *Petty Federal Offenses and the Constitutional Guarantee of Trial by Jury*, 39 Harv. L. Rev. 917, 933, 935-36 (1926); Rossman, *supra* note 155, at 529, 530, 539-40; Bane, *supra* note 121, at 33-35. These historical justifications, however, are outdated. *See, e.g.*, Bing & Rosenfeld, *supra* note 115, at 39-40; Rossman, *supra* note 155, at 540.
205. *See* Bing & Rosenfeld, *supra* note 115, at 24-27; Robertson, *supra* note 10, at xvii. Note, however, that some of the same problems highlighted in this section of text appear even in misdemeanor and petty offense courts in which judicial review is available. Bing & Rosenfeld, *supra* note 115, at 27-28; Francis Allen, *Small Crimes and Large Problems: Some Constitutional Dimensions*, in Mass Production Justice and the Constitutional Ideal (Charles H. Whitebread ed.,

1970). These authors attribute the problems found in lower courts without the de novo feature to the apathy and lack of influence of the lawyers who practice in these court and the lack of political and economic power of the defendants who pass through them. While apathy and lack of influence and power may cause problems, de novo court systems suffer from the same lack of influence and power compounded by the lack of judicial accountability that is built into the de novo system. Judges in lower courts in de novo court systems are implicitly instructed that regardless of what happens in their courts, no matter who should pass through them, their rulings will never be reviewed.

206. Use of traditional appellate review in de novo systems would, of course, require that the lower court generate a record of the proceedings. *See infra* notes 259-61 and accompanying text.

207. Bing & Rosenfeld, *supra* note 115, at 97.

208. *See* Rossman, *supra* note 155, at 519 (lack of review creates "unacceptable risk of jeopardizing defendants' rights to life and liberty . . . .").

209. Albert W. Alschuler, *Mediation with a Mugger: The Shortage of Adjudicative Services and the Need for a Two-Tier Trial System in Civil Cases*, 99 Harv. L. Rev. 1808, 1850 (1986).

210. Rossman, *supra* note 155, at 518.

211. *Id.*

212. *Id.* at 519.

213. *Id.* at 549.

214. *Id.;* Pound, *supra* note 204, at 153.

215. Rossman, *supra* note 155, at 530, 533.

216. Bing & Rosenfeld, *supra* note 115, at 26-27.

217. *Id.* at 27.

218. *Id.* at 26.

219. Rossman, *supra* note 155, at 519 (without review, "each lower court judge would possess absolute, unreviewable discretion over the legal issues at trial").

220. A recent study of magistrates in England illustrates the point. Howard Parker et al., Unmasking the Magistrates (1989). The study shows that among England's magistrates who preside over juvenile offenses and whose sentencing decisions are not reviewed by higher courts, personal feelings about what the right result should be, including the magistrates' "own moral assessments," received a "surprising" amount of consideration. *Id.* at 114. This led the researchers to conclude that cases were "not decided only on criteria which are open to scrutiny," *id.*, that is, criteria mandated by law. These findings are ironic in light of the Supreme Court's approving reference to the English use of lay judges in North v. Russell, 427 U.S. 328, 333, n.4. (1976).

221. *See, e.g.*, Bing & Rosenfeld, *supra* note 115, at 26; Katz, *supra* note 166, at 91, n.11; *see also* Robertson, *supra* note 10, at xvii.

222. John Paul Ryan & James H. Guterman, *Lawyer versus Nonlawyer Town Justices: An Empirical Footnote to* North v. Russell, 60 Judicature 272 (1977). Ryan and Guterman's article indicates that there is, indeed, cause for concern. Their study indicates that judges without legal training perceive criminal proceedings and the participants therein differently than judges with legal training, resulting in an appreciable tilting of the balance of due process of law away from defendants. *Id.* at 280. Thus, what happens in court may have less to do with the law than the identity of the judge. At the very least, the judge's lack of training influences her perceptions, and thus cannot help but to influence her judgment. *See also* John M. Conley & William M. O'Barr, *Fundamentals of Jurisprudence: An Ethnography of Judicial Decision Making in Informal Courts*, 66 N.C. L. Rev. 467, 504-07 (1988) (decision making in informal courts in civil cases in North Carolina shows great judge-to-judge divergence, which springs from differing "conceptions of the judges's role and the nature of legal decision making").

223. *See, e.g.*, Md. Cts. & Jud. Proc. § 1-601 (1973) ("The District Court of Maryland is established. It is the court of limited jurisdiction created by Article IV, §§ 1 and 41A-411 of the Constitution. It is a court of record and shall have a seal."); Md. Cts. & Jud. Proc. § 12-401(d) (right to trial de novo).

224. Note, *Jury Trials for Misdemeanants in New York City: The Effects of* Baldwin, 7 Columbia J.L. & Soc. Probs. 173, 191-92 (1971). This study showed that use of juries in misdemeanor cases noticeably improved not only the decorum of the cases in which the jury sat, but the decorum in nonjury cases as well. The researchers conclude that this improvement results, at least in part, from the more moderate pace that the presence of the jury forces on the court.

225. Harry Kalven, Jr. & Hans Zeisel, The American Jury 56-59 (1966).

226. *Id.* at 182.

227. *Id.* at 318-23.

228. Duncan v. Louisiana, 391 U.S. 145, 155-56 (1968).

229. *See* National Inst. of Law Enforcement and Criminal Justice, United States Department of Justice, Courts of Limited Jurisdiction: A National Survey v (Karen Markle Knab ed., 1977). This work lists all the administrative regulations for all misdemeanor courts around the country, including lower courts in de novo systems. The entry for Alabama's lower courts is typical: "*Reporting Duty of Court:* All court officials, including judges, clerks, and reporters are required to supply statistics and information on the business of the courts to the chief justice of the supreme court in his capacity as head of the Judicial Conference." *Id.* at 3. Thus, while Alabama's lower court judges receive no review on their performance as jurists, they are required to report to the chief justice on their performance as administrators and processors of cases.

230. *See* Robertson, *supra* note 10, at xviii-xix.

231. *See* John Paul Ryan et al., American Trial Judges—Their Work Styles and Performance 243 (1980) (predicting that judges will be evaluated increasingly on managerial and administrative skills, perhaps to exclusion of "other skills essential to judging"); *see also* National Advisory Comm'n on Criminal Justice Standards and Goals. Courts 171 (1973) [hereinafter National Advisory Comm'n].

232. *See supra* note 10 and accompanying text; Feeley, *supra* note 10, at 5; National Advisory Comm'n, *supra* note 231, at 161; Robertson, *supra* note 10, at xxiii; Kalodner, *supra* note 128, at 320.

233. Feeley, *supra* note 10, at 5; Robertson, *supra* note 10, at xxiii; Kalodner, *supra* note 128, at 320.

234. Feeley, *supra* note 10, at 5; Robertson, *supra* note 10, at xx; Kalodner, *supra* note 128, at 320.

235. National Advisory Comm'n, *supra* note 231, at 161.

236. *See, e.g.*, National Advisory Comm'n, *supra* note 231, at 161 (lower courts inferior not only in name but in "financing, facilities, rehabilitative resources, and quality of personnel"); Katz, *supra* note 166, at 98-100 (noting that defendants are herded through these courts without courtesy or respect); Knab & Lindberg, *supra* note 121, at 417 (noting rapid rate of case processing, incomprehensible proceedings, lack of decorum, delay, and poor scheduling procedures).

237. Alfini, *supra* note 122, at 8; *see also* Barkai, *supra* note 164, at 270-71.

238. Schulhofer, *supra* note 152, at 591.

239. Edward L. Barrett, Jr., *Criminal Justice: The Problem of Mass Production, in* The Courts, the Public, and the Law Explosion 85, 115 (Harry W. James ed., 1965).

240. Robertson, *supra* note 10, at xx.

241. Indeed, the temptation is more than superficial: Some research suggests that judges, among others, prefer many of the unsavory practices that have become identified with lower courts and would retain them regardless of caseload or resources. Knab & Lindberg, *supra* note 121, at 422. Some would argue that this makes abolition of these lower courts the only solution.

242. The history of efforts to improve lower courts should give reformers pause. Professor John Barkai has identified at least three distinct waves of interest in reform of lower criminal courts with and without the de novo feature in the first seventy-five years of this century. Barkai, *supra* note 164, at 273. The results of each set of efforts are dishearteningly similar: lower courts remain

almost untouched by any kind of reform. In Professor Barkai's words, "America's lower criminal courts have proved virtually impervious to any attempt at principled reform. . . . Despite the apparent unanimity of criticism, little or no change in the operation of the lower courts has occurred." *Id.* at 272; *see also* Feeley, *supra* note 10, at 292-97; Robertson, *supra* note 10, at xx-xxii; Schulhofer, *supra* note 152, at 520-21. Given this resistance to change in lower courts in general, a call for the outright abolition of de novo systems seems doomed from the outset. Even suggestions for incremental changes must be tendered with humility.

243. Indeed, states may receive proposals for incremental change in de novo systems with more enthusiasm than the past experience of reformers of general misdemeanor courts would suggest. There are a number of reasons to retain properly reformed de novo systems that would utilize bench trials to try a significant portion of cases, since this would allow the savings of time and resources for states through legitimate means.

First, not all cases require juries. In fact, a jury often is the least desirable factfinder from the defendant's point of view, for example, in cases that center around legal, as opposed to factual, issues. Second, bench trials consume less time and fewer resources than jury trials. Thus, bench trials are bound to result in efficiencies if such trials are properly conducted, and if the sentences received are not so severe as to guarantee requests for new trials. Surprisingly, bench trials do not consume much more time than guilty pleas. Schulhofer, *supra* note 7, at 1084-85. Third, a bench trial can provide an adequate adversarial test of the state's case. Contrary to expectations, many misdemeanor cases present real and complex questions of law and fact. Argersinger v. Hamlin, 407 U.S. 25, 33 (1972); Sibron v. New York, 392 U.S. 40, 52 (1968). Professor Schulhofer's work offers reliable evidence that bench trials can be "genuinely contested, with vigorous efforts by opposing counsel and decisions based on applicable law and the testimony given in court." Schulhofer, *supra* note 7, at 1073, 1086; *see also* Schulhofer, *supra* note 152, at 524, 563-66; Alschuler, *supra* note 6, at 1033-40. Thus, a bench trial need not be regarded as a poor substitute for a "real" trial. Further, bench trials also result in acquittals, or partial acquittals, in a significant percentage of cases. Schulhofer, *supra* note 152, at 566-67. If bench trials are retained in some measure in reformed de novo systems and revitalized by the recommendations of this Article, *see infra* text accompanying notes 244-84, defendants may choose bench trials because they are simpler, cheaper, better suited to individual cases, and do not cost the defendant important rights: the state, for its part, would gain efficiency and economy.

244. *See supra* note 42 and accompanying text. Bing and Rosenfeld recommended that the legislature of Massachusetts make a similar change. Bing & Rosenfeld, *supra* note 115, at 114.

245. Colten v. Kentucky, 407 U.S. 104, 119 (1972). Note that the now defunct Kentucky de novo system that the Supreme Court reviewed in *Colten* had the very feature advocated here. *Id.* at 113.

246. *See supra* note 42 and accompanying text.

247. Whether a person is free or not pending trial has a measurable effect on the person's chances to win an acquittal, or, if convicted, to avoid incarceration. *See supra* notes 158-61 and accompanying text.

248. *See supra* notes 158-61 and accompanying text.

249. *See supra* note 161 and accompanying text.

250. Feeley, *supra* note 10, at 10.

251. *Id.* at 205-06.

252. *See* Bing & Rosenfeld, *supra* note 115, at 114.

253. This review obviously requires that all lower courts generate a record of each proceeding. *See infra* text accompanying notes 259-61; *see also* Katz, *supra* note 166, at 117.

254. Ala. Code § 12-12-72 (1986). Bing and Rosenfeld made a similar suggestion, in the form of enhancing the availability and utility of the writ of error. Bing & Rosenfeld, *supra* note 115, at 112-14.

Alabama's use of such a system means that further research can test these hypotheses.

255. *See supra* notes 244-52 and accompanying text.

256. *See, e.g.*, Alschuler, *supra* note 209, at 1850; *see also supra* note 234 and accompanying text.
257. *See supra* notes 203-23 and accompanying text.
258. *See supra* notes 203-23 and accompanying text.
259. *See supra* notes 196-99 and accompanying text.
260. *See supra* notes 196-99 and accompanying text.
261. *See supra* notes 162-69 and accompanying text.
262. North v. Russell, 427 U.S. 328, 329-30, 332 (1976). One commentator has expressed the hope that *North* did not foreclose any requirement of legal training for judges. Abraham S. Goldstein, *The Search Warrant, the Magistrate, and Judicial Review*, 62 N.Y.U. L. Rev. 1173, 1185 (1987) ("*North* left open the question whether there are issues which, because of their complexity, can be decided only by a judicial official trained in the law.").
263. *See* Alfini, *supra* note 122, at 6-8; Ryan & Guterman, *supra* note 222, at 280; *see also North*, 427 U.S. at 340 n.1 (Stewart, J., dissenting) and studies cited therein; National Advisory Comm'n, *supra* note 231, at 164-66; Kalodner, *supra* note 128, at 324 ("the lawyer's training may give the advantage of impartiality").
264. *See* Colten v. Kentucky, 407 U.S. 104, 118-19 (1972).
265. *See supra* notes 37-39 and accompanying text; *see also* Alfini, *supra* note 122, at 13.
266. Feeley, *supra* note 10, at 242.
267. *Contra* Kalodner, *supra* note 128, at 337-38 (recommending enlargement of lower court jurisdiction to include misdemeanors with the goal of increasing quality of judges and proceedings).
268. Some states advise defendants of their rights at their first appearance before a judicial officer. *E.g.*, Md. Rules Code Ann. 4-213(a)(1), (2), (4) (1991). Certainly, it is feasible to advise a defendant of her right to a new trial *after* the first trial.
269. *E.g.*, Md. R. Code Ann. 4-202(a), 4-213(a)(1) (1991).
270. *See* Mileski, *supra* note 164, at 482-83.
271. States with sentencing guidelines include Maryland, Maryland Sentencing Guidelines, *supra* note 176; Minnesota, Minn. Stat. Ann. § 244.App (West Supp. 1992); Pennsylvania, 204 Pa. Code § 303.1 (1988), *reprinted in* 42 Pa. Const. Stat. Ann. § 9721 (Supp. 1991); and Utah, Utah Comm'n on Criminal and Juvenile Justice, Utah Sentence and Release Guidelines (1986).
272. Sentencing Guidelines for United States Courts, 18 U.S.C.S. app. A (Law. Co-op. 1991). The guidelines resulted from the Sentencing Reform Act of 1984, 18 U.S.C. §§ 3551-742. 28 U.S.C. §§ 991-998 (1988).
273. Purposes range from the explicit control of prison populations, Rodgers, *supra* note 116, at 311, 340-41 (urging the manipulation of Utah's sentencing guidelines to control the number of the state's inmates), to the elimination of sentencing disparities.
274. *E.g.*, Maryland Sentencing Guidelines, *supra* note 176, at 4.
275. This could be done by averaging data from superior court sentencing for the same types of crimes and offenders that appear in lower courts. For states with guidelines in place in the superior court, such as Maryland, lower courts simply could begin to use the superior court guidelines, provided that the superior court guidelines include the offenses that the lower court handles. *See* Maryland Sentencing Guidelines, *supra* note 176.
276. Uniformity is a goal shared by many commentators who have considered the sentencing process. *See, e.g.*, Marvin E. Frankel, Criminal Sentences: Law Without Order 3-8 (1972) (the arbitrariness of the then-current federal sentencing process led to such great and inexplicable disparities that they violate constitutional guarantees of due process of law); William F. Weld, *Foreward* to Criminal Div., U.S. Dep't of Justice, Prosecutors Handbook on Sentencing Guidelines and Other Provisions of the Sentencing Reform Act of 1984, at i (1987) (federal guidelines sought to eliminate sentence disparities and uncertainty).

277. Such a practice runs contrary to the idea of a freely available new trial in the superior court, in which the actions of the lower court have no relevance. Yet this practice exists and in some jurisdictions flourishes. Interview with Assistant Public Defender Mark J. Kappelhoff, Montgomery County, Maryland, in Washington, D.C. (July 25, 1991) (confirming the common use of this technique). One may take a cynical view and assert that superior court judges simply want to discourage appeals to cut down on institutional and personal workloads. It may also be the case, however, that the practice stems from respect for fellow judges, or that some superior court judges began judicial careers in the lower court. Use of sentencing guidelines in the manner suggested here means that when superior court judges impose the same or very similar sentences on defendants who were sentenced in the lower court, those sentences will already be consistent with the practices of judges of the superior court, who have legal training and are consistently subjected to oversight through the traditional appellate process.
278. *E.g.*, Rodgers, *supra* note 116, at 338 ("Existing sentencing commission systems demonstrate that the sentencing commission model cannot be effective unless the guidelines are binding . . . .") and other materials cited therein.
279. *See id.*
280. *See supra* notes 224-28 and accompanying text.
281. Ludwig v. Massachusetts, 427 U.S. 618, 635 (1976) (Stevens, J., dissenting) ("[W]hy does the [state] insist on the *requirement* that the defendant must submit to the first trial? . . . [T]he very purpose of the requirement is to discourage jury trials by placing a burden on the exercise of the constitutional right."); *see also* Bane, *supra* note 121, at 59.
282. *See, e.g.*, Md. Cts. & Jud. Proc. § 4-302(e) (1989).
283. Abuse also could take the form of using a request for a jury trial as a delaying tactic to discourage witnesses, to cause their memories to become stale, and to put off the day of reckoning. *See supra* notes 117-22 and accompanying text.
284. *See, e.g.*, Herb Cohen, You Can Negotiate Anything 101-13 (1982).

2

Drug Diversion Courts: Are They Needed and Will They Succeed in Breaking the Cycle of Drug-Related Crime?

James R. Brown

I. INTRODUCTION

Contemporary concerns about the impact of drugs in our society result in large measure from the increases in crime and violence relating to drug use.[1] For the past three decades, increases in crime rates provided ample reason for Americans to conclude that crime in the United States has been largely uncontrollable.[2] Understandably, they looked to the causes of crime in search of a solution. In the 1960s, Americans first looked at "root causes" of crime, including poverty, unemployment, and illiteracy.[3] The publicity surrounding the violence of drug-related crime and the fear of crack cocaine, however, soon forced public attention to shift to a new focus.[4] The public became fixated upon the nexus between crime and drugs. Once it became apparent that this relationship existed, Americans demanded that their government concentrate efforts to reduce drug-related crime by dealing with drug-abusing criminals.[5] Eradicating drug-related crime proved to be a daunting task for officials that governed a society that has only 4.5% of the world's population[6] but consumes 60% of the illicit drugs.[7]

The consequences of the "war on drugs"[8] fell most heavily on the nation's criminal justice system, especially on the courts and prisons.[9] Faced with unprecedented increases in incarceration rates of drug offenders, prisons became overcrowded. Recognizing that the traditional approach of incarcerating nonviolent drug offenders failed to reduce drug-related crime, innovative criminal justice professionals determined that, in order to break the cycle of drugs and crime, drug abusers must receive intensive, supervised treatment.[10] Traditionally, this type of treatment was not available to incarcerated drug abusers.[11]

One exciting and innovative approach to addressing drug-related crime has been the establishment of "drug diversion courts."[12] These courts differ from traditional trial courts[13] in that their primary focus is to keep nonviolent, drug-abusing offenders out of prison and in treatment programs mandated and monitored by the courts.[14] If

Reprinted by permission of the *New England Journal on Criminal and Civil Confinement* from vol. 23 (1997), pp. 63-99.

drug courts prove successful, both the nation's criminal justice system and American society will encounter far-reaching benefits.

Part II of this Note discusses the close nexus between drug abuse and crime. Violent crime, especially murder and gang-related crimes, while only a small percentage of all felonies, has a major influence on the public's perception of drug abuse and crime. Given this close nexus, the public understandably demanded that government reduce crime by controlling the drug-abusing criminal.

The government responded aggressively to the demand that it punish drug offenders.[15] Part III describes the increase in drug-related arrests, convictions, and sentence lengths of drug offenders. These aggressive strategies have had a disproportionate negative impact on minorities and women.[16]

Part IV examines the consequences of increased numbers of drug offenders in the criminal justice system. The two most significant consequences are the overcrowding of prisons and the failure to control recidivism rates. Prison overcrowding has many negative consequences for the entire criminal justice system.[17]

The importance of treatment in reducing drug dependency is discussed in Part V. Due to prison overcrowding and other factors, however, effective treatment is not available to most incarcerated drug abusers.[18] This Note discusses why the incarceration of nonviolent drug offenders has not been successful in reducing drug-related criminal activities.

Part VI details the objectives and general structure of drug diversion courts. The most important dimension of drug courts is the use of court power to direct nonviolent drug offenders to intensive court monitored treatment in lieu of incarceration.[19] By using a combination of sanctions and incentives, judges carefully direct defendants toward the ultimate goal of freeing drug-abusing criminals from the chains of substance abuse.[20]

Part VII then describes two operating drug courts. The Miami drug court is the nation's oldest, while the Boston court is the most recent. This Note will discuss their similarities and differences and explain why each court is important to future development of drug diversion courts.

The past fifteen years have witnessed a great evolution in the criminal justice system. Today, the system has arrived, albeit reluctantly, at an important threshold. If the system is to endure as an effective force for improving society, it must be willing to support innovations like drug diversion courts.

II. THE NEXUS BETWEEN DRUGS AND CRIME

In the United States, drugs and crime are closely related.[21] Prior to the mid-1980s, determining the magnitude of drug use by criminals was primarily achieved through information provided by the offenders themselves.[22] Data from drug-testing programs, implemented in the past decade, however, has revealed the true dimensions of the relationship between drugs and criminals.[23]

A. The Impact of Drug Users Upon American Crime

Given the economic pressures resulting from the need to purchase addictive drugs, it is not surprising that an estimated 17% of state prison inmates reported that they committed their offenses to obtain funds for drug purchases.[24] Similarly, studies demonstrate conclusively that many convicted criminals, regardless of their crime, were under the influence of drugs at the time of the crime.[25] Up to 50% of prison inmates reported using drugs in the month before the offense.[26]

The percentage of drug use by criminals is higher in urban areas.[27] The National Institute of Justice reported that in sampled urban areas, up to 82% of arrestees tested positive for drug use at the time of their criminal activity.[28] These included criminals involved in both drug and nondrug offenses.[29] In another sampled population, drug-testing showed that 80% of the 400 subjects booked for various crimes used cocaine.[30]

"Involvement with substance abuse has been found to accelerate the level of criminal activity."[31] In California, prison and jail inmates addicted to heroin committed up to fifteen times as many robberies and twenty times more burglaries as those who did not use drugs.[32] Drugs also contribute to many domestic problems including spousal and child abuse.[33]

While not related directly to crime, one can see an indication of the widespread use of illicit drugs in hospital emergency room reports of annual increases in drug-related admissions.[34] From 1990 to 1993, emergency room reports indicated that drug-related admissions increased from 635,460 to 808,233.[35]

It is important that society approach the relationship between crime and drugs cautiously.[36] There is little contention with the argument that many factors other than drugs influence criminals.[37] As discussed throughout this section, however, it is apparent that drugs play a major role in the lives of many criminals and serve as the primary motivation for their ongoing criminal activities.[38] While studies show that drug abuse in both adults and youths peaked during the 1980s, the number of abusers is still daunting.[39] "In 1993, an estimated 4,530,000 persons used cocaine, including crack cocaine, at least once in the previous year."[40]

B. Drug-Trafficking and Violent Crime

Criminal justice experts often associate drug-trafficking with violent crime.[41] The publicity generated by drug-related homicides often reinforces the public's perception of the seriousness of drug-related crime.[42] While the number of homicides is small compared to other crimes, the impact on public perception is large. Homicides often involve drugs or drug-trafficking.[43] Homicides that occur during the commission of felony narcotics offenses comprise 5.6% of all homicides.[44] In 7% of homicides, both victims and killers were at the scene because of a drug relationship; of homicide victims, 12% were "involved with their killer in a drug relationship."[45]

C. Drugs, Gangs, and Youth

There also exists a close relationship between gangs and drugs. Approximately 6% of state prison inmates belonged to gangs.[46] Among inmates who were gang members, 81% reported previous drug abuse and 69% said they manufactured or sold drugs.[47] School age youths also are likely to be confronted with the presence of illicit drugs.[48] In 1992, 70% of public school students reported that drugs were available at their school.[49] The fact that 15% of students aged twelve to nineteen reported the presence of gangs at their school[50] is even more troubling to a society concerned about the exposure of school aged children to illicit drugs. For example, one sample of urban areas reported that 54% of juvenile arrestees tested positive for at least one drug.[51] In a two year period, a sample of juveniles booked for all crimes and who tested positive for cocaine use increased from 28% to 71%.[52]

III. AGGRESSIVE GOVERNMENT RESPONSE TO THE DRUG CRISIS

A. Public Opinion and the War on Drugs

During the 1980s, Americans became convinced that illicit drug abuse represented a grave threat to their well-being.[53] The wanton brutality associated with illicit drug-trafficking, "continual media exposure of the link between drugs and crime, the dramatic increas[e] in the number of drug arrests, and the political emphasis on the war on drugs, suggested to the public that drug use and related crime remained uncontrollable."[54] In 1985, only 2% of Americans responding to a poll indicated that drug abuse was the most important problem facing this country.[55] By 1989, this percentage increased to 63%.[56] Government officials at all levels followed this trend closely, and responded with the so-called war on drugs.

B. The War on Crime

In 1967, the federal government began a war on crime.[57] This war has taken two forms. The "war on poverty" (1967–1980) attacked the economic and social root causes of crime.[58] Programs emphasized offender rehabilitation, constitutional rights, and humane treatment of those falling outside the law.[59] In 1980, the focus of the campaign changed[60] to targeting criminals by focusing upon detection, arrest, and incarceration.[61] In response to a growing retributive public mood, criminal justice agencies of all levels engineered and implemented an intensive and aggressive campaign to combat both crime and criminals associated with drug abuse.[62] Strategies to accomplish the war on drugs involved law enforcement agencies attacking the supply of drugs, dramatically increasing the arrest and conviction of drug offenders, sending more drug offenders to jail for longer sentences, and building prisons at a record pace.[63]

C. Funding the War on Drugs

The federal government funded the attack on drug abuse with a massive infusion of federal dollars.[64] In 1981, the total drug enforcement budget was $1.5 billion; by fiscal year 1995, this budget had grown to $13.1 billion.[65] In the early Reagan administration, federal spending for drug enforcement and interdiction jumped 50%.[66] President Bush continued to emphasize control of the drug supply by allocating 70% of the federal drug budget to this objective.[67] "Resources for domestic law enforcement, the largest component of the National Drug Control Budget, increase[d] 9.3% in [fiscal year] 1997 (from $7.6 billion in [fiscal year] 1996 to $8.3 billion in [fiscal year] 1997)."[68]

D. The Increase in Arrests of Drug Offenders

Assuming that arrest and incarceration rates of drug abusers are a proper gauge, the war on drugs has been a major success.[69] Beginning in the 1980s, the number of drug arrests increased dramatically.[70] In 1993, 1,126,300 arrests were made for drug abuse violations,[71] compared to 661,400 in 1983.[72] The magnitude of over one million drug arrests becomes apparent when compared to the 38,420 arrests for forcible rape and 23,400 arrests for murder during 1993.[73]

Drug-related arrests changed the criminal justice system in less than a decade.[74] As the war on drugs gained momentum, increases in drug arrests occurred even though drug use in the general population declined.[75] Police departments devoted considerable resources to accomplish this dramatic increase in drug-related arrests.[76] For example, the majority of law enforcement agencies serving 50,000 or more citizens established special drug enforcement units.[77]

Increases in the arrests of drug abusers did not occur in a vacuum. Each arrest had an impact on police, courts, and prisons. The following sections will discuss this impact.

E. The Increase in Convictions of Drug Offenders

Courts responded to increased arrests by convicting more drug offenders.[78] From 1985 to 1992, the number of drug defendants convicted in federal courts increased 82%.[79] This compared to an increase of 31% for violent offenders.[80] Given the highly addictive nature of heroin and cocaine, it is not surprising that the majority of drug defendants were involved with these drugs.[81] State courts convicted 280,231 individuals of drug offenses during one twelve-month period.[82] Among all categories of convicted felons, drug traffickers experienced the highest increase in the rate of convictions.[83] In 1992, state courts convicted 170,806 drug traffickers, an increase of 116% from 1986.[84]

F. The Increase in Incarceration Rates of Convicted Drug Offenders

Courts are sending more convicted drug offenders to prison.[85] In the federal system, courts incarcerated 88% of convicted drug offenders in 1992, compared to 76% in 1985.[86] From 1980 to 1992, the rate at which drug offenders were sent to state prison rose from nineteen per thousand adult arrests to 104 per thousand.[87]

In 1980, 6.8% of new court commitments to state prisons were for drug offenses.[88] The percentage increased to 30% in 1992.[89] If the total number of defendants before the state court systems in this period had remained constant, this percentage change would be dramatic. Given that the number of court commitments for all crimes increased from 159,286 in 1980 to 480,675 in 1992,[90] however, the total number of drug-related commitments had an even greater impact on an already troubled system.

G. The Increase in Prison Term Lengths for Convicted Drug Offenders

In addition to more arrests for drug violations and increased conviction and incarceration rates, courts are sentencing drug felons to longer terms of incarceration.[91] In federal courts, the average length of sentences for drug felons increased from forty-seven months in 1980 to eighty-two months in 1992.[92] In the same period, however, the average sentences for violent offenders decreased from 125.4 months to 88.5 months.[93] The average percentage of the sentence actually served by drug offenders also increased.[94] In state courts, the average maximum drug offense sentence to state prison was sixty-four months for first time offenders and seventy-two months for criminals with previous convictions.[95]

H. The Effect of the War on Drugs on Minorities and Women

The war on drugs disproportionately impacts African-Americans,[96] Latinos,[97] and women.[98] While the total number of federal and state prisoners serving sentences of more than a year increased by over 616,292 (195%) between 1980 and 1993,[99] this increase was not proportional to the racial or gender make-up of the prison population in 1980, nor to the general population changes of the United States from 1980 to 1993.[100] From 1980 to 1993, the number of white males in prison grew 163%, while the number of black males increased by 217%.[101] By the end of 1993, black males comprised 50.8% of all federal and state incarcerated prisoners.[102] In New York State, young Latino men are eleven times more likely to go to jail than white males, and an estimated 6% of all young Latino men are incarcerated.[103] The minority male prison population is comprised mostly of unemployed and undereducated offenders.[104]

Drug-abusing women of all races constitute the fastest growing segment of incarcerations.[105] The incarceration rate of black women, compared to white women, is even more disturbing.[106] The nexus between these increases and drug abuse is indisputable.[107] In a two year period, the percentage of the female inmate population incarcerated for drug offenses increased from 42% to 66.1% of the total female prison population.[108]

The profile of female drug offenders raises serious questions as to the value of incarceration.[109] Many drug-abusing women suffer from physical or mental illness,[110] and over half are victims of physical abuse.[111] Most drug-abusing women are likely to have children already.[112] Perhaps the greatest tragedy is the frequency with which their children become drug abusers, thus perpetuating the problems from one generation to another.[113] The percentage of women incarcerated for nonviolent crimes is growing at a faster rate than that of nonviolent males.[114]

Regardless of the crime, the majority of females arrested test positive for drugs.[115] This fact is not surprising since a high proportion of crimes committed by women are to support their habits.[116] Treatment for incarcerated female drug abusers is an area of particular concern because often it is developed as an afterthought.[117] Treatment is usually limited in both intensity and duration.[118]

While states are becoming more concerned about providing treatment for incarcerated female drug abusers, increases in programming have failed to reduce the difference between those who need services and those who actually receive treatment.[119] Overcrowding in prisons, combined with the dramatic increase in drug-abusing female inmates, is cause for significant alarm. Given the importance of women in single parent households and the nonviolent nature of their crimes, an alternative response to traditional incarceration has great potential for an immediate impact. One such alternative is the drug diversion courts discussed in Part VI.

IV. THE CONSEQUENCES OF INCREASED NUMBERS OF DRUG OFFENDERS IN THE PRISON SYSTEM

The consequences of arresting, convicting, and sentencing more drug offenders has had a dramatic negative effect on the nation's prison system.[120] The increase in drug offenders admitted to prison accounted for nearly 46% of the total growth in new court commitments.[121] For example, in Florida, prison admissions for drug offenders increased by 942% in eight years,[122] while during the past decade, the number of drug offenders in Massachusetts state prisons tripled.[123] In 1980, drug offenders accounted for 25% of inmates sentenced to federal prisons.[124] By 1993, this figure rose to 61%.[125] Drug offenders constituted an estimated 21% of state prison inmates in 1991, up from 9% in 1986.[126]

A. Prison Overcrowding

Sending more drug offenders to prison has caused the most serious prison overcrowding in American penal history.[127] This overcrowding has resulted in more than just unpleasantness to inmates. Rather, it has significantly altered sentencing for violent offenders, diverted funds for corrections away from other needs, and most importantly, failed to stem the crime wave associated with drug abuse.[128]

The United States is currently in the midst of the longest and most intense prison population explosion ever.[129] The total prison population has increased from 329,821 in state and federal prisons in 1980, to 1,053,738 in 1994.[130] Texas' prison population has the distinction of having the nation's largest annual increase at 28.5%.[131] Forty-one states are operating at or above their capacity,[132] while the federal system is operating at 125% of capacity.[133]

This overcrowding has serious consequences, many of which are not obvious to the general public. When state prisons become crowded, prisoners are often held in local jails.[134] In 1994, states housed 48,949 prisoners originally sentenced to state prisons in local and county jails.[135] This has resulted in states either releasing offenders originally sentenced to jails early, or not incarcerating them at all in order to provide room for state prison inmates.

B. Prison Health Issues Are Often Related to Drug Abuse

The influx of drug offenders has affected the prison system in ways beyond that which population figures indicate. A substantial number of drug offenders in state prisons were tested for HIV, and 3.2% (78,729) were HIV-positive.[136] Of drug offenders who used needles to inject drugs, 4.9% tested HIV-positive, while approximately 15% of drug offenders who shared needles also tested HIV-positive.[137] Since AIDS victims have a higher incidence of health problems, and drug users have a higher incidence of AIDS, the link between drugs and prison health costs is apparent. The prison hospital system is collapsing under the pressure of treating more prisoners with serious health problems.[138] Keeping nonviolent drug offenders out of jail would ameliorate a significant portion of this crisis. The justice system must seek alternatives to keep nonviolent drug abusers out of the prison system. One answer is the drug diversion courts discussed in Part VI.

C. Incarceration of Drug Offenders Has Not Improved Crime or Recidivism Rates

After spending billions of dollars on law enforcement,[139] doubling the number of arrests and incarcerations,[140] and building prisons at a record pace,[141] the system has failed to decrease the level of drug-related crime.[142] Placing people in jail at increasing rates has had little long-term effect on the levels of crime.[143] In fact, wholesale incarceration may actually increase recidivism and corresponding crime rates.[144] Cocaine abusers will be arrested an average of 1.5 times per year when they are not incarcerated.[145] Among drug offenders rearrested for a drug offense, police arrested 21% within one year after release from prison.[146] In the 1980s, California's prison population increased by a staggering 450% with no apparent effect on the number of crimes.[147] Considering that prisons still primarily emphasize security over rehabilitation, the reason for this increase becomes obvious.[148]

High recidivism among drug abusers results from the view that prisons serve to incapacitate and punish, and accordingly, rarely function as effective treatment centers.[149] It is indisputable that a person in prison will not, at least temporarily, commit crimes against society. It is clear, however, that when they return to society, there is a high likelihood they will return to illicit drug use, crime, arrest, and finally reincarceration. When they return to illegal activity, the amount of crime caused by individual drug abusers is staggering.[150]

The nation's correctional institutions have failed society in at least one way. They have failed to provide nonviolent prisoners who suffer from substance abuse problems an experience that could help them overcome the obstacles that initially led them to prison.[151] Parolees depart from their prison experience with no marketable skills, little formal education, and most likely, an existing drug problem.

There has been increased recognition that the construction of additional jails that serve only to incapacitate drug offenders has not provided an effective, economical method to reduce the social and economic costs of drug-related crime.[152] In large measure, this failure is understandable given the increased influx of drug-abusing felons into prisons. It is difficult to criticize officials confronted by prisons so overcrowded that, in meeting the daily challenges of their systems, they are unable to focus on long-term treatment programs.

Americans need not believe, however, that the incarceration of drug traffickers and violent drug offenders should be considered a failure since many Americans support the continuation of an aggressive campaign to incarcerate the most dangerous members of our society.[153] It is apparent, however, that incarcerating drug abusers who have committed nonviolent crimes has little likelihood of successfully reducing drug-related crime patterns.[154] Americans concerned about drug-related crime need to consider two approaches. The first is to continue to support efforts to arrest, convict, and incarcerate violent criminals and drug traffickers. The second is to seek alternatives to the incarceration of nonviolent, drug-abusing criminals who, time and time again, will return to crime unless they eliminate their drug dependency. The system must provide intensive treatment that has a higher potential of long-term success when compared to traditional methods of treatment in prisons and jails.

Illicit drug abuse remains the cause of many economic and social problems.[155] Drug abuse has cost over $300 billion and as many as 375,000 babies are born exposed to the harmful effects of their mother's drug habits.[156] These are just two examples of the magnitude of the drug problem. Rather than incarceration, society must realize that keeping nonviolent drug abusers out of jail and placing them into effective treatment programs is both cost-effective and more likely to succeed than traditional approaches.

D. Violent Felons Are Often the Undeserving Beneficiaries of Incarcerating Nonviolent Drug Offenders

Incarcerating increasing numbers of drug offenders has led to keeping other offenders, many of whom may be violent, out of jail or reducing the traditional length of time served. Prison overcrowding has had a direct result on the percentage of violent offenders in prisons and on the length of time they serve.[157] In 1980, violent offenders comprised 48.2% of new commitments to state prisons, but decreased to 28.5% by 1992.[158] A Massachusetts survey found that criminals sent to prison for armed robbery, armed assault, or rape will serve substantially less time than those sentenced for the same crimes a decade earlier.[159] This can be attributed directly to significant overcrowding in Massachusetts prisons.[160] In the federal system, the length of time served for violent offenses decreased, while the time served for drug offenses increased.[161] This is occurring when the fastest growing segment of inmates is first time offenders.[162]

E. Building Prisons

The most visible response to increased numbers of convicted felons has been the construction of new prisons.[163] "New York State opened twenty-seven prisons between 1983 and 1990."[164] Texas alone has 155,000 prison beds. The cost to build a prison bed ranges from \$42,000 to \$100,000.[165] To house an inmate costs an average of \$23,000 annually.[166] Nationally, the total cost of incarceration exceeds \$20 billion.[167] These costs have not been without sacrifice to other segments of our society. In 1990, California, the nation's largest prison system at the time, added more beds than any other jurisdiction, while cutting educational spending by \$2 billion.[168]

F. Drug Cases Have Heavily Burdened the Court System

The volume of criminals who have committed a drug-related crime or who have a drug abuse problem has placed unprecedented workload increases on trial courts.[169] In every court system in the United States, the drug case volume has increased substantially.[170] The Cook County Illinois court system "is the largest single location felony trial court system in the United States."[171] Consistent with courts nationwide, it was "inundated with drug cases, which pushed judges' caseloads to unmanageable levels."[172] Judges have become increasingly alarmed at the impact of drug-related suspects on the judicial system.[173] The negative impact on courts includes: "(1) the movement of resources to drug cases and away from other court priorities . . . ; (2) a dramatic alteration of traditional plea bargaining polices; (3) increased prosecutorial power; (4) escalation of already serious jail overcrowding; and (5) diminished credibility of the justice system among Americans."[174]

V. TREATMENT

While the war on drugs focussed heavily on reducing the supply of drugs and incapacitating drug offenders, there has been increased awareness that building additional prisons has provided neither an effective nor economical solution to the massive drug problem.[175] States have initiated several approaches to alleviate the burden of drug addicts on prisons. These include house arrest, intensive probation supervision, and correctional treatment programs.[176]

There has been a significant increase in funding for the treatment of drug offenders.[177] This reflects the general acceptance that treatment is more effective than incarceration.[178] Studies consistently demonstrate that, without treatment, drug offenders will likely return to drugs and crime.[179] "Without treatment, 90% of incarcerated drug offenders will renew a career of addiction and crime within three years of release. . . ."[180]

When evaluating prison treatment programs, there are two important considerations. First, it is important to recognize that to achieve even modest success there must be intensive treatment.[181] Studies have proven that intensive treatment reduces recidivism rates.[182] But, "the effectiveness of many surveyed programs that provide treatment of relatively short duration to a population with multiple needs, particularly programs that provide only a few hours per week is questionable."[183] Second, given the unprecedented increase in inmates with drug abuse problems, even when there is considerable allocation of resources, it has only met a small percentage of the need.[184] Even as the federal government doubled treatment funding between 1988 and 1993, treatment efforts failed to reach at-risk populations, including inmates, and failed to reduce the level of drug-related crime.[185]

Recognizing the need for effective treatment and confronted with a lack of alternatives, prisons have attempted to provide substance abuse treatment.[186] In 1979, approximately 4% of prison inmates received substance abuse treatment.[187] By 1987, the percentage increased to 11%.[188] While this increase is an encouraging trend indicating augmented and improved substance abuse treatment, it has not remotely addressed the total need.[189] A further complication is the wide disparity of treatment plans among local and county jails, which are least likely to have effective drug abuse treatment programs.[190]

Given the magnitude of the need combined with the limits on resources, it is likely that prison systems cannot provide intensive treatment programs to those who need them. The criminal justice system has failed to provide intensive drug abuse treatment. This has resulted in higher recidivism rates among drug abusers and has led to the inability of prisons to provide effective treatment programs. Therefore, the goal of the criminal justice system should be to keep nonviolent drug offenders out of prison and in effective treatment programs. If alternatives to incarceration include intensive treatment, the opportunity to reduce drug-related crime has a greater chance of success than incarceration.

VI. DRUG DIVERSION COURTS

A. The Evolution of Drug Diversion Courts

Many factors contributed to the origin of drug diversion courts.[191] The primary impetus for their development, however, "grew out of a sense of frustration that law enforcement and imprisonment policies were not having the impact on drug supply or demand that proponents of the war against drugs of the 1980s had hoped for."[192]

After almost two decades of using the traditional methods of arrest and incarceration with little likelihood of effective treatment, the American criminal justice system was faced with a multitude of problems. These problems included: unprecedented drug-related crime,[193] staggering increases in the number of drug offenders,[194] high rates of incarceration of first-time nonviolent offenders,[195] prison overcrowding,[196] high recidivism rates of drug abusers,[197] increased workloads on the courts,[198] an acceptance that most treatment approaches have failed to respond to the drug problems of incarcerated prisoners,[199] the existence of drug treatment plans that do work and can only meet a small percentage of the need,[200] a disproportionate impact on minorities and women,[201] and continuing public pressure to do something about drug-related crime.[202]

Criminal justice professionals, especially experienced members of the judiciary, searched for solutions that would be cost-effective, politically acceptable, and successful in reducing illicit drug abuse.[203] Beginning in the late 1980s, there was an "unprecedented experimentation among state courts with incorporating drug treatment programs into the adjudication process."[204] One result of this experimentation has been the establishment of treatment-based drug diversion courts.

B. Goals of Drug Diversion Courts

1. *Treatment Goals*

Given the complexity and difficulty of dealing with long-term drug addictions, drug court treatment objectives are designed to be realistic. The most important goals are: to improve the rate of abstention among drug abusers compared with traditional approaches; to improve the capabilities of drug court clients to function in society; to create the situation in which, when relapses occur, they occur with less frequency and with longer periods of sobriety; and, to provide clients with employment, education, and life skills.[205]

2. *Criminal Justice Goals*

If the system realizes the treatment goals outlined above, the achievement of the general objectives of the criminal justice system, especially prisons and courts, will have a higher likelihood of success. These general goals are: to reduce the level of criminal activity related to drug abuse; to reduce recidivism rates of drug offenders; to reduce the impact on the nation's prisons and jails by reducing the percentage of nonviolent drug offenders incarcerated; to reduce the number of offenders failing to appear for trials, sentencing, and probation supervision; to improve the caseload of the trial courts; and, to achieve meaningful cost savings within the entire criminal justice system.[206]

C. Major Characteristics of Drug Diversion Courts

Treatment-based courts "are as varied as the jurisdictions in which they exist."[207] The ultimate structure of each court depends on the "character of a jurisdiction," state laws, financial and other available resources, and individual characteristics of each court's judges and personnel.[208] "Although they vary greatly in operation, there are elements which are common to all treatment-based drug courts which contribute to their success."[209]

Drug diversion courts are different from traditional trial courts.[210] Their uniqueness stems from the nonadversarial nature of the proceedings and the active participation of the judge.[211] Another distinguishing feature is the level of support and willing participation of prosecutors, defense attorneys, probation departments, and treatment providers.[212]

Drug diversion courts have three major characteristics. First, they treat offenders with illicit drug abuse problems differently from traditional courts by focusing on treatment rather than punishment. Second, clients[213] who successfully complete a drug court treatment program will likely have their current charges dismissed or mitigated in some other way. Finally, the courts use "*judicial* authority (rather than a probation officer's) to directly supervise and support the . . . [client's] performance in treatment and rehabilitation programs."[214]

1. The Role of the Judiciary in "Drug Courts"

The establishment of drug diversion courts required judges to view themselves in a new role.

> Traditionally, judges have played the passive role of objective, impartial referee, only reluctantly stepping beyond the boundaries of their own courtroom. However, when the fair and effective administration of justice is threatened (as [by] . . . an exploding drug problem), the court has the responsibility to come forward and become a leader and active participant in the organization and implementation of coordinated criminal justice and community-wide drug control efforts.[215]

Unlike a traditional trial court judge, drug offenders may appear before the drug diversion court judge twenty to thirty times during the course of the treatment plan.[216] Judges must deal both with successes and failures, often with the same client, and must understand the delicate balance that exists between punishment and treatment.[217] Often receiving conflicting advice, judges must make rapid decisions about sanctions, suspensions from the program, or incarcerations.[218] Miami's drug court justice is "fatherly, supportive, sarcastic, or stern" as the case requires.[219] The Boston drug court's judge makes a special effort to reward and encourage clients who give up their drug abuse even for a short time.[220]

The judge does more than just place a drug offender into a program for treatment.[221] His or her involvement includes an active hands-on approach.[222] The client's treatment plan carries the full authority of the judge.[223]

2. *Collaboration Among Criminal Justice Agencies*

Drug court judges are actively involved with treatment providers, court administrators, and probation officers.[224] Dealing with the conflicts among these diverse groups requires both the appropriate judicial temperament, strong interpersonal skills, and significant administrative abilities.

Judges must also understand the importance of community involvement. The judge is often the most visible component of the drug court and his or her participation is critical to the flow of information into the community. Generally, the public's desire is to keep drug offenders incarcerated, and it may view skeptically any program that works to keep drug felons in the community. Additionally, the drug court cannot achieve any of its goals without the successful integration of education, housing, vocational training, and most importantly, employment counseling and job placement.[225] The drug court judge, or his or her delegates, represent the critical link to these vital components of a comprehensive and long-term treatment program.[226]

3. *Selection of "Clients" for Participation in Drug Court Programs*

One critical component of all drug diversion programs is the identification of appropriate candidates. Almost all drug courts seek offenders with no history of violent behavior.[227] Treatment-oriented drug courts usually will not accept any type of drug-trafficking offender.[228] Unfortunately, many drug abusers also are involved in minor drug transactions; however, this type of "drug selling" may not necessarily bar participation in a program.[229] Almost all offenders accepted for participation will have a criminal record.[230]

A major concern of drug courts must be public safety.[231] It is impossible to identify specific drug offenders as being likely to commit another crime while in a treatment program.[232] If a client is arrested for another crime, dismissal from the drug court program is likely.[233]

Drug treatment will best succeed if it begins when the "defendant is most motivated."[234] Drug felons will likely respond positively to intervention when they are in crisis. This often "occurs at arrest and continues to a lesser extent through the initial court appearance."[235]

To have the greatest chance of success, courts must identify the drug offender and place him or her into the treatment program as soon after arrest as possible. To locate appropriate candidates, an initial screening must be performed soon after arrest.[236] The trial court's probation department often coordinates the screening process.[237] When the court identifies a nonviolent offender, the defendant and his or her attorney must have the options described.[238] The drug court carefully explains the components of the system to candidates.[239]

While the threat of incarceration is a powerful weapon used to induce drug offenders into an intensive treatment program, defense attorneys may not be so fast to endorse this entry.[240] Defense attorneys may object to a client's waiving a right to a speedy trial, anticipating the client will "fail" the program.[241] Additionally, defense attorneys may recognize that the drug court program may involve, from their perspective, "a more onerous disposition in terms of the length of time [the client] is subject to court control."[242] This may pose a dilemma for defense counsel who believe that their client abuses drugs and requires intensive treatment.[243]

Also, prosecutors must adjust to a new role.[244] Perhaps the most difficult challenge is reorienting prosecutors to the treatment approach of the drug court.[245] The prosecutor must be able to distinguish between cases in which treatment is the appropriate response and others where "full prosecution and firm punishment" is appropriate.[246]

Clients agreeing to participate in a drug court treatment program waive their right to trial.[247] Some courts find the defendants guilty of the crime for which they have been arrested and place them on probation; in others, the court defers prosecution for those who agree to participate.[248] Regardless of the method of adjudication, the client will avoid incarceration by successfully completing the treatment program but will face a jail sentence if the judge determines that the client has failed to comply with a court-mandated treatment plan.[249]

4. Treatment Is the Most Important Component of Drug Court Programs

The treatment component of drug diversion court programs ultimately will determine success or failure. Failure of the client to complete a treatment plan means incarceration and most likely a return to the previous pattern of criminal activity.[250] Drug court treatment plans are different because they are court-mandated and reviewed periodically by the court.[251] The judge makes ongoing determinations based on the input of both probation and treatment personnel.[252] The client who is not progressing as required faces the immediate threat of incarceration for the original offense.[253] This threat provides a powerful tool for treatment providers. Anecdotal evidence supports the belief that drug offenders consider incarceration the worst alternative, and they will make every attempt to avoid going to jail.

The treatment program for a typical drug court client consists of various phases.[254] A court-supervised treatment plan lasts approximately one year.[255] Beginning with the initial phase, and continuing throughout all subsequent phases, the court requires clients to submit to urine-testing.[256] Urine-testing has given treatment providers a powerful weapon to combat ongoing drug use.[257] Clients, aware that testing occurs frequently and on a random basis, recognize that repeated failures may result in incarceration.[258]

The initial step in a treatment plan is an intake which determines the client's substances of choice, educational background, and employment history.[259] If it is apparent that the extent of the problem is of such a magnitude that detoxification is required the judge may order placement in a residential detoxification facility.[260] If detoxification is not required, or, if it is required and is successfully completed, clients usually participate in an orientation component that lasts one or two weeks.[261] During orientation, the counselor and client prepare the treatment plan jointly.[262] The treatment plan contains realistic and measurable goals and lists strategies that the client will utilize to overcome barriers they face.[263]

Each subsequent phase lasts approximately twelve weeks.[264] Phase one, the most intensive phase,[265] meets at least four days per week and involves group and individual counseling.[266] Frequent urine-testing and weekly appearances before the court are also part of this phase.[267] The program may also refer clients to community support groups including Alcoholics Anonymous and Narcotics Anonymous.[268]

One unusual component of drug court treatment plans is acupuncture.[269] Acupuncture is offered primarily as an aid in detoxification.[270] This treatment may alleviate withdrawal symptoms and "ease the anxiety that clients typically experience during the first . . . weeks after they stop using drugs."[271]

A second phase meets three days per week for approximately twelve weeks and includes group and individual counseling, less frequent urine-testing, and introductory employment and parenting counseling.[272] The courts also require appearances on a weekly basis.[273]

The third phase also lasts twelve weeks but requires less frequent meetings, usually two days per week, with less frequent urine-testing.[274] A final phase focuses on aftercare and transition issues.[275] In the final phase, which concentrates on gaining employment, clients often meet with employment counselors.[276]

5. *Relapses and Sanctions*

Drug court programs are designed to allow for client relapses.[277] Drug diversion courts are based on several philosophies: that "drug dependency is a disease," that the courts must expect relapses as well as progress, and that by treating the disease, the system will have stemmed future criminal activity.[278]

Clients may revert to substance use, fail to attend required treatment components, or be arrested for another crime.[279] Even though anticipated, a drug court participant who relapses can expect a series of increased sanctions.[280] The drug courts employ sanctions as a weapon to keep clients on the road to success.[281] Sanctions may include detoxification,[282] increased urine-testing, repetition of a phase, or a short period of incarceration.[283] The most serious sanction is dismissal from the program which results in incarceration for the original crime.[284]

Given the philosophy of drug courts, the active involvement of drug court judges, the expected relapses, the personal connection between the judge and the client, and the active input of treatment providers, it is not surprising to find a high rate of "second chances."[285] While a flexible and individualized approach to dealing with clients is a key component of the program, commentators have criticized this approach when taken to what may be an extreme.[286] Critics chastised a Broward County drug court judge, for instance, for allowing one defendant to continue in the program after failing seventy-one urine tests.[287]

Judicial monitoring continues throughout the process.[288] In some courts, clients make weekly appearances before the judge, along with treatment and probation officials, to report on the client's status and progress.[289] Because of judicial monitoring and effective cooperation and communication among criminal justice components, arrestees and program participants almost always discover that they "cannot manipulate the [drug] court system" in ways that may have worked in traditional court systems.[290]

D. Drug Courts Are Cost-Effective

Treating drug offenders in court-mandated programs is more cost-effective than incarceration.[291] The average cost for treating participants in a court-mandated treatment program "ranges between $900 and $1,600 per participant."[292] For each client not incarcerated, jurisdictions save over $5,000 in jail costs alone.[293] If the courts sent these clients to state or federal prison, the costs would exceed $20,000 per prisoner.[294] Police overtime, witness costs and trial court expenses are other cost savings associated with drug court programs. The savings realized as a result of dealing with drug offenders, who, without this option would have been dealt with in a traditional manner, provides support for the maintenance and expansion of drug courts.[295]

In addition to direct dollar savings, drug courts have provided an opportunity for all components of the criminal justice system to allocate scarce resources more efficiently.[296] Staff and services, previously required to adjudicate drug offenders, are now directed to more serious offenders including those who "present greater risks to society."[297]

E. Drug Courts Have Improved the Recidivism Rate of Drug Offenders

Since drug courts are recent innovations, one cannot yet accurately determine the long-term effect on drug-related crime. Preliminary evaluations, however, indicate beneficial results.[298] "Recidivism has been significantly reduced for offenders participating in a drug court program."[299] In Florida's Broward County, a preliminary study found that 90% of the first group of clients to complete the program had not been rearrested.[300] In Oregon's drug court, preliminary studies are also positive: police arrested 6% of clients who completed the program after six months compared to 24% of those who did not complete the program.[301] After twelve months, the rearrest rate for program graduates was 15% compared to 54% for program drop-outs.[302]

F. Additional Benefits of Drug Courts

In addition to the significant impact of drug courts on both recidivism rates and costs, there are other important but less noticed benefits. One unanticipated result of drug court treatment programs has been "the birth of a significant number of drug-free babies to women enrolled in the programs."[303]

VII. TWO DRUG COURT MODELS

To understand their workings fully, this Note will look at two drug diversion courts. Miami's court was the first treatment court established. The drug diversion court in Massachusetts is the latest.

A. Miami's Drug Court: The Nation's First

In 1989, faced with an unprecedented growth in drug-related crime,[304] then State Attorney General Janet Reno,[305] Florida's judiciary, and the Dade County public defender combined efforts to establish the first drug diversion court in the United States.[306] The Miami court has since become the model for courts in jurisdictions across the country.[307]

The Miami drug court's one year treatment component consists of three phases: detoxification, stabilization, and aftercare (testing and other monitoring occurs in all phases).[308] The judge serves as the model for active judicial participation and leadership.[309] The Miami court has a significant case volume of approximately eighty defendants per day.[310]

The Miami drug court is important because, as the nation's longest operating court, it is not only the best known, but it is the most intensely studied. Preliminary studies are encouraging.[311] An initial eighteen month study concluded that drug court defendants had less frequent rearrests,[312] and significantly longer periods between rearrest than comparable non-drug court defendants.[313] The length of time until rearrest best demonstrates the positive impact of the drug court program on both the criminal justice system and public safety.[314] Drug court participants who were rearrested had a median time of 235 days until first rearrest after entering the drug court program.[315] This compares to control groups that had a median rearrest period of forty-five to 115 days.[316] This difference in rearrest rates is important. If the national system can achieve this same success, there will be a significant impact on caseloads, prisons, and drug-related crime rates.

The Miami court had a significantly larger "failure to appear rate" than other, traditional court drug defendants.[317] This is likely attributed, however, to the requirement that defendants appear before the court many times more than defendants before a traditional court. The Miami drug court has been a success. Most importantly, it has demonstrated that given the right judge, close collaboration with treatment and criminal justice agencies, and support of judicial and political leaders, the system can break the cycle of drug dependency and crime.

B. Boston's Drug Diversion Court

The Boston drug diversion court[318] was established in response to the impact drug-related crime had upon an already over-burdened criminal justice system[319] and represents the most recent evolution of drug courts.[320] The Boston court built upon the experiences of other jurisdictions but has many unique components which will allow it to serve as a model for future courts, both within and outside the commonwealth.

1. The Boston Drug Diversion Program Benefitted From a Strong Coalition

The successful establishment of the Boston drug court was due in large measure to the development of a broad and influential coalition. The Boston Coalition, a task force on criminal justice and law enforcement initiated by the Boston Bar Association and the United Way, led the effort to establish a drug court.[321] Throughout the planning process, the Boston Coalition convened and met with the agencies and key individuals crucial to the success of the drug diversion program.[322] These agencies and officials included court and probation officers, judges, public health officials, the District Attorney and Sheriff of Suffolk County, the Boston Police Commissioner, and the Mayor of Boston.[323]

In subsequent stages, the coalition actively involved community groups, treatment providers, and business leaders in the planning and implementation process.[324]

The importance of collaboration and cooperation cannot be overestimated. Often competing for scarce resources, including space, staff, and money, criminal justice agencies have rarely cooperated at the level demonstrated by the coalition that supported Boston's drug court. Through this heightened level of cooperation, the coalition was able to secure funding and other resources from federal, state, municipal, and private sources.[325]

The input of the judiciary to this process was a major factor in the successful implementation of the drug diversion program. The planners utilized the knowledge of two experienced trial judges in designing the drug court.[326] Additionally, the project received the endorsement of the task force appointed by the Massachusetts Supreme Judicial Court.[327]

The Boston court is a pilot project which other trial courts in Suffolk County, or perhaps throughout the commonwealth, should emulate. The court has intentionally limited its number of clients in the first year to ensure that it gives ample opportunity to both the development of protocols and evaluation of results. But, most importantly, the backing of the Coalition ensures that whatever direction this court or other future courts may take, there is a broad and experienced partnership acting on its behalf. Courts in other jurisdictions will have a significantly better opportunity for success if a strong and supportive coalition is built before the establishment of a drug diversion court.

2. *The Court Is Located on a Public Health Campus*

While the court is similar to other drug courts in overall philosophy, general treatment approaches, and sanctions, the Boston drug court has one very important and unique feature which will serve as a model for future courts. The court was established directly on the grounds of a health care campus.[328] The court, and a large component of the treatment resources, are within the same physical facility.[329] Treatment providers are literally outside the courtroom doors. The decision to locate the court on a rehabilitation hospital reflects the philosophy that treatment is the central theme of a drug court.[330] Additionally, the court planners assumed that drug court clients are traditionally "underserved by the healthcare system."[331] The court location "will help the drug diversion court to connect its clients to public health, primary care systems, and a rich network of social service and supportive agencies."[332]

One major benefit of this approach is to facilitate communication between treatment providers and the criminal justice personnel, including the judge. Because the initial stages of the Boston Court are shorter than most other courts, the judge is able to be more actively involved with treatment providers. Every orientation and "Phase I" client must appear before the judge each week. This does not present difficult logistic or scheduling problems since group and individual counseling takes place in the same facility.

The judge meets with both treatment and probation personnel prior to the weekly court session. In the courtroom, both probation and treatment providers are present. This unified and coordinated approach has an impact on the clients, who recognize that the system will not tolerate manipulation. As is true in Miami and other jurisdictions, the Boston judge uses the full scope of his authority to reward or sanction clients based on their individual needs and performance.

VIII. CONCLUSION

The criminal justice system is collapsing under the deluge of drug offenders entering the system. Increased arrests, convictions, and sentences of drug offenders, especially nonviolent drug offenders, do little to break the cycle that returns released prisoners to drug dependency and crime. While it would be far better to deal with the "root causes" of drug related crime including poverty, lack of education and housing, widespread unemployment, and domestic violence, it is not realistic to assume that society will resolve these problems in the near future.

Treatment is the only approach that will break the cycle of drug dependency. To be effective, the treatment must be intensive and of sufficient length to have lasting effect. Due to prison overcrowding, however, caused ironically in large part by drug offenders, there is little opportunity for an incarcerated drug offender to receive effective treatment in prison.

Treatment-based drug diversion courts have all the mechanisms required to provide this treatment. First, they come in contact with the drug abuser at a time when he or she is most susceptible to entering a treatment plan: at the time of arrest with the likelihood of incarceration. Second, the treatment is court-supervised and clients are individually monitored. Third, the threat of sanctions provides a powerful weapon to force clients to remain in the program. Finally, compared to incarceration, the drug diversion courts are cost-effective.

To have a successful drug diversion court, three vital components are required: an acceptance by the criminal justice and political communities that a new philosophy is required if our courts are to play a major role in breaking the nexus between crime and drugs; an innovative and dedicated judiciary willing to assume a new role far removed from that of a traditional trial judge; and a committed broad-based coalition that provides knowledge, support, and long-term commitment to a drug court and its aims. Additionally, the Boston Court moved the treatment concept one step further by locating on a public health campus. The Boston drug court can serve as a model system which has achieved its goals.

Given the rate with which communities are establishing drug courts, their impact on drug-related crime, and thus on the criminal justice system, will be significant. Ultimately, society in general will benefit. Accordingly, criminal justice professionals should encourage the development of drug courts in their jurisdictions.

Furthermore, drug courts can serve as models for other treatment-based specialty courts. Domestic violence is one area in which a comprehensive court-supervised intensive treatment program, modeled on the drug court concept, may have positive results when compared with traditional approaches. Drug courts represent an opportunity finally to succeed in an arena in which successes have been far too infrequent.

NOTES

1. *See* Jerome H. Skolnick, *A Critical Look at the National Drug Strategy*, 8 Yale L. & Pol'y Rev. 75, 94 (1990).

2. From 1975 to 1994, violent crimes increased by 79%. *See* Federal Bureau of Investigation, U.S. Dep't of Justice, Crime in the United States 1994 58 tbl.1 (1995) [hereinafter Crime in the United States].

3. *See* John J. DiIulio, Jr., *Rethinking the Criminal Justice System: Toward a New Paradigm, in* Bureau of Justice Statistics, U.S. Dep't of Justice, Performance Measures for the Criminal Justice System 1, 7 (1993).

4. "The probability of being addicted to crack cocaine is high" and more users become addicted to crack than users of powdered cocaine. Skolnick, *supra* note 1, at 98.

5. *See* Peter Reuter, *Drug Data and Policy: Hawks, Doves, and Owls, in* U.S. Dep't of Justice, Enhancing Capacities and Confronting Controversies in Criminal Justice 7, 9 (1994).

6. *See* Census Bureau, Census of the United States 1990.

7. *See* Panel Discussion, *The Drugging of the Courts: How Sick is the Patient and What is the Treatment*?, 73 Judicature 314 (1990).

8. The war on drugs is the general term employed by both the media and politicians describing the government's response to the drug crisis beginning in the 1980s. Virtually any program that deals with drugs or drug abusers could be included as a component of the war on drugs.

9. *See infra* notes 120-35, 185-90 and accompanying text.

10. *See infra* notes 191-204 and accompanying text.

11. *See infra* notes 191-204 and accompanying text.

12. These courts provide intensive supervised treatment as an alternative to the traditional method of incarceration, and are referred to as "drug diversion courts," "drug courts," or "treatment-based courts."

13. *See infra* notes 210-12 and accompanying text.

14. *See* National Institute of Justice, U.S. Dep't of Justice, Searching for Answers, Annual Evaluation Report on Drugs and Crime: 1992 53-56 (June 1993) [hereinafter Searching for Answers].

15. *See infra* notes 57-63 and accompanying text.

16. *See infra* notes 96-119 and accompanying text.

17. *See infra* notes 127-35 and accompanying text.

18. *See infra* note 127-28 and accompanying text.

19. *See* John S. Goldkamp, U.S. Dep't of Justice, Justice and Treatment Innovation: The Drug Court Movement 6 (1994).

20. *See id.*

21. *See* Bureau of Justice Statistics, U.S. Dep't of Justice, Fact Sheet: Drug-Related Crime 1 (1994) [hereinafter Drug-Related Crime]. "It is a crime in all jurisdictions to use, sell, possess, manufacture, or distribute a broad spectrum of drugs." *Id.*

22. *See* Mary G. Graham, U.S. Dep't of Justice, Controlling Drug Abuse and Crime: A Research Update 1 (1987). Studies have confirmed "that without drug-testing most drug use will go undetected. Only half of those who tested positive actually admitted using drugs." *Id.*

23. *See id.*

24. *See* Drug-Related Crime, *supra* note 21, at 3. Those guilty of burglary, robbery, and larceny/theft were most disposed to committing the crime to obtain funds for later drug purchases. *See id.*

25. *See id.* at 2. The percentage of prison inmates reporting that they were under the influence of drugs included 38.9% for drug crimes, 30.9% for property crimes, and 24.5% for violent crimes. *See id.* at 2, fig.1.

26. *See* Bureau of Justice Statistics, U.S. Dep't of Justice, Drugs and Crime Facts, 1993 5 (1994) [hereinafter Drugs and Crime Facts].

27. *See* National Institute of Justice, Drug Use Forecasting, 1994 Annual Report 11-46 (1995) [hereinafter Drug Use Forecasting 1994].

28. "The percentage of male booked arrestees testing positive for illicit drug use ranged from 48% in Houston to 82% in Manhattan." Drug Use Forecasting 1994, *supra* note 27, at 7. For female arrestees, the range was 32% in New Orleans to 90% in Manhattan. *See id.* at 8.

29. *See id.* at 47.
30. *See* Graham, *supra* note 22, at 2.
31. Roger H. Peters, *Substance Abuse Services in Jails and Prisons*, 17 L. & Psychol. Rev. 85 (1993). "Findings indicate that a diagnosis of substance abuse . . . was the most important predictor of recent violence." *Id.*
32. *See* Graham, *supra* note 22, at 2-3.
33. *See* Supreme Judicial Court, A Matter of Just Treatment: Substance Abuse and The Courts 6 (1995) [hereinafter Just Treatment]. "Substance abuse operates at the threshold of almost all criminal cases and is a significant factor in the explosion of domestic and family violence, sexual and physical abuse and parental neglect." *Id.*
34. *See* Bureau of Justice Statistics, U.S. Dep't of Justice, Fact Sheet: Drug Use Trends 4 tbl.5 (1995) [hereinafter Drug Use Trends].
35. *See id.*
36. *See* Drug-Related Crime, *supra* note 21, at 3.
37. *See id.*
38. *See supra* notes 24-35 and accompanying text; *see also infra* notes 40-50 and accompanying text.
39. *See* Drug Use Trends, *supra* note 34, at 1-2.
40. *Id.*
41. *See* Drug-Related Crime, *supra* note 21, at 3. "Reasons for this relationship include the competition for drug markets, the disputes among people involved in the drug trade, the likelihood that drug traffickers are prone to violence, and that drug-trafficking takes place in locations where social controls against violence tend to be ineffective." *Id.* "The recent proliferation of guns is also a factor." *Id.*
42. "Of the fourteen million arrests in 1994, 22,100 were for murder and 36,610 were for forcible rape." Crime in the United States, *supra* note 2, at 217 tbl. 29.
43. *See* Drug-Related Crime, *supra* note 21, at 3. "Over 18% of defendants in homicide cases were involved in drug manufacturing, a dispute over drugs, theft of drugs or drug money, a drug scam, punishment for drug theft, or illegal use of drugs." *Id.*
44. *See* Crime in the United States, *supra* note 2, at 21 tbl.2.14.
45. Drugs and Crime Facts, *supra* note 26, at 9.
46. *See id.* at 27.
47. *See id.*
48. *See id.* at 25.
49. *See id.*
50. *See id.*
51. *See* National Institute of Justice, U.S. Dep't of Justice, Drug Use Forecasting, 1993, 3 (1994) [hereinafter Drug Use Forecasting 1993].
52. *See* Graham, *supra* note 22, at 2.
53. *See generally* Bureau of Justice Statistics, U.S. Dep't of Justice, Drugs, Crime, and the Justice System 95 (1992) [hereinafter Drugs, Crime, and the Justice System].
54. John A. Martin, *Drugs, Crime, and Urban Trial Court Management: The Unintended Consequences of the War on Drugs*, 8 Yale L. & Pol'y Rev. 117, 134 (1990).
55. *See* Drugs, Crime, and the Justice System, *supra* note 53, at 95.
56. *See id.*
57. *See* DiIulio, *supra* note 3, at 7.
58. *See id.*
59. *See id.*
60. *See id.*
61. *See id.*

62. *See* Reuter, *supra* note 5, at 9.

63. These are important components of the war on drugs but not a complete listing. The interdiction of drug supplies is a major thrust of the government's efforts to control drug abuse, and the government has devoted substantial resources to this effort (including the use of the armed forces). *See generally* Drugs, Crime, and the Justice System, *supra* note 53, at 141-51. While large quantities of drugs have been seized, illicit drugs remain readily available and the price has remained low. William Rhodes et al., ONDCP, What America's Users Spend on Illegal Drugs, 1988–1993 18 (1995).

64. *See* Bureau of Justice Statistics, U.S. Dep't of Justice, Fact Sheet: Drug Data Summary 5 (1995) [hereinafter Drug Data Summary].

65. *See id.*

66. *See* Mathea Falco, *Toward a Rational Drug Policy, Toward a More Effective Drug Policy*, 1994 U. Chi. Legal F. 9, 11.

67. *See id.* at 11.

68. ONDCP, Executive Off. of the President, The National Drug Control Strategy: 1996 60 (1996) [hereinafter Drug Strategy]. "In total, resources for domestic law enforcement comprise 55% of the total drug control budget in Fiscal Year 1997. These resources support activities such as investigations, prosecutions, corrections, state and local law enforcement assistance . . . and other law enforcement efforts." *Id.* Interdiction spending accounts for 10% ($1.4 billion) of the fiscal year 1997 drug control budget. *See id.* Resources for demand reduction increased by 8.7% to $5 billion. *See id.* Demand reduction includes treatment, prevention, education, and research. *See id.* Demand reduction comprises 33% of the budget. *See id.*

69. *See infra* notes 71-73.

70. *See infra* notes 71-73.

71. *See* Crime in the United States, *supra* note 2, at 217.

72. *See* Drugs and Crimes Facts, *supra* note 26, at 10.

73. *See* Crime in the United States, *supra* note 2, at 216.

74. *See generally* Drug Data Summary, *supra* note 64, at 1-5.

75. *See* Drug Use Trends, *supra* note 34, at 1.

76. *See* Drugs and Crime Facts, *supra* note 26, at 13.

77. *See id.* Eighty-five percent of state police departments and over 90% of local police departments serving populations of 50,000 or greater have special drug units. *See id.*

78. *See* Bureau of Justice Statistics, U.S. Dep't of Justice, Federal Drug Case Processing, 1982–91 with Preliminary Data for 1992 5 tbl.7a. (1994) [hereinafter Drug Case Processing].

79. *See id.*

80. *See id.*

81. *See id.*

82. *See* Patrick A. Langan & Helen A. Graziadel, U.S. Dep't of Justice, Felony Sentences in State Courts, 1992 9 tbl.9 (1995).

83. *See id.* at 8.

84. *See id.* at 8-9 tbl.9.

85. *See* Allen J. Beck & Darrell K. Gilliard, U.S. Dep't of Justice, Prisoners in 1994 10 (1995).

86. *See* Drug Case Processing, *supra* note 78, at 9 tbl.10d.

87. *See* Beck & Gilliard, *supra* note 85, at 3 tbl.18. In the same period, commitments to prison for murder decreased from 621 per thousand to 521 per thousand. *See id.*

88. *See* Darrell K. Gilliard & Allen J. Beck, U.S. Dep't of Justice, Prisoners in 1993 7 (1994).

89. *See id.*

90. *See id.* at 7 tbl.10.

91. *See* Drug Data Summary, *supra* note 64, at 2.

92. *See id.* This compares with an increase in sentence length of all federal offenders from 44 months to 62 months. *See id.*
93. *See id.*
94. *See* Drugs and Crime Facts, *supra* note 26, at 16. "The average percent of [federal prison] sentences served until first release increased from 60% in 1985 to 68% in 1990. Contributing to these increases are the sentencing guidelines that went into effect . . . which proscribe stiffer sentences and mandatory minimum incarceration." *Id.*
95. *See* Langan & Graziadel, *supra* note 82, at 9 tbl.8.
96. *See* Elaine R. Jones, *The Failure of the "Get Tough" Crime Policy*, 20 U. Dayton L. Rev. 803, 804 (1995). Prior to the full implementation of the war on drugs, the number of black juveniles arrested for drug violations was actually lower than whites. *See id.* After 1981, however, the rates changed dramatically. *See id.*
97. *See* David C. Leven, *Curing America's Addiction to Prisons*, 20 Fordham Urb. L.J. 641, 645 (1993).
98. *See* Jean Wellisch et al., U.S. Dep't of Justice, Drug Abusing Women Offenders: Results of a National Survey 1 (1994).
99. *See* Beck & Gilliard, *supra* note 85, at 9.
100. *See id.* at 8 tbl.10.
101. *See id.* at 9.
102. *See id.*
103. *See* Leven, *supra* note 97, at 645.
104. *See id.* at 646. Forty percent of all state prison inmates are unable to read or write and only 33% were employed at the time of arrest. *See id.*
105. *See* Wellisch, et al. *supra* note 98, at 1; Leven, *supra* note 97 at 647. From 1983 to 1994, women arrested for drug abuse violations increased by 91.8%. *See* Crime in the United States, *supra* note 2, 222 tbl.33.
106. *See* Beck & Gilliard, *supra* note 85, at 8 tbl.11. The incarceration rate of black females is 165 per 100,000; for white females it is 23 per 100,000. *See id.*
107. *See* Leven, *supra* note 97, at 647. The period was 1987 to 1989. *See id.* In New York, the women prison population increased 450% in the decade ending 1990. *See id.*
108. *See id.*
109. *See infra* notes 110-14 and accompanying text.
110. *See* Wellisch, et al., *supra* note 98, at 2.
111. *See* Leven, *supra* note 97 at 647.
112. *See* Wellisch, et al., *supra* note 98, at 2.
113. *See id.*
114. *See* Leven, *supra* note 97, at 647.
115. *See* Wellisch, et al., *supra* note 98, at 1.
116. *See id.* at 1.
117. *See id.* at 5.
118. *See id.*
119. *See id.*
120. *See infra* notes 127-38 and accompanying text.
121. *See* Gilliard & Beck, *supra* note 88, at 7-8.
122. *See* Jeff Potts, *American Penal Institutions and Two Alternative Proposals For Punishment*, 34 S. Tex. L. Rev. 443, 449 (1993).
123. *See* Bruce Butterfield & Dick Lehr, *Criminal Justice/Overdosing on the Drug War*, Boston Globe, Sept. 24, 1995, at 31-32.
124. *See* Drugs and Crime Facts, *supra* note 26, at 19.

125. *See id.*
126. *See id.*
127. *See* Beck & Gilliard, *supra* note 85, at 4.
128. *See id.* at 5.
129. *See id.* at 4.
130. *See id.* at 1.
131. *See id.* at 5. Other states with a large annual increase in 1994 include: Georgia (20.3%) and Nevada (16%). *See id.* at 5. States with the largest five year increase from 1989–94 are: New Hampshire (73.3%) and Connecticut (66.4%). *See id.* The national prison system increased by an average 1,162 per week for all five years. *See id.*
132. *See id.* at 8.
133. *See* Beck & Gilliard, *supra* note 85, at 8.
134. *See id.* at 6.
135. *See id.*
136. *See* Drugs and Crime Facts, *supra* note 26, at 20.
137. *See id.*
138. *See* Potts, *supra* note 122, at 469.
139. *See supra* notes 64-67 and accompanying text.
140. *See supra* notes 71-77, 85-90 and accompanying text.
141. *See infra* notes 167-68 and accompanying text.
142. *See infra* notes 143-50 and accompanying text.
143. *See* Potts, *supra* note 122, at 457.
144. *See id.* at 458.
145. *See* John P. Walters, *Race and the War on Drugs*, 1994 U. Chi. Legal F. 107, 122.
146. *See* Steven Belenko et al., *The Effects of Legal Sanctions of Recidivism in Special Drug Courts*, 17 Just. Sys. J. 53, 57 (1994).
147. *See* Leven, *supra* note 97, at 649. In 1980, index crimes reported by California police totaled 1,118,417. *See id.* Despite the increase in incarcerations, by 1990 reported crimes climbed to 1,965,237. *See id.* In the same period, however, the population only increased 25%. *See id.*
148. *See id.* at 641.
149. *See id.*
150. *See* Searching for Answers, *supra* note 14, at 54. "A mid 1980s study of 573 substance abusers in Miami found that . . . they committed 6,000 robberies and assaults, 6,700 burglaries, 900 auto thefts and 25,000 acts of shoplifting . . . ." *Id.*
151. *See* Leven, *supra* note 97, at 641.
152. *See generally* Drug Strategy, *supra* note 68, at 41-51.
153. *See generally*, Reuter *supra* note 5, at 9.
154. *See supra* notes 139-48 and accompanying text.
155. *See generally* Falco, *supra* note 66, at 9.
156. *See id.*
157. *See* Butterfield & Lehr, *supra* note 123, at 30.
158. *See* Gilliard & Beck, *supra* note 88, at 10, app. tbl.1.
159. *See* Butterfield & Lehr, *supra* note 123, at 30.
160. *See id.*
161. *See* Drug Case Processing, *supra* note 78, cit.10, tbl.11a. Federal murder sentences decreased from 133 months to 88.5 months in seven years (1985–92). *See id.*
162. *See* Butterfield & Lehr, *supra* note 123, at 20.
163. *See infra* notes 164-68 and accompanying text.
164. Leven, *supra* note 97, at 643.
165. *See* Jones, *supra* note 96, at 80.

166. *See id.*
167. *See* Carol Vance, *To Achieve Law and Order, People Must be Changed*, 29 Prosecutor 28 (May/June 1995). The cost of building prison space and housing an inmate for 30 years exceeds $1 million. *See id.*
168. *See* Leven, *supra* note 97, at 644.
169. *See* Searching for Answers, *supra* note 14, at 88.
170. *See id.* "Court reports of increases in drug caseloads from 45% to 70% . . . are common." *Id.*
171. Barbara E. Smith et al., *Burning the Midnight Oil: An Examination of Cook County's Night Drug Court*, 17 Just. Sys. J. 41, 42 (1994).
172. *Id.* From 1988 to 1989, drug cases in Cook County increased by 77%, while non-drug cases increased only 5%. *See id.*
173. *See* Martin, *supra* note 54, at 135.
174. *Id.* It is important to note that the Detroit court has responded to increased drug-related caseloads effectively and efficiently. *See* Barry Mahoney, *Drug Courts: What Have We Learned So Far?*, 17 Just. Sys. J. 127, 128 (1994). Felony drug-related arrests in Detroit increased 157% from 1985 to 1988, but there was no sense of crisis. *See id.* The Detroit court continued to handle its felony cases expeditiously by using systems developed in response to earlier increases in caseloads. *See id.*
175. *See generally* Peters, *supra* note 31.
176. *See id.* at 86. Many states, in order to reduce recidivism rates among participants, especially first time offenders, have introduced boot camps (shock incarceration). *See* Ernest L. Cowles et al., U.S. Department of Justice, "Boot Camp" Drug Treatment and Aftercare Interventions: An Evaluation Review (July 1995). However, "substance abuse programming [often] appears to have been introduced in the shock incarceration . . . as an afterthought" *Id.* at 6. Since drug abuse treatment has to be intensive and "boot camps" are often of short duration, this treatment may not have long-term success in dealing with a drug addiction. *See id.*
177. *See* Drug Strategy, *supra* note 68, at 57-69 (1992). Treatment funding increased from $487 million in 1981, to $2,908 billion in fiscal year 1997. *See id.* at 67.
178. *See* Falco, *supra* note 66, at 21.
179. *See id.* at 17.
180. Fred Setterberg, *Oakland Tries a Carrot and Stick Approach to Keeping First-Time Drug Offenders Out of Jail*, California Lawyer, May 14, 1994, at 93.
181. *See* Wellisch, et al., *supra* note 98, at 5.
182. *See* Falco, *supra* note 66, at 16.
183. Wellisch, et al., *supra* note 98, at 5 (referring to a survey of treatment directed towards women drug abusers).
184. *See* Gregory P. Falkin et al., *Drug Treatment in the Criminal Justice System*, 58 Fed. Probation 31, 32 (1994). In surveyed urban areas, "the number of arrestees who need treatment relative to the number enrolled in treatment, is about 16 to 1" for cocaine abusers. *Id.*
185. *See* Walters, *supra* note 145, at 121.
186. *See generally* Peters, *supra* note 31, at 97-98.
187. *See id.* at 106.
188. *See id.* at 107.
189. *See* Falkin, *supra* note 184, at 32.
190. *See* Peters, *supra* note 31, at 98. Only 28% of jails have treatment programs other than detoxification, and only 18% of those are funded. *See id.* Additionally, even where there are programs, they are often not as comprehensive as intensive outpatient programs. *See id.*
191. *See* Goldkamp, *supra* note 19, at i.
192. *Id.*
193. *See supra* notes 24-33 and accompanying text.

194. *See supra* notes 69-73 and accompanying text.
195. *See supra* notes 127-33 and accompanying text.
196. *See supra* notes 127-33 and accompanying text.
197. *See supra* notes 139-50 and accompanying text.
198. *See supra* notes 185-90 and accompanying text.
199. *See supra* notes 175-79 and accompanying text.
200. *See supra* notes 181-84 and accompanying text.
201. *See supra* notes 96-119 and accompanying text.
202. *See supra* notes 4, 53-56 and accompanying text.
203. *See* Robert C. Davis et al., *Court Strategies To Cope With Rising Drug Caseloads*, 17 Just. Sys. J. 1, 2 (1994).
204. Caroline S. Cooper & Joseph A. Trotter, Jr., The American University, Drug Case Management and Treatment Intervention Strategies in the State and Local Courts 20 (1994).
205. *See generally* Jamey H. Weitzman, Drug Courts: A Manual for Planning and Implementation (Robin J. Kimbrough ed.) (1995).
206. *See id.*
207. *Id.*
208. *See id.*
209. *Id.*
210. *See* Cooper & Trotter, *supra* note 204, at 20.
211. *See id.*
212. *See id.*
213. Further highlighting the difference between traditional courts, offenders before drug courts are often referred to as "clients." *See generally* Peter Finn & Andrea K. Newlyn, *Miami Drug Court Gives Drug Defendants a Second Chance*, 77 Judicature 268, 269 (1994).
214. Cooper & Trotter, *supra* note 204, at 21 (emphasis in original).
215. Pamela Casey, *Court Enforced Drug Treatment Programs: Do They Enhance Court Performances?*, 17 Just. Sys. J. 118-19 (1994) (quoting Jeffrey S. Tauber, A Judicial Primer on Unified Drug Courts and Court Ordered Rehabilitation Programs, Paper presented at California Continuing Education Society (August 20, 1993)).
216. *See* Cooper & Trotter, *supra* note 204, at 27; *see also* Weitzman, *supra* note 205.
217. *See generally* Weitzman, *supra* note 205.
218. *See* Peter Finn & Andrea K. Newlyn, U.S. Dep't of Justice, Dade County Diverts Drug Defendants to Court Run Rehabilitation Program 9-10 (1993).
219. *See id.* at 4.
220. This assertion is based upon direct observations of the author.
221. *See* Goldkamp, *supra* note 19, at 11.
222. *See id.*
223. *See id.*
224. *See generally* Weitzman, *supra* note 205.
225. *See* Drug Court Implementation Initiative 14 (May 23, 1995) (application for federal assistance, filed in support of the Boston Drug Diversion Court) [hereinafter Drug Court Initiative].
226. *See* Goldkamp, *supra* note 19, at 7.
227. *See* Cooper & Trotter, *supra* note 204, at 22. A number of programs are available only to first offenders; others allow for some prior criminal activity. *See id.* Some courts target all drug offenders but may include incarceration as a component. *See id.* at 22 n.15. The Boston Drug Court will not accept offenders who have a violent conviction within five years. *See* Dorchester District Court, The Drug Diversion Court Program 2 (1995) (brochure describing the Boston Drug Court) [hereinafter Drug Diversion Court Program].
228. *See* U.S. Dep't of Justice, Bureau of Justice Assistance, Special Drug Courts, Program Brief 10 (1993).

229. *See id.*
230. *See* Searching for Answers, *supra* note 14, at 51. This is not surprising since evidence consistently shows that drug offenders frequently repeat the cycle of crime, conviction, sentence, release, and a return to crime.
231. *See* Goldkamp, *supra* note 19, at 18.
232. *See id.*
233. *See* Finn & Newlyn, *supra* note 218, at 10.
234. *See* Cooper & Trotter, *supra* note 204, at 21.
235. *See generally*, Weitzman, *supra* note 205.
236. *See* Cooper & Trotter, *supra* note 204, at 23.
237. *See* Drug Court Initiative, *supra* note 225, at 8.
238. *See id.*
239. *See* Finn & Newlyn, *supra* note 218, at 4.
240. *See* Goldkamp, *supra* note 19, at 11.
241. *See id.*
242. *Id.*
243. *See id.*
244. *See id.*
245. *See id.* at 16. Prosecutors also may be concerned about drug court eligibility, nondrug abusers using the system to avoid incarceration, and retaining the discretion to prosecute cases of individuals failing the program. *See id.* at 15-16.
246. Goldkamp, *supra* note 19, at 16.
247. *See* Cooper & Trotter, *supra* note 204, at 24.
248. *See id.* at 22-23.
249. *See* Finn & Newlyn, *supra* note 218, at 10.
250. *See infra* notes 277-90 and accompanying text.
251. *See* Goldkamp, *supra* note 19, at 14.
252. *See* Drug Court Initiative, *supra* note 225, at 21.
253. *See id.* at 21-22.
254. Courts may break treatment into phases, stages, or steps. While individual courts may vary as to length of each phase, the number of phases, and the name of the phase, most courts have the same substantive treatment approaches.
255. *See* Finn & Newlyn, *supra* note 218, at 3.
256. *See id.* at 5.
257. *See id.* at 5-9.
258. *See id.* at 5.
259. *See* Drug Court Initiative, *supra* note 225, at 18.
260. *See* Finn & Newlyn, *supra* note 218, at 5. Detoxification generally lasts about two weeks but can be adjusted as required. *See id.* The judge may order detoxification at any point during treatment if he or she believes it necessary. *See id.*
261. *See* Drug Court Initiative, *supra* note 225, at 19.
262. *See* Finn & Newlyn, *supra* note 218, at 5.
263. *See id.*
264. *See* Drug Court Initiative, *supra* note 225, at 20.
265. *See* Cooper & Trotter, *supra* note 204, at 28.
266. *See* Finn & Newlyn, *supra* note 218, at 6.
267. *See id.*
268. *See id.*
269. *See id.*
270. *See id.*
271. *Id.*

272. *See* Drug Court Initiative, *supra* note 225, at 20.
273. *See id.*
274. *See id.*
275. *See id.*
276. *See id.*
277. *See* Cooper & Trotter, *supra* note 204, at 29.
278. *See id.* at 21.
279. The Boston Drug Court lists over twenty possible reasons, ranging from drug use to inappropriate behavior in the courthouse, for which a client may be sanctioned. Dorchester District Court, Drug Diversion Court Program, Client's Orientation Brochure (1995). Clients accepted for participation are informed of the reasons for sanctions. *See id.* Arrest for a new crime or refusal to participate in a urine test are the most serious infractions resulting in sanctions. *See id.*
280. Florida's Broward County drug court has specific guidelines for increased sanctions for clients failing urine analysis. Ronnie Green, *Drug Court Audit Praises 'Favorable Results,' But Pans Judge*, The Herald, Feb. 18, 1995, at 1BR, 3BR. Clients with two failed tests may receive weekend incarceration. *See id.* Ten or more failed tests may result in dismissal from the program and lead to incarceration for the original offense. *See id.* The system is designed, however, to allow the judge to respond to the circumstances of individual clients. *See id.*
281. *See id.*
282. In Massachusetts, a judge may invoke Chapter 123, Section 35 of the Penal Code and, upon advice of a medical consultant, remand an individual to a detoxification center. *See* Mass. Gen. Laws ch. 123, 35 (1994 & Supp. 1996).
283. *See* Finn & Newlyn, *supra* note 218, at 10. In Miami's drug court, as many as 60% of the clients spend a short time in jail for failing to adhere consistently to their treatment plan. *See id.*
284. *See id.*
285. *See id.* at 9-10.
286. *See generally* Green, *supra* note 280.
287. *See* Green, *supra* note 280, at 3BR.
288. *See* Goldkamp, *supra* note 19, at 6.
289. *See* Drug Court Initiative, *supra* note 225, at 21.
290. Finn & Newlyn, *supra* note 218, at 4.
291. *See* Drug Court Resource Center, U.S. Dep't of Justice, Preliminary Assessment of the Drug Court Program Experience 1 (1995) [hereinafter Preliminary Assessment].
292. *Id.*
293. *See id.*
294. *See supra* notes 165-66 and accompanying text.
295. *See* Preliminary Assessment, *supra* note 291, at 1.
296. *See id.*
297. *See id.*
298. *See GAO and American University's Drug Court Resource Center Release Drug Court Reports*, NADCP News, June, 1995, at 2.
299. *Id.*
300. *See* Green, *supra* note 280, at 3BR.
301. *See* Mark Curriden, *Drug Courts Gain Popularity*, 80 A.B.A. J. 16, 18 (May 1994).
302. *See id.*
303. Preliminary Assessment, *supra* note 291, at 1. On September 24, 1996, the Boston Drug Court held a graduation for the first clients to complete the program. It was noted that one of the clients gave birth to a "crack free baby" while in the program (ceremony attended by author).
304. *See* John S. Goldkamp, *Miami's Treatment Drug Court for Felony Defendants: Some Implications of Assessment Findings*, 73 Prison J. 110, 112 (1994). From 1985 to 1989, arrests in

Florida for drug-related crimes increased to 93%, and 83% of felons either were involved in a drug-related crime or tested positive for an illicit drug. *See id.*

305. U.S. Attorney General Janet Reno not only adopted the drug court concept, she proposed the "carrot and stick" philosophy of dealing with drug offenders. *See* Finn & Newlyn, *supra* note 218, at 12. This approach presented the offender with a simple choice, either "accept and complete treatment and [the] . . . case will be dismissed . . . [or,] refuse or fail and . . . be prosecuted." *Id.* Attorney General Reno also pushed for expanding the program. *See id.* She subsequently raised concerns that the program did not reach enough offenders. *See id.* Attorney General Reno continues to speak out on the need for drug courts as an alternative to traditional methods of dealing with drug offenders. *See id. See generally*, Attorney General Janet Reno, Address at the 1996 New England School of Law Barrister's Ball (May 20, 1996), *in* 31 New Eng. L. Rev. 159 (1996) (discussing alternative avenues by which to accomplish the goals of the criminal justice system).

306. *See* Goldkamp, *supra* note 19, at 3.

307. *See* Searching for Answers, *supra* note 14, at 56. From 1991 to 1993, over twenty jurisdictions established drug courts based on the Miami court model. *See* Goldkamp, *supra* note 19, at ii.

308. *See* Searching for Answers, *supra* note 14, at 54.

309. *See* Finn & Newlyn, *supra* note 218, at 3.

310. *See id.*

311. "The oldest drug court has only been in existence since 1989." *Id.* at 2. Therefore, long-term results will not be known for many years. *See id.* Thus, definitive conclusions cannot be made.

312. *See* Searching for Answers, *supra* note 14, at 55. In 1990, only 32% of drug court defendants were rearrested during an eighteen month observation period. *See id.* This compares to 50% for drug offenders not in a drug court program. *See id.*

313. *See id.*

314. *See* Goldkamp, *supra* note 304, at 126-27.

315. *See id.* at 130.

316. *See id.*

317. *See* Searching for Answers, *supra* note 14, at 55.

318. The Boston drug court is a session of the Dorchester District Court. *See* Just Treatment, *supra* note 33, at 38.

319. *See id.* at 60. An estimated "62% of the total state inmate population used drugs on a regular basis before they were arrested." *Id.* The number of estimated juvenile drug offenders in Massachusetts has tripled since 1984. *See id.* at 59.

320. The court held its first session June 1, 1995. The author of this Note attended this session.

321. *See* Just Treatment, *supra* note 33, at 38.

322. *See* Drug Court Initiative, *supra* note 225, at 1.

323. *See id.*

324. *See id.*

325. *See id.* The list of financial supporters included the Massachusetts Trial Court, the Office of the Probation Commissioner, the City of Boston, the Boston Police Department, the Massachusetts Committee on Criminal Justice, the Robert Wood Johnson Foundation, The Boston Foundation, The Boston Bar Foundation, W.K. Kellogg, the Gardiner Howland Shaw Foundation, The Hymans Foundation, and the American Bar Foundation. *See generally* Drug Diversion Court Program, *supra* note 227.

326. *See* Drug Court Initiative, *supra* note 225, at 8. Judge Robert Ziemian was actively involved in designing the project. *See id.* Judge Ziemian, prior to his judicial appointment, was Director of Drug Enforcement for the Commonwealth of Massachusetts. *See id.* Judge James Dolan, Former First Justice of the Dorchester District Court, was involved with the project from its inception. *See id.* Judge Ziemian was appointed as judge of the drug court. *See id.*

327. *See* Just Treatment, *supra* note 33, at 38-39. The Supreme Judicial Court Substance Abuse Task Force reported to the Chief Justice that the drug court proposal "offers an innovative and potentially effective approach that realistically recognizes the dynamics of substance abuse and criminal conduct." *Id.* at 39.
328. *See* Drug Court Initiative, *supra* note 225, at 15.
329. *See id.*
330. *See id.*
331. *Id.*
332. *Id.*

3

Pregnancy, Drugs, and the Perils of Prosecution

Wendy K. Mariner, Leonard H. Glantz, George J. Annas

In the war on drugs an offensive has been launched against pregnant women who use drugs. Over the past four years, prosecuting attorneys have been indicting women who use drugs while pregnant. In South Carolina alone, eighteen women who allegedly took drugs during pregnancy were indicted last summer for criminal neglect of a child or distribution of drugs to a minor.[1] In the only successful prosecution so far, Jennifer Johnson was convicted in Florida for delivering illegal drugs to a minor via the umbilical cord in the moment after her child was born and before the cord was clamped.[2] No one seriously maintains that the transitory "delivery" was the conduct on trial. Rather, the crime was the mother's use of illegal drugs during pregnancy. But the indictment contorted the statute's prohibition against drug "delivery" to characterize as criminal the kind of conduct that could not have been considered within its scope by the enacting legislature.

No new law had been passed making it a special criminal offense to use drugs during pregnancy. Rather, the prosecutions have been based on obviously strained interpretations of existing law, such as child endangerment or delivery of drugs to a minor. Since both drug use and criminal laws prohibiting sale, distribution, or possession of drugs have been with us for decades, why should prosecuting attorneys be searching the statute books today for creative ways to prosecute pregnant women who use drugs? The answer may lie in a peculiar confluence of changing attitudes towards pregnancy and drug use. Public attitudes are pro-natalist in the broad sense of supporting efforts to overcome infertility and to have children.[3] Advances in medical technology have produced new methods for detecting and sometimes correcting fetal abnormalities,[4] which enables us to think of fetuses as "patients" separately from their mothers. Public health studies have found that pregnant women can have a positive impact on the outcome of their pregnancies through prenatal care, improved nutrition, and the avoidance of teratogenic or toxic substances like alcohol and drugs. This had led to a close scrutiny of the behavior of pregnant women. Finally, the war on illegal drugs announced by the Reagan Administration has spurred intense publicity about the dangers of drug use and has tended to legitimize virtually any action to suppress drugs.[5] Indeed, the civil liberties of individuals are often seen as a hindrance to winning the

Reprinted by permission of the Institute for Criminal Justice Ethics and the authors from *Criminal Justice Ethics,* from vol. 9 (1990), pp. 30-41.

"war." Media reports of increases in the number of infants born with traces of drugs in their systems have linked the horrors of drugs with our concern for healthy babies.

The influence of changing knowledge and values has led us to see the mother as responsible for many ills that befall her newborn. If she did not receive prenatal care, ate poorly, drank too much, or took drugs, she is assumed to be the cause of any injury to the baby—she is a bad mother. It is easy to feel outrage at behavior that seems avoidable and that risks injury to a newborn. So it is understandable that many have argued for controlling women to protect a fetus.[6] Few would argue that a pregnant woman has no moral responsibility to her developing fetus. However, violation of this moral responsibility not to harm is being transformed into a punishable crime.

Prosecuting women for prenatal drug use offers immediate and visible action against an identifiable "wrong-doer." It is always a news story. Unable to make significant inroads against drug traffickers, prosecutors can appear to take a strong stand against illegal drugs and for protecting children. The alternatives—intercepting the drug supply, finding effective treatment for drug dependency, and providing drug treatment programs—are tedious, expensive, and rarely newsworthy.

No one really disagrees that drug use, among other things, risks jeopardizing fetal health, and that, ideally, such drug use should be eliminated. The question is who should be responsible for, and who will be effective in, taking steps to protect fetal health—the public health community or the criminal justice system?

This article examines the assumptions that underlie current prosecutions of pregnant women who use drugs. It argues that the professed goals of such prosecutions cannot be achieved through the criminal law. The offense that pregnant women are thought to commit cannot be defined in terms of any intelligible duty enforceable by the criminal law. Prosecuting pregnant women for drug use is unlikely to alter the spread of drugs or the health prospects of children. Instead, it is likely to threaten the rights of women as autonomous individuals and, ultimately, the future of their children.

THE GOAL OF PROSECUTION

Most prosecutors argue that their actions are not intended to punish women. For example, one prosecutor was reported to say, "We are not really interested in convicting women and sending them to jail. We're just interested in getting them to stop using drugs before they do something horrible to their babies."[7] If the goal is to stop drug use, there is no need to resort to rationalizations about protecting the fetus in order to prosecute. In virtually all states, the manufacture, delivery, or possession of controlled substances (illicit drugs) is already a criminal offense.[8] This applies to everyone, not just pregnant women. Women are not immune from prosecution for these crimes merely because they are pregnant. Few pregnant women, however, are involved in drug trafficking. At most they might be guilty of illegal drug possession. Yet because they are not ordinarily discovered until their children are born and drug metabolites are found in the newborn's system, there is not likely to be proof sufficient to permit a conviction for the offense of possession. Thus, as a practical matter, pregnant women are not likely to be successfully prosecuted for drug possession.

Drug use, by itself, is not ordinarily a criminal offense,[9] largely because of the difficulty of proof and because offenders can ordinarily be charged with possession.

Moreover, if drug use results in harm to another person, such as an assault, the undesirable behavior is ordinarily proscribed by another criminal statute, such as that making assault a criminal offense. In such cases, however, the prosecution is limited to the crime of assault, independent of drug use. Thus, drug use that results in harm to a fetus cannot be prosecuted unless either drug use alone or harm to the fetus by itself is an independent crime. If neither is punishable as a crime, their co-existence should not constitute a crime. If drug use alone is not a criminal offense, then what is being punished is the status of being pregnant.[10] This makes pregnancy a necessary element of a remarkable new criminal offense: pregnancy by a drug-dependent person, or drug use by a pregnant woman.[11]

There are instances in which two lawful activities constitute an offense when combined. Driving while intoxicated is the most obvious example. Yet this offense does not automatically justify criminalizing the combination of pregnancy and drug use. It is not the act of drinking that offends but the condition of intoxication that precludes the driver from safely managing a vehicle. After all, motor vehicles are inherently dangerous objects. It is for this reason that driving itself is regulated. Driving is not permitted without a license, obtainable only upon demonstration of at least a minimal level of competence and skill. Pregnancy, in contrast, is not deemed a privilege for which licensure is required.[12] Pregnancy is a condition, not an activity, and while it poses some risks to the pregnant women, it is not inherently dangerous to *others.* Prosecutions for drug use during pregnancy appear to enforce an implied license, one that stipulates the conduct required of those granted the privilege of pregnancy. Yet pregnancy is unlike driving in more fundamental ways. Pregnancy is symbolic of the continuation of the human race. For individuals, it is, ideally, a time of joy, of preparing for an expanded family. It involves nurturing and growth. To convert it into a symbol of woman as threat is likely to profoundly affect the way society views women in general and to transform pregnant women from nurturers into suspects.

The justifications for wanting to stop pregnant women from taking drugs have to do with preventing harm to the fetus and insuring the birth of a health baby. This raises several questions. What is the harm to be prevented? What acts or omissions cause the harm? What kind of duty can a pregnant woman have to prevent the harm? Can the duty be enforced and the harm prevented by prosecuting pregnant women under the criminal law?

DUTY

Criminal prosecutions of women's conduct during pregnancy assume that women have a special duty to the fetus.[13] But precisely what is this duty? And what qualifies as a violation of the duty? General discussions of the subject appear to assume that women have a legal duty not to *harm* the fetus. (In this article, we discuss only duties arising in existing *law*, not moral obligations that may exist in the absence of any legal duty.

One of the truisms of criminal law is that it exists to prevent harm. What is the harm to be prevented in the case of pregnant women who use drugs? The most extreme case of harm would be the death of the fetus. Criminal law governing killing a fetus is already in place. In most states, homicide can be committed against the fetus, but only if it dies after live birth.[14] A few states have made feticide a crime if someone other than the mother intentionally kills the fetus. Convictions have been sustained in cases of brutal attacks upon the woman, often by men who specifically intended to kill the fetus. Unintentional or negligent killing of a fetus by one unaware of the pregnancy, however, is not even manslaughter in most states.[15] There are good reasons why the criminal law has treated feticide differently from homicide. The harm ordinarily sought to be prevented is that directed against the pregnant women herself. Ascribing legal personhood to fetuses for purposes of applying homicide laws would unnecessarily subject most stillbirths to criminal investigation. It could also create two independent rights-holders within the body of one pregnant woman—the woman and the fetus—with controversial implications for both criminal and civil law that society has not yet agreed on and is not likely soon to accept.

Even so, one might argue that a woman has a duty not to cause the death of her fetus.[16] If the duty is to guarantee the fetus's survival to live birth, then no harm occurs when the baby is born alive. It should be evident that there is no general duty to guarantee survival to birth. However, women have been prosecuted when their babies have been born alive. So death is not the harm—or at least not the only harm—being targeted.

In the absence of fetal death or stillbirth, the harm might be any physical or developmental damage that the living child suffers. If so the duty is to guarantee the child optimal or at least normal mental and physical health. Or it might be the seemingly lesser duty of preventing avoidable injury. But this is not a duty imposed generally on pregnant women. And with good reason. First, before the state can accuse one of a criminal offense, it must define the crime in an understandable way. How would we define the degree of health or well-being that a woman should have a duty to produce? How would we define the degree of health or well-being that a woman should not adversely affect?

Second, there is the problem of determining the cause of any harm. The physical and mental status of a child is affected by a multitude of actors, some genetic, some gestational, some perinatal, some environmental in the postnatal period, many unknown.[17] Many of these lie outside a woman's control, such as her genetic contribution to the child or her exposure to rubella or toxic air pollutants. How is the state or anyone else to know whether and when a crime has been committed? Must every birth with an Apgar score of less than 10 be investigated? There is no general duty to produce a perfect or even a healthy or "normal" child. Thus, this cannot be the duty that pregnant women are said to violate. Moreover, any general duty to perform or refrain from specific acts that harm the fetus in some clearly identifiable way would be derivative of a more general duty not to harm the fetus.[18]

Interestingly, few prosecutions of drug-using women have demonstrated that a drug actually caused harm to a newborn. The offense that is prosecuted is not the materialization of harm at birth. It is the conduct that exposes the child to risk. This conduct takes place during pregnancy, not after birth.[19] This suggests that it is not enough to avoid harm. The duty implied is really a duty to prevent any *risk* of harm. Since the fetus is integrally connected to the pregnant woman, preventing risks of harm to the fetus requires caring for the woman's body or at least preventing harm to her. Thus, the woman's duty to the fetus is necessarily a duty to protect her own body, for she cannot take proper care of the fetus unless she cares properly for her own body. This duty to prevent risk to the fetus amounts to imposing on a pregnant woman a state-defined standard of care for her own body, or conduct toward herself. It is noteworthy that while the state justifies its prosecutions on the basis of its interest in protecting the fetus, it does not undertake any duty to ensure the necessary care for the woman's body. Instead, it imposes that duty on the pregnant woman.

The *Johnson Controls* case[20] now before the United States Supreme Court will decide whether a company can impose controls on women employees to protect a future fetus—excluding those without proof of sterility from higher-paying jobs that expose them to lead. If criminal prosecutions are acceptable, it would follow that not only *may* employers impose such controls, they *must* do so, and women must abide by them.

CAUSATION

The evidence that drug use harms the fetus is suggestive but problematic as a basis for criminal offense. The harmful effects of heroin and alcohol when taken frequently in very large quantities are well known. Yet a surprising number of children of substance abusers escape damage. For example, the Public Health Services has estimated that 86 percent of women drink at least once during pregnancy, with 20 to 35 percent drinking regularly.[21] Most of their children are born quite healthy. Alcohol appears to be teratogenic only if used on a few specific days of gestation.[22] Different substances have different effects on the fetus at different times during pregnancy. For example, significant damage to organs generally occurs early in pregnancy; birth weight problems happen later; there is still uncertainty about when brain damage can occur. Given the difficulties in estimating gestation in general, how are we to know whether a particular substance caused a particular harm in one infant?

The evidence with respect to cocaine use is still being accumulated. Women who use cocaine have newborns with low birth weight (5.5 pounds or less), reduced head circumference, some congenital malformations, and an increased risk of premature birth and of *abruptio placentae* resulting in stillbirth.[23] However, cocaine's precise contribution to these and other risks remains uncertain and under study. The effect of occasional as opposed to regular heavy use is unclear. Studies indicate that the health of women who used cocaine during pregnancy is often impaired by other factors, such as poor nutrition and the use of alcohol, cigarettes, marijuana, and other drugs.[24] Some researchers studied only poor minority women, who typically have poorer prenatal health than the general population. Poverty, poor nutrition, lack of prenatal care, and even stress adversely affect fetal development.[25] One of the most important determinants of low birth weight (itself a major risk factor for infant mortality) is inadequate prenatal care.[26] Thus, drug use may not be the primary determinant of poor birth outcomes. Stopping drug use during pregnancy will not guarantee a healthy baby. Continued drug use does not always cause damage. Moreover, the long-term effects of drug use are still under study. The degree to which children who are born prematurely, or with low birth weight or small head size, are actually prejudiced in their development remains to be seen.[27] Caretaking and their environment contribute significantly to their developmental functioning.

Women who use drugs typically are beset with problems in addition to substance abuse—from lack of housing and income to family difficulties—that contribute to poor birth outcomes. Yet, when a bad outcome occurs, it is easier to blame it on a drug the women took during pregnancy than to recognize the constellation of possible causes. As a practical matter, it seems almost impossible to satisfy the standard of proof of causation in a criminal prosecution, given the complexity of fetal development and the multiplicity of factors that affect it. While drug use is certainly a risk factor, focusing on drugs draws attention away from the much more global problem of inadequate prenatal care.

SOURCES OF HARM

If harm is what is to be prevented, then the source of the harm should not matter. Anything that causes serious harm should be the subject of prosecution. Women who fail to get adequate prenatal care or proper nourishment should be prosecuted. This approach was used in California when Pamela Rae Stewart's baby died six weeks after birth. She was prosecuted not just for taking amphetamines but also for disregarding her physician's advice to refrain from sex with her husband and to get to the hospital at the first sign of bleeding.[28] The court dismissed the criminal action on the grounds that the child support statute under which it was brought was not intended to apply to refusals to follow physician's orders.[29] Amending the statute to prohibit pregnant women from having sex with their husbands might protect some fetuses from harm but would be seen by most people as an outrageous violation of liberty.

A recent study compared the neurological development of children born prematurely whose heart rates were monitored electronically before and during delivery with children (also born prematurely) whose heart rates were checked periodically by auscultation or "listening" through the pregnant woman's abdomen.[30] Children who were monitored with state-of-the-art electronic fetal monitors had cerebral palsy 2.9 times as often as children monitored by ordinary auscultation. After adjustment for other risks factors, the risk of cerebral palsy was 3.8 higher for the electronically monitored children than the other group. Does this mean that the use of electronic fetal monitors is or should be a criminal offense? Such a law would merely require women and physicians to avoid using something that creates a risk of fetal harm.

Variations in medical practice should make us wary of relying on current medical standards as ideal pregnancy care. Over the decades, women have been alternately praised and chastised for gaining more than ten pounds during pregnancy. Attitudes toward giving birth outside the hospital have varied from acceptance as normal to rejection as dangerous or crazy. A former president of a state chapter of the American College of Obstetrics and Gynecology reportedly said that people who have home births are "kooks, the lunatic fringe, people who have emotional problems they're acting out."[31] Physicians in Alaska even requested the attorney general to charge a physician with murder after a baby died following a home birth he attended.[32] Such incidents are reminders of the fallibility of medical opinion and how quick some are to equate unfashionable conduct with crime.

There is little doubt that drug use during pregnancy presents a risk of harm to the fetus. But it is hardly the only risk. How are we to distinguish the harm from drug use from harm arising from poor nourishment during infancy and childhood, from poor parenting practices such as emotional detachment, excessive discipline, or lack of supervision? What kind of duty will prevent such similar harms? Should we require a license to have children, as some have suggested,[33] obtainable upon proof of adequate parenting capabilities? How will we define these? Can they be predicted before one has a child?

The duty pregnant women who use drugs are assumed to have cannot, in fact, be explained in terms of the harm to the fetus or child or even risk of harm. Harm can be caused by more than just drug use. Thus, the duty cannot be justified by the desire to prevent the harm itself. It must be justified, if at all, by the need to proscribe specific drug use that causes harm that does not result from other sources. The only distinction between cases of possible harm to a child from drug use and cases of harm arising from alcohol, tobacco, malnutrition, lack of prenatal care, and physical trauma is the assumed source of the harm—the drugs. The duty that is really imposed here is the duty not to use drugs, a duty that may already exist regardless of pregnancy. If the real concern is to avoid fetal harm, there is no principled way to distinguish between harm caused by drugs and harm caused by these other avoidable factors, and, therefore, no principled way to limit prosecutions to drug using pregnant women.

But, it might be argued, the harm from drug use can be singled out because drug use is already illegal in some states or could be made unlawful. Certainly drug use could be prosecuted as an offense. But its illegality does not distinguish it from other risks of harm to a fetus. Anyone—male or female—could be prosecuted for illegal drug use. Prosecuting *only* pregnant women for drug use requires a justification beyond illegality based on harm to the fetus that other risk factors do not create.

DUTY TO WHOM?

The idea of a duty raises the additional question of to whom the duty is owed. If the law is criminal, then the duty is owed to the state. This transforms any normal desire to avoid harm to the fetus into an obligation to the government.

Parents do have obligations to their children. Analogizing to child abuse and neglect laws, some commentators have argued that pregnant women should have an enforceable duty not to take drugs that risk harm to the fetus.[34] This notion of "fetal abuse" however, treats the fetus better than a child. The harm to children prohibited by civil child abuse laws is both greater in degree and easier to identify than the more general risk of harm to a fetus. While drug use may expose a fetus to risk, harm occurs only in a proportion of cases. The fetus is also at risk from other factors. Child abuse intervention ordinarily occurs only when a child has suffered real injury. Only in the most extreme cases of intentional, long-lasting injury are parents charged with a crime. Even then, the crime is not a special offense of child abuse but ordinary homicide or assault.

Child abuse laws are most active—and most successful—in the civil sphere. They create a system of social services intended to enable the family to provide adequate care for a child. This is a social service model; the intervention is directed at the family unit, parents and child together. If the parents refuse to cooperate, the state may take custody of the child, but this is not automatic and is ordinarily viewed as a last resort. Children who are abused can be removed from parental custody because they are physically separate persons.[35] "Fetal abuse," however, cannot be stopped without physically intervening on the mother, or at the least, seriously restricting her liberty. As long as the two are physiologically united, such an intervention subordinates the woman to the fetus. The concept of fetal abuse can be justified only by granting to the fetus rights of an independent live-born person and denying such rights to the woman. Pregnant women would be treated as chattel, as inert "fetal containers."[36] Even temporary denial of the rights of personhood to women is incompatible with the fundamental principles of individual autonomy and equal respect for persons that form the core of our law.[37] If there is a duty to the fetus, it cannot be bootstrapped into a fetal abuse hypothesis.[38]

INTENT

Attaching criminal liability to drug use raises the issue of criminal intent—whether, in taking drugs, the woman could be said to have intended the harm in question. Criminal intent is sometimes attributed to reckless conduct, in which the risk of harm is consciously disregarded, even though the actor has no reason or desire to cause harm. What is often thought to provide an explanation or reason for the action—the motive—is generally considered to be irrelevant. Were motive relevant, the absence of any purpose to harm would render many reckless actions nonculpable.[39]

Motive and intention are not always easily distinguished in fact.[40] Indeed, culpability of drug-using pregnant women seems predicated on the motives attributed to them rather than on their intention, as construed in the traditional sense just described. If intent were all that were at issue, then *any* act that produced harm to a fetus could be declared a criminal offense. The source of the harm should not matter. And if intent includes reckless behavior, then any thoughtless behavior that causes harm to the fetus would entail the requisite *mens rea.*[41] A pregnant woman who intentionally walked on an icy sidewalk might be said to have acted criminally if a fall causes injury or death to the fetus. Indeed, if the goal is to prevent any *risk* of fetal harm, then the crime is committed once the woman sets foot on the ice, even if no injury results. Similarly, a pregnant woman who has sex with her husband could be guilty of endangering her fetus. In fact, when such an event results in injury, it is considered a tragedy and not a crime. This suggests that it is not the behavior alone that determines liability. Rather, it is society's perception of the behavior as desirable or undesirable that controls. From the fetus's perspective, walking on ice and taking drugs may have the same unwanted consequences. The only explanation for making the latter a crime is that we think drug use is bad.

The focus on pregnant women who use illegal drugs is best explained by societal disapproval of mothers who need or want to get high, an attitude that "betrays a profound suspicion of pregnant women."[42] It is as though we believe that women are taking a drug for the purpose of harming the fetus. Yet it is doubtful that any woman has taken any drug for the express purpose of harming her fetus. However the initial use of a drug might be characterized, its continued use by addicts is rarely, if ever, truly voluntary. Drug addiction tends to obliterate rational, autonomous decision making about drug use. Drugs become a necessity for dependent users, even when they would much prefer to escape their addiction. In virtually all instances, a user specifically does *not* want to harm her fetus. Yet she cannot resist the drive to use the drug. Thus, it is not plausible to attribute to drug-using women a motive of causing harm to the fetus. The only intent the women form is to take the drug. But this is the traditional definition of intent merely to do the act, which is not sufficient to define *this* crime.

CRIMINALIZING DRUG USE IS COUNTERPRODUCTIVE

Even if one could plausibly argue that pregnant women have a duty to have healthy children, and that they intend by drug use to injure a child, and even if the causal link between drug use and harm to the fetus could be proved beyond a reasonable doubt, use of the criminal law to protect fetuses from their drug-using mothers should still be opposed because it will be counterproductive.

One of the goals of prosecuting women who use drugs seems to be to create an incentive for pregnant women to stop using drugs, as by entering a drug treatment program. But treatment is rarely available to pregnant women.[43] Dr. Chavkin's survey showed that about 54 percent of New York City's drug treatment programs excluded pregnant women.[44] Moreover, 67 percent refused to admit pregnant women whose source of payment was Medicaid. Eighty-seven percent excluded pregnant Medicaid patients who used crack.[45] In Massachusetts, there are only thirty state-funded residential beds for pregnant women in drug treatment programs.[46] Ten of these are in a new program that opened only last year; fifteen are in the women's correctional facility.

In part, the scarcity of treatment for pregnant women reflects a history of ignoring drug treatment for women.[47] Even now, little is known about how to eliminate drug dependence among women. The absence of child care has made it impossible for many women to enter or remain in treatment. Also, few programs deal with the problems of domestic violence or husbands or partners who introduce women to drugs, so that women return to circumstances that foster drug use.

In addition, there continues to be considerable uncertainty about *how* to treat drug-dependent women. Medical opinion has both recommended and cautioned against methadone detoxification during pregnancy over the years.[48] There is little successful experience in treating dependency on cocaine and crack, the drugs that appear to be increasingly used by women. A handful of residential programs that provide comprehensive medical services and job training, and help women learn how to care for their children have had some success.[49] But these are labor intensive and expensive.

The general absence of drug treatment programs for pregnant women means that there is little likelihood that women who want to get off drugs will be able to.[50] In these circumstances, there is little justification for making the pregnant woman's drug use a crime. The woman would be punished for society's more general failure to provide treatment. Some prosecutors have claimed that they prosecuted women in order to get them into treatment, and indeed, have recommended sentencing them to a treatment program instead of prison.[51] This type of sentence assumes an obligation on the part of drug users to join a treatment program, an obligation they cannot meet because of the woefully inadequate treatment facilities available. The irony of requiring a criminal conviction in order to gain access to treatment is apparent. Prosecutions cannot be justified as long as there are insufficient treatment programs to meet the needs of pregnant women.

Finally, criminalizing drug use during pregnancy is likely to be counterproductive in protecting the fetus. There is reason to believe that women will avoid prenatal delivery care if detection of their drug use could lead to their arrest or loss of child custody. Several states currently require that health care providers report to the state women or their newborns who are drug dependent or exhibit drug withdrawal symptoms. The state may act to take custody of the newborn and may notify the district attorney to initiate criminal charges.

Newborns are rarely protected by such a system. If women avoid prenatal care for fear of losing their babies or going to jail, the child's birth weight and development are likely to be prejudiced. Removing the child from the mother after birth compounds the injury. There are already too few foster homes available without adding more children to the system. Many of these children languish as boarder babies in hospitals waiting for placement.[52] The emotional deprivation that is necessarily typical of institutional care may harm these children more than living at home with their mothers. The paucity of resources devoted to caring for children belies the assertion that the purpose of separating mother and child is to protect the child. William Bennett, the Bush Administration's "drug czar," has recommended removing children from every woman who uses drugs. But prenatal drug use, by itself, does not predict postnatal abuse or neglect. If the mother demonstrates conduct sufficient to constitute child abuse or neglect after birth, existing law is more than adequate to take the child into custody for its own protection.

It seems clear that punishment is the only goal that is served by defining drug use by pregnant women as a crime. No one can seriously maintain that prosecution serves the traditional goal of deterrence. Existing prohibitions and increased penalties have not stopped the distribution or use of drugs. In the absence of adequate treatment programs, "rehabilitation" cannot be provided. Rehabilitation is generally conceived as appropriate for recalcitrant offenders who have refused to comply with the law. Creating a new crime for the sole purpose of getting pregnant women into treatment stands the goal of rehabilitation on its head. Jennifer Johnson was unable to get into a drug treatment facility when she became pregnant. After she was convicted, she was sentenced, in part, to a treatment program. This is not rehabilitation. It is using the criminal law to gain access to social services. Why should a pregnant woman have to be convicted of a crime in order to enter a social program that is, in theory, open to anyone? While some prosecutors may think of themselves as heroes because their conviction forced a treatment program to accept a woman (no longer pregnant), in reality the government is giving its stamp of approval to a barrier that keeps pregnant women out of treatment programs.

If neither deterrence nor rehabilitation is served by prosecuting pregnant women, only punishment remains. Pregnant women who use drugs need help, not punishment. But all that prosecution can accomplish is conviction and punishment.

CONCLUSION

Prosecutions of drug-using pregnant women are based on an illusion, and a dangerous one at that. They foster the illusion that society is protecting its future generations. In reality, such prosecutions substitute punishment for protection. By treating women as threats to their own progeny, society rejects the only source of fetal sustenance. It separates mother and child at the time the child most needs a mother, and relegates the child to the woefully inadequate system of institutional or foster care.

Criminal prosecutions assume that women have a special duty to the fetus that men do not have. But when they are examined closely, that duty cannot be found. Any duty not to harm the fetus would cover a wide range of concededly lawful behavior. The more expansive duty to avoid any risk to the fetus would prohibit an even larger sphere of ordinary conduct. A pregnant woman might be assured of satisfying such a duty only by having an abortion.

Singling out pregnant women highlights the fact that they are being punished not for any act harming the fetus but because they are pregnant and use drugs. Making pregnancy one of the elements of a crime is disturbing. It affects the way we think about pregnancy, making all pregnant women suspect. Moreover, punishment cannot remotely be believed to deter either drug use or pregnancy.

Imposing a legal duty on pregnant women to protect the fetus—especially one enforceable by criminal law—requires stripping women of their status as rights-bearing persons. It is dangerous because it would create a precedent for controlling pregnancy and women in general. Any rationale that justifies prosecuting pregnant women for risking harm to a fetus may be used to justify controlling all behavior of pregnant women. If the goal is to protect the fetus, then there would be no impediment to controlling the behavior of all women of childbearing age.[53]

Finally, criminalizing certain conduct by pregnant women is likely to be counterproductive, deterring women not from drug use but from prenatal care and other services that have a realistic probability of improving the health of their children.

The effects of drug use are tragic for women, children, and society Injecting the criminal law can only deepen the tragedy. The answer lies not in punishing women but in helping them to emerge from their own misery. It is an expensive and lengthy process requiring better education about pregnancy care, expansion of prenatal care facilities, research into addiction treatment, and the creation of treatment facilities. It won't get headlines, but it can work. Drug use during pregnancy is a *real* problem. It is a public health problem that can only be compounded by treating it as a crime.

NOTES

1. *Pregnant and Newly Delivered Women Jailed on Drug Charges*, 2 Reproductive Rights Update, Feb. 2, 1990, at 6.

2. Johnson v. State, No. 89-1765 (Fla. Dist. Ct. App., 5th Dist., 1989). Johnson was convicted and sentenced to 15 years on probation, and required to abstain from drug and alcohol use if pregnant and to comply with prenatal care recommendations.

3. Robertson draws upon this general feeling to support a right to procreate. *See* Robertson, *The Right to Procreate and In Utero Fetal Therapy*, 3 J. Legal Med. 333 (1982).

4. S. Elias & G.J. Annas, Reproductive Genetics and the Law (1987).

5. Glantz, *A Nation of Suspects: Drug Testing and the Fourth Amendment*, 79 Am. J. Public Health 1427 (1989).

6. Criminal prosecutions are not the only forms of control being advocated. Physicians and hospitals, among others, have endorsed requiring women to undergo caesarean section delivery in lieu of vaginal birth when physicians believe the fetus might be in distress. *See* Kolder, Gallagher & Parsons, *Court-Ordered Obstetrical Interventions*, 316 New Eng. J. Med. 1192-96 (1987). Others suggest requiring pregnant women to comply with their physicians' recommendations for prenatal care, including limitations on exercise and marital sex. Some heads of Maternal-Fetal Medicine Departments would detain women who fail to abide by their physicians' "orders." *Id. See generally*, Field, *Controlling the Women to Protect the Fetus*, 17 Law, Med. & Health Care 114 (1989); Rhoden, *The Judge in the Delivery Room: The Emergence of Court-Ordered Cesareans*, 75 Calif. L. Rev. 1951 (1987). The increasing availability of prenatal diagnosis and screening for genetic abnormalities suggests requiring women to undergo testing and surgery, if not abortion, to correct fetal problems. On the scope of genetic screening, *see generally*, S. Elias & G.J. Annas, *supra* note 4; Annas, *Who's Afraid of the Human Genome*? 19 Hastings Center Rep. 19 (1989). One need not even wait until pregnancy to avoid such problems. Commercial industry has excluded women of childbearing capacity from jobs that could expose them to teratogens. *See, e.g.*, Wright v. Olin Corp., 697 F. 2d 1172 (4th Cir. 1982); International Union v. Johnson Controls Inc., 886 F.2d 871 (7th Cir. 1989), cert. granted, _U.S_ (1990). *See generally*, Becker, *From Muller v. Oregon to Fetal Vulnerability Policies*, 53 U. Chi. L. Rev. 1219-73 (1986). Yet making undesirable behavior a criminal offense, putting a new mother in prison, or depriving her of custody of her child, goes beyond controlling women's behavior or excluding them from certain jobs or activities.

7. Lewin, *Drug Use in Pregnancy: New Issues for the Courts*, N. Y. Times, Feb. 5, 1990, at A14.

8. Unif. Cont. Subst. Act §401, 9 U.L.A. 91 (1988) makes it unlawful for any person to manufacture, deliver, or possess with intent to manufacture or deliver, a controlled substance (the trafficking crimes), or knowingly or intentionally to possess a controlled substance. Distribution to persons under age eighteen is also an offense. The Act has been adopted by forty-eight states, the District of Columbia, Guam, Puerto Rico, and the Virgin Islands.

9. Mere *use*—as opposed to possession or trafficking—is not included as an offense in the Uniform Act. However, a few states, such as California, have made drug use a crime. *See, e.g.*, In re Orosco, 82 Cal. App. 3d 924, 147 Cal. Rptr. 463 (1978). However, use refers to a present state of being under the influence of a controlled substance, not use in the past. *See* People v. Spann, 1987 Cal. App. 3d 400, 232 Cal. Rptr. 31 (1986).

10. Note, *Maternal Rights and Fetal Wrongs: The Case Against the Criminalization of "Fetal Abuse,"* 101 Harv. L. Rev. 995, 1007 n. 79 (1988).

11. Criminalizing pregnancy by a drug-dependent person creates a crime dependent on status, the status of being pregnant and the status of drug dependency. Since Robinson v. California, 370 U.S. 660 (1962), criminalization of drug addiction has been recognized as impermissible punishment of status in violation of the eighth amendment. There does not appear to be any basis for squaring the criminalization of pregnancy with the teachings of *Robinson*.

12. For an argument that parents *should* be licensed before having children, *see* McIntire, *Parenthood Training or Mandatory Birth Control: Take Your Choice*, Psychology Today, Oct. 1973, at 34. McIntire's argument, however, applies evenhandedly to both men and women. Licensure of pregnancy would burden only women.
13. Alternatively, they may assume that the fetus is entitled to legal status as a person. However, ascribing personhood to the fetus is a much harder case to make than imposing a duty to the fetus regardless of whether it is considered a person with all the rights and privileges granted to those already born. This discussion focuses on the nature of the duty rather than the legal status of the fetus because it is the duty, if any, that is the critical element of the crime.
14. Kahn, *Of Woman's First Disobedience: Forsaking a Duty of Care to Her Fetus—Is This a Mother's Crime?*, 53 Brooklyn L. Rev. 807, 818-20 (1987).
15. *But see* Commonwealth v. Cass, 392 Mass. 799, 467 N.E.2d 1324 (1984) (holding that a fetus was a "person" for purposes of vehicular homicide statute).
16. Any duty not to cause the death of the fetus is obviously complicated by lawful abortion and would require some principle to distinguish lawful abortion from lawful killing. This can be and has been accomplished when the person doing the killing is a third party, such as a felon who assaults the mother and causes the death of the fetus. But defining the duty on the part of the pregnant women requires more.
17. S. Elias & G.J. Annas, *supra* note 4.
18. It thus depends for its justification on the justification for any duty to the fetus. In addition, it requires an empirical basis for claiming that specific acts or omissions harm the fetus in particular, avoidable ways.
19. *See* Reyes v. Superior Ct, 75 Cal. App. 3d 214, 217, 141 Cal. Rptr. 912 (1977).
20. International Union v. Johnson Controls Inc., 886 F.2d 871 (7th Cir 1989), cert. granted _U.S._ (1990).
21. Rosenthal, *When a Pregnant Woman Drinks*, N. Y. Times, Feb. 4, 1990, §6 (Magazine), at 30, 49, 61.
22. S. Elias & G.J. Annas, *supra* note 4.
23. Chasnoff, *Perinatal Effects of Cocaine*, Contemporary Ob/Gyn 164 (1987); Zuckerman, Frank, Hingson, Amaro, Levenson, Kane, Parker, Vinci, Aboagye, Fried, Cabral, Timperi & Bauchner, *Effects of Maternal Marijuana and Cocaine Use on Fetal Growth*, 320 New Eng. J. Med. 762 (1989) [hereinafter cited as *Effects*]; Petitti & Coleman, *Cocaine and the Risk of Low Birth Weight*, 80 Am. J. Public Health 25 (1990).
24. Frank, Zuckerman, Amaro, Aboagye, Bauchner, Cabral, Fried, Hingson, Kane, Levenson, Parker, Reece & Vinci, *Cocaine Use During Pregnancy: Prevalence and Correlates*, 82 Pediatrics 888 (1988); *Effects*, *supra* note 23.
25. Binsacca, Ellis, Martin & Petitti, *Factors Associated with Low Birthweight in an Inner City Population: The Role of Financial Problems*, 77 Am. J. Public Health 505 (1987); Leveno, Cunningham, Roarke, Nelson & Williams, *Prenatal Care and the Low Birth Weight Infant*, 66 Obst. & Gyn. 599 (1985); Miller, *Infant Mortality in the U.S.*, 253 Sci. Am. 31 (1985).
26. U.S. General Accounting Office, Prenatal Care: Medicaid Recipients and Uninsured Women Obtain Insufficient Care, Sept., 1987, at 13, 31.
27. *Drug Babies: An Ethical Quagmire for Doctors*, Medical World News, Feb. 12, 1990, at 39, 43, 45.
28. Stewart had placenta previa which separated from the uterus causing hemorrhaging and severe damage to the fetus. Her husband was not prosecuted for having sex with his wife or failing to take her to the hospital.
29. People v. Stewart, No. M598097, slip op. (San Diego Co. Ct., Feb. 23, 1987). In Reyes v. Superior Court, 75 Cal. App. 3d 214, 141 Cal. Rptr. 912 (1977), Margaret Reyes was charged with felony child endangerment for using heroin and failing to seek prenatal care, against the advice of a

public health nurse. She gave birth to twins who were addicted to heroin and suffered withdrawal. The prosecution was prohibited because the court found that the statute did not apply to unborn children and was not intended to apply to prenatal conduct. Similarly, in Baby X v. Misiano, 373 Mass. 265, 266, 366 N.E.2d 755 (1977), the father's duty of support under the Massachusetts child support statute was held to extend only to a child, and not to an unborn fetus.

30. Shy, Luthy, Bennett, Whitfield, Larson, van Belle, Hughes, Wilson & Stencher, *Effects of Electronic Fetal-Heart-Rate Monitoring, as Compared with Periodic Auscultation, on the Neurologic Development of Premature Infants*, 322 New Eng. J. Med. 533 (1990).

31. Harvey, *Homebirths*, Boston Globe, Oct. 16, 1977 (Magazine), at 18, quoted in Annas, *Legal Aspects of Home Birth*, in S.E. Sagov, R.I. Feinbloom, P. Spindel, A. Brodsky, Home Birth: A Practitioner's Guide to Birth Outside the Hospital 51-63, 54 (1984).

32. *Id.* at 56.

33. *See, e.g.*, McIntire, *supra* note 12.

34. Myers, *Abuse and Neglect of the Unborn: Can the State Intervene*? 23 Duquesne L. Rev. 1 (1984); Robertson, *Legal Issues in Fetal Therapy*, 9 Seminars in Perinatology 136 (1985).

35. A few states deem a medical diagnosis of drug addiction or fetal alcohol syndrome in a newborn to be prima facie evidence of neglect for purposes of determining whether parents are fit to retain custody of the child after birth. Ill. Rev. Stat. ch. 37, § 704-6(c) (d); Utah Code Ann. § 78-36.5; In re Smith, 128 Misc.2d 976, 492 N.Y.S.2d.331 (Fam. Ct. 1985); In re Baby X, 97 Mich. App. 111, 293 N.W.2d 736. (1980). Still, the determination focuses on whether the parents will be able to care for the child after it is born. The termination of custody or parental rights remains a civil proceeding consistent with the purposes of child abuse laws. It does not entail criminal prosecution for acts committed before birth.

36. Annas, *Women as Fetal Containers*, 16 Hastings Center Rep. 13 (1986). *See generally*, Johnsen, *The Creation of Fetal Rights: Conflicts with Women's Constitutional Rights to Liberty, Privacy, and Equal Protection*, 95 Yale L. J. 599 (1986).

37. Criminal laws prohibiting drug use only by pregnant women would single out pregnant women for punishment solely on the basis of their sex and reproductive capacity. It is the drug use, not the harm to the fetus, that is the conduct being proscribed. Sex is not a sufficient justification for making it a crime for pregnant women, but not men, to take drugs. The argument that this is permissible because only women can harm the fetus by drug use only underscores the discriminatory nature of the purported law. Men can cause harm to a fetus by using drugs or alcohol that affect the sperm and ultimately the delivered child, or by physically injuring a pregnant woman, for example. On the effects of drug and alcohol use by males on reproduction, *see generally*, Soyka & Joffe, *Male Mediated Drug Effect on Offspring*, Drug and Chemical Risks to The Fetus and Newborn (1980); and Abel & Lee, *Paternal Alcohol Exposure Affects Offspring Behavior but not Body or Organ Weights in Mice*, 12 Alcoholism Clinical & Experimental Research (May/June 1988). Environmental exposure to lead and other hazards can cause genetic damage prior to conception. *See, e.g.*, Occupational Safety & Health Administration, *Final Standard for Occupational Exposure to Lead*, 43 Fed. Reg. 52959 (1978); United Nations Scientific Committee on the Effects of Atomic Radiation, Sources and Effects of Ionizing Radiation (1977). What men cannot do, of course, is transmit drug metabolites to a fetus via the placenta. Allocating duties and punishments on the basis of sex is fundamentally at odds with the concept of equal protection. The United States Supreme Court has not recognized this degree of equal protection for pregnant women. *See* General Electric v. Gilbert, 429 U.S. 125 (1976), Geduldig v. Aiello, 417 U.S. 484 (1984). The Pregnancy Discrimination Act of 1978, 42 U.S.C. sec. 2000E (k), was enacted to protect pregnant women from the kind of workplace discrimination that the Court found the Constitution did not forbid. Still, the Court has not addressed the question whether the equal protection clause allows pregnant women to be burdened with criminal punishments to which men are not subject.

38. If a breach of this "duty" is punishable in criminal law, it should be remediable by a civil action for damages brought by the infant. In Curlender v. Bio-Science Laboratories, 106 Cal. App. 3d 811, 165 Cal. Rptr. 477 (1980), the Court recognized an infant's cause of action for wrongful life where a laboratory was alleged to have incorrectly notified the parents that they were not carriers of the gene for Tay-Sachs disease. The court also suggested that had the parents been warned, and then "made a conscious choice to proceed with a pregnancy, with full knowledge that a seriously impaired infant would be born . . . we see no sound public policy which should protect those parents from being answerable for the pain, suffering and misery which they have wrought upon their offspring." 106 Cal. App. 3d at 829. Thus, the court indicated its willingness to recognize a cause of action by an infant against its parents where the parents knew that the infant would suffer serious injury and failed to prevent it. In a much criticized decision, Grodin v. Grodin, 102 Mich. App. 396, 301 N.W. 2d 869 (1980), a Michigan court permitted a cause of action in negligence for the mother's use, during pregnancy, of tetracycline, which discolored the child's teeth.

39. "Hardly any part of penal law is more definitely settled than that motive is irrelevant." J. Hall, General Principles of Criminal Law 88 (2d ed. 1960), quoted in Husak, *Motive and Criminal Liability*, 8 Crim. Just. Ethics, 3, (Winter/Spring 1989). Husak criticizes this statement as an inaccurate description of the definition of many offenses. More importantly, he argues that motive cannot be divorced from intention on defensible principles in a significant proportion of cases and is thus a relevant factor in determining criminal liability, as well as punishment.

40. Husak, *supra* note 39.

41. We ignore here the possibility of defenses such as necessity or self-defense that might excuse otherwise reckless behavior.

42. Annas, *Protecting the Liberty of Pregnant Patients*, 316 New Eng. J. Med. 1213 (1987).

43. Treatment is generally scarce in the United States. A National Institute on Drug Abuse official said that only 338,365 public and private drug treatment slots were available in 1987 (the most recent figures) for an estimated 4 million addicts. Malcolm, *In Making Drug Strategy, No Accord on Treatment*, N. Y. Times, Nov. 19, 1989, §1, at 1. The majority of these serve men only. *See, e.g., Help is Hard to Find for Addict Mothers*, L.A. Times, Dec. 12, 1986, at J1.

44. Chavkin, *Drug Addiction and Pregnancy: Policy Crossroads*, 80 Am. J. Public Health 483 (1990).

45. *Id. See, also*, Atters, *Women and Crack: Equal Addiction, Unequal Care*, Boston Globe, Nov. 1, 1989, at 1, 4.

46. Malaspina, *Clean Living: An Innovative Residential Program Helps Pregnant Women with Drug Problems Take Control of Their Lives.* Boston Globe, Nov. 5, 1989 (Magazine), at 20.

47. Chavkin, *supra* note 44.

48. *Id.*

49. Malaspina, *supra* note 46.

50. About 375,000 infants are born to drug-using mothers each year in the United States, according to a 1988 study by the National Association for Perinatal Addiction Research and Education. *Id.* at 20. That exceeds the total number of treatment slots for all addicts—male and female—in the country.

51. A prison sentence would make clear that the prosecution was intended to punish, not to help, the woman because drugs are easy to get in most prisons.

52. Forty percent of the more than 300 hospitals boarder babies awaiting placement daily in New York City were there because of maternal drug use. C. Driver, W. Chavkin & G. Higginson, Survey of Infants Awaiting Placement in Voluntary Hospitals 1986–87 (New York City Dept. of Health, New York, NY 1987).

53. Field, *supra* note 6; Johnsen, *supra* note 36.

4

The Criminal Defense Lawyer: Zealous Advocate, Double Agent, or Beleaguered Dealer?

Rodney J. Uphoff*

In theory, the criminal defense lawyer is called to be a zealous advocate vigorously representing those persons accused by the state of violating the law.[1] As the champion of the accused, the criminal defense lawyer plays an essential role in the adversary system by challenging the prosecution's efforts to secure a conviction.[2] Defense counsel's responsibility is to probe and test the state's evidence to ensure that the accused is convicted only if the prosecution can muster sufficient evidence to prove the defendant's guilt beyond a reasonable doubt.[3] Moreover, it is counsel's duty to defend the accused zealously, even if counsel knows the defendant is guilty.[4]

In principle, therefore, a criminal defense lawyer, through counsel's legitimate efforts, may actually frustrate the search for the truth. Indeed, defense counsel may be ethically required to do so.[5] Defense counsel's zealous representation of a client is not, of course, without bounds. As an officer of the court, a defense lawyer's advocacy is constrained by various ethical rules.[6] Nevertheless, although disagreement exists as to how far a criminal defense lawyer may go on behalf of a client in certain tough ethical situations,[7] there is little question that defense counsel is required to be an able, devoted defender standing with the accused in an adversarial struggle with the state.[8]

However, is defense counsel, in practice, really a zealous advocate striving to provide a vigorous defense to the accused? Or is defense counsel too often a "double agent" merely seeking to persuade the client to accept a plea bargain, which is designed primarily to redound to the benefit of the lawyer and the criminal justice system?[9] Is there, in fact, a significant gap between the theoretical role of defense counsel and the actual practices of most criminal defense lawyers? To answer these questions, the first section of this article explores the observations made by Abraham Blumberg in 1967 that led him to conclude that defense lawyers were co-opted by the criminal justice system to serve organizational ends rather than their clients' interests.[10] The second section examines the behavior of defense lawyers in three counties

Reprinted by permission of West Group from the *Criminal Law Bulletin,* vol. 28 (1992), pp. 419-456.
*Lori Ketner's assistance in the preparation of this article is greatly appreciated.

to ascertain whether Blumberg's portrayal of defense counsel as double agent indeed is accurate. After discussing a number of important systemic variables that adversely affect the behavior and zeal of criminal defense lawyers, the second section concludes that "beleaguered dealer" more aptly describes the role of defense counsel in these counties. Finally, the third section considers the extent to which strengthening the system for the delivery of indigent defense services will enhance zealous advocacy and improve the quality of representation provided to most criminal defendants.

DEFENSE LAWYER AS "DOUBLE AGENT"

In his oft-cited article "The Practice of Law as Confidence Game: Organization Co-optation of a Profession," Abraham Blumberg turned his attention to the question of whether the traditional legal conception of the role of a criminal defense lawyer actually squared with social reality.[11] Blumberg correctly noted that the traditional view was based on the notion of a criminal case as an adversary, combative proceeding in which defense counsel zealously defended the accused. In fact, Blumberg stated, few cases actually are decided by trial.[12] Rather, the vast majority of cases are resolved by the plea-bargaining process, a process dictated by the organizational structure of criminal courts.[13] This court organization has its own set of goals and discipline, which in turn impose certain demands and conditions of practice on the actors in the system, including defense counsel.[14] As a result of organizational pressure, defense lawyers abandon their ethical commitment to their clients and instead "help the accused redefine his situation and restructure his perceptions concomitant with a plea of guilty."[15]

According to Blumberg, the formal and informal relations of all of the various actors in the criminal justice system were more important than the needs of any client.[16] Hence, in order to ensure continued positive relations and to cope with an intolerably large number of cases, these actors were bound together in "an organized system of complicity."[17] Blumberg described a variety of different systemic practices and institutional evasions that serve to pressure the accused to plead guilty while permitting the system to maintain an outward commitment to due process.[18] Defense lawyers were key players in the successful operation of the system. Owing their primary allegiance to the system, defense lawyers, whether public defenders or retained counsel, were concerned largely with strategies designed to manipulate clients into pleading guilty.[19]

Blumberg focused much of his attention on the efforts of criminal defense lawyers to "con" their clients.[20] To pull off this con, the criminal defense lawyer had to collect a fee, convince the client to accept a guilty plea, and still terminate the litigation as quickly as possible.[21] Counsel was a double agent because she pretended to help the client when, in fact, her main objective was to limit the scope and duration of the client's case, not to do battle.[22] Thus, defense counsel utilized her unique role in the organization to persuade or cajole the client to accept a result—a plea bargain—that served the interests of the organization and the lawyer above those of the client.[23]

But do Blumberg's damning observations about criminal defense lawyers really reflect the reality of the contemporary criminal justice system? To address this question, this article examines the practices of criminal defense lawyers in three counties: Milwaukee County, Wis., Dane County, Wis., and Cleveland County, Okla.[24] There is no methodological significance to the selection of these three counties. They were selected simply because the author has been a participant observer in each.[25] As with Blumberg's article, no emperical data supports the author's observations about the behavior of criminal defense lawyers in these counties. Nonetheless, the picture of the criminal defense bar portrayed in this article is quite similar to that painted by others looking at defense lawyers in other criminal justice systems.[26]

DEFENSE LAWYER AS BELEAGUERED DEALER: OBSERVATIONS OF LAWYERS AT WORK

Blumberg presented a very cynical, negative picture of criminal defense lawyers and of their relationships with their clients. With broad strokes, Blumberg painted the portrait of the criminal defense lawyer as a manipulative con artist who succumbs to the pressures of making a living in a closed community by "duping" clients to enter pleas that benefit the system more than the clients.[27] Although it is true, as it was in 1967, when Blumberg's article appeared, that the vast majority of clients in Milwaukee, Dane, and Cleveland Counties plead guilty instead of going to trial.[28] Nevertheless, it does not follow that the large number of guilty pleas is simply the product of defense lawyer double-dealing. Rather, numerous factors, including some of the systemic pressures described by Blumberg, affect a defendant's plea decision and the behavior of a criminal defense lawyer. Indeed, the varied conduct of defense lawyers in these three counties confirms that Blumberg's premise that court organization dictates defense counsel's role, that of double agent, is suspect.

Admittedly, many of Blumberg's observations about certain systemic pressures and practices accurately reflect similar aspects of the criminal justice systems in Milwaukee, Dane, and Cleveland Counties. In all three counties, private defense lawyers almost always want their fees in advance and routinely look to the client's family and friends to contribute to the client's defense.[29] Certainly, there are lawyers in each county who prey on the ignorance or anxieties of their clients and their clients' families to increase their fees and to enhance the collection of those fees.[30] At times, court personnel, prosecutors, or judges will aid defense counsel's efforts to collect a fee, and this assistance may subsequently be used to pressure defense counsel.[31] And there are lawyers who manipulate their clients by lying to them about the complexity of the case, the working of the system, or the dangers of going to trial in order to maximize the lawyer's financial return on a particular case.[32] There are, therefore, lawyers in each county who fit Blumberg's double agent profile.

Simply to characterize all criminal defense lawyers as double agents, however, grossly distorts the overall picture of the criminal defense bar in these counties. Not all defense lawyers "ultimately are concerned with strategies which tend to lead to a plea."[33] Nor is it true that "it is the rational, impersonal elements involving economics of time, labor, expense and a superior commitment of the defense counsel to these rationalistic values of maximum production of court organization that prevail, in his relationship with a client."[34] If Blumberg's image of defense counsel is entirely accurate, what explains those cases that do go to trial: stubborn clients, bad salesmanship by the lawyers, ideological zealots, or desire to deflect "outside" scrutiny?[35] Blumberg's analysis offers no explanation.

Unquestionably, however, each county has a number of criminal defense lawyers, especially public defenders in Dane and Milwaukee Counties, who are committed professionally and ideologically to obtaining the best possible results for their clients.[36] Although heavy case loads affect the ability of public defenders—and, in some instances, their willingness and enthusiasm—to go to trial, most public defenders in Milwaukee and Dane Counties bargain as aggressively as possible on behalf of their clients. These public defenders, in turn, usually advise their clients of the available, albeit often quite limited, options, in an honest, unbiased manner.

Moreover, in each county there are private lawyers specializing in criminal cases who can and will aggressively defend those clients with the economic resources to pay for a zealous defense. Instead of seeking to limit the litigation, some lawyers file numerous motions in an effort to wear down the prosecution and achieve a favorable outcome for their clients.[37] Finally, there are lawyers in each county who have zealously defended their clients at great personal sacrifice. Dedication, commitment to principle, and personal values, not financial gain, drive some criminal defense lawyers.[38]

Blumberg posited that criminal defense lawyers function as double agents because conning the client into a quick plea ensured that a case would be profitable and enabled counsel to serve the ends of a complicitous, closed system.[39] Yet, if court structure and organization dictate defense counsel's role, why is it that not all defense lawyers in Milwaukee, Dane, and Cleveland Counties behave alike? Why do only some criminal defense lawyers in these counties succumb to personal or systemic pressure and function as double agents while others do not? Why is it that some defense lawyers in these counties conduct vigorous defenses and others put up only a staged or token resistance?

There is no single explanation for why criminal defense lawyers play their role so differently. Nor is there a simple answer as to why some public defenders and private lawyers operate some of the time as double agents.[40] A public defender may be lazy, inexperienced, incompetent, overwhelmed, burned out, focused on a particularly difficult and time-consuming case, subject to personal problems, or distracted by a combination of such factors.[41] Private lawyers must not only cope with these factors but also try to earn a living. Only infrequently does a criminal defense lawyer command a fee commensurate with the time it takes to investigate and defend a criminal case fully and competently. Simply put, most people accused of a crime cannot afford to pay for effective assistance of counsel.[42] Most low-income defendants who do not qualify for public defenders in Wisconsin or for court-appointed counsel in Cleveland County cannot obtain adequate legal representation.[43] It is these defendants in all three counties who face the real prospect of being represented by double agents. Although, at times, a defendant will be advised by defense counsel that the meager retainer paid will only cover a negotiated plea, too often the accused neither understands nor ever learns of the real limits of counsel's representation. Unhappily, it may not be until the client insists on a trial that the defense lawyer's limited zeal becomes obvious.[44]

Often, however, it is not defense counsel's lack of zeal but the defendant's lack of money that dictates counsel's actions. Often a defendant who wishes to hire a own lawyer can only raise a minimal retainer. Once retained, the lawyer may prod and push the prosecutor for a dismissal or a favorable plea bargain, but if the prosecutor refuses, the client is often left with an unhappy choice: Accept the negotiated deal or go to trial. Even if the lawyer wants to fight the charge and is willing to go to trial for an additional $1,500, the client rarely chooses to do so. The economic realities of the system, not counsel's lack of zeal, frequently pressure the defendant to accept a plea.[45]

In Milwaukee, Dane, and Cleveland Counties, there also are some defense lawyers who are afraid of trying cases, view trials personally as losing ventures, or do not want to alienate a judge or prosecutor by refusing a settlement. These lawyers are not really responding to economic forces or case load pressure but to personal needs or psychological limitations that interfere with their ability to perform in accordance with their professional responsibilities.[46] For many defense lawyers, however, the spirit is willing, but the resources are lacking.

What is clear, then, is that most criminal defense lawyers in Milwaukee, Dane, and Cleveland Counties cannot be characterized simply as double agents. Systemic pressures and organizational obligations certainly influence but do not dictate the behavior of the criminal defense lawyer. As with many of his observations, Blumberg's generalizations about defense lawyers as double agents simply sweep too broadly.[47]

Are most defense lawyers, then, zealous advocates? If so, why is it that the vast majority of cases end in guilty pleas?[48] Blumberg's focus on the role played by defense lawyers in producing guilty pleas underplays the fact that a defendant's decision to plead guilty is shaped by a variety of individual factors and systemic features.[49] For many defendants, the plea decision has little to do with the zeal or even the availability of defense counsel. Rather, a significant number of defendants simply want to plead guilty. Some defendants plead guilty because they really are willing to accept responsibility for their actions. Others want to end the matter quickly and see a guilty plea as the fastest way out of a bothersome predicament. Still other defendants engage in their own simple cost-benefit analysis and conclude that fighting the charge is not worth the time, money, or risk.[50] For some defendants, then, the decision to plead guilty does not depend on the availability or actions of defense counsel.

Nonetheless, for other defendants, various systemic factors, including the availability, cost, and quality of counsel, profoundly influence the plea-bargaining process and, ultimately, the plea decision.[51] A comparison of the features and the culture of the criminal justice system in Milwaukee, Dane, and Cleveland Counties reveals many striking similarities in the plea-bargaining process. However, that comparison also reveals significant differences in the delivery of indigent defense services, local bail practices, and the workings of the local prosecutor's office. These systemic variations not only have an impact on the plea-bargaining process in each county, but also affect the general zeal of the local defense bar.

The most significant systemic feature distinguishing Cleveland County from the two Wisconsin counties is the absence of a public-defender system in Cleveland County. Rather, Cleveland County uses an assigned-counsel system to provide representation to indigent defendants.[52] An indigent defendant in Cleveland County obtains representation, therefore, only if the court chooses to appoint counsel. Only those defendants able to retain counsel are represented at their initial appearance. Defendants unable to make bail generally must wait at least three weeks before the court will act on their application for court-appointed counsel.[53] Those defendants who bail out or have a bond posted for them are presumed to be able to afford counsel.[54] Hence, no lawyer is appointed until the defendant appears before the court and demonstrates an inability to hire counsel. Even then, the defendant is generally denied appointed counsel, told to make additional efforts to secure retained counsel, and threatened with bail revocation if counsel is not obtained. Defendants have had their bail revoked and been forced to return to jail in order to secure appointed counsel.

Felony defendants who remain in jail for at least three weeks are usually deemed indigent, and counsel is appointed. Appointments are made by the local judges from a list of all of the lawyers in the county who practice criminal law.[55] Appointed lawyers in Cleveland County are not paid on an hourly basis. Rather, defense lawyers are paid at a fixed rate of $250 for a misdemeanor case and $500 for a felony.[56] Except in a capital case, therefore, a lawyer will not be compensated more than $500 regardless of the amount of time devoted to a case. Any appointed lawyer wishing an investigator or expert assistance must apply to the judge. Judicial approval of such litigation expenses, however, is very rare.[57]

Milwaukee and Dane Counties have local public-defender offices that are part of a statewide program.[58] Public-defender staff attorneys are state employees with salaries and benefits comparable to those provided to the lawyers in the Wisconsin Attorney General's Office.[59] These staff lawyers answer to the lawyer who directs their office, not to the local judges. Moreover, indigency determinations are made not by the judges but by the local public defender's office. Hence, any person charged with a crime will obtain representation as long as that person meets the eligibility standards set by statute.[60] The public defender's office then assigns the indigent defendant a staff attorney or a private lawyer from a list maintained by the local office. Some clients secure representation even prior to charges being issued.[61]

Although public defenders represent the majority of indigent defendants in Milwaukee and Dane Counties, private lawyers in each county defend roughly 25 percent of the clients served by the public-defender program.[62] Private lawyers presently are paid $45 dollars per hour for in-court time and $35 dollars per hour for out-of-court work with no specified limit on the number of hours to be spent on a case.[63] The bills generated by private lawyers handling assigned cases are paid by the public-defender program. In addition, private lawyers can also obtain funds for investigative and expert services from the local office.[64] Finally, the Milwaukee and Dane County offices have their own investigative staff, some access to social workers, and the ability to fund expert services. Even though the Wisconsin public-defender program definitely needs increased funding, the funding problem is not at the same crisis level experienced by Cleveland County and numerous other jurisdictions.[65]

Many indigent defendants in Milwaukee and Dane Counties are in custody at the time of their initial appearance, but, unlike in Cleveland County, defendants usually are represented by counsel at that court appearance. Not only does defense counsel's early intervention allow him to argue about bail but it enhances counsel's ability to mount an effective defense. Finally, in stark contrast with the judicial reluctance to appoint assigned counsel in Cleveland County, judges in Milwaukee and Dane Counties actively encourage defendants to seek legal assistance from the public defender's office. As a result, many more defendants come to court with a lawyer in these Wisconsin counties than in Cleveland County. Thus, the system's structure for delivering indigent defense services encourages representation in Milwaukee and Dane Counties while discouraging it in Cleveland County. Unrepresented defendants in Cleveland County have little ability to do more than just accept whatever plea bargain is offered to them.[66] Easy access to free defense services or the imposition of barriers to obtaining such representation substantially affects the plea-bargaining process and the actors involved in that process.

A second significant systemic difference between Cleveland County and the two Wisconsin counties is Cleveland County's more limited use of personal recognizance bonds and its heavy reliance on bail bondsmen. When a person is arrested, that person's family and friends generally make every effort to post bail. Unable to raise sufficient funds on their own, many people in Cleveland County turn to a bail bondsman to obtain the needed bond. Money paid to a bail bondsman, however, is no longer available to secure counsel, pay fines, or satisfy court costs. For many defendants and their families, the lack of additional funds compels them either to forgo defense counsel or hire counsel at a bargain price. Unfortunately, it is defense counsel retained for an inadequate fee who is least likely to act as a zealous advocate and most likely to function as a double agent.[67]

In addition, those defendants who do not secure a bond prior to their initial court appearance rarely are represented at that initial appearance. Without counsel to make a bail argument on their behalf, fewer defendants in Cleveland County are released on their own recognizance than in Milwaukee or Dane County. Continued incarceration increases the pressure on defendants to use a bail bondsman or plead guilty to obtain their release. In Cleveland County, defendants unable to make bail at times are provided counsel solely to facilitate the entry of a guilty plea. At other times, defendants will languish in jail for periods well beyond the normal sentence meted out for a particular charge simply because counsel is never appointed and the matter is not brought to the attention of the judge or prosecutor. When the case finally surfaces, the defendant is allowed to plead guilty for time served.[68]

Although, infrequently, a defendant unable to post low bail in Milwaukee or Dane County will be held for an inordinate length before the case is located and resolved, the system generally operates to avoid such cases. Indeed, the Wisconsin bail provisions specifically "are designed to see that a maximum number of persons are released prior to trial with a minimum of financial burden upon them."[69] A sizable number of persons arrested for a misdemeanor are given a citation and released.[70] If the person is detained and the accused's family or friends cannot post the necessary cash bail, the defendant will remain incarcerated until the initial court appearance. Fortunately, most defendants have an initial court appearance within twenty-four hours of their arrest. Moreover, most defendants in Milwaukee and Dane Counties are represented at the initial appearance, usually by a public defender.

Counsel's bail arguments regularly lead either to a recognizance bond or a reduction in the amount of bail.[71]

Some defendants in Milwaukee and Dane Counties fail to make bail and are subject, therefore, to some of the same pressure experienced by detainees in Cleveland County. Nevertheless, these defendants at least have had a lawyer assigned to them who now is working on their behalf. For the unrepresented defendant in Cleveland County, the pressure is much greater.[72]

Finally, for those defendants in Milwaukee or Dane Counties who do post cash bail, that money will be returned to the person posting it unless the defendant fails to appear for a court appearance. Sometimes a defendant can retain counsel by offering the lawyer a lien on this bail money. Often the bail money can be used to pay a fine, restitution, or court costs. In short, a comparison of Milwaukee, Dane, and Cleveland Counties demonstrates that the bail practices in a given community have a considerable impact on the plea decisions of many defendants in that community.[73]

The operation of the district attorney's office in Milwaukee, Dane, and Cleveland Counties represents the third significant systemic feature affecting defendants' plea decisions and the behavior of criminal defense lawyers in these three counties. There are many similarities in the attitude of the staff and in the workings of the three offices,[74] but there also are some significant differences. With over ninety attorneys, the size of the Milwaukee office allows for more specialization and more overall expertise. Nevertheless, the volume of cases handled by the system and each prosecutor, the number of courts, and the greater time it takes for cases to work through the system increase the opportunity for defense counsel in Milwaukee to "shop" for a better plea bargain, to leverage defense strengths to the defendant's advantage, and to resist prosecutorial pressure to "play ball."

In contrast to Milwaukee's large staff, Dane County has twenty-six prosecutors and Cleveland County nine. Operating in smaller, more closed courthouse communies than in Milwaukee County, the prosecutors in Dane and Cleveland Counties tend to be more cohesive and communicative about defense lawyers and their practices. Because they know most defense lawyers very well, Dane and Cleveland County prosecutors have an edge over their Milwaukee counterparts.

Although news travels faster in the courthouse communities of Dane and Cleveland Counties, the systemic pace is slower than in Milwaukee County. Thus, prosecutors in Dane and Cleveland Counties seemingly have more time to spend on minor charges and are less willing either to divert cases from the system or dismiss them once they are filed.[75] This reluctance to divert or dismiss charges in part reflects the fact that Dane and Cleveland Counties rely on a deputy district attorney to issue virtually all charges.[76] Accordingly, once charges have been issued, most assistant district attorneys are very hesitant to dismiss a case. This is so even though the initial charging decision rested primarily on the deputy's review of police reports with little opportunity to evaluate the strengths or weaknesses of the case or the existence of any mitigating factors. This is particularly so in Cleveland County because the office relies on law student interns to handle almost the entire misdemeanor case load.[77] The interns' limited discretion makes it difficult to negotiate the dismissal of any issued charge or to secure a significant reduction in the standard offer for a particular offense.

In Milwaukee County, however, charges generally are issued following a charging conference in which one of the prosecutors on duty that week meets with the complainant, police officers, witnesses, and, at times, the defendant and defense counsel, before deciding what, if any, charges to file.[78] Although the charging system used in Milwaukee County involves an enormous front-loading of prosecutorial resources, the system produces better-informed and more accurate charging decisions. This charging process also eliminates many weak or unsubstantiated cases that otherwise would clog the system.

There are several lessons to be learned in studying the systems in Milwaukee, Dane, and Cleveland Counties. First, variations in significant systemic features influence the behavior of a system's defense lawyers. In Cleveland County, for example, the system for appointing counsel works to discourage defendants from actually obtaining counsel. Defendants are pressured to waive their rights and plead guilty without the assistance of counsel. In other cases, the delay in appointing a lawyer or the system's bail practices pressure the defendant simply to "get it over with." Once a lawyer finally is appointed, the client may instruct the attorney simply to obtain the best plea bargain possible.[79] The defense lawyer may be very willing to challenge the state's case and even argue with the defendant about the shortsightedness of a guilty plea.[80] Nonetheless, if the client persists in wanting a plea bargain, defense counsel may be left simply securing the best deal possible, even though counsel believes a conviction is unjust and a guilty verdict unlikely.

Second, a criminal justice system driven by plea bargaining exerts substantial pressure on a criminal defendant not to go to trial. Defendants face considerable moral, psychological, physical,[81] and economic pressure to plead guilty. Many defendants confess and few suppression motions are granted, so that most defendants battle tough odds should they choose to go to trial. Even if the evidence is less than overwhelming, a defendant may be reluctant to risk trial because of numerous prior convictions, the fear of judicial retaliation for going to trial, or the amount of pretrial incarceration to be endured before a trial will occur. Above all, the prosecutor usually has a wide range of bargaining threats—charging additional offenses, adding sentence enhancers, and including a charge with a mandatory minimum sentence, to name a few—that also deter defendants from turning down proposed deals.[82]

Although most defendants want to plea bargain, they often are not satisfied with the deals they receive. Yet, few defendants actually want to go to trial. For criminal defense lawyers, then, much of their time is spent negotiating a deal against an adversary who generally can dictate the terms. Under such circumstances, defense counsel is not a double agent but a beleaguered dealer negotiating from a position of weakness. It is not defense counsel's profit motive but the structure of the system that primarily influences the decision of many defendants to accept a plea bargain.

Third, because so many defendants are unable to afford counsel, the local structure for delivering indigent defense services largely determines the overall quality of representation provided to criminal defendants in a particular community. Thus, the existence of a reasonably well-funded public-defender program in Milwaukee and Dane Counties explains in large part why more defendants in these counties receive competent, zealous representation than in Cleveland County. As full-time criminal practitioners, the Wisconsin public defenders are better trained and have more resources than the appointed lawyers in Cleveland County. It is not surprising, then, that these public defenders generally pursue more aggressive defense tactics.[83] Moreover, by filing motions, taking cases to trial, and disseminating information to private lawyers who do not specialize in criminal law, the public defenders encourage and educate other defense lawyers to be more zealous. In addition, retained counsel in these two counties tend to be more aggressive, knowing that they will not be singled out by the prosecutor's office and retaliated against for taking cases to trial. Finally, not only do appointed lawyers in Wisconsin have access to experts and investigative assistance but they also receive adequate compensation without imposed limits. Private lawyers appointed to represent indigent defendants in Wisconsin, therefore, are provided with a financial incentive to prepare adequately and to take cases to trial.[84]

On the other hand, the appointed-counsel system in Cleveland County, based on a fixed flat-compensation scheme, serves to encourage the very behavior by defense counsel condemned by Blumberg.[85] A defense lawyer earns a modest or, at times, even a decent fee if the client enters a quick plea. There is, however, an economic disincentive to investigate, to research, or, above all, to take a case to trial. A lawyer who chooses to spend time, energy, and money in the defense of a case does so at his own expense. In Cleveland County, as in other jurisdictions around the country, not enough lawyers are willing to make that personal sacrifice.[86] Defense counsel may not be a con but feels pressure to strike a deal. Frequently, appointed counsel enters the negotiation process without much leverage. In fact, the prosecutors in Cleveland County know full well the economic realities confronting appointed counsel.

Nonetheless, it is not just profit motive or financial pressure that causes some criminal defense lawyers to be less than zealous. Heavy case loads create time pressure and stress that can overwhelm even the best-intentioned, most competent defense lawyer.[87] Certainly there are some public defenders in Milwaukee and Dane Counties who respond to case load pressures by cajoling, threatening, or manipulating their clients into pleading guilty.[88] Like private lawyers who accept an insufficient retainer and then force a plea bargain on a unwitting client, some public defenders will oversell the advantages of a plea bargain, conduct an inadequate investigation, or fail to prepare properly for trial, thereby coercing guilty pleas from reluctant defendants.

Most public defenders in Milwaukee and Dane Counties, however, do not respond to heavy case loads by operating as double agents. Rather, they attempt to cope with their heavy case loads by allocating their time and limited investigative resources in the best possible way.[89] Consequently, some cases are not adequately researched or investigated. Some defendants, therefore, receive better representation at the expense of others. Moreover, overworked public defenders have less time to spend with their clients and this hampers their ability to develop trusting, meaningful attorney-client relationships.[90] Absent a good attorney-client relationship, the defendant is even more susceptible to buckle under the pressure to plead guilty.

Despite serious time pressure and heavy case loads, the public defenders in Milwaukee and Dane Counties, for the most part, bargain effectively for many of their clients. They know the system well and thus are able to evaluate the worth of a proposed plea bargain and the merits of taking a case to trial.[91] In addition, faced with their own case load pressures and the knowledge that these public defenders generally have the capacity and willingness to fight if an acceptable deal is not struck, the prosecutors in these counties have some incentive to bargain reasonably. Unlike appointed counsel in Cleveland County, defenders of the indigent in Wisconsin, albeit beleaguered, pose a credible threat.

But as their resources become increasingly strained, overburdened public defenders in Milwaukee and Dane Counties are more vulnerable to prosecutorial pressure and less able to use tactics, such as filing a well-briefed motion, that apply pressure on the prosecutor.[92] In short, the final lesson to be learned from examining these three counties is that even the lawyers in a well-structured indigent defense system will find it difficult to act aggressively without adequate time and resources. Large case loads exert added pressure on public defenders to obtain acceptable plea bargains for most of their clients. There is that subtle but constant pressure when negotiating numerous cases not to push a prosecutor too hard in one case so that counsel will obtain favorable consideration in other cases.[93] And there is real pressure to avoid antagonizing prosecutors because of the tremendous discretion they have to reward or punish defendants in the plea bargain process. Faced with these pressures, the overworked public defender may produce the same results as the underpaid private lawyer: "plea bargains too easily accepted by one-shot clients on the advice of lawyers trying, either out of self-interest or for the good of their clients *as a class*, to maintain good personal relations with the judges and prosecutors with whom they must regularly work."[94]

DEFENSE LAWYER AS EFFECTIVE ADVOCATE: STRUCTURING THE SYSTEM TO ENHANCE ZEAL

Criminal defense lawyers in Milwaukee and Dane Counties appear to defend their clients more zealously and effectively than lawyers in Cleveland County primarily because of the superior resources allotted to the representation of indigent defendants in Wisconsin. Simply put, zealousness comes with a price tag. Until society is prepared to increase the resources allocated to the defense of persons accused of crimes, few defendants will receive effective zealous assistance of counsel.

Because most criminal defendants are indigent, improving the delivery of indigent defense services in a local system constitutes the best means of enhancing the overall quality of representation in that system. Moreover, improving the indigent defense system in a community heightens the zeal and effectiveness of the private defense bar. This improvement, however, cannot be attained simply by sleight of hand or minor structural tinkering. In most jurisdictions, substantial resources are needed to correct serious shortcomings in the delivery of indigent defense services.[95] In light of the keen competition for dollars in austere state budgets and the incessant clamor for a war on crime, the prospects for major funding increases for defense services are dim. And yet, increased funding is imperative if the crisis in the delivery of indigent defense services occurring in many counties across the United States is to be adequately addressed.[96]

Assuming, therefore, that some additional funds are made available for indigent defense services, how must the system be structured for delivering those services to ensure that more defendants are provided a zealous defense? Again, there is no simple answer. It is clear, however, that if the system truly is to enhance zeal and effective advocacy, it must lessen defense counsel's vulnerability to the pressures inherent in the plea-bargain-driven criminal justice system.[97]

An adequately funded, independent, "mixed" statewide program of salaried public defenders and assigned private counsel represents the indigent defense system least susceptible to these insidious pressures.[98] First, a mixed system is desirable because it blends experienced, well-trained criminal law specialists together with private lawyers who may bring fresh, creative approaches to systemic problems as a result of their civil experience. In addition, a strong assigned-counsel component of the program ensures that the local defense bar will continue to play an active role in criminal defense litigation. If the private bar lacks an investment in the indigent defense program, the organized bar may not rally enthusiastically behind the program. Without the vigorous support of the bar, the public-defender program will have difficulty garnering legislative votes for needed funding.[99] Finally, the continued involvement of private lawyers in the criminal justice system lessens the institutionalization of criminal defense work with its concomitant dangers.[100]

Next, this mixed public-defender program must be structured to insulate defense counsel from direct economic pressure. Counsel should not have to curry favor with the judiciary to be appointed to cases or face economic retaliation for not settling or defending a case as a judge sees fit. The program must control the hiring and firing of its staff lawyers as well as the selection of appointed counsel. Neither the judiciary nor any local government entity should control the salaries or compensation paid to indigent defenders.[101] Economic control includes the real threat of interference with counsel's representation.[102] Defense counsel's independence must be respected and encouraged.

So, also, assigned counsel must be adequately compensated. Flat, fixed fees, especially with low maximum limits, discourage lawyers from being effective advocates. Instead, lawyers are rewarded for resolving cases as quickly as possible without an adequate inquiry into the merits of the case. Any contract or assigned-counsel system relying on a fixed-fee method of compensation builds into the system an economic disincentive to take cases to trial.[103] This does not mean that many cases should or would be tried even under this proposed public-defender system. Indeed, the systemic pressures that already coerce many defendants into pleading guilty will continue to force most defendants to accept plea bargains. But the indigent defense system should not add to that pressure. Rather, the system must be structured to facilitate access to counsel. As in the Wisconsin public-defender system, defendants must get representation early with as few procedural hurdles as possible.[104]

Early representation is meaningless, however, unless defense counsel has ready access to the resources needed to mount a vigorous defense. Adequate support staff and investigative resources are crucial if effective representation is to be provided.[105] Care must be taken to ensure that assigned counsel as well as staff lawyers have sufficient access to investigators and expert services. Moreover, adequate training must be provided for public-defender staff lawyers, and low-cost continuing education programs must be developed for assigned counsel.[106] A lawyer cannot practice criminal law competently without keeping current on changes in substantive law and criminal procedure.[107]

In addition, this public-defender system must provide reasonable salaries with manageable case loads. Excessive case loads create undue pressure to settle, not to try jury trials. The public defender's compensation package must be designed to reward effective, aggressive lawyering, not to encourage the mere processing of a set number of cases. Adequate performance measures together with merit raise incentives[108] improve the likelihood that public defenders will act zealously.[109]

A statewide public-defender program must secure adequate funding if it is to provide competent defense services. Given the budget pressures confronting virtually every state legislature, however, even an adequately funded program will still face tough choices on allocating funds.[110] The history of the Wisconsin public-defender program since 1977 suggests that it is extremely difficult to balance reasonably high salaries, excellent benefits, good working conditions, and strong support and litigation services with reasonable case loads.[111] In striking an appropriate balance, program administrators must bear in mind that together with the lawyer actually handling a case, they are responsible for the quality of representation ultimately provided.[112] Administrators and legislators also must remember that requiring public defenders to handle too many cases invariably results in deficient representation.

The top priority for a public-defender program, therefore, must be to keep case loads at a level that allows staff attorneys to perform in accordance with the standards of a competent criminal defense lawyer.[113] This means, in part, developing a mechanism to divert cases to assigned counsel when case loads get too heavy. In addition, this means giving public defenders sufficient time to interview their clients, to investigate, to research, and to prepare adequately for negotiations, trials, and sentencings.[114]

There is no cost-free method for generating more time. Faced with the challenge of keeping case loads light while providing quality representation to an increasing number of clients, the program may have to use a salary structure that is unlikely to produce career public defenders. Thus, it may be necessary to keep salaries fairly low and hire more new law school graduates, thereby creating more positions but with fewer cases per attorney. Staff lawyers would earn less money but have improved working conditions, less stress, and more job satisfaction.[115] Any loss of expertise due to increased lawyer turnover would arguably be offset by the increased zeal of the larger staff and the greater use of senior staff lawyers as supervisors.[116]

Moreover, some additional time may be created by providing staff lawyers with better litigation support. It may be desirable to spend more money on investigators or paralegals, who could assume many of the tasks that are often inefficiently handled by lawyers. Finally, difficult and complex cases often strain the resources of a small public-defender office. One advantage of a statewide program would be the central administration's ability to shift resources or use special units to defend selected cases efficiently and effectively.[117]

Yet, even though improving the indigent defense system in a community would affect the quality of representation afforded many defendants, a significant number of low-income defendants would remain largely unaffected. The working poor, many making only minimum wage, do not qualify under existing indigency standards for an indigent defender.[118] Unable to afford to hire a zealous advocate, the low-income defendant is forced to take whatever bargain the prosecutor proffers.

The prospects for improving the representation of these defendants are particularly bleak. It may be that a percentage of low-income defendants could qualify as partially indigent and, therefore, for a small retainer, receive the same representation provided to other defendants by the public-defender program.[119] Expanding the number of indigent clients served by the program, however, increases case load pressure and decreases the time available to provide zealous representation to others in the program. In light of the substantial financial needs already facing most jurisdictions, expansion of the program to cover more low-income people is highly unlikely.[120]

There are limits, then, to the extent to which dramatic change can occur in the criminal justice system. Undoubtedly, improving indigent services will lead to greater zeal and more effective lawyering. And yet, even though the overall zeal of the defense bar may increase, the nature of the plea-bargaining process and the system itself substantially limit a dramatic difference in the role of the criminal defense lawyer. That is because in most cases, the defendant, the case itself and the system substantially limit the options available to the defendant and to counsel.

Given the pressure that the prosecutor and the system bring to bear on criminal defendants, even zealous defense lawyers generally will be beleaguered dealers. If negotiations fail, however, the zealous advocate must have the will and ability to fight on behalf of a client. Unless we give defense lawyers the necessary resources and incentives to challenge the state, our adversary system indeed will drift further toward the co-optative system Blumberg described.

NOTES

1. "The basic duty defense counsel owes to the administration of justice and as an officer of the court is to serve as the accused's counselor and advocate with courage and devotion, and to render effective, quality representation." ABA, *Standards for Criminal Justice* Standard 4-1.2(b) (3d ed. 1991). The ethics codes enshrine the principle of zealous partisanship. See, e.g., *Model Code of Professional Responsibility* DR 7-101, EC 7-1, EC 7-4, EC 7-19 (1981); *Model Rules of Professional Conduct* Preamble (1983). As Charles Wolfram observes, "[T]he American lawyer's professional model is that of zeal: a lawyer is expected to devote energy, intelligence, skill and personal commitment to the single goal of furthering the clients' interests as those are ultimately defined by the client." C. Wolfram, *Modern Legal Ethics* 585 (1986). Moreover, numerous cases trumpet the lawyer's obligation to be a vigorous defender. See, e.g., Von Moltke v. Gillies, 332 U.S. 708, 725-726 (1948) (the right to counsel demands undivided allegiance and service devoted solely to the interests of the client).

2. As Justice Powell has noted:

> In our system a defense lawyer characteristically opposes the designated representative of the State. The system assumes that adversarial testimony will ultimately advance the public interest in truth and fairness. But it posits that a defense lawyer best serves the public not by acting on behalf of the State or in concert with it but rather by advancing "the undivided interests of his client."

Polk County v. Dodson, 454 U.S. 312, 318-319 (1981). For an excellent summary of the basic principles of the U.S. adversary system of criminal justice, see W. LaFave & J. Israel, *Criminal Procedure* 24-32 (1985).

3. Justice White eloquently summarized the role of the criminal defense lawyer:

> But defense counsel has no comparable obligation to ascertain or present the truth. Our system assigns him a different mission . . . . Defense counsel need present nothing, even if he knows what the truth is. He need not furnish any witnesses to the police, or reveal any confidences of his client, or furnish any other information to help the prosecution's case. If he can confuse a witness, even a truthful one, or make him appear at a disadvantage, unsure or indecisive, that will be his normal course. Our interest in not convicting the innocent permits counsel to put the State to its proof, to put the State's case in the worst possible light, regardless of what he thinks or knows to be the truth. Undoubtedly there are some limits which defense counsel must observe, but more often than not, defense counsel will cross-examine a prosecution witness, and impeach him if he can, even if he thinks the witness is telling the truth, just as he will attempt to destroy a witness who he thinks is lying. In this respect, as part of our modified adversary system and as part of the duty imposed on the most honorable defense counsel, we countenance or require conduct which in many instances has little, if any, relation to the search for truth.

United States v. Wade, 388 U.S. 218, 256-258 (1967) (White, J., dissenting in part and concurring in part).

4. *Id.* See also C. Wolfram, note 1 *supra*, at 586-587.

5. "The procedural and legal system are supposedly designed to produce results based on just laws fairly applied on the basis of accurate facts; but a lawyer's objective within that system is to achieve a result favorable to the lawyer's client, possibly despite justice, the law, and the facts." C. Wolfram, note 1 *supra*, at 585. Because defense counsel must be a zealous partisan, counsel's efforts may well interfere with the search for the truth. M. Freedman, *Understanding Lawyers' Ethics* 161-171 (1990); A. Amsterdam, *Trial Manual for the Defense of Criminal Cases* 2-237 (1984); C. Wolfram, note 1 *supra*, at 588-589, 641, 650-651. Even commentators critical of the legal profession's commitment to the principles of partisanship and nonaccountability generally recognize that the criminal defense lawyer must pursue the defendant's interests even at the expense of an accurate outcome. D. Luban, *Lawyers and Justice: An Ethical Study* 58-63 (1988).

6. As Chief Justice Burger noted in Nix v. Whiteside, 475 U.S. 157 (1986), the lawyer's "overarching duty" to advocate and advance the client's interests is limited by the lawyer's "equally solemn" responsibilities and duties as an officer of the court. *Id.* at 166-168. In certain situations, ethical provisions require defense counsel to take action or to disclose information adverse to the interests of the client. See J. Burkoff, *Criminal Defense Ethics* ch. 6 (1986). Nonetheless, there is considerable disagreement regarding the extent to which defense counsel's advocacy must be tempered by his duties as an officer of the court. Compare Chief Justice Burger's view in Nix v. Whiteside, *supra*, at 157, 168 (emphasizing defense counsel's role as an officer of the court) with that of Justice Brennan in Jones v. Barnes, 463 U.S. 745, 761-762 (1983) (Brennan, J., dissenting) (stressing that counsel must function as an advocate as opposed to a friend of the court). See also Justice White in United States v. Wade, note 3 *supra*, at 218, 257-258 (White, J., dissenting in part and concurring in part) (defense lawyer's mission is not to ascertain or present the truth); Justice Black in Von Moltke v. Gillies, note 1 *supra*, at 708, 725-726 (right to counsel demands undivided allegiance and service devoted solely to the interests of the client); Justice Powell in Polk County v. Dodson, note 2 *supra*, at 312, 318 (defense counsel best serves the public by advancing the individual interests of the accused); Commission on Professional Responsibility of Roscoe Pound-Am Trial Lawyers Found., *The American Lawyer's Code of Conduct* preamble (1982) ("It is clear that the lawyer for a private party is and should be an officer of the court only in the sense of serving a court as a zealous, partisan advocate of one side of the case before it, and in the sense of having been licensed by a court to play that very role.").

7. Even after Nix v. Whiteside, note 6 *supra*, at 157, for example, there is a continuing controversy as to how the criminal defense lawyer should respond when counsel knows or suspects that the client is going to testify falsely. Lefstein, "Client Perjury in Criminal Cases: Still in Search of an Answer," 1 Geo. J. Legal Ethics 521 (1988). For a discussion of various resolutions to the perjury issue, see M. Freedman, note 5 *supra*, at 109-141.

8. As Justice Powell observed:

> "[T]he duty of the lawyer, subject to his role as an "officer of the court," is to further the interests of his clients by all lawful means, even when these interests are in conflict with the interests of the United States or of a State. But his representation involves no conflict of interest in the invidious sense. Rather, it casts the lawyer in his honored and traditional role as an authorized but independent agent acting to vindicate the legal rights of a client, whoever it may be.

In re Griffiths, 413 U.S. 717, 724 n. 14 (1973).

To vindicate the rights of an accused, a lawyer must be an effective as well as loyal advocate. Polk County v. Dodson, note 2 *supra*, at 312, 322. At a minimum, therefore, a criminal defendant is guaranteed the right to "reasonably effective assistance of counsel." Strickland v. Washington, 466 U.S. 668, 687 (1984). The line between ineffective and adequate assistance of counsel is difficult to draw. See Mounts, "The Right to Counsel and the Indigent Defense System." 14 N.Y.U. Rev. L. & Soc. Change 221-241 (1986). Yet, unquestionably, defense counsel is ethically bound to provide competent, timely, and informed representation. See *Model Rules of Professional Conduct* Rule 1.1, 1.3, 1.4 and commentary (1983); *Model Code of Professional Responsibility* DR 6-101, DR 7-101 (1981); ABA, note 1 *supra*, Standard 4-1.3.

9. See Blumberg, "The Practice of Law as Confidence Game: Organizational Co-optation of a Profession," 1 Law & Soc'y Rev. 15, 28-31 (1967) (describing criminal defense lawyers as double agents because they serve organizational ends while appearing to help their clients).

10. *Id.* at 15-39. See also M. Heumann, *Plea Bargaining* 80 (1978) (concluding that defense lawyers ultimately succumb to the culture of the court system, a culture that rewards cooperation and sanctions a formal adversarial approach).

11. Blumberg, note 9 *supra*, at 18. Blumberg's work continues to be cited regularly. See, e.g., D. Luban, note 5 *supra*, at 60-61; Schneyer, "Sympathy for the Hired Gun," 41 J.L. Educ. 11, 23-24 (1991).

12. Blumberg indicated that usually over 90 percent of criminal convictions followed a negotiated guilty plea. Blumberg, note 9 *supra*, at 18.

13. Intolerably large case loads must be disposed of by a court system lacking sufficient resources. As a result, "the principals, lawyer and assistant district attorney, rely upon one another's cooperation for their continued professional existence, and so the bargaining between them tends usually to be 'reasonable' rather than fierce." *Id.* at 22-23.

14. *Id.* at 19.

15. *Id.* at 20.

16. Blumberg reasoned:

> Accused persons come and go in the court system schema, but the structure and its occupational incumbents remain to carry on their respective career, occupational and organizational enterprises. The individual stridencies, tensions, and conflicts a given accused person's case may present to all the participants are overcome because the formal and informal relations of all the groups in the court setting require it. The probability of continued future relations and interaction must be preserved at all cost.

Id.

17. *Id.* at 22.

18. *Id.* at 22-23.

19. *Id.* at 23. See also Sudnow, "Normal Crimes: Sociological Features of the Penal Code in the Public Defender's Office," 12 Soc. Probs. 255-277 (1965) (public defenders are mere functionaries primarily concerned with quickly disposing of cases).

20. Blumberg detailed at length the nature of this "confidence game," in which the criminal defense lawyer manipulated the client into accepting a guilty plea that the client was "conned" into believing was the desirable fruit of counsel's vigorous efforts on the client's behalf. Blumberg, note 9 *supra*, at 24-31.

21. *Id.* at 27.

22. *Id.* at 28-29.

23. Blumberg expressed this conclusion in the following language:

> [T]he lawyer's role as agent-mediator may be seen as unique in that he is in effect a double agent. Although, as "officer of the court" he mediates between the court organization and the defendant, his roles with respect to each are rent by conflicts of interest. Too often these must be resolved in favor of the organization which provides him with the means for his professional existence. Consequently, in order to reduce the strains and conflicts imposed in what is ultimately an over-demanding role obligation for him, the lawyer engages in the lawyer-client "confidence game" so as to structure more favorably an otherwise onerous role system.

Id. at 38.

24. Milwaukee County is a large urban county of 959,275 people, most of whom live in the city of Milwaukee. Dane County's population of 367,085 is concentrated in Madison, the capital of Wisconsin. Like Dane, Cleveland County is a moderate-size county of 174,253 people. Norman, the home of the University of Oklahoma, is the largest city in Cleveland County.

25. The author practiced law in Milwaukee from 1978 to 1984 as a public defender and in a private firm from 1988 to 1990. He directed a clinical program at the University of Wisconsin in Dane County from 1984 to 1988. The students in this program defended indigent clients charged with misdemeanor offenses. Since joining the faculty at the University of Oklahoma College of Law in 1990, he has supervised law students handling criminal cases in the Cleveland County courts. His comments, therefore, are based on his own observations as a participant in each system as well as discussions with and observations of third-year law students working in these three systems. He also interviewed criminal defense lawyers, prosecutors, and judges in each county.

Similarly, Blumberg's article was "based upon observations made by the writer during many years of legal practice in the criminal courts of a large metropolitan area." Blumberg, note 9 *supra*, at 18.

26. See, e.g., L. McIntyre, *The Public Defender* (1987); J. Casper, *Criminal Courts: The Defendant's Perspective* (1978); Coyle, Strasser & Lovelle, "Fatal Defense," Nat'l L.J. June 11, 1990, at 30; Alschuler, "The Defense Attorney's Role in Plea Bargaining," 84 Yale L.J. 1179 (1975); Skolnick, "Social Control in the Adversary System," 11 J. Conflict Resolution 52 (1967); R. Herman, E. Single & I. Boston, *Counsel for the Poor* (1977); Arthur Young & Co., *Seattle–King County Public Defender Association Evaluation Project: Final Report* (1975).

Moreover, many of the author's observations about the representation provided by assistant public defenders in Milwaukee and Dane Counties mirror those of the Spangenberg Group, a nationally recognized consulting firm offering technical assistance and research concerning indigent defense systems. See Spangenberg Group, *Caseload/Workload Study for the State Public Defender of Wisconsin, Final Report* (1990).

27. Blumberg, note 9 *supra*, at 18-38.

28. It is difficult to obtain exact figures on the percentage of cases actually tried in each jurisdiction. In Cleveland County, 38 cases were tried in 1989 and 29 in 1990. In comparison, 5,724 criminal cases were disposed of by guilty pleas in Cleveland County in 1989 and 5,029 in 1990. In Dane County, 165 cases were decided by trial in 1989 and 141 in 1990. This compares with 5,095 cases disposed of by guilty pleas in Dane County in 1989 and 6,184 in 1990. The Director of State

Courts Office for Wisconsin does not maintain statistics on the manner in which cases were disposed of in Milwaukee County. The statistics maintained by the Milwaukee County Clerk of Courts Office reflect that in 1989 there were 428 criminal jury trials out of 14,756 cases that either were pleaded out or dismissed. In 1990, there were 461 criminal jury trials held in Milwaukee County while 16,029 cases were pleaded out or dismissed.

29. These observations are borne out not only by the author's experiences and conversations with defense lawyers but also by clients unable to raise sufficient funds to retain or keep private counsel, who subsequently looked to the public-defender office or the author's clinical program for assistance.

30. For a similar observation, see Alschuler, note 26 *supra*, at 1190-1194.

31. *Id.* at 1195. See also M. Mayer, *The Lawyers* 161-162 (1967) (reporting that the courts commonly grant postponements to private lawyers to aid them in collecting fees). Judicial willingness to tolerate numerous continuances is not surprising given the willingness of many of these lawyers to contribute to judicial reelection campaigns.

32. Unfortunately, it is not only defense lawyers who sometimes lie to their clients. Others have observed that both civil and criminal lawyers lie to their clients for reasons of self-interest. See Lerman, "Lying to Clients," 138 U. Pa. L. Rev. 659 (1990); Hellman, *"The Effects of Law Office Work on the Formation of Law Students' Professional Values: Observation, Explanation, Optimization,"* 4 Geo. J. Legal Ethics 537 (1991); Alschuler, note 26 *supra*, at 1194-1198.

33. Blumberg, note 9 *supra*, at 23.

34. *Id.*

35. According to Blumberg, the criminal justice system shrouds itself in secrecy to avoid close scrutiny, which would reveal the complicitous nature of the system. *Id.* at 22. See also A. Dershowitz, *The Best Defense* (1982).

36. In their study of the Wisconsin public-defender program, the Spangenberg Group was particularly impressed with the quality and dedication of the public defenders in the Milwaukee office. See Spangenberg Group, note 26 *supra*, at 39. For a similar positive reaction to the lawyers in the Cook County public defender office, see McIntyre, note 26 *supra*, at 172-173.

37. Good criminal defense lawyers frequently use an aggressive motion practice to further their clients' interests. *The Champion*, a monthly magazine put out by the National Association of Criminal Defense Lawyers, regularly contains articles urging defense lawyers to file a variety of different motions. See, e.g., Hingson, "State Constitutions and the Criminal Defense Lawyer: A Necessary Virtue," 14 The Champion 6 (Dec. 1990); Preiser & Swisher, Aggressive Defense of White Collar Clients, 15 The Champion 6 (June 1991).

38. Not all lawyers are willing to make a financial sacrifice like that of Connecticut lawyer Chester Fairlie, who ruined his private practice and exhausted his own savings by spending over 650 hours to defend an accused murderer. See ABA & National Legal Aid & Defender Ass'n, Gideon *Undone: The Crisis in Indigent Defense Funding* 11, 14-15 (1982).

Nonetheless, there are numerous examples in all three counties of lawyers who have unselfishly made personal and financial sacrifices on behalf of their clients. See also Spangenberg, "Why We Are Not Defending the Poor Properly," 1 Crim. Just. 48 (1986) (noting that despite many problems, many public defenders and private lawyers were dedicated to providing quality representation to indigent defendants).

39. Blumberg, note 9 *supra*, at 28.

40. Indeed, as Ted Schneyer suggests, there are many forces and pressures at work that discourage zealousness and tempt the criminal defense lawyer to be an indifferent advocate. Schneyer, note 11 *supra*, at 23-24. See also Alschuler, note 26 *supra*, at 1180 (nature of plea-bargaining system necessarily tempts lawyers to make decisions not really in their clients' interest).

41. A number of commentators complain that public defenders provide perfunctory representation. See, e.g., Sudnow, note 19 *supra*. Many have linked the public defender's cooperative approach to defending their clients to the defender's deferential attitude toward the

judiciary. See M. Levin, *Urban Politics and the Criminal Court* (1977); Dimock, "The Public Defender: A Step Towards a Police State," 42 A.B.A.J. 219-221 (1965); C. Silverman, *Criminal Violence, Criminal Justice* (1978); G. Robin, *Introduction to the Criminal Justice System* (1984). More commonly, inadequate representation by public defenders has been traced to excessive case loads and underfunded programs. See, e.g., Klein, "The Emperor Gideon Has No Clothes: The Empty Promise of the Constitutional Right to Effective Assistance of Counsel," 13 Hastings Const. L.Q. 625, 661-662 (1986). Other commentators as well as numerous empirical studies suggest, however, that defendants represented by public defenders fare no worse that those represented by retained private counsel. See, e.g., J. Casper, note 26 *supra*; Herman, Single & Boston, note 26 *supra*; L. McIntyre, note 26 *supra.* Nonetheless, these commentators report that public-defender clients often mistrust their lawyers and believe they receive inadequate representation. See also note 90 *infra* and accompanying text.

42. As overhead costs and inflation drive legal costs up, few defendants are able to raise sufficient money to pay a significant retainer. Even fewer are able to afford the cost of the investigator or expert needed to mount an effective defense.

43. The problem is particularly acute in Cleveland County because the judges apply such a low indigency standard that few defendants qualify for court-appointed counsel. See notes 52-57, 60 *infra* and accompanying text.

44. On numerous occasions, defendants would come to the Milwaukee public-defender office seeking assistance after their lawyer successfully withdrew from a case. The lawyer would have claimed irreconcilable differences as the basis for the motion to withdraw. In reality, however, it was the defendant's insistence on a trial and counsel's unwillingness to go to trial for the meager retainer the defendant could scrape up that prompted the motion to withdraw.

45. Alschuler, note 26 *supra*, at 1203.

46. Trial work is often incredibly stressful. Stress, fear, and personal convenience shape the behavior of some lawyers and influence the recommendations made to their clients. See L. McIntyre, note 26 *supra*, at 150-151. Moreover, given the uncertainty of predicting trials, the cautious nature of most lawyers, and the fear of a severe sentence after a guilty verdict, even well-intentioned lawyers may present clients with their options in a manner that influences them to plead guilty rather than go to trial. See Alschuler, note 26 *supra*, at 1205-1206.

47. For a similar conclusion based on her study of the Cook County public defender, see L. McIntyre, note 26 *supra*, at 47-48.

48. Although statistics vary from jurisdiction to jurisdiction, most studies indicate that over 90 percent of the convictions in the state courts are the result of guilty pleas. See Bureau of Justice Statistics, U.S. Dep't of Justice, *Bulletin: Felony Sentences in the State Courts*, 1988, at 6 (1990). Undoubtedly, the percentage of misdemeanor cases disposed of by a guilty plea is even higher. See Smith, "Forgotten in the Courts," 2 Crim. Just. 14, 17 (1987). In Milwaukee County, for example, out of 38,202 misdemeanor cases disposed of during 1986, there were only 114 trials. See G. Barczak, *Milwaukee County Circuit Court Annual Report* (1986).

49. To Alschuler, the whole plea-bargaining system is structured to coerce guilty pleas and thereby to deprive defendants of their right to trial. See Alschuler, note 26 *supra*, at 1199-1206, 1306-1314.

50. The author shares Malcolm Feeley's observation that most defendants are concerned primarily with resolving their cases quickly with a minimal expenditure of time and money. See generally M. Feeley, *The Process Is The Punishment: Handling Cases in a Lower Criminal Court* (1979). Indeed, one of the most common observations of the clinical students both at the University of Wisconsin and the Oklahoma College of Law is that so many defendants are uninterested in their own cases. Often, the students were frustrated by clients indifference and decision to just get the matter over with despite the weakness of the state's case.

51. Numerous variables affect the working of a criminal justice system. The local crime rate, funding for the different systemic actors, effectiveness of the local police, arrest policies, economic

health of the local community, and availability of social services and treatment programs are among the many factors contributing to the number of cases in the system and the manner in which these cases will be handled. Also, events and decisions at the state and national level influence the local system. For example, statewide prison overcrowding and parole release policies may influence local plea-bargaining practices and sentencing decisions. Or federal funding for the war on drugs may mean an additional position in the district attorney's office, allowing for more aggressive prosecution of defendants charged with drug offenses.

52. There are four primary systems for the delivery of defense services to indigent defendants:

1. A public-defender program, in which full-time or part-time salaried staff attorneys handle cases as part of a public or private nonprofit agency;
2. An assigned-counsel system, in which the court appoints a private attorney from a list of available attorneys to handle a particular case;
3. A contract system, in which an individual attorney, a group of attorneys, or a bar association agrees to provide defense services for a fixed amount; and
4. A mixed system, in which both salaried and public defenders and assigned counsel represent a significant number of indigent defendants.

See N. Lefstein, *Criminal Defense Services for the Poor* 7-8 (1982); Bureau of Justice Statistics, U.S. Dep't of Justice, *Special Report, Criminal Defense Systems—A National Survey* 3 (1984).

As of 1988, sixty-eight of Oklahoma's seventy-seven counties used the assigned-counsel method. Oklahoma's two largest counties had public defender agencies, and seven counties used a contract system. See Spangenberg Group, *Oklahoma Indigent Defense Systems Study Final Report* 9-10 (1988).

53. Prior to July 1991, however, defendants who appeared at their initial arraignment without counsel were to be informed of their right to counsel and assigned a lawyer if they were financially unable to employ counsel. Okla. Stat. tit. 22, § 464 (Supp. 1985).

54. This practice is inconsistent with McCraw v. State, 476 P.2d 370 (Okla. Crim. App. 1970), in which the court held that the fact that defendant was free on bond did not preclude a finding that he lacked the financial ability to retain counsel. As the court noted, "[I]t is understandable that an accused with limited resources might use them to pay for a bond to secure his freedom rather than paying a lawyer's fee." *Id.* at 373. It appears that the problem of denying counsel to persons who make bail may be widespread in Oklahoma. See Spangenberg Group, note 52 *supra*, at 50-51. It also is not uncommon for judges around the country to view the defendant's ability to post bond as a significant factor in determining indigency. See National Legal Aid & Defender Ass'n, *The Other Face of Justice: A Report of the National Defender Survey* 60-61 (1973). According to Alschuler, Texas trial judges apply the same "unfair and unrealistic" test: Anyone who can make bond is not indigent. See Alschuler, note 26 *supra*, at 1257 no.214. But see ABA, note 1 *supra*, Standard 5-6.1 ("counsel should not be denied because of a person's ability to pay part of the cost of representation, because friends or relatives have resources to retain counsel, or because bond has been or can be posted.").

55. The judges insist that any lawyer with any criminal experience who practiced in Cleveland County take several criminal appointments each year. Given the minimal compensation available for handling these cases, many lawyers consider these cases a financial burden. The burden becomes very onerous in serious felony or capital cases. See State v. Lynch, 796 P.2d 1150 (Okla. 1990) (holding that Oklahoma's statutory scheme for compensating lawyers appointed to represent indigent defendants provides an unreasonable, arbitrary rate of compensation).

56. Prior to July 1, 1991, the maximum fees by statute that an appointed Oklahoma lawyer could receive were as follows: Title 22, Section 1271 of the Oklahoma Statutes provided that compensation should be "reasonable and just" but should not exceed $500 per case, regardless of the severity of the charges; Title 22, Section 464 of the Oklahoma Statutes provided that fees for services rendered until the defendant is discharged or bound over after a preliminary hearing were not to exceed $100; Title 22, Section 701.4 of the Oklahoma Statutes provided for "reasonable and

just" compensation in capital cases with a maximum of $200 for services prior to a preliminary hearing, $500 for the preliminary hearing, and $2,500 for services from the time a defendant is bound over through final disposition in trial court.

For administrative ease, Cleveland County judges for years have simply awarded lawyers the set amount of $250 for a misdemeanor and $500 for a felony, regardless of the actual time spent. The judges assume that most lawyers in most cases put in a sufficient number of hours of work that it is unlikely that any lawyer will reap a significant financial windfall from handling these cases. The judges recognize, however, that in some cases, especially ones that go to trial, lawyers are grossly undercompensated.

In State v. Lynch, note 55 *supra*, at 1164, the Oklahoma Supreme Court recognized the inadequacies of Oklahoma's statutory scheme and set up guidelines for compensating appointed counsel based on the hourly rate of prosecutors and the public defenders in Oklahoma's two largest counties. It held off implementing these guidelines in noncapital cases until August 24, 1992 to give the legislature an opportunity to address the problem.

In response to *Lynch*, the Oklahoma legislature passed the Indigent Defense Act, Okla. Stat. tit. 22, § 1355 (Supp. 1990). Pursuant to this statute, each judicial district is to develop its own system for delivering indigent defense services. This legislation is still being implemented, and its effects on Cleveland County have yet to be felt.

57. Throughout Oklahoma, courts seldom approve requests for investigators, forensic testing, or experts. See Spangenberg Group, note 52 *supra* at 46-48. Lack of access to investigative assistance or expert services is a common weakness of many indigent defense systems, especially assigned counsel or contract systems. See Mounts & Wilson, "Systems for Providing Indigent Defense: An Introduction," 14 N.Y.U. Rev. L. & Soc. Change 193, 199 n.33 (1986); Coyle, Strasser & Lavelle, note 26 *supra*, at 30; Smith, note 48 *supra*, at 17.

58. In 1977, The Wisconsin legislature created the Office of the State Public Defender, an independent agency under the direction of the Public Defender Board. Wis. Stat. 15.78 (1989). The governor, with the advice and consent of the Senate, appoints the nine members of the board, who, in turn, select the state public defender. The state public defender supervises the operation of the program, which is divided into two divisions: appellate and trial. As of September 1990, there were 258 staff attorneys located in 37 offices throughout Wisconsin and approximately 1,400 private lawyers certified to accept appointment cases. See Office of the State Pub. Defender, *1989–91 Biennial Report* (1991). The Milwaukee trial office had 46 staff lawyers compared with 18 in the Dane County office.

59. In most jurisdictions, salaries of public defenders lag behind those of their prosecutorial counterparts. In Wisconsin, however, public defenders as state employees generally earned more during the past decade than most assistant district attorneys with comparable experience. This lack of salary parity led the Wisconsin District Attorneys Association to push for legislation that created state funding for the operation of all local district attorney offices and made assistant district attorneys state rather than county employees. See Wis. Stat. Ann. § 978.001-978.14 (West 1991).

60. Wis. Stat. § 977.07(2) (1989) provides:

> If the person's assets, less reasonable and necessary living expenses, are not sufficient to cover the anticipated cost of effective representation when the length and complexity of the anticipated proceedings are taken fully into account, the person shall be determined to be indigent in full or in part. The determination of the ability of the person to contribute to the cost of legal services shall be based upon specific written standards relating to income, assets and the anticipated cost of representation.

The specific written standards are set forth by administrative rule. See Wis. Admin. Code § S.P.D. 3.01 (1990).

In Cleveland County, on the other hand, judges determine the defendant's right to appointed counsel based on their subjective assessment of the defendant's indigency. The judges use the pauper's affidavit set forth in Okla. Ct. Crim. App. R. 1.14 to obtain information, but no guidelines exist as to how that information is to be analyzed. Accordingly, there is considerable variance in indigency determinations. This problem is not unique to Cleveland County. See Spangenberg Group, note 52 *supra*, at 49-51. For an extended discussion of the need to develop specific eligibility criteria that compares liquid assets with the anticipated cost of counsel, including litigation expenses, and the merits of removing the eligibility determination from judicial control, see National Study Comm'n on Defense Servs. *Guidelines for Legal Defense Systems in the United States* 72-96 (1976).

61. Section 969.06 of the Wisconsin Statutes, read in conjunction with Section 977.05(b) of the Wisconsin Statutes, provides for representation of an indigent "as soon as practicable after a person has been detained or arrested." In practice, however, the public defender's office represents eligible persons seeking assistance even before any arrest or detention. For a discussion of the importance of early representation, see ABA, note 1 *supra*, Standard 5-5.1 and commentary (2d ed. 1980); National Study Comm'n on Defense Servs., note 60 *supra*, at 48-71.

62. In his last report to Governor Thompson and the Wisconsin legislature, State Public Defender Nicholas Chiarkas noted that the public-defender trial staff was now handling 62.3 percent of all indigent cases statewide, with the remainder handled by assigned private lawyers. See Office of State Pub. Defender, note 58 *supra*, at 5-6. Since 1977, staff lawyers in the Milwaukee and Dane County offices generally have defended about 75 percent of the program's clients in each county.

63. As of December 1, 1992, the rate will be $50 per hour for in-court work and $40 for other work. *Id.* at 15.

64. Private lawyers must seek prior approval from the local public-defender office before hiring an expert or investigator. See Wis. Admin. Code § S.P.D. 2.12 (1990).

65. For a discussion of the Wisconsin funding needs, see Spangenberg Group, note 26 *supra*, at 28-49. Clearly, there are other jurisdictions, including Cleveland County, where the funding shortfalls are much worse. See, e.g., Coyle, Strasser & Lavelle, note 26 *supra*, at 30-44; Special Comm. on Criminal Justice in Free Soc'y, Criminal Justice Section, *Criminal Justice in Crisis* (1988). For a discussion of the serious funding crisis in Oklahoma, see Spangenberg Group, note 52 *supra*, at 30-46.

As Spangenberg noted in the fall of 1989, "[T]he problem has grown substantially worse for most indigent defense systems since 1986. With a few exceptions, indigent defense delivery in the country once again has reached a crisis stage." Spangenberg, "We Are Still Not Defending the Poor Properly," 4 Crim. Just. 11 (1989). Norman Lefstein detailed the extent of the national crisis in his study done at the behest of the American Bar Association. See N. Lefstein, note 52 *supra.* For other accounts of the continuing crisis in the delivery of indigent defense services in this country, see Spangenberg, note 38 *supra*, at 13-15, 48; Murphy, "Indigent Defense and the U.S. War on Drugs," 6 Crim. Just. 14, 14-20 (1991); Monahan, "Who Is Trying to Kill the Sixth Amendment," 6 Crim. Just. 24, 24-28, 51-52 (1991).

66. Some unrepresented defendants do obtain better plea bargains by negotiating their own deals. Like Alschuler, this author has observed some sympathetic prosecutors make offers to unrepresented defendants that went well below the norm given the person's record and the charge. See Alschuler, note 26 *supra*, at 1274-1278. If the unrepresented defendant wants to contest the charge or the prosecutor's initial offer is harsh, however, the defendant has little leverage or ability to obtain the desired result.

67. Many commentators have decried the inadequate representation provided by poorly paid courthouse "regulars" or "pleaders," who turn over cases as quickly as possible to maximize their profits. See, e.g., Bazelon, "The Defective Assistance of Counsel," 42 U. Cin. L. Rev. 1, 8-11 (1973); Alschuler, note 26 *supra*, at 1182-1186.

68. After the arraignment, the next court appearance in Cleveland County is referred to as the call docket. At the call docket, each defendant must announce whether he wants a jury trial, court

trial, or date to plead guilty. Call dockets are held roughly six weeks apart. At the call docket on November 19, 1991, it was "discovered" that seven misdemeanor defendants had each been incarcerated for almost six weeks because of their inability to post minimal bond. Each was charged with public intoxication in violation of Title 37, Section 8 of the Oklahoma Statutes (1990), which carries a maximum jail sentence of thirty days. The usual disposition for this offense is a small fine, some community service, or a weekend in jail. Upon learning that these defendants were still incarcerated—the jail was checked when the defendants did not appear in person at the call docket—the cases were set for disposition. Each defendant pleaded guilty for time served.

This problem is, of course, not unique to Cleveland County. For a brief look at the problems with "forgotten" detainees in the Baltimore city jail, see Presser, "Lost and Found," A.B.A.J., Nov. 1991, at 42.

69. Wis. Stat. Ann. § 969.03 comment L. 1969, ch. 255 (West 1985). Sections 969.02 and 969.03 of the Wisconsin Statutes spell out the procedures for releasing persons charged with misdemeanors and felonies. Although surety bonds by individuals or corporate sureties are still permitted, such bonds are rarely used.

70. See Wis. Stat. § 968.085 (1989).

71. Moreover, in Milwaukee County there is a nonprofit social service agency, the Wisconsin Correctional Service, which runs various programs for the Milwaukee court system. These programs further facilitate the pretrial release of a number of defendants, especially those with drug, alcohol, or mental health problems, who would otherwise remain incarcerated. Success on a release program enchances a defendant's chance to obtain a favorable outcome. Dane County has some similar programs, but they are not as structured or as extensive as those of Milwaukee County. Cleveland County does not have any agency involved in a pretrial release program.

72. The pressure on indigent defendants is compounded by the policy of the Cleveland County sheriff not to permit pretrial detainees any visitors except for a lawyer for their first seven days in jail.

73. For an article making the same point based on a study of the pretrial detention practices in Houston, Texas, see Wheeler & Wheeler, "Reflections on Legal Representation of the Economically Disadvantaged: Beyond Assembly Line Justice," 26 Crime & Delinq. 319 (1982). See also H. Zeisel, *The Limits of Law Enforcement* 47-49 (1982) (discussing the inequities of a bail system that exerts undue pressure on incarcerated defendants to plead guilty).

74. None of the offices adheres to a policy of no plea bargaining. Presumably, a major policy decision such as this would have a substantial impact on the behavior of defendants and their lawyers. See Spangenberg, note 65 *supra*, at 12 (policies of limited or no plea bargaining have great impact on indigent defense resources).

75. Although assistant district attorneys in all three counties complained of heavy case loads and serious time pressures, the prosecutors in Milwaukee County seemingly labored under heavier work loads. As a result, the Milwaukee prosecutors were more responsive when defense counsel demonstrated the weakness of the state's case. Prosecutors in both Dane and Cleveland Counties routinely filed and then more aggressively pursued cases that either would not have been issued or would have been quickly dismissed in Milwaukee County.

76. Dane County has two deputy district attorneys, while Cleveland County has one. In both counties, the district attorney is also involved in charging decisions in certain cases. Additionally, in Cleveland County, all drug charges are filed by one assistant district attorney and all child molestation cases by another. Occasionally, the deputy district attorney will speak to the complainant, other witnesses, the arresting officers, or the suspect in making a charging decision. Charges usually are issued, however, based on a review of the police reports and the suspect's criminal record.

77. The law student interns are authorized to practice pursuant to Okla. Sup. Ct. R. 2. Although the intern program is designed to give the students "real-world" experience under the supervision of

an experienced lawyer, the students are all supervised by one prosecutor who rarely appears with them in court. The interns generally seek advice from their supervisor, however, before reducing or dismissing a charge.

78. This charging conference procedure is used in all felony and serious misdemeanor cases. All other misdemeanor charges are filed based on the prosecutor's review of police reports and rap sheets.

79. Generally, a lawyer should not even begin plea negotiations without the consent of the client. See ABA, note 1 *supra*, Standard 4-6.1(b) (2d ed. 1980). In the latest edition of the *Standards for Criminal Justice*, Standard 4-6.1(b) has been modified by the deletion of the phrase "although ordinarily the client's consent to engage in such discussions should be obtained in advance." Because the commentary to this standard has yet to be published, the rationale for this change is unclear. Nevertheless, because a lawyer may find it necessary to discuss information revealed by the client while plea bargaining, counsel generally should secure the client's permission before negotiating with the prosecutor. Compare *Model Code of Professional Responsibility* DR 4-101(B), DR 4-101(C) (1981) with *Model Rules of Professional Conduct* Rule 1.6 (1983).

80. Because the defendant ultimately controls the decision whether to plead guilty or to go to trial, defense counsel should present the available options as clearly and as objectively as possible. See Jones v. Barnes, note 6 *supra*, at 745, 751; *Model Rules of Professional Conduct* Rule 1.2 (1983); ABA, note 1 *supra*, Standard 4-5.2(a). Even when the defendant is anxious just to plead guilty to get the matter over with, counsel must ensure that the defendant is cognizant of the consequences of a guilty plea. This is particularly so when representing young defendants, who often do not recognize the potential impact of a criminal conviction on their employment opportunities, eligibility for military service, or insurance rates. Like Feeley, this author has frequently seen public defenders or clinical law students attempt to dissuade defendants who are anxious to get their cases over quickly from pleading guilty. See M. Feeley, note 50 *supra*, at 222. See also ABA, note 1 *supra*, Standard 4-4.1 (defense counsel's duty to investigate exists regardless of defendant's admission of guilt or stated desire to plead guilty).

81. Unquestionably, the deplorable conditions in many county jails, including the real risk of physical harm to pretrial detainees, spur some defendants to plead guilty. For a brief look at some of the hardships endured by pretrial detainees, see Wallace v. Kern, 371 F.Supp. 1384 (E.D.N.Y. 1974), *rev'd*, 499 F.2d 1345 (2d Cir. 1974).

82. There is little question to anyone familiar with the criminal justice system that the prosecutor wields extraordinary power and has enormous discretion. See ABA, note 1 *supra*, Standard 3-1.1, at 3-7 (2d ed. 1979). For a summary of the scope of the prosecutor's discretion, see W. LaFave & J. Israel, note 2 *supra*, at 559-594. Moreover, the "give and take" of plea bargaining gives the prosecutor considerable leverage to coerce a guilty plea. See Bordenkircher v. Hayes, 434 U.S. 357 (1978) (not improper for prosecutor to carry out threat to prosecute defendant as a habitual offender because of defendant's unwillingness to plead to underlying felony).

83. Not all public defenders have a reputation for providing aggressive, zealous representation. See Klein, note 41 *supra*, at 657-663. For a thorough and damning account of the abysmal quality of representation provided to indigents in New York by both assigned counsel and the Legal Aid Society, see McConville & Mirsky, "Criminal Defense of the Poor in New York City," 15 Rev. of L. & Soc. Change 581 (1986–1987). See also Sudnow, note 19 *supra.* Most of the criticism leveled against public defenders, however, springs from underfunded, overloaded programs that provide substandard representation. Adequately funded programs tend to get high marks for the quality of representation delivered to the program's clients. See, e.g., U.S. Dep't of Justice, *An Exemplary Project: The D.C. Public Defender Service* (1975); Arthur Young & Co., note 26 *supra.*

84. Arguably, the reasonable rates paid by the Wisconsin public-defender program provide a financial incentive for lawyers to spend unnecessary time defending a case, turn down reasonable plea offers, or go to trial on hopeless cases. Admittedly, some lawyers may overwork a case. While

at the Milwaukee public-defender office, the author reviewed a private lawyer's voucher that included twenty-five hours for time spent calling every Brown in the Milwaukee phone book trying unsuccessfully to make initial contact with his newly assigned client. The public-defender program would selectively cut bills such as the one submitted in Brown's case. Although this power is used sparingly, it does discourage abuse. See Wis. Stat. § 977.08(4) (1989) (Public Defender Board reviews decisions of the state public defender regarding payment of private lawyer vouchers). Finally, the client makes the ultimate decision on pleading guilty or going to trial. The client's reluctance to go to trial, fear of an increased sentence, and interest in a quick resolution generally will override the desire of an overzealous assigned lawyer looking to make some extra money by "milking" an appointed case.

85. See State v. McKenny, 582 P.2d 573, 577 (Wash. 1978) (compensation scheme unrelated to work actually performed creates "an economic disincentive against satisfactory representation"); ABA, note 1 *supra*, Standard 5-2.4, at 5-33 (2d. ed. 1979) (flat payment rates should be discouraged because the inevitable result is lawyers doing only what is minimally necessary to qualify for flat payment). For a chilling study of the inadequate representation provided to many capital defendants in several Southern states using an assigned-counsel method, see Coyle et al., note 26 *supra*, at 30-44. A number of courts have struck down statutory schemes for compensating assigned counsel with low maximum awards on the ground that as administered, such systems unfairly and arbitrarily compelled some lawyers to shoulder a heavy financial burden that properly should be borne by the state. See, e.g., State v. Lynch, note 55 *supra*, at 1150; State v. Smith, 242 Kan. 336, 747 P.2d 816 (1987).

Nevertheless, it is evident that in many jurisdictions, the compensation provided to appointed lawyers in an assigned-counsel system still is woefully inadequate. Unfortunately, too often these assigned lawyers also provide woeful representation. See N.Lefstein, note 52 *supra*, at 17-24; McConville & Mirsky, note 83 *supra*, at 899-901; Smith, note 48 *supra*, at 17; Herman, Single & Boston, note 26 *supra*, at 161.

86. See Mounts & Wilson, note 57 *supra*, at 194; N. Lefstein, note 52 *supra*, at 19-20. For personal accounts of private lawyers laboring under financial pressure to induce clients to plead guilty and not go to trial, see ABA & National Legal Aid & Defender Ass'n, note 38 *supra*, at 10-11, 14-15. As Dean Paul Carrington observed, "while there will be admirable exceptions of lawyers laboring to do what few will ever know or care about, a system that desires zealous advocacy on the whole will have to reward it." Carrington, "The Right to Zealous Counsel," 1979 Duke L.J. 1291, 1294. See also Spangenberg Group, note 52 *supra*, at 37-46 (commending Oklahoma lawyers for continuing to take indigent appointments despite inadequate compensation but noting that experienced lawyers increasingly were opting out of such appointments).

87. "No attorney, no matter how skilled, trained, and committed, can provide competent representation under working conditions which do not allow such skill, training, and commitment to be practiced." Mounts, note 8 *supra*, at 221. See also ABA, note 1 *supra*, Standard 5-4.3, at 5-48 (2d ed. 1979); ABA & National Legal Aid & Defender Ass'n, note 38 *supra*, at 5.

88. For a summary of the adverse effects of an excessive case load on a public defender's ability to prepare, investigate, research, and consult with clients, see Klein, note 41 *supra*, at 662-675.

89. In his recent report, Spangenberg praised the Wisconsin public defenders for their dedication and quality. Yet, he concluded that an increasing number of the public defenders' clients were suffering because the lawyers were laboring under the strain of an excessive case load and work load. See Spangenberg Group, note 26 *supra*, at 32-49.

90. See Mounts, *"Public Defender Programs, Professional Responsibility and Competent Representation,"* 1982 Wis. L. Rev. 473, 486. As many commentators have noted, defendants often mistrust their lawyer, especially when counsel is appointed, not retained. See Jones v. Barnes, note 6 *supra*, at 745, 761 (Brennan, J., dissenting); Herman, Single & Boston, note 26 *supra*, at 153. For a detailed account of the reasons clients mistrust their lawyers, especially public defenders, see J. Casper, note 26 *supra*; L. McIntyre, note 26 *supra*, at 62-73.

91. Like any experienced criminal practitioner, most public defenders can assess realistically the value of a proffered plea bargain because they know the prosecutor's standard offers and the judge's sentencing proclivities. See Alschuler, note 26 *supra*, at 1229-1230.

92. See Spangenberg Group, note 26 *supra*, at 34.

93. "Defense counsel should not seek concessions favorable to one client by any agreement which is detrimental to the legitimate interests of a client in another case." ABA, note 1 *supra*, Standard 4-6.2(d). Although public defenders probably do not often explicitly "trade off" one client to secure a favorable deal for another, the give-and-take process involved in bargaining numerous cases with a handful of prosecutors invariably works to the advantage of some clients and the disadvantage of others. For a brief look at this troublesome and, perhaps, unresolvable problem, see Alschuler, note 26 *supra*, at 1210-1224.

94. Schneyer, note 11 *supra*, at 24 (emphasis in the original). See also Alschuler, note 26 *supra*, at 1254-1255; Klien, note 41 *supra*, at 669-673.

95. See note 65 *supra.*

96. As Mounts and Wilson point out, there are many political factors contributing to this serious underfunding of defense services. Mounts & Wilson, note 57 *supra*, at 200-201. Because increased spending for defense services is so politically unpopular, the litigation model may well be one of the most effective means of securing additional funding. See Wilson, "Litigative Approaches to Enforcing the Right to Effective Assistance of Counsel in Criminal Cases," 14 N.Y.U. Rev. L. & Soc. Change 203 (1986). In Oklahoma, for example, it was not until the Supreme Court of Oklahoma forced the legislature's hand by adopting its own statewide compensation scheme for court-appointed counsel in State v. Lynch, note 55 *supra*, at 1150, that the Oklahoma legislature finally passed a measure creating the Indigent Defense Act. See note 56 *supra.*

97. Alschuler argues that the intolerable nature of the plea-bargaining system is such that all defense lawyers are "subject to bureaucratic pressures and conflicts of interest" that can only be avoided by "restructur[ing] our criminal justice system to eliminate the overwhelming importance of the defendant's choice of plea." Alschuler, note 26 *supra*, at 1313. He calls, therefore, for the abolition of the plea-bargaining system and sufficient resources to pay for the added costs of more trials. *Id.* at 1180, 1314.

While the author of this article concurs with many of Alschuler's observations, especially his descriptions of the destructive impact of plea bargaining on the attorney-client relationship, the author does not agree that the abolition of plea bargaining is either feasible or desirable. Given the existing crisis in the criminal justice system at all levels, with only a small percentage of cases going to trial, the resources needed to adequately fund this restructured system would be staggering. Moreover, the working poor and many middle-class defendants would be unable to afford aggressive advocacy under this restructured system. In a system devoid of plea-bargaining, these defendants may face far harsher dispositions. It is more desirable, therefore, to expand and adequately fund defense services and, thus, permit defense lawyers to function as effective adversaries of the state. See also Mounts, note 90 *supra*, at 488 (suggesting that budgetary problems are the primary stumbling block to a public defender's ability to provide quality representation).

98. In a mixed system, both staff public defenders and assigned private lawyers represent a "substantial number" of indigent clients. N. Lefstein, note 52 *supra*, at 8. For an excellent summary of the advantages of a mixed system, see ABA, note 1 *supra*, Standard 5-1.2 and commentary (2d. ed. 1979). See also National Study Comm'n on Defense Servs. note 60 *supra*, at 124-136 (recommending mixed defender and assigned-counsel system, with each handling a substantial share of cases) 144-180 (recommending a state defender office to organize, coordinate, and monitor the delivery of defense services throughout each state).

99. See Spangenberg, note 38 *supra*, at 15; National Study Comm'n on Defense Servs., note 60 *supra*, at 134-135. In Wisconsin, the support of the state bar has been instrumental in enabling the Wisconsin public-defender program to avert financial crisis. See Gimbel, "The Public Defenders' Changing Image," Wis. B. Bull., Sept. 1985, at 9, 10.

100. Echoing earlier observations by Alschuler, Spangenberg noted that a substantial diminution of the role of the private bar in the criminal system raised the specter of a system dominated by institutional lawyers too comfortable and too cooperative to protect their clients' rights. See Spangenberg, note 38 *supra*, at 14-15; Alschuler, note 26 *supra*, at 1210-1222. For an extended look at the dangers of an institutional defender program primarily committed to the cost-efficient processing of defendants, see McConville & Mirsky, note 83 *supra*, at 582-695.
101. The ethics codes clearly require a defense lawyer to exercise independent judgment on behalf of a client without allowing an employer or administrator to direct or regulate counsel's advocacy. See *Model Code of Professional Responsibility* DR 5-107(B) (1981); *Model Rules of Professional Conduct* Rule 5.4(c) (1983). See also Polk County v. Dodson, note 2 *supra*, at 312, 321-322 (concluding that the state must respect the professional independence of the individual public defender, who, in turn, must make case decisions free from administrative control). There is little question that assistant public defenders and appointed counsel are unlikely to feel free to engage in legitimate but judicially unpopular defense tactics if they are economically dependent on the judicairy. See National Study Comm'n on Defense Servs., note 60 *supra*, at 218-221; ABA, note 1 *supra*, Standards 5-1.3, 5-3.1 and commentary (2d. ed. 1979).

Similarly, a county's interest in obtaining defense services at the lowest possible cost cannot be permitted to compromise defense counsel's independence and the quality of representation provided by counsel. See State v. Smith, 140 Ariz. 355, 681 P.2d 1374 (1984).
102. To guarantee the professional independence of the defender program, most commentators urge the creation of a board that sets general policies for the operation of the program but is removed from the day-to-day operation of the program and precluded from interfering in any cases. See ABA, note 1 *supra*, Standards 5-1.3, 5-1.6, 5-2.4; National Study Comm'n on Defense Servs., note 60 *supra*, at 224-231.
103. "Since a primary objective of the payment system should be to encourage vigorous defense representation, flat payment rates should be discouraged. The inevitable effect of such rates is to discourage lawyers from doing more than what is minimally necessary to qualify for the flat payment." ABA, note 1 *supra*, Standard 5-2.4, at 5-33 (2d. ed 1979). See also notes 85-86 *supra* and accompanying text. For an unduly optimistic view of the contract system, see Spears, "Contract Counsel: A Different Way to Defend the Poor," 6 Crim. Just. 24-31 (1991) (arguing that quality criteria in the initial bidding process, prior approval by the funding agency of any change in the lawyers in the contracting firm, and a noncause termination clause in the contract ensures quality representation by the contracting firm). Most commentators, however, believe that the contract system provides an economic incentive to turn over cases quickly without regard for quality representation. See, e.g., National Study Comm'n on Defense Servs., note 60 *supra*, at 169-170; Wilson, *Contract Bid Programs: A Threat to Quality Indigent Defense Services* (Mar. 1982) (unpublished report for National Legal Aid and Defender Association). See also State v. Smith, note 101 *supra* (finding that contract system in Mohave County based on flat payment for one-fourth of county's total case load militated against adequate representation by overburdened defense counsel).
104. See notes 61-66 *supra* and accompanying text.
105. As a national study has concluded:

> Quality representation is not only related to the compensation of counsel. It also depends upon the availability of supporting services and facilities as these are not only vital to the presentation of the defense's case, they are often required to disprove the prosecution's case. Since the state already has the police to conduct investigations and supply expert testimony, assigned counsel would be forced to operate under a distinct disadvantage without the availability of necessary supporting services and facilities. This is an inequity which no system of justice should tolerate.

National Study Comm'n on Defense Servs., note 60 *supra*, at 272. See also ABA, note 1 *supra*, Standard 5-1.4.

Although it is evident that defense counsel can seldom function effectively without adequate support, it is abundantly clear that support services are virtually nonexistent or badly underfunded in most jurisdictions. See N. Lefstein, note 52 *supra*, app. at F-1-F-68. Even though the Wisconsin public-defender program is better funded than most, it is seriously deficient in investigative and support services. See Spangenberg Group, note 26 *supra*, at 33, 43-44.

106. See ABA, note 1 *supra* Standard 5-1.5.

107. "The practice of criminal law has become highly specialized in recent years, and only lawyers experienced in trial practice, with an interest in and knowledge of criminal law and procedure, can properly be expected to serve as assigned counsel." ABA, note 1 *supra*, Standard 5-2.2, at 5-27 (2d ed. 1979). Many courts and commentators have noted the increased complexity of handling a criminal case. See, e.g., State v. Smith, note 85 *supra*; N. Lefstein, note 52 *supra*, at 18; National Study Comm'n on Defense Servs., note 60 *supra*, at 433-439.

108. My experience as the chief staff attorney of the Milwaukee office confirms that to encourage zeal and productivity, merit raises are essential. See also Carrington, note 86 *supra*, at 1305-1307 (arguing for bonus system for staff attorneys to inspire zeal together with the right to fire one's appointed lawyer); National Study Comm'n on Defense Servs., note 60 *supra*, at 454-458.

109. Developing adequate performance measures poses a serious problem for any public defender administrator or board. There are national case load standards, but they are only a crude starting point for assessing the adequacy of a staff lawyer's performance. Local case load standards must be tailored to reflect local variations such as the prosecutor's charging system, local plea-bargaining practices, and court congestion. For a detailed look at one approach to developing case load standards weighted to reflect various local factors, see Spangenberg Group, note 26 *supra*, at 16-93.

Setting reasonable case load standards, however, only solves part of the problem. A public defender may meet case load requirements and handle a prescribed number of cases but provide poor representation. An effort must be made to ensure that aggressive, competent lawyering is rewarded and that quality representation is not sacrificed at the altar of case load statistics. Supervision and evaluation by experienced senior lawyers constitutes the best mechanism for ensuring quality representation. See National Study Comm'n on Defense Servs., note 60 *supra*, at 440-441.

110. Given the demonstrated inability of local government to fund indigent defense services adequately, the author assumes that this proposed program is state funded and administered as an independent state agency. For the advantages of this approach, see National Study Comm'n on Defense Servs., note 60 *supra*, at 242-258.

111. See Spangenberg Group, note 26 *supra*, at 1-15. For additional background on the often heated political battles over the budget for the Wisconsin public-defender program, see Phelps, "Dust Settles After Legislative Battle," Wis. B. Bull., Sept. 1985, at 20-23; Phelps, "Mounting Stress on Wisconsin's Justice System," Wis. B. Bull., Mar. 1987, at 32.

112. Program administrators who are lawyers are bound to ensure that the lawyers in their program are not violating the rules of professional conduct. Model Rules of Professional Conduct Rule 5.1 (1983). If the supervising lawyers know that their lawyers are handling so many cases that they are neglecting the rights of their clients, these supervisors as well as the staff lawyers are in violation of their ethical responsibilities. For a further discussion of the ethical problems confronting supervisors and staff lawyers grappling with excessive case loads, see Klein, "Legal Malpractice, Professional Discipline, and Representation of the Indigent," 61 Temp. L.Q. 1171 (1988); Mounts, note 90 *supra*, at 473.

113. See note 109 *supra.*

114. Public defenders also must recognize the importance of spending more time talking with their clients about their cases and then devote the necessary time. See, e.g., Wilkerson, "Public Defenders as Their Clients See Them," 1 Am. J. Crim. L. 141, 142 (1972) (most widely shared grievance among public-defender clients is lack of contact with or visits from their lawyer). Absent

increased and improved communications, public defenders will not be able to overcome the mistrust most clients feel toward their assigned lawyers. See, e.g., J. Casper, note 26 *supra*, at 36 (lack of time spent with clients is a significant factor contributing to the poor image of public defenders).

115. Keeping salaries low is not a desirable solution, but it is preferable to making do with inadequate support services or excessive case loads, both of which compromise the quality of defense services. The issue in part turns on whether good lawyers could still be attracted to and retained by the program if salaries were not comparable to those in the prosecutor's office as recommended by the National Study Commission. See National Study Comm'n on Defense Servs., note 60 *supra*, at 278-284. Given the poor job market, the increased number of clinical students anxious to get into defender programs, and the attractiveness of a public-defender job for lawyers looking for litigation experience, attracting good candidates is unlikely to be a problem. A loan forgiveness program for students going to a public defender's office or doing other public service work would encourage even more quality graduates to apply for public-defender positions.

Although it is possible that a lower salary structure will lead to increased turnover, the job market and enhanced job satisfaction may counter that trend. Moreover, it is clear that many lawyers do public-defender work for reasons other than money. See L. McIntyre, note 26 *supra*, at 80-84, 89. Finally, it is not clear that higher turnover and loss of experience necessarily results in lower-quality representation. That depends on the extent of the turnover, the quality of the training programs, and the zeal and quality of the new recruits.

116. For a discussion of the importance of monitoring training and supervision, see National Study Comm'n on Defense Servs., note 60 *supra*, at 434-447.

117. Not only does a statewide program best serve the goal of quality representation, it "offers the most efficient and flexible means of allocating available resources." National Study Comm'n on Defense Servs., note 60 *supra*, at 175.

118. Even using the Wisconsin indigency test, which is more generous than the standardless determinations made in Cleveland County and many other jurisdictions, see note 59 *supra*, many people on small fixed incomes do not qualify for public-defender representation. Realistically, however, a person receiving a monthly Social Security benefit cannot hire counsel. Unfortunately, public-defender administrators facing case load increases on top of existing crushing case loads are not inclined to argue for a loosening of indigency standards. In fact, the Wisconsin public-defender office continues to use outdated figures as to the anticipated cost of retaining counsel in applying their indigency test to hold down their case load. See Wis. Admin. Code § S.P.D. 3.02(1). See also State v. Dean, 163 Wis. 2d 503, 471 N.W.2d 310 (Wis. Ct. App. 1991) (Wis. Admin. Code § S.P.D. 3.02 use $300 for cost of hiring lawyer in criminal traffic case when evidence suggests real cost is $500 to $1,000). The use of outdated figures works to deny counsel to low-income persons who really cannot afford representation. As a result, some low-income defendants are challenging the public defender's denial of counsel. In *State v. Dean*, the Wisconsin Court of Appeals held that the trial court should have exercised its inherent power to appoint counsel despite the indigency determination of the public defender. Most needy defendants, however, do not challenge the public defender's denial of counsel but simply go without counsel.

119. Such an approach was recommended by the National Study Commission in its 1976 report on defense services. See National Study Comm'n on Defense Servs., note 60 *supra*, at 104-122.

120. Indeed, it already appears that overtaxed indigent defense systems are being asked to handle more indigent cases each year, this exacerbating existing case load problems. See Spangenberg Group, note 26 *supra*, at 4. Budgetary pressures are likely to produce a tightening of indigency standards rather than an expansion of coverage to include the working poor. In fact, the drive toward a tightening of eligibility requirements is already under way in many states. See Spangenberg, note 38 *supra*, at 48. The problem, of course, is that people squeezed out of the indigent defense system usually are left with two bad alternatives: pro se representation or hiring a cheap lawyer.

Some public-defender programs have urged decriminalization as a means to retard case load growth and the spiraling costs both of the public-defender program and the criminal justice system as a whole. See Phleps, "Mounting Stress on Wisconsin's Justice System," Wis. B. Bull., Mar. 1987, at 33-34. As Nicholas Chiarkas noted in his agency's annual report, the public defender's office achieved several major goals with the enactment of the latest Wisconsin biennial budget: Various misdemeanor offenses were decriminalized and the line between misdemeanor and felony property offenses was raised from $500 to $1,000. See Office of State Pub. Defender, note 58 *supra*, at 7, 9. While these legislative changes are desirable from the standpoint of many defendants, the result will be the greater use of civil forfeiture actions where no right to counsel exists.

5

Juvenile (In)Justice and the Criminal Court Alternative

Barry C. Feld

The Supreme Court's decision in *In re Gault* (1967) began transforming the juvenile court into a very different institution than the Progressives contemplated. Progressive reformers envisioned an informal court whose dispositions reflected the "best interests" of the child. The Supreme Court engrafted formal procedures at trial onto juvenile courts' individualized treatment sentencing schema. Although the Court's decisions were not intended to alter the juvenile courts' therapeutic mission, legislative, judicial, and administrative responses to *Gault* have modified the courts' jurisdiction, purpose, and procedures (Feld 1984, 1988b). The substantive and procedural convergence between juvenile and criminal courts eliminates most of the conceptual and operational differences between social control strategies for youths and adults. With its transformation from an informal, rehabilitative agency into a scaled-down, second-class criminal court, is there any reason to maintain a separate punitive juvenile court whose only distinction is its persisting procedural deficiencies?

Three types of reforms—jurisdictional, jurisprudential, and procedural—reveal the transformation of the contemporary juvenile court (Feld 1991b). Recognizing that juvenile courts often failed to realize their benevolent purposes has led to two jurisdictional changes. Status offenses are misconduct by juveniles, such as truancy or incorrigibility, that would not be a crime if committed by an adult. Recent reforms limit the dispositions that noncriminal offenders may receive or even remove status offenses from juvenile court jurisdiction. A second jurisdictional change is the criminalizing of serious juvenile offenders. Increasingly, courts and legislatures transfer some youths from juvenile courts to criminal courts for prosecution as adults (Feld 1987). As jurisdiction contracts with the removal of serious offenders and noncriminal status offenders, the sentences received by delinquents charged with crimes are based on the idea of just deserts rather than their "real needs." Proportional and determinate sentences based on the present offense and prior record, rather than the best interests of the child, dictate the length, location, and intensity of intervention (Feld 1988b). Increased emphasis on formal procedures at trial has accompanied the enhanced role of punishment in sentencing juveniles (Feld 1984). Although, theoretically, juvenile courts' pro-

Reprinted by permission of Sage Publications from *Crime & Deliquency,* vol. 39 (1993), pp. 403-424.

cedures closely resemble those of criminal courts, in reality, the justice routinely afforded juveniles is lower than the minimum insisted upon for adults.

The Progressive Juvenile Court

Prior to the creation of the juvenile court, the only special protections received by youths charged with crimes were those afforded by the common law's infancy *mens rea* defense, which conclusively presumed that children less than 7 years old lacked criminal capacity, those 14 years old or older were responsible, and those between 7 years old and 14 years old were rebuttably irresponsible (Fox 1970b). Changes in the cultural conception of children and in strategies of social control during the 19th century led to the creation of the juvenile court (Fox 1970a; Feld 1991b). By the end of the century, children increasingly were seen as vulnerable, innocent, passive, and dependent beings who needed extended preparation for life (Ainsworth 1991; Sutton 1988). The ideology of crime causation changed, as positivistic criminology, which regarded crime as determined rather than chosen, superseded classical explanations that attributed crime to free-willed actors (Allen 1981). Attributing criminal behavior to antecedent causes reduced offenders' moral responsibility, focused efforts on reforming rather than punishing them, and fostered the "rehabilitative ideal." At the dawn of the 20th century, Progressive reformers used the new theories of social control and the new ideas about childhood to create a social welfare alternative to criminal courts to treat criminal and noncriminal misconduct by youths.

By redefining social control, Progressive reformers removed children from the adult criminal system and achieved greater flexibility and supervision of children (Platt 1977; Sutton 1988). Progressives envisioned the juvenile court as a welfare agency in which an expert judge, assisted by social workers and probation officers, made individualized dispositions in a child's best interests (Rothman 1980). The inquiry into the "whole" child accorded minor significance to crime because the specific offense indicated little about a child's real needs. They maximized discretion to provide flexibility in diagnosis and treatment and focused on the child's character and lifestyle. Because juvenile courts separated children from adults and provided an alternative to punishment, they rejected procedural safeguards of criminal law such as juries and lawyers. Informal procedures, euphemistic vocabularies, confidential and private hearings, limited access to court records, and findings of "delinquency" eliminated any stigma or implication of a criminal proceeding. Indeterminate, nonproportional dispositions continued for the duration of the minority, because each child's "treatment" needs differed and no limits could be defined in advance.

THE CONSTITUTIONAL DOMESTICATION OF THE JUVENILE COURT

The Supreme Court's *Gault* (1967) decision mandated procedural safeguards in delinquency proceedings and focused judicial attention initially on whether the child committed an offense as prerequisite to sentencing (Feld 1984, 1988b). In shifting the focus of juvenile courts from real needs to legal guilt, *Gault* emphasized two crucial gaps between juvenile justice rhetoric and reality: the theory versus practice of rehabilitation, and the differences between the procedural safeguards afforded adults and those available to juveniles (Feld 1990b). The *Gault* Court emphasized that juveniles charged with crimes who faced institutional confinement required elementary procedural safeguards, including notice of charges, a hearing, assistance of counsel, an opportunity to confront and cross-examine witnesses, and a privilege against self-incrimination.

In *In re Winship* (1970), the Court concluded that the risks of erroneous convictions required delinquency to be proven by the criminal standard "beyond a reasonable doubt" rather than by a lower civil standard of proof. In *Breed v. Jones* (1975), the Court posited a functional equivalence between criminal trials and delinquency proceedings and applied the ban on double jeopardy to delinquency convictions.

In *McKeiver v. Pennsylvania* (1970), however, the Court denied juveniles the constitutional right to jury trials and halted the extension of full procedural parity with adult criminal prosecutions. Although *Gault* and *Winship* recognized the need for procedural safeguards against governmental oppression, *McKeiver* denied the need for such protections, invoked the mythology of benevolent juvenile court judges, and justified the procedural differences of juvenile courts by their treatment rationale (*McKeiver* 1970, pp. 550-51; Feld 1988b).

TRANSFORMATION OF THE JUVENILE COURT: REFORMED BUT NOT REHABILITATED

Gault (1967), *Winship* (1970), and *McKeiver* (1970) precipitated a procedural and substantive revolution in juvenile justice that unintentionally but inevitably transformed its Progressive conception. By emphasizing criminal procedural regularity in determining delinquency and formalizing the connection between crime and sentence, the Court made explicit a relationship previously implicit and unacknowledged. Legislative and judicial responses to those decisions—decriminalizing status offenders, waiving serious offenders, punitively sentencing delinquents, and formalizing procedures—further the convergence between criminal and juvenile courts.

Noncriminal Status Offenders

The definition and administration of status jurisdiction has been criticized extensively in the post-*Gault* decades. The President's Crime Commission (President's Commission on Law Enforcement and Administration of Justice 1967) recommended narrowing the grounds for juvenile court intervention, and many professional organizations subsequently have advocated reform or elimination of status jurisdiction (American Bar Association [ABA] 1982). Some critics focused on its adverse impact on children because, traditionally, status offenses were a form of delinquency and status offenders were detained and incarcerated in the same institutions as criminal delinquents (Handler and Zatz 1982). Others noted its disabling effects on families and other sources of referral, as parents overloaded juvenile courts with intractable family disputes and schools and social agencies used the court as a "dumping ground" to coercively impose solutions (Andrews and Cohn 1974). Legal critics contended that it was "void for vagueness," denied equal protection and procedural justice, and had a disproportionate impact on poor, minority, and female juveniles (Rubin 1985).

Diversion

Disillusionment with juvenile courts' coercive treatment of noncriminal youths led to efforts to divert, deinstitutionalize, and decriminalize them. The Federal Juvenile Justice and Delinquency Prevention Act (1974) required states to begin a process of removing noncriminal offenders from secure detention and correctional facilities and provided an impetus to divert status offenders from juvenile court and decarcerate those remaining in the system (Handler and Zatz 1982).

Progressives created the juvenile court to divert youths from criminal courts and deliver services; now diversion exists to shift otherwise eligible youths away from juvenile court to provide services on an informal basis. Many question whether diversion programs have been implemented coherently or effectively (Klein 1979). Rather than reducing the court's client population, diversion may have had a "net widening" effect, as juveniles who previously would have been released now are subject to informal intervention (Klein 1979).

Deinstitutionalization

Although the numbers of status offenders in secure facilities declined by the mid-1980s, those efforts were frustrated by amendments to the Federal Juvenile Justice Act (1974) in 1980, which weakened the restrictions on secure confinement and allowed youths who ran away from nonsecure placements or violated court orders to be charged with contempt of court and incarcerated (Schwartz 1989). Although subsequent probation violations may result in confinement, juveniles adjudicated for status offenses often receive fewer procedural rights than do youths charged with delinquency (Smith 1992).

Decriminalization

Almost every state "decriminalized" conduct that is illegal only for children by creating nondelinquency classifications such as Persons or Children in Need of Supervision (PINS or CHINS) (Rubin 1985). Such label changes simply shift youths from one jurisdictional category to another without significantly limiting courts' dispositional authority. Using labels of convenience, officials may relabel former status offenders downward as dependent or neglected youths, upward as delinquent offenders, or laterally into a "hidden system" of control in chemical dependency facilities and mental hospitals (Weithorn 1988).

Sentencing Juveniles

Historically, juvenile courts imposed indeterminate and nonproportional sentences to achieve the delinquent offender's best interests. In the post-*Gault* era, a fundamental change in the jurisprudence of sentencing occurred as the offense rather than the offender began to dominate the decision (Von Hirsch 1976). A shift in sentencing philosophy from rehabilitation to retribution is evident in the response to serious juvenile offenders and in routine sentencing of delinquent offenders.

Waiver of Juvenile Offenders to Criminal Court

Whether to sentence persistent or violent young offenders as juveniles or adults poses difficult theoretical and practical problems and implicates the relationship between juvenile and adult court sentencing practices. Virtually every state has a mechanism for prosecuting some juveniles as adults (Feld 1987). Two types of statutes—judicial waiver and legislative offense exclusion—illustrate the alternative mechanisms and changes in juvenile sentencing philosophies. With judicial waiver, a judge may transfer jurisdiction on a discretionary basis after a hearing to determine whether a youth is "amenable to treatment" or a "threat to public safety" (Feld 1987). With legislative offense exclusion, by statutory definition, youths charged with certain offenses simply are not within juvenile court jurisdiction.

Judicial Waiver

Judicial waiver embodies the juvenile court's approach to individual sentencing. In *Kent v. United States* (1966), the Court mandated procedural due process at a waiver hearing where a judge assesses a youth's amenability to treatment or dangerousness. But, if there are no effective treatment programs for serious juvenile offenders, no valid or reliable clinical tests with which to diagnose youths' treatment potential, and no scientific bases by which accurately to predict future dangerousness, then judicial waiver statutes are simply broad grants of standardless discretion (Feld 1978, 1987; Zimring 1991). The inherent subjectivity of discretionary waiver results in racial disparities (Fagan, Forst, and Vivona 1987), and "justice by geography" as different courts within a single state interpret and apply the law inconsistently (Feld 1990a).

Treatment as a juvenile or punishment as an adult is based on an arbitrary line that has no criminological significance other than its legal consequences. There is a relationship between age and crime, and crime rates for many offenses peak in mid- to late adolescence. Rational sentencing requires a coordinated response to active young offenders on both sides of the juvenile/adult line. Because offenders are not irresponsible children one day and responsible adults the next, except as a matter of law, juvenile and criminal courts may work at cross-purposes when juveniles make the transition to criminal courts. Most juveniles judicially waived are charged with property crimes like burglary, rather than with serious offenses against the person; when they appear in criminal courts as adult first offenders, typically they are not imprisoned (Feld 1987; Hamparian et al. 1982).

Legislative Exclusion of Offenses

Legislative waiver simply excludes from juvenile court jurisdiction youths charged with certain offenses (Feld 1987). Because legislatures create juvenile courts, they may modify their jurisdiction as they please. Increasingly, legislatures use offense criteria either as dispositional guidelines to limit judicial discretion or to automatically exclude certain youths (Feld 1987). Some states amended their judicial waiver statutes to use offense criteria to structure discretion, to reduce inconsistency, and to improve the fit between juvenile waiver and adult sentencing practices. More states reject the juvenile court's individualized sentencing philosophy, at least in part, emphasize retributive policies, and exclude some youths from juvenile court. Exclusion statutes remove judicial sentencing discretion entirely and base the decision to try a youth as an adult on the offense. These statutes emphasizing offenses provide one indicator of the "get-tough" mentality and the shift from a treatment philosophy to a more retributive one. Punishing serious young offenders as adults exposes some youths to the death penalty for the crimes they commit as juveniles (*Stanford v. Kentucky* 1989).

Punishment in Juvenile Courts

McKeiver denied jury trials and justified a juvenile system separate from the adult one by invoking distinctions between punishment and treatment (Feld 1988b). Whether juvenile courts punish or treat may be determined by examining (a) legislative-purpose clauses and court opinions, (b) juvenile court sentencing statutes and practices, and (c) conditions of confinement and evaluations of treatment effectiveness (Feld 1990b). Despite rehabilitative rhetoric, treating juveniles closely resembles punishing adult criminals.

Purpose of Juvenile Court

Although 42 states' juvenile codes contain statements of legislative purpose, within the past decade, about one quarter of them have redefined their juvenile codes to de-emphasize rehabilitation and the child's best interest and to assert the importance of public safety and punishing youths for their offenses (Feld 1988b, 1990b). Courts considering these changes in purpose clauses recognize that they signal a basic philosophical reorientation in juvenile justice, even as they endorse punishment as an appropriate juvenile disposition (Feld 1990b).

Juvenile Court Sentencing Statutes

Sentencing statutes provide another indicator of whether juvenile courts punish or treat. Whereas most states' sentencing statutes are indeterminate and nonproportional to achieve a child's best interests, about one third of the states use present offense and/or prior record to regulate some sentencing decisions through determinate or mandatory minimum-sentencing statutes (Feld 1988b, 1990b). Washington state created a juvenile sentencing guidelines commission and based presumptive "just deserts" sentences on a youth's age, present offense, and prior record (Feld 1988b; Walkover 1984). In other states, juvenile court judges consider offense, criminal history, and statutory "aggravating and mitigating" factors when imposing determinate sentences on juveniles (Feld 1988b, 1990b). Some states' mandatory minimum sentences for serious offenses impose terms of confinement ranging from 12 to 18 months up to the age of 21 or to the adult limit for the same offense (Feld 1990b).

Juvenile Court Sentencing Practices

Juvenile court judges enjoy great discretion because of paternalistic assumptions about children and the need to look beyond the offense to their best interests. The exercise of judicial discretion raises concerns about its discriminatory impact, however, because poor and minority youths are disproportionately overrepresented in juvenile correctional institutions (Pope and Feyerherm 1990a, 1990b; Krisberg et al. 1987).

Although evaluations of juvenile court sentencing practices are contradictory, two general findings emerge. First, present offense and prior record account for most of the variance in sentencing that can be explained (McCarthy and Smith 1986; Fagan, Slaughter, and Hartstone 1987; Feld 1989). Second, after controlling for present offense and prior record, individualized discretion is often synonymous with racial disparities in sentencing juveniles (Pope and Feyerherm 1990a, 1990b; Krisberg et al. 1987; Fagan, Slaughter, and Hartstone 1987). A comprehensive review of the influence of race on juvenile sentencing concluded that "race effects may occur at various decision points, they may be direct or indirect, and they may accumulate as youths are processed through the system" (Pope and Feyerherm 1990a, p. 331). Although offense variables exhibit a stronger relationship with dispositions than do social variables, most of the variance in sentencing juveniles remains unexplained. The recent changes in juvenile court sentencing statutes may reflect disquiet with individualized justice, idiosyncratic exercises of discretion, and the inequalities that result (Feld 1988b).

Conditions of Juvenile Confinement

Gault (1967) belatedly recognized the longstanding contradictions between rehabilitative rhetoric and punitive reality; conditions of confinement motivated the Court to insist upon minimal procedural safeguards for juveniles. Contemporary evaluations of juvenile institutions reveal a continuing gap between rehabilitative rhetoric and punitive reality (Feld 1977, 1981). Simultaneously, lawsuits challenged conditions of confinement, alleged that they violated inmates' "right to treatment," inflicted "cruel and unusual punishment," and provided another outside view of juvenile corrections. A number of courts found inmates beaten by staff, injected with drugs for social control purposes, deprived of minimally adequate care and individualized treatment, routinely locked in solitary confinement, forced to do repetitive and degrading make-work, and provided minimal clinical services (Feld 1990b). The reality for juveniles confined in many treatment facilities is one of violence and punishment.

Effectiveness of Treatment

Evaluations of juvenile treatment programs provide scant support for their effectiveness (Whitehead and Lab 1989; Lab and Whitehead 1988). Empirical evaluations question both the efficacy of treatment programs and the scientific underpinnings of those who administer the enterprise. Although the general conclusion that "nothing works" in juvenile corrections has not been persuasively refuted (Melton 1989), it has been strenuously resisted by those who contend that some types of programs may have positive effects on selected clients under certain conditions (Palmer 1991).

The critique of the juvenile court does not rest on the premise that nothing works or ever can work. Even if some demonstration model programs produce positive changes for some youths under some conditions, after a century of unfulfilled promises, a continuing societal unwillingness to commit scare resources to rehabilitative endeavors, and treatment strategies of dubious efficacy, the possibility of effective treatment is inadequate to justify an entire separate justice system.

PROCEDURAL CONVERGENCE BETWEEN JUVENILE AND CRIMINAL COURTS

A strong nationwide movement, both in theory and in practice, away from therapeutic, individualized dispositions and toward punitive, offense-based sentences eliminates many of the differences between juvenile and adult sentencing practices (Feld 1988b, 1990b). These changes repudiate juvenile courts' original assumptions that youths should be treated differently than adults, that they operate in a youth's best interest, and that rehabilitation is indeterminate and cannot be limited by fixed-time punishment.

The emphasis on punishment contradicts *McKeiver's* (1970) premise that juveniles require fewer safeguards than do adult defendants and raises questions about the quality of procedural justice (Feld 1990b). Under *Gault's* (1967) impetus, the formal procedures of juvenile and criminal courts increasingly converge (Feld 1984). There remains, however, a substantial gulf between theory and reality, between the law on the books and the law in action. Theoretically, delinquents are entitled to formal trials and the assistance of counsel. In actuality, juvenile justice is far different. Nearly 3 decades ago, the Supreme Court observed that "the child receives the worst of both worlds: he gets neither the protections accorded to adults nor the solicitous care and regenerative treatment postulated for children" (*Kent v. United States* 1966, p. 556). Despite criminalizing juvenile courts, most states provide neither special procedures to protect juveniles from their own immaturity nor the full panoply of adult procedural safeguards. Instead, states treat juveniles like adult defendants when equality redounds to their disadvantage and use less adequate juvenile court safeguards when those deficient procedures provide an advantage to the state (Feld 1984).

Jury Trials in Juvenile Court

Procedural safeguards are critical when sentences are punitive rather than therapeutic. In denying juries to juveniles, *McKeiver* (1970) posited virtual parity between the accuracy of judges and juries when finding facts. But juries provide special protections to assure factual accuracy, use a higher evidentiary threshold when they apply *Winship's* (1970) "proof beyond a reasonable doubt" standard, and acquit more readily than do judges (Feld 1984; Ainsworth 1991).

Moreover, *McKeiver* (1970) simply ignored that juries prevent governmental oppression by protecting against weak or biased judges, injecting the community's values into law, and increasing the visibility and accountability of justice administration (Feld 1984; *Duncan v. Louisiana* 1968). Such protections are even more crucial in juvenile courts, which labor behind closed doors immune from public scrutiny.

The Right to Counsel in Juvenile Court

Gault (1967) established a constitutional right to an attorney in delinquency proceedings. Despite formal legal changes, the actual delivery of legal services in juvenile courts lags behind; it appears that in many states, half or less of all juveniles receive the assistance of counsel (Feld 1988a, 1989). One study (Feld 1988a) reported that in three of the six states surveyed, only 37.5%, 47.7%, and 52.7% of juveniles charged with delinquency and status offenses were represented. Research in Minnesota (Feld 1989, 1991a) indicates that most juveniles are unrepresented and that many youths removed from their homes or confined in correctional institutions lacked counsel.

The most common explanation for why so many juveniles are unrepresented is that they waive their right to counsel. Courts use the adult standard—"knowing, intelligent, and voluntary" under the "totality of the circumstances"—to assess the validity of juveniles' waivers of constitutional rights (*Fare v. Michael C.* 1979). The crucial issue for juveniles, as for adults, is whether waiver of counsel can be knowing, intelligent, and voluntary when it is made by a child alone without consulting with an attorney. Because juveniles are not as competent as adults, commentators criticize the "totality" approach to waivers as an instance of treating juveniles like adults when equality puts them at a disadvantage (Grisso 1980, 1981).

THE FUTURE OF THE JUVENILE COURT: THREE SCENARIOS

For several decades, juvenile courts have deflected, co-opted, ignored, or accommodated constitutional and legislative reforms with minimal institutional change. The juvenile court remains essentially unreformed despite its transformation from a welfare agency into a scaled-down, second-class criminal court. Public and political concerns about drugs and youth crime encourage repressing rather than rehabilitating young offenders. Fiscal constraints, budget deficits, and competition from other interest groups reduce the likelihood that treatment services for delinquents will expand. Coupling these punitive policies with societal unwillingness to provide for the welfare of children in general, much less those who commit crimes, is there any reason to believe the juvenile court can be rehabilitated?

What is the justification for maintaining a separate court system whose only distinction is that it uses procedures under which no adult would consent to be tried (Feld 1988b; Ainsworth 1991)? Whereas most commentators acknowledge the emergence of a punitive juvenile court, they recoil at the prospect of its outright abolition, emphasize that children are different, and strive to maintain separation between delinquents and criminals (Melton 1989; Rosenberg 1993). Most conclude, however, that juvenile courts need a new rationale that melds punishment with reduced culpability and procedural justice.

There are three plausible responses to a juvenile court that punishes in the name of treatment and simultaneously denies young offenders elementary procedural justice: (a) juvenile courts could be "restructured to fit their original [therapeutic] purpose" (*McKeiver* 1970, p. 557); (b) punishment could be accepted as appropriate in delinquency proceedings but coupled with all criminal procedural safeguards (Melton 1989; ABA 1980c); or (c) juvenile courts could be abolished and young offenders tried in criminal courts with certain substantive and procedural modifications (Feld 1984, 1988b; Ainsworth 1991).

RETURN TO INFORMAL, REHABILITATIVE JUVENILE JUSTICE

Proponents of informal, therapeutic juvenile courts contend that the experiment should not be declared a failure because it has never been implemented effectively (Ferdinand 1989, 1991). From its inception, juvenile courts and correctional facilities have had more in common with penal facilities than welfare agencies (Rothman 1980). Despite its long-standing and readily apparent failures of implementation, proposals persist to reinvigorate the juvenile court as an informal, welfare agency (Edwards 1992).

Even if a flood of resources and a coterie of clinicians suddenly inundated a juvenile court, it would be a dubious policy to recreate it as originally conceived. Despite formal statutes and procedural rules, the "individualized justice" of juvenile courts is substantively and procedurally lawless. To the extent that judges individualize decisions in offenders' best interests, judicial discretion is formally unrestricted. But without practical scientific or clinical bases by which to classify or treat, the exercise of sound discretion is simply a euphemism for judicial subjectivity. Individualization treats similarly situated offenders differently on the basis of personal characteristics and imposes unequal sanctions on invidious bases.

Procedural informality is the concomitant of substantive discretion. If clinical decision making is unconstrained substantively, then it cannot be limited procedurally either, because every case is unique. Although lawyers manipulate legal rules for their clients' advantage, a court without objective laws or formal procedures is unfavorable terrain. But without lawyers to invoke laws, no mechanisms exist to make juvenile courts conform to legal mandates. Closed, informal, confidential proceedings reduce visibility and accountability and preclude external checks on coercive intervention.

Subordinating Social Welfare to Social Control

Focusing simply on failures of implementation, inadequate social services or welfare resources, abuses of discretion, and persisting procedural deficiencies, however, systematically misleads both proponents and critics of the juvenile court and prevents either from envisioning alternatives. The fundamental shortcoming of the juvenile court is not just its failures of implementation, but a deeper flaw in its basic concept. The original juvenile court was conceived of as a social service agency operating in a judicial setting, a fusion of welfare and coercion. But providing for the social welfare of young people is ultimately a societal responsibility rather than a judicial one. It is simply unrealistic to expect juvenile courts, or any other legal institution, either to alleviate the social ills afflicting young people or to have a significant impact on youth crime.

Despite claims of being a child-centered nation, we care less about other people's children than we do our own, especially when they are children of other colors or cultures (National Commission on Children 1991). Without a societal commitment to adequately meet the minimum family, medical, housing, nutritional, and educational needs of all young people on a voluntary basis, the juvenile court provides a mechanism for imposing involuntary controls on some youths, regardless of how ineffective it may be in delivering services or rehabilitating offenders.

Juvenile Courts' Penal Emphasis

When social services and social control are combined in one setting, as in juvenile court, custodial considerations quickly subordinate social welfare concerns. Historically, juvenile courts purported to resolve the tension between social welfare and social control by asserting that dispositions in a child's best interests achieved individual and public welfare simultaneously. In reality, some youths who commit crimes do not need social services, whereas others cannot be meaningfully rehabilitated. And, many more children with social service needs do not commit crimes.

Juvenile courts' subordination of individual welfare to custody and control stems from its fundamentally penal focus. Delinquency jurisdiction is not based on characteristics of children for which they are not responsible and for whom intervention could mean an improvement in their lives—their lack of decent education, their lack of adequate housing, their unmet medical needs, or their family or social circumstances (National Commission on Children 1991). Rather, delinquency jurisdiction is based on criminal law violations that are the youths' fault and for which the youths are responsible (Fox 1970b). As long as juvenile courts emphasize criminal characteristics of children least likely to elicit sympathy and ignore social conditions most likely to engender a desire to nurture and help, they reinforce punitive rather than rehabilitative impulses. Operating in a societal context that does not provide adequately for children in general, intervention in the lives of those who commit crimes inevitably serves purposes of penal social control, regardless of the court's ability to deliver social welfare.

Due Process and Punishment in Juvenile Court

Acknowledging that juvenile courts punish imposes an obligation to provide all criminal procedural safeguards because "the condition of being a boy does not justify a kangaroo court" (*Gault* 1967, p. 28). Although procedural parity with adults may end the juvenile court experiment, to fail to do so perpetuates injustice. Punishing juveniles in the name of treatment and denying them basic safeguards fosters injustice that thwarts any reform efforts.

Developing rationales to respond to young offenders requires reconciling contradictory impulses engendered when the child is a criminal and the criminal is a child.

If juvenile courts provide neither therapy nor justice, then the alternatives are either (a) to make juvenile courts more like criminal courts, or (b) to make criminal courts more like juvenile courts. Whether young offenders ultimately are tried in a separate juvenile court or in a criminal court raises basic issues of substance and procedure. Issues of substantive justice include developing and implementing a doctrinal rationale to sentence young offenders differently, and more leniently, than older defendants (Feld 1988b). Issues of procedural justice include providing youths with *all* of the procedural safeguards adults receive *and* additional protections that recognize their immaturity (Rosenberg 1980; Feld 1984).

Most commentators who recoil from abolishing juvenile court instead propose to transform it into an explicitly penal one, albeit one that limits punishment based on reduced culpability and provides enhanced procedural justice (Melton 1989; ABA 1980a). The paradigm of the "new juvenile court" is the American Bar Association's Juvenile Justice Standards. The Juvenile Justice Standards recommend repeal of jurisdiction over status offenders, use of proportional and determinate sentences to sanction delinquent offenders, use of offense criteria to regularize pretrial detention and judicial transfer decisions, and provision of all criminal procedural safeguards, including nonwaivable counsel and jury trials (Flicker 1983; Wizner and Keller 1977). Although the ABA's "criminal juvenile court" combines reduced culpability sentencing and greater procedural justice, it fails to explain why these principles should be implemented in a separate juvenile court rather than in a criminal court (Melton 1989; Gardner 1989). The ABA's Juvenile Justice Standards assert that "removal of the treatment rationale does not destroy the rationale for a separate system or for utilization of an ameliorative approach; it does, however, require a different rationale" (ABA 1980b, p. 19, note 5). Unfortunately, although the ABA standards virtually replicate the adult criminal process, they provide no rationale for a separate juvenile system.

Some commentators contend that maintaining a separate punishment system for juveniles may avoid some stigmatic effects of a "criminal" label (Gardner 1989). Others speculate that because some specialized juvenile procedures and dispositional facilities will remain, it is more practical and less risky to retain than to abolish juvenile courts (Rubin 1979). Some emphasize criminal courts' deficiencies—overcrowding, ineffective counsel, insufficient sentencing alternatives—as a justification for retaining juvenile courts, even while acknowledging that these are characteristics of juvenile courts as well (Dawson 1990). Given institutional and bureaucratic inertia, however, it might be that only a clean break with the personnel and practices of the past would permit the implementation of procedural justice and sentencing reforms.

The only real difference between the ABA's criminal juvenile court and adult criminal courts is that the former would impose shorter sentences (ABA 1980c; Wizner and Keller 1977). Particularly for serious young offenders, the sanctions imposed in juvenile court are less than those of criminal courts, and a separate court might be the only way to achieve those shorter sentences and insulate youths from criminal courts.

But, recent research suggests that there might be a relationship between increased procedural formality and sentencing severity in juvenile courts. Despite statutes and rules of statewide applicability, juvenile courts are highly variable. Urban courts, which typically are the most formal, also detain and sentence more severely than do their more traditional, rural counterparts (Feld 1991a). If procedural formality increases substantive severity, could a separate criminal juvenile court continue to afford leniency? Will juvenile courts' procedural convergence with criminal courts increase repressiveness and erode present sentencing differences? Can juvenile courts only be lenient because discretion is hidden behind closed doors? Would imposing the rule of law prevent them from affording leniency to most youths? The ABA Standards do not even recognize, much less answer, these questions.

Young Offenders in Criminal Court

If the primary reason a child is in court is because he or she committed a crime, then the child could be tried in criminal courts alongside adult counterparts. Before returning young offenders to criminal courts, however, a legislature must address issues of substance and procedure in order to create a juvenile criminal court. Substantively, a legislature must develop a rationale to sentence young offenders differently and more leniently than older defendants. Procedurally, it must afford youths full parity with adults and additional safeguards.

Substantive Justice—Juveniles' Criminal Responsibility

The primary virtue of the contemporary juvenile court is that young serious offenders typically receive shorter sentences than do adults convicted of comparable crimes. One premise of juvenile justice is that youths should survive the mistakes of adolescence with their life chances intact, and this goal would be threatened by the draconian sentences frequently inflicted on 18-year-old "adults." However, even juvenile courts' seeming virtue of shorter sentences for serious offenders is offset by the far more numerous minor offenders who receive longer sentences as juveniles than they would as adults.

Shorter sentences for young people do not require that they be tried in separate juvenile courts. Criminal law doctrines and policies provide rationales to sentence youths less severely than adults in criminal courts (Feld 1988b; Melton 1989). Juvenile courts simply extended upward by a few years the common law's infancy presumptions that immature young people lack criminal capacity (Fox 1970b). "Diminished responsibility" doctrines provide additional rationale for shorter sentences for youths, because within a framework of "deserved" punishments, it would be unjust to sentence youths and adults alike (ABA 1980c). Although an offender's age is of little relevance when assessing harm, youthfulness is highly pertinent when assessing culpability.

Developmental psychological research confirms that young people move through developmental stages with respect to legal reasoning and ethical decision making akin to the common law's infancy defense. Even youths 14 years of age or older, who abstractly may know "right from wrong," might still not be as blameworthy and deserving of comparable punishment as adult offenders. Families, schools, and communities socialize young people and share some responsibility for their offenses (Twentieth Century Fund 1978). To the extent that the ability to make responsible choices is learned behavior, the dependent status of youths systematically deprives them of opportunities to learn to be responsible (Zimring 1982).

The Supreme Court in *Thompson v. Oklahoma* (1988) provided additional support for lesser sentences for reduced culpability even for youths above the common-law infancy threshold of 14 years of age. In vacating Thompson's capital sentence, the Court noted that even though he was criminally responsible, he should not be punished as severely. Despite a later decision upholding the death penalty for 16-year-old or 17-year-old youths (*Stanford* 1989), the Court has repeatedly emphasized that youthfulness is an important mitigating factor at sentencing. The argument for shorter sentences for reduced culpability is not a constitutional claim because the Supreme Court consistently has resisted developing a criminal law mens rea jurisprudence (Rosenberg 1993). Rather, like the juvenile court itself, it is a matter of state legislative sentencing policy.

"Youth Discount"

Shorter sentences for reduced culpability is a more modest rationale to treat young people differently from adults than the juvenile court's rehabilitative claims. Criminal courts can provide shorter sentences for reduced culpability with fractional reductions of adult sentences in the form of an explicit "youth discount." For example, a 14-year-old might receive 33% of the adult penalty, a 16-year-old 66%, and an 18-year-old the adult penalty, as is presently the case (Feld 1988b). Of course, explicit fractional youth discount sentence reductions can only be calculated against a backdrop of realistic, humane, and determinate adult sentencing practices. For youths younger than 14 years old, the common-law mens rea infancy defense acquires a new vitality for shorter sentences or even noncriminal alternative dispositions (Fox 1970b).

A graduated age-culpability sentencing scheme avoids the inconsistency and injustice played out in binary either/or juvenile versus adult judicial waiver determinations (Feld 1987). Sentences that young people receive might differ by orders of magnitude, depending upon whether or not transfer is ordered. Because of the profound consequences, waiver hearings consume a disproportionate amount of juvenile court time and resources. Abolishing juvenile court eliminates waiver hearings, saves resources that are ultimately expended to no purpose, reduces the "punishment gap" when youths cross from one system to the other, and assures similar consequences for similar offenders.

Trying young people in criminal courts with full procedural safeguards would not appreciably diminish judges' sentencing expertise. Although Progressives envisioned a specialist juvenile court judge possessing the wisdom of a "kadi" (Matza 1964), judges increasingly handle juvenile matters as part of the general docket or rotate through juvenile court on short-term assignments without acquiring any particular dispositional expertise. In most juvenile courts, social services personnel advise judges and possess the information necessary for appropriate dispositions.

Punishing youths does not require incarcerating them with adults in jails and prisons. Departments of corrections already classify inmates, and existing juvenile detention facilities and institutions provide options for age-segregated dispositional facilities. Insisting explicitly on humane conditions of confinement could do as much to improve the lives of incarcerated youths as has the "right to treatment" or the "rehabilitative ideal" (Feld 1977, 1981). Recognizing that most young offenders return to society imposes an obligation to provide resources for self-improvement on a voluntary basis.

Procedural Justice for Youth

Since *Gault*, most of the procedures of criminal courts are supposed to be routine aspects of juvenile courts as well. Generally, both courts apply the same laws of arrest, search, identification, and interrogation to adults and juveniles, and increasingly subject juveniles charged with felony offenses to similar fingerprinting and booking processes as adults (Feld 1984; Dawson 1990). The more formal and adversarial nature of juvenile court procedures reflects the attenuation between the court's therapeutic mission and its social control functions. The many instances in which states treat juvenile offenders procedurally like adult criminal defendants is one aspect of this process (Feld 1984). Despite the procedural convergence, it remains nearly as true today as 2 decades ago that "the child receives the worst of both worlds" (*Kent* 1966, p. 556). Most states provide neither special safeguards to protect juveniles from the consequences of their immaturity nor the full panoply of adult procedural safeguards to protect them from punitive state intervention.

Youths' differences in age and competence require them to receive more protections than adults, rather than less. The rationales to sentence youths differently and more leniently than adults also justify providing them with *all* of the procedural safeguards adults receive *and* additional protections that recognize their immaturity. This dual-maximal strategy explicitly provides enhanced protection for children because of their vulnerability and immaturity (Feld 1984; Rosenberg 1980; Melton 1989). As contrasted with current practices, for example, a dual-maximal procedural strategy produces different results with respect to waivers of constitutional rights. Although counsel is the prerequisite to procedural justice for juveniles, many youths do not receive the assistance of counsel because courts use the adult standard and find they waived the right in a "knowing, intelligent and voluntary" manner under the "totality of the circumstances." The Juvenile Justice Standards recognize youths' limitations in dealing with the law and provide that the right to counsel attaches when a youth is taken into custody, that it is self-invoking and does not require an affirmative request as is the case for adults, and that youths must consult with counsel prior to waiving counsel or at interrogation (ABA 1980a).

Providing youths with full procedural parity in criminal courts and additional substantive and procedural safeguards could afford more protection than does the juvenile court. A youth concerned about adverse publicity could waive the right to public trial. If a youth successfully completes a sentence without recidivating, then expunging criminal records and eliminating collateral disabilities could avoid criminal labels and afford as much relief from an isolated act of folly as does the juvenile court's confidentiality.

The conceptual problems of creating a juvenile criminal court are soluble. The difficulty is political. Even though juvenile courts currently provide uneven leniency, could legislators who want to get tough on crime vote for a youth-discount sentencing provision that explicitly recognizes youthfulness as a mitigating factor in sentencing? Even though young people presently possess some constitutional rights, would politicians be willing to provide a justice system that assures those rights would be realistically and routinely exercised? Or, would they rather maintain a juvenile system that provides neither therapy nor justice, that elevates social control over social welfare, and that abuses children while claiming to protect them?

Abolishing juvenile court forces a long overdue and critical reassessment of the meaning of "childhood" (Ainsworth 1991). A society that regards young people as fundamentally different from adults easily justifies an inferior justice system and conveniently rationalizes it on the grounds that children are entitled only to custody, not liberty (*Schall v. Martin* 1984). The ideology of therapeutic justice and its discretionary apparatus persist because the social control is directed at children. Despite humanitarian claims of being a child-centered nation, cultural and legal conceptions of children support institutional arrangements that deny the personhood of young people. Rethinking the juvenile court requires critically reassessing the meaning of childhood and creating social institutions to assure the welfare of the next generation.

REFERENCES

Ainsworth, Janet. 1991. "Re-imagining Childhood and Reconstructing the Legal Order: The Case for Abolishing the Juvenile Court." *North Carolina Law Review* 69:1083–1133.

Allen, Francis A. 1981. *The Decline of the Rehabilitative Ideal: Penal Policy and Social Purpose.* New Haven, CT: Yale University Press.

American Bar Association—Institute of Judicial Administration. 1980a. *Juvenile Justice Standards Relating to Counsel for Private Parties.* Cambridge, MA: Ballinger.

———. 1980b. *Juvenile Justice Standards Relating to Dispositions.* Cambridge, MA: Ballinger.

———. 1980c. *Juvenile Justice Standards Relating to Juvenile Delinquency and Sanctions.* Cambridge, MA: Ballinger.

———. 1982. *Juvenile Justice Standards Relating to Noncriminal Misbehavior.* Cambridge, MA: Ballinger.

Andrews, R. Hale and Andrew H. Cohn. 1974. "Ungovernability: The Unjustifiable Jurisdiction." *Yale Law Journal* 83:1383–1409.

Dawson, Robert. 1990. "The Future of Juvenile Justice: Is It Time to Abolish the System?" *Journal of Criminal Law & Criminology* 81:136–55.

Edwards, Leonard P. 1992. "The Juvenile Court and the Role of the Juvenile Court Judge." *Juvenile and Family Court Journal* 43:1–45.

Fagan, Jeffrey, Martin Forst, and Scott Vivona. 1987. "Racial Determinants of the Judicial Transfer Decision: Prosecuting Violent Youth in Criminal Court." *Crime & Delinquency* 33:259–86.

Fagan, Jeffrey, Ellen Slaughter, and Eliot Hartstone. 1987. "Blind Justice? The Impact of Race on the Juvenile Justice Process." *Crime & Delinquency* 33:224–58.

Feld, Barry C. 1977. *Neutralizing Inmate Violence: Juvenile Offenders in Institutions.* Cambridge, MA: Ballinger.

———. 1978. "Reference of Juvenile Offenders for Adult Prosecution: The Legislative Alternative to Asking Unanswerable Questions." *Minnesota Law Review* 62:515–618.

———. 1981. "A Comparative Analysis of Organizational Structure and Inmate Subcultures in Institutions for Juvenile Offenders." *Crime & Delinquency* 27:336–63.

———. 1984. "Criminalizing Juvenile Justice: Rules of Procedure for Juvenile Court." *Minnesota Law Review* 69:141–276.

———. 1987. "Juvenile Court Meets the Principle of Offense: Legislative Changes in Juvenile Waiver Statutes." *Journal of Criminal Law and Criminology* 78:471–533.

———. 1988a. "*In re Gault* Revisited: A Cross-State Comparison of the Right to Counsel in Juvenile Court." *Crime & Delinquency* 34:393–424.

———. 1988b. "Juvenile Court Meets the Principle of Offense: Punishment, Treatment, and the Difference it Makes." *Boston University Law Review* 68:821–915.

———. 1989. "The Right to Counsel in Juvenile Court: An Empirical Study of When Lawyers Appear and the Difference They Make." *Journal of Criminal Law and Criminology* 79:1185–1346.

———. 1990a. "Bad Law Makes Hard Cases: Reflections on Teen-Aged Axe-Murderers, Judicial Activism, and Legislative Default." *Journal of Law and Inequality* 8:1–101.

———. 1990b. "The Punitive Juvenile Court and the Quality of Procedural Justice: Disjunctions Between Rhetoric and Reality." *Crime & Delinquency* 36:443–66.

———. 1991a. "Justice by Geography: Urban, Suburban, and Rural Variations in Juvenile Justice Administration." *Journal of Criminal Law and Criminology* 82:156–210.

———. 1991b. "The Transformation of the Juvenile Court." *Minnesota Law Review* 75:691–725.

Ferdinand, Theodore N. 1989. "Juvenile Delinquency or Juvenile Justice: Which Came First?" *Criminology* 27:79–106.

———. 1991. "History Overtakes the Juvenile Justice System." *Crime & Delinquency* 37:204–24.

Flicker, Barbara. 1983. *Standards for Juvenile Justice: A Summary and Analysis.* 2nd ed. Cambridge, MA: Ballinger.

Fox, Sanford J. 1970a. "Juvenile Justice Reform: An Historical Perspective." *Stanford Law Review* 22:1187–1239.

———. 1970b. "Responsibility in the Juvenile Court." *William & Mary Law Review* 11:659–84.

Gardner, Martin. 1989. "The Right of Juvenile Offenders to be Punished: Some Implications of Treating Kids as Persons." *Nebraska Law Review* 68:182–215.

Grisso, Thomas. 1980. "Juveniles' Capacities to Waive Miranda Rights: An Empirical Analysis." *California Law Review* 68:1134–66.

———. 1981. *Juveniles' Waiver of Rights.* New York: Plenum.

Hamparian, Donna, Linda Estep, Susan Muntean, Ramon Priestino, Robert Swisher, Paul Wallace, and Joseph White. 1982. *Youth in Adult Courts: Between Two Worlds.* Washington, DC: Office of Juvenile Justice and Delinquency Prevention.

Handler, Joel F. and Julie Zatz, eds. 1982. *Neither Angels Nor Thieves: Studies in Deinstitutionalization of Status Offenders.* Washington, DC: National Academy Press.

Klein, Malcolm W. 1979. "Deinstitutionalization and Diversion of Juvenile Offenders: A Litany of Impediments." Pp. 145–201 in *Crime and Justice: An Annual Review*, edited by M. Tonry and N. Morris. Chicago: University of Chicago Press.

Krisberg, Barry, Ira Schwartz, Gideon Fishman, Zvi Eisikovits, Edna Guttman, and Karen Joe. 1987. "The Incarceration of Minority Youth." *Crime & Delinquency* 33:173–205.

Lab, Steven P. and John T. Whitehead. 1988. "An Analysis of Juvenile Correctional Treatment." *Crime & Delinquency* 34:60–83.

Matza, David. 1964. *Delinquency and Drift.* New York: Wiley.

McCarthy, Belinda and Brent L. Smith. 1986. "The Conceptualization of Discrimination in the Juvenile Justice Process: The Impact of Administrative Factors and Screening Decisions on Juvenile Court Dispositions." *Criminology* 24:41–64.

Melton, Gary B. 1989. "Taking *Gault* Seriously: Toward a New Juvenile Court." *Nebraska Law Review* 68:146–81.

National Commission on Children. 1991. *Beyond Rhetoric: A New American Agenda for Children and Families.* Washington, DC: U.S. Government Printing Office.

Palmer, Ted. 1991. "The Effectiveness of Intervention: Recent Trends and Current Issues." *Crime & Delinquency* 37:330–46.

Platt, Anthony. 1977. *The Child Savers.* 2nd ed. Chicago: University of Chicago Press.

Pope, Carl E. and William H. Feyerherm. 1990a. "Minority Status and Juvenile Justice Processing: An Assessment of the Research Literature (Part I)." *Criminal Justice Abstracts* 22:327–35.

———. 1990b. "Minority Status and Juvenile Justice Processing: An Assessment of the Research Literature (Part II)." *Criminal Justice Abstracts* 22:527–42.

President's Commission on Law Enforcement and Administration of Justice. 1967. *The Challenge of Crime in a Free Society.* Washington, DC: U.S. Government Printing Office.

Rosenberg, Irene M. 1980. "The Constitutional Rights of Children Charged with Crime: Proposal for a Return to the Not So Distant Past." *University of California Los Angeles Law Review* 27:656–721.

———. 1993. "Leaving Bad Enough Alone: A Response to the Juvenile Court Abolitionists." *Wisconsin Law Review* 1993:163–85.

Rothman, David J. 1980. *Conscience and Convenience: The Asylum and Its Alternative in Progressive America.* Boston: Little, Brown.

Rubin, H. Ted. 1979. "Retain the Juvenile Court? Legislative Developments, Reform Directions and the Call for Abolition." *Crime & Delinquency* 25:281–98.

———. 1985. *Juvenile Justice: Policy, Practice, and Law.* 2nd ed. New York: Random House.

Schwartz, Ira M. 1989. *(In)Justice for Juveniles: Rethinking the Best Interests of the Child.* Lexington, MA: Lexington Books.

Smith, Erin. 1992. "In a Child's Best Interest: Juvenile Status Offenders Deserve Procedural Due Process." *Journal of Law & Inequality* 10:253–303.

Sutton, John R. 1988. *Stubborn Children: Controlling Deliquency in the United States.* Berkeley: University of California Press.

Twentieth Century Fund Task Force on Sentencing Policy Toward Young Offenders. 1978. *Confronting Youth Crime.* New York: Holmes & Meier.

Von Hirsch, Andrew. 1976. *Doing Justice.* New York: Hill and Wang.

Walkover, Andrew. 1984. "The Infancy Defense in the New Juvenile Court." *University of California Los Angeles Law Review* 31:503–62.

Weithorn, Lois A. 1988. "Mental Hospitalization of Troublesome Youth: An Analysis of Skyrocketing Admission Rates." *Stanford Law Review* 40:773–838.

Whitehead, John T. and Steven P. Lab. 1989. "A Meta-Analysis of Juvenile Correctional Treatment." *Journal of Research in Crime and Delinquency* 26:267–95.

Wizner, Steven and Mary F. Keller. 1977. "The Penal Model of Juvenile Justice: Is Juvenile Court Delinquency Jurisdiction Obsolete?" *New York University Law Review* 52:1120–35.

Zimring, Franklin. 1982. *The Changing Legal World of Adolescence.* New York: Free Press.

———. 1991. "The Treatment of Hard Cases in American Juvenile Justice: In Defense of Discretionary Waiver." *Notre Dame Journal of Law, Ethics and Public Policy* 5:267–80.

CASES

Breed v. Jones, 421 U.S. 519 (1975).

Duncan v. Louisiana, 391 U.S. 145 (1968).

Fare v. Michael C., 442 U.S. 707 (1979).

In re Gault, 387 U.S. 1 (1967).

Kent v. United States, 383 U.S. 541 (1966).

McKeiver v. Pennsylvania, 403 U.S. 528 (1970).

Schall v. Martin, 467 U.S. 260 (1984).

PART TWO

Pretrial Procedures and Evidentiary Issues

"The typical method of conviction is by the accused's plea of guilty. Mostly, therefore, the system of administering criminal justice in the United States is a system of justice without trial."

—Jerome H. Skolnick, 1966

INTRODUCTION

Following an arrest, a defendant may be subjected to a lineup, pretrial motions, arraignment, and a bail hearing. The defendant may also enter into plea negotiations with the prosecutor. Although the media tends to direct the public's attention on elaborate jury trials with their interesting participants and majestic settings, the pretrial processing of criminal defendants is extremely important because most criminal cases are resolved before trial. As a consequence, anyone wishing to acquire a realistic view of the criminal court process must have an understanding of the events that occur prior to trial.

There are a number of reasons why most criminal cases are resolved before a formal trial. First, the prosecutor may decide to drop the charges against a criminal defendant because of insufficient evidence to obtain a conviction or because the victim decides not to proceed with the case. The prosecutor may also opt against pursuing a case in order that the defendant may receive drug treatment or participate in another type of diversion program. Finally, the defendant may agree to plead guilty in exchange for certain leniencies. Although plea bargains usually involve an offer by the prosecutor to recommend a more lenient punishment in exchange for a guilty plea, the prosecutor does have the ability to reduce the defendant's original charge, drop any additional charges, or forego the prosecution of pending cases against the defendant. For many defendants, the decision to plead guilty in exchange for leniency concludes their involvement in the criminal justice system. For others, however, the acceptance of a plea bargain simply results in a shorter prison sentence or, in extreme instances, a life rather than a death sentence. Because most defendants never experience a formal trial, the major challenge for our criminal courts is to ensure that justice prevails during pretrial processing.

This section examines several important factors that influence the processing of criminal defendants, including bail guidelines, pretrial drug testing programs, and plea bargaining. In addition, some of the controversies surrounding eyewitness identification, lineups, and the use of DNA evidence in the prosecution of defendants are discussed.

In the first article, "The Bail Guidelines Experiment in Dade County, Miami," Peter R. Jones and John S. Goldkamp discuss the development and implementation of a voluntary bail guideline system in two large, urban court jurisdictions. After a brief review of the conceptual rationale underlying bail guidelines, the authors present the results of a pioneering bail guidelines experiment conducted in Philadelphia. Additionally, they evaluate the impact of a recent attempt in Miami to replicate the Philadelphia guidelines experiment. The authors conclude their article by discussing the policy implications of bail guidelines, as well as the problems associated with their widespread implementation.

In the second article, "Pretrial Drug Testing: Panacea or Pandora's Box?," Christy A. Visher observes that the pretrial drug testing of arrestees and defendants released before trial is being implemented with increasing frequency at both the state and local levels. The federal courts are also considering whether pretrial drug testing should be initiated at the federal level. Nevertheless, debate continues among researchers and policymakers regarding the merits and drawbacks of pretrial drug-testing programs. Critics contend that these programs are difficult to implement, are too expensive, and have little measurable impact on criminal behavior and illegal drug use. Proponents counter by arguing that pretrial drug testing enables criminal justice officials to reliably detect drug use among pretrial defendants, to effectively supervise drug-involved defendants before trial, and to encourage defendants to seek appropriate treatment. This article reviews both state and local experiences with pretrial drug testing programs, discusses the evaluations that have been conducted, and offers some suggestions as to the role that pretrial drug testing should play in our nation's drug control policy.

In the third article, "Is a Ban on Plea Bargaining an Ethical Abuse of Discretion? A Bronx County, New York Case Study," Ronald Acevedo argues that the Bronx District Attorney's decision to ban plea bargaining has affected adversely the Bronx criminal justice system. After discussing the problems related to the ban on plea bargaining, Acevedo proposes two courses of action to avoid further deterioration and damage to the Bronx criminal justice system.

First, he proposes that criminal defendants be given additional time when deciding whether or not to plead guilty. Second, he recommends that the plea bargaining process should be governed by written guidelines to prevent abuses of discretion and to ensure that appropriate sentences are imposed on defendants. In the absence of these modifications, Acevedo believes that the Bronx plea bargaining ban is destined to fail and that the Bronx District Attorney will eventually be forced to rescind his ban and restore plea bargaining, as was done in Alaska and El Paso County, Texas.

The scientific basis of eyewitness identification—what is commonly termed the psychology of perception—has become the subject of contentious debate in recent years. In the belief that scientific information is important to judges, prosecutors, and criminal defense lawyers, Marvin Zalman and Larry Siegel discuss some of the controversies that relate to eyewitness identification and offer a few practical suggestions to improve the detection of the guilty and to minimize the misidentification of the innocent. Their specific recommendations are outlined in their article, "The Psychology of Perception, Eyewitness Identification, and the Lineup." First, they argue that there should be statewide standardization of court instructions, mandated interview training at state-chartered police academies, and prosecution standards and training. Relevant training for defense attorneys and judges is also warranted. Second, recently developed computerized face-drawing programs, using a virtually infinite range of shapes, features, colors, and hairstyles, should be made readily available to police agencies. Finally, they suggest that the National Institute of Justice should devote the necessary resources to assess the current "state of the art" in the psychology of perception. These resources will aid in the rapid dissemination of relevant information to the justice community. The authors conclude by arguing that the implementation of these policy initiatives will go a long way to furthering one of the major goals of the criminal justice system: acquitting the innocent and convicting the guilty.

In the final article in this section, "DNA (Deoxyribonucleic Acid) Evidence, Criminal Law, and Felony Prosecutions: Issues and Prospects," G. Larry Mays, Noreen Purcell, and L. Thomas Winfree, Jr. examine how courts respond to new strategies applied to the analysis of physical evidence, using as a case in point the potential effect of DNA-testing technology. The authors maintain that forensic scientists have made significant strides, with the use of lasers, complex computer software programs, and genetic engineering, in their crime-related analyses of physical evidence (that is, weapons, drugs, fingerprints, etc.). As a consequence, physical evidence now plays an important role in the criminal justice system. However, while physical evidence can answer many questions about a crime scene, such evidence can also have unintended consequences in the processing of criminal defendants. The exact scope and nature of these unintended consequences are the focus of this article.

6

The Bail Guidelines Experiment in Dade County, Miami: A Case Study in the Development and Implementation of a Policy Innovation

Peter R. Jones, John S. Goldkamp*

In 1985 Goldkamp and Gottfredson reported on the success of an experiment testing the efficacy of a voluntary guidelines approach to pretrial release decisionmaking in the Phildelphia Municipal Court (Goldkamp and Gottfredson, 1985). As a follow-up to this work the National Institute of Justice funded a second round of projects to determine whether the initial success could be replicated in other, quite different, jurisdictions. The aim of this article is to assess efforts to develop and introduce pretrial release guidelines in one of these 'second round' sites—Dade County, Florida. More specifically, the article discusses the need for a guidelines approach to pretrial decisionmaking and examines the problems of implementing innovative policy changes within a court system.

EVALUATING A POLICY INNOVATION

There is nothing more sobering in the field of social science research than the 'quantum leap' from the niceties of theoretical research design to the pragmatic realities of a complex evaluative study. Certainly, the problems and pitfalls of inadequately designed evaluative research have been well described in the literature (Austin and Krisberg, 1982; Posavac and Carey, 1985; Boyum, 1987). Austin and Krisberg (1982) strike a common chord when they argue that progress in policy innovations (developing alternatives to incarceration in their particular case) will remain frustrated until reforms are more carefully implemented and until proponents of the policies are willing to test their ideologies through rigorous research.

Reprinted by permission of the National Center for State Courts from the *Justice System Journal*, vol. 14-15 (1991), pp. 445-476.

At a minimum, evaluation of the impact of a policy change has to begin with the program itself: its goals, its implementation, and its content. Whereas discussion of the latter two components forms the bulk of the present article, the goals of the present study can be briefly summarized. We sought to undertake the development of guidelines in the Dade County jurisdiction, to implement them once they were developed, and to evaluate their impact so that they might be modified as necessary. In doing this, the overarching question was whether or not the lessons, if not the detail, of the Philadelphia research can be applied to other jurisdictions with equally satisfactory results.

PRETRIAL DECISIONMAKING—THE NEED FOR REFORM

Bail reform efforts in the United States have long targeted the reliance by judges on the requirement of financial assurances for the pretrial release of the criminally accused. The controversy over the central role of financial conditioning of pretrial release has been fueled by a number of concerns, such as the disadvantage suffered by poor defendants, the unfairness of detention determined by the defendant's financial background, the lack of accountability of dollar-based decisionmaking, the opportunity for corruption, the inappropriateness of commercial bondsmen in the justice process, and, frankly, the value of cash as an incentive to return a defendant to court or prevent further crime.[1]

In questioning traditional, cash-based bail practices reformers were questioning both the motivations behind the judicial decisionmaking process and its methods. Although it is not our purpose here to review the progress of bail reform over the last three decades, legislative and programmatic reform initiatives have focused, though in a rather piecemeal fashion, on clarification of goals (witness the debate over public danger and preventive detention in America), the development of nonfinancial alternatives and means for improving the efficacy of the pretrial release determination.

The beginnings of bail reform are often identified with the work of Arthur Beeley, who argued in his 1920's research that a large proportion of defendants in the Cook County Jail, Chicago, were needlessly detained because judges did not employ a full array of information to determine a defendant's "dependability" for pretrial release. However, the major initiative to reform bail in the United States was launched by the Vera Institute in New York during the early 1960's (Ares, Rankin, and Sturz, 1963). That reform, which was widely emulated across the United States during the 1960's and early 1970's, sought to encourage judges to employ nonfinancial release options (ROR) more often based on a recommendation scheme taking into account the defendant's "community ties" as an alternative to the traditional focus on the seriousness of criminal charges. Thus, the goal was to encourage greater release of more dependable (lower risk) defendants by providing the judge with an informational resource.[2]

In focusing on the provision of more and better information (Vera developed a "point scale" which was advertised as "objectifying" the recommendation process), the Vera ROR reform was underscoring dissatisfaction with the conduct of judicial decisionmaking at the bail stage. Similarly, landmark legislation—such as the Federal Bail Reform Act of 1966, the District of Columbia's Preventive Detention Act of 1970 and the Federal Bail Reform (Preventive Detention) Act of 1984—was offering directions for the improvement of decision practices in the clarification of goals (the prevention of defendant danger and flight), the provision of non-financial release options according to a least restrictive principle) and the specification of the kinds of information judges ought to take into account in weighing defendants' release prospects at the bail stage. In fact, the furor in the 1970's and 1980's over jail overcrowding and the public safety threat posed by released defendants represented—as two sides to the same coin—a widespread public policy concern that bail/pretrial release decisionmaking by the judiciary was ineffective. On the one hand, the jails were being needlessly filled with defendants before trial; on the other, too many "dangerous" defendants were being released to prey once again on the public.

BAIL GUIDELINES

The bail decision is a difficult, possibly high risk (to the judge) decision that occurs in a very short period of time with little reliable information. Frequently, its goals are argued and operationalized *sub rosa*, there are few release options in most places to offset the traditional recourse to cash bail, and there is little opportunity for review (for defendant or decisionmakers). Bail guidelines are intended to assist a court in coming to grips with the various problems associated with this situation—from unfairness to ineffectiveness.

Against the background of reform in the areas of parole and sentencing in the United States, Goldkamp and Gottfredson (1979; Goldkamp, 1979) proposed that problems with the bail system might best be viewed as an overall problem with judicial decisionmaking. They argued that, although the Vera-type and legislative reforms had touched upon aspects of changing judicial decision practices, judges had never been sufficiently engaged in the reform process. While welcoming the additional information provided by a pre-bail, Vera-type screening interview, for example, judges were not necessarily led to change their traditional decision practices.

Borrowing from the development of decision guidelines in the area of sentencing and parole (Gottfredson, Wilkins and Hoffman, 1978), Goldkamp and Gottfredson (1985) further argued that the problems with bail—visibility, equity, rationality and effectiveness—were normal problems associated with risky (i.e., predictive) decisions that could be addressed by the development of a decisionmaking resource that would spell out the decision goals, provide a range of decision options and be built upon demonstrably relevant criteria (information about the defendant). This approach attempts to come to grips with a number of troublesome aspects of bail/pretrial release decisionmaking—predicting flight or crime, equity—in a balanced and explicit fashion by means of a policy tool to be used by the judiciary as a compass for bail decisionmaking.

The guidelines approach comprises two quite discrete, though interrelated, elements. That is, guidelines represent both a policy tool and a day-to-day decisionmaking aid. Consequently, the development of guidelines would need to involve careful review of a court's current practices and their consequences. Using empirical methods it is possible to contrast beliefs about how the system should work with data on operational themes and real outcome measures. Furthermore, detailed evaluation of current law, policy and programs both in the United States and elsewhere would enable some critical appraisal of current goals. Having discussed goals and mapped out the nature of current practice, the next stage would require the court to utilize this information in shaping its own prospective policy. Thus, once the shape and substance of guidelines are decided upon, we have a self-help tool tailored to the court's particular needs and concerns in the bail area. The court is then responsible for ensuring that individual judges follow the "presumptive" suggestions in a majority of cases, have the opportunity to note reasons for their departures, and receive periodic feedback of information.

Guidelines can be seen to represent a means for identifying and describing, through an iterative process of policy formulation and review, some balance between the conflicting goals of equity and effectiveness. They are meant to provide explicit rules for deciding cases while simultaneously offering the flexibility necessary for individualized decisionmaking. The original guidelines research (Gottfredson, Wilkins and Hoffman, 1978) assumed that if patterns and regularities could be found that explain decisions for a large proportion of cases then these factors may be seen to constitute an operating court policy. While judges might be charged with arbitrary and capricious decisionmaking, strong themes of some sort are likely to influence decisionmaking. While these themes may well be informal and idiosyncratic, and may or may not reflect the appropriate legal "rules" governing bail, they will nevertheless be identifiable. They may be undesirable also, from the standpoint of the court, or even legally inappropriate. Furthermore, deviations from these themes will exist, some justified by special circumstances in individual cases, others perhaps wholly unwarranted. Guidelines offer a means for reviewing operating policy and making explicit its guiding principles. Properly designed and implemented guidelines will permit legitimate deviations and minimize inappropriate departures from court policy.

It should be noted that the guidelines "process" is as important as the guidelines "product." The methodology, beginning with a careful empirical review of the court's current practices and their consequences, enabled decisionmakers to view "what is," and use this information as a springboard for debate about "what ought to be." The court's central participation in the developmental process is viewed as essential to the production of a decisionmaking resource that will be valued for its policy guidance as well as its assistance for the bail decisionmakers. Further, when the guidelines are implemented, the court's leadership continues to play an important part in ensuring that its purposes and use are understood by the relevant decisionmakers.

THE PHILADELPHIA BAIL EXPERIMENT

The Philadelphia bail experiment from 1978-83 (Goldkamp and Gottfredson, 1985) adapted the concept of voluntary decision guidelines (Gottfredson, Wilkins and Hoffman, 1978) to pretrial decisionmaking. Undertaken in collaboration with the judges of the Philadelphia Municipal Court and its pretrial services program, the experiment sought to determine whether guidelines could offer a resource for developing an explicit policy framework and thereby improve the overall rationality, equity and effectiveness (measured in terms of appearance rates, pretrial crime and detention) of bail decisions in the city. The experiment also questioned the willingness and ability of judges and researchers to collaboratively review and debate bail policy and to examine its practice through empirical means. Perhaps most intriguing of all was the question of whether or not judges in Philadelphia would make use of the guidelines in the manner intended.

The study involved a lengthy period of policy review (in Philadelphia and other jurisdictions), empirical study of bail practices within the city and policy debates. The importance of these procedural aspects of guidelines development cannot be overemphasized, for they serve to distinguish between a well-conducted, self-help guidelines application and the poorly conceptualized, non-empirical applications which frequently are mis-represented as 'guidelines.'

Having identified the major correlates of pretrial decisionmaking, the researchers, in collaboration with a 'Steering and Policy Committee,' developed a guidelines matrix combining the two dimensions of charge seriousness and individual risk. Again, it is worth emphasizing that both these dimensions were the product of considerable review of court developed policy and were, therefore, prescriptive rather than recommended or imposed. The guidelines represented the court's strong suggestion to its members deciding bail. The presumptive range of options permitted disagreement when based on sound reason, but requested that judges note their reasons. The Philadelphia study was clearly testing more than the guidelines concept; it was testing whether such a rational policy development could possibly work within a large court of highly individual judges.

The guidelines were implemented in a controlled experiment. Briefly, the guidelines operated as follows. Prior to the bail hearing, staff of the Pretrial Services Agency gather information on the defendant, identify the appropriate "cell" on the guidelines grid and produce a presumptive bail decision. With the guidelines form and the defendant file at their disposal judges are then free to make their decision. If this differs from the presumptive bail decision judges are expected to note the reasons for their departure.

The findings from the Philadelphia study were promising. They confirmed that the process of empirical research and policymaking could be successfully combined to produce a guidelines tool. Furthermore, judges complied with the guidelines (the guidelines were followed in about 75% of cases) and frequently gave reasons for their departures, thus increasing the visibility of the whole process.

The guidelines increased also the equity of pretrial decisionmaking in Philadelphia while simultaneously maintaining its effectiveness. With the guidelines categories offering a benchmark for the identification of 'similarly situated' defendants, it was evident that one of the most significant contributions of the guidelines was to reduce disparity in bail and pretrial detention and to increase the equitable treatment of defendants overall. This was achieved without any growth in pretrial flight or crime.

While the findings of the Philadelphia study were encouraging, it was difficult to assess the generalizability of the guidelines approach. The Municipal Court in Philadelphia was in many ways, akin to lower courts throughout urban America. However, Goldkamp noted also that the Philadelphia Courts had "a unique sociopolitical climate" in which the leadership was at that time "strong and progressive" and the court as a whole "relatively sophisticated concerning the developments in criminal justice" (Goldkamp and Gottfredson, 1988). Equally important to the successful implementation of the experiment was the fact that Goldkamp had already established a strong, positive working relationship with key personnel in the court. The key question, therefore, was whether the guidelines principle would be accepted and successfully implemented elsewhere.

DEVELOPMENT OF THE GUIDELINES

The present study was funded by the National Institute of Justice and began in 1984, three years after the implementation of the Philadelphia experiment.[3] Since the Philadelphia study, the kinds of issues which guidelines were designed to address had become even more prominent in public policy debate. Jail overcrowding had worsened considerably and the proportion of unconvicted defendants in those jails had risen by almost half. Questions about the appropriateness of a public safety orientation to the pretrial release decision had been addressed in caselaw and in many state laws (Goldkamp, 1985).

The developmental stage took almost two years to complete and revealed an enormously challenging situation. Dade County Jail, a predominantly pretrial institution, had been the target of litigation in Federal Court since 1975[4] because of crowding. The recently revised Florida law governing bail and pretrial release explicitly stated that the purpose for bail was to assure the appearance of the criminal defendant at subsequent proceedings and to protect the community against unreasonable danger from the criminal defendant.[5] The strong public safety orientation of Florida's bail statute is reflected in the fact that the primary consideration in bail proceedings is stated as being "the protection of the community from risk of physical harm."[6] The corollary of this is a significant dilution in the principles of presumed release on personal recognizances or release under least drastic conditions. Because cash bond is retained under Florida law, both the traditional *sub rosa* means of securing detention and the more recent, formal preventive detention procedures (requiring a hearing, etc.) exist side by side.

Details of the analysis of bail practices and procedures in Dade are presented in Goldkamp and Gottfredson (1988). Here, we restrict the discussion to some of the more significant results. First, it soon became clear that the bond schedule[7] dominated pretrial release decisionmaking. This was particularly intriguing given the subsequent finding that general seriousness of criminal charges was not found to be a predictor of either pretrial flight or crime. A second important finding was that differences between detained and released defendants could not be explained at all by multivariate analysis, suggesting that pretrial detention is used inconsistently. Given these and other findings it was surprising to discover that Dade actually released a sizeable number of felony defendants with average failure (rearrest and/or failure to appear (FTA)) rates.

The descriptive research and rounds of group discussions led to the next, more complex step of trying to devise decision guidelines which would prove helpful in establishing both an overall policy frame and a day-to-day decisionmaking tool. Inevitably, the debate became more pointed as its focus shifted from a review and critique of past bail practices to consideration of a tool for shaping future practices. Several possible guidelines 'models' were considered[8] and the judges eventually agreed to adopt the Philadelphia model incorporating the two dimensions of risk and seriousness of the criminal charges.

A risk classification based on empirical analysis of past bail practices identified several variables which were weakly associated with pretrial flight (including prior FTA's, felony 2 charges (generally theft related), having a telephone and living with spouse and/or child) and two variables more strongly associated with pretrial rearrest (arrests within last 3 years and prior felony convictions). Using both groups of variables it was possible to classify defendants into one of four risk categories.

The second dimension, seriousness of the offense, proved a little more straightforward. In contrast to both Boston and Phoenix,[9] where ranking the severity of defendants' charges was extremely difficult, Miami had already an elaborate charge severity ranking in its bond schedule. Under this schedule, each possible criminal charge was assigned a dollar amount by a committee of judges. Thus, using the bond schedule as a measure of charge severity eight groups of charges were identified.

Figure 1 describes the guidelines matrix which resulted from this process. In Miami, as in Boston and Phoenix, the court valued the development of an empirically derived risk classification but was not prepared to let it dominate the guidelines. In general, the risk dimension represents the odds that categories of defendants would fail to appear or be rearrested before trial if released.[10] The severity dimension provides an, albeit crude, measure of the possible costs of decisions going awry within specific categories.[11]

Having designated a two-dimensional guidelines format that effectively classified defendants into one of 32 cells, the next major step was to determine the range of appropriate options. This is a crucial decision stage since it defines the point at which a court might decide simply to continue with recent practice (easily determined through empirical analysis) or to devise presumptive decisions which would introduce change in decision practices intended to achieve specific, agreed upon goals such as the reduction of pretrial detention or of defendant flight. The procedure followed was for research staff to review decisions and pretrial performances of prior defendants who could be retrospectively classified into each of the cells. The first draft of decision options was generally based on the court's past practices (using alternatively the modal decisions or an average of past decisions). Through an iterative procedure of revision and discussion based on consideration of differing policy factors the draft guidelines were continually revised until it seemed that they met the concerns expressed by the court.

IMPLEMENTATION

Background

Implementation of the project began at an inauspicious time. The jail population had just exceeded the federally established ceiling and two key figures—the director of pretrial services and the administrative judge for the Criminal Division—had only

CORRECTIONS & REHABILITATION DEPARTMENT
METROPOLITAN DADE COUNTY, FLORIDA
PRETRIAL SERVICES

UNIFORM BOND STANDARDS – DADE COUNTY CIRCUIT COURT

DATE ______________

DEFENDANT'S NAME ______________________________ JAIL # ______________

SECTION A: SUGGESTED DECISION

Less serious ← Severity ranking → More serious

Relative Risk (Lowest ↕ Highest)

	1	2	3	4	5	6	7	8
I	PTS/ Nonfinancial	PTS/ Nonfinancial	PTS/ Nonfinancial B D	PTS/ Nonfinancial	PTS/ Nonfinancial	PTS/ Nonfinancial	PTS/ Nonfinancial D	500 to 2,000
II	PTS/ Nonfinancial	PTS/ Nonfinancial B D	PTS/ Nonfinancial B	PTS/ Nonfinancial B	PTS/ Nonfinancial	PTS Special	PTS Special	1,500 to 3,000
III	PTS Special D	PTS Special D	PTS Special B X	PTS Special B X	PTS Special B	PTS Special to 500 B	PTS Special to 1,000	2,500 to 5,000
IV	PTS Special B D	PTS Special D	PTS Special to 750	PTS Special to 1,500	1,500 to 3,500	2,500 to 4,500	3,000 to 5,000	6,000 to 11,000

NOTE: X = higher risk B = higher than average probability of bind down
D = higher than average dropout rate

SECTION B: UNUSUAL CIRCUMSTANCES

____
____
____
____

SECTION C: SUGGESTED SPECIAL CONDITIONS

____
____
____
____

SECTION D: JUDGE'S DECISION

Check

- [ ] PTS/ NONFINANCIAL

or

- [ ] FINANCIAL $ ______________ (amount of bond)

PTS/ CONDITIONS: ______________________________

- [ ] FALLS WITHIN UNIFORM BOND STANDARDS

or

- [ ] DIFFERS FROM SUGGESTED DECISION

Reasons (for deciding out of UBS range):

- [ ] Currently on Felony Bond
- [ ] Probation/Parole Hold
- [ ] Fugitive
- [ ] A/C, Outstanding Warrants or Detainers
- [ ] Physical or Mental Health
- [ ] Added Charges
- [ ] Other (please specify) ______________________________

____
Judge's signature

FIGURE 1 Pretrial Release Guidelines for Dade County Circuit Court

recently taken up their appointments. The need for a strong leadership role within the court was clear, given that the guidelines required several significant changes to normal procedures. Prior to the study, pretrial services staff had traditionally gathered defendant information with a view to a subjective recommendation to the bond hearing judge. The type of information collected and the form of the recommendation were broadly discretionary. Guidelines required a change in procedure such that a predetermined body of information would routinely be collected and presentation to the judge would be systematized through use of the guidelines matrix. In addition, the judge was now being asked to replace the bond schedule (based entirely on charge seriousness) with guideline recommendations as the basis for decisionmaking. This required judges to actually consider pertinent defendant data (other than charge) and to follow or depart (noting reasons) with the presumptive guidelines decisions.

Even at the outset of the study, it was clear that the courtroom working environment in Dade County was not overly susceptible to innovation. Goldkamp et. al. (1988) noted that judges showed little interest in reviewing descriptive information on defendant profiles, or in knowing the reasons for pretrial services recommendations in individual cases. Indeed, it was soon apparent that the success of the guidelines experiment rested very much on the efforts of the judicial working committee established to supervise the development and initial implementation of the guidelines. Unfortunately, several crucial changes in personnel (unforeseen deaths and promotions) resulted in the dissolution of the committee prior to full implementation. At a stroke, this removed the main source of support for the research and, *de facto*, handed to pretrial services the responsibility for implementing guidelines and "educating" new bond hearing judges.

Implementation began in mid-June 1987 and, initially, resulted in complaints by pretrial services staff that data collection and guidelines completion were taking more time than anticipated. These were soon superseded by more intractable problems. First, the appropriate bond schedule amount continued to be announced formally at the beginning of each defendant's appearance and seemed to dominate the judges' considerations at the hearings. Second, bond hearing judges began to instruct pretrial services staff not to reveal the guidelines information and reverted back to the pre-guidelines custom of requesting whether or not pretrial services would "accept" the defendant (i.e. agree to non-financial release without consideration of conditions at this point). Equally as frustrating was the tendency for judges to ignore the agreement that they would provide reasons for any departures from the guidelines presumptive decision.

Methods

The research funding period required a prompt evaluation of initial implementation and, consequently, data collection in Miami began almost immediately after implementation. Recognizing the problems inherent in such an approach, it was decided also to study a much reduced number of defendants entering the process several months after implementation. Data describing pretrial release decisions and a 90 day follow-up were collected on approximately 3,000 felony defendants entering Dade County Circuit Court during June-July 1987 (the first two months of guideline use).

All defendants securing release were followed for a period of 90 days (or less, if adjudication of the charges had occurred) to determine whether any failures to appear in court (FTA's) or rearrests for crimes occurring during pretrial release were recorded. The second data set of approximately 470 cases was developed for a one week period in November, 1987. Separate analysis of the cases within this sample offer some insight on changes that occurred as use of the guidelines became more established. To compare pretrial decisions once guidelines had been implemented to decisions pre-guidelines, a third sample of approximately 2,000 felony defendants entering between April-October, 1984 was utilized.

It should be noted that, although each of the samples are likely to be comparable they could not be exactly comparable.[12] Analysis of the data contrasting the charge and risk characteristics of the three samples suggests that the 1987 cases involve somewhat more seriously charged cases. Moreover, the 1987 samples have fewer defendants in both the lowest and the highest risk category than the 1984 sample. While the overall differences are slight they present the possibility that reported differences in outcome may be due, in part, to differences in the make-up of the samples rather than to differences in decisionmaking practices as a result of the guidelines. For that reason, we have more confidence in comparisons between subcategories of defendants when the key characteristics—risk and severity—of cases are controlled. Guidelines enable a relatively straightforward exercise of such control through the comparison of specific cells or zones within the guidelines matrix.[13]

Comparison of the defendant samples based on specific guideline zones suggests that, for the most part, the distribution of defendants does not vary dramatically across the three samples (Figure 2). Similar comparison by cell[14] indicates very little significant variation across the samples.

RESULTS

We described above the three goals of the study: the development of guidelines in Dade County, their successful implementation and an assessment of their impact. Each goal is discussed in detail below.

Guidelines Development

A key question posed by this research was whether it would be possible to persuade the court to participate in any review of practices which required empirical research, let alone agree to utilize the information collected to develop a policy and decision-making tool. The general response was positive. There was, in each of the three sites, a considerable amount of participation, debate, refinement of goals and ideas and, eventually, a generally acceptable product. However, several key changes in personnel—particularly the appointment of the present judge to the Florida Supreme Court—served notice that past agreements might not translate into current consensus.

Before considering the results of the implementation, it is worth emphasizing the fact that the process of guidelines development is, in itself, vitally important. Indeed,

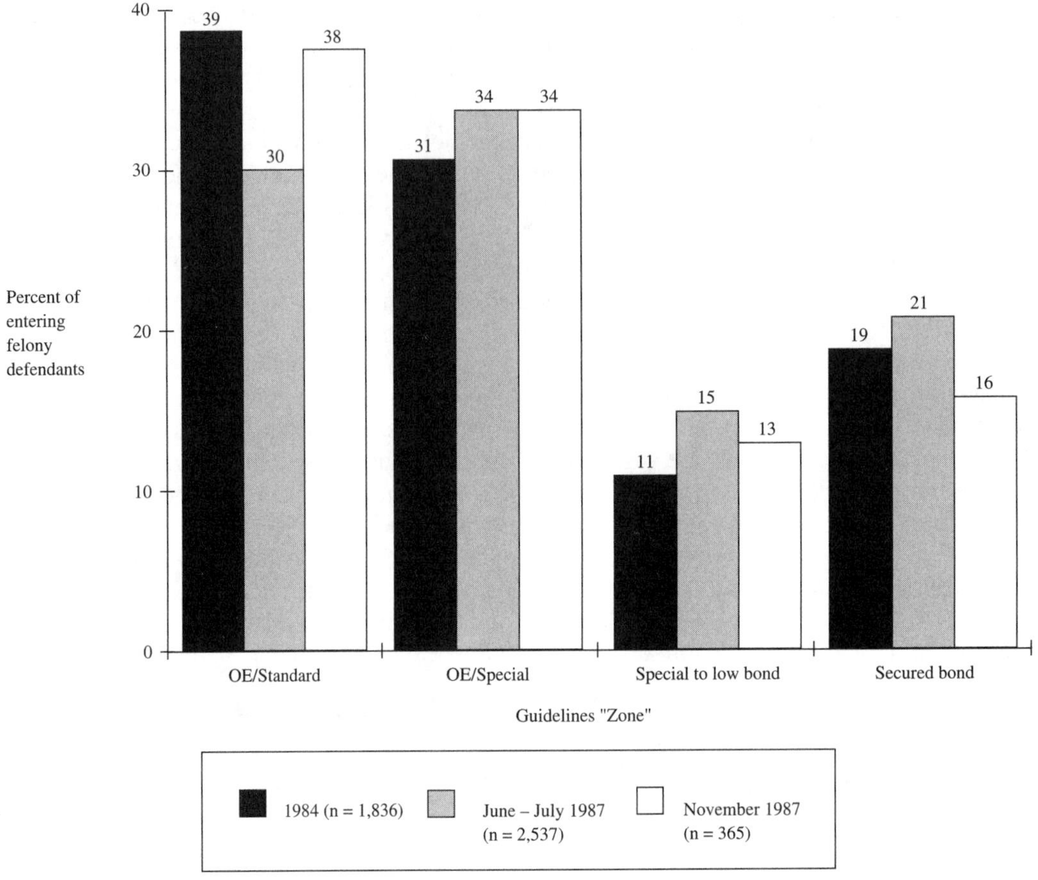

FIGURE 2 The Classification of Felony Defendants Entering Dade County Circuit Court, By Guidelines Zone, By Sample

one might suggest that many courts would be satisfied with the developmental phase alone, since it represents such a dramatic policy advance over the totally discretionary bail systems of the past.

Guidelines Implementation

Implementation of the guidelines is essentially dependent on two groups of people; the staff of pretrial services (the guidelines preparers), and the judges (the consumers of the tool). Examination of the extent to which guidelines materials were actually prepared by pretrial services staff revealed totally incomplete cases for about 29 percent of defendants in both 1987 samples. Furthermore, guidelines materials were begun but not completed in another 10 percent of the June-July 1987 sample and another 37 percent of the one week November sample. Frequently, the reason for non-completion was clear. For example, in cases with extremely high bond schedule amounts pretrial services assumed that it was highly unlikely the judge would consider the guidelines recommendation. Materials were frequently not prepared also for defendants who were on probation/parole at the time of their arrest because of the court's policy of denying bond to these individuals until the former sentencing judge could review the case. In both these instances it is worth noting that such defendants would generally be considered non-bondable and ordinarily excluded from an analysis of the effect of guidelines on the cases of bondable felony defendants. Finally, it is not surprising that an evaluation which started coincident with program implementation would face some procedural difficulties.

Even in cases where guidelines materials were prepared, it was possible for pretrial services staff to make mistakes in the coding of risk, charge severity, or the subsequent classification into guideline cell. In approximately 15 percent of June-July cases and 19 percent of November cases for which classifications were prepared, pretrial services incorrectly ranked charge severity.[15] The classification of defendant risk offered greater potential for error since it was possible to err on the classification of any individual risk characteristic and on the computation of the overall risk score. Overall, only 55 percent of completed June-July felony cases and 48 percent of completed November cases were assigned to the correct risk category.[16]

The errors of classification on either/both risk and severity inevitably translate into misclassification of defendants within the guidelines. Comparisons of actual and "corrected"[17] guidelines classifications by zone and cell were possible in all cases where guidelines materials were prepared. Among the June-July 1987 defendants, 64 percent were classified by pretrial services into the correct guidelines zone and 44 percent classified into the correct guidelines cell. Results for the November sample were worse, with 61 and 40 percent of defendants respectively, classified correctly. Unfortunately, the misclassification erred more often than not in the direction of more restrictive guidelines recommendations. This not only may have resulted in inappropriate decisions but severely limited the potential for guidelines to impact on the jail overcrowding problem it was designed to address.

Given the immediacy of the evaluation, it was no surprise to find many implementation problems. The severe time constraints of a large, busy, urban court system leave little opportunity to reach and gather information on all bailable defendants. Indeed, the jail overcrowding crisis in Dade occasionally required expedited release procedures permitting no time at all for guidelines preparation or use. Less expected was the scale of guideline preparation errors identified for both 1987 samples. These problems, if left uncorrected, would seriously undermine the efficacy of guidelines. nevertheless, they offer a cogent illustration of the need for, and value of, a mechanism for the feedback of information to the court.

The problems of implementation make it difficult to gauge the willingness of judges to adopt guidelines as well as the impact guidelines had on judicial decision-making. It is conceivable that the errors of classification lead judges to believe that guidelines placed a defendant in a less, or more restrictive, decision category than they felt appropriate. If such situations arose frequently they might easily give way to disenchantment with the whole guidelines approach. While recognizing the existence of this problem, the present analysis reasonably assumes that a large majority of classification errors were unnoticed by the judges. Consequently, the analysis proceeds on the working assumption that the judges believed the guidelines to be appropriately prepared.

It was never expected that judges would universally adopt the guidelines decisions. However, it was felt that an agreement rate approximating 75 percent was necessary if guidelines were to have a measurable impact on bail practices. As Figure 3 shows, the overall agreement rate fell far below the desired level. In both 1987 samples the judicial agreement rate was just 30 percent. Since the actual decisions of judges in 1984 agreed with the guidelines (which, of course, they did not see) in 36 percent of cases, we have to conclude that judges in 1987 did not change their decision practices despite the experiment. Furthermore, where disagreement with the guidelines occurred, the actual decision was generally more restrictive than that suggested (see Figure 3). Analysis by zone and cell revealed some variation in the agreement rates and identified particular types of cases where agreement was virtually nonexistent. For example, cell 8 of the guidelines (see Figure 1 above) contained bondable defendants ranked highest on the charge seriousness dimension and lowest

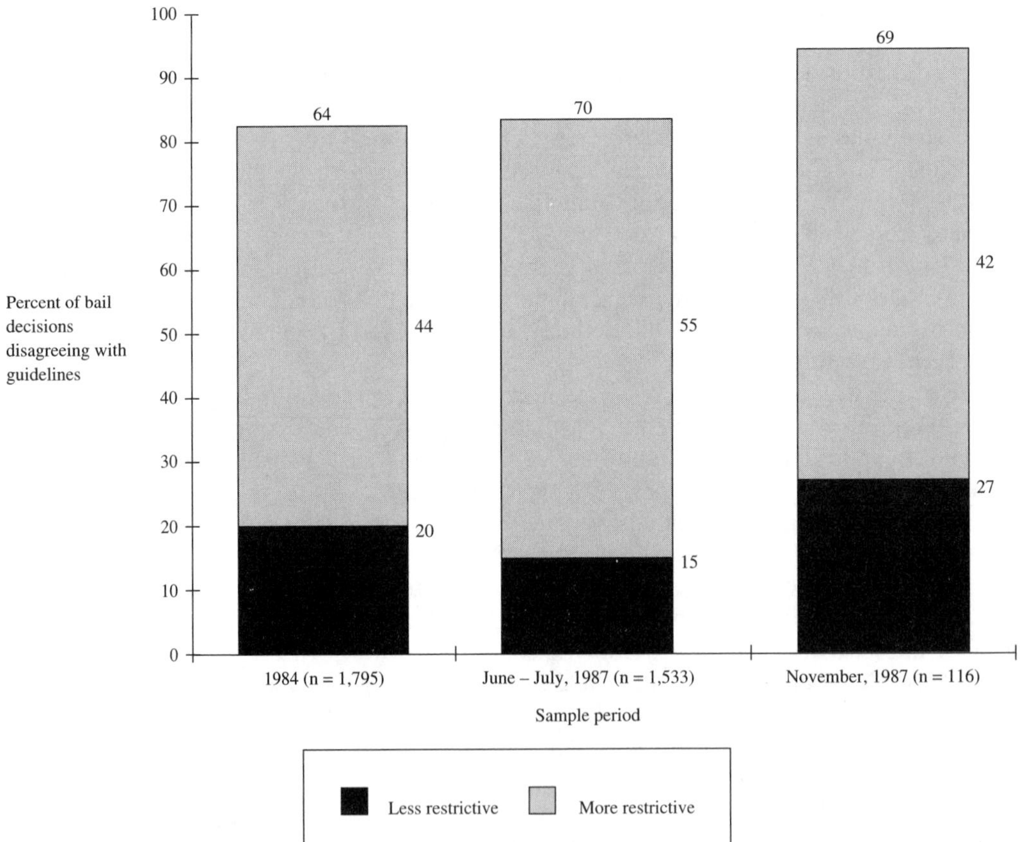

FIGURE 3 Disagreement Between Judicial Decisions at Bond Hearing and the Guidelines Suggestions Among Felony Defendants Entering Dade County Court, By Sample

on the risk dimension. The guidelines suggested cash bond in the range $500 to $2,000. There were no cases in which the judge agreed with the guidelines decision but, interestingly, the judges were almost equally divided in the direction of their disagreement (43% favoring less restrictive decisions—less cash bond or non-financial release; 57% favoring a more restrictive decision).

The judges in Miami clearly did not make use of the guidelines to the extent we expected. Furthermore, they rarely specified the reasons for their disagreement with the presumptive decisions. Given the feedback function of the early guidelines results it would appear that the most significant problem to solve in Miami is to determine why judges did not participate in the guidelines program. Several possible reasons present themselves. First, the loss of several key supervising judges just prior to implementation created a situation in which it was necessary to "educate" the judges about the goals and advantages of the guidelines. Alternatively, Dade County judges might have understood perfectly well the meaning of the guidelines and simply rejected them. Finally, as with any innovation, there is always the issue of inertia. Judges in Dade appear wedded to the bond schedule as a means for determining bail and it is probable that their underlying assumptions are to follow the schedule unless pretrail service could persuade them otherwise.

Impact

Given the exceptionally low utilization of the guidelines by judges in Dade County there can be no meaningful impact consequent upon the experiment. However, a comparison of decisionmaking and case outcome data for 1984 and 1987 will at least reveal changes occurring during this period. Figure 4 shows a substantial reduction in the use of ROR between 1984 and the first sample period (69% and 47% respectively) but a return to 1984 levels by the November 1987 sample (65%). The corollary of this was an increase in the use of cash bond, from 31 percent in 1984 to 53 percent in June-July 1987 (then to 35% in November 1987) and an increase in the amount of bond required (for example, the median bond for zone 4—secured bond on the guidelines grid—increased from $4,000 to $9,250).

Comparison of the three samples reveals a similar pattern of results in the use of pretrial detention (Figure 5).[18] Overall, use of pretrial detention increased from 36 percent of the 1984 cases to 53 percent of guidelines prepared cases in June-July 1987, before returning almost to the 1984 rate during the November period (39%). Had judges employed the guidelines at the anticipated rate these pretrial detention rates would be very disconcerting. However, as the judges generally failed to adopt the guidelines we conclude that the increased use of pretrial detention is due to a combination of different sample compositions and an apparent trend toward more restrictive bond decisions among Dade judges during the study period.[19]

THE EFFECTIVENESS OF BAIL PRACTICES, 1984 AND 1987

If the sole purpose of guidelines were to reduce pretrail misconduct (FTA and/or rearrest) there would be need only for the risk classification dimension. However, for many reasons (see Goldkamp and Gottfredson, 1985) a severity dimension (not

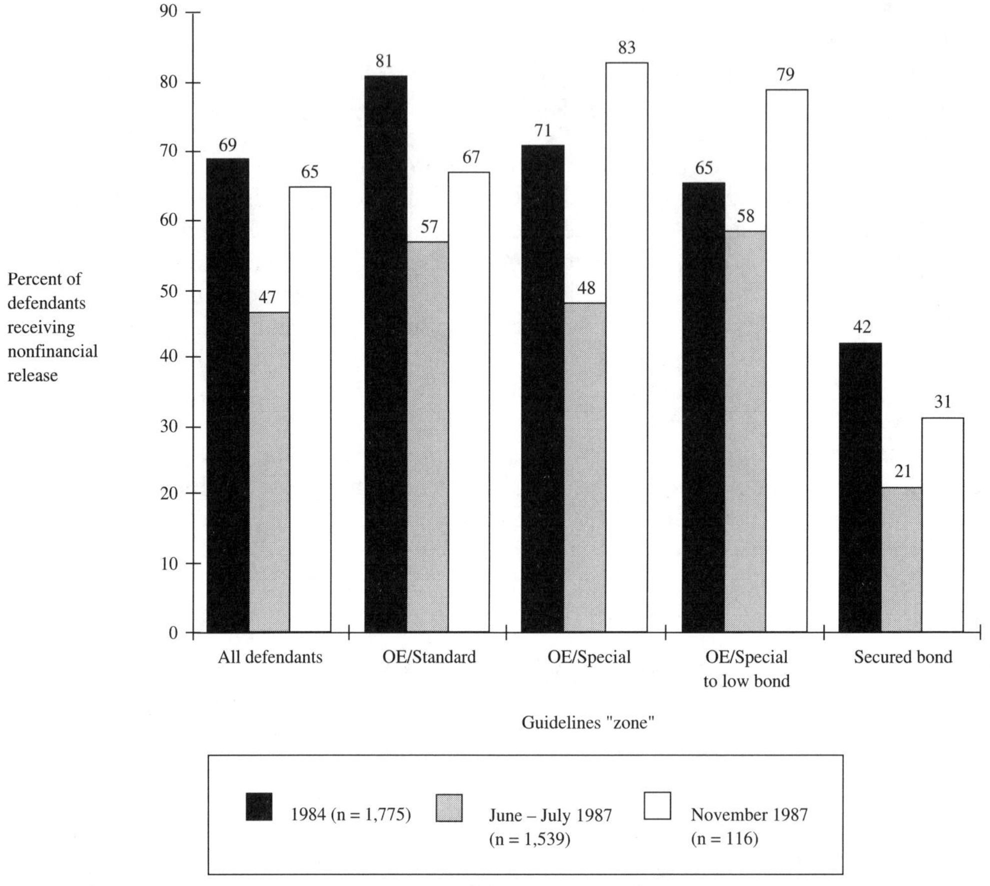

FIGURE 4 Change in the Use of Nonfinancial Release (OR) Among Decisions for Entering Felony Defendants in Dade County Circuit Court from 1984 to 1987, By Guidelines Zone

related to either flight or rearrest) was incorporated into the guidelines format. Consequently, guidelines do not offer an optimum test of our ability to affect pretrail misconduct. The fact that judges failed to follow the guidelines further weakens any expectations we might have had in this direction. Having entered these caveats, Figures 6 and 7 present data on FTA and rearrest for the 1984 and 1987[20] samples. It appears that pretrail misconduct increased markedly between the two sample years, FTA's from 12 to 17 percent, and rearrest from 7 to 17 percent.

Comparison of FTA's and/or rearrest as misconduct rates must be undertaken cautiously since they are ultimately dependent on the proportions and types of defendants actually released (the lowest misconduct rate would be achieved through the pretrial detention of all defendants). A preferable measure of the effectiveness of pretrial release decisionmaking would take into account both the use of pretrail detention and misconduct rates for those released pretrial.[21] Given the legal presumption in favor of release under the least restrictive of alternatives, "effectiveness" of pretrial

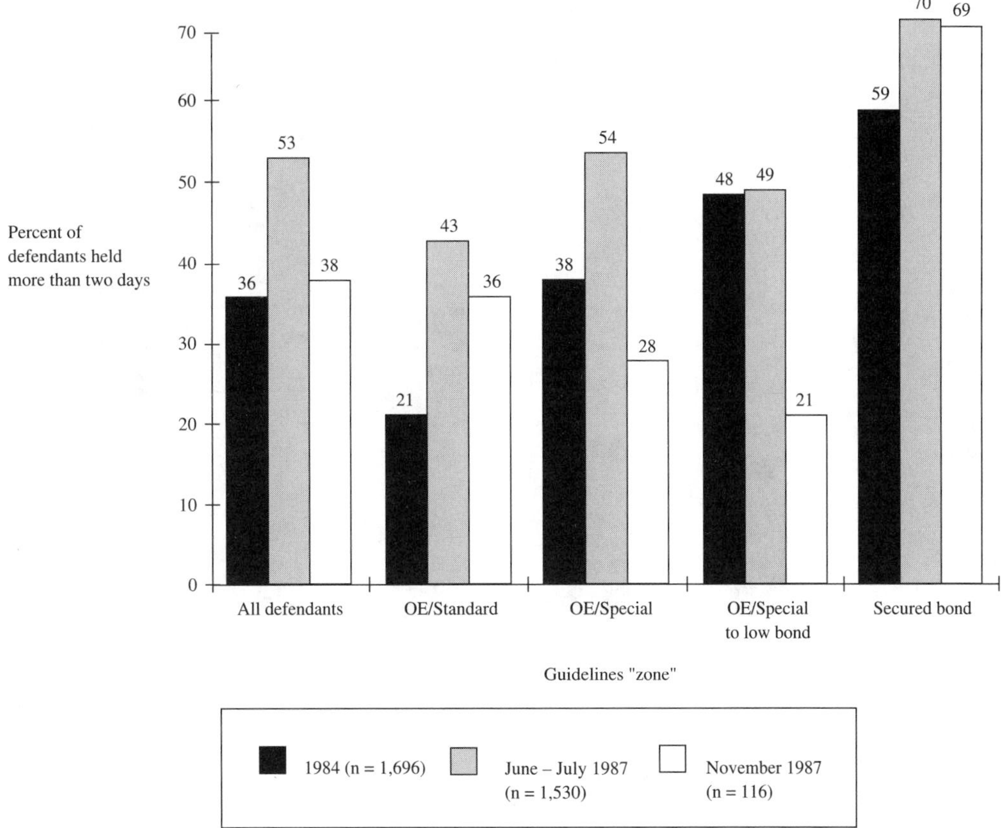

FIGURE 5 Change in the Use of Pretrial Detention (Held More Than Two Days) For Entering Felony Defendants in Dade County Circuit Court from 1984 to 1987, By Guidelines Zone

decisionmaking can be conceptualized as the release of as many defendants as possible without increasing the threat to public safety or risk of defendant flight. Conversely, "ineffectiveness" is generated by either not releasing defendants or inappropriately releasing defendants who commit new crimes or fail to appear in court. Figure 8 compares the effectiveness rates associated with the 1984 and 1987 samples of Dade defendants. Overall, effective release decreased from 53 percent of cases in 1984 to just 35 percent in 1987.

THE EQUITABLE TREATMENT OF OFFENDERS, 1984 AND 1987

One of the most important philosophical concerns with bail decisionmaking is the question of equity. Very often this is assessed by the comparison of bail decisions for defendants facing charges of similar severity (much like the logic underlying the

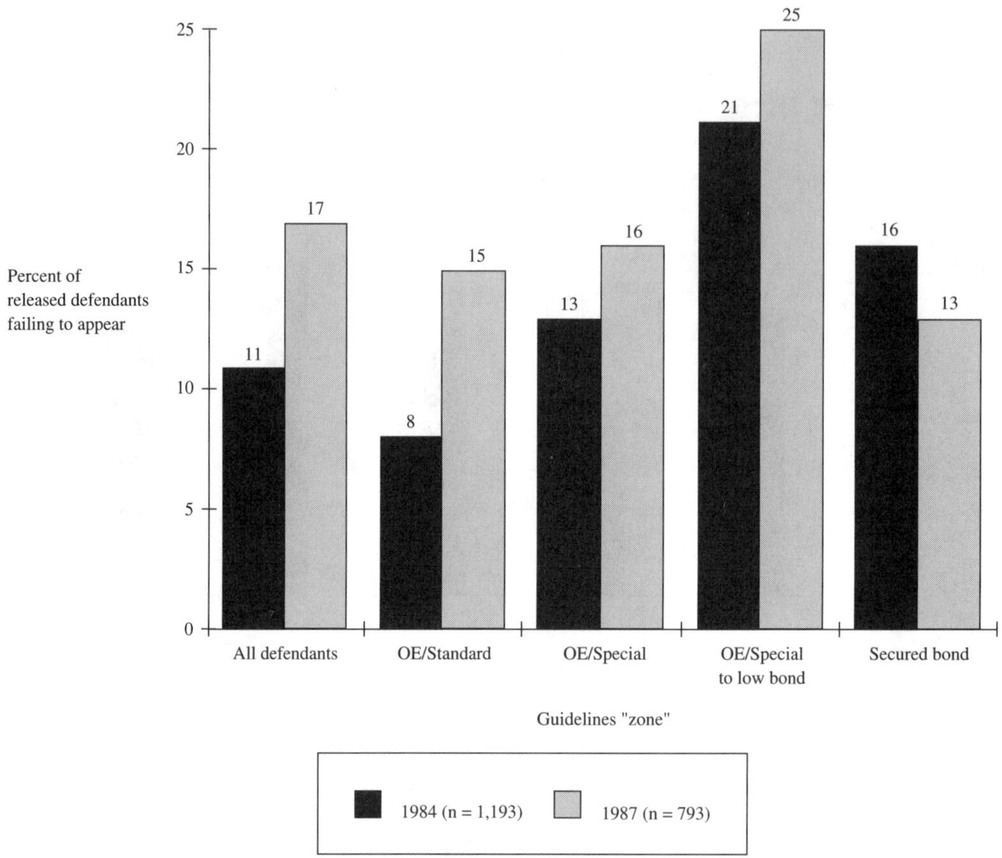

FIGURE 6 Change in Defendant Failure to Appear Rates for Entering Felony Defendants in Dade County Court from 1984 to 1987, By Guidelines Zone

bond schedule). The guidelines, based as they are on a set of policy decisions concerning the desired aims and practices of bail decisionmaking in each particular court, offer a more relevant and valid gauge by which equity can be evaluated. The guidelines based measure of equity is straightforward: defendants located in cell 1 of the guidelines matrix should—except in unusual circumstances—receive decisions comparable with other defendants with cell 1 attributes. In essence, we would expect more within-cell consistency under guidelines (at least if utilized) than non-guidelines systems.

Figure 9 suggests that, overall, equity remained very much the same in both sample years. Considered by zone, it appears that equity decreased between 1984 and 1987 for zone 2 defendants (OR/Standard Conditions) but increased for zone 3 defendants (OR/Special Conditions to low cash bond). Again, interpretation of these findings is complicated by the fact that judges did not utilize the guidelines. It is safe to conclude, however, that trends in equity, like effectiveness, appear to have occurred

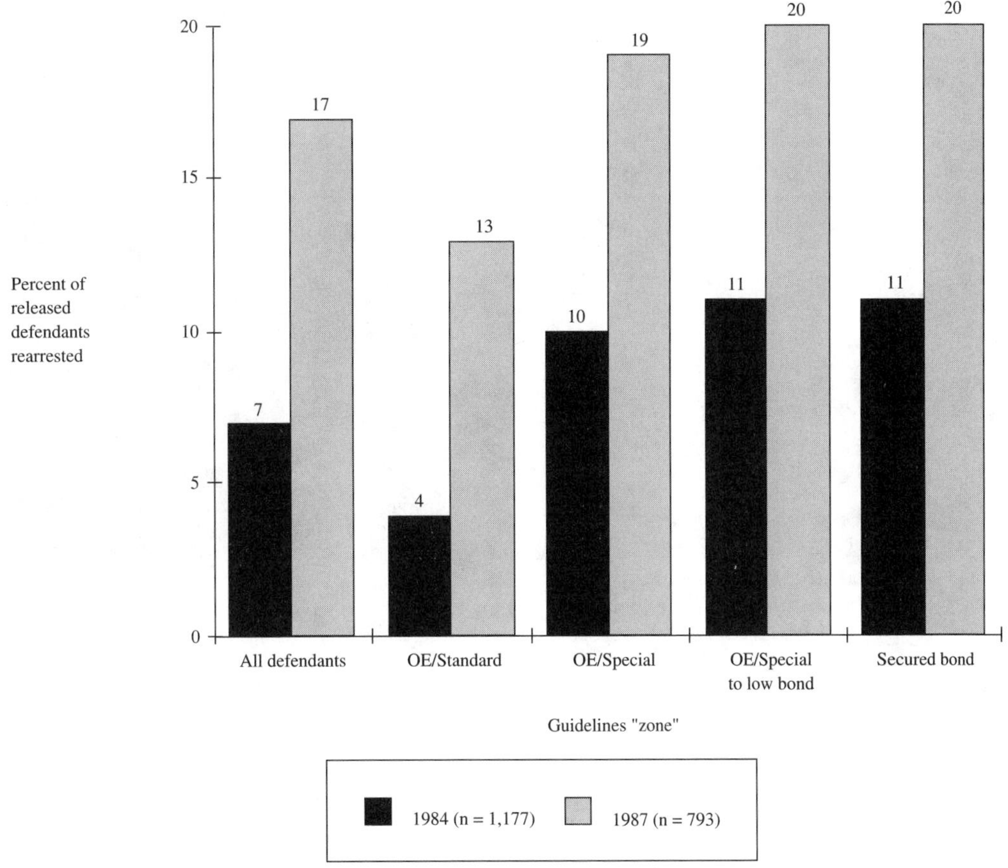

FIGURE 7 Change in Defendants Rearrest Rates for Entering Felony Defendants in Dade County Circuit Court from 1984 to 1987, By Guidelines Zone

in the Dade County Circuit Court regardless of guidelines. Unfortunately, it is precisely these sorts of deteriorating conditions that the guidelines were originally designed to address.

SUMMARY

The descriptive stage of the research revealed a jurisdiction faced with enormous jail overcrowding pressures, a strong public safety orientation to bail decisionmaking and a continued reliance on the bond schedule as the *de facto* guidelines for decisionmaking.

The developmental stage produced a guidelines format comprising two dimensions: individual risk and seriousness of the criminal charges. Through a process of drafting, revision and discussion appropriate options were assigned to each of the

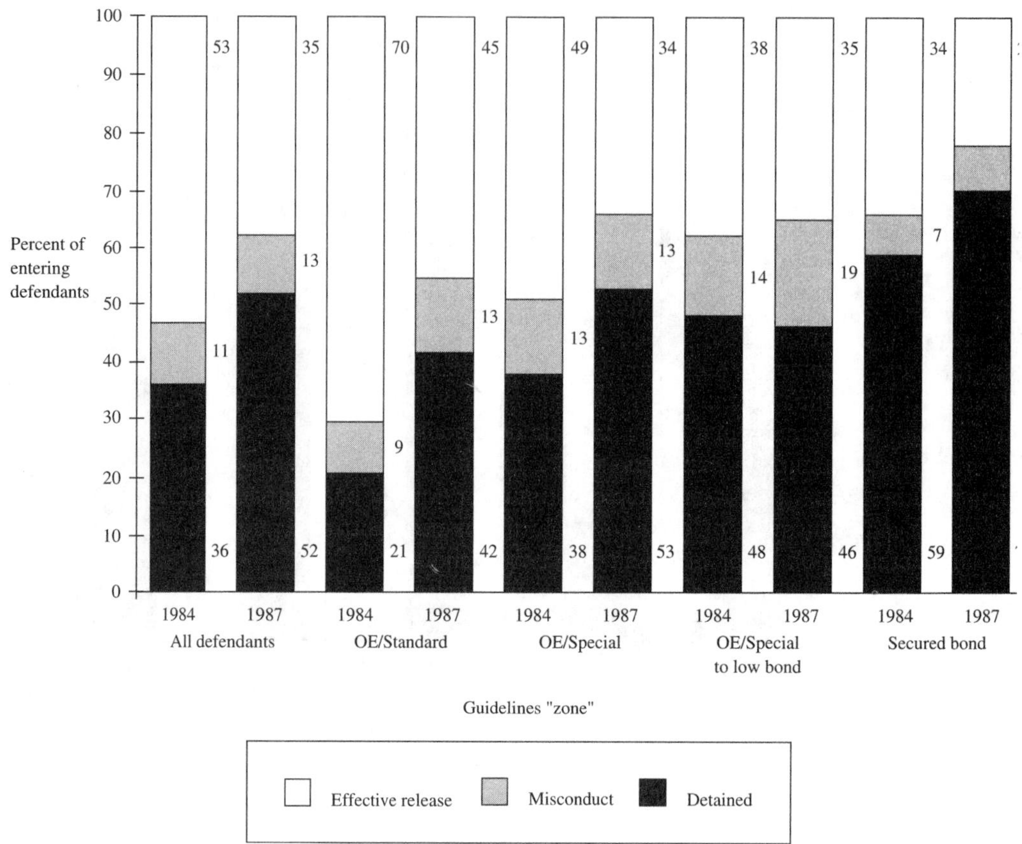

FIGURE 8 Change in the Misconduct Effectiveness of Pretrial Release for Felony Defendants Entering Dade County Circuit Court from 1984 to 1987, By Guidelines Zone

individual guideline cells. Throughout this process, the emphasis was on the development of a judicial tool, not merely on the updating of information that is collected and presented to judges, or the refurbishing of pretrail service procedures.

The results of the implementation stage seriously question whether or not it is appropriate to consider the guidelines system as having been implemented at all in Dade. The problem of uncompleted and mistakenly completed guidelines forms was, in part, to be expected. Certainly, it was something that could be improved. However, the fact that judges in Dade never really adopted the guidelines—despite the fact that it was established in collaboration with the Court as a decisionmaking tool—means that we cannot rigorously test the theoretical value of the guidelines as well as hoped. It is difficult to conclusively identify reasons why the guidelines failed to engage judges in the way intended. The inopportune loss of the supervisory group has been noted. Even though every effort was made to distinguish between legislatively imposed guidelines and the court-developed, self-help version involved in the present

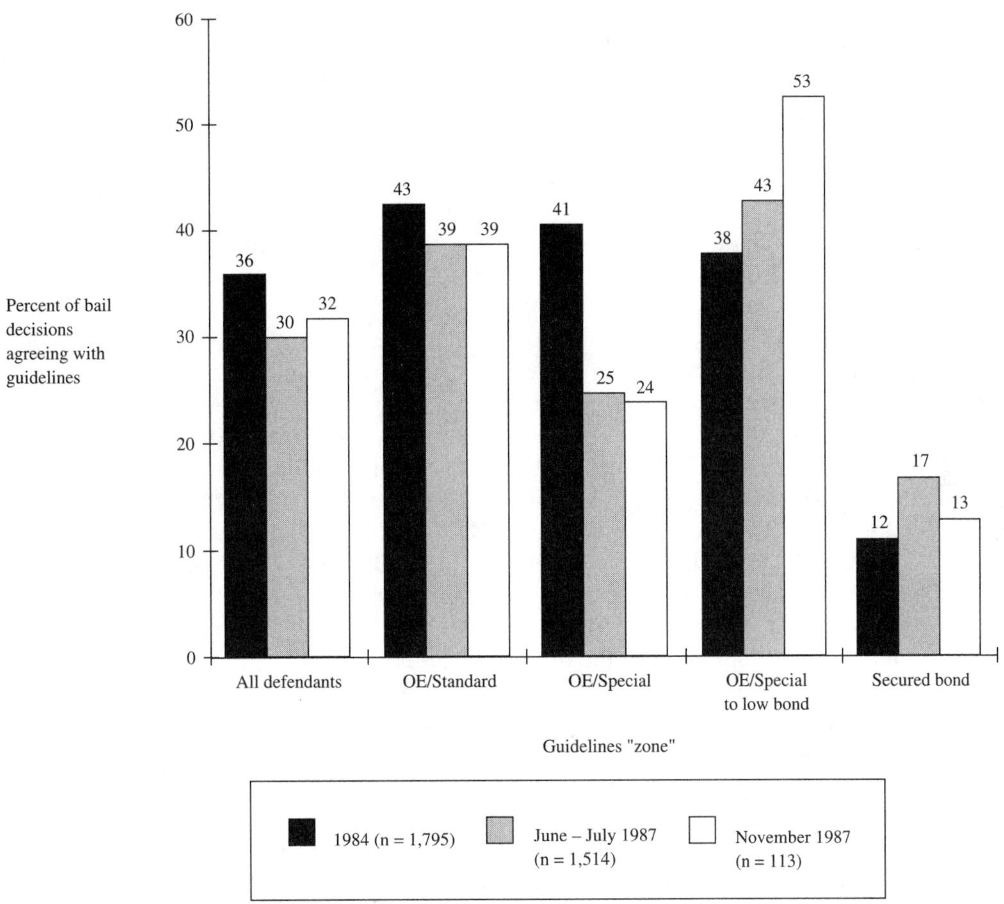

FIGURE 9 Equity as Consistency: Comparing Agreement with Guidelines, By Zone, By Sample

study, it seems that prior experience with sentencing guidelines (rumored to have been particularly frustrating) set the wrong tone for our experiment. Finally, it is possible that we underestimated the power of tradition or inertia. The bond schedule was, and is, a central feature of bail decisionmaking in Dade and judges clearly found it difficult to perceive guidelines as a new, more rational basis for decisionmaking.

DISCUSSION

This research set out to examine several fundamental questions about the process as well as the product of developing/implementing bail guidelines. Consequently, it would be wrong to dismiss the study because the judges never fully adopted the guidelines. Similarly, the negative (or no-difference) findings reported should not be interpreted as indicative of the failure of the guidelines approach. Indeed, given the considerable common sense plausibility of the guidelines the results would argue for the intensification of such research rather than its abandonment.

Even though the Dade implementation findings are relatively inconclusive, the larger research process itself surfaced several important practical and policy issues. Perhaps most important is the issue of informed decisionmaking. Courts in the United States and elsewhere might regard guidelines as impractical because of informational inadequacies at the bond hearing stage. Our argument would be that the availability of relevant information is not an issue for consideration solely in the context of guidelines—it is a fundamental requirement of any decisionmaking process. One of the requirements of the guidelines program, therefore, is a commitment on the part of the Court to improving their information capacity. Where no pretrial services agency exists this commitment will necessarily need to be translated into new resource allocation. Undoubtedly, the substance of guidelines comprises the in-depth review and re-organization of how information should be used in light of the goals of the pretrial release decision and the decision options available.

The enhanced visibility of bail decisions—both the broad policies underlying bail decisionmaking, as well as the specific criteria upon which decisions are to be made—is another major benefit of the guidelines process. The interactive process of guidelines development and the iterative nature of implementation (involving continual feedback of information and, where necessary, modification) permit explicit consideration of policy aims, program goals and objective review of performance. Importantly, the guidelines should not be perceived as eliminating discretion. The combination of discretion within each guidelines cell, and the opportunity for judicial decisions which depart from the guidelines, ensure that discretion exists and yet is structured, measurable and open to review. Furthermore, policymakers always have the option of modifying the guidelines themselves at any time.

In Dade County, as in each of the other jurisdictions involved in the wider research project, the majority if the judiciary believed that voluntary guidelines would be good for their court. There was full and committed participation in all aspects of the developmental stage. However, implementation was, at best, fragmentary. Guidelines directly effect judges by structuring their discretion and enhancing their accountability (by requiring reasons for any departures from presumptive outcomes). Understandably, some judges feel these requirements go too far or, at least, defeat the principal of individual responsibility for decisionmaking, by relegating the task to the group.

One lesson to be learned from the research in Dade County is that implementation of voluntary guidelines depends largely on the degree to which court authority is centralized, such that collective decisions can be subsequently carried out. Furthermore, the success of the guidelines depends very much on the court's willingness and ability to monitor the system in operation. The present study suggests that individual judges vary considerably in their compliance with the guidelines and the requirements that they provide reasons for their departures from the presumptive decisions. The uneven compliance rates again point to the need for strong central authority within the court. However, such centralized authority is a necessary rather than sufficient prerequisite for successful guidelines implementation. The experience of Dade shows unequivocally that large, urban courts need also to have in place modern, efficient information systems to enable successful implementation of voluntary guidelines. Finally, and despite the experience of Dade County, we remain convinced of the need to involve judges in the process of policy and practice review as well as in the design of the decisionmaking resource. The interactive process of guidelines development and the iterative nature of implementation (involving continual feedback of information and, where necessary, modification) is crucial to the explicit consideration of policy aims, program goals and objective review of performance. While discussion of guidelines implies dissatisfaction with court practices this should not prompt researchers to avoid confrontation, or even collaboration, with court authorities. The consequence of such avoidance is a program deprived of its most important source of guidance, destined to remain on the periphery of power and authority and unlikely to significantly impact on current bail decisionmaking.

The pretrail decision, like most decision stages in the criminal justice system, has traditionally been individualized. Judges seek to take into account the "totality of the circumstances" in any given case. The guidelines concept, with its emphasis on structured discretion, inevitably causes a tension. The experience of conducting the present study reinforces our belief in the guidelines concept. Judges continue to make subjective decisions, sometimes based on a *sub rosa* agenda, and in virtual ignorance of their consequences. The components which buttress the guidelines philosophy—information, rationality, feedback—offer an opportunity for more effective decisionmaking.

*The research studies described in the paper were supported with grants from the National Institute of Justice, U.S. Department of Justice. An earlier version of this paper was presented at the British Society of Criminology Conference, Bristol, 1989.

NOTES

1. The history and agenda of bail reform in the United States which has criticized financial bail decisions is lengthy, dating back at least to the 1920's (Pound and Frankfurter, 1922; Beeley, 1927) and reaching its peak ferment in the late 1950's (Foote, 1954) and 1960's (Ares, Rankin and Sturz, 1963). For a review of the debate on the constitutional purposes of bail see Goldkamp (1979; 1984).
2. The terminology employed in the study was "pretrial parole", meaning release on one's promise to appear without any requirement of a cash bond.
3. While the present paper focuses solely on Dade County, Miami, the overall research project comprised evaluation of two other site—Maricopa County, Phoenix and Boston Municipal Court.
4. Bridges v. Sandstrom, F.Supp., U.S. District Court for So. Fla., No. 79-994, Jan 2, 1975.
5. Fla. Stat. Ch. 903.046.
6. Ibid.
7. A bond schedule sets fixed bond amounts for each offense according to its seriousness at booking only.

8. See Chapter 10 of Goldkamp and Gottkamp and Gottfredson (1988) for a discussion of alternative guideline models.

9. Boston and Phoenix were the other two cities chosen in the second round of NIJ funding.

10. See Goldkamp and Gottfredson (1988) for a detailed description of the statistical analyses of defendant performance during pretrial release as well as a discussion of the strengths and weaknesses of prediction as a tool for decisionmakers.

11. Judges are well aware that making a "mistake" in releasing a low-risk alleged rapist (low risk/high severity) who then commits another crime is quite a different scenario to making a similar mistake with a high risk alleged petty thief. The costs of these possible mistakes for given categories of defendant are quite different, and the juxtaposition of risk and severity reasonably depicts that difference for the decisionmaker.

12. For a detailed description of methodology see Goldkamp and Gottfredson, 1988; Goldkamp, Gottfredson and Jones, 1988).

13. "Zone" means the broad area of the guidelines grid defined by the four types of suggested decision options: OR/Standard (conditions of release), OR/Special (restrictive conditions of release), OR/Special to low bond (a choice of restrictive conditions or low amounts of secured bond), and various ranges of cash bond. "Cell" means the specific decision associated with a particular severity/risk intersection. See Figure 1.

14. The comparisons by cell are limited to those cells with sufficient cases.

15. Two-thirds of misclassified June-July and almost one half of November of misclassified. November cases had the charge severity ranked too high.

16. Of those defendants incorrectly assigned to a risk category 60 percent were overclassified (placed in a more serious risk category).

17. The data collection instrument permitted direct checks of all severity and risk items with the exception of "living arrangements." Thus, a "correct" classification based on this alternative source of information was generally possible.

18. Pretrial detention is defined as detention for more than 48 hours following booking.

19. This view is supported when data from cases decided during the same period but not processed for the guidelines are compared with the guidelines cases.

20. The 1987 samples are combined in this analysis due to the small number of November, 1987 cases.

21. See Goldkamp and Gottfredson (1985; 1988) for a discussion of this version of "effectiveness."

REFERENCES

Ares, Charles, Ann Rankin, and H. Sturz (1963) The Manhattan Bail Project: An Interim Report on the Use of Pre-Trial Parole, 38 *New York University Law Review,* 67.

Austin, James and Barry Krisberg (1982) The Unmet Promise of Alternatives to Incarceration. 28(3) *Crime and Delinquency,* 374.

Beeley, Arthur (1927) The Bail System in Chicago. Chicago: University of Chicago Press.

Boyum, Keith O. (1987) The Politics of Court Reform: A Review Essay, 12(3) *Justice System Journal,* 406

Feeley, Malcolm (1983) Court Reform on Trial: Why Simple Solutions Fail. New York: Basic Books.

Fisher, Franklin M. and Joseph B. Kadane (1983) "Empirically Based Sentening Guidelines and Ethical Considerations." In Alfred Blumstein, Jacqueline Cohen, Susan E. Martin and Michael H. Tonry (Eds.) Research on Sentencing: The Search For Reform: Vol. II. Washington D.C.: National Academy Press.

Foote, Caleb, J. Markle and E. Woolley (1954) "Compelling Appearance in Court: Administration of Bail in Philadelphia." 102 *University of Pennsylvania Law Review,* 1031.

Freed, Daniel and Patricia Wald (1964) Bail in The United States: 1964. Washington, D.C.: U.S. Department of Justice and the Vera Foundation.

Goldkamp, John S. (1979) Two Classes of Accused: A Study of Bail and Detention in America, Cambridge, Mass: Ballinger.

———(1985) Danger and Detention: A Second Generation of Bail Reform, 76(1) *The Journal of Criminal Law and Criminology,* 1–74.

Goldkamp, John S. and Michael R. Gottfredson (1985) Policy Guidelines for Bail: An Experiment in Court Reform. Philadelphia, PA: Temple University Press.

———(1988) Guidelines for Bail and Pretrail Release in Three Urban Courts (Volume I). Unpublished Report, Department of Criminal Justice, Temple University, Philadelphia.

Goldkamp, John S., Michael R. Gottfredson and Peter R. Jones (1988) Guidelines for Bail and Pretrail Release in Three Urban Courts (Volume II). Unpublished Report, Department of Criminal Justice, Temple University, Philadelphia.

Gottfredson, Don M., Leslie T. Wilkins and Peter B. Hoffman (1978) Guidelines For Parole and Sentencing. Lexington, Massachusetts: Lexington Books.

Gottfredson, Michael R. and Don M. Gottfredson (1984) Guidelines for Incarceration Decisions: A Partisan Review, 2 *University of Illinois Law Review*.

Gottfredson, Michael R. (1984) An Empirical Analysis of Pretrial Release Decisions, 2 *Journal of Criminal Justice,* 287.

Gottfredson, Michael R. and Don M. Gottfredson (1988) Decisonmaking in Criminal Justice: Toward the Rational Exercise of Discretion. New York: Plenum.

Posavac, Emil J. and Raymond G. Carey (1985) Program Evaluation: Methods and Case Studies. New Jersey: Prentice-Hall.

Pound, Roscoe and F. Frankfurter (1922) Criminal Justice in Cleveland. Cleveland: Cleveland Foundation; reprint ed., Montclair, N.J.: Patterson Smith, 1968.

Rich William D., L. Paul Sutton, Todd D. Clear and Michael J. Saks (1982) Sentencing by Mathematics: An Evaluation of the Early Attempts to Develop and Implement Sentencing Guidelines. Williamsburg, VA:National Center for State Courts.

Roth, Jeffrey A. and Paul B. Wice (1978) Pretrial Release and Misconduct in The District of Columbia, Promis Research Project Publication 16. Washington D.C.: Inslaw.

Sparks, Richard F. (1983) "The Construction of Sentencing Guidelines: A Methodological Critique," In Alfred Blumstein, Jacqueline Cohen, Susan E. Martin and Michael H. Tonry (Eds.) Research on Sentencing: The Search For Reform: Vol. II. Washington D.C.: National Academy Press.

Thomas, Wayne H., (1976) Bail Reform in America. Berkeley:University of California Press.

7

Pretrial Drug Testing: Panacea or Pandora's Box?*

Christy A. Visher**

In the 1980s, rising public awareness of the drug abuse problem in all sectors of society led to a variety of strategies for reducing and controlling illicit drug consumption. A principal strategy in the workplace, the military, and the criminal justice system has been an increased emphasis on the detection of persons who use illegal drugs. Since drug users may not show any overt symptoms of use and will often conceal illegal drug use if asked about it directly, urinalysis technologies have emerged as a convenient tool for identifying users of illegal drugs.

Drug testing has been used for decades in drug abuse treatment programs to monitor clients' drug use during treatment. Drug testing also has a long history in the military and in professional sports. Probation and parole agencies in a few states—notably California—and in the federal system have had drug-testing programs in place for more than a decade. In the last several years, drug testing has become a common requirement for persons convicted of drug offenses or suspected of using drugs who are placed on probation or parole. Drug testing is also gaining the attention of national policymakers. The President's Office of National Drug Control Policy has recommended that states implement comprehensive drug-testing programs—from arrest through post-conviction supervision—as part of their criminal justice programs.[1]

Pretrial drug testing of suspected offenders at arrest and during the period before trial, however, is a relatively new practice. After the arrest and arraignment of suspected offenders, judges must make bail and pretrial-release determinations and set any conditions of release. The principal concern in this decision-making process is the defendant's risk of flight and potential danger to the community, which are the only statutory reasons for deciding whom to release before trial. In 1984, the Federal Bail Reform Act urged that a defendant's drug involvement be considered in these risk assessments. Washington, D.C., has put this suggested policy into practice and operates the most comprehensive pretrial drug-testing program in the country. Arrestees are asked to submit to a drug test at arrest, and those testing positive for illegal drugs may be released before trial with the condition that they enter a monitoring or treatment program involving regular drug testing.

Both state and federal criminal justice systems are now debating the merits and drawbacks of establishing similar pretrial testing programs. Among the concerns

Reprinted by permission of Sage Publications from the *Annals of the American Academy of Political & Social Science,* vol. 521 (1992), pp. 112–131.

raised about pretrial drug testing are the utility of the program in minimizing the risk of releasing drug-using defendants by reducing pretrial rearrests and increasing court appearances, the accuracy of the testing procedures, possible constitutional challenges to drug testing at the pretrial stage, and the costs associated with operating a pretrial testing program.

A series of studies funded by the National Institute of Justice and the Bureau of Justice Assistance of the U.S. Department of Justice provides empirical and practical information about the utility of pretrial drug testing. Drawing on these studies, this article discusses the current debates within research and policy on pretrial drug testing. First, it describes the Washington, D.C., pretrial testing program, the longest-running such program in the country, and several studies of that program. Second, it reviews additional research on the use of drug-testing results as a predictive indicator of pretrial misconduct. Third, it relates the experiences and findings of six other jurisdictions that attempted to replicate the District of Columbia program. Finally, it considers the future of pretrial drug testing and whether pretrial testing programs have a place in our national drug policy.

PRETRIAL DRUG TESTING IN WASHINGTON, D.C.

Pretrial drug testing has existed in Washington, D.C., since the 1970s. The early phase of the program referred suspected drug-involved offenders to a local treatment agency for testing, and results were delivered to the courts. But in 1984, this testing program was transferred to the criminal justice system, and the Pretrial Services Agency (PSA) of Washington, D.C., launched an expanded, comprehensive program for all arrestees and released drug-involved offenders.[2] The basis for the new program arose from research that has consistently shown that the most frequent, serious offenders are also the heaviest drug users.[3] Moreover, for many drug-involved offenders, criminal activity appears to rise or decline with level of drug use.[4] In practical terms, the identification of drug-involved offenders and the potential control of their drug use appeared to be a useful approach to managing high-risk defendants at the earliest stage of the criminal justice process.

The pretrial testing program in the District of Columbia has two components: (1) drug testing of arrestees prior to the initial court appearance and release decision,[5] and (2) regular monitoring of drug use through testing as a condition of release. Testing is completed before arraignment in a facility within the courthouse and results are made available to the judge before the initial court appearance. The PSA uses the EMIT (enzyme multiplied immunoassay test) to screen arrestees for five drugs: cocaine; opiates—primarily heroin; phencyclidine (PCP); methadone; and amphetamines. The initial drug test is voluntary, but high compliance is achieved because, before granting nonfinancial release, judges will often order testing of those who refuse. Test results are not used in prosecution or adjudication decisions.

In most state and federal courts, judges may set release conditions to minimize the safety threat posed by high-risk defendants and to ensure appearance at trial. The second component of the Washington, D.C., testing program, drug monitoring during release, provided judges with a new option for handling drug-involved offenders who were thought to pose increased risk if released. Arrestees who test positive for drugs at arrest are placed in a regular drug-testing or treatment program as a condition of release. Defendants must report at least weekly for testing; all tests are recorded in an automated information system. Violations—positive test results or nonappearance for testing—are met with a system of graduated sanctions, including more frequent testing, detention for three to five days, and, in extreme cases, being held in jail until trial. Some judges use performance in the monitoring program in sentencing convicted defendants.

Evaluation of the Washington, D.C., Testing Program

It was hoped that the Washington, D.C., program would provide local criminal justice officials with objective information about drug use. Such information would then be used in pretrial-release decisions as a possible risk factor for assessing defendant suitability for release. Legally, the likelihood of rearrest before trial and failure to appear for scheduled court appearances (FTA) are the primary concerns. District of Columbia officials also hoped that a pretrial monitoring program might help control drug use among released defendants, which in turn might lead to reductions in pretrial misconduct—either rearrest or FTA—in this high-risk group. One comprehensive evaluation and several other analyses examined whether the program was accomplishing these two objectives in its first two years of operation by the D.C. PSA.

Persons who tested positive for drugs at arrest were more likely to be rearrested and miss scheduled court appearances than those who did not test positive for drugs, according to data from the program.[6] Indeed, the risk of rearrest in the early weeks after release was about four times higher for drug users than nonusers, even after taking into account defendant attributes usually associated with pretrial rearrest.[7] Moreover, the results of the drug test at arrest appeared to add significantly to the assessment of pretrial risk, over and above the typically collected information on defendant's employment, prior convictions, and pending case status.[8] In particular, multiple drug use increased the risk of pretrial misconduct.

Thus, in Washington, D.C., drug test results seem to improve a judge's ability to reliably assess defendant risk of pretrial misconduct. But does regular testing reduce rearrest and FTA rates for all released drug users? An evaluation of the monitoring component of the program indicated that about two-thirds of the defendants assigned to drug monitoring during release stayed with the program for at least three tests. These defendants had lower rates of rearrest and FTA than did those who never showed up for testing or who dropped out of the program before the third test.[9] But an experimental evaluation of the effects of the monitoring program, in which eligible defendants were randomly assigned to either regular drug testing, community drug treatment, or a control group, found no differences between the three groups in rearrest or FTA rates.[10] Implementation problems, however, may have compromised the experimental design.

Taken together, evaluations of the Washington, D.C., program indicate that some drug users were better risks than others and that a monitoring program may help to sort out the good and bad risks. A small group of drug users did not comply with the program, and their noncompliance was a strong indicator of their high risk for pretrial rearrest and FTA. In another study of the program, defendants who did not report for their first post-release test had a much greater risk of rearrest and FTA than those who reported for the test.[11] In summary, in the Washington, D.C., program, a large group of released drug users who were regularly tested for drug use had lower than average rearrest and FTA rates, actually similar to those who did not use drugs. It is difficult to determine, however, whether regular testing encouraged good behavior or whether this group of released drug users would have been low risks without the testing program.

Drug Tests and Risk Management

Independent research conducted in Manhattan and in Dade County, Florida, provides additional information on whether drug tests at arrest might improve judges' assessments of defendant risk for pretrial rearrest or FTA if the defendant is released before trial. Pretrial testing programs were not operational at these sites, but both jurisdictions were considering the implementation of testing programs and allowed researchers to gather data on defendants being considered for release, including the results of voluntary drug testing at arrest. Since these were exploratory studies, judges were not informed of the drug test results, and defendants were assured that the results would be used only for research purposes.

At both sites, released defendants who tested positive for illegal drugs had higher rates of pretrial misconduct than did defendants similar in all respects but who had not tested positive. In Manhattan, both pretrial rearrest and FTA rates were higher among those testing positive, especially for those testing positive for more than two drugs.[12] But a separate analysis of the Manhattan data concluded that urine testing was not a feasible policy alternative because assessment of individual risk of failure to appear was not measurably improved by drug test results.[13] In Dade County, drug test results were statistically related to the risk of pretrial rearrest, especially rearrest for serious crimes, but not to FTA.[14] Some drug-specific results—for example, that PCP use affected rearrest, but not FTA, in Manhattan—also existed, but no clear patterns emerged in the two jurisdictions.[15]

The issue of whether drug test information is a strong indicator of pretrial misconduct or whether the statistical relationship is substantively significant is addressed in all reports, albeit using different approaches that are difficult to compare. But other defendant characteristics used in predicting pretrial misconduct, such as community ties, have rarely, if ever, been held to this rigorous standard to justify their predictive utility in judges' pretrial-release decisions. In any event, a statistical relationship between drug test results and pretrial misconduct is only one of many factors involved in debates about the merits of a pretrial drug-testing program in a particular jurisdiction.

In summary, drug test results appear to improve the classification of defendants according to the risk of pretrial misconduct in three sites—Washington, D.C., Manhattan, and Dade County—but the improvement by drug test results of individual predictions of risk is not necessarily guaranteed. In illustrating this concept, the Manhattan study used the example of releasing 100 defendants testing positive for PCP and 100 defendants who tested negative for PCP but who were similar to the first group on all other characteristics. The analysis showed that 37 would be expected to be rearrested in the first group, but among the defendants who had not used PCP, only 25 would be expected to be rearrested.[16] Choosing which PCP user would be rearrested is a much more difficult task, and determining whether drug test results would in fact improve such individual predictions requires a different type of analysis from that used in existing studies.[17]

REPLICATIONS OF THE WASHINGTON, D.C., PROGRAM

In an effort to gain further insight into whether pretrial testing programs would be useful in other jurisdictions, the Bureau of Justice Assistance funded six sites to implement programs modeled on the one in the District of Columbia. The six jurisdictions were Prince George's County, Maryland, a suburb of Washington, D.C.; Milwaukee County, Wisconsin; Multnomah County, Oregon, the county that includes Portland; Pima and Maricopa counties, Arizona, the counties that include, respectively, Tucson and Phoenix; and New Castle County, Delaware, which includes Wilmington.[18] The Bureau of Justice Assistance funded evaluations of four of these programs, and the National Institute of Justice funded evaluations of the two programs in Arizona. The evaluations were to address the two questions raised in the previous studies: (1) are the results of drug tests at arrest significantly related to pretrial rearrest and FTA? and (2) does regular drug testing during pretrial release reduce pretrial rearrest and FTA among released drug users?[19]

Implementing Pretrial Drug Testing

The six demonstration sites experienced varying levels of difficulty in the implementation of a pretrial drug-testing program, and these difficulties had implications for the evaluations. In two sites—Multnomah County and New Castle County—the severity of the problems meant that a reasonable evaluation of the program could not be conducted during the time allotted for the evaluation by the funding agency. Table 1 summarizes both the implementation problems and the results of the evaluations. Among the most serious implementation problems occurring at the six sites were

- inability of two sites to test the majority of defendants at arrest for illegal drug use;
- the lack of support among pretrial staff in recommending eligible defendants—usually those with positive test results—for the monitoring program;
- the failure to provide the arraignment judge with initial drug test results before the hearing;
- the arraignment judge's low rate of referring eligible defendants to the monitoring program;
- high rates of noncompliance—not showing up—for testing among the released defendants in the monitoring program;
- the inability of some sites to randomly assign defendants to experiment, or monitoring, and control groups without bias;

TABLE 1 Implementation Issues and Evaluation Results for the Six Demonstration Sites

Program Site	*Implementation Issues*	*Evaluation Results*
Prince George's County, Maryland	40 percent of the defendants eligible for monitoring program were assigned cash bail. Pretrial staff did not recommend the monitoring program. Test results were not reported to the arraignment judge. Testing center was inconveniently located. There was a high no-show rate for monitoring program. Only 17 percent of eligible defendants were referred to program. Sanctions were not applied as proposed. The information system for tracking defendants was delayed.	Drug test results did not improve assessment of risk of pretrial rearrest or FTA. Monitoring program did not reduce rearrests or FTAs.
Pima County, Arizona	There were low rates of rearrest or FTA during evaluation. There was a very small number of cases for monitoring experiment ($n = 222$). 30 percent of the monitored group was never tested.	Drug test results did not improve assessment of risk of pretrial rearrest or FTA. Monitoring program reduced rearrests, especially for drug crimes, but not FTAs.
Maricopa County, Arizona	Target sample ($n = 500$) of tested arrestees could not be achieved; final sample = 284. Randomization into experiment was faulty. Number of cases in experiment was small ($n = 234$). 30 percent of the monitored group was never tested.	Drug test results improved assessment of risk of pretrial rearrest, but not of FTA. Monitoring program modestly reduced FTAs, but not rearrests.
Milwaukee County, Wisconsin	50 percent of arrestees were not tested. Only 19 percent of eligible defendants were referred to monitoring program. There was weak support for program among pretrial staff and judges. Sanctions were not applied as proposed.	Drug test results improved assessment of risk of FTA, but not of rearrests. The monitoring program did not reduce rearrests or FTAs.

Continued

TABLE 1 Implementation Issues and Evaluation Results for the Six Demonstration Sites *Continued*

Program Site	*Implementation Issues*	*Evaluation Results*
Multnomah County, Oregon	Only 30–50 percent of arrestees were tested. There was a low program referral rate—10–40 percent of eligible defendants—by judges. The structure of pretrial release system impeded coordination. 54 percent of the monitored group was never tested. The testing center was inconveniently located. The information system did not permit adequate tracking of released defendants.	Insufficient data were collected to assess the effect of drug test results on pretrial misconduct. Evaluation of the monitoring experiment was unreliable because of implementation problems.
New Castle County, Delaware	Lengthy delays were encountered in logistical planning for the program. Initial lack of community support for the program existed. There was a lack of support from pretrial services staff for implementing program. The information system did not permit adequate collection of data for evaluation. There was lack of support among judiciary. Funding was terminated by the federal agency before evaluation.	No data were collected to assess the effect of drug test results on pretrial misconduct. There were insufficient cases in monitoring program for evaluation.

Sources: Stefan Kapsch and Louis Sweeny, "Multnomah County DMDA Program Evaluation Final Report" (Final report, Bureau of Justice Assistance, U.S. Department of Justice, 1990); idem, "Multnomah County DMDA Project Implementation Report" (Final report, Bureau of Justice Assistance, U.S. Department of Justice, 1990); John S. Goldkamp, Peter Jones, and Michael Gottfredson, "Measuring the Impact of Drug Testing at the Pretrial Release Stage: Pretrial Drug Testing in Milwaukee County, New Castle County and Prince George's County, Preliminary Report" (Report, Bureau of Justice Assistance, U.S. Department of Justice, 1989); idem, "Measuring the Impact of Drug Testing at the Pretrial Release Stage: Experimental Findings from Prince George's County and Milwaukee County, Final Report" (Report, Bureau of Justice Assistance, U.S. Department of Justice, 1990); Michael Gottfredson, Chester L. Britt, and John Goldkamp, "Evaluation of Arizona Pretrial Services Drug Testing Programs, Final Report" (Report, National Institute of Justice, U.S. Department of Justice, 1990); *Pretrial Reporter* (Oct., Dec. 1988; Feb., Apr., June, Aug. 1989; Feb. 1991).

- difficulty in maintaining current information about test results, sanctions pending, and so forth for defendants in the monitoring program; and
- the lack of judicial support for the sanctioning plan, a lack that led to high violation rates—no-shows and positive tests—among defendants in the testing program.

Some sites were able to correct most of these problems as the programs continued—in some cases, after the evaluation was completed—but the quality of the data collected during the early phase of the programs was clearly affected by the implementation problems. The impact of these problems on the evaluation results will be discussed shortly. In general, the practical problems of implementing pretrial drug-testing programs were related to support for the program within the local criminal justice community and the cognizant agencies and were also related to the logistical capability of the jurisdiction to implement the program. Legal considerations arose in the planning stage at several demonstration sites, although none seriously impeded the implementation of the programs.

Implementation of a pretrial testing program modeled after the Washington, D.C., program demands the involvement of all agencies within a local criminal justice system. The pretrial services agency often must coordinate its efforts with the police or sheriff's department responsible for detaining the arrestees until testing can take place. In Milwaukee, implementation of the program was delayed until the police department consented to drug testing of arrestees being held until arraignment. In Prince George's County, bail magistrates at local police stations released 40 percent of eligible defendants on cash bail with no other release conditions before testing could occur. These defendants were not considered for release supervised by the pretrial services agency, hence they were not placed in the monitoring program.

Other problems surfaced when private agencies with important roles in the pretrial release system were involved in the demonstration program. Initially in Maricopa County, few arrestees agreed to be tested; it was later determined that a private agency, the Treatment Assessment Screening Center, not previously involved with interviewing arrestees, was not correctly explaining the nature of the pretrial testing program. In Multnomah County, one private agency interviewed and tested arrestees before the release hearing, and three other agencies—public and private—supervised released defendants. Difficulties in coordinating the efforts of these organizations led to considerable interagency diversity in the implementation of the monitoring program and to problems in tracking defendants during release.

Support from the judiciary was particularly crucial to the implementation of the program. Judges were supposed to use drug test results in determining pretrial release, assigning eligible drug users to the drug-monitoring program, and imposing sanctions on defendants who failed to comply with the monitoring program. Although the chief judge or magistrate at all demonstration sites had indicated support for the program before federal funding, individual judges at some sites apparently did not support the program's goals. Thus, at some sites, relatively few eligible defendants were referred to the monitoring program, and sanctions for program violations were not consistently carried out. In Multnomah County, when it became apparent that judges were not using the program as a release condition, the chief judge issued a court order directing referral to the monitoring program as a condition of release for eligible defendants, and program referral rates improved dramatically.

Logistical problems in implementing the pretrial testing program at a few sites proved as serious as did system support problems. Among the most common problems were (1) integrating the program within an existing structure of pretrial-release procedures; (2) creating a computerized information system that would allow the efficient tracking of defendants and the collection of data for the evaluation; (3) locating a testing facility that was accessible to defendants during release; (4) informing new and rotating pretrial personnel and judges about the testing program and its operations; and (5) scheduling court hearings for defendants who did not comply with the testing program. Solving logistical issues surrounding the day-to-day operation of a pretrial drug-testing program requires the involvement of many different agencies, whose actions must be coordinated.

At most sites, one or more of these implementation problems seriously affected the collection of the data necessary for an adequate evaluation of the pretrial testing program. The interpretation of these data is addressed in the next section. But in New Castle County, the problems encountered in commencing and managing the program were so profound that the program was never fully implemented and federal funds for program operation and evaluation were terminated.[20] In Multnomah County, the program eventually overcame most of the implementation problems, but data for one portion of the evaluation were never collected and faulty procedures during the experimental phase of the evaluation raise serious doubts about the available data.

Results of the Evaluations

In four of the six sites, the evaluators were able to collect the necessary data for an assessment of whether the program was meeting its stated goals. Recall that the two questions at issue were (1) whether drug abuse detection—using urinalysis—at arrest might provide additional information about the risk of pretrial rearrest or FTA for released defendants, and (2) whether drug use monitoring—regular urinalysis—during release might reduce pretrial rearrest and FTA.

At two of these four sites, defendants who tested positive for illegal drugs at arrest were at significantly greater risk of pretrial rearrest or FTA, after taking into account factors usually considered by the arraignment judge. In Milwaukee and Maricopa counties, positive drug test results increased risk of FTA and rearrest, respectively. As to the experimental evaluation of the drug-monitoring component, again, two of the four sites—Pima and Maricopa counties—concluded that the program significantly reduced, respectively, rearrest and FTA for released drug-involved defendants. The impact of the program was not large at these sites, however, and the evaluators concluded that the program had only modest effects on pretrial misconduct.[21]

Interpreting these evaluation results is difficult, and caution is urged for a number of reasons. First, the implementation problems discussed earlier reduced the quality of the evaluation data at several sites. Consider those sites that tested only half of the eligible defendants at arrest. If, for example, the defendants who refused the test were at greater risk of pretrial misconduct than those who agreed to be tested, then the evaluation results were based on a relatively low-risk group and it is not surprising that the drug tests results did not add to the risk assessment of pretrial misconduct. As another example, for sites that had low referral rates of eligible defendants to the monitoring program—referred defendants may have differed in important respects from defendants not referred—the experimental evaluation cannot effectively assess the program's impact on pretrial misconduct for the total eligible population. Also, for sites where many monitored defendants did not appear for testing or were not sanctioned for violations, the evaluation is not of the program that was planned.

Second, and equally important, were serious anomalies in some of the statistical analyses, which make valid interpretation of the results highly questionable.[22] Small sample sizes, especially for the experimental evaluation, also hindered convincing analyses at several of the sites. Moreover, it is difficult to compare the evaluation results across sites because of different analytic procedures, especially the measurement of drug test results. For example, the number of drugs for which an arrestee tested positive increased the likelihood of pretrial rearrest and FTA in the earlier studies in Washington, D.C., and Manhattan. Unfortunately, the evaluations of the demonstration sites did not always include this measure.

In summary, the serious implementation problems encountered at some demonstration sites coupled with analytic problems in the evaluation analyses complicate our understanding of whether pretrial testing programs might be beneficial for release decisions or as a supervisory tool in those sites. A review of the evaluation results published in the *Pretrial Reporter* concluded that "the question of pretrial drug testing should not be considered answered," largely because of the implementation issues.[23] That review also suggested that a more current evaluation of existing programs be undertaken now since many of the problems have been overcome and some sites report clear benefits of the programs.

ASSESSING THE UTILITY OF PRETRIAL DRUG TESTING

Studies from nine jurisdictions—Washington, D.C.; Dade County; Manhattan; and the six demonstration sites—have examined the practical utility of pretrial drug testing for release decisions or pretrial supervision of drug-involved offenders. At five of the seven sites that collected data on release decisions, drug test results provided additional information about the defendant's potential risk of rearrest or FTA but not always about both types of misconduct. Thus drug tests at arrest are likely to be useful in pretrial-release decision making, but drug test results may not be equally predictive of rearrest and FTA in all jurisdictions.

The drug-monitoring program for released drug users, however, reduced rearrests or FTAs—and these were modest effects—in only two of the five jurisdictions that implemented the monitoring experiment, in Pima and Maricopa counties. Even though regular drug testing during release may not decrease pretrial misconduct for all released drug users, some types of drug-involved offenders appear to benefit. At three demonstration sites—Pima County, Prince George's County, and Milwaukee—a reasonable minority of released drug users consistently tested negative while in the monitoring program: one-third or more of those assigned to regular drug testing during pretrial release had no positive tests.[24] This group of drug-involved offenders may have been infrequent drug users, or the enforced nature of the program may have deterred them from illegal drug use while awaiting trial.

Other data suggest that compliance with drug-monitoring programs may serve as an early-warning system for pretrial misconduct among released drug users. This signaling effect, described by the evaluators of the Washington, D.C., program,[25] appeared to have some support from three sites that reported detailed data on defendant performance in the monitoring program (see Tables 2 and 3). For example, in Prince George's County, defendants who missed less than 25 percent of their tests were much less likely to be rearrested than those who missed more than 75 percent of their tests; 4.6 percent of the former compared to 14.5 percent of the latter were rearrested. A similar pattern was found in Milwaukee County (see Table 2). In Pima County, defendants with few positive tests during monitoring were less likely to be rearrested or to fail to appear than defendants with more positive tests (see Table 3).[26] Thus a pretrial drug-monitoring program can be a useful strategy for supervising some offenders. Pretrial drug testing may reduce drug use, and perhaps related criminal activity, for one group of released drug-involved offenders, and it provides the courts with information on high-risk releasees who are not complying with the monitoring program.

The pretrial drug-testing program in the District of Columbia faced some of the problems that the demonstration sites experienced, but these problems were eventually resolved. When judges and hearing commissioners in Washington, D.C., were interviewed about their opinions of the program, most responded that they used the

TABLE 2 Defendant Behavior in Drug-Monitoring Programs, Pretrial Rearrests, and Failure to Appear

Site	*Percentage of Scheduled Drug Tests Missed by Defendants*	N	*Percentage of Defendants Who Were Rearrested*	*Percentage of Defendants Who Failed to Appear*
Prince George's County, Maryland	0–25	43	4.6	2.3
	26–50	80	11.2	35.0
	51–75	87	13.8	32.2
	76+	69	14.5	27.5
Milwaukee County, Wisconsin	0–25	132	10.6	8.3*
	26–50	62	21.3	19.4
	51–75	71	23.9	45.1
	76+	67	22.3	56.7

Sources: Adapted from data presented in John S. Goldkamp, Peter Jones, and Michael Gottfredson, "Measuring the Impact of Drug Testing at the Pretrial Release Stage: Experimental Findings from Prince George's County and Milwaukee County, Final Report" (Report, Bureau of Justice Assistance, U.S. Department of Justice, Nov. 1990), pp. 92, 114, tabs. 5.15, 6.9.

*The rates of failure to appear (FTA) for Milwaukee include failure to appear for scheduled drug tests, which complicates the interpretation of whether noncompliance with the drug-testing program—here, percentage of scheduled drug tests missed by defendants—was related to other FTAs.

TABLE 3 Pretrial Misconduct and Defendant Behavior in the Drug-Monitoring Program, Pima County, Arizona

Positive Test Results	N	*Percentage of Defendants with Rearrests or FTAs*
None	45	8.8
1–2	37	10.8
3–9	35	28.6
10 or more	6	—*
Missed all tests	30	50.0
Total	153	15.0

Source: Tabulated from data presented in Michael Gottfredson, Chester L. Britt, and John Goldkamp, "Evaluation of Arizona Pretrial Services Drug Testing Programs, Final Report," (Report, National Institute of Justice, U.S. Department of Justice, 1990), pp. 41–42.
Note: Pretrial misconduct is measured by defendant's positive test results; defendant behavior is measured by number of rearrests or FTAs.
*Too few cases to compute a meaningful percentage.

information generated by the testing program a great deal and that it represented a substantial improvement over previous practices.[27] Clearly, one key to the success of the pretrial testing program in Washington, D.C., has been the willingness of the judges to impose sanctions on defendants who failed to comply with the monitoring program.[28] Judges in the District of Columbia believe that accurate information about drug use is vital to their decisions regarding pretrial release and supervision of released drug-involved offenders. The Washington, D.C., program was recently expanded to include testing of juvenile offenders.

In some sense, an overall assessment of the usefulness of both components of a pretrial testing program is akin to interpreting a picture of a partially filled glass of water: is the glass half empty or half full? Opponents of pretrial drug testing view the inconsistent evaluation results as primarily showing small benefits of drug testing at the pretrial stage and propose that decisions about such programs be based on issues of cost and convenience. Proponents of the program minimize the logistical and financial issues and point to the utility of the program in raising community awareness about illegal drug use and providing much-needed alternatives, albeit incomplete ones, to assist in the control of drug-involved offenders. Researchers have focused on rearrest and FTA as evaluation outcomes because of the statutory requirements that underlie judges' pretrial-release decisions. But there may be other practical, nonlegal benefits, including the ability to detect drug abusers and send them to treatment.

THE FUTURE OF PRETRIAL DRUG TESTING

Pretrial drug-testing programs present many challenges to jurisdictions considering the implementation of drug testing for detection and supervision of drug-involved offenders at the pretrial stage. At least two obstacles to such programs have largely disappeared, however: concerns about the accuracy of drug tests and legal issues. Despite some claims to the contrary, immunoassay urinalysis technologies are widely regarded as very accurate,[29] and the accuracy of the most commonly used test in criminal justice operations, EMIT, has been upheld in numerous court decisions.[30]

A recent study by the National Institute of Justice evaluated the accuracy of four commonly used drug-testing urinalysis technologies.[31] The study concluded that immunoassays are much more accurate than thin-layer chromatography, which was commonly used in the 1970s. Drug testing using immunoassay methods correctly identifies 98 to 99 percent of negative urine specimens—that is, it yields few false positive results—and correctly identifies about 80 percent of positive urine specimens, that is, it yields a moderate number of false negative results. The study recommended that positive results be confirmed by a highly accurate method if the test result is contested by the defendant and could be used for punitive action.

Several legal issues concerning the constitutionality of pretrial drug testing were discussed at length at most of the demonstration sites. Among the issues raised was whether pretrial drug tests violate Fourth Amendment protections against unreasonable searches, Fifth Amendment guarantees against self-incrimination, or Fourteenth Amendment protections pertaining to equal treatment and substantive and procedural due process requirements.[32] Two recent legal analyses of the existing case law disagree as to whether pretrial drug testing will withstand these constitutional challenges.[33]

Nonetheless, the only formal legal challenge to pretrial drug testing occurred in Washington, D.C., in *Berry v. District of Columbia.*[34] In general, the U.S. Court of Appeals for the District of Columbia upheld the constitutionality of the monitoring program but sent the case back to the lower court for more specific information about its operation before a final ruling. In 1990, the case was dismissed, basically for lack of response by the plaintiff to the appeal court's ruling. The constitutionality of voluntary testing of arrestees before arraignment had not come before the courts in the eight years of the program's operation in Washington, D.C. Hence, as of this writing, there are no pending legal challenges to pretrial drug testing in either state or federal courts.

More serious potential obstacles to pretrial drug testing are the problems that can arise in the actual implementation of a program. As discussed earlier, these problems can spell the difference between a successful program and an unsuccessful one. Internal and external support for pretrial testing is critical to its effectiveness. The introduction of a new operation into an existing system of procedures often meets with resistance from staff, and building support among the staff involved in the implementation of a pretrial testing program is essential to its success. Moreover, in the jurisdictions that have experimented with pretrial drug testing, the judiciary significantly influenced the program's operation. Invariably, lack of support by the judiciary impeded any successful implementation of the program. But, at the same time, judges have individual philosophies about the use of drug test results, and jurisdictions should expect judges to differ in their application of the testing program.

The successful operation of pretrial drug-testing programs is also dependent on other local circumstances. Jurisdictions vary widely in patterns of criminal behavior and drug use, which may affect how such programs are best utilized. For example, jurisdictions with small criminal caseloads, such as New Castle County, Delaware, may not benefit as much from program implementation as would a jurisdiction with a greater caseload. As another example, Pima County experienced very low rates of pretrial misconduct during the evaluation phase of the project. If such low rates are typical, then a large-scale drug-monitoring program may not be able to improve behavior of defendants on release sufficiently to justify its costs. The drug detection component of the program might be useful, however, for tracking drug use in the offender population, identifying drug-involved offenders, and encouraging drug-positive arrestees to seek treatment.

Conversely, jurisdictions with high rates of drug use in the arrestee population may find that initial drug test results cannot improve release decisions significantly since the vast majority of arrestees will test positive for drug use. In this situation, the screening component might be used to identify users of multiple drugs—users at highest risk if released—and a drug-monitoring program might help the supervising agency differentiate those drug users who are likely to engage in pretrial misconduct while on release from those who are good risks. Moreover, as some of the demonstration programs showed, 30 to 40 percent of those who tested positive for illegal drugs at arrest had no positive tests while in a drug-monitoring program. For many drug-involved offenders, reductions in drug use may lead to reductions in criminal activity. More research is needed on identifying those drug-involved offenders who might benefit from drug monitoring.

Costs associated with pretrial drug-testing programs also vary with local circumstances. Particular policy and procedural decisions about the program, such as staffing patterns, choice of testing equipment, number of drugs being tested for, and size of target population, can substantially affect operating costs. For example, these types of factors resulted in more than a threefold difference in estimated, first-year costs for operating both components of a pretrial testing program in two jurisdictions with the same annual arrestee population.[35]

Policymakers and criminal justice officials must weigh all of these considerations—expected utility, implementation issues, local circumstances, value to the community, and costs—in making decisions about the implementation of pretrial drug-testing programs. Information gained from pretrial testing can also be useful for assessing drug treatment needs, tracking local changes in drug use preferences, and documenting need for state and federal assistance for drug enforcement and treatment programs. Pretrial testing, both at arrest and during release, is also one component of the comprehensive drug-testing program recommended by the President's Office of National Drug Control Policy for state and local criminal justice agencies.

As a first step, the testing of arrestees can provide valuable information about the nature and extent of drug use among the offender population, which can be used in planning both comprehensive drug-testing and treatment programs. This type of approach would probably be a suitable initial stage for most jurisdictions and could be modeled after the National Institute of Justice's Drug Use Forecasting program.[36] Drug testing as a supervision tool, whether during pretrial release or as a post-conviction option, requires considerable additional planning, and favorable outcomes may require a year or more of cooperative effort. Examining and understanding the problem is always much easier than devising solutions to it.

CONCLUSION

At the present time, pretrial drug-testing programs are under considerable scrutiny. As more jurisdictions implement such programs, more will be learned about how and under what circumstances pretrial testing can improve the management of drug-involved defendants in the community. In the meantime, evaluations are needed of established programs, even though these programs may have been studied in the past. A 1990 nationwide survey of state and local pretrial service programs found that 72 programs were conducting pretrial testing at some level, usually selectively as a condition of release.[37] Little is known about these programs, however.

Many criminal justice officials are uncertain about whether pretrial drug testing would be useful for their jurisdiction. But much of this uncertainty is based on misinformation or lack of information about the operations, practicality, and utility of pretrial drug testing. It is hoped that this article has illuminated some of these issues. Nevertheless, it is also apparent that pretrial drug testing will fail when local criminal justice officials have not adequately planned for its implementation. Officials involved in ongoing pretrial testing programs and other experts can provide practical information and technical assistance in designing programs.

Pretrial drug-testing programs can be adapted to local circumstances and can play an important role in the detection and supervision of drug-involved offenders. The utility of specific components of pretrial testing may vary from one jurisdiction to another. What works in one jurisdiction may not work elsewhere. Moreover, these programs do not necessarily lead to a Pandora's box of problems and difficulties, although they do require careful planning and continual attention. With strong internal and external support, pretrial testing programs can form a key element in a jurisdiction's criminal justice policy on drug abuse and drug-related crime.

NOTES

*NOTE: Points of view expressed in this article do not necessarily represent the official position of the National Institute of Justice or the U.S. Department of Justice.

**Dr. Visher conducts research on issues related to criminal justice policy and provides advice and support to Institute management on research issues. Her recent research interests include drug testing, the relationship between illegal drug use and criminal behavior, violent offending, and criminal careers.

1. U.S., Office of National Drug Control Policy, *National Drug Control Strategy* (Washington, DC: Government Printing Office, 1989), p. 26.

2. John Carver, "Drugs and Crime: Controlling Use and Reducing Risk through Testing," *NIJ Reports* no. 199 (Sept.–Oct. 1986).

3. Jan Chaiken and Marcia Chaiken, *Varieties of Criminal Behavior* (Santa Monica, CA: RAND, 1982); Eric Wish and Bruce Johnson, "The Impact of Substance Abuse on Criminal Careers," in *Criminal Careers and "Career Criminals,"* vol. 2, ed. A. Blumstein et al. (Washington, DC: National Academy Press, 1986).

4. J. C. Ball et al., "The Criminality of Heroin Addicts When Addicted and When off Opiates," in *The Drugs-Crime Connection,* ed. J. A. Inciardi (Beverly Hills, CA: Sage, 1981); Bruce Johnson et al., *Taking Care of Business: The Economics of Crime by Heroin Users* (Lexington, MA:

Lexington Books, 1985); Ko-lin Chin and Jeffrey Fagan, "Impact of Crack on Drug and Crime Involvement" (Paper delivered at the annual meeting of the American Society of Criminology, Baltimore, MD, 1990).

5. Arrestees who are charged with minor crimes—for example, misdemeanors and traffic violations—are often released at a district police station. Since they are not brought to the central booking facility, they are not tested for drug use.

6. Mary Toborg et al., *Assessment of Pretrial Urine Testing in the District of Columbia* (Washington, DC: National Institute of Justice, 1989); Christy A. Visher and Richard L. Linster, "A Survival Model of Pretrial Failure," *Journal of Quantitative Criminology,* 6:153-84 (1990).

7. Visher and Linster, "Survival Model of Pretrial Failure," p. 167, tab. 5.

8. Toborg et al., "Assessment of Pretrial Urine Testing," p. 10.

9. Ibid., pp. 13-14. Surprisingly, this finding was independent of whether those who showed up for testing were positive or negative for illegal drugs.

10. Ibid., pp. 23-24. This type of evaluation is the strongest statistical test of whether regular drug testing during release might reduce pretrial misconduct. Such experiments, however, are difficult to carry out successfully in an actual criminal justice environment, and implementation problems usually occur.

11. Christy A. Visher, "Using Drug Testing to Identify High-Risk Defendants on Release: A Study in the District of Columbia," *Journal of Criminal Justice,* 18:321-32 (1990).

12. Douglas A. Smith, Eric Wish, and G. Roger Jarjoura, "Drug Use and Pretrial Misconduct in New York City," *Journal of Quantitative Criminology,* 5:101-26 (1989); Eric Wish, Mary Cuadrado, and Stephen Magura, "Drug Abuse as a Predictor of Pretrial Failure-to-Appear in Arrestees in Manhattan" (Final report submitted to the National Institute of Justice, U.S. Department of Justice, 1988).

13. S. Belenko and I. Mara-Drita, "Drug Use and Pretrial Misconduct: The Utility of Prearraignment Drug Tests as a Predictor of Failure-to-Appear" (Manuscript, Criminal Justice Agency, New York, 1988). These results were based on a slightly different sample and different analytic methods from those of the analysis reported in the published study of the Manhattan data by Smith, Wish, and Jarjoura, "Drug Use and Pretrial Misconduct in New York City." The study by Belenko and Mara-Drita analyzed only failure to appear and did not adjust for sample-selection effects or time at risk.

14. John Goldkamp, Michael Gottfredson, and Doris Weiland, "Pretrial Drug Testing and Defendant Risk," *Journal of Criminal Law and Criminology,* 81:585-652 (Fall 1990). The Dade County study appears to be seriously flawed, however. It is difficult to interpret the results because of the simultaneous inclusion of four measures of the drug test results—namely, positive for marijuana, positive for cocaine, positive for either, and positive for both—in the logit analysis. Ibid., p. 624 (tab. 7), p. 626 (tab. 9). These measures are likely to be highly correlated—one did not pass tolerance—which would cause unstable and unreliable coefficient estimates. These problems raise serious doubts about substantive conclusions based on this analysis.

15. Comparisons of empirical studies carried out by different investigators in different jurisdictions are inherently difficult. These two studies had many important differences: they were carried out in different years—1984 in Manhattan and 1987 in Dade County—during a period when illegal drug use was experiencing rapid change; they measured variables differently, especially the drug test results; and they used dissimilar analytic techniques. The overall rearrest rate in Manhattan was 25 percent compared to 15 percent in Dade County; the FTA rates were 33 percent and 9 percent in Manhattan and Dade County, respectively—these differences are probably related, in part, to the length of the follow-up period in the two studies. Opiate use, a characteristic of serious drug use and criminal behavior, was practically nonexistent in Dade County, whereas 21 percent of the Manhattan sample tested positive for opiates. Finally, 56 percent tested positive for drugs in general in Manhattan compared to 80 percent in Dade County.

16. Smith, Wish, and Jarjoura, "Drug Use and Pretrial Misconduct in New York City," p. 119.
17. The statistical determination of whether specific information predicts individual criminal behavior is a two-step analytic task. Initially, a prediction instrument using the information is developed, and then a second analysis, with a different sample or with the same sample at a later point in time, is used to confirm the instrument's accuracy. The analyses reported here are only the first step in this process. For further discussion, see, for example, Don Gottfredson and Michael Tonry, eds., *Prediction and Classification: Criminal Justice Decision Making* (Chicago: University of Chicago Press, 1987), esp. pp. 21-52, 201-48.
18. The federal court system also implemented a demonstration pretrial testing program in several sites without the monitoring component, but an evaluation of its effectiveness was not conducted. See U.S., Administrative Office of the United States Courts, *The Demonstration Program of Mandatory Drug Testing of Criminal Defendants* (submitted to the U.S. Congress, 1991).
19. The implementation issues and evaluation results of the six sites are discussed in a series of reports to the funding agencies: Stefan Kapsch and Louis Sweeny, "Multnomah County DMDA Program Evaluation Final Report" (Final report, Bureau of Justice Assistance, U.S. Department of Justice, 1990); idem, "Multnomah County DMDA Project Implementation Report" (Final report, Bureau of Justice Assistance, U.S. Department of Justice, 1990); John S. Goldkamp, Peter Jones, and Michael Gottfredson, "Measuring the Impact of Drug Testing at the Pretrial Release Stage: Pretrial Drug Testing in Milwaukee County, New Castle County and Prince George's County, Preliminary Report" (Report, Bureau of Justice Assistance, U.S. Department of Justice, 1989); idem, "Measuring the Impact of Drug Testing at the Pretrial Release Stage: Experimental Findings from Prince George's County and Milwaukee County, Final Report" (Report, Bureau of Justice Assistance, U.S. Department of Justice, Nov. 1990); Michael Gottfredson, Chester L. Britt, and John Goldkamp, "Evaluation of Arizona Pretrial Services Drug Testing Programs, Final Report" (Report, National Institute of Justice, U.S. Department of Justice, 1990). Additional reports on the pretrial demonstration programs are available in seven issues of the *Pretrial Reporter,* the newsletter of the National Association of Pretrial Services Agencies (Oct., Dec. 1988; Feb., Apr., June, Aug. 1989; Feb. 1991).
20. Goldkamp, Jones, and Gottfredson, "Measuring the Impact of Drug Testing at the Pretrial Release Stage: Pretrial Drug Testing," pp. 81-96.
21. In the Pima County experiment, 4 percent of the drug-monitored group was rearrested compared to 12 percent of the control group ($p = .06$). In the Maricopa County experiment, the drug-monitored group had a 29 percent FTA rate whereas the control group had a 39 percent FTA rate ($p = .11$). Sample sizes in both analyses were small, which reduced the likelihood of finding large statistically significant differences between the groups.
22. In particular, the analyses of the release decisions in Prince George's County and Milwaukee (Goldkamp, Jones, and Gottfredson, "Measuring the Impact of Drug Testing at the Pretrial Release Stage: Experimental Findings," p. 27, tabs. 2.7 and 2.8) suffer from the problems raised earlier about the Dade County study (Goldkamp, Gottfredson, and Weiland, "Pretrial Drug Testing and Defendant Risk," n. 12). The simultaneous inclusion of multiple measures of drug test results—namely, positive for any drug, positive for cocaine, and number or positive test results—in the multivariate analysis confounds any substantive interpretation of the results.
23. National Association of Pretrial Services Agencies, "Pretrial Drug Testing: A Review of Three Evaluations," *Pretrial Reporter,* Feb. 1991, p. iv.
24. Specifically, in Pima County, 29 percent of the defendants in the monitoring program had no positive tests during monitoring, in Prince George's County 36 percent had no positive tests, and in Milwaukee 32 percent had no positive tests. Similar data from Maricopa County and Washington, D.C., are not presented in available sources.
25. Toborg et al., *Assessment of Pretrial Urine Testing,* pp. 12-16.

26. Data from Prince George's County and Milwaukee on positive test results and pretrial misconduct are difficult to interpret because of analytic problems. The analysis unfortunately combined defendants who had no positive tests with those who missed all tests, the latter being a group likely to comprise drug users. Thus the reported high FTA rates for those with no positive tests in Prince George's County and Milwaukee are not surprising since many of the defendants in that group had missed all tests. See Goldkamp, Jones, and Gottfredson, "Measuring the Impact of Drug Testing at the Pretrial Release Stage: Experimental Findings," p. 92 (tab. 5.15), p. 114 (tab. 6.9).
27. Mary A. Toborg and John P. Bellassai, "Assessment of Pretrial Urine Testing in the District of Columbia: The Views of Judicial Officers" (Final report, National Institute of Justice, U.S. Department of Justice, 1988), pp. 4, 10.
28. Ibid., pp. 5-9.
29. See, for example, Kenneth Davis and Richard Hawks, *Urine Testing for Drugs of Abuse,* Research Monograph no. 73 (Rockville, MD: National Institute on Drug Abuse, 1973); David Hoyt et al., "Drug Testing in the Workplace—Are Methods Legally Defensible?" *Journal of the American Medical Association,* 258:504-9 (July 1987).
30. See the review of drug-testing case law in U.S., Department of Justice, Bureau of Justice Assistance, *American Probation and Parole Association's Drug Testing Guidelines and Practices for Adult Probation and Parole Agencies* (Washington, DC: Bureau of Justice Assistance, 1991), pp. 87-108.
31. Christy Visher and Karen McFadden, *A Comparison of Urinalysis Technologies for Drug Testing in Criminal Justice,* National Institute of Justice Research in Action (Washington, DC: Department of Justice, National Institute of Justice, June 1991); Christy Visher, *A Comparison of Urinalysis Technologies for Drug Testing in Criminal Justice* (Washington, DC: Department of Justice, National Institute of Justice, 1991).
32. National Association of Pretrial Services Agencies, "Pretrial Drug Testing in Six Jurisdictions: Legal Issues in Pretrial Urinalysis," *Pretrial Reporter,* June 1989, pp. i-iv.
33. Cathryn Jo Rosen and John S. Goldkamp, "The Constitutionality of Drug Testing at the Bail Stage," *Journal of Criminal Law and Criminology,* 80:114-76 (1989); Reggie B. Walton, Gary J. Peters, and J. Anthony Towns, "Pretrial Drug Testing—An Essential Component of the National Drug Control Strategy," *Brigham Young University Law Journal,* in press.
34. *Berry v. District of Columbia,* 833 F.2d 1031, 1034-36 (D.C. Cir. 1987).
35. U.S., Department of Justice, Bureau of Justice Assistance, *Estimating the Costs of Drug Testing for a Pretrial Services Program* (Washington, DC: Bureau of Justice Assistance, 1989), p. 17.
36. The Drug Use Forecasting program obtains voluntary and anonymous urine specimens and interviews from a sample of arrestees in 24 cities each quarter. For more information about the program, see Joyce Ann O'Neil and Virginia Baldau, *Drug Use Forecasting: 1990 Annual Report* (Washington, DC: Department of Justice, National Institute of Justice, 1991).
37. Discussed in Walton, Peters, and Towns, "Pretrial Drug Testing."

8

Is a Ban on Plea Bargaining an Ethical Abuse of Discretion? A Bronx County, New York Case Study

Roland Acevedo*

INTRODUCTION

Plea bargaining[1] is an essential[2] and important[3] component of the American criminal justice system. The significance of plea bargaining within our criminal justice system is readily revealed by a single statistic—plea bargaining accounts for ninety percent of all criminal convictions in the United States.[4] As the principal means of resolution in criminal cases, plea bargaining is no longer "some adjunct to the criminal justice system; it *is* the criminal justice system."[5] Nonetheless, although plea bargaining has gained near unanimous acceptance among scholars and practitioners[6] and its use is encouraged by the United States Supreme Court,[7] a number of jurisdictions have banned the practice.

In 1975, in an attempt to restore the public's confidence in the existence of a system in which defendants could be fairly charged, tried, and sentenced,[8] Alaska became the first state to ban plea bargaining.[9] The Alaskan ban remained in effect for a decade, until plea bargaining resumed in 1985.[10] El Paso County, Texas implemented a second but shorter lived ban in 1978.[11] The El Paso County ban, designed to bring about sentence uniformity among defendants,[12] was in effect for six years before the county restored plea bargaining.[13] At least three other jurisdictions have implemented experimental[14] or limited[15] plea bargaining bans that also proved ineffective.[16]

The latest jurisdiction to ban plea bargaining is Bronx County, New York ("Bronx"). In November, 1992, Bronx County District Attorney Robert Johnson[17] announced that his office would no longer plea bargain with criminal defendants who had been indicted for felony offenses.[18] While the Bronx District Attorney's decision was portrayed by the press as a ban on plea bargaining,[19] the term ban is a misnomer when used in the context of the Bronx plea bargaining policy. The Bronx District Attorney did not ban plea bargaining totally; the practice is still permitted with defendants who have not been indicted.[20] Once the grand jury indicts a defendant on a felony offense, however, no plea bargaining is permitted.[21] Under the new plea pol-

Reprinted by permission of the *Fordham Law Review* from vol. 64 (1995), pp. 987–1013.

icy, an indicted defendant must plead guilty to the highest count of the indictment or face a trial.[22]

The Bronx District Attorney's plea bargaining ban "shocked" the entire legal community.[23] In the Bronx, a county that prosecutes more than 10,000 felonies annually and where the rate of felony prosecution has increased fifty percent since 1985,[24] plea bargaining appeared to be an indispensable tool of the criminal justice system.[25] Indeed, prior to the implementation of the ban, plea bargaining accounted for resolutions in approximately eighty-five percent of all Bronx felony prosecutions.[26]

Not surprisingly, the imposition of the ban set off a furor among judges, defense attorneys, and other officials[27] who feared a "catastrophic backlog of cases,"[28] "unfair" treatment of defendants,[29] "jail overcrowding,"[30] and "violations of a federal court order"[31] that could expose New York City to fines and force the release of prisoners.[32] Three years have elapsed since the Bronx plea bargaining ban went into effect and many of the expressed fears are now realities.[33] While there is little doubt that the Bronx plea bargaining ban is legal,[34] its harsh impact upon the Bronx criminal justice system raises serious ethical concerns.[35] This Note will examine and address some of these ethical concerns.

Part I of this Note discusses the advantages and criticisms of plea bargaining and the prosecutor's role in the plea bargaining process. Part II examines the origin of the Bronx plea bargaining ban and the effects that the ban has had on the Bronx criminal justice system. Part III examines the prosecutor's ethical duties and discusses whether the Bronx District Attorney's behavior violated those ethical duties when he banned plea bargaining. Part IV suggests possible methods of tailoring the Bronx plea bargaining ban to lessen its adverse impact, while still allowing the ban to accomplish its goal. This Note concludes that while the Bronx plea bargaining ban does not violate any specific ethics rules, it raises serious concerns that must be addressed before the Bronx criminal justice system suffers irreparable harm.

I. PLEA BARGAINING IN THE AMERICAN CRIMINAL JUSTICE SYSTEM

Plea bargaining has its proponents and its critics. This section discusses the reasons for the popularity of plea bargaining, as well as the criticisms that have been leveled against the practice. This section also examines how the exercise of prosecutorial discretion makes the District Attorney the principal player in the plea bargaining process.

A. The Mutual Advantages of Plea Bargaining

Criticized harshly in the past,[36] plea bargaining has gained the imprimatur of our courts[37] and has become the most prevalent form of case resolution in the American criminal justice system.[38] The popularity of plea bargaining stems from its "mutuality of advantage"[39]—the process offers advantages to defendants, prosecutors, defense counsel, judges, victims, and the public alike.

Plea bargaining allows defendants, in exchange for the surrender of certain constitutional rights,[40] to gain prompt and final dispositions of their cases,[41] "avoid the anxieties and uncertainties of a trial,"[42] and escape the maximum penalties authorized by law.[43] Prosecutors, by agreeing to reduce charges[44] or to recommend lower sentences,[45] avoid costly, time consuming trials and, thus, conserve vital and scarce prosecutorial resources.[46] Defense counsel, most of whom are court appointed public defenders, dispose of cases quickly and reduce overwhelming caseloads through plea bargaining.[47] Judges ameliorate congested court calendars and conserve judicial resources through the speedy dispositions attributed to plea bargaining.[48] Victims may benefit by avoiding the rigors of a trial and by not having to relive the horrors of their victimization in the presence of the defendant and the public.[49] Finally, the public is protected from the risks posed by defendants who are free on bail while awaiting completion of the criminal proceedings against them.[50]

B. Criticisms of Plea Bargaining

While plea bargaining is often praised for the advantages it offers, the process is also sharply criticized at times. A large portion of the public disapproves of plea bargaining because it perceives the process as being too lenient on defendants.[51] Statistics support public perception—the average sentence for defendants convicted of serious felonies after pleading guilty was one-half that of defendants convicted after trials in state courts.[52] In addition to viewing plea bargaining as too lenient, many commentators believe the process undermines legislative intent.[53] These commentators argue that plea bargaining allows prosecutors to circumvent sentencing statutes that fix the punishment for certain crimes.[54]

Another criticism of plea bargaining is that its *sub rosa* nature has led to a decline of public confidence in the criminal justice system.[55] Because plea bargaining takes place in private and is not open to public scrutiny, the public is suspicious of the secretive nature of the process.[56] The public's confidence is further eroded because plea bargaining circumvents the trial process.[57] Trials allow the public to participate directly in the criminal justice process and the high visibility of criminal trials serves as a check on government oppression and misconduct.[58] The absence of trials deprives the public of the opportunity "to restore [a] sense of equilibrium to . . . communit[ies] defaced by . . . criminal act[s]."[59]

Removing criminal cases from the trial process through plea bargaining also circumvents the "rigorous standards of due process and proof imposed during trials."[60] Plea bargaining permits the defendant's fate to be determined without a full investigation, presentation of testimony and evidence, and impartial fact finding.[61] The absence of these procedural safeguards presents a possibility that the prosecution will coerce innocent defendants into pleading guilty.[62] The law recognizes this possibility and allows courts to accept guilty pleas containing protestations of innocence;[63] an admission of guilt is not "a constitutional requisite to the imposition of criminal penalty."[64]

C. Prosecutorial Discretion and Plea Bargaining

Both proponents and critics of plea bargaining agree that the prosecutor is the central and controlling figure in the plea bargaining process.[65] Because defendants do not have a constitutional right to plea bargain,[66] the decision whether to permit plea bargaining in any particular case is solely a matter of prosecutorial discretion.[67] In exercising this discretion, prosecutors can refuse to plea bargain entirely,[68] or can set the terms and conditions on any offer made.[69] This absolute control over the plea bargaining process has led to characterizations of the prosecutor as an "unregulated monopoly," capable of changing at will the "going rate" for a particular category of crime.[70] The reluctance of courts to interfere in the process further buttresses the prosecutor's monopoly over plea bargaining.[71] Courts presume that prosecutors exercise their discretionary powers in good faith[72] and require a strong showing of proof before inferring that a prosecutor has abused his discretion.[73] This high standard of proof affords prosecutors tremendous leeway in exercising their discretionary powers.[74]

D. The Limited Judicial Review of Prosecutorial Discretion

Prosecutors' decisions are not immunized from judicial scrutiny.[75] Recognizing that prosecutorial discretion carries with it the potential for "individual and institutional abuse,"[76] appellate courts regularly review defendants' claims of alleged abuse of prosecutorial discretion during the plea bargaining process.

Most courts use one of two tests in reviewing claims of alleged abuse of prosecutorial discretion. Claims of individual abuse of prosecutorial discretion are reviewed under a motive test.[77] The motive test examines a prosecutor's subjective reasons for acting against a particular defendant.[78] If the court determines that the prosecutor had an improper motive for his actions, it will deem his otherwise authorized behavior impermissible.[79] The motive test, however, focuses on the behavior of individual prosecutors, and thus is inadequate to evaluate an institutional prosecutorial practice such as the Bronx plea bargaining ban.[80]

In evaluating institutional practices which do not involve fundamental rights, courts employ a rational basis test.[81] Under the rational basis test, courts will uphold an institutional practice and not find an abuse of discretion as long as some relationship exists between the challenged practice and a legitimate state interest.[82] At least one New York court employed the rational basis test to reject a challenge to a plea bargaining practice similar to that in use in the Bronx.[83] Thus, according to current jurisprudence, the Bronx District Attorney did not abuse his discretion in implementing a plea bargaining ban.

II. ORIGIN AND EFFECTS OF THE PLEA BARGAINING BAN

This part examines the Bronx District Attorney's reasons for banning plea bargaining. This part also discusses the adverse and beneficial effects the plea bargaining ban has had on the Bronx criminal justice system.

A. The Origins of the Ban

Contending that "society [had] ceded control" of the criminal justice system to those accused of violating the law and that it was time for the "system to take stock of itself,"[84] the Bronx District Attorney banned plea bargaining in all indicted felony cases.[85] In addition to causing the criminal justice system "to slow down, take a breather and refocus,"[86] the Bronx District Attorney intended the ban to increase the severity of punishment judges imposed on defendants by, in effect, socializing judges into imposing harsher sentences acceptable to the District Attorney.[87] The District Attorney claimed that this socialization was necessary because judges' sentencing practices were responsible for a case backlog and the resulting disproportionate acquittal rate in the Bronx.[88] According to the District Attorney, judges in the Bronx created a disincentive to plead guilty by not adhering to a policy of sentence disparity.[89] Because defendants had no incentive to plead guilty in the absence of sentence disparity,[90] their cases languished, created a backlog in the Bronx, and made it more difficult for the prosecutor to obtain a conviction.[91]

In an effort to reverse this trend, the District Attorney banned plea bargaining with indicted defendants and thereby eliminated a judge's opportunity to impose a lesser sentence for a reduced charge.[92] Under the new plea policy, judges are required by law to impose the mandatory minimum sentence[93] under the highest count of the indictment.[94] The District Attorney surmised that judges faced with the plea bargaining ban would be forced to revive sentence disparity rather than risk a greater backlog of pending cases and an increase in the number of trials.[95] This situation, in turn, would create an incentive to plea bargain and allow plea bargaining to return to the Bronx.[96]

B. The Effects of the Ban

The plea bargaining ban has not had its intended effect of reforming the sentencing practices of Bronx judges. Under the ban, Bronx judges have become more lenient and appear to be imposing shorter sentences on the highest counts of indictments.[97] According to the Bronx District Attorney's theory,[98] this additional leniency should result in a further disincentive to plea bargain and an increase in the backlog of cases. Indeed, since the imposition of the ban, guilty pleas have decreased by eleven percent,[99] and the backlog of pending cases in the Bronx has increased by twenty-four percent.[100] As a direct result of the increase in the backlog of pending cases, the average time defendants remain in custody has also increased. Since the imposition of the ban, Bronx defendants average in excess of 160 days in custody, compared to the 120 day average for other New York City boroughs.[101] There has also been a forty-seven percent increase in the number of Bronx defendants incarcerated for over one year.[102] These additional days of incarceration cost New York City taxpayers three to four million dollars annually.[103]

The increase in the average time defendants remain in pre-trial custody has also had a substantial effect on the dismissal rate in the Bronx. Dismissals have increased twenty-one percent since the prohibition of plea bargaining in the New York Supreme Court.[104] Presently, one out of every ten criminal cases filed in the Bronx is dismissed.[105] This marked increase is primarily attributed to two factors: (1) the weakening of the prosecutor's case with the passage of time;[106] and (2) constitutional and statutory speedy trial provisions.[107]

More troubling than the rise in the dismissal rate and the concomitant threat posed to society by the release of potentially guilty defendants is the probability that innocent defendants are being convicted because of the Bronx ban.[108] This probability results from a combination of three factors. First, under the new plea policy, defendants must usually decide within six days, before they are indicted, whether to accept a prosecutor's offer and plead guilty.[109] This time limit places tremendous pressure on a defendant who, from a jail cell, must attempt to contact and consult with family and counsel before making a decision that could affect him for the rest of his life. Furthermore, not only must a defendant make this crucial decision within a few days, he must do so without the benefit of necessary information to assist him.[110] Finally, because innocent defendants are highly risk averse,[111] they will likely succumb to the pressure of making a rushed decision without adequate information. These defendants will often conclude that their interests are best served by pleading guilty, accepting the certainty of a lesser punishment, and avoiding the risk of a longer period of incarceration.[112]

While more innocent defendants will be pressured into pleading guilty because of the Bronx ban, others will continue to maintain their innocence and proceed to trial. Innocent defendants have strong reasons for going to trial because they have a greater chance of success.[113] Nonetheless, "convicting innocents [after a trial would] likely be easier in a no-bargaining world"[114] because of deterioration in the trial process caused by the plea bargaining ban. To compensate for the additional requests for trials[115] without a corresponding increase in resources,[116] the trial process in the Bronx will become more "casual."[117] The relaxation of the trial process will result in higher error rates and in a greater number of innocent defendants being convicted.[118] Thus, regardless of the means of obtaining a conviction—by guilty plea or trial—innocent defendants will have a greater chance of being convicted under the new ban.

Another adverse effect of the plea bargaining ban is the erosion of a defendant's constitutional right to be prosecuted by indictment.[119] The New York State Constitution provides that "[n]o person shall be held to answer for . . . [an] infamous crime . . . unless on indictment of a grand jury."[120] This constitutional guarantee is aimed at preventing potentially oppressive prosecutorial behavior by requiring that, before an individual is publicly accused of a crime, the state must convince a grand jury that sufficient evidence exists for it to believe that the accused is guilty.[121] This important constitutional right has eroded due to the tremendous increase in the use of Superior Court Informations ("SCI").

The SCI is essentially a waiver of indictment by a defendant that permits the prosecutor to forego the grand jury process and proceed in the New York Supreme Court on the basis of a written accusation drafted by the prosecutor.[122] While the legislature hoped that the use of SCIs would result in "speedier and equally fair dispositions" for defendants,[123] it did not intend to eliminate the grand jury process and its inherent protections.[124] The right to be prosecuted by indictment is so vital to our criminal justice system that a defendant can only waive the right in open court in the presence of an attorney.[125] Even then, a defendant's waiver is subject to approval by the court.[126]

Prior to the imposition of the plea bargaining ban, approximately twenty-five percent of the cases filed in the Bronx were disposed of by defendants pleading guilty to reduced felony charges in SCIs.[127] The ban has resulted in a sixty percent increase in the use of SCIs.[128] Now, forty percent of Bronx cases are disposed of with SCIs.[129] The dramatic increase in the use of SCIs indicates that the locus of plea bargaining in the Bronx has moved away from the New York Supreme Court to the New York City Criminal Court.[130] Recognizing this, defendants are pressured into waiving the constitutional protections of the grand jury process and agreeing to be prosecuted by SCI to avoid the strict no bargaining policy that applies to indicted defendants.[131]

An examination of two hypothetical defendants, A and B, charged with murder in the second degree reveals why increasing numbers of Bronx defendants are electing to be prosecuted by SCI to circumvent the plea bargaining ban. In New York, second degree murder is a class A-I felony,[132] carrying a minimum indeterminate[133] sentence of fifteen years[134] to life imprisonment[135] and a maximum indeterminate sentence of twenty-five years[136] to life imprisonment[137] upon conviction.

Defendant A is arraigned on a felony complaint charging second degree murder and elects not to plead guilty because she feels that the state's case against her is weak. Defendant A is subsequently indicted for second degree murder. Under the Bronx plea bargaining ban, once defendant A is indicted she must plead guilty to the highest count of the indictment,[138] second degree murder, or attempt to vindicate herself at trial. If defendant A decides to plead guilty, the court must impose an indeterminate sentence with a minimum term of at least fifteen years[139] and a maximum term of life imprisonment.[140] If defendant A refuses to plead guilty, elects to proceed to trial and is convicted, she will be subject to an indeterminate sentence with a minimum term of as much as twenty-five years[141] and a maximum term of life imprisonment.[142]

Defendant B, like defendant A, is also arraigned on a felony complaint charging second degree murder. Defendant B, however, feels that the state's case against her is strong and attempts to circumvent the Bronx plea bargaining ban by waiving her right to be prosecuted by indictment and consenting to be prosecuted by SCI.[143] Because the plea bargaining ban only applies to indicted defendants and defendant B is being prosecuted by SCI,[144] defendant B will still be permitted to plea bargain. Under this scenario, the District Attorney offers to allow defendant B to plead guilty to a reduced charge, second degree manslaughter, a class C felony.[145] If defendant B consents and pleads guilty, her potential exposure to imprisonment will be greatly reduced because the permissible sentence for a class C felony conviction ranges from a definite term of one year in prison to an indeterminate term of five to fifteen years imprisonment.[146] Thus, by waiving her right to be prosecuted by indictment and consenting to be prosecuted by SCI, defendant B circumvented the Bronx ban and secured a plea bargain offer from the District Attorney that guarantees that the minimum and maximum terms of imprisonment to which she would be subject are well below that of her counterpart, defendant A.

While the plea bargaining ban has severely impacted the Bronx criminal justice system, not all of its effects have been adverse. As a result of the ban, the Bronx is now the New York City borough with the highest percentage of defendants convicted on the highest count of indictments charging felonies.[147] The Bronx also boasts a dramatic increase in the number of people convicted of low level drug offenses.[148] Overall, however, these positive effects are greatly outweighed by the adverse effects of the ban, resulting in a deterioration of the quality of justice in the Bronx.

III. AN EXAMINATION OF THE EFFECTS OF THE BAN UNDER ETHICS RULES

While the Bronx District Attorney's exercise of discretion in imposing a plea bargaining ban appears to pass judicial muster,[149] his behavior still raises serious ethical questions.[150] Behavior that is legal can nonetheless be unethical.[151] Prosecutors, like all members of the bar, must conform their behavior to the professional rules of ethics.[152] The role of prosecutors significantly differs from that of other attorneys,[153] however, and a number of particularized ethics rules govern their behavior.[154] These particularized rules provide guidance in determining whether the Bronx District Attorney abused his discretion and acted unethically in implementing a plea bargaining ban.

A. THE BRONX DISTRICT ATTORNEY'S DUTY TO "SEEK JUSTICE"

Foremost among the special ethics rules governing the Bronx District Attorney's conduct is N.Y. Code EC 7-13, which states that prosecutors have a "duty to seek justice [and] not merely to convict."[155] In seeking justice, the prosecutor performs an "oversight function"[156] and must be mindful of his responsibilities to the community, victim, defendant, and state.[157] The prosecutor must protect the community, quench the victim's desire for vengeance, safeguard the defendant's rights, and ensure that the state has a fair and efficient criminal justice system.[158] An examination of the effects of the Bronx plea bargaining ban suggests that the District Attorney may have neglected his obligation to certain constituencies.

While the community and victims are applauding the plea bargaining ban because felons are being increasingly convicted on the highest counts of indictments,[159] defendants are lamenting its effects. The ban has not only resulted in a substantial increase in the average length of defendants' pre-trial detention,[160] but has also heightened the possibility that innocent defendants are being unjustly convicted.[161] Additionally, the increased reliance on SCIs as a means of prosecution deprives defendants of the constitutional protections afforded by the grand jury process.[162]

The state also suffers as a result of the Bronx District Attorney's failure to maintain a fair and efficient criminal justice system. The large increase in the backlog of pending cases[163] and the number of dismissals[164] undermines the efficiency of the system. Further, a system that convicts innocent defendants[165] and holds others in lengthy pre-trial detention[166] leads the public to question its fairness. In sum, the effects of the Bronx ban strongly suggest that the District Attorney is failing to seek justice for segments of society that he is responsible for representing.

Nonetheless, the effects of the Bronx ban alone are insufficient to substantiate a finding that the District Attorney is acting unethically by failing to seek justice. First, the duty to seek justice standard is too nebulous to be enforceable.[167] In fact, no prosecutor has ever received a disciplinary sanction for failing to comply with the duty to seek justice standard.[168] Instead, if the Bronx District Attorney was faced with disciplinary action for failing to seek justice based on his plea bargaining ban, he would probably be charged under a New York disciplinary rule prohibiting "[e]ngag[ing] in conduct that is prejudicial to the administration of justice."[169] While some of the ban's effects have clearly prejudiced the administration of justice in the Bronx,[170] the prejudicial standard is also nebulous[171] and provides no parameters by which to judge behavior. Thus, this standard would most likely not support a finding that the Bronx District Attorney acted unethically.[172]

Although the District Attorney must seek justice and refrain from engaging in conduct prejudicial to the administration of justice, these two standards alone do not guide his behavior. In exercising his discretionary powers, the Bronx District Attorney must also attempt to discern the needs of the public and must avoid being guided by improper motivation.[173] The District Attorney should have banned plea bargaining only if he "conscientiously believe[d it] to be in the public interest."[174] Accordingly, if the Bronx District Attorney "conscientiously believe[d]" that a ban on plea bargaining would reform sentencing practices and benefit the criminal justice system,[175] his decision was well within ethical bounds. If, however, the Bronx District Attorney banned plea bargaining because of his personal dissatisfaction with a specific judge's ruling, as a number of newspapers have reported,[176] his behavior was unethical.[177]

B. The Prosecutor's Duty to Identify and Correct Deficiencies in the Criminal Justice System

As a key player in the criminal justice system, the Bronx District Attorney also has an ethical duty to "recognize deficiencies in the legal system and to initiate corrective measures therein."[178] This ethical obligation to innovate[179] imposes a duty on the Bronx District Attorney to encourage and aid in making needed changes in the legal system.[180] Arguably, the Bronx District Attorney was implementing needed changes when he banned plea bargaining. First, restrictive plea bargaining policies are associated with efforts to crack down on crime by refusing to offer lenient sentences.[181] In a borough that has sixteen percent of New York City's population yet twenty-five percent of its homicides, twenty-two percent of its drug arrests, and twenty percent of its rapes,[182] the public may perceive the plea bargaining ban as a welcome and needed change to combat the disproportionate amount of crime in the Bronx.[183] The public may also perceive the Bronx ban as an innovative attempt to secure desperately needed additional courtrooms and judges from the state.[184] While some may view the Bronx ban as an innovative corrective measure designed to improve the legal system, others perceive it as a death knell for criminal justice in the Bronx.[185] The plea bargaining ban has not only increased the backlog of pending cases[186] and the number of dismissals,[187] but has also forced defendants to remain in pre-trial detention longer[188] and has cost the state millions of extra dollars.[189] In light of these results,[190] there is support for the proposition that the Bronx District Attorney is impairing the quality of justice rather than fulfilling his ethical obligation to improve the legal system.

C. The Bronx District Attorney Did Not Violate Ethics Rules

Unquestionably, the plea bargaining ban has adversely affected the Bronx criminal justice system. The adverse effects of the ban, however, are not enough to substantiate a finding that the Bronx District Attorney acted unethically by abusing his discretion. First, the nebulous standards governing the Bronx District Attorney's behavior make it nearly impossible to define exactly what constitutes unethical behavior in these circumstances.[191] Second, many ethics rules are couched in subjective terms,[192] providing the Bronx District Attorney with tremendous leeway to decide what is right and wrong.[193] Moreover, absent an admission by the District Attorney, this subjectivity makes it impossible to ascertain whether or not he was improperly motivated, and thus acting unethically,[194] in banning plea bargaining. Third, the adverse effects of the Bronx ban cannot be viewed in isolation. The ban has resulted in a number of positive changes in the Bronx,[195] suggesting that the District Attorney exercised "sound discretion"[196] in his attempt to change a system in dire need of reform. In sum, the vague, subjective ethical standards governing a prosecutor's behavior and the mixed effects of the Bronx ban do not support a conclusion that the District Attorney abused his discretion and acted unethically in implementing a plea bargaining ban.

IV. MODIFYING THE BRONX BAN

An examination of the effects of the Bronx ban under existing case law and ethics rules does not support a conclusion that the District Attorney acted illegally or unethically. Rather, it indicates the need to modify the plea bargaining ban to avoid irreparable harm to the Bronx criminal justice system. This part proposes two possible modifications: (1) extending the time in which to allow plea bargaining; and (2) using written guidelines in the plea bargaining process.[197]

A. Extending the Time in Which to Plea Bargain

A major criticism of the Bronx ban is that its coercive nature pressures defendants into making hasty, uninformed decisions.[198] Under the ban, defendants must make crucial decisions on plea offers within six days, before the grand jury indicts them and the New York City Criminal Court transfers their cases to the New York Supreme Court.[199] Defendants often make these decisions without any relevant information[200] or sound legal advice.[201] To temper the coercive nature of the Bronx ban and to allow for more informed decisions by defendants, the District Attorney should extend the time period in which the state will plea bargain with indicted defendants.

A reasonable time limit on plea bargaining is not a novel idea. In 1977, the National District Attorneys' Association recommended that individual jurisdictions "set a time limit after which plea negotiations may no longer be conducted."[202] More recently, a pilot program commenced in Brooklyn, New York, under which time limits are imposed on plea bargaining.[203] The pilot program allows defendants to engage in plea bargaining for sixty days.[204] On the sixty-first day, the District Attorney makes a final plea offer.[205] If the defendant refuses the offer, the case is immediately scheduled for trial.[206] The results of the program are phenomenal—judges have shaved an average of sixty-five days off the time it takes to dispose of a case; twenty-seven percent more indictments have been disposed of; and there has been a seventy-eight percent increase in guilty pleas to the severest charge against a defendant.[207]

The Brooklyn pilot program provides concrete proof that a prosecutor can restrict plea bargaining, be tough on crime, and yet still treat defendants fairly and reform the criminal justice system. The Bronx District Attorney should follow Brooklyn's lead and replace the plea bargaining ban in the New York Supreme Court with a policy that permits bargaining for a reasonable but limited period of time.

B. Guidelines for Plea Bargaining

Another method of reforming the Bronx plea bargaining ban is through the use of written guidelines.[208] Like most jurisdictions, the Bronx does not employ guidelines to regulate plea bargaining.[209] The adverse effects of the Bronx ban, however, demonstrate the need to adopt such guidelines in the near future.[210] Implementing plea bargaining guidelines in the Bronx would serve two purposes. First, guidelines would impose structure on, and control over, the prosecutor's discretion without eliminating the prosecutor's ability to treat each defendant as an individual.[211] Second, guidelines would "limit the opportunities for any of the actors [in the criminal justice system] to stonewall the system at the expense of . . . others."[212]

The use of written guidelines in New York State's criminal justice system is not new. In 1978, the New York State Board of Parole implemented written guidelines to control the discretion of parole commissioners and to aid them in determining when to release inmates from state prisons.[213] Under the parole guidelines, inmates are given numerical scores in two categories—offense severity[214] and prior criminal history.[215] The two scores are then added together and matched against a guideline time range which indicates the suggested time an inmate should serve in prison.[216] Inmates who commit serious crimes and have lengthy criminal histories receive high scores under the guidelines and are severely penalized by the Parole Board by being forced to serve lengthy periods of incarceration.[217] Conversely, inmates who commit less serious crimes and have no criminal histories benefit most from the guidelines by being released early from prison by the Parole Board.[218]

Guidelines similar to those governing parole could be implemented easily and efficiently in the Bronx to regulate the plea bargaining process. Under such a guideline system, the District Attorney could restrict or refuse to plea bargain with career criminals charged with serious offenses—defendants who score high under the guideline system. On the other hand, defendants who score low under the guidelines—those charged with less serious offenses and who do not have lengthy criminal histories—would be given reasonable plea offers by the District Attorney.

By implementing guidelines, the Bronx District Attorney could restore plea bargaining and ameliorate the harsh effects of the ban, maintain a tough stance on crime, and reinstill a sense of fairness in the criminal justice system.

CONCLUSION

The ban on plea bargaining has severely impacted the Bronx criminal justice system. The overall adverse effects of the plea bargaining ban suggest that the Bronx District Attorney may be acting unethically. An examination of the relevant ethics rules, however, reveals that the standards governing the Bronx District Attorney's behavior are nebulous, provide no concrete standards upon which to judge his behavior, and afford him tremendous latitude in exercising his discretion. This discretion makes the Bronx District Attorney's behavior nearly irreproachable under ethical standards. Furthermore, not all of the effects of the Bronx plea bargaining ban have been adverse. The few positive effects of the plea bargaining ban could lead one to conclude that the Bronx District Attorney was being innovative in his attempt, through the ban, to pressure the state to provide much needed additional courtroom space and judges.

But while the Bronx District Attorney's behavior does not appear to violate any ethics rules, his behavior is nonetheless adversely impacting the Bronx criminal justice system. To avoid further deterioration and possible irreparable harm to the Bronx criminal justice system, the Bronx District Attorney needs to take prompt and definitive action. Two possible courses of action are available. First, the District Attorney could expand the time allotted for plea bargaining so that defendants would have sufficient time to secure the information necessary to assist them in deciding whether or not to plead guilty. Second, the District Attorney could implement written guidelines governing the plea bargaining process to prevent abuses of discretion and to ensure that appropriate sentences are imposed on defendants.

In the absence of modifications, the Bronx plea bargaining ban is destined to fail, and the Bronx District Attorney will be forced to rescind his ban and restore plea bargaining, as was done in Alaska and El Paso County, Texas. The Bronx ban should serve as a model to other jurisdictions that are contemplating banning plea bargaining, alerting them to the dangers of banning the principal means of resolution in our criminal justice system. If plea bargaining bans like the Bronx ban are to succeed, controls are needed to guide prosecutors in exercising their discretion.

NOTES

*I would like to thank Professor Bruce A. Green for his advice and guidance in the preparation of this Note. I am also grateful to the Stein Scholars Program for providing the academic climate in which I was able to explore these issues of legal ethics.

1. Plea bargaining is defined as "[t]he process whereby the accused and the prosecutor in a criminal case work out a mutually satisfactory disposition of the case subject to court approval." Black's Law Dictionary 1152 (6th ed. 1990).

2. Santobello v. New York, 404 U.S. 257, 260 (1971) (noting that plea bargaining is essential because it allows the states and the federal government to save resources by avoiding full-scale trials).

3. Bordenkircher v. Hayes, 434 U.S. 357, 361-62 (1978); Blackledge v. Allison, 431 U.S. 63, 71 (1977).

4. Albert W. Alschuler, *The Prosecutor's Role in Plea Bargaining*, 36 U. Chi. L. Rev. 50, 50 (1968) [hereinafter *The Prosecutor's Role*]; Susan E. Gegan & Nicholas E. Rodriguez, Note, *Victims' Roles in the Criminal Justice System: A Fallacy of Victim Empowerment?*, 8 St. John's J. Legal Comment. 225, 229 n.16 (1992); *see also* Bruce A. Green, *"Package" Plea Bargaining and the Prosecutor's Duty of Good Faith*, 25 Crim. L. Bull. 507, 509 (1989) ("The overwhelming majority of criminal cases in this country are resolved by guilty pleas, most of which are the product of plea bargaining." (citation omitted)).

5. Robert E. Scott & William J. Stuntz, *Plea Bargaining As Contract*, 101 Yale L.J. 1909, 1912 (1992).

6. Robert A. Weninger, *The Abolition of Plea Bargaining: A Case Study of El Paso County Texas*, 35 UCLA L. Rev. 265, 265 (1987).

7. Santobello v. New York, 404 U.S. 257, 260 (1971) ("Properly administered, [plea bargaining] is to be encouraged.").

8. Teresa White Carns & John A. Kruse, *Alaska's Ban on Plea Bargaining Reevaluated,* 75 Judicature 310, 310-11 (1992).

9. *Id.* at 311.

10. *Id.* at 317.

11. *See* Weninger, *supra* note 6, at 270.

12. *See id.* at 275-76.

13. *Id.* at 270.

14. *See* Carns & Kruse, *supra* note 8, at 311 n.11 (discussing an experimental plea bargaining ban on drug trafficking cases prosecuted in a Michigan County).

15. *Id.* (discussing Detroit, Michigan's ban on plea bargaining with defendants charged with felony firearm offenses); Jeff Brown, *Proposition 8: Origins and Impact—A Public Defender's Perspective*, 23 Pac. L.J. 881, 939 (1992) (discussing California's ban on plea bargaining with defendants charged with "serious" offenses).

16. *See e.g.*, Brown, *supra* note 15, at 941-42 (discussing how plea bargaining still occurs with defendants charged with "serious" crimes despite a ban prohibiting the practice).

17. Robert Johnson was elected to the Bronx County District Attorney's Office in November 1988 in a special election held to fill the vacancy created by the death of long time Bronx District Attorney Mario Merola. Telephone Interview with Office of Public Affairs, Bronx County District Attorney's Office (Nov. 8, 1995). Mr. Johnson was reelected to new four year terms in 1991 and 1995. *Id.*

18. Anthony M. DeStefano, *DA: No Deals—Bronx No Plea Bargain Order Shocks Judges Lawyers*, N.Y. Newsday, Nov. 24, 1992, at 3, 3 [hereinafter *DA: No Deals*]; Martin Fox, *Problems Seen with Johnson's End to Plea Bargains*, N.Y. L.J., Nov. 25, 1992, at 1 [hereinafter *Problems Seen*].

19. Anthony M. DeStefano, *Court Clog in Bronx: DA Plea Bargain Ban has Backlog at 10-Year High*, N.Y. Newsday, Jan. 13, 1993, at 29 [hereinafter *Court Clog in Bronx*].

20. *DA: No Deals*, *supra* note 18, at 3.

21. *See id.*

22. *Id.*

23. *Id.*

24. Bernice Kanner, *Rough Justice: A Young Prosecutor and Her Team Battle the Odds in the Bronx*, New York, May 10, 1993, at 46, 48.

25. *Problems Seen, supra* note 18, at 5 ("Plea negotiations are as important to the [Bronx] court system as breathing, sleeping and eating are to human[s] . . ." (quoting Bronx Administrative Judge Burton B. Roberts)).

26. Anthony M. DeStefano, *No-Plea Policy Draws Fire*, N.Y. Newsday, Nov. 25, 1992. at 23 [hereinafter *Policy Draws Fire*]; *Problems Seen, supra* note 18, at 1.

27. *Court Clog in Bronx, supra* note 19, at 29.

28. *See Policy Draws Fire, supra* note 26, at 23.

29. Martin Fox, *Next Six Weeks Seen Critical in Bronx Courts: No Impact Yet from Bar on Plea Bargaining*, N.Y. L.J., Jan. 4, 1993, at 1, 2 [hereinafter *Next Six Weeks*]. According to Irwin Shaw, Supervising Attorney at The Legal Aid Society's Bronx Criminal Defense Division, the Bronx plea bargaining ban is "philosophically wrong," "a mistake," and "unfair" because it does not look at each case individually. *Id.*

30. *See Problems Seen, supra* note 18, at 5. Declaring that the Bronx lacked sufficient court resources to try a large number of additional cases. Administrative Judge Burton B. Roberts warned that New York City's jails would become "overcrowd [ed]." *Id.*

31. *Id.* Matthew T. Crosson, Chief Administrator of the New York State Courts, voiced concern that a sharp rise in the number of inmates awaiting trial at Rikers Island could "trigger violations of a federal court order that limits the number of prisoners in city jails and thereby requires additional facilities or release of the detainees on constitutional grounds." *Id.*

32. *Id.* In 1978, New York City entered into a stipulation ("Benjamin Stipulation") in which it acknowledged that pretrial detainees were being confined in overcrowded facilities that violated the detainees' constitutional rights. *See* Benjamin v. Malcolm, 495 F. Supp. 1357, 1359 (S.D.N.Y. 1980) *modified* 646 F. Supp. 1550, 1554 (S.D.N.Y. 1986). In that stipulation the City agreed to allow the district court to impose appropriate remedies to correct the overcrowding. 495 F. Supp. at 1359. Among the remedies imposed was a cap on the number of pretrial detainees that could be housed in certain New York City jails. 495 F.Supp. at 1365. A sharp rise in the number of pretrial detainees resulting from the Bronx ban could trigger violations of the Benjamin Stipulation, expose the city to fines, and force the release of prisoners to relieve the overcrowding. *See Problems Seen, supra* note 18, at 5.

33. *See* Anthony M. DeStefano, *No Place Like Rikers-Bronx Inmates Staying Longer*, N.Y. Newsday, May 27, 1993, at 35 ("An increase in the percentage of Bronx prisoners waiting a year or more on Rikers Island for trial is apparently traced to a tougher no-plea-bargain policy. . . ."); *Plea Bargains Expedite Our System of Justice*, Buffalo News (Editorial), June 12, 1993, at C2 (noting that the trial case load in the Bronx has skyrocketed by 24% because of the plea bargaining ban); Kathleen Lynch, Remarks at a Panel Discussion on Ethical Issues in Plea Bargaining, Stein Center for Ethics and Public Interest Law, Stein Scholars Program (Oct. 13, 1993) ("A prosecutor's role is to look for justice. If you have a policy whereby everyone charged with a crime gets the same exact plea, then he is not doing justice."); Chester Mirsky, The Bronx Plea Bargaining Ban: Contradictions and the Continued Need for Reform, Address at the Alan Fortunoff Criminal Justice Colloquium on Evaluating the Plea Bargaining Ban in Bronx County 8 (Oct. 25, 1993) (transcript available at New York University School of Law) (stating that there has been a 24% increase in indictments pending over six months in the Bronx, despite a 7.5% reduction in the total number of indictments and informations filed since the implementation of the ban).

34. At least one New York court recently rejected a challenge to a plea bargaining policy similar to that in place in the Bronx. *See e.g.*, People v. Cohen, 588 N.Y.S.2d 211, 212 (App. Div. 1992) (holding that defendant's constitutional right to equal protection was not violated by District Attorney's policy not to accept pleas to less than the highest count of an indictment). Courts have also held that defendants do not have a right to engage in plea bargaining. *See* Weatherford v. Bursey, 429 U.S. 545, 561 (1977) (holding that defendants do not have a constitutional right to plea bargain); People v. Harmon, 586 N.Y.S.2d 922, 925 (App. Div. 1992) ("The People . . . are not

obliged to make any offer in any case. . . ."); People v. Memminger, 469 N.Y.S.2d 323, 324 (Sup. Ct. 1983) ("[D]efendants have no constitutional entitlement to a plea offer."). In the absence of a constitutional right to plea bargain, it appears that a ban on the process would comport with the law. Furthermore, plea bargaining bans are not novel and have been implemented and accepted in other jurisdictions. *See supra* notes 8-16 and accompanying text.

35. While seemingly a paradox, behavior that is legal in the eyes of a court can still be unethical. The gap between legal and ethical conduct exists because courts do not equate professional codes or canons of ethics with decisional and statutory law. *See* Nix v. Whiteside, 475 U.S. 157, 189-90 (1986) (Blackmun, J., concurring) (noting that the time had not yet arrived for the Court to specify the weight to be assigned to professional codes or canons of ethics in defining attorney performance); Paretti v. Cavalier Label Co., 722 F. Supp. 985, 986 (S.D.N.Y. 1989) ("[T]he Model Code does not have the force of legislation or decisional law, [but only] provides guidance on issues of professional conduct."); S & S Hotel Ventures Ltd. Partnership v. 777 S.H. Corp., 508 N.E.2d 647, 650 (N.Y. 1987) ("The Code of Professional Responsibility establishes ethical standards that guide attorneys in their professional conduct . . . [T]he Code provisions cannot be applied as if they were controlling statutory or decisional law."). Thus, while at least one New York court has upheld a plea bargaining policy similar to that in place in the Bronx, and a number of other jurisdictions have approved plea bargaining bans, *see supra* note 34, the effects of the Bronx ban could still lead to the conclusion that Robert Johnson abused his prosecutorial discretion and acted unethically when he banned plea bargaining.

36. *See* National Prosecution Standards 218 (Nat'l District Att'ys Ass'n 1st ed. 1977) (noting that the first American court confronted with a guilty plea expressed strong opposition); Thomas J. Gardner, Criminal Evidence—Principles. Cases and Readings 28 (1978) (noting that American courts have historically discouraged plea bargaining, with a number of courts calling the practice "corrupt" and "immoral"); Albert W. Alschuler, *Implementing the Criminal Defendant's Right to Trial: Alternatives to the Plea Bargaining System*, 50 U. Chi. L. Rev. 931, 970 (1983) ("For many centuries, Anglo-American courts did not encourage guilty pleas but actively discouraged them."); *The Prosecutor's Role supra* note 4, at 50 (stating that American courts have actively discouraged guilty pleas for most of the history of the common law).

37. *See* United States v. Goodwin, 457 U.S. 368, 378 (1982) (stating that the Supreme Court has accepted plea bargaining as "constitutionally legitimate"); Corbitt v. New Jersey, 439 U.S. 212, 222 (1978) (recognizing the state's interest in facilitating plea bargaining); Santobello v. New York, 404 U.S. 257, 260 (1971) (noting that plea bargaining is an essential component of the administration of justice and is to be encouraged).

38. Donald G. Gifford, *Meaningful Reform of Plea Bargaining: The Control of Prosecutorial Discretion*, 1983 U. Ill. L. Rev. 37, 37.

39. Bordenkircher v. Hayes, 434 U.S. 357, 363 (1978); Brady v. United States, 397 U.S. 742, 752 (1970).

40. *Santobello*, 404 U.S. at 264 (Douglas, J., concurring); People v. Taylor, 478 N.E.2d 755, 757 (N.Y. 1985). Among the rights a defendant surrenders when he pleads guilty are the right to confront one's accusers, the right to present witnesses in one's defense, and the right to be convicted on proof beyond a reasonable doubt. *Santobello*, 404 U.S. at 264.

41. *Santobello*, 404 U.S. at 261.

42. Blackledge v. Allison, 431 U.S. 63, 71 (1977).

43. *See Brady*, 397 U.S. at 752.

44. Prosecutors engage in two types of plea bargaining—charge bargaining and sentence negotiation. In charge bargaining, the prosector agrees to reduce the charges against a defendant in exchange for a guilty plea. By pleading guilty to reduced charges, a defendant reduces the maximum time of incarceration to which he will be subject by the sentencing judge. *See* Weninger, *supra* note 6, at 279.

45. In sentence negotiation, the second type of plea bargaining, the prosecutor agrees to recommend a specific term of incarceration or probation to the sentencing judge in exchange for a guilty plea. *Id.* at 279-80. Sentence negotiation is the more prevalent form of plea bargaining. *Id.* at 279.

46. *Blackledge*, 431 U.S. at 71; *Brady*, 397 U.S. at 752.

47. Richard Klein, *The Relationship of the Court and Defense Counsel: The Impact on Competent Representation and Proposals for Reform*, 29 B.C.L. Rev. 531, 550 (1988) ("Public defenders often use plea bargaining . . . [as] 'a necessary technique to deal with an overwhelming caseload.'"). At least one study conducted in Michigan concluded that court appointed counsel submitted guilty pleas for their clients more than twice as frequently as privately retained counsel. *Id.* at 550-51 n.140.

48. *See Blackledge*, 431 U.S. at 71.

49. Carolyn E. Demarest, *Plea Bargaining Can Often Protect the Victim*, N.Y. Times, Apr. 15, 1994, at A30.

50. *Blackledge*, 431 U.S. at 71; Santobello v. New York, 404 U.S. 257, 261 (1971).

51. Eric Felten, *Crime and Punishment: Disorder in the Court*, Insight, Feb. 15, 1993, *available in* WESTLAW, 1993 WL 7511408, at *1-2; Scott & Stuntz, *supra* note 5, at 1909-10 n.4.

52. Scott & Stuntz, *supra* note 5, at 1909 n.2; *see also* Gifford, *supra* note 38, at 66 ("[D]efendants who plead guilty receive an average sentence of either probation or less than one year's imprisonment, while those convicted after trial received a typical sentence of three or four years.").

53. *See* Gifford, *supra* note 38, at 66-70.

54. *Id.* at 68.

55. *Id.* at 71.

56. *Id.*

57. *Id.*

58. *Id.*

59. *Id.* at 70. While the absence of trials can disrupt an entire community's sense of equilibrium, crime victims are particularly affected. Trials have cathartic effects on victims by providing outlets for feelings of retribution and the psychological need to participate in the societal condemnation of a defendant. *See id.* at 72-73; *see also* Maria L. Imperial & Jeanne B. Mullgrav, *The Convergence Between Illusion and Reality: Lifting the Veil of Secrecy Around Childhood Sexual Abuse*, 8 St. John's J. Legal Comment. 135, 146 (1992) (discussing how civil actions further a victim's healing process and allow society to publicly denounce unacceptable behavior).

60. Alissa Pollitz Worden, *Policymaking By Prosecutors: The Uses of Discretion in Regulating Plea Bargaining*, 73 Judicature 335, 336 (1990).

61. *See* Scott & Stuntz, *supra* note 5, at 1912; *see also* ABA Comm. on Ethics and Professional Responsibility, Informal Op. 1043 (1968) (finding that it is not unethical for a defense attorney to advise his client to plead guilty without first examining the government's case).

62. Felten, *supra* note 51, at *2; *see* Frank H. Easterbrook, *Plea Bargaining as Compromise*, 101 Yale L.J. 1969, 1975 (1992). It is no surprise that innocent defendants may buckle under the emotional strains of the criminal justice system. The criminal justice process has been known to destroy marriages and cause alienation or emotional disturbance among a defendant's children. *See* Monroe H. Freedman, Understanding Lawyers' Ethics 218 (1990). The financial burden of paying legal fees can be tremendous, especially if a defendant has been fired from his job due to the stigma associated with allegations of criminal activity or extended absenteeism because of pretrial confinement. *Id.*

63. North Carolina v. Alford, 400 U.S. 25, 37 (1970).

64. *Id.;* Freedman, *supra* note 62, at 220-21 ("The law, in its even-handed majesty, permits the innocent as well as the guilty to plead guilty in order to avoid the coercive threat of extended imprisonment.").

65. *See* Weatherford v. Bursey, 429 U.S. 545, 561 (1977) (stating that a prosecutor need not plea bargain if he prefers to go to trial); United States v. Dockery, 965 F.2d 1112, 1116 (D.C. Cir. 1992) ("The prosecutor generally is free to refuse to plea bargain or, having made a plea offer, to withdraw it at any time."); People v. Harmon, 586 N.Y.S.2d 922, 925 (App. Div. 1992) ("The People . . . may set the terms and conditions of their consent to a guilty plea to a lesser charge."); Gifford, *supra* note 38, at 45 (noting that a prosecutor can refuse to plea bargain or set the terms and conditions on any offer); Judge Burton B. Roberts, Remarks at the Alan Fortunoff Criminal Justice Colloquium on Evaluating the Plea Bargaining Ban in Bronx County (Oct. 25, 1993) ("No judge can take a lesser plea unless the District Attorney recommends the lesser plea.").

66. *See Weatherford*, 429 U.S. at 561; *Harmon*, 586 N.Y.S.2d at 925.

67. *See Dockery*, 965 F.2d at 1116; People v. Cohen, 588 N.Y.S.2d 211, 212 (App. Div. 1992); People v. Memminger, 469 N.Y.S.2d 323, 324 (Sup. Ct. 1983); W.J. Michael Cody, *Special Ethical Duties for Attorneys Who Hold Public Positions*, 23 Mem. St. U. L. Rev. 453, 456 (1993).

68. *Weatherford*, 429 U.S. at 561; *Dockery*, 965 F.2d at 1116.

69. *Harmon*, 586 N.Y.S.2d at 925.

70. Gifford, *supra* note 38, at 45.

71. *See* Bordenkircher v. Hayes, 434 U.S. 357, 362-64 (1978) (holding that due process is not violated when a prosecutor carries out a threat made during plea bargaining); People v. Lofton, 366 N.Y.S.2d 769, 776-77 (Sup. Ct. 1975) (noting that the remedy against a prosecutor who abuses his discretion is his removal from office or the election of a successor, both of which are beyond the power of the court).

72. *In re* Delicati v. Schechter, 157 N.Y.S.2d 715, 721 (App. Div. 1956); *Lofton*, 366 N.Y.S.2d at 776; People v. Anonymous, 481 N.Y.S.2d 987, 991 (Crim. Ct. 1984).

73. *See* McClesky v. Kemp, 481 U.S. 279, 297 (1987) ("Because discretion is essential to the criminal justice process, we would demand exceptionally clear proof before we would infer that the discretion has been abused.").

74. *See Lofton*, 366 N.Y.S.2d at 776 (stating that a prosecutor has wide latitude in determining when and how to prosecute); *see also In re* Holtzman v. Goldman, 523 N.E.2d 297, 303 (N.Y. 1988) ("District Attorneys . . . possess[] broad discretion in determining when . . . [to prosecute.]"); People v. DiFalco, 377 N.E.2d 732, 735 (N.Y. 1978) (commenting on prosecutor's broad discretion); *The Prosecutor's Role*, *supra* note 4, at 105 (noting that courts have sanctioned the prosecutor's discretionary powers).

75. State v. Freeland, 667 P.2d 509, 512 (Or. 1983) (en banc).

76. Bordenkircher v. Hayes, 434 U.S. 357, 365 (1978); Bennett L. Gershman, *The New Prosecutors*, 53 U. Pitt. L. Rev. 393, 408-09 (1992); Green, *supra* note 4, at 530 n.80.

77. William J. Genego, *The New Adversary*, 54 Brook. L. Rev. 781, 840 (1988).

78. *Id.*

79. *Id.* For example, a prosecutor cannot use his charging authority to retaliate against a defendant who exercises his right to trial. *Id.* Nor can a prosecutor subpoena a defendant's lawyer to testify merely to disqualify the lawyer from the case. *Id.; see* Richard P. Adelstein, *The Negotiated Guilty Plea: A Framework for Analysis*, 53 N.Y.U. L. Rev. 783, 829 (1978) (examining a prosecutor's improper motives during plea bargaining).

80. *See* Genego, *supra* note 77, at 841.

81. People v. Cohen, 588 N.Y.S.2d 211, 212 (App. Div. 1992); New York State Soc'y of Enrolled Agents v. New York State Div. of Tax Appeals, 559 N.Y.S.2d 906, 910 (App. Div. 1990); People v. Elliby, 436 N.Y.S.2d 784, 786 (App. Div. 1981); People v. Robert Z., 511 N.Y.S.2d 473, 476 (Civ. Ct. 1986); Dranzo v. Winterhalter, 577 A.2d 1349, 1355 (Pa. Super. Ct. 1990).

82. *See Dranzo*, 577 A.2d at 1355.

83. *See Cohen*, 588 N.Y.S.2d at 212. In *Cohen,* the defendant challenged the District Attorney's plea bargaining ban on equal protection grounds, arguing that his rights were violated because

defendants in other New York counties were still permitted to plea bargain while he was prohibited from doing so. *Id.* Noting that neither a fundamental right nor a suspect classification was involved, the court employed a rational basis test in analyzing the defendant's argument. *Id.* In rejecting the defendant's argument, the court held that it was rational to have different plea bargaining policies in different counties because prosecutorial caseloads and staffing varied throughout the state. *Id.*

84. *Next Six Weeks, supra* note 29, at 2. Although Robert Johnson publicly stated that he banned plea bargaining to reform the Bronx criminal justice system, a number of newspapers reported that the District Attorney banned plea bargaining because he was angered by a judge's decision to hold an evidentiary hearing over the prosecutor's objections. *See Problems Seen, supra* note 18, at 5 (reporting that Robert Johnson decided to end plea bargaining "out of pique" with a decision by a Supreme Court judge to hold an evidentiary hearing over the prosecutor's objections); *Policy Draws Fire, supra* note 26, at 23 (reporting that the Bronx District Attorney was motivated by "pique" over the actions of one trial judge).

85. Mirsky, *supra* note 33, at 3.

86. Shaun Assael, *Driving a Tough Bargain in the Bronx*, N.Y. Newsday, Apr. 8, 1993, at 99.

87. *See* Mirsky, *supra* note 29, at 3, 5.

88. *Id.* at 4. The acquittal rate in the Bronx in November 1992—the month in which the District Attorney implemented the ban—exceeded 40%. *Id.* at 5.

89. *Id.* at 4. Sentence disparity refers to the practice in which judges impose markedly different sentences on defendants convicted following a trial, compared to defendants convicted upon guilty pleas. For example, defendants A and B are charged with first degree robbery, a class B felony carrying a maximum term of imprisonment of twenty-five years upon conviction. *See* N.Y. Penal Law § 70.00(2)(b), 160.15 (McKinney 1992). Defendant A believes that the state's case against him is weak, rejects a plea bargaining offer by the prosecutor, and elects to proceed to trial. Defendant A is convicted of first degree robbery after a trial and is sentenced to twenty-five years in prison, the maximum term allowed by law. *Id.* § 70.00(2)(b). Defendant B, on the other hand, feels that the state has a strong case against him and elects to plead guilty to first degree robbery in exchange for a recommendation by the prosecutor to the sentencing judge that the defendant be sentenced to nine years in prison. *See* N.Y. Crim. Proc. Law § 220.50(5) (McKinney 1992) (requiring that the agreed upon sentence be made "orally on the record, or in writing filed with the court" as a condition of the plea bargain). The court accepts the prosecutor's recommendation and sentences defendant B to a maximum term of imprisonment of nine years. In this example, the court adhered to a policy of sentence disparity by sentencing the defendant who pled guilty to a much shorter term of imprisonment than the defendant who elected to have his guilt determined following a trial. The defendant who pleads guilty and saves the prosecutor and the court valuable resources by allowing them to dispose of a case quickly and efficiently is thus rewarded with a less severe sentence. According to the Bronx District Attorney, a policy of sentence disparity induces defendants to plead guilty to avoid the more severe sentences that are imposed following a conviction after a trial. *See* Mirsky, *supra* note 33, at 4.

90. In the absence of sentence disparity, defendants have no incentive to plead guilty because they receive the same sentence regardless of whether they are convicted upon a plea of guilty or after a trial. *See supra* note 89.

91. It is axiomatic that the longer a case languishes, the more difficult it is for a prosecutor to obtain a conviction. With the passage of time, witnesses may die or disappear, memories may fade, evidence may disappear or be inadvertently destroyed, needed trial resources may become scarcer, and statutory speedy trial provisions may mandate that the charges against a defendant be dismissed. *See* Anthony M. DeStefano, *Letting 'Em Go in the Bronx*, N.Y. Newsday, Sept. 23, 1993, at 36, 36 ("The longer cases stay around, the more chance there is of [a] witness becoming unavailable, the more chance there is of a witness becoming intimidated and the more chance there is of a witness' recollection becoming dimmed." (quoting Bronx Administrative Judge Burton B.

Roberts)); Mirsky, *supra* note 33, at 6 ("[A]s cases age, the ability to prosecute successfully is reduced . . .").

92. In New York State, the consent of both the prosecutor and the court is required before a defendant is permitted to enter a plea of guilty to a lesser included offense. *See* N.Y. Crim. Proc. Law § 220.10(3)-(4) (McKinney 1992). In the absence of the prosecutor's consent, a defendant may plead guilty as a matter of right only to the entire indictment. *Id.* § 220.10(2); *see also supra* notes 18-22 and accompanying text.

93. Judges are required under New York State law to impose mandatory minimum sentences on defendants convicted of certain classes of crimes. *See* N.Y. Penal Law §§ 70.00(3)(a)-(b), 70.02(4), 70.04(4), 70.06(4)(a)-(b), 70.08(3)(a)-(c) (McKinney 1992).

94. Mirsky, *supra* note 33, at 3.

95. *Id.* at 4.

96. *Id.* at 4-5.

97. Richard H. Girgenti, Remarks at the Alan Fortunoff Criminal Justice Colloquium on Evaluating the Plea Bargaining Ban in Bronx County, (Oct. 25, 1993) ("Bronx County judges [have been] more lenient [since] the policy went into effect.").

98. *See supra* notes 89-91 and accompanying text.

99. Mirsky, *supra* note 33, at 9.

100. *Plea Bargains Expedite Our System of Justice*, *supra* note 33, at C2; Mirsky, *supra* note 33, at 8.

101. Mirsky, *supra* note 33, at 11; *cf.* Girgenti, *supra* note 97 ("The average days of incarceration [for defendants] increased overall but the average time for violent felonies has decreased.").

102. Mirsky, *supra* note 33, at 11.

103. Roberts, *supra* note 65 (stating that New York City will have to spend an additional three to four million dollars on incarceration because of the Bronx plea bargaining ban).

104. Mirsky, *supra* note 33, at 10; *see also* Girgenti, *supra* note 97 ("We do see the percentage of disposed indicted dismissals has increased.").

105. Mirsky, *supra* note 33, at 10.

106. *See supra* note 91.

107. The Sixth Amendment of the United States Constitution, made applicable to the states through the Fourteenth Amendment, guarantees defendants the right to a speedy trial. *See* U.S. Const. amends. VI, XIV. This guarantee is codified at N.Y. Crim. Proc. Law §§ 30.20, 30.30 (McKinney 1992 & Supp. 1995). The New York State speedy trial provisions provide that a defendant's motion to dismiss a criminal prosecution must be granted where the People are not ready for trial within a certain amount of time. *Id.* § 30.30(1)(a)-(d).

108. Lynch, *supra* note 33 ("I think there are some innocent people taking pleas as a result of pressure from the [Bronx] system.").

109. This six-day window of opportunity to plead guilty is based on N.Y. Crim. Proc. Law § 180.80, which requires that defendants held in custody on felony complaints be given a preliminary hearing within 144 hours (six days) to determine if reasonable cause exists to believe that the defendant committed the offense charged. *See* N.Y. Crim. Proc. Law § 180.80 (McKinney 1992). Because New York City prosecutors do not have the resources to conduct thousands of preliminary hearings every year, they circumvent the hearing requirement by having defendants indicted. New York State law does not require preliminary hearings for defendants who have been indicted. *Id.* § 180.80(2)(a)-(b). Indictments are normally not filed by the Grand Jury until the sixth day, and thus a defendant usually has up to six days to engage in plea bargaining while the New York City Criminal Court still has jurisdiction over his case. *Id.* § 10.30(1)(a)-(b), (2). Once an indictment is filed, however, the New York Supreme Court acquires jurisdiction of the case. *Id.* §§ 10.20(1)(a), 210.10. At this point, plea bargaining is no longer permitted.

110. *See* Lynch, *supra* note 33 ("The Legal Aid Society has no information other than what the District Attorney gives them. We don't have any police reports by the [N.Y. Crim. Proc. Law §] 180.80 day. We have nothing."); *A Plea for Better Justice in the Bronx—The DA's Plan Is No Bargain*, N.Y. Newsday, July 29, 1993, at 54 ("It's especially tough [for a person to consider a plea] when police reports, medical records and the like are unavailable."). Indicted defendants in New York State are not provided with detailed information concerning the charges against them until they make specific written requests or file motions. *See* N.Y. Crim. Proc. Law §§ 200.95(1),(3), 240.20(1)(a)-(j), 240.80(1), 240.90(2), 255.20(1)-(2) (McKinney 1992). These requests and motions cannot be made or filed until after a defendant has been arraigned on the indictment. *Id.* §§ 200.95(3), 240.80(1), 240.90(2), 255.20(1). Thus, a defendant will usually not be provided with detailed information about the charges against him until weeks after he has been arraigned in Supreme Court.

111. *See* Scott & Stuntz, *supra* note 5, at 1943 (noting that innocent defendants are less prone to take risks than guilty defendants). As a class, criminal defendants are usually prone to take risks. *Id.* A criminal history strongly suggests that the defendant is willing to take risks and fears punishment less than most people. *Id.* "But risk aversion is a much more plausible assumption where innocent defendants are concerned. . . ." *Id.*

112. *See* Gifford, *supra* note 38, at 58-59; *see also* Felten, *supra* note 51, at *2 ("Under pressure to cop a plea, innocent people may opt for punishment, deciding that the time, expense and risk of going to trial is too great.").

113. *See* Easterbrook, *supra* note 62, at 1969-70.

114. Scott & Stuntz, *supra* note 5, at 1933.

115. It can be assumed that in the absence of plea bargaining in the Bronx, an increased number of defendants will exercise their constitutional right to trial. In at least one jurisdiction where plea bargaining was banned, El Paso County, Texas, the proportion of cases disposed of by trial doubled following the implementation of the ban. *See* Weninger, *supra* note 6, at 276-77.

116. The Bronx criminal justice system's budget would need to double to pay for the costs of additional trials if plea bargaining was reduced by only 10 percentage points—from 85% to 75%. *See* Felten, *supra* note 51, at *7. Unfortunately, the New York City criminal justice system is already broke, as is evidenced by the condition of facilities. *Id.; see also* Stephen J. Schulhofer, *Is Plea Bargaining Inevitable?*, 97 Harv. L. Rev. 1037, 1040 (1984) ("A reduction from 90 per cent to 80 per cent in guilty pleas requires the assignment of twice the judicial manpower and facilities. . . ." (quoting Chief Justice Burger)).

117. Scott & Stuntz, *supra* note 5, at 1916 ("If plea bargaining were abolished—if, that is, the system had to process many more cases by trial than it presently does—one might reasonably suppose that the trial process would be more casual than it is now."). To accommodate a substantial increase in trials without additional resources, the trial process would also have to be "truncated." *Id.* at 1950. Shortening the trial process would also increase the error rate. *Id.; see also* National Prosecution Standards, *supra* note 36, at 223 (noting that an increased reliance on trials would lower the quality of justice administered).

118. *See* Scott & Stuntz, *supra* note 5, at 1932-33.

119. This Note posits that the grand jury process affords defendants valuable constitutional protections. Courts and commentators, however, have been highly critical of the grand jury process. *See* People v. Carter, 566 N.E.2d 119, 124 (N.Y. 1990) (Titone, J., dissenting) (repeating former Chief Judge Sol Wachtler's criticism that the grand jury would indict a ham sandwich); Ronald F. Wright, *Why Not Administrative Grand Juries?*, 44 Admin. L. Rev. 465, 514 (1992) (describing the grand jury as a rubber stamp and not a valid protector of liberty).

120. N.Y. Const. art. 1, § 6.

121. People v. Ford, 465 N.E.2d 322, 325-26 (N.Y. 1984); People v. Iannone, 384 N.E.2d 656, 660 (N.Y. 1978).

122. N.Y. Crim. Proc. Law § 200.15 (McKinney 1992); People v. Burke, 432 N.Y.S.2d 832, 832-33 (Sup. Ct. 1980).
123. *Burke*, 432 N.Y.S.2d at 833.
124. *See* N.Y. Const. art. 1, § 6; N.Y. Crim. Proc. Law § 195.20(a) (McKinney 1992).
125. N.Y. Crim. Proc. Law § 195.20 (McKinney 1992).
126. *Id.* § 195.30.
127. Mirsky, *supra* note 33, at graph T1M1.XLC.
128. *Id.*
129. *Id.*
130. *Id.* at 9. The New York City Criminal Court is the forum in which defendants are usually arraigned on criminal complaints or prosecuted on misdemeanors. *See* N.Y. Crim. Proc. Law § 10.30(1)(a)-(b), (2) (McKinney 1992). Once the grand jury indicts a defendant on a felony offense, however, the New York City Criminal Court transfers jurisdiction of the case to the Supreme Court. *See id.* §§ 10.20(1)(a), 210.10.
131. The ability of defendants to circumvent the ban by pleading guilty to SCIs led Bronx Administrative Judge Burton Roberts to declare that the "[no plea bargaining] policy is as phony as a three-dollar bill. It's a bunch of smoke and mirrors." *See* Roberts, *supra* note 65; *see also supra* notes 18-22 and accompanying text.
132. N.Y. Penal Law § 125.25 (McKinney 1992).
133. New York law provides for the imposition of two types of sentences upon defendants convicted of a criminal offense—indeterminate sentences and definite sentences. N.Y. Penal Law § 70.00(1), (4) (McKinney 1992). With indeterminate sentences, the length of imprisonment "is not fixed by the court but is left to the determination of penal authorities within minimum and maximum time limits fixed by the court of law." Black's Law Dictionary 771 (6th ed. 1990). For example, a defendant sentenced to an indeterminate term of 5 to 15 years imprisonment must serve at least 5 years in prison and cannot serve in excess of 15 years. Penal authorities, however, can release the defendant on parole as a reward for exemplary behavior anytime after he has served 5 years. Penal authorities can also penalize a recalcitrant defendant who habitually violates prison rules by holding him in prison for up to 15 years. With definite or determinate sentences, the length of imprisonment is specified by the court and penal authorities have no discretion in deciding when to release the defendant. *Id.* at 450. For example, a defendant sentenced to two years in prison would have to be released by penal authorities after serving two years.
134. N.Y. Penal Law § 70.00(3)(a)(i) (McKinney 1992).
135. *Id.* § 70.00(2)(a).
136. *Id.* § 70.00(3)(a)(i).
137. *Id.* § 70.00(2)(a).
138. *See supra* notes 18-22, 93-94 and accompanying text.
139. N.Y. Penal Law § 70.00(3)(a)(i) (McKinney 1992).
140. *Id.* § 70.00(2)(a).
141. *Id.* § 70.00(3)(a)(i).
142. *Id.* § 70.00(2)(a).
143. *See supra* note 122 and accompanying text.
144. *See supra* notes 18-22, 92 and accompanying text.
145. N.Y. Penal Law § 125.15 (McKinney 1992).
146. *Id.* § 70.00(2)(c), (3)(b), (4).
147. Girgenti, *supra* note 97 ("Bronx County convicted the highest percentage of defendants charged with [class] B, C, D, and E felonies—the top count that is.").
148. *Id.* ("With low level drug offenses there has been a dramatic increase of people convicted of the top count that they were indicted for.").
149. *See supra* notes 81-83 and accompanying text.

150. This Note will examine the Bronx District Attorney's behavior under the Model Code of Professional Responsibility (1981) [hereinafter Model Code], the Model Rules of Professional Conduct (1983) [hereinafter Model Rules], the New York Code of Professional Responsibility (1990) [hereinafter N.Y. Code], and the ABA Standards Relating to the Administration of Criminal Justice (1992) [hereinafter Standards for Criminal Justice]. While this Note will examine the Bronx District Attorney's behavior under all of the above provisions, only the N.Y. Code has been adopted in New York and can serve as the basis of a disciplinary action against the Bronx District Attorney. Both the Model Code and the N.Y. Code employ the designations Disciplinary Rules ("DR"), Ethical Considerations ("EC"), and Canons. Their purposes are as follows:

> The Canons are statements of axiomatic norms, expressing in general terms the standards of professional conduct expected of lawyers in their relationships with the public, with the legal system, and with the legal profession. They embody the general concepts from which the Ethical Considerations and the Disciplinary Rules are derived.
>
> The Ethical Considerations are aspirational in character and represent the objectives toward which every member of the profession should strive. . . .
>
> The Disciplinary Rules . . . are mandatory in character. [They] state the minimum level of conduct below which no lawyer can fall without being subject to disciplinary action.

Model Code, *supra*, *Preliminary Statement;* N.Y. Code, *supra*, *Preliminary Statement.* The Standards for Criminal Justice are intended as a guide to professional conduct and in New York cannot serve as the basis for disciplinary action against a prosecutor. *See* Standards for Criminal Justice, *supra*, Standard 3-1.1.

151. *See* United States v. Babb, 807 F.2d 272, 279 (1st Cir. 1986) (upholding defendant's conviction despite unprofessional conduct of prosecutor "worthy of severe condemnation"); United States v. Modica, 663 F.2d 1173, 1174 (2d Cir. 1981) (per curiam) (affirming conviction despite unprofessional conduct of prosecutor), *cert. denied*, 456 U.S. 989 (1982); *cf.* Eleanor Holmes Norton, *Bargaining and the Ethic of Process*, 64 N.Y.U. L. Rev. 493, 506 (1989) ("[Behavior that] appears strategically sound during the course of bargaining may not be ethically . . . appropriate.").

152. *See* Raphael v. Shapiro, 587 N.Y.S.2d 68, 70 (Sup. Ct. 1992) ("The integrity of our legal system and the fair administration of justice mandates [sic] strict adherence to the Code of Professional Responsibility by all members of the Bar."); Grunberg v. Feller, 505 N.Y.S.2d 515, 517 (Civ. Ct. 1986) ("Every attorney admitted to the Bar must strictly follow and subscribe to the provisions of the Code of Professional Ethics. . . ." (citations omitted)); *see also* Cody, *supra* note 67, at 464 (noting that "[a]ttorneys in government service are bound by two sets of ethics"—ethical principles governing public officials and the codes of ethics for attorneys). Every state except California has adopted either the Model Rules or the Model Code with some minor variation to govern the conduct of attorneys. *See* Thomas D. Morgan & Ronald D. Rotunda, 1993 Selected Standards on Professional Responsibility 127-32 (1993). California developed its own specific code: California Business and Professions Code. *Id.* at 300-25.

153. The role of the prosecutor differs from that of an attorney representing an individual in a number of ways. First, a prosecutor represents a powerful sovereignty and not an ordinary party in a controversy. Berger v. United States, 295 U.S. 78, 88 (1935). Second, "[t]he prosecutor's freedom from client control gives rise to vast discretion in making decisions." Fred C. Zacharias, *Structuring the Ethics of Prosecutorial Trial Practice: Can Prosecutors Do Justice?*, 44 Vand. L. Rev. 45, 58 (1991). The attorney representing an individual client is required to consult with the client concerning decisions. *See e.g.* Model Rules, *supra* note 150, Rule 1.4(a)-(b) (requiring a lawyer to keep a client reasonably informed to permit the client to make informed decisions). Third, the prosecutor simultaneously represents the often conflicting interests of the community, victim, defendant, and the state. *See* Zacharias, *supra*, at 57-59. The attorney representing an individual is normally prohibited from representing conflicting interests. *See* Model Code, *supra* note 150, DR 5-105(A)-(B); Model Rules, *supra* note 150, Rule 1.7(a)-(b).

154. *See* Cody, *supra* note 67, at 456; Freedman, *supra* note 62, at 213.
155. N.Y. Code, *supra* note 150, EC 7-13; Model Code, *supra* note 150, EC 7-13; *see Berger*, 295 U.S. at 88; People v. Brown, 412 N.Y.S.2d 522, 525 (App. Div. 1979); Model Rules, *supra* note 150, Rule 3.8 cmt.; Standards for Criminal Justice, *supra* note 150, Standard 3-1.2(c).
156. Zacharias, *supra* note 153, at 110.
157. *Id.* at 57; *see also* N.Y. Code, *supra* note 150, EC 7-13(2) (stating that decisions made by the prosecutor affecting the public interest should be fair to all).
158. Zacharias, *supra* note 153, at 57.
159. *See supra* note 147 and accompanying text.
160. *See supra* notes 101-02 and accompanying text.
161. *See supra* notes 108-18 and accompanying text.
162. *See supra* notes 119-29 and accompanying text.
163. *See supra* note 100 and accompanying text.
164. *See supra* notes 104-07 and accompanying text.
165. *See supra* notes 108-18 and accompanying text.
166. *See supra* notes 101-02 and accompanying text.
167. *See* Gershman, *supra* note 76, at 445; *see also* Zacharias, *supra* note 153, at 48 ("The 'do justice' standard . . . establishes no identifiable norm.").
168. Zacharias, *supra* note 153, at 105. In New York, the seek justice standard could not form the basis of a disciplinary action because it is an ethical consideration which is aspirational in nature. *See supra* note 150.
169. N.Y. Code, *supra* note 150, DR 1-102(A)(5); *see also* Model Code, *supra* note 150, DR 1-102(A)(5) ("A lawyer shall not: Engage in conduct that is prejudicial to the administration of justice."); Model Rules, *supra* note 150, Rule 8.4(d) ("It is professional misconduct for a lawyer to: Engage in conduct that is prejudicial to the administration of justice. . . .").
170. *See supra* notes 97-131 and accompanying text.
171. *See e.g.* H. Richard Uviller, *The Virtuous Prosecutor in Quest of an Ethical Standard: Guidance from the ABA*, 71 Mich. L. Rev. 1145, 1153 (1973) (stating that "justice in the criminal process . . . [is] a matter of myth").
172. An exhaustive search failed to discover a single instance in which a prosecutor was sanctioned for engaging in conduct prejudicial to the administration of justice. The only discovered disciplinary sanction of a prosecutor in relation to plea bargaining dated back to 1914. *See* Romualdo P. Eclavea, Annotation, *Disciplinary Action Against Attorney for Misconduct Related to Performance of Official Duties as Prosecuting Attorney*, 10 A.L.R.4th 605, 630 (1981) (discussing a one-year suspension of a prosecutor for inducing three young boys who proclaimed their innocence into pleading guilty).
173. *See* Uviller, *supra*, note 171, at 1152-53; *see also* Norton, *supra* note 151, at 531 ("The purpose of ethics . . . is to curb excessive self-interest and to encourage regard for the rights of others.").
174. N.Y. Code, *supra* note 150, EC 8-4; Model Code, *supra* note 150, EC 8-4.
175. *See supra* notes 84-96 and accompanying text.
176. *See supra* note 84.
177. *See* N.Y. Code, *supra* note 150, DR 5-101(A), EC 5-1 Model Code, *supra* note 150, DR 5-101(A), EC 5-1 (requiring an attorney to exercise independent professional judgment on behalf of a client and not to be influenced by personal interests or desires); *see also* Model Rules, *supra* note 150, Rule 1.7 cmt. [6] ("The lawyer's own interests should not be permitted to have adverse effect on representation of a client.").
178. N.Y. Code, *supra* note 150, EC 8-1; Model Code, *supra* note 150, EC 8-1; *see also* Model Rules, *supra* note 150, pmbl. [5] ("A lawyer should be mindful of deficiencies in the administration of justice . . . ."); Standards for Criminal Justice, *supra* note 150, Standard 3-1.2(d) ("It is an

important function of the prosecutor to seek to reform and improve the administration of criminal justice."). *But cf.* Cowles v. Brownell, 538 N.E.2d 325, 327 (N.Y. 1989) (stating that a prosecutor's duty is to represent the people and not to insulate the criminal justice system from civil liability).

179. Richard H. Kuh, *Professional Responsibility of the Lawyer in Government Service*, Remarks at the Association of the Bar of the City of New York (Jan. 28, 1975), *in* Professional Responsibility of the Lawyer: The Murky Divide Between Right and Wrong 93, 105 (1976) ("I am talking about an *ethical obligation* of the lawyer in government *to rock the boat to innovate to improve.*").

180. *See* N.Y. Code, *supra* note 150, EC 8-9; Model Code, *supra* note 150, EC 8-9. Both the N.Y. Code and the Model Code provide that "[t]he advancement of our legal system is of vital importance in maintaining the rule of law and in facilitating orderly changes; therefore, lawyers should encourage, and should aid in making, needed changes and improvements." N.Y. Code, *supra* note 150, EC 8-9; Model Code, *supra* note 150, EC 8-9; *see also* Standards for Criminal Justice, *supra* note 150, Standard 3-1.2(d) ("When inadequacies or injustices in the substantive or procedural law come to the prosecutor's attention, he or she should stimulate efforts for remedial action."); Cody, *supra* note 67, at 456 (stating that the prosecutor's duty extends beyond merely seeking convictions).

181. *See* Worden, *supra* note 60, at 340.

182. Kanner, *supra* note 24, at 48.

183. *See* Bertram R. Gelfand, *Pleas Are No Bargain*, N.Y. Newsday, Mar. 3, 1993, at 86, 86.

184. *See* Assael, *supra* note 86, at 99 ("'If we continue to plea-bargain because the system is crowded, we won't address the real issue: getting more courtrooms and judges.'" (quoting Bronx District Attorney Robert Johnson)). One effect of the El Paso County plea bargaining ban was a greatly expanded and restructured court system to counteract the adverse effects of the ban. *See* Weninger, *supra* note 6, at 305-06.

185. *See Next Six Weeks*, *supra* note 29, at 2 ("[I]f the policy of no plea bargaining . . . remains in effect, '[a]fter the new year, we'll begin to die a slow death.'" (quoting Justice Eggert, Acting Bronx County Administrative Judge)).

186. *See supra* note 100 and accompanying text.

187. *See supra* notes 104-07 and accompanying text.

188. *See supra* notes 101-02 and accompanying text.

189. *See supra* note 103 and accompanying text.

190. A study of other plea bargaining bans would have alerted the Bronx District Attorney to the adverse effects associated with such bans. For instance, following a ban on plea bargaining in El Paso, Texas, the number of requests for trials doubled, resulting in a 250% increase in the number of pending cases. *See* Weninger, *supra* note 6, at 277-78. The increase in pending cases delayed the start of the average trial by one hundred days. *Id.* at 305 tbl. 5. As a result, incarcerated defendants were required to remain in jail longer while awaiting their day in court. *Id.*

191. *See supra* notes 167-72 and accompanying text.

192. The seek justice standard is an example of an ethics rule couched in subjective terms. *See supra* note 155 and accompanying text. The absence of objective criteria in the seek justice standard makes the rule nebulous and impossible to enforce. *See supra* note 167 and accompanying text. A second ethics rule couched in subjective terms is N.Y. Code EC 8-4, which prohibits a prosecutor from acting unless he "conscientiously believes [his action] to be in the public interest." N.Y. Code, *supra* note 150, EC 8-4; *see also supra* notes 174-75 and accompanying text. This rule establishes an entirely subjective standard since it is impossible to determine if a prosecutor actually believed he was acting in the public's interest. *Id.* The requirement that a prosecutor exercise sound discretion in the performance of his duties is a third rule couched in subjective terms. *See infra* note 196. Actions seemingly "sound" to one prosecutor may appear foolish to another.

193. *See supra* notes 72-74 and accompanying text.

194. *See supra* notes 77-80 and accompanying text.

195. *See supra* notes 147-48 and accompanying text.
196. *See* Standards for Criminal Justice, *supra* note 150, Standard 3-1.2(b) ("[T]he prosecutor must exercise sound discretion in the performance of his or her functions.").
197. Although these proposed modifications are discussed separately, they are not mutually exclusive and could be implemented jointly.
198. *See, e.g.*, Lynch, *supra* note 33 ("The Bronx District Attorney's policy is onerous. It makes sometimes for uninformed decisions.").
199. *See supra* note 109 and accompanying text.
200. *See supra* note 110 and accompanying text.
201. *See* Lynch, *supra* note 33 ("How can we give good advice to the client when we have no information?"); *see also supra* note 110 (commenting on how defendants must decide whether to plead guilty without the benefit of police reports and other vital information).
202. *See* National Prosecution Standards, *supra* note 36, Standard 16.7.
203. *See* Anthony M. DeStefano & Patricia Hurtado, *B'klyn Makes Case for Faster Trials*, N.Y. Newsday, Apr. 23, 1993, at 8.
204. *Id.*
205. *Id.*
206. *Id.*
207. *Id.*
208. The use of written guidelines for prosecutors is not novel. The Standards for Criminal Justice list seven factors to guide prosecutors in exercising their discretion when deciding whether to initiate criminal charges against a defendant. *See* Standards for Criminal Justice, *supra* note 150, Standard 3-3.9(b)(i)-(vii).
209. *See* Mirsky, *supra* note 33, at 2.
210. *Id.*
211. *See* Weninger, *supra* note 6, at 283-85. *But cf.* Terence Dunworth & Charles D. Weisselberg, *Felony Cases and the Federal Courts: The Guidelines Experience*, 66 S. Cal. L. Rev. 99, 125-40 (1992) (discussing how the use of guidelines in the federal courts has not controlled prosecutorial discretion but has resulted in disparate treatment of certain classes of offenders).
212. Mirsky, *supra* note 33, at 3.
213. N.Y. Exec. Law § 259-c(4) (McKinney 1991); N.Y. Comp. Codes R. & Regs. tit. 9, §§ 8001.3, 8002.3(a)-(b) (1991).
214. N.Y. Comp. Codes R.& Regs. tit. 9, § 8001.3(b)(3) (1991); Revised Guidelines for Parole Board Decision Making, N.Y.S. Div. of Parole (Oct. 1978) [hereinafter Revised Guidelines]. In the offense severity category, inmates receive scores in the following three subcategories: (1) felony class of conviction; (2) weapon involvement; and (3) forcible contact. *Id.* at 3. In New York State, felonies are classified from A through E, with A felonies being the most serious. N.Y. Penal Law §§ 55.00(1)(a)-(e), 70.00(2)(a)-(e) (McKinney 1992). Under the guidelines, inmates convicted of class A felonies receive a score of five; inmates convicted of class B felonies receive a score four, and so on. Revised Guidelines, *supra*, at 3. After receiving a score on the class of felony for which they were convicted, inmates are scored on weapon possession. If a weapon was possessed during the commission of the crime, the inmate receives one point. If no weapon was possessed, the inmate does not receive any points. *Id.* Next, the inmate receives a score on the amount of forcible contact he had with the victim. Physical injury to the victim results in one point, serious injury results in two points, and death results in three points. *Id.* The higher an inmate scores in these three categories, the more likely he will be penalized by the Parole Board under the guideline system. N.Y. Comp. Codes R. & Regs. tit. 9, § 8001.3(b)(3); Revised Guidelines, *supra*, at 2.
215. N.Y. Comp. Codes R. & Regs., tit. 9 § 8001.3(b)(3) (1991); Revised Guidelines, *supra* note 214, at 4. In the prior criminal history category, inmates receive scores in the following six subcategories: (1) number of prior misdemeanor convictions; (2) number of prior felony

convictions; (3) number of prior jail terms; (4) number of prior prison terms; (5) prior probation/parole revocations; and (6) whether the inmate was on probation/parole at the time he committed the current offense. *Id.* For instance, an inmate with up to two prior misdemeanor convictions will receive zero points, while an inmate with three or more misdemeanor convictions will receive one point. *Id.* Likewise, an inmate with one prior felony conviction will receive one point, while an inmate with three or more prior felony convictions will receive three points. *Id.* Again, the higher an inmate scores in these categories, the more likely he will be penalized by the Parole Board under the guidelines. N.Y. Comp. Codes R. & Regs. tit. 9, § 8001.3(b)(3); Revised Guidelines, *supra* note 214, at 2.

216. N.Y. Comp. Codes R. & Regs. tit. 9, § 8001.3(b)(3) (1991); Revised Guidelines, *supra* note 214, at 2. A point system similar to that used by New York State's Division of Parole was used in El Paso, Texas to determine if defendants were eligible for probation. Weninger, *supra* note 6, at 286 n.90.

217. *See* N.Y. Comp. Codes R. & Regs. tit. 9, § 8001.3(b)(3) (1991); Revised Guidelines, *supra* note 214, at 2; *see also supra* notes 214-15 (explaining the guidelines used by the New York State Board of Parole); Weninger, *supra* note 6, at 286-89 (commenting on the judicial guidelines used in plea bargaining in El Paso, Texas).

218. *See* N.Y. Comp. Codes R. & Regs., tit. 9, § 8001.8(b)(3) (1991); Revised Guidelines, *supra* note 214; *supra* notes 214-15.

9

The Psychology of Perception, Eyewitness Identification, and the Lineup

Marvin Zalman, Larry Siegel

In the past century, psychologists have built up a substantial body of knowledge about human sensory perception[1] that is relevant to the question of eyewitness testimony. This body of knowledge, of course, is continuously subjected to more refined analysis so that our understanding of perception, memory, and attention is not final.[2] Nevertheless

> [E]yewitness research retains a broad range of implications for the criminal justice system. We have, for example, become quite sophisticated in our ability to evaluate the fairness of a photo spread or lineup. . . . Much of this knowledge is new and not accessible to the police or trier of fact.[3]

Perhaps the most important practical, if not theoretical, starting point is the wide agreement in perception research that to a substantial extent eyewitness testimony can be unreliable. The proper appreciation of this knowledge is so important to a knowledge of the courts' response to eyewitness testimony that it will be returned to when the possible bias of researchers is discussed. This knowledge is considered first because it contradicts the beliefs of many people and the experience of jurors:

> [E]yewitness testimony is likely to be believed by jurors, especially when it is offered with a high level of confidence, even though the accuracy of an eyewitness and the confidence of that witness may not be related to one another at all. All the evidence points rather strikingly to the conclusion that there is almost nothing more convincing than a live human being who takes the stand, points a finger at the defendant, and says, "That's the one!"[4]

UNRELIABILITY OF EYEWITNESSES

But just how accurate are eyewitnesses? The possibility of over 5,000 wrongful convictions in the United States annually and the steady trickle of news accounts of innocent persons imprisoned alert us to the fact that the human and legal process of iden-

Reprinted by permission of West Group from the *Criminal Law Bulletin,* vol. 27 (1991), pp. 159–176.

tification contains risks of error.[5] This conclusion is amply supported by research. Under experimental conditions, such as a staged crime before a class or a television audience, "witnesses have been proven to be remarkably inaccurate."[6] One authority performed an experiment in which a New York television news program ran a staged robbery that lasted for twelve seconds. A six-man lineup was then shown, and viewers were invited to call a number to pick out the perpetrator. Over 2,000 viewers called in, and only 14.1 percent picked the correct man, a result that was no better than a random guess.[7] Because psychological experiments can vary the elements of perception and recall in many ways, the percent of recall in various experiments has varied from no better than chance to 90 percent.[8]

Another interesting field experiment assessed the accuracy of facial recall in a real-life setting.[9] Two casually dressed male "confederates," one white and one black, ages 19 and 23, entered different convenience food stores within five minutes of one another, posing as customers. One would pay for a pack of cigarettes entirely with pennies and then would ask for directions to a location, such as an airport, that was fairly distant from the store. The other would also ask for directions after fumbling around for change. These encounters were designed to be plausible and to require the clerk to focus on the person somewhat longer than usual. Two hours after the second "customer's" visit, two males pretending to be law interns asked the clerk to identify each "customer" from two photo arrays, one of six whites and the other of six blacks. A total of seventy-three convenience store clerks in the Tallahassee area were thus questioned. The overall rate of accurate identifications was 34.2 percent, which increased to 46.8 percent when instances of "no identification" were omitted. While this figure is significantly higher than the 16.7 percent rate (one out of six) that would be expected by random guessing, it also points to a large number of incorrect identifications. The experimenters, incidentally, found in a pilot study that the correct recall of convenience store clerks under these conditions fell to the level of chance guessing when the "law interns" presented the photograph arrays more than twenty-four hours after the "customers" left the store. This study also found, in accord with other research, that identification accuracy of a person of one's own race is higher and that the ability of white clerks to identify the black "customer" was significantly related to the amount of cross-racial experience of the white clerk.[10] The black clerks in this study had higher accuracy rates than the white clerks: They were 13 percent more accurate in identifying the white "customer" and 23 percent more accurate in identifying the black "customer."[11] As expected, recognition was higher for the "customers" who were more attractive or distinctive and for lineups using larger pictures. A finding contradicting prior research was a positive relationship between the clerks' identification confidence and their accuracy. Commenting on the overall accuracy of findings, given the nature of the field setting, the authors suggested that a higher accuracy rate is expected if the clerks were victims of robberies because their attention to the face of the suspect would have been higher.[12]

One writer has summarized many of the pre-1980 research findings:

> When we experience an important event, we do not simply record that event in memory as a videotape recorder would. The situation is much more complex. Nearly all of the theoretical analyses of the process divide it into three stages. First, there is the *acquisition*

> stage—the perception of the original event—in which information is encoded, laid down, or entered into a person's memory system. Second, there is the *retention* stage, the period of time that passes between the event and the eventual recollection of a particular piece of information. Third, there is the *retrieval* stage during which a person recalls stored information.[13]

SELECTIVITY OF MEMORY PROCESS

Selectivity is a central fact about the memory process. A complex event consists of vast amounts of information, and the perceiving individual's sensory mechanism selects certain aspects from the total visual and aural stimuli. This generalization is supported by research findings that show that people are much better at remembering the salient facts of an event than peripheral details.[14] As a result, the core action of a crime is more likely to be "encoded" and retained in memory than are details regarding the features of a perpetrator. A factor such as a gun is likely to be "better attended" and thus better remembered than less central factors, such as the color of articles of clothing, and "[f]or some reason, the upper part of the face (e.g., eyes and nose) appears to be more salient than the lower part (e.g., mouth and chin)."[15] Selectivity is also affected by the expectations and interpretations of the event by the witness. Unfortunately, it is difficult to establish an unambiguous rule because "expectations can either enhance or impede accurate perception and memory."[16] Thus, if a witness expects a particular event, details that do not fit the expectation may be omitted. On the other hand, a predictable event allows for its rapid encoding and recall. Thus, "expectations can bias perception. When an event is not ambiguous or does not occur too rapidly, however, expectations typically support rather than hamper perception."[17]

Event Factors

Information acquisition is affected by event factors: retention time and frequency (the longer or more frequently something is viewed, the more information is stored); the type of fact observed (people have great difficulty in assessing speed and time; violent and emotional events produce lower accuracy of memory).[18] "Studies also show that the amount of time perceived as going by is overestimated under conditions of danger and that the overestimation tends to increase as the stress increases."[19] Thus, a witness may report viewing a crime scene for a lengthy period, and this report could be accepted as a factor that enhances reliability. Nevertheless, "since there is a pervasive human tendency to overestimate the duration of criminal events," the acceptance of a single witness's estimation of the time span of a criminal event ought to be subjected to testing.[20]

Witness Factors

Witness factors also affect observation. Thus, the "role that stress plays at the time a witness is perceiving a complex event is captured in the Yerkes-Dodson Law . . . that strong motivational states such as stress or other emotional arousal facilitate learning and performance up to a point, after which there is a decrement."[21] Although psychologists generally support the Yerkes-Dodson Law, its application to the evaluation of eyewitness testimony is far from precise because numerous studies vary considerably in the amount of stress that is reported as an experimental condition.[22] An experiment using children as subjects indicated that children who must identify individuals to whom they have been previously exposed (in an in-school, rather than a criminal, setting) in a lineup procedure experience higher levels of anxiety than children who make identifications from photographs or from lineups where they viewed the lineup persons through a one-way vision screen. Furthermore, this experiment produced higher levels of accurate identification with the low-stress identification methods but no reduction in the proportion of incorrect identifications.[23]

A review of research discloses that children are not necessarily worse witnesses than adults. Thus, while children generally recall less information than adults do, they are less likely to innocently invent information that was not present in the encounter situation. Research findings also indicate that child witnesses are somewhat more suggestible than adults, thus making it imperative that interviewers avoid leading questions.[24] The attention recently given by the United States Supreme Court to confrontation clause issues that have arisen from special procedures for the testimony of child witnesses in sexual abuse cases indicates an awareness of the heightened suggestibility of children.[25] Also, a great deal of social-psychological research has demonstrated that individual bias affects perception, whether the bias is a result of situational expectations, personal or cultural prejudice, or expectations from past experience.[26]

Retention Stage

The retention stage can be affected by factors such as the time elapsed between viewing the event and the time of recall. The most unnerving aspect of this process is that memory of an event can change. It is not simply a matter of a subject remembering less of what "actually" happened since "[p]ostevent information can not only enhance existing memories but also change a witness's memory and even cause nonexistent details to become incorporated into a previously acquired memory."[27] This finding is of great importance for appreciating the danger of suggestibility, the reason for the rules of the *Wade*, *Gilbert*, and *Stovall* cases.[28]

Thus, various studies have shown that (1) the likelihood of recall of an event is enhanced simply by mentioning it; (2) postevent suggestion can cause the memory to compromise between what was originally seen and what is reported; and (3) mentioning a nonexistent object to a witness can cause the witness to later report having seen it. It is not only simple facts that can be modified by postevent suggestion; subjective recollections (e.g., about how noisy or violent an event was) have been so modified.

Memory consists of both original information and external information that is acquired after the event, and both kinds of information become merged into one memory. Memory can also be influenced by the way an item or a situation is labeled and by the practice of witnesses to guess at information if they are not sure of their original memory. The dangers of the fragile process of memory retention is made worse by a "freezing effect." When a person makes a statement about an event, that statement tends to be more strongly remembered at a later time, and this tendency applies both to objectively true elements of the original event as well as false information.[29]

Retrieval Stage

Just as the memory of an event can be modified during retention by external information, the report of one's memory can be modified during the retrieval stage by factors such as the status of the person asking for the information, the form in which information is requested (i.e., narrative (free report) or controlled narrative questions (interrogatory form)), the retrieval environment, and, of course, the way in which questions are worded. Generally, the increased status of a questioner enhances the quantity and accuracy of responses; more errors occur when witnesses are forced to answer questions; and accuracy increases when a person relays it in a familiar and comfortable setting. The wording of questions raises issues similar to the injection of information at the retrieval stage by suggestion. One experiment indicates that the difference between the words "a" and "the" in a question precipitate different expectations about the existence of an event in the witness, and use of "the" significantly increases the percent who say that they saw something that was not, in fact, present in a film.[30]

Thus, since the individual is not a recording device but instead remembers selectively and since the individual is subject to suggestion during the retention and at the retrieval of information in memory, there are numerous variables at each stage that may contribute to producing a recollection that is not a true reflection of the underlying event. When this distortion occurs not in the psychology laboratory but during police interrogation or at a lineup, the potential for injustice is real.

A balanced view of the accuracy of perception, then, is that "[E]yewitness reports contain accuracies but inaccuracies as well."[31] The published research tends to indicate that commonsense evaluations of the accuracy of particular eyewitness situations may or may not be valid guides as to their reliability. This awareness should lead to at least two practical conclusions: that practicing trial attorneys must maintain familiarity with the recent developments in the field of perceptions research and that courts should be more open to the introduction of expert testimony regarding this particular branch of psychology.

ROLE OF PSYCHOLOGICAL EXPERTS AT TRIAL

The admission of the testimony of psychologists as experts has been a contested legal issue in cases where an eyewitness's testimony is critical.[32] Most psychologists who work in this field favor the use of expert testimony, although some have questioned it.[33] Aside from a concern that experts on both sides of an issue will further confuse the jury, the use of psychologists raises the question of whether psychology-of-perception findings seem to favor only the criminal defendant. Does the extensive use of expert testimony lead to the release of many guilty parties in return for ensuring that relatively few innocent defendants are freed?

Countering Defense Bias

Undoubtedly, many specific findings about the accuracy of eyewitness identification tend to favor defendants. For example, several studies show little or no correlation between the confidence that witnesses express in their certainty and the accuracy of their observations while some show such a relationship.[34] The lack of a confidence-accuracy correlation is counterintuitive; indeed, the U.S. Supreme Court in *Manson v. Brathwaite*[35] relied on witness confidence as one of five indicia of certainty, thus possibly injecting an element of factual injustice into some cases. Another factor used by the Court in *Neil v. Biggers*[36] as evidence of lineup accuracy is that the witness had previously described the suspect. Yet, studies have found that "accuracy of prior facial description was at best weakly related to identification accuracy. . . ."[37] Finally, most of the findings regarding perception reviewed in this article can be put to use by defense attorneys utilizing expert witnesses to raise the jury's level of skepticism about eyewitness testimony. While such knowledge may be used unfairly, it is the responsibility of the trial judge to ensure the fairness of the overall proceedings. In any event, sober skepticism should be the attitude of a jury to all evidence, and the indication that juries accept eyewitness testimony uncritically may require special counterbalancing in order to ensure truthful verdicts.

There are other ways in which knowledge of perception psychology can be used by the prosecution of ensure fairness. The fact that witnesses focus on central, rather than peripheral, facts of an incident[38] can be used by prosecutors on cross-examination if the defense attempts to show poor memory of a witness by drawing attention to peripheral facts. The environmental context, which indicates that witnesses remember facts better in familiar surroundings, should encourage police to question witnesses at home or work and motivate courts to allow questioning at crime scenes that may evoke memories of the event.

One authority has expressed concern that the literature in this field is "negative in its approach to the eyewitness."[39] Yet he suggests that several critical questions have not been fully aired. First, the selection of first-year college students as subjects for a study differs radically from real witnesses who "step forward" to volunteer information to the police. Perhaps those who become witnesses voluntarily in real cases are likely to be more accurate. Nothing is known about this relationship at present. Second, the staged nature of most psychological experiments may make the subjects less reluctant to risk misidentification when compared to real witnesses. Little is known about this point, and it is difficult to study. Third, it may be that researchers are more likely to report studies that show low accuracy rates as more interesting and socially important. Despite these risks and potentially biasing factors that may undervalue the strengths of eyewitness testimony, it has been noted that without the input of experts, juries and judges in individual cases may continue to rely on evidence that is clearly biasing.[40] A court may avoid pro-expert bias by cautioning the jury that the expert's testimony is only one element of proof and not decisive of the issue of guilt or for the court to limit expert testimony to statements "based on solid scientific data and cover only those studies bearing on the case [that] will minimize any prejudicial effects that the testimony might have."[41] While such elements are important in maintaining the fairness of trials in the search for truth, they are partial solutions to the larger problem of mistaken eyewitness identification.

Support for Use of Testimony

Two other researchers conducted a sophisticated "meta-analysis" of 190 studies, reported in 128 research articles, analyzing 960 experimental conditions, utilizing over 16,950 subjects, and generating more than 713,600 separate subject judgments in order to (1) determine how much has been "learned about the factors that affect facial identification" and (2) identify areas for further research. The basic concern of this meta-analysis was whether a sufficient scientific basis existed to "justify the courtroom appearance of expert witnesses to testify about these factors."[42] Following a complex two-stage analytic process, involving quantitative effect size analyses[43] and study characteristics analyses,[44] the authors concluded that the studies suggest three psychological processes that encompass many of the results of the reanalyzed studies:

1. *An encoding specificity principle:* "Performance is enhanced when the target at the encoding stage matches the target at the recognition stage." Variables such as context reinstatement,[45] target distinctiveness, target present/absent, transformation, and pose were significant to this principle.
2. *An elaboration principle:* "[T]he more processing the target prompts, the better performance will be." Variables included under this principle included encoding instructions, target distinctiveness, target present/absent, cross-race identification, and subject age.
3. *Viewing conditions and identification procedures:* "The third principle is that performance will be increased to the extent that the *viewing conditions and identification procedures* make more information available at identification." Relevant variables include exposure time and retention interval.[46]

This analysis indicates that a substantial body of information exists that justifies the use of expert witnesses on the issue of eyewitness identification.

IMPROVING THE ACCURACY OF LINEUPS

In recent years, finely honed studies have suggested specific ways in which the accuracy of the lineup itself can be improved. For example, as nonsuspects ("foils") in a lineup come to resemble the suspect more, more witnesses can be expected to identify the foils erroneously, suggesting a trade-off between a high probability of selecting the suspect in unfair (low similarity) lineups and a high probability of selecting an innocent person in high similarity lineups. Using experimental lineups with a "criminal" present and a "criminal" absent, studies[47] have found that the choice of a "guilty" suspect fell from 71 percent to 58 percent when going from unfair to fair lineups in the criminal-present mode. The choice of the "innocent suspect" (a look-alike to the "criminal"), however, fell from 70 percent to 31 percent in the criminal-absent mode. The same studies have developed diagnosticity ratios that indicate mathematically that the fair lineups improve the relative quality of both identifications and no-identifications over the unfair lineups. The practical value of this experiment is to dissuade police from setting up unfair lineups in the hope of highlighting suspects who they are "certain" are guilty. After all, since the conviction of an innocent person leaves the real criminal at large, law enforcement and prosecution have as real a legitimate desire to make lineups fairer as do defendants.

It has also been noted that although "there is abundant research evidence that recognition of same-race faces tends to be more accurate than recognition of other-race faces when large groups of photographs or slides are used,"[48] little thought has been given to the race of the lineup constructor in relation to the race of the suspect. This research application is complex as it "implies interactions between the race of the witness, race of the suspect, *and* the race of the person who constructs the lineup."[49] If it is true that other-race faces tend to look similar, then there is a risk that, for example, a white police officer who constructs a lineup of a black suspect and black foils for witnesses who are black may construct a lineup of faces that look alike to him but will appear dissimilar to the witnesses. This intriguing conjecture has not been subjected to experimental manipulation, but it does suggest one way in which a police department could attempt to ensure greater lineup fairness.

An experiment that has garnered some public interest is one that intentionally manipulated elements of the presentation of lineups to see if these manipulations would increase the accuracy of witness identification.[50] The overall conclusion was that techniques of lineup construction and presentation can significantly increase the accuracy of lineup identification. An important finding is that when a lineup or photograph array is presented *simultaneously* (i.e., the suspects and foils are presented at the same time), the proportion of false identifications increased, both in criminal-present and criminal-absent ("blank") lineups. False identifications were reduced when the suspect and foils were presented *sequentially* with instructions to make a yes-no decision as to each and not to compare one photograph to another. Although simultaneous presentation increased identification accuracy in the criminal-present lineups, the increase was not large nor statistically significant.[51] Additionally, "lineup context cues" were found to improve the accuracy of lineup identifications. As a result, the authors of the study recommended:

> [L]ineup procedures should ensure the use of voice samples and should show the lineup members from three-quarter poses and, whenever possible and appropriate, allow the witness to watch the lineup members walking in and out of the observation room. Such cues should also be taken into consideration when photographs are taken for the purpose of mug books.[52]

A news article calling attention to these sequential presentation findings noted the use of "cognitive interview" techniques by some law-enforcement agencies: Police in some cities were using several other applications of memory research, such as multiple-interview sessions, while using memory research to question the validity of others, such as interviews under hypnosis.[53] This change seems a welcome extension of the use of scientific tools for enhancing the accuracy of identifications.

Whether such information will be put to use in field settings is another matter. Law-enforcement agencies for the most part are not organized to conduct research and development (R&D) independently. Innovations in a variety of police procedures often occur on a "snowball" basis and may be adopted without rigorously testing underlying assumptions. This situation is often the case with crime-reduction strategies, and few police agencies are likely to experiment with identification procedures to determine which methods yield the best results. Yet, given the dynamic nature of the field of perception psychology, it is apparent that the continuous monitoring of research in this field is necessary if law-enforcement departments are to utilize such information. As the volume of academic research continues, some findings and techniques will have an influence on the police at the operational level. But the fact that most police agencies do not maintain an R&D function is an argument for allowing defense counsel to bring experts into the courtroom. In addition to serving the immediate ends of justice, such expert testimony may also serve a broader social function of educating police departments in recent findings.

EYEWITNESS IDENTIFICATION, ACCURACY, AND JUSTICE

Eyewitness identification, essential to the prosecution of criminals, is a process fraught with variation and uncertainty. The findings of psychology aid in an understanding of the reasons for instances of mistaken identity. Psychologists may be able to enhance the fairness of trials by explaining biasing factors to juries and working to improve the accuracy and fairness of identification techniques. The subtlety and complexity of both the psychology of perception and the operation of the criminal justice system show the limits of the law. Constitutional rules controlling the presence of attorneys at lineups and after-the-fact due process review are helpful but are of limited utility in maximizing the fairness and accuracy of identification.

Mistaken identification is one part of a broader misidentification problem. A comprehensive public policy approach must suggest several techniques for lessening the incidence of wrongful convictions.[54] For example, where guilt is based entirely on eyewitness testimony, extraordinary attention must be paid to the general and specific questions of reliability. Expert witnesses must always be allowed to testify on the issue of reliability and special training be given to police officers and to high-risk employees (e.g., of banks and convenience stores) on observation and documentation during criminal incidents. Police and prosecutors should also be given some sensitivity training on the dangers of wrongful conviction. Instances of deliberate fabrication of evidence or perjury by police and prosecutors should result in permanent removal of such officers or disbarment of attorneys. Special training for defense attorneys on the issues of identification is also important.

In view of the special seriousness of erroneous felony convictions, authorities in this field have recommended that states adopt a law, such as the one pioneered in Ohio,[55] that would streamline and routinize the compensation of those wrongfully convicted. At common law, there is no action for compensation of a person who is completely exonerated of a crime by a governor's pardon or by court action. Compensation, if it comes at all, must be through a "private bill" of the legislature. The Ohio law replaces the cumbersome procedure of seeking a special bill from the legislature with a special civil lawsuit. In this lawsuit, a plaintiff may prove exoneration from crime on the grounds that he did not commit the crime or any lesser included element or that the alleged crime, in fact, never occurred. Once this exoneration is proven, the plaintiff is entitled to receive the amount of any fines imposed and court costs or attorney fees paid for trial or appellate work; $25,000 for each year of imprisonment in a state institution (prorated for parts of years); any loss of wages, salary, or other earned income that resulted from the prosecution and imprisonment; and reasonable attorney fees for the civil suit to get compensation for the wrongful conviction. In calculating this amount, the court may not subtract the cost of arrest, prosecution, or imprisonment of the claimant.

In conclusion, it may also be worthwhile for appropriate state agencies to engage in the testing and dissemination of techniques designed to enhance the accuracy and fairness of identification techniques and lineups. These may include statewide standardized court instructions (such as those published by the Michigan State Bar Association),[56] mandated interview training through state-chartered police academies, prosecution standards and training through statewide prosecutors' associations, and relevant training for defense attorneys and judges. Recently available computerized face-drawing programs, utilizing a virtually infinite range of, for example, shapes, features, colors, and hairstyles, could be made available to police agencies, combined with adequate training and support. Those few states with central criminal justice information offices or perhaps the National Institute of Justice could devote some resources to assessing the current "state of the art" in the psychology of perception with the aim of disseminating relevant information to the justice community as quickly and as fully as is practically possible. Such activity would be in line with one of the ultimate goals of criminal justice: acquitting the innocent and convicting the guilty.

NOTES

1. According to Shapiro & Penrod, "Meta-Analysis of Facial Identification Studies," 100 Psych. Bull. 139, 140 (1986), many research volumes have been published on this area: B.R. Clifford & R. Bull, *The Psychology of Personal Identification* (1978); G.M. Davies, H.D. Ellis & J.W. Shepherd, *Perceiving and Remembering Faces* (1981); S. Lloyd-Bostock & B.R. Clifford, *Evaluating Witness Evidence* (1983); E.F. Loftus, *Eyewitness Testimony* (1979); J.W. Shepherd, H.D. Ellis & G.M. Davies, *Identification Evidence* (1982); *Eyewitness Testimony: Psychological Perspectives* (G.L. Wells & E.F. Loftus eds. 1984); A.D. Yarmey, *The Psychology of Eyewitness Testimony* (1979).

   For a useful review article with an extended bibliography, see Goodman & Hahn, "Evaluating Eyewitness Testimony," in *Handbook of Forensic Psychology,* at 258-292 (I. Weiner and A. Hess eds. 1987).

   Two earlier books on this topic are still useful: J. Marshall, *Law and Psychology in Conflict* (1966); P.M. Wall, *Eye-Witness Identification in Criminal Cases* (1965).
2. One observer points out that a century of experimentation on the eyewitness phenomenon, although yielding many findings, has failed to provide an integrated theoretical structure about perception, memory, and attention. Yuille, "A Critical Examination of the Psychological and Practical Implications of Eyewitness Research," 4 L. & Hum. Behav. 335-345 (1980).
3. *Id.* at 340. The relevant research is conducted under two overlapping headings: *facial identifications* usually conducted by cognitive psychologists and *eyewitness identification research* usually conducted by social and cognitive psychologists. Shapiro & Penrod, note 1 *supra*, at 139.

As Shapiro & Penrod also note, facial identification studies (which simply study the recognition of faces shown at an earlier time) do not encompass "studies that use descriptions of an event, the estimated time of an event, multiple-choice questions concerning the event," and so forth, all of which have important practical application in the law. *Id.*

4. E.F. Loftus, note 1 *supra*, at 19.

5. Huff, Rattner & Sagarin, "Guilty Until Proven Innocent: Wrongful Conviction and Public Policy," 32 Crime & Delinq. 518-544 (1986).

6. Yuille, note 2 *supra*, at 336.

7. Buckhout, "Nearly 2,000 Witnesses Can Be Wrong," *in* E.F. Loftus, note 1 *supra*, at 135-136.

8. Thus, an experiment where trained and untrained subjects were told to "take a 'good hard look' " at twenty-four photographs of faces because they would later be asked to recall them from a larger set of portraits produced recognition results of 80 percent to 90 percent correct identification of undisguised faces over a four-day postviewing period. Interestingly, those subjects who underwent intensive training on face recognition by remembering particular facial features did no better in recalling the faces than untrained subjects. E.F. Loftus, note 1 *supra*, at 166-170.

9. Brigham, Maass, Snyder & Spaulding, "Accuracy of Eyewitness Identifications in a Field Setting," 42 J. Personality & Soc. Psych. 673-681 (1982) (hereinafter Brigham et al.).

10. "White targets are more easily identified" than black targets. Shapiro & Penrod, note 1 *supra*, at 145. This conclusion is not undermined by the overall results of their regression analysis in the "study characteristics analysis" (see the detailed discussion of their study at note 43 *infra*) that "the target race main effect is essentially a cross-racial identification effect" (Shapiro & Penrod, note 1 *supra*, at 149) because most of their studies involved white subjects, and only a few cross-racial studies (4 percent) were included in their set of studies.

11. The authors suggested that one possible explanation might be that the black clerks worked in stores in higher-crime areas, but this situation was not shown to exist. On the other hand, black clerks who had been robbed had a 100 percent accuracy rate in this experiment while no such rate was found for white clerks who had been previously robbed. An explanatory factor not suggested by the authors is that minority group members may have more cross-racial experience than whites. *Id.* at 677.

12. *Id.* at 679.

13. E.F. Loftus, note 1 *supra*, at 21 (citations omitted).

14. *Id.* at 21, 25-27.

15. Goodman & Hahn, note 1 *supra*, at 261 (citation omitted). Indeed, there is some evidence that the focus in a weapon may detract from a witness's ability to encode and recall the description of a perpetrator. *Id.* at 265.

16. *Id.* at 262.

17. *Id.* at 263.

18. E.F. Loftus, note 1 *supra*, at 23-32.

19. A.D. Yarmey, note 1 *supra*, at 52.

20. Goodman & Hahn, note 1 *supra*, at 260 (citing primary sources).

21. E.F. Loftus, note 1 *supra*, at 33.

22. Goodman & Hahn, note 1 *supra*, at 263-264.

23. Dent & Stephenson, "Identification Evidence: Experimental Investigations of Factors Affecting the Reliability of Juvenile and Adult Witnesses," in *Psychology, Law and Legal Processes,* 195-206 (D. Farrington, K. Hawkins & S. Lloyd-Bostock eds. 1979).

24. Goodman & Hahn, note 1 *supra*, at 277-278. A journalist's account of a day-care center sexual molestation trial in New Jersey that led to a conviction reported that a determined investigator ignored denials of sexual abuse by the children interviewed and continued interviewing the children with leading questions until the "right" answers were obtained. See Rabinowitz, "From

the Mouths of Babes to a Jail Cell," Harper's, May 1990, at 52-63. Whether or not such techniques are prevalent in such cases, it would appear that investigators should keep detailed records of the interviews that should be available to the court in a trial.

25. In Maryland v. Craig (110 S. Ct. 3157 (1990)), the U.S. Supreme Court upheld the use of trial testimony by a child sex abuse victim via one-way closed-circuit television where certain procedural safeguards were established and where the determination of necessity was made on a case-by-case basis. The Maryland statute posited that children may be more susceptible to mental trauma by the experience of testifying such that they could not reasonably communicate in a face-to-face confrontation. More to the point of the special susceptibility to suggestion of children was Idaho v. Wright (110 S. Ct. 3139 (1990)), which held that, in a child sexual abuse case, the hearsay testimony of a pediatrician that did not have "circumstantial guarantees of trustworthiness" was inadmissible as a confrontation clause violation. The physician who interviewed the victimized children, aged 2½ and 5½ years old at the times of the crimes charged, failed to keep a picture that he drew during the interview, and did not keep detailed notes recording changes in the child's affect or attitude. The Court affirmed the Supreme Court of Idaho, which ruled the pediatrician's testimony inadmissible. Referring to the holding, Justice Sandra Day O'Connor stated:

> The statements also lacked trustworthiness, according to the court, because "this interrogation was performed by someone with a preconceived idea of what the child should be disclosing. . . ." Noting that expert testimony and child psychology texts indicated that children are susceptible to suggestion and are therefore likely to be misled by leading questions, the court found that "[t]he circumstances surrounding this interview demonstrate dangers of unreliability which, because the interview was not [audio or video] recorded, can never be fully assessed."

Id. at 3145.

26. E.F. Loftus, note 1 *supra*, at 32-51.

27. *Id.* at 55.

28. United States v. Wade, 388 U.S. 218, 87 S. Ct. 1926 (1967); Gilbert v. California, 388 U.S. 263, 87 S. Ct. 1951 (1967); Stovall v. Denno, 388 U.S. 293, 87 S. Ct. 1967 (1967). *Wade* and *Gilbert* required that counsel be present at lineups in order to counteract or observe any behavior likely to be suggestive to witnesses while *Stovall* held that unfair lineups or that inherently suggestive one-on-one showups violate due process. In *Kirby v. Illinois* (406 U.S. 682, 92 S. Ct. 1877 (1972)), the U.S. Supreme Court limited the *Wade-Gilbert* rule to preindictment lineups only.

29. E.F. Loftus, note 1 *supra*, at 52-87.

30. *Id.* at 88-104.

31. Goodman & Hahn, note 1 *supra*, at 258.

32. See United States v. Alexander, 816 F.2d 164 (5th Cir. 1987).

33. E.g., E.F. Loftus, note 1 *supra*, at 191-203; A.D. Yarmey, note 1 *supra*, at 196-198; Cutler, Penrod & Martens, "The Reliability of Eyewitness Identification: The Role of System and Estimator Variables," 11 L. & Hum. Behav. 233-258 (1987) (hereinafter Cutler et al.).

34. A.D. Yarmey, note 1 *supra*, at 150-151, 156; E.F. Loftus, note 1 *supra*, at 100-101; Brigham et al., note 9 *supra*.

35. 432 U.S. 98, 97 S. Ct. 2243 (1977).

36. 409 U.S. 188, 93 S. Ct. 375 (1972).

37. Cutler et al., note 33 *supra*, at 233-258.

38. E.F. Loftus, note 1 *supra*, at 63.

39. Yuille, note 2 *supra*, at 338-339.

40. *Id.* at 338-339, 341-342; see E.F. Loftus, note 1 *supra*, at 171-177.

41. E.F. Loftus, note 1 *supra*, at 197.

42. Shapiro & Penrod, note 1 *supra*, at 139.

43. These studies involved analyses of nineteen independent variables (factors usually manipulated by experimenters) and sixteen study characteristics (factors such as sex and race of the target, retention interval, pose at recognition stage, and number of targets) on four dependent variables: (1) correct "hits"; (2) false alarms (incorrect identifications); (3) sensitivity (the ability to detect the target when it is present and missing); and (4) decision criteria (the willingness to guess). Context reinstatement (the use of techniques and cues at the retrieval stage that were previously associated with the targets or the incidents in the study phase) emerged as an important variable, enhancing "hits" and suppressing false alarms, suggesting a technique to enhance the accuracy of lineups. Yet the effect of context reinstatement was smaller in lifelike situations than in laboratory studies. Training was a perplexing variable because extensive training failed to improve identification performance. Target-absent lineups produced a significant effect on false alarms. Shapiro & Penrod, note 1 *supra*, at 141-146.

44. *Id.* at 146-151. A factor analysis and a regression analysis were conducted to study the influence of study characteristics on performance. The most salient factor could be called "optimality of viewing" or "type of study," reflecting an important peculiarity of this entire research area. Although the policy concern of the legal world fastens on eyewitness identification in the lineup situation, researchers are concerned also with the theory of facial recognition. Thus, the studies may be broadly divided into (1) laboratory experiments where subjects are presented with facial views at the encoding stage and later are asked to identify the correct face at the retrieval stage and (2) experiments that attempt to simulate crimes or observation events followed by some test of eyewitness identification procedure (including lineups). Shapiro and Penrod review both kinds of studies in their meta-analysis.

Substantively, Shaprio and Penrod conclude from this part of their study: "The regression analysis results suggest that within our set of studies, the quality of viewing is the most important determinant of facial identification performance, followed by pose, target race, and gender." *Id.* They suggest that information on false alarms is important to policymakers (*id.* at 150), and this importance should also be the case for attorneys and experts in litigation.

45. It has been found that memory is improved when the context of the event is recreated or "reinstated" by recalling contextual factors (e.g., the time of day or the voice of the suspect).

46. Shapiro & Penrod, note 1 *supra*, at 152.

47. Lindsay & Wells, "What Price Justice? Exploring the Relationship of Lineup Fairness to Identification Accuracy," 4 L. & Hum. Behav. 303-313 (1980).

48. Brigham, "Perspectives on the Impact of Lineup Composition, Race, and Witness Confidence on Identification Accuracy," 4 L. & Hum. Behav. 315-321, 318 (1980).

49. *Id.*

50. Cutler & Penrod, "Improving the Reliability of Eyewitness Identification: Lineup Construction and Presentation," 72 J. Applied Psych. 281-290, 288 (1988).

51. *Id.* at 284, 287. This finding supported an earlier study by Lindsay & Wells, "Improving Eyewitness Identifications From Lineups: Simultaneous Versus Sequential Presentation," 70 J. Applied Psych. 556-564 (1985).

52. Cutler & Penrod, note 50 *supra*, at 289.

53. Leary, "Novel Methods Unlock Witnesses' Memories," N.Y. Times, Nov. 15, 1988, at 25 (national edition).

54. C.R. Huff, A. Rattner & E. Sagarin, *Convicted but Innocent: Wrongful Conviction and Public Policy* (forthcoming 1991).

55. Ohio H.B. 609 of 1986 (effective Sept. 23, 1986) (sponsored by Ohio Rep. Vernon L. Sykes).

56. See E.F. Loftus, note 1 *supra*, 189.

10

DNA (Deoxyribonucleic Acid) Evidence, Criminal Law, and Felony Prosecutions: Issues and Prospects*

G. Larry Mays, Noreen Purcell, L. Thomas Winfree, Jr.

INTRODUCTION

Forensic evidence is an integral part of criminal investigation. The use of new scientific techniques for analysis is a constant challenge to our justice system. The development and utilization of new procedures will enhance the importance of forensic evidence and facilitate the processing of specific cases through the courts. However, each new scientific advancement will bring with it legal and operational problems. For example, DNA (deoxyribonucleic acid) testing, one of the newest of the forensic techniques, is likely to have an impact on all parts of the criminal justice system.

As a result of the recent endorsement of DNA testing by the National Research Council (see "Genetic fingerprinting reliable . . . ," 1992), the use of forensic evidence has gained national attention. This review essay examines how the courts respond to new strategies applied to the analysis of physical evidence, using as a case in point the potential effect of DNA-testing technology. Modern forensic scientists have progressed in their crime-related analyses of physical evidence (that is, weapons, drugs, fingerprints, etc.) with advances such as lasers, complex computer software programs, and genetic engineering. Physical evidence plays a very significant role in the criminal justice system. Yet, the history of forensic science tells us that physical evidence not only can answer many legal questions surrounding a crime scene but can also influence the processing of defendants through the system. At times, these effects are not always intended or desired. Just how much of an influence, and in what areas, specific physical evidence has is the focus of this review essay.

FORENSIC ANALYSIS

As a rule, crime scenes are complex puzzles, where the pieces are supplied by witnesses, victims, suspects, and physical evidence. The evidence at crime scenes is

Reprinted by permission of the National Center for State Courts from the *Justice System Journal,* vol. 16 (1992), pp. 111–122.

unstable and everchanging. As time passes, witnesses disappear, die, or forget, and evidence is destroyed or misplaced. Police officers, in their zeal to provide a timely response to a call for assistance, may destroy, alter, or add unnecessarily to evidence at a crime scene. Physical evidence is also subject to the forces of nature.

Investigators and forensic analysts must work together to accomplish the objectives of criminal investigation. With each new scientific advancement, forensic analysts are better able to connect the pieces of the crime scene puzzle together to help solve the questions surrounding the criminal investigation—questions that supply form and substance to the *corpus delicti.* It is the job of the crime scene investigator to collect and preserve the physical evidence so that forensic analysts can examine it and determine its potential for use in court (Kirk, 1974). Physical evidence can establish that a crime has been committed, place the suspect at the scene or with the victim, corroborate witnesses' testimony, and exonerate innocent persons (Fisher, 1987). More important, physical evidence can establish the identity of the person responsible for the crime.

Personal identification has become the primary goal of forensic scientists, since it is imperative for effective law enforcement (Hicks, 1988). Different identification methods have been used over the past century. For example, in the late 1800s Alphonse Bertillon, the chief of the Judicial Identification Service in France, devised a systematic method of human identification. The Bertillon method utilized measurements of an individual's size, coloring, and markings. More specifically, this method of human identification took into account physical and verbal characteristics (Bertillon, 1896). That is, a man would have his height and the diameters of his head, right ear, left foot, and fingers measured. He also would have the coloring of the iris of his left eye and hair noted. Finally, a verbal portrait of the type and manner of his speech would be noted and photographs would be taken. The Bertillon system was used worldwide until the 1930s, when two individuals at Leavenworth prison were found to have the same measurements (Lambourne, 1984).

Although his system was flawed, Bertillon previously had alluded to the usefulness of the patterns of ridges on the tips of the fingers (Bertillon, 1896). However, Bertillon was not convinced that the statistician Frances Galton had provided sufficient proof for the primacy of fingerprinting: "[T]hese designs taken by themselves do not present elements of variability sufficiently well-defined to serve as a basis of classification of several hundred thousand cases" (Bertillon, 1896: 14).

In spite of Bertillon's reservations, fingerprint identification has become perhaps the best known way of identifying suspects. Just over 100 years ago, fingerprints were determined to be individualistic, permanent, and classifiable. However, it was not until the early 1900s that the usefulness of fingerprinting as a means of identification became apparent. In 1902 the first system of fingerprinting in the United States was implemented by the New York Civil Service Commission. By 1933 a latent fingerprint section was established in the identification division of the Federal Bureau of Investigation (FBI). This section of the FBI specializes in individual examinations of latent or inked prints. Today, the Identification Division of the FBI utilizes computer-aided identification procedures (Federal Bureau of Investigation, 1977).

Unfortunately, fingerprints often are not detected at the scenes of some violent crimes (Hicks, 1988). A far more frequent occurrence is that the physical evidence found at violent crime scenes consists of biological materials (for example, blood, hair, and semen). Until recently, this type of evidence could only make a limited trace association to the suspect or exclude him or her completely as a potential suspect (Fisher, 1987).

The application of advanced scientific techniques enables law enforcement professionals to be more effective in solving crimes. Historically, this can be seen by the development of dyes sensitive to gunshot residue, cameras to photograph latent prints, and equipment to separate components of biological evidence. The methods of human identification have gone from outward physical features, such as the Bertillon system, to minute genetic identifiers, such as blood enzyme types and DNA tests.

DNA AND CRIME SCENE INVESTIGATIONS

In 1985 Dr. Alec J. Jeffreys, of Leicester University (England), announced a new genetic-engineering technique that could positively identify an individual by a process he termed "DNA fingerprinting" (Jeffreys et al., 1985). DNA (deoxyribonucleic acid) is a molecule that carries the genetic information that makes each person unique, and it is found in every nucleated cell in the body (Gebreth, 1988). The first DNA criminal case on record involved a multiple rapist/killer in the English Midlands, who claimed at least two victims between 1983 and 1986 (Franklin-Barbajosa, 1992: 118–119). Criminal investigators, trying to determine if a suspect was indeed the killer, asked Jeffreys in 1987 to apply his DNA technique. The man who confessed was shown to be innocent, and after "blooding" by 4,500 men in the Midlands, a suspect was identified by police investigations; his identity as the killer was confirmed by DNA fingerprinting.

DNA testing involves a procedure by which DNA is extracted from a sample (for example, blood, tissue, or semen), cut up, and separated into a gel. The next step entails the introduction of alkaline chemicals to split the DNA fragments apart and the attachment of radioactive probes. These probes—synthetic DNA segments of known sequence—bond to a specific strand or sequence. Finally, a print (x-ray) is made of the radioactive probes on a nylon sheet, and a technician compares sample banding patterns. The specific banding pattern observed from the radioactive assay is unique to each individual: like fingerprints, DNA banding patterns are highly characteristic of the source.

There are currently four major private laboratories in the United States conducting DNA tests for law enforcement agencies.[1] The FBI has produced several publications and has implemented a DNA-testing section in the federal crime laboratory at Quantico, Va. (Budowle et al., 1988). The FBI also has been instrumental in assisting state agencies interested in initiating DNA-testing laboratories.

A great deal has been written about the specific analytical techniques involved in DNA testing. However, the focus of the remainder of this review essay is on the operational and legal issues raised by the use of DNA evidence testing in criminal trials. It should be immediately obvious that these two areas are really inseparable. Nevertheless, to fully elucidate the range of issues raised by DNA testing, operational and legal concerns will be treated separately.

OPERATIONAL ISSUES

There are two types of operational issues involved in DNA evidence testing: laboratory or "technical" concerns, and probability or statistical concerns. Both types of issues will be treated in this section and this, in turn, will lay the foundation for discussion of the legal issues.

LABORATORY STANDARDS

As with any new forensic technique, DNA evidence testing has raised questions about the laboratory techniques employed in the analysis and what the appropriate standards are for the laboratories undertaking such analyses. Several states (Minnesota, New York, and Virginia), along with the FBI's national crime laboratory, have been dealing with the issue of lab standards. In fact, an organization called the Technical Working Group for DNA Analysis Methods (composed of FBI and state crime lab scientists) has been working "to identify existing problems in the field of DNA analysis and to standardize protocols" (McDonald, 1991: 34). Likewise, the Bureau of Criminal Apprehension in Minnesota "has been mandated to develop uniform procedures and protocol for collecting and preserving specimens for analysis" (McDonald, 1991: 34). As laboratories, both public and private, move toward standardizing DNA-testing procedures, greater confidence can be placed in the reliability of the analyses themselves and the interpretations of those analyses. While the genetic principles upon which DNA fingerprinting are based are reasonably well established, it is fair to characterize the forensic applications as still in their nascent stage.

Accuracy and reliability are far from given, even when the FBI laboratory is involved. Edwards (1991: 8) cited one laboratory as reporting a 50 percent failure rate in correctly identifying rape suspects; the FBI cannot reach a definitive evaluation in between 25 and more than 30 percent of the DNA samples it analyzes. Ultimately, a match, using current technology and equipment, relies upon the individual and subjective evaluation of the DNA lab technician.

PROBABILITY CONCERNS

Because the population database for DNA comparisons is really just being formed, perhaps the fiercest debate is raging over the probability estimates of identical matches (see Chakraborty and Kidd, 1991; Lewontin and Hartl, 1991; Roberts, 1991). In other words, what are the chances that a DNA sample belongs to one individual, to the exclusion of all others, and how confident are we about those probabilities? Early estimates of DNA samples matching by chance were from 1 in 500,000 to 1 in 738 trillion (Roberts, 1991: 1721). Recent estimates, based on the fact that sexual unions resulting in live births do not occur randomly in the world population, dip as low as 1 in 100,000 (Franklin-Barbajosa, 1992: 119). However, as Lewontin and Hartl (1991: 1749) note, there are really two problems in making these estimates: "First, the probability estimates are unduly influenced by VNTR (variable number of tandem repeat) patterns that are uncommon in the reference database, and it is precisely the uncommon VNTR patters whose frequencies are most difficult to estimate accurately. . . . Second, the current method often confronts the very real dilemma of not being able to specify a suitable reference base."

To counter what they believe to be the undue caution expressed by Lewontin and Hartl, Chakraborty and Kidd (1991: 1735) emphasize that we are dealing with "valid estimates" rather than "exact values." Their conclusion is that DNA evidence is reliable and that excluding it will substantially diminish "the prospect of convicting true criminals, as well as exonerating the falsely accused" (Chakraborty and Kidd, 1991: 1739).

The debate over probability estimates is more than a case of mental gymnastics involving arcane issues: it has very real consequences for criminal case processing. When scientists disagree over procedures, interpretations, and probabilities, the courts are less willing to accept as definitive the laboratory analyses of DNA evidence. Thus, the operational issues have clear implications for the legal issues concerned as well.

LEGAL ISSUES

There are several aspects to DNA-testing implementation that are of immediate concern to the legal community. As with any new scientific discovery that has a justice system application, there must be a thorough review to determine what effects it may have on the legal system. The legal issues associated with DNA testing include invasiveness, the standards of proof, the probative value of the evidence, privacy concerns, and admissibility.

Invasiveness

There are several constitutional questions that are relevant to DNA testing. One of the primary concerns raised by both advocates and opponents of DNA testing is the question of invasiveness (sometimes expressed as intrusiveness). For example, a report prepared by the SEARCH Group for the Bureau of Justice Statistics (1991: 11) suggests that obtaining a known biogenic sample to compare with an unknown sample may involve the "compulsory taking of a specimen." The Fourth Amendment protects against unreasonable searches and seizures. The question arises as to whether the taking of a sample from a suspect, for the purpose of DNA testing, is an unreasonable search and seizure. As the BJS report notes: "The Supreme Court has held [in *Schmerber v. California*, 384 U.S. 757 (1966)] that the compulsory withdrawal of blood constitutes a search within the meaning of the Fourth Amendment. Accordingly, law enforcement officials may be required to obtain a search warrant prior to obtaining a blood sample." The report goes on to add that "in order to obtain a search warrant, law enforcement officials are required to show that they have probable cause to believe that the suspect has committed a crime" (Bureau of Justice Statistics, 1991: 11).

The Fifth Amendment protects individuals against self-incrimination. If a suspect is court ordered to give a sample for DNA testing, the question of self-incrimination may be raised. Both the Fifth and Fourteenth amendments protect against deprivation of life, liberty, or property without due process of law (Williams, 1987–1988). Thus far, no DNA case based on these or any other grounds has reached the United States Supreme Court.

It is unlikely that an argument of a constitutional nature will result in any significant change due to previous rulings on similar scientific techniques. For example, the Supreme Court has ruled that the "function of the Fourth Amendment is to protect personal privacy and dignity against unwarranted governmental intrusion" [*Wolf v. Colorado*, 338 U.S. 25, 27 (1949)]. The Court further has required that the police find a "clear indication"; that is, they must have probable cause that incriminating evidence would be found before they can search beyond the surface of the body (Williams, 1987–1988: 22).

The Supreme Court has held that under the Fifth Amendment, the collection and use of blood for the purpose of chemical analysis does not violate the privilege against self-incrimination. Justice Holmes said that the Fifth Amendment protects only communications and not bodily evidence [*Holt v. U.S.*, 218 U.S. 245 (1910)]. More recently, cases, such as *State v. Washington*, 622 P. 2d 986 (Wash. 1981) and *U.S. v. Brown*, 557 F. 2d 541 (6th Cir. 1977) particularly, have involved bodily fluids. It was also noted that the distinction between testimonial and physical evidence may not be valid in all circumstances. That is, when the evidence is procured by coercion or a false confession is given due to fear of the testing, the evidence is not admissible (Williams, 1987–1988).

According to the Supreme Court, the taking of a blood sample for chemical analysis does not violate the Fourteenth Amendment, either. However, there is a difference between the normal taking of a blood sample and the method of extraction used by the police in *Rochin v. California*, 342 U.S. 165 (1952). In the *Rochin* case the police used extreme methods (doctors forced a solution into the suspect so that he would vomit the evidence) to obtain the incriminating evidence. To the contrary, in most instances the collection of blood for analysis has been found to be reasonable because the methods are well known and effective (Williams, 1987–1988).

Standards of Proof

A second legal issue deals with the standards or levels of proof. Roberts (1991: 1721) says that for many individuals on both sides of the DNA-evidence issue "the debate is not about right and wrong but about different standards of proof, with the purists on one side demanding scientific accuracy and the technologists on the other saying approximations are good enough." The standard of proof is related to two key concerns for the courts: probative value and admissibility. Probative value will be addressed here, and admissibility will be discussed at length later.

Probative Value

White (1990: 12) observes that "probative value refers to how much evidence proves. In the context of the prosecution's burden of proving the defendant guilty, it refers to how far a piece of evidence goes towards meeting that burden of proof." Roberts

(1991: 1721), in dealing with DNA evidence, alludes to the issue of probity. She says that when DNA evidence is introduced, the courts must make certain to tell "the jury how much weight to give this new type of scientific evidence." In other words, the jury should be instructed that DNA evidence should not be considered more important than other evidence and that the time it takes to introduce such evidence is not indicative of its significance.

Privacy

The fourth legal concern deals with privacy. Privacy is really a threefold matter. First, obtaining blood and other biogenic samples (as discussed in relation to intrusiveness), clearly is a privacy concern (Bureau of Justice Statistics, 1991; see also, Edwards, 1991). Second, even more complex and troubling, however, may be some of the questions facing the courts: from whom may samples be taken, under what circumstances, and for what purposes? Some states (New York and Virginia, for example) already require the extraction of biogenic samples for DNA testing and databank storage from convicted felons (see Greenspan, 1991; Kolmetz, 1991). Questions then arise about whether noncriminal DNA samples can be included in state databanks in the same way noncriminal sets of fingerprints can be retained on file. And finally, to what extent will DNA databanks be open files? Currently, some states grant public access (under clearly specified conditions) to criminal history information (Bureau of Justice Statistics, 1991; Edwards, 1991). Will the same be true for DNA files? In some cases, this question has not been answered.

Admissibility

Perhaps the major issue facing the courts is the admissibility of new technological advances. If technology provides reliable and accurate evidence and it is admissible, then the preservation of constitutional rights must be examined (Williams, 1987–1988).

There are two standards that both state and federal courts can use to determine if evidence is admissible: the *Frye* test of general acceptance and the Federal Rules test (Beeler and Wiebe, 1988). The *Frye* test is the most commonly used standard of admissibility, and it provides that before scientific evidence will be admissible at trial the procedures generally must be accepted by the scientific community from which it is generated (del Carmen, 1991).[2] The purpose of the *Frye* test is to ensure sufficient technical expertise to accurately evaluate the technique's reliability (Beeler and Wiebe, 1988). The reliability of a new technology is best accomplished by peer review and the acceptance of adequate empirical testing. The *Frye* test often has been pivotal in cases that involve such diverse techniques as breath analysis and blood proteins. It has been used to attack every aspect of forensic scientific technology from specific scientific procedures, to the technical theory of reliability and validity, to persons who perform the examination and their knowledge and expertise.

The *Frye* test has been referred to as the "general acceptance test." However, a difference has arisen between the "general acceptance test" and a liberalized "substantial acceptance test": the former implies acceptance by a majority, and the latter permits admissibility when acceptance is recognized by a minority (Wright, 1970). The *Frye* test was crafted in such a way to assure scientific reliability should continue to be followed.

Unlike the *Frye* test, the Federal Rules are designed to eliminate extreme expense and delay and to strengthen the fairness of scientific evidence. The Federal Rules of Evidence are a broad set of instructions that cannot encompass every situation that may arise. Thus, the Rules are set forth to allow the courts discretion in an effort to establish the truth. The Rules use "reasoning by analogy to cover new or unanticipated situations" (Wright, 1970: 43). The Federal Rules describe relevant evidence as evidence of consequence, having any tendency to make the existence of a fact of the action more or less probable than it would be without the evidence (Wright, 1970). Results of experiments are substantive evidence, admissible to show cause and effect, characteristics, and the like. For example, DNA-testing results show the characteristics of identity. Experiments generally are conducted out of court, and the results are reported in court by either the presenters of fact or an expert witness. Evidence found sufficiently reliable to be admitted nevertheless may be excluded under Rule 403.

Rule 403 describes the exclusion of relevant evidence on the grounds of prejudice, confusion, or waste of time. Relevant evidence is to be excluded only if its probative value is substantially outweighed by any of the factors mentioned previously, alone or in combination. Since the burden of proof is on the objecting party, Rule 403 involves a subjective evaluation by the judge, which often favors inclusion. For example, the judge must decide to what extent inclusion of a piece of evidence would constitute a "waste of time." This type of exclusion is an extraordinary remedy and can be prevented by other avenues (Farley and Harrington, 1991).

Confusion is said to exist when the jury loses sight of the main issue and the evidence becomes a mass of confused data from which it will be difficult to extract essential information. Confusion results in new issues arising, and this often leads to new and different kinds of additional issues.

A jury may be misled by the amount of time spent upon a question; they may believe the issue to be of major importance and accordingly attach too much significance to it in determining the factual issues involved. The *Frye* test imposes the requirement with respect to the admissibility of scientific evidence that the particular technique be shown to have gained "general acceptance in the particular field to which it belongs," in an attempt to prevent jurors from being unduly swayed by unreliable scientific evidence (Wright, 1970: 49). It is important to note here that the judge must apply the *Frye* test before the jury can hear the evidence. The judge might consider this evidentiary issue on a motion from either party dealing with the lack of general acceptance, or the judge might simply rule in due course of having the evidence presented. The essential point is that this is an area in which especially defense attorneys may contest the nature of the evidence, its analysis or evaluation, and the expert witnesses called to present the evidence. From a legal perspective, part of DNA testing's impact will result from the education of justice system personnel (judges and attorneys) in the technique. Efficient implementation will require the development of standardization and enhanced peer review (Peterson, 1989).

In most cases, the attorney representing the prosecution or defense must present the DNA evidence along with the testimony of the technician and one or more scientific experts at a *Frye* hearing to determine the validity and reliability of the procedure. This process must be followed, except in states that allow judicial notice. The validity of the principle or technique is either assumed in subsequent cases, or it may be established through judicial notice. However, every judge may decide evidentiary questions differently, so judicial notice may apply only to a given judge who has decided a particular issue previously. In many cases, when a new technology is introduced the parties are not evenly matched on the procedural issues. Until both prosecutors and defense attorneys can be equally armed on a new procedure, judges may choose to apply the rules in a very technical fashion.

The courts overwhelmingly have accepted DNA evidence due to the path established by other serological techniques, such as enzyme typing, that have been in practice for well over two decades (Fisher, 1987; Thompson and Ford, 1989). This is true even though there are lingering questions about whether DNA testing produces reliable and reproducible results with forensic samples. Still, many of the procedures employed by DNA testing are also used in enzyme typing (such as electrophoresis), and these techniques have been tested and presented numerous times in courts and forensic journals. This type of scrutiny can only enhance the acceptance of DNA testing.

The dangers of admitting scientific evidence include unfair prejudice or confusion. The courts that apply both the *Frye* test and the Federal Rules of Evidence rely on safeguards (for example, discovery, cross-examination of experts, opposing experts, and cautionary instructions to the jury) to negate the possible dangers that can arise. However, Beeler and Wiebe (1988) contend that courts applying the Federal Rules test will be more likely to admit the results of DNA testing than courts that apply the *Frye* doctrine, due to its less stringent format.

To date, two DNA testing cases (*Florida v. Andrews*, 533 So. 2d 841 [1987] and *Maryland v. Coby*, 559 A. 2d 391 [Md. Ct. Special Appeals 1989]) have reached the appellate courts, and both convictions have been upheld (Giles, 1989). The *Andrews* decision was based on an evidentiary hearing at the trial court level in which there were no defense witnesses (Thompson and Ford, 1989). Andrews was convicted in the Circuit Court of Orange County, Florida, and appealed his conviction on the grounds that DNA evidence testing was inadmissible and that separate convictions or punishments arose from charges stemming from one criminal act. The District Court of Appeal found DNA testing admissible because of its proven scientific principles and because it was shown to be valid and reliable.

In the *Coby* case, the decision was based on admissibility of DNA and was found by the court to be well received (White, 1990). The defendant appealed a conviction from the Circuit Court in Montgomery County, Maryland. The court of special appeals reversed and remanded the case; on remand, Coby was again convicted. Coby appealed a second time to the court of special appeals on the grounds that DNA testing was inadmissible and that extraction of the defendant's blood was done without a search warrant. The court found in favor of the admissibility of DNA testing due to its meeting the *Frye* guidelines. The court found that DNA testing is accepted by the scientific community. The defendant also appealed on the grounds of a Fourth Amendment violation. It was determined that the defendant consented to the blood test through his attorney. The decision was affirmed (559 A. 2d 391 [Md. App. 1989]). DNA testing has been deemed valid and reliable in some courts using both the Federal Rules of Evidence and the *Frye* tests. Unless it is otherwise determined unsatisfactory, expanded applications of DNA testing should enhance its admissibility.

CONCLUSIONS

As del Carmen (1991: 271) notes, "the jury is still out" on DNA fingerprinting. Particularly troubling to many DNA experts, including a number who serve as expert witnesses in trials, are the unanswered problems of reliability and validity. While most of the estimates of identical matches are incredibly high, it is difficult to assess the accuracy of those estimates and to know against what population base to compare the estimates. As with most new scientific advances, further research will vindicate the proponents or the skeptics of DNA identification, but at this point both sides agree that "genetic techniques . . . could be improved by setting a national standard for laboratory techniques and by the certification of lab personnel" ("Genetic fingerprinting reliable . . . ," 1992).

Many of the legal issues remain unresolved. Some of the key concerns seem to be (1) to what extent will courts allow the forcible (nonconsensual) taking of physical evidence (hair, blood, etc.) from a suspect to facilitate DNA testing and (2) in these cases, what are the applicable search warrant requirements, if any?

Perhaps one of the major legal and procedural issues involving DNA testing is: Will it inform the trier of fact? Related to this, will expert witnesses presenting DNA evidence overwhelm a jury with statistical arguments? And, finally, will it clarify the questions surrounding guilt or innocence, or will it merely serve to further confuse the decision-making process?

In addressing these and other issues, the courts must resolve the role to be played by DNA evidence. Does this evidence have sufficient validity and reliability to stand on its own, or must it be used with other forms of evidence? Will DNA testing be established as one of the major forensic standards in the courts, or will it go the way of physiognomy and the Bertillon method?

For DNA evidence to be widely accepted, access to data (laboratory analyses and expert witnesses) may be as important as admissibility. Additionally, as the intrusiveness of the process increases, the courts may require increased levels of proof (such as probable cause). However, only additional research and extensive laboratory testing can answer these and other questions about one of forensic sciences's latest innovations.

NOTES

*An earlier version of this article was presented at the annual meeting of the Western Social Science Association, Denver, Colorado, April 22-25, 1995. The authors gratefully acknowledge the assistance of Dr. Peter Gregware in reviewing and commenting on earlier drafts of the article.

1. The four private United States laboratories are CellMark Diagnostics, in Germantown, Md.; LifeCodes Corporation, in Valhalla, N.Y.; GeneScreen, in Texas; and Forensic Science Associates, in Richmond, Calif. These are in addition to state and federal labs that do DNA testing (Bureau of Justice Statistics, 1991: 9).
2. The so-called *Frye* test is based on *Frye v. United States*, 293 F. 1013 (D.C. Cir. 1923), a case dealing with polygraph examinations, which provided the rule that a scientific principle must cross the line from experimentation to demonstration. The Court of Appeals for the District of Columbia noted: "Just when a scientific principle or discovery crosses the line between the experimental and demonstrable stages is difficult to define. Somewhere in this twilight zone the evidential force of the principle must be recognized, and while courts will go a long way in admitting expert testimony deduced from a well-recognized scientific principle or discovery, the thing from which the deduction is made must be sufficiently established to have gained general acceptance in the particular field in which it belongs" [293 F. 1014 (1923); see also White, 1990].

REFERENCES

Beeler, L. and Wiebe, W. R. (1988) "DNA (Deoxyribonucleic Acid) Identification Tests and the Courts," *Washington Law Review*, 63(4): 903–55.

Bertillon, A. (1896) *The Bertillon System of Identification.* Chicago: The Wierner Company.

Budowle, B., H. A. Deadman, R. S. Murch, and F. S. Baechtel (1988) "An Introduction to the Methods of DNA Analysis Under Investigation in the FBI Laboratory," *Crime Laboratory Digest*, 15(1): 8–21.

Bureau of Justice Statistics (1991) *Forensic DNA Analysis: Issues.* Washington, DC: U.S. Department of Justice.

Chakraborty, R., and K. K. Kidd (1991) "The Utility of DNA Typing in Forensic Work," *Science*, 254 (December 20): 1735–39.

del Carmen, R. V. (1991) *Criminal Procedure: Law and Practice*, 2nd ed. Pacific Grove, CA: Brooks/Cole.

Edwards, Rep. Don (1991). "DNA Tests: Privacy, Civil Liberties Implications," *Interface*, Spring: 8–9, 31.

Farley, M. A. and J. J. Harrington, (1991) *Forensic DNA Technology.* Chelsea, MI: Lewis Publishers, Inc.

Fisher, B. A. (1987). *Techniques of Crime Scene Investigation.* New York: Elsevier Science Publishing.

Florida v. Andrews, 533 So. 2d 841 (1987).

Franklin-Barbajosa, Cassandra (1992) "DNA Profiling: The New Science of Identity," *National Geographic* 181(5): 112–123.

Frye v. United States, 293 F. 1013 (D.C. Cir. 1923).

Gebreth, V. J. (1988) "DNA (Deoxyribonucleic Acid) Print Identification Test Provides Crucial Evidence in Lust Murder Case," *Law and Order*, 36(7): 22–28.

"Genetic fingerprinting reliable in criminal cases, scientists say," (1992), *El Paso (Texas) Times*, April 15, p. 2A.

Giles, B. (1989) "DNA Fingerprinting Meets Courtroom Challenges," *The Texas Prosecutor*, July/August: 11–16.

Greenspan, O. (1991) "Criminal Justice DNA Analysis Issues Challenge New York," *Interface*, Spring: 13, 36.

Hicks, J. W. (1988) "DNA Profiling: A Tool for Law Enforcement," *FBI Law Enforcement Bulletin*, 57(8): 1–5.

Holt v. United States, 218 U.S. 245 (1910).
Jeffreys, A. J., V. Wilson, and S. L. Thein (1985) "Individual-specific 'Fingerprints' of Human DNA," *Nature*, 316: 76–79.
Kirk, P. L. (1974) *Criminal Investigation*, 2nd ed. New York: John Wiley & Sons.
Kolmetz, Paul F. (1991) "Virginia Enacts Comprehensive DNA Program," *Interface*, Spring: 13, 37.
Lambourne, G. (1984) *The Fingerprint Story.* Great Britain: Harrays Limited.
Lewontin, R. C., and Daniel L. Hartl (1991) "Population Genetics in Forensic DNA Typing," *Science*, 254 (December 20): 1745–50.
Maryland v. Coby, 559 A. 2d 391 (Md. Ct. Special Appeals 1989).
McDonald, Karen R. (1991) "Minnesota Laws Allow State to Collect, Analyze, Store DNA," *Interface*, Spring: 12, 34–35.
Neufeld, P. J., and N. Colman (1990) "When Science Takes the Witness Stand," *Scientific American*, 262(5): 46–53.
Peterson, J. L. (1989) "Impact of Biological Evidence on the Adjudication of Criminal Cases: Potential for DNA Technology," in *DNA Technology and Forensic Science.* Cold Spring Harbor: Laboratory Press, pp. 55–70.
Roberts, Leslie (1991) "Fight Erupts Over DNA Fingerprinting," *Science*, 254 (December 20): 1721–23.
Rochin v. California, 3342 U.S. 165 (1952).
Schmerber v. California, 384 U.S. 757 (1966).
State v. Washington, 622 P. 2d 986 (Wash. 1981).
Thompson, W. C., and S. Ford (1989) "DNA Typing: Acceptance and Weight of the New Genetic Identification Tests," *Virginia Law Review*, 75(1): 45–108.
United States v. Brown, 557 F. 2d 541 (6th Cir. 1977).
Wambaugh, J. (1989) *The Blooding.* New York: Perigord Press.
White, Stephen R. (1990) "DNA 'Identification': Some Practical Questions." Paper presented at the annual meeting of the Academy of Criminal Justice Sciences, Denver, Colorado, March.
Williams, C. L. (1987–1988) "DNA Fingerprinting: A Revolutionary Technique in Forensic Science and Its Probable Effects on Evidentiary Law," *Drake Law Review*, 37(1): 1–32.
Wolf v. Colorado, 338 U.S. 25 (1949).
Wright, C. (1970) *Handbook of the Law of Federal Courts*, 2nd ed. St. Paul, MN: West Publishing Co.

PART THREE

The Criminal Trial

"The jury has spoken, and we, as well as our client, respect its labors and enormously difficult decision. However, a not guilty verdict does not equate to innocence."

—Attorney David Roth, on the verdict of William Kennedy Smith, 1991

INTRODUCTION

One of the most distinctive and interesting features of our criminal justice system is the jury trial. Highly visible and public, jury trials attract attention with their captivating drama and sometimes gruesome details of horrific crimes and brazen murderers. Although fewer than five percent of all criminal cases end in jury trials, they provide one of the few opportunities for public scrutiny of the judicial process. However, it is important to recognize that actual criminal trials are usually much less entertaining than the fictional trials portrayed on television or in the movies. Most trials are fairly routine and highly regulated by specific procedures and rules. The typical criminal trial is usually completed within a matter of hours or days. Only the most complex and celebrated cases may take a week or longer to conclude.

Because criminal trials are adversarial in nature, they are thought to provide the best forum currently available for determining the truth in a given case. The adversaries are the prosecutor and the defense attorney. The burden of proof rests squarely on the shoulders of the prosecutor. It is his or her responsibility to represent the state and to present evidence that shows that the defendant is guilty of the crime beyond a reasonable doubt. The primary objective of the defense counsel is to discredit the prosecution's case by creating a reasonable doubt about the defendant's alleged guilt. It is the responsibility of the jury or the judge (in bench trials) to determine and assign guilt. Although trials are rare events, serious cases in which either the facts or the law remain unclear are the mostly likely to result in a trial.

This section focuses on the most engaging aspects of the trial process, such as the role of jury science, nonevidentiary social influences on the jury, and judicial misconduct during jury deliberations. This section also addresses some of the controversies regarding the use of cameras in the courtroom and whether jury deliberations should be recorded.

In the first article in this section, "The Jury is Still Out: The Role of Jury Science in the Modern American Courtroom," Jeremy W. Barber observes that legal scholars and judges have paid relatively little attention to the phenomenon of jury science. This dearth of attention is disturbing given the potential that this science, which has been employed with remarkable success in a number of high profile criminal cases, has for undermining the fundamental values that our jury system is supposed to exemplify. The need for attention and study becomes particularly important if we accept the aphorism with which this article begins: ". . . every case has been won or lost when the jury is sworn in." Barber strongly believes that the legal community must develop a broad analytic framework to address the important questions that the use of jury science raises. By adopting a framework similar to the one he outlines in his article, Barber is convinced that the legal community can ensure that this science is applied equitably without damaging the legitimacy of the jury system.

In his article, "The American Jury: Handicapped in the Pursuit of Justice," Saul K. Kassin examines nonevidentiary social influences on the jury. He argues that these influences, which emanate from various trial practices, threaten to compromise a defendant's right to a fair trial. According to Kassin, there are two phases in the jury's decision-making task that are at jeopardy from nonevidentiary social influences. First, it has become increasingly difficult for individual jurors to make accurate judgments about the complex evidence frequently presented to them. Second, the process by which individual jury members contribute independently and equally to a joint outcome is also being endangered. Kassin concludes that jurors must base their decisions on the actual evidence presented in the case rather than on nonevidentiary sources of information such as newspapers or television.

In the third article, "Judicial Misconduct During Jury Deliberations," Bennett L. Gershman considers the two major types of improper judicial behavior that might occur during the jury deliberation process. First, judicial conduct that attempts to place undue pressure on a jury to reach a verdict may include verdict-urging instructions, threats and intimidation, and inquiry into the numerical division of the jury on the merits of the verdict. Second, judicial participation in private, ex parte communications with jurors may also subvert orderly trial procedures and undermine the impartiality of the jury. Gershman contends that neither type of judicial conduct should be allowed to compel a jury to reach a verdict.

Largely because of the O.J. Simpson murder case, many commentators have questioned the televising of criminal trials. In his article, "Time, TV, and Criminal Justice: Second Thoughts on the Simpson Trial," Samuel H. Pillsbury argues that television broadcasts probably did impinge negatively on the justice process in the Simpson case. Even so, he believes that the real problem in this case resulted from live broadcasts of the proceedings. The author proposes a general rule granting electronic access to the courtroom, but allowing the trial judge to order a delay in video broadcast for up to 24 hours after the court session. He argues that in high-profile cases like the Simpson trial, such a delay represents the best accommodation of the public's need for electronic access and the judicial system's need for relief from the "spotlight" effects of in-court television coverage.

In the final article in this section, "Cameras in the Jury Room: An Unnecessary and Dangerous Precedent," Abraham Abramovsky and Jonathan I. Edelstein argue that although there are compelling arguments favoring the recording of jury deliberations, both as a one-time-only educational project and as a routine means of ensuring jury accountability, the arguments against such a practice far outweigh those favoring it. The recording of jury deliberations are of dubious educational value for two specific reasons. First, the prospect of recording may contaminate the jury pool. Second, the monitoring of a jury may alter the manner in which it deliberates a case. Furthermore, because of the careful selection of cases to be recorded and because of the selective editing of jury deliberation footage to fit documentary film length, the trial process may not be portrayed accurately. Abramovsky and Edelstein believe that if jury deliberations are routinely recorded, any gain in accountability will be offset by the damage to free debate in the jury room, jury privacy, and the centuries-old tradition of jury deliberation in secrecy. They also note that the CBS recording of a Wisconsin jury's deliberations is available to those who feel that taped deliberations are a valid means of studying the jury process; repeating the experiment serves no further educational purpose and sets a potentially dangerous precedent. Despite the insights that might have resulted from CBS's documentary, the authors urge that courts and lawmakers not allow cameras to delve any deeper into the American justice system. The potential negative impact is far too great.

11

The Jury is Still Out: The Role of Jury Science in the Modern American Courtroom

Jeremy W. Barber*

"Never forget, almost every case has been won or lost when the jury is sworn."[1]

I. INTRODUCTION

In the aftermath of the Rodney King and Reginald Denny trials and in the lengthening shadow of astronomical jury product liability awards, the American jury has come under increasing examination and assault. Despite all of this attention on the jury as an institution, there is little debate about jury science, a phenomenon that has ballooned over the past twenty years and threatens to undermine the basic values of our jury system. Many questions surround this science which, today, shapes many major trials. Where did it come from? What are its implications for the fundamental assumptions and models of American jury trials? And why has the science escaped public scrutiny?

This Note will first explore three distinct historical justifications for jury trials. Two of these rationales[2] appear to be irreconcilable.[3] This Note will analyze the tension between the ideals of an impartial jury and a jury of one's peers and discuss the effect of jury science on these values. The Note then will trace the evolution of jury science;[4] examine what this science accomplishes and where it is used; analyze the arguments for and against the use of jury science; and make limited recommendations about how best to manage a jury system which increasingly makes use of and relies on this science. Further, the Note will explore the impact jury science has had upon both our rationales for juries and our perception of juries.[5] Finally, this Note will suggest an analytic framework for the use of jury science.

II. THREE HISTORICAL RATIONALES FOR JURY TRIALS

A. The Sixth Amendment Impartial Jury Mandate

The first model for a jury trial is found in the Sixth Amendment, which calls for an impartial jury in a criminal trial.[6] The Sixth Amendment guarantee of an "impartial jury"[7] was

Reprinted by permission of Georgetown University and the *American Criminal Law Review* from vol. 31 (1994), pp. 1225–1252.

intended to ensure the impartiality of the individual juror as well as the process by which the jurors are selected. The Due Process Clause has been construed to require an impartial tribunal, but not an impartial jury.[8] The Supreme Court has defined an impartial juror as one who is able to base a verdict on the evidence developed at trial and not on any preconceived notion or bias about the defendant's innocence or guilt.[9]

Prosecutors have relied on the impartial juror mandate of the Sixth Amendment to justify selecting jurors who come from backgrounds different from that of the defendant, in order to ensure that the jury is not overly sympathetic with the defendant.[10] Despite the Sixth Amendment's edict, the adversarial climate of our legal system encourages neither defense nor prosecution attorneys to truly seek an impartial jury.[11] Instead, our system assumes that the adversarial struggle itself will foster a climate that produces impartial juries. The hope is that both the defense and prosecution will aggressively seek partial jurors and that this process will balance out, leading to the eventual empaneling of an impartial jury.

B. A Jury of One's Peers

The second conception of jury trials comes from the historical notion of a jury composed of one's peers. The First Continental Congress in 1774 asserted that the colonists had the right to be "tried by their peers."[12] However, the definition of "peers," like the definition of "impartial," has caused the Supreme Court some difficulty. Although the term is not directly included in either the Sixth or the Seventh Amendment right to a jury trial, it is clearly part of the historical understanding of the notion of a jury trial.[13]

At the time of the Magna Carta, "peer" probably meant "equal."[14] A baron's peer was a baron, a knight's peer was a knight, and a Jew's peer another Jew.[15] In American trials, the definition of "peer" has expanded to encompass members of the defendant's community. The Supreme Court has defined "peers" to mean "neighbors, fellows, associates, [and] persons having the same legal status in society as that which he holds."[16] However, the definition of community is malleable; for example, a defendant who was raised in poverty in a broken home may be entitled to a jury composed of others from the same background. The Supreme Court has rejected this notion,[17] but the expansive reading is not an implausible construction of "peer" or "community."

The concept of "a jury of peers" developed to assure empathy for the accused.[18] However, the concept is often relied upon by defense attorneys to assure that the defendant be tried not by an impartial jury, but rather by one partial to the defendant.[19] We must determine if our jury system anticipates and relies on this maneuvering, or if it is ignorant and thus may be undermined by such practices.

At first glance, there appears to be a contradiction between the requirement that a jury be impartial and that it be composed of one's peers. The dilemma is whether a jury of a defendant's peers can be impartial, in the sense of being free of sympathy for the defendant. However, the goals of impartiality and representativeness can be viewed as compatible. A peer need not be one whose plight and station in life is a mirror reflection of the defendant's, but rather one who is similarly enough placed, in socio-economic and geographic terms, to be able to see the defendant's act in context.

An impartial juror might be capable of judging a case on the evidence presented, rather than on a special understanding of the defendant's behavior.

C. Juries as a Bulwark of Democracy

The final justification for juries is that they play a significant role in America's democratic and pluralistic tradition. Alexis DeTocqueville illuminated the empowering effect of jury participation upon the citizens of a democracy:

> He who punishes infractions of the law is therefore the real master of society. Now, the institution of the jury raises the people itself, or at least a class of citizens, to the bench of judicial authority. The institution of the jury consequently invests the people, or that class of citizens, with the direction of society.[20]

The society is given the opportunity to apply its values and participate in the administration of justice through jury service.

Moreover, jury service delivers an even larger democratic good. Sharing in the administration of justice as a juror gives the public confidence in the administration of justice.[21] Juror participation in the administration of justice also "enlarges the human matrix of diffusion of responsibility through which people more easily make the difficult decisions that somehow must be made."[22] For example, the public met the jury's decision that John Hinckley was not guilty by reason of insanity for his attempted assassination of President Reagan with relative calm. The public may perceive otherwise controversial decisions as fair because they know their peers have considered the problem carefully.

The infusion of laymen into the criminal justice system legitimizes the administration of justice and bolsters democracy. It counters the professional desensitization that is inevitable in those who confront the criminal justice system daily.[23] Through juror nullification, a jury has the power to mitigate some of the harshness of the numb, professional administration of justice and to provide some clemency and mercy. This role of the jury strengthens the administration of the law by ensuring that the community can always breathe its own values and insight into the dispensation of justice.

Finally, jury service fortifies America's populist tradition. Unlike many more elitist governmental bodies, the venire is drawn from the community at large.[24] Jury decision making, more than any other form of government in our representative democracy, is "literally the *vox populi*—the voice of the people."[25]

III. JURY SCIENCE

If it is true that every case "has been won or lost when the jury is sworn," then the introduction of a scientific method of selecting juries should send a tremor through the legal world.[26] However, the American legal community appears unimpressed by the introduction of jury science.[27] One must assume that this wan reaction arises either from a perception that the science does not really work and that juries cannot be rigged, or from a reluctance to admit that it does work and then face the consequences for jury trials. Either way, any new technology that potentially allows attorneys and parties to tamper with the construction of juries and the outcome of trials merits serious scrutiny.

Attorneys who have begun to use the social sciences to assess jurors are dissatisfied with the speculative approach to jury selection.[28] Jury science is designed to replace the attorney's guesses and intuitions about members of the venire with empirical studies that connect expected biases with actual data about the jury pool.[29] Under the old regime of jury selection, an attorney would usually rely on personal biases to determine the types of people who would make sympathetic jurors. Often the hunches used to select sympathetic jurors are based on gross stereotypes.[30] Jury selection in a jury science regime is based upon community surveys; the numerical values assigned to different types of people, depending on their responses to detailed questionnaires, guide the attorney to select potential jurors likely to be sympathetic to a particular defendant.[31]

There is little consensus regarding the efficacy of these sciences. Moreover, experts assert that the "overwhelming majority of jury verdicts is decided by the direction and strength of the evidence and not by the personal characteristics of triers-of-fact."[32] Nonetheless, leading practitioners of jury science boast that they can predict with greater than ninety percent certitude the outcomes of trials before the evidence has been heard.[33] Recognizing that such claims may be little more than self-promotion, there is a patent need to examine their accuracy and credibility.

A. The Origin and Evolution of Jury Science

Jury science first appeared in the fall of 1970. J. Edgar Hoover was locked in a battle with an anti-war group called the "East Coast Conspiracy to Save Lives," made up of Catholic priests.[34] The leaders of this group were two well-known Catholic priests, Philip and Daniel Berrigan, who had actively opposed the war in Vietnam since the mid-1960s.[35] In November 1970, the government indicted Philip Berrigan and six others for conspiring to blow up heating tunnels in Washington, smuggling letters in and out of prison, and various other counts. Although it had a choice of a number of different locations within the United States, the government brought the indictment in politically conservative Harrisburg, Pennsylvania.[36] Into this fray stepped Jay Schulman, a New York sociologist and anti-war activist who believed the "scales of justice were by no means balanced in this case."[37] Schulman had concluded that the government's pre-trial publicity, its reliance on informers, its choice of Harrisburg as the venue, and its attempts to discredit anti-war activists all made a fair trial for the defendants unlikely.[38] For these reasons, Schulman offered the defense team his services in helping to define the characteristics for the ideal jury, which he believed would be "critical to the outcome of the trial."[39] Although initially skeptical and resistant to Schulman's offer of help, the defense team eventually yielded.[40] Schulman introduced the notion of a partnership between the social sciences and the law in order to correct, or at least balance, what he viewed to be the state's inordinate advantage in trying the "Harrisburg-Seven" trial.

Schulman designed a survey of the federal judicial district that included Harrisburg. With the help of associates, he interviewed 840 people over the telephone and followed up with an additional 252 in-depth face-to-face interviews.[41] Schulman and his associates questioned the respondents about their attitudes towards such issues as religion, education, books and magazines, government, and war resistance.[42] They then rated the potential jurors on a scale of desirability from one to five. The defense then sought to remove the "fives" during voir dire, either for-cause or by using its peremptory strikes.[43] One of Schulman's most important and counter-intuitive findings was that in Harrisburg, college-educated people tended to be conservative, and hence poor defense jurors.[44] Schulman concentrated not only on the characteristics of the individual jurors, but also on potential group dynamics, such as who would make a good jury foreman, and which factions might work together.[45]

Ultimately, the jury hung on all of the most serious charges. J. Edgar Hoover suffered the "greatest Federal fizzle of recent years,"[46] and as word spread of Jay Schulman's success, modern jury science was born.[47]

Ironically, despite its liberal origins, jury science has become the province of high-priced civil litigation and high-profile defendants. Schulman anticipated this danger:

> The second ethical question concerns who will benefit from our procedures in the long run. We depended upon energetic volunteers. In less celebrated cases, most defendants would lack the organization and money required to apply social research to jury selection. The Justice Department might also adopt our methods, thus turning our efforts into a weapon against defendants.[48]

The use of jury science has increased dramatically. Today, there are over 250 members of the American Society of Trial Consultants.[49] When the Society was founded in 1983 there were only nineteen. Services may cost anywhere from $150 an hour to hundreds of thousands of dollars.[50] Litigation Sciences Inc., the market leader, boasts annual revenues of approximately $25 million.[51] From its public interest beginnings, jury science has become high stakes poker. Today, those litigants most likely to be confronted by the type of stacked deck that initially concerned Jay Schulman, are least likely to be able to afford the minimum $10,000 price tag of a jury consultant.[52]

However, there might be hope on the cost of jury science front. In the Reginald Denny trial, Los Angeles Superior Court Judge John W. Ouderkirk appointed Jo-Ellan Dimitrius of Litigation Sciences Inc. at $175 an hour to assist the defense.[53] Whatever one thinks about the utility or danger of jury science, Judge Ouderkirk's appointment of Dimitrius in the Reginald Denny trial signals a potential return to Schulman's initial goal of leveling the legal playing field.

B. What Is Jury Science?

At its core, jury science is little more than a social scientific or psychological attempt to compile and implement the "ideal" juror profile. Its effective use depends on the ability to conduct a voir dire of the venire, or at least to submit questions to the judge, and then to remove members of the venire either for-cause or through the use of peremptory challenges. This section of the Note will briefly review the most popular and frequently applied methods of jury science.

1. *Ranking Scales*[54]

In the Harrisburg-Seven trial, Schulman ranked potential jurors from one to five based on a number of characteristics that he had determined, through his telephone and in-person surveys, to be critical in determining a juror's potential sympathy for the defendant. The defense would use its peremptories to strike the "fives," the jurors least likely to be sympathetic to the defendant. Schulman assumed the prosecution would remove most of the "ones," the jurors most likely to favor the defendant. Schulman hoped that the defense would be able to prioritize the "twos," "threes," and "fours," or those jurors who might be acceptable to both sides. Most attorneys now use this type of ranking before they select a jury.

Before the introduction of science to this procedure, attorneys relied on their instincts and popular stereotypes to select a jury.[55] Ranking scales are vulnerable to the charge that they are little more than a continuation of this practice, an assignment of preferences and numeric values to instincts and stereotypes. The difference, however, is that the ranking scales are based on information gathered in scientific community attitudinal surveys and are, thus, more likely to be accurate than preferences based on generalizations and stereotypes.

2. *Community Attitudinal Surveys*[56]

Community attitudinal surveys are employed to "get a feel for local biases. . . . [to] get[ ] beneath the Darrow-Leibowitz[57] stereotyping and discover[ ] the local pressures and conditions that may be at work on the personalities of the prospective jurors in [a] geographical area."[58] Community attitudinal surveys also help address the problem that potential jurors are prone to lie about their biases.[59] When a potential juror of certain demographic characteristics answers questions during the voir dire which are not consistent with the answers given by a large percentage of her socioeconomic group, an attorney armed with this information can either pursue the questioning more assertively, or exclude this juror on the basis of the attitudinal survey. It is often difficult, for example, for a potential juror to stand up in court and admit to being a bigot. Attitudinal surveys might allow an attorney to ferret out such unspoken, yet potentially harmful, biases. On the other hand, the strategy denies the autonomy and agency of the juror, who is reduced to his or her group characteristics.

3. *Juror Investigations*[60]

The two most common types of juror investigations are community network models and home surveillance of potential jurors. Community network models combine general neighborhood demographic information and aggregate interview responses; this model is, therefore, merely derivative of the other survey methodology. Home surveillance, on the other hand, is exactly what it sounds like: watching a juror's home.[61] These sorts of practices no doubt existed before formal jury science was introduced into the process of selecting juries and gave this practice a formal nomenclature.

4. In-Court Assessment of Juror Non-Verbal Communication[62]

In-court assessment, perhaps more formalized in a jury science regime, is not that different from the way in which attorneys have always selected jurors. However, unlike the days when attorneys made these decisions alone, now attorneys are accompanied by sociologists or psychologists who have made a career out of studying human mannerisms. The potential juror who sits rigidly and responds in a laconic tone with monosyllabic answers to the voir dire might be an "authoritarian" personality and thus likely to side with the prosecution.[63] The potential juror who looks into the attorney's eyes and smiles engagingly when answering the voir dire will probably be malleable and open to the defense's case.[64] Jury scientists carefully craft voir dire questions in an attempt to evoke certain physical responses from the members of the venire on the basis of which juror attitudes can be assessed.

5. Group Dynamic Analysis[65]

Group dynamic analysis was another jury science technique used in the Harrisburg-Seven trial. In that case, Schulman chose a subgroup of young women whom he posited would function as a faction, supporting and strengthening a pro-defense position. Many attorneys will also try to establish a special rapport with one juror who appears to have the typical characteristics of a foreperson.[66] A committed foreperson can often make the difference in the outcome of a jury's deliberations.[67]

6. Focus Groups[68]

Focus groups are drawn from the area where the case is pending. The attorneys present one or two issues or approaches to the group to gauge its response. For example, an opening statement may be simulated before the mock jurors who will then be divided into small response groups. After the focus group responds, the individual members are questioned in great detail about which factors weighed in their decision, what they liked or disliked, and what they understood. This information is then assimilated and identified with corresponding personalities and demographic types. Attorneys can use this information to remove potential jurors who may jeopardize a case or clash with the attorney's idiosyncracies.[69]

Focus groups have the advantage of being far more flexible and much less expensive than a full mock trial. Focus groups also may be guided to deliberate on specific issues. However, these advantages are offset by the fact that the focus group environment is less formal than an actual trial, and thus its deliberations may be less than truly representative.[70]

7. Mock Trial[71]

Mock trials, as dry runs of the upcoming trial, are expensive, time-consuming endeavors. Unlike the other new methodologies discussed above, mock trials reach far into the trial itself and shape it beyond the selection of the jurors. A mock trial allows attorneys to see the potential pitfalls in their case long before the first witness takes the stand. After the mock trial has finished, the jurors deliberate and the attorneys analyze their discussion. It is through mock trials that actual trial strategy is formed.[72]

A mock jury was used with great success in MCI Communication Corporation's antitrust suit against AT&T.[73] Through the use of mock juries, MCI's trial team was able to develop a strategy which raised the mock jury damages from an initial $100 million to $900 million—the figure ultimately awarded by the actual jury.[74]

8. *Shadow Juries*[75]

Shadow juries, like mock juries, reach beyond the selection of jurors to the course of the trial itself. Unlike mock juries, however, shadow juries play no role in the selection of actual jurors. Shadow juries are groups of six to twelve people selected to match the demographic characteristics and background of the actual jury panel. This mirror jury is then hired to attend the trial and to behave like the actual jury, including leaving the room when the actual jury does. The shadow jury deliberates each evening, and trial consultants and attorneys examine its deliberations to check the ongoing status of the trial. The use of shadow juries gives the attorney the ability to address unwitting errors or misconceptions that arise during the course of the trial.

In sum, the tools of jury science are neither revolutionary nor particularly innovative. Rather, they represent an attempt to give systematic and scientific grounding to techniques that trial attorneys have used in an ad hoc fashion for many years. However, refining these techniques, basing them in science, packaging and marketing them, and then selling them for hundreds of thousands of dollars raises a number of public policy concerns. The adoption of this science by segments of the legal community raises significant questions about the three rationales for jury trials: impartiality, judgment by peers, and democracy.[76] The inexorable growth of jury science over the past decade seems to have ramifications for the fundamental fairness of our jury system.

C. Negative and Positive Aspects of Jury Science

Many of the methods employed by trial and jury consultants give the impression that the rules of the game are being changed or that the trial process is being corrupted. Perhaps, these methods could just be considered good old-fashioned adversarial tactics, especially if both sides were endowed with the financial resources to hire firms like Litigation Sciences Inc. However, all too often, only the wealthiest litigants or the state can afford these services. At first blush, the idea of scientific jury selection appears to be "antithetical to the juridical practice of picking an impartial body of citizens to judge a case involving a member of the same community."[77] Despite this kind of criticism, a warning bell has not sounded; perhaps because we are too accustomed to a system in which the rich and powerful get a different brand of justice than the common man or, perhaps we are not convinced of the efficacy of jury science.

This section of the Note will focus on the arguments for and against the use of jury science and will illuminate the question of whether scientific jury selection is indeed antithetical to the rationales for our jury system.

1. Concerns Raised by Jury Science

a. Jury science—A misnomer?

The fundamental conundrum of proponents of jury science is that this system might not be scientific or any more effective than choosing jurors based on Darrow's stereotypes.[78] The science of selecting jurors has been compared to "predicting the future from tea leaves."[79] One of the reasons for the skepticism is the indeterminacy of the social sciences on which it rests.[80] Some observers question the reliability of current social science research and others doubt whether social science inquiry can ever be scientific.[81] Many commentators see jury science as something less than science and something more than guesswork. However, despite skepticism about its reliability, many think that some competitive edge can be gained through the use of jury science and its selection methods.[82]

With an unclear picture of its effect, it is difficult to know the degree to which the use of jury science should be monitored and regulated. The uncertainty about the impact of jury science is not a concern for those who market jury science because it allows them to speculate regarding their own success rate.[83] However, for those who attempt to assess the impact of the science, its indeterminacy is problematic.

b. Faulty correlation between juror characteristics and juror verdict

Potentially the most significant dilemma for advocates of jury science is the fact that the whole system may be posited upon a faulty assumption: that there is a correlation between juror characteristics and the favoring of one party, and that a particular juror in the jury box will behave according to this relationship. This assumption is not necessarily warranted.[84] A number of experts have demonstrated that the "relationship between background characteristics and verdict preference is too weak to be of real use to the trial lawyer."[85]

However, even if jury science lacks predictive value, it remains a valuable weapon in a trial attorney's arsenal. The extra information culled by the science gives additional insight into the biases and dynamics within a particular judicial district. While not determinative, this information may help tilt the balance of a trial if used by only one side. Most experts, including proponents of jury science, continue to claim that trials are determined by the quality of the evidence and not by the quality of the people hearing the evidence.[86] The fact that groups, like Litigation Sciences, boast of success rates around ninety percent should give some pause to one who is certain that the evidence governs a trial's outcome.

If jury science is indeed posited upon a faulty correlation, then there is less reason to be concerned about its detrimental effects or unfair advantage. The uncertainty surrounding jury science is one of its main detriments. Ironically, however, the fact that jury science can hide behind this uncertainty might be one factor that ultimately assures that it infiltrates our legal system unchecked.

c. Jury science is only available to the wealthy

The first two concerns raised about jury science relate to its effectiveness. The third major problem, the potential advantage to the wealthy, was identified by Schulman at the birth of jury science with the Harrisburg-Seven trial.[87] Schulman worried that the science would not always be used to balance the inequities between the state and the defendant, but rather, would become a tool for the state. Michael Saks echoes this concern by pointing out that the "realities of justice in America" make it so that only the "wealthy and celebrated have such help [as jury science], and tomorrow the additional people to have it will be prosecutors, and they will use it routinely."[88]

In a 1984 Georgia murder case,[89] the defendant asked the court to provide funds to hire experts to assist in jury selection. When the trial court denied his request, the defendant appealed to the Georgia Supreme Court, claiming that the ruling had violated his rights to equal protection, due process, and effective assistance of counsel. The Georgia Supreme Court rejected his claims.

This is not always the case. As previously stated, Los Angeles Superior Court Judge Ouderkirk did appoint a trial consultant in the Reginald Denny case.[90] It is ironic that a tool created to level the playing field may now be just one more weapon for the government.[91] But perhaps Judge Ouderkirk's decision marks a judicial turn to protect defendants' rights.

d. Jury science as high-tech jury tampering

Finally, the new jury science has been lambasted by some prominent social scientists as high-tech jury tampering.[92] Attorneys can empanel a biased, partial, or predetermined jury under a jury science regime, undermining the Sixth Amendment's impartiality mandate. Others have predicted that if the "outcome of a trial can be manipulated simply by choosing jurors labeled acceptable by social scientists, then trial by jury would cease to function impartially and ultimately have to be abandoned."[93] This second charge goes beyond the mandate of impartiality and states that jury science threatens to eviscerate the role of the jury in our democratic government. If these allegations can be substantiated, jury science might be more clearly in the public eye and subject to greater scrutiny and regulation.

The two main complaints about jury science—on the one hand, that it does not work and, on the other hand, that it does work and, therefore, disadvantages the indigent or effectively tampers with the impartial jury—are in tension with each other. If jury science is ineffective, then the fairness and jury tampering concerns dissipate. If the science is effective, then the claim that jury science is not truly a science or that it is posited upon a faulty assumption loses its sting. Given the limited critical data currently available about jury science, it is almost impossible to resolve this tension. However, regardless of its efficacy, jury science is arguably potentially detrimental simply because it creates a perception of unfairness or tampering.

2. *Benefits of Jury Science*

a. Rooting out bias

Perhaps the central benefit of jury science is that it helps attorneys see through dishonest answers by potential jurors during the voir dire. Many studies have shown, "when people are questioned before an authority figure (the judge) and a number of strangers, they tend to give socially acceptable answers to conceal or deny their prejudices."[94] Through the use of demographic correlation of attitudes related to the trial, obtained from questionnaires and in-person interviews, attorneys can remove potential jurors during the voir dire whom they believe to be cloaking biases.[95] In addition, psychological studies indicate that jurors biased toward one side tend to react in telling ways when questioned by attorneys.[96] For example, a juror biased against the defense might become "tense, evasive, or hostile when questioned by the defense lawyer."[97] Jury science thus helps implement the Sixth Amendment's impartiality mandate. Of course, as previously noted, these tools can also be used to privilege bias, rather than to root it out.[98]

b. Countering the juror misconception that a defendant is guilty as charged

A second benefit of jury science, at least for defendants and defense attorneys, is that it may counter the tendency of juries to believe that a defendant in a criminal case is most likely guilty.[99] The use of demographic characteristics allows an attorney to identify traits of people likely to prejudge a defendant's guilt and then either educate these venire members during the voir dire or remove them. Assuming that jury science is effective, biases may be countered and the Sixth Amendment's impartiality edict may be fostered.

c. Decreasing stereotyping by attorneys

Jury science might cause some attorneys to abandon the use of antiquated stereotypes in selecting a jury. For example, Schulman's detailed research of the Harrisburg community revealed that one's education level or the type of book one read was more relevant to the defense than one's class or race. On the other hand, one could argue that jury science actually reinforces these stereotypes by placing the imprimatur of science on these findings. But jury science, and the highly refined and nuanced demographic information it provides, supplant the stereotypes and in many cases prove them to be outmoded and wrong.[100] It seems likely that the science will provide a more textured view of the characteristics that would make one either a biased or unbiased juror.

The old stereotypes and rules of jury selection may also foster undemocratic discrimination.[101] To the extent that jury science provides some other means of selecting a juror from the venire, beyond religion, race, gender, or age, it may achieve an egalitarian and democratic good.

d. Balancing the powerful arsenal of the state

Finally, Schulman hoped to balance the inequity between the powerful state and the weak defendant. For the most part, history has not delivered Schulman's jury science to the aid of indigent criminal defendants as he had hoped. Instead, the science has become the tool of the rich and powerful. However, jury science remains a potentially powerful method for balancing the inequities. The origins of jury science, along with Judge Ouderkirk's appointment of a jury consultant to the defense in the Reginald Denny trial, provide some grounds of hope for indigent defendants seeking jury experts in their cases.[102]

Jury science roots out bias, corrects misperceptions, rebuts stereotypes, and potentially balances the advantages of the state. However, these advantages only arise where both sides have equal access to the use of the science. Moreover, the above benefits do not address concerns about the unquantifiable nature of the results or the negative perceptions of jury tampering.

D. Managing a Jury System That Relies on Jury Science

There are a number of changes that could be made which would both recognize the integral part that jury science has come to play in America's major litigation[103] and make its use more equitable. These changes could be made relatively inexpensively and expeditiously.

1. *Equal Access to Data*

Where juror questionnaires or other community attitudinal surveys are used by either the defense or the prosecution, the raw data should be made available to both sides.[104] While each side could do its analysis of the raw data independently, the starting ground would be more equal. Given the adversarial nature of litigation, there is sure to be much objection to this suggestion,[105] but it seems to address one of the most cogent criticisms of jury science: the fact that it unfairly favors the wealthy and the state. This suggestion would also reorient jury science towards its original function—leveling the legal playing field.

2. *State Funding for Indigent Defendants*

As demonstrated by Judge Ouderkirk's appointment of a jury consultant, state funding of jury experts might be available in the future. However, given current budget constraints, government largesse in this area is unlikely. There is precedent for providing this kind of assistance to indigent defendants in the form of investigators and experts,[106] but, given the uncertainty and cost of the science, it may not make sense for the state to spend the few dollars it has on jury consultants for indigent defendants.

3. *Prohibit the Use of Jury Science*

To the extent that firms like Litigation Sciences Inc. can determine the outcomes of trials with a ninety percent success rate and that jury science is outcome-determinative, jury science has undermined a fundamental reason for having jury trials. The Sixth Amendment's "impartial jury" is neither being impartial nor administering justice. If jury science can actually manipulate the outcomes of trials with great certainty, then the Due Process Clause would likely demand that it be abolished; otherwise, a defendant's due process rights would be violated.[107] There can be no due process of law where the outcome of the trial is predetermined. However, as noted above, given the social science foundation of jury science, it is unlikely that there will ever be sufficient evidence to prove that jury science is outcome-determinative, implicating the Due Process Clause and giving a court the constitutional power to ban the science. To the extent that this science becomes equally available to both parties, the fairness and policy rationales for banning jury science are mitigated.

4. *Judge-Conducted Voir Dire or Abolition of Peremptory Challenges*

With the exception of shadow juries and perhaps mock trials, most jury research aims at selecting favorable jurors or weeding out biased ones. If judges conduct the voir dire, much of the abuse or even use of jury science would be removed. However, placing voir dire in the hands of the judge places great faith in judges and in their ability to be unbiased or impartial.

Another solution less likely to vest so much power in judges is to follow Justice Marshall's suggestion that peremptory strikes be abolished.[108] However, many sound arguments can be made that peremptories are needed to remove biased jurors who cannot be removed for-cause so as to guarantee impartial juries.

5. *Attack Structural Biases in Jury Selection*

Rather than relying on jury science to root out biased jurors from the venire at the time of trial, one could seek a venire that is more representative of the American landscape. Although the case law already requires the venire to be representative,[109] in reality, bias persists because of the way jury lists for the venire are compiled. While making the venire as reflective of the community as possible is a sensible idea, this suggestion may fail to detect the subtler forms of bias that must be eradicated in order to ensure a fair trial.

6. *Disclosure of Use of Jury Science*

Requiring litigants to inform the court and the members of the venire that they are using jury science may also be a sensible suggestion. Such disclosure would provide the opposing party the opportunity to hire its own consultant, and the indigent defendant the opportunity to ask the court to appoint one. This might also facilitate study into the frequency and depth of the use of jury science. Finally, disclosure would be inexpensive and provide neither side with a competitive edge, except perhaps by reducing the advantage of stealth strategies and tactics.

7. *Maintain the Status Quo*

In the case of jury science, perhaps all that is needed is to continue to study its impact and frequency of its use. If jury science does have a significant effect on a large number of trials, then courts may need to establish controls over the practice beyond those which currently exist.[110] However, if the science is infrequently used and when used is ineffective, the courts need not act. If the answer is ambiguous or perceptions must be taken into account, then minor adjustments like equal access, state funding for indigents, and disclosure might be in order.

IV. JURY SCIENCE AND THE FAIRNESS OF THE JURY SYSTEM

A. An Analytic Framework

When the legal profession and the judiciary begin to examine the effects of jury science on the fairness of the American jury system, they might best conduct the examination by following a two-prong analytic framework. The first prong focuses on whether jury science works, while the second prong focuses on perceptions of the science, regardless of whether it works. The analysis would be as follows: first, one would ask if jury science is likely to be effective in a particular case or class of cases. If it is, then fairness concerns are raised. If the science is likely to be effective and not implemented equitably, then the use of the science should be presumptively unfair and should not be sanctioned. However, if both sides have equal access to the science, then fairness concerns dissipate and one can turn to the second prong of the analysis.

Even if jury science does not have a significant effect on the outcome of trials, questions remain about how jury science affects societal perceptions of the jury system. Not all of the potentially negative perceptions engendered by jury science relate to fairness between actual parties. The public perception of juries, as an integral part of a fair justice system, could be seriously undermined by the use of jury science and, therefore, should be carefully monitored.

The above framework establishes a series of rebuttable presumptions. Any jury science method that is likely to be effective would create a presumption that unfairness exists, but this presumption may be rebutted by showing that both sides have equal access to jury science, or by showing that the state will appoint a jury consultant where an indigent defendant requests one and the state is using jury science. Where application of jury science is ineffective, the trial is presumed to be fair.

However, equitable application of the science does not answer all of the concerns of the perception prong. The second prong presents a more formidable barrier for proponents of jury science because the question of perception is more amorphous and open to general questions regarding policy and community values. In order for jury science to be used fairly, it must either be ineffective and engender no negative community perception about the jury system, or be effective, applied equitably, and foster no negative community perception.

Underlying the above analysis is a problematic question for jury science as a whole: whether and how its effectiveness can be measured. Because jury science is based on social science and psychological tenets, its effectiveness is difficult to quantify.[111] Given the limited information that exists about the efficacy of jury science, the inquiry really turns on the second part of the analysis: assuming the science is effective, what steps have been taken to assure that its use is fair? Many of the negative perceptions of jury science may be tempered by its fair and equal application.

Finally, regardless of the even-handedness of the use of jury science and regardless of its efficacy, the use of the science may still foster the negative societal perception that the jury system is being undermined or rigged. Using the science might imply that jurors are incapable of drawing conclusions based on the evidence that they see and hear at trial. In contrast, rationality and the autonomy of jurors are fundamental to the American jury system. Moreover, the use of the science might discredit the verdict in the eyes of the public. For these reasons, the judicial system must be vigilant in monitoring the growth of jury science. Depending on what is learned from the above analysis, the legal profession and the judiciary might want to change its Rules of Procedure in order to account for the impact of jury science.[112]

B. Reconciling Jury Science with the Rationales for Jury Trials

The analytic framework helps reconcile jury science with the rationales for jury trials. The efficacy prong is directly relevant to the Sixth Amendment's impartiality mandate and to history's "peer" mandates. The perception prong is more pertinent to the democracy-reinforcing value of jury trials.

1. The Sixth Amendment's Impartial Jury Mandate

Jury science poses the greatest threat to the Sixth Amendment's impartiality dictate. Where one party uses the science and the other does not, impartiality has been sacrificed for one party. If the science is ineffective, then neither party is put at a competitive disadvantage by the use of jury science. If the science is effective, under this Note's proposed analytic framework, the science should only be used if both parties have equal access. This outcome will ensure that neither side is put at a disadvantage in the jury selection process and that a relatively impartial jury is empaneled.

2. A Jury of One's Peers

Similarly, although jury science is less threatening to the notion of a trial by one's peers, threats still exist. If the science is evenly applied, then neither side is placed at a disadvantage in its endeavor to define "peer" as innovatively or broadly as possible. If the science is ineffective, then it has no effect on the notion of peer. Yet, where jury science is effective, it can be used to define "peer" so broadly that the term loses its original meaning of a person from the same socio-economic station. However, the potential harm to the original meaning of "peer" can be controlled under the perception prong of the above framework. If the community or the defendant no longer believes that a trial by peers is possible when a broader application of the term is applied, then the use of the science would engender negative community perception and the science should not be exploited.

C. Resolving the Impartiality/Peer Tension

The proposed analytic framework might help resolve the tension between the notions of impartiality and peer. This tension is inherent in the difficulty of reconciling a jury composed of one's peer group or community with an impartial panel free from undue sympathy for the defendant. Assuming the science is effective and can be equitably applied, it might help weed out hidden bias and thus empanel a more impartial jury. Moreover, to the extent that the science allows "peer" to be defined more broadly, an attorney can seek to empanel impartial jurors from a wider community of peers. If both of these eventualities were to occur, then there would be few negative perceptions accompanying the use of jury science. By narrowing bias while expanding the concept of peer, jury science might diminish the tension between impartiality and peer.

D. Juries as a Bulwark of Democracy

Finally, questions of perception go directly to our vision of jury trials as a bulwark of democracy. To the extent that jury science counters the stereotypes that have for so long guided attorneys in jury selection and replaces them with scientific demographic analysis, the science opens the doors of jury service to more Americans. America's pluralistic society reaps the indirect benefit of having sometimes racist, and often malevolent, stereotypes rebuffed. On the other hand, by defining some characteristics and individuals as undesirable, jury science continues to exclude some Americans from jury service.

Moreover, the science might create the impression that juries can be manipulated and that their actions can be predicted. To this end, jury science eliminates the legitimacy that jurors otherwise bring to the administration of justice. If the legal community believes this to be true, then the science should not be used. Finally, by selecting jurors who will behave in a predictable fashion, the science may hamper the instillation of a broad range of community values or the ability of jurors to nullify the law.

The proposed analytic framework thus addresses the two most problematic aspects of jury science: its effect on the fairness of trials and the negative perceptions of justice that the science fosters. By examining the above questions, the legal system can begin to create sound parameters for applying jury science.

V. CONCLUSION

Legal scholars and judges have paid little attention to the phenomenon of jury science which accompanies many of America's highest profile trials.[113] The lack of attention is disturbing given the potential for this science to undermine some of the fundamental values that our jury system is supposed to perpetuate. It is time for the legal community to begin to question the role that jury science should play in our justice system.

One commentator has warned that as "increasingly sophisticated marketing techniques meet decreasingly sophisticated jurors, the jury of the future might be highly susceptible to manipulation."[114] Another expert admonishes that jury science will potentially undermine the moral values of our current system:

> If we come to perceive jurors not as independent moral agents but as creatures whose behavior, determined by social and psychological forces, is more or less predictable, we undercut the fundamental belief in rationality and responsibility that justifies the process of trial by jury.[115]

Further, some scholars have cautioned that "those who ignore the laws of science will be controlled by those who understand them."[116]

Jury science has arrived on the legal landscape with minimal scrutiny. Given its potential to fundamentally alter the system, it makes sense to begin to focus on the full extent and impact of this science. The need for attention and study becomes particularly acute if we accept the aphorism with which this Note began: that "every case has been won or lost when the jury is sworn in." To this end, the legal community needs to pursue some sort of broad analytic framework for addressing the questions that the use of jury science raises. By adopting a framework similar to the one suggested in this Note, the legal community can ensure that the science is applied equitably without damaging the legitimacy of the jury system.

NOTES

*I would like to thank Professor David D. Cole of the Georgetown University Law Center for his direction and guidance, Cara Miller for her insight and assistance, and Benjamin Barber for his helpful comments.

1. Clarence Darrow, Warshaw, *Voir Dire*, Trial Dipl. J., Fall 1986, at 2, *quoted in* Emily M. DeFalla, Note, *Voir Dire for California's Civil Trials: Applying the Williams Standard*, 39 Hastings L.J. 517, 517 (1988).

2. The models that have evolved to support our vision of the traditional American jury trial might be better denominated by the less rigid term "rationales."

3. The three rationales for jury trials are: the Sixth Amendment's impartial jury mandate, the historical notion of a jury of one's peers, and the Anglo-American tradition of the jury as a bulwark of democracy.

4. This Note will use the term "jury science" to include juror questionnaires, jury polling, mock juries, and a number of other devices designed to assist in the selection of jurors during voir dire. This new science derives from the nexus of the social sciences and the law. Jury science attempts to give some quantifiable foundation to the stereotyping and intuition that, until recently, formed the basis for a lawyer's selection of a particular juror. It might be a misnomer to label such endeavors to select a sympathetic jury as "science." Often the line between the "scientific" and "unscientific" is murky. Science's distinguishing characteristic is its "obsess[ion] with systematic empirical verification of its hypotheses." Michael J. Saks, *Social Scientists Can't Rig Juries*, *in* In the Jury Box 48, 53 (Lawrence S. Wrightsman et al. eds., 1987). The process of using social science to

select jurors is not itself science, but rather is the application of findings obtained through the use of the scientific method. *Id.* Saks points out that "[a]lmost of necessity, applications [of science] themselves cannot be science." *Id.* Therefore, this type of jury selection might more accurately be called an art.

5. For example, jury science has different implications for the criminal and the civil domains. In civil litigation, especially where corporate titans are doing battle, fairness concerns are diminished compared to the situation of an indigent defendant in a criminal proceeding, who is unable to afford jury science but is prosecuted by a state that is armed with the science. The Constitution is, likewise, more vigilant in policing the criminal proceeding, despite the fact that the use of jury science does raise similar concerns in the civil and criminal contexts regarding society's perception of the roles of and rationales for jury trials. A full discussion of the distinction between the civil and criminal contexts is beyond the scope of this Note.

6. The Sixth Amendment provides: "In all criminal prosecutions, the accused shall enjoy the right to a speedy and public trial, by an impartial jury of the State and district wherein the crime shall have been committed, which district shall have been previously ascertained by. . . ." U.S. Const. amend. VI.

7. *See* Toni M. Massaro, *Peremptories or Peers? Rethinking Sixth Amendment Doctrine, Images and Procedures*, 64 N.C. L. Rev. 501, 542 (1986)(discussing meaning of "impartial" within context of Sixth Amendment).

8. *See, e.g.*, Withrow v. Larkin, 421 U.S. 35 (1975) (holding fair trial in fair tribunal to be basic requirement of due process).

9. *See* Irvin v. Dowd, 366 U.S. 717, 722 (1961)(impartial juror must not have formed opinion prior to trial and must base verdict on evidence developed at trial).

10. *See* Hiroshi Fukurai et al., Race and the Jury 142 (1993) (discussing goals of both prosecution and defense in jury selection).

11. Herald Price Fahringer, a prominent New York attorney, has stated that "[t]here isn't a trial lawyer in this country who wouldn't tell you—if he were being honest—'I don't want an impartial jury. I want one that's going to find in my client's favor.'" Saul M. Kassin & Lawrence S. Wrightsman, The American Jury on Trial 50 (1988) (citing Morton Hunt, *Putting Juries on the Couch*, N.Y. Times, Nov. 28, 1982. (Magazine), at 70, 86). It has also been argued that:

> Ostensibly, a jury is selected for the primary purpose of seeking justice. Therefore, lawyers, as officers of the court, should ideally present all pertinent evidence in the forum of justice with the hope that truth will prevail. If this were so, any jury would be proper so long as it could objectively and fairly listen to both sides and, in the end, render a just verdict. Unfortunately, the practice of law forces those who wish to survive in the continuing contest to be much more realistic. It is not enough just to present a good case effectively; the payoff comes in the winning. In the harsh reality of life, a lawyer gets paid for a victory—and he knows it. With this thought in mind, the successful trial lawyer bends every effort to achieve victory. It is not enough just to have a good case, a good preparation, and good ability. He must also have a good jury. This means a jury good to his cause, having inherently a tendency to favor him.

Marcus Gleisser, Juries and Justice 223 (1968).

12. *See infra* note 14 and accompanying text.

13. The history of the debate surrounding the adoption of the Sixth Amendment and the corresponding question of the geographical area from which a jury should be drawn reflects the colonists' concern that a jury be composed of members of one's community and that justice be delivered by that same community. Massaro, *supra* note 7, at 550.

14. The Magna Carta provided that "'we will not set forth against him (any freeman) nor send against him unless by the lawful judgment of his peers.'" This provision demonstrated that as early as the thirteenth century, English freemen were entitled to jury trials by their peers, however "peers" might be defined. At that time, the term probably refered to other freemen who were part of the same community. Gleisser, *supra* note 11, at 39.

15. Paula Diperna, Juries on Trial 79 (1984).

16. Strauder v. West Virginia, 100 U.S. 303 (1880). However, it should be noted that this decision probably applies to the composition of the venire and not the petit jury.

17. *See* Diperna, *supra* note 15, at 79-84 (discussing evolution of the meaning of "peer").

18. Massaro, *supra* note 7, at 552.

19. *See* Fukurai et al., *supra* note 10, at 142 ("[T]he defense wants to exclude jurors from wider geographic and socioeconomic boundaries who do not necessarily share the standards of life and morals that may have been underlying factors in the alleged crime.").

20. Alexis Clerel DeTocqueville, Democracy in America 282 (George Adlard, 3d Am. ed. 1839), *quoted in* Lloyd E. Moore, The Jury: Tool of Kings, Palladium of Liberty 182 (1973).

21. *See* Shirley S. Abrahamson, *Justice and Juror*, 20 Ga. L. Rev. 257, 259 (1986) (discussing legitimization of administration of justice through juror participation).

22. Michael J. Saks, *Blaming the Jury*, 75 Geo. L.J. 693, 702 (1986) (reviewing Valerie P. Hans & Neil Widman, Judging the Jury (1986)).

23. G.K. Chesterton described this professional numbness:

> And the horrible thing about all legal officials, even the best, about all judges, magistrates, barristers, detectives, and policemen, is not that they are wicked (some of them are good), not that they are stupid (several of them are quite intelligent), it is simply that they have got used to it. . . . They do not see the awful court of judgment; they only see their own workshop.

G.K. Chesterton, *The Twelve Men, in* Tremendous Trifles 80, 85-86 (1909), *quoted in* Abrahamson, *supra* note 21, at 277.

24. Selection biases can exist in the compilation of juror lists. For example, relying on voter registration lists excludes from jury service large segments of the population who are not registered to vote. Nevertheless, it is likely that more Americans will be called for juror service than for any other form of government service.

25. James P. Levine, Juries and Politics 17 (1992).

26. David S. Davis, who heads the Boston offices of the jury selection firm Litigation Sciences Inc. said, after jury selection in a tobacco liability case in federal district court, "[a]fter the jury was picked I felt we couldn't lose." He won. John H. Kennedy, *Pretrial Studying of Jurors Becomes a Key to the Case*, Boston Globe, Feb. 19, 1990, Metro, at 1. Dr. Robert Minick, also with Litigation Sciences Inc., stated that he believed the Manuel Noriega case would be won or lost during jury selection. Minick called jury selection possibly "the only chance that the defendant has." *Jury Selection Key Issue in Noriega Trial, Experts Say*, Cleveland Plain Dealer, Aug. 25, 1991, at A22.

27. The above inference is based on the paucity of either case law or scholarly work regarding the impact of jury science on the jury system.

28. Levine, *supra* note 25, at 55.

29. *Id.* Professor Alan Dershowitz summed up this outlook:

> Lawyers' instincts are often the least trustworthy basis on which to pick jurors. All those neat rules of thumb, but no feedback. Ten years of accumulated experiences may be ten years of being wrong. I myself, even when I trust my instincts, like to have them scientifically confirmed.

Hunt, *supra* note 11, at 82.

30. *See infra* note 55 and accompanying text (discussing possible stereotypes used in jury selection).

31. The methodologies of jury science are discussed at length in the next section of this Note.

32. Walter F. Abbott, Surrogate Juries 2 (1990). Other writers have reached the same conclusion. *See, e.g.*, Harry Kalven, Jr. & Hans Zeisel, The American Jury (1966); M.J. Saks & R. Hastie, Social Psychology in Court (1978).

33. Jo-Ellan Dimitrius, a leading jury consultant who has recently worked on both the Rodney King and the Reginald Denny trials, claims a 90 percent success rate in the more than 100 cases she

has worked on since 1984. Philip M. Gollner, *Consulting by Peering Into Minds of Jurors*, N.Y. Times, Jan. 7, 1994, at A23. Litigation Sciences Inc., the most prominent jury consulting firm in the country with revenues of over $25 million per annum, "boasts a 96 percent accuracy rate in predicting the final outcome of its clients' cases that go to trial." Michele Galen, *The Best Jurors Money Can Pick*, Bus. Wk., June 15, 1992, at 108.

34. For a detailed account of this story, see Jay Schulman et al., *Recipe for a Jury*, *in* In the Jury Box 13, 13-47 (Lawrence S. Wrightsman et al. eds., 1987).

35. *Id.* at 14.

36. *Id.* at 15. Even within the middle district of Pennsylvania, the government had a choice between Harrisburg, Lewisburg, and Scranton. Lewisburg is a college town and Scranton had a large number of Catholics and Democrats. The government chose Harrisburg, which had twice as many Republicans as Democrats and which had few Catholics. Harrisburg also contained the highest proportion of fundamentalist religious sects, an active Klu Klux Klan, and war related industries. *Id.*

37. *Id.* at 16.

38. *Id.* at 16-17. Schulman stated that by "fair," he meant a trial in which the "jury would assume [the defendants] innocent unless proven guilty beyond a reasonable doubt." *Id.* at 17.

39. *Id.* at 17. Schulman said, "I kept thinking there must be something I, as a social scientist, can do to help my friends. But what?" Hunt, *supra* note 11, at 72.

40. Hunt, *supra* note 11, at 82.

41. Schulman, *supra* note 34, at 18.

42. *Id.* at 18-19.

43. *Id.* at 23.

44. Schulman found that the liberal college graduates tended to leave Harrisburg. Hunt, *supra* note 11, at 82.

45. Schulman and the defense team successfully chose a cluster of young women who formed such a faction, who arrived at a more lenient view of the defendants than did other members of the jury and who supported each other during jury deliberations. Schulman et al., *supra* note 34, at 44.

46. *Id.* at 16.

47. After the "Harrisburg-Seven" trial, jury science was next used frequently in the 1970s. It was applied in the Angela Davis trial in 1972, as well as the Daniel Ellsberg and Anthony Russo trials that same year, and in the Watergate trials of Maurice Stans, John Mitchell, and Robert Vesco. John Guinther, The Jury in America 55 (1988). Schulman proceeded to work with Indian militants of Wounded Knee, South Dakota, the Attica prison rioters, radical feminist Susan Saxe, and Joan Little, an African-American woman who was accused of murdering a white prison guard. In 1975, Schulman established the National Jury Project, a non-profit organization, which carried on the liberal battle against the establishment and assisted those defendants who seemed to have the deck stacked against them. Sheryl Seyfert, *The New Science of Jury Selection*, Boston Globe, Aug. 5, 1984, (New England Magazine).

48. Schulman, *supra* note 34, at 46.

49. Galen, *supra* note 33, at 108.

50. *Id.*

51. *Id.*

52. This $10,000 figure was quoted by Ross Laguzza, managing director of Litigation Sciences Inc. in Houston. Diane Burch Beckham, *The Art of the Voir Dire: Is it Really a Science?* N.J. L.J., July 5, 1990, at 5. However, other practitioners estimate that the bare minimum needed for adequate research is $50,000. Hunt, *supra* note 11, at 72.

At least one commentator has noted the irony that "[a] method that originated in the 1960s to help downtrodden defendants faced with potentially hostile juries is now more commonly used by affluent litigants in civil cases and is sometimes even employed by prosecutors in criminal cases." Levine, *supra* note 25, at 57.

53. Gail Diane Cox, *King Trial: The Real Story*, Nat'l L.J., May 3, 1993, at 38.

54. Margaret Covington, *Jury Selection: Innovative Approaches to Both Civil and Criminal Litigation*, 16 St. Mary's L.J. 575, 591 (1985).

55. "Never take a German; they are bullheaded. Rarely take a Swede; they are stubborn. Always take an Irishman or a Jew; they are the easiest to move to emotional sympathy. Old men are generally more charitable and kindly disposed than young men; they have seen more of the world and understand it." Clarence Darrow, *quoted in* The Oxford Book of Legal Anecdotes 101 (Michael Gilbert ed., 1986).

One of the benefits of the introduction of jury science is its attempt to move away from these sorts of gross generalizations and stereotypes. However, the science also brings a corresponding danger of stamping the imprimatur of science on these stereotypes.

56. Covington, *supra* note 54, at 591.

57. *See supra* note 55 (discussing Darrow's stereotypes).

58. Robert F. Hanley, *Getting to Know You*, 40 Am. U. L. Rev. 865, 871 (1991).

59. Saks, *supra* note 4, at 51.

60. Covington, *supra* note 54, at 593-94.

61. *See The Fine Art of Selecting a Jury: Attorneys Have Conflicting Ideas About Panelists*, Phila. Inquirer, Oct. 31, 1983, at B5 [hereinafter *Fine Art of Selecting Jury*] ("Occasionally, attorneys hire detectives to do research on potential jurors by interviewing their neighbors and by delving into their records.").

62. Covington, *supra* note 54, at 591.

63. *See, e.g.*, Peskin, *Non-Verbal Communication in the Courtroom*, Trial Dipl. J., 1980, at 6.

64. *Id.*

65. Covington, *supra* note 54, at 595.

66. The typical jury foreperson in 1982 was a college-educated, white male professional who earned about $35,000 per year and was a political centrist. Edward Burke Arnolds & Thomas Sannito, Ph.D., *Jury Study Results Part II: Making Use of the Findings*, Trial Dipl. J., Summer 1982, at 13, 15.

67. Kassin & Wrightsman, *supra* note 11, at 179.

68. *See* Covington, *supra* note 54, at 595-96.

69. *See* Hanley, *supra* note 58, at 870-71 (discussing focus groups).

70. Covington, *supra* note 54, at 596.

71. *Id.* at 596-98.

72. *Id.*

73. MCI won a verdict of $1.8 billion, the largest in antitrust history, from a six-person jury. Abbott, *supra* note 32, at 1.

74. The first mock jury awarded MCI only $100 million, far less than the $900 million requested. After examining the jury's deliberations, the attorneys learned that the jury was uncomfortable with the existing law that AT&T had to share its telephone lines and that the jury had based its damage assessment on MCI's actual damages as stated by MCI's attorneys. Based on these findings, the second mock jury was told to apply the law regardless of its feelings about the law, and the $100 million lost-profit figure was not introduced. This jury, as did the real jury, awarded MCI $900 million. *Id.* at 2.

75. *See* Covington, *supra* note 54, at 598.

76. The concerns might take the following form: Does this science refine an attorney's ability to empanel a truly impartial jury by uncovering hidden bias? Alternatively, does the science provide one side with an unfair ability to empanel partial jurors, thereby undermining the adversarial process? Does it become easier to empanel a jury composed of a defendant's peers because the

science allows an unexpected group or party to be defined as a peer and sympathize with the plight of the defendant? Or, does the definition of "peer" become so broadly construed by jury science that it loses its original meaning of a juror who shares a common heritage with the defendant? Finally, does the science enhance the democratic function of a jury trial by not selecting jurors on the basis of stereotypes? Or, does the science undermine the democratic function of juries by acknowledging jury tampering, thus validating our former practice of selecting jurors on the basis of stereotypes?

Given the amorphous character of jury science, it is unclear whether any of the above concerns can be answered satisfactorily. To a large extent, the conclusions one reaches will be shaped by one's instincts about jury science and the role that juries ought to play. Minimally, jury science would seem to call into question the rationales that undergird the jury system, and to impinge on the system's autonomy and fairness.

77. Fukurai et al., *supra* note 10, at 141. The authors continue in the same vein:

> The practice of carefully selecting a jury favorable to the case seems calculated, not to render the justice that a court system is supposed to award, but to provide counsel with a kind of leverage that has little or nothing to do with the guilt or innocence of the defendant.

78. *Id.* Scientific jury selection has been called "voodoo jury selection." Abrahamson, *supra* note 21, at 292. However, as Abrahamson points out, "[some] believe in voodoo." *Id.* After an extensive study of over 800 jurors, Reid Hastie concluded that scientific jury selection techniques are "not an impressively powerful lever for use in courtroom selection procedures." Elizabeth F. Loftus & Edith Greene, *Twelve Angry People: The Collective Mind of the Jury, Inside the Jury*, 84 Colum. L. Rev. 1425, 1430 (1984) (reviewing Reid Hastie, Steven D. Penrod, & Nancy Pennington, Inside the Jury, (1983)).

79. *Fine Art of Selecting Jury*, *supra* note 61, at B5.

80. The place where social science and law meet has been described by one commentator as being similar to "the parlor in the Victorian home in which the girl and her suitor can get together—but not get together too much." Riesman, *Some Observations on Law and Psychology*, 19 U. Chi. L. Rev. 30, 32 (1951).

81. *See* David L. Faigman, *To Have or Have Not: Assessing the Value of Social Science to the Law as Science and Policy*, 38 Emory L.J. 1005, 1008 (1989) (discussing indeterminacy of social science).

82. *See infra* note 90 and accompanying text (discussing Judge Ouderkirk's appointment of jury consultant in Reginald Denny trial).

83. *See supra* note 33 (discussing success rate of jury consultants).

84. *See*, e.g., Abrahamson, *supra* note 21, at 292 (explaining that some smokers who have higher asbestos cancer risk may nonetheless favor an asbestos-producing corporation if exposed person knew about risk).

85. Loftus & Greene, *supra* note 78, at 1431.

86. Saks, *supra* note 4, at 60.

87. As noted above, the bare minimum that must be spent to obtain the assistance of a jury consultant is somewhere between $10,000 and $50,000. Justice Abrahamson raises the concern of the "inability of the poor to obtain [such surveys]." Abrahamson, *supra* note 21, at 292.

88. Saks, *supra* note 4, at 55. *See also* Collins v. United States, 972 F.2d 1385 (5th Cir. 1992), *cert. denied*, 113 S. Ct. 1812 (1993) (raising constitutional and other concerns, defense unsuccessfully challenged government's use of jury science).

89. Spivey v. State, 319 S.E.2d 420 (Ga. 1984). The court noted that the defendant had received the assistance of at least one member of the National Jury Project during jury selection.

90. Judge Ouderkirk provided no reasoning for the appointment of a jury consultant. While probably not constitutionally mandated, the high-profile nature of the Reginald Denny trial and the

combustible state of Los Angeles in the aftermath of the first Rodney King trial may have led the judge to provide the defense with every tool possible to ensure a fair trial. Regardless of the reasons for this appointment, it may serve as precedent for other defendants in their endeavors to balance the scales of justice.

91. James P. Levine asks:

> Perhaps it is all right for both sides to have access to similar weapons for fighting courtroom battles, but it is open to question whether it is ethically proper to permit those who already have the upper hand to extend their advantage by employing science for the purpose of stacking the jury.

Levine, *supra* note 25, at 57.

92. Amitai Etzioni has said, "[a]ll this is just a form of tampering with the jury, and I would prohibit it." Galen, *supra* note 33, at 108.

93. Saks, *supra* note 4, at 49.

94. Hunt, *supra* note 11, at 86.

95. Saks, *supra* note 4, at 51 (discussing use of this technique during the Harrisburg-Seven trial to remove jurors who were perceived to be biased).

96. Seyfert, *supra* note 47, at 3.

97. *Id.*

98. As stated earlier in this Note, the legal system assumes that through a voir dire process, in which both sides try to empanel their own partial jurors while removing the other side's partial jurors, the most biased jurors will be removed and an impartial jury will be empaneled. However, it is unclear if the system imagined this battle occurring under the guidance of experts or if the system considered the impact of one side being armed with an expert while the other is left to its own devices.

99. According to The National Jury Project, Jurywork, Systematic Techniques (1979), a third or more of Americans consider a criminal defendant probably guilty, but few would admit this in the courtroom.

100. *See* Schulman, *supra* note 34, at 19.

101. A manual used to instruct Dallas, Texas prosecutors provides that:

> You are not looking for a fair juror, but rather a strong, biased and sometimes hypocritical individual who believes that defendants are different from them in kind, rather than degree. You are not looking for any member of a minority group which may subject him to oppression—they almost always empathize with the accused.
>
> I don't like women jurors because I can't trust them.
>
> Extremely overweight young men, indicates a lack of self-discipline and often time instability. I like the lean and hungry look.
>
> Hunters always make good State's jurors.
>
> Jewish veniremen generally make poor State's jurors. Jews have a history of oppression and generally empathize with the accused.

Albert W. Alschuler, *The Supreme Court and the Jury: Voir Dire Peremptory Challenges, and the Review of Jury Verdicts*, 56 U. Chi. L. Rev. 153, 156 (1989). These types of stereotypes are clearly antithetical to our pluralistic, egalitarian tradition.

102. *See infra* note 106 (citing cases supporting appointment of experts and investigators to some indigent defendants).

103. "By the end of the century . . . every lawyer will hire a jury consultant for major trials." James F. McCarty, *Jury Expert Puts Solid Record Behind Unusual Methods*, Cleveland Plain Dealer, Feb. 21, 1993, at 2B (quoting Robert Hirschhorn).

104. Norbert L. Kerr & Robert J. MacCoun, *The Effects of Jury Size and Polling Method on the Process and Product of Jury Deliberation, in* In the Jury Box 209 (Lawrence S. Wrightsman et al. eds., 1987).

105. Indeed, our legal system already tolerates gross mismatches in the talent of attorneys. For example, it is not a constitutional violation for one side to be represented by Edward Bennett Williams and the other to be represented by an overworked public defender straight out of law school. *See* Gideon v. Wainright, 372 U.S. 335 (1963) (holding that indigent defendant in criminal trial has fundamental right to assistance of counsel).
106. *See, e.g.*, Ake v. Oklahoma, 470 U.S. 68 (1985) (holding that when state brings judicial power to bear on defendant, it must take steps to assure that defendant has fair opportunity to present defense). In *Ake*, the Court held that where sanity is a significant factor at trial, the state must provide an indigent with a competent expert witness and examination. *See also* Smith v. McCormick, 914 F.2d 1153 (1990) (due process mandates not met where state failed to provide indigent with psychiatric expert prior to trial); State v. Brooks, 385 S.E.2d 81 (Ga. 1989) (criminal defendant not precluded from obtaining public funds for investigative or expert assistance on theory that overwhelming evidence would be presented at trial).
107. "[N]owhere in the guarantees for due process is there any rule regarding jury research—at least not yet." DiPerna, *supra* note 15, at 131.
108. "The decision today will not end the racial discrimination that peremptories inject into the jury selection process. That goal can be accomplished only by eliminating peremptory challenges entirely." Batson v. Kentucky, 476 U.S. 79, 102-03 (1986) (Marshall, J., concurring). *See also* Alschuler, *supra* note 101, at 208 (endorsing Justice Marshall's conclusion that peremptories should be abolished); Jeff Rosen, *Jurymandering: A Case Against Peremptory Challenges*, New Republic, Nov. 30, 1992, at 15 (same).
109. *Batson*, 476 U.S. at 89 (holding that state denies an African-American defendant equal protection when it puts him or her on trial before a jury from which members of his or her race have purposely been excluded).
110. Presently, there are no real controls on jury research. The only minimal guideline is that no one may talk to a potential juror directly before the case begins or to a sworn juror during the case. Diperna, *supra* note 15, at 130.
111. There is only a paltry amount of research on the use, effect, and success of jury science in trials.
112. The two most important changes would be either to require equal access to information garnered by the science or to require state funding of jury consultants for indigent parties when the other side uses the science.
113. Robert Hirschhorn, a leading jury consultant, has said that by the end of the century "[jury consultants] will be as indispensable as a lawyer's computer, private investigator and secretary." McCarty, *supra* note 103, at 2B.
114. DiPerna, *supra* note 15, at 149.
115. Hunt, *supra* note 11, at 83.
116. Loftus & Greene, *supra* note 78, at 1431.

12

The American Jury: Handicapped in the Pursuit of Justice

Saul M. Kassin

Whether it is true or not, the story is a favorite among students of trial advocacy: Clarence Darrow, smoking a cigar during the presentation of his opponent's case, stole the jury's attention by inserting a thin wire into the cigar and producing an ash that grew like magic with every puff.[1] In a more recent case involving personal injury in which the plaintiff had lost a leg, Melvin Belli carried into court a large L-shaped package wrapped in yellow butcher paper and tied with a white string, and placed it on counsel's table as a visible reminder. Then during his closing argument, Belli unwrapped the package, only to reveal a prosthesis.[2] These courtroom pranks as well as other, more common trial practices, are clever, entertaining, and perhaps even effective. But at what cost to the jury's pursuit of justice?

This Article examines nonevidentiary social influences on the jury, influences that emanate from various trial practices and threaten to compromise a litigant's right to a fair trial. Broadly defined, there are two phases in the jury's decision-making task that are at risk. The first is the factfinding competence of *individual jurors*—that is, their ability to make accurate judgments of the evidence (*e.g.*, by distinguishing among witnesses of varying credibility), and disregard information that is not in evidence (*e.g.*, material received from the news media, voir dire questions, opening statements, closing arguments, and inadmissible testimony). The second phase of a jury's task is the deliberation of the *jury as a group*—that is, the process by which individual members contribute independently and equally to a joint outcome, exerting influence over each other through information and rational argument rather than heavy-handed social pressure.[3]

The following evaluation of juries is based on the results of controlled behavioral research, not on abstract legal theory, isolated case studies, or trial anecdotes. The reader should thus be mindful of both the strengths and weaknesses inherent in this approach. The most appropriate way to obtain a full and rich understanding of how juries function is to observe the decision-making process in action. Juries, however, deliberate in complete privacy, behind closed doors. Unable to observe or record actual jury deliberations, researchers have had to develop alternative, less direct strategies (*e.g.*, analysis of court records in search of statistical relationships between various trial factors and jury verdicts; post-trial interviews with jurors, alternates, and

Reprinted by permission of the *Ohio State Law Journal* and the author from vol. 51 (1990), pp. 687–711.

other trial participants; jury simulation experiments). Most of the research reported in this paper was conducted within a mock jury paradigm.[4]

I. FACTFINDING COMPETENCE OF INDIVIDUAL JURORS

As individual factfinders, jurors must competently process all evidence and instructions, disregard information that is not in evidence, and reconstruct disputed events by distinguishing among witnesses of varying credibility. We will see that the task is difficult, and that it is complicated even further by various questionable practices.

A. Jurors as Arbiters of Truth and Deception

Confronted with opposing sides and inevitably conflicting testimony, jurors must accept the testimony of some witnesses, and reject others. Toward this end, the courts instruct jurors to pay close attention not only to the content of the witness's testimony but to his or her demeanor while testifying. Indeed, many judges prohibit jurors from taking notes for fear that they will overlook informative nonverbal cues.[5]

Unfortunately, psychological research suggests that people perform at only slightly better than chance levels in evaluating truth and deception. Even individuals who make these judgments for a living (*e.g.*, customs inspectors, law enforcement officers) are prone to error.[6] Based on a review of over thirty studies, Miron Zuckerman and others conclude that there is a mismatch between the nonverbal behaviors actually associated with deception and those cues used by perceivers.[7] People tend to focus on a speaker's face, for example, even though facial expressions are under conscious deceptive control.[8] At the same time, there is a tendency to overlook kinesic and paralinguistic cues, even though they are more revealing.[9] In short, there is reason to believe that jurors tune into the wrong channels of communication. Seduced by the silver tongue and the smiling face, they may fail to notice the restless body and the quivering voice.[10]

Human imperfections aside, the rules of evidence and trial procedure that guide the questioning of witnesses are intended to facilitate the jury's quest for the truth.[11] In theory, direct and cross examination should thus enhance the credibility of witnesses who are accurate and honest, while diminishing the credibility of those who are inaccurate or dishonest—in other words, it should heighten the jury's factfinding competence. There is no way to know how frequently the law's objectives are actually achieved. While much is written about effective questioning techniques, surprisingly little research has examined their prevalence or their impact on the jury.[12] One problem, however, seems evident. Even though trial attorneys are expected to adhere to rules of evidence and keep their trial strategies within the boundaries of ethical conduct,[13] they often bend the rules and stretch the boundaries.[14] Thus we ask, to what extent can the examination of witnesses be used to subvert a jury's quest for the truth?

There are several ethically questionable trial practices, or "dirty tricks," that could make it difficult for jurors to make sound credibility judgments. Coaching witnesses, leading their testimony in court, distracting the jury at critical moments in an opponent's case, making frivolous objections, and asking questions that invite the leakage of inadmissible evidence, are among the possibilities.[15] In this section, two such practices are evaluated: the presentation of deposition testimony, and the use of presumptuous cross-examination questions.

B. Deposition Testimony and the Surrogate Witness

As difficult as it is to evaluate witnesses by their demeanor, the task is needlessly complicated when jurors must make judgments of credibility without ever seeing the actual witness. Often, people who are scheduled to testify are not available to appear in court.[16] In order to secure the substance of what these prospective witnesses have to say, counsel may take a deposition and enter that deposition into the trial record.

The use of deposition testimony in lieu of the live witness raises an interesting procedural question: How is such testimony entered into the trial record? How is the information presented, and what effect does it have on the jury's ability to evaluate the witness? In most courts, depositions are transcribed and then read aloud from the witness stand by a clerk or by an individual appointed by the witness's attorney. Usually, the clerk reads the answers, while the attorney reads the questions; sometimes, the attorney reads the entire script.

As one might expect, the practice of using what I call "surrogate witnesses" in an adversarial context paves the way for abuse. In one case, for example, I observed pretrial auditions of more than thirty professional actors and actresses who were called to play the roles of various absent witnesses who had been deposed. The actors all read the transcripts flawlessly. What distinguished those who were hired from those who were not was their ability to project through subtle nonverbal behaviors—crossing legs, rolling eyes, smiling, or sighing at a critical moment—specific impressions of the witnesses they were supposed to represent.[17]

It should not be permissible to use surrogates in this manner. Indeed, deposition readers should not unduly emphasize any words or engage in suggestive conduct. Nevertheless, many litigators appreciate the potential for gain in this procedure. For example, one trial advocate advises that "whoever is playing the part of the witness on the stand will, most assuredly, be identified with that witness. True, he is nothing more than an actor, but human beings tend to associate a voice with a person; so be certain that the 'actor' projects a favourable image."[18] It is even suggested that when faced with a witness with undesirable characteristics, the "imaginative" lawyer should consider taking a deposition and then replacing that witness with an attractive surrogate.[19] Research on the social psychology of persuasion offers little guidance. It is clear that audiences are influenced by the *source* of a communication,[20] but do characteristics of the *messenger* have the same effect? Is it truly possible to alter the impact of a deposition and mislead the jury by manipulating the surrogate's demeanor?

To test this hypothesis, I conducted the following mock jury experiment.[21] Eighty-eight subjects read a summary of a case in which the plaintiff sought damages from a security company because he had been harassed and then shot by one of its guards. The defense claimed the plaintiff was drunk and had inadvertently shot himself in a scuffle with their guard. There were no eyewitnesses to the shooting, and the physical evidence was ambiguous. For all practical purposes, a jury's verdict would thus hinge on the relative credibility of opposing witnesses, the plaintiff and the guard. After reading a summary of the case, subjects watched a carefully staged videotape of the plaintiff's testimony. An actor was hired to play this critical witness in two contrasting roles. In one tape, he was attentive, polite, cooperative, and unhesitating in his response to questions; in the other, he read the same testimony, but was impolite, often annoyed, cautious and fumbling in his style. The actor read exactly the same transcript in both conditions, varying only his tone of voice, facial expressions, and body language.

Since a witness's demeanor is considered relevant, one would expect that even though subjects heard the same testimony read by the same actor, those who viewed the positive-demeanor witness would prove more favorable to the plaintiff than those who viewed the negative-demeanor witness. This expectation was confirmed. Subjects rated the positive witness as more likeable, sincere, and trustworthy, and his testimony as more believable, accurate, and persuasive. Seventy-two percent of those in the positive-demeanor group voted for the plaintiff, compared to only twenty-two percent in the negative-demeanor group. But what if subjects were told—both before and after watching the tape—that they were not seeing the actual witness, but an individual assigned to read the witness's deposition? Since the demeanor of a surrogate is not relevant to judging the credibility of a witness, and since the two tapes were identical in verbal content, jurors should not be affected by what they saw. But they were. Even though subjects were aware that they were merely watching a clerk reading from a transcript, those who watched the positive- rather than negative-demeanor tape rated the witness and the testimony itself as more credible, and were more likely to return a verdict for the plaintiff—sixty-one percent to thirty-three percent.

As noted earlier, deposition readers are not supposed to embellish their performances. But can judges necessarily detect the subtle nuances and manipulations of a professional actor? People are often not conscious of the nonverbal cues that guide their impressions. Moreover, what about *nonbehavioral* sources of bias such as the deposition reader's physical appearance? Persuasion researchers have found that communicators who are attractive elicit a greater change in attitudes and behavior than those who are not.[22] To examine whether jurors are likewise influenced by the physical appearance of a surrogate, I conducted an experiment similar to the one just described.[23] Mock jurors read about a criminal conspiracy case, and then listened to an audiotape of the testimony of a female witness accompanied by a series of slides taken in a courtroom. All subjects heard the same tape, but viewed slides of either an attractive or unattractive woman who was believed to be either the witness or a deposition reader.[24] Paralleling the results of the first study, perceptions of the witness's credibility were affected not only by the physical attractiveness of the witness, but by the surrogate's appearance as well.

Taken together, these studies suggest that jurors may be unable to separate a witness and his or her testimony from the messenger who delivers it. Thus, it seems that jurors—despite their best efforts to make sound credibility judgments—may be seriously misled by the behavior and appearance of those who read depositions. The solution to this problem is clear, and easily implemented: videotaped depositions. Since the opportunity for mischief is inherent in the mere substitution of one individual for another, videotape should be used to preserve the witness's demeanor for the record without introducing additional extraneous information. Jurors would then watch these tapes on a monitor stationed in the courtroom.[25]

C. Presumptuous Cross-Examination Questions and the Power of Conjecture

The opportunity to confront opposing witnesses through cross-examination is an essential device for safeguarding the accuracy and completeness of testimonial evidence. What impact does cross-examination have on the jury's ability to reconstruct the truth about an event? What are the dangers? Ideally, cross-examination should enhance a jury's factfinding competence by increasing the credibility of witnesses who are accurate and honest relative to those who are not. To be sure, cross-examination is an indispensable device. Many a mistaken and deceptive witness has no doubt fallen from the stand, exposed, scarred, and discredited from the battle of cross-examination. But cross-examination can also be used to exert an influence over the jury in a way that subverts its quest for truth.

Asking questions provides more than simply a mechanism for eliciting answers. Leading questions in particular may impart information to a listener through imagery, implication, and conjecture.[26] Carefully chosen words can obscure and even alter people's impressions, as when tax increases are called "revenue enhancements," and the strategic defense initiative is referred to as "star wars." Consider the following exchange between an attorney and the defendant in an illegal abortion case:

> *Q:* You didn't tell us, Doctor, whether you determined that the *baby* was alive or dead, did you Doctor?
>
> *A:* The *fetus* had no signs of life.[27]

In this example, the witness resisted the lawyer's imagery. Often, however, answers can be shaped by how a question is worded. In a classic experiment on eyewitness testimony, for example, Elizabeth Loftus and John Palmer had subjects watch films of an automobile collision. Those who were subsequently asked, "About how fast were the cars going when they *smashed* into each other?" estimated an average speed of forty-one miles per hour; those who were asked "About how fast were the cars going when they *hit* each other?" estimated an average of only thirty-four mph.[28] In fact, the wording of this critical question had a lasting effect on subjects' memories of the event. When asked one week later whether they could recall broken glass at the scene of the accident (there was none), only fourteen percent of those previously asked the hit question said they did, compared to thirty-two percent of those who had been asked the smash question. Once the seed of misinformation was planted, it took on a life of its own.

Even when a question does not mislead its respondent, it may still mislead the jury. When a question implies something that is never explicitly stated, for example, the listener may confuse what is said with what is only implied. Cognitive studies of pragmatic implications reveal that such confusion is common. In one study, mock jurors listened to an excerpt of testimony and indicated whether certain statements were true or false. After hearing the statement, "I ran up to the burglar alarm," for example, most subjects recalled that the witness had said, "I *rang* the burglar alarm." Apparently, people process information between the lines and assume they heard what was only implied.[29]

Due to the nearly unrestricted use of leading questions, cross-examination provides additional opportunity to influence jurors through questions that are designed to impart misleading information to the jury. In *Trial Ethics*, Underwood and Fortune note that "one of the most common abuses of cross-examination takes the form of a question implying a serious charge against the witness, for which counsel has little or no proof. All too often, trial attorneys ask such questions for the sole purpose of wafting unwarranted innuendo into the jury box."[30] When lawyers ask questions that suggest their own answers, are jurors influenced by the information implied by those questions? Is cross-examination by innuendo an effective device?

Research in non-legal settings tentatively suggests an affirmative answer. For example, William Swann and his colleagues examined the effects of hearing an interview in which the questioner implies that the respondent has certain personal characteristics.[31] They had subjects listen to question-and-answer sessions in which the interviewer probed for evidence of either extroverted behavior (*e.g.*, "What do you do when you want to liven things up at a party?") or introverted behavior (*e.g.*, "Have you ever felt left out of some social group?"). One-third of the subjects heard only the questions, one-third heard only the answers, and one-third heard both sides of the interview. When subjects heard only the questions, they inferred that the respondent had the traits sought by the interviewer (*i.e.*, they assumed that the interviewer knew enough to ask extroverts about parties and introverts about difficult social situations). Suggestive questions thus serve as proof by conjecture.

In the context of a trial, of course, jurors hear not only the questions asked but the answers they elicit. It stands to reason that under the circumstances, conjectural evidence may be buried under the weight of the witness's testimony. Yet those subjects in the Swann study who—like jurors—heard both sides of the interview, were also misled. Consider the implications. The respondents in these experimental interviews did not actually possess the implied traits, so it seems odd that their answers did not override the effects of the interviewers' questions. In fact, however, the result makes sense. Limited to answering specific questions, respondents provided evidence to confirm the interviewers' conjecture. Subjects who heard the full interview were thus left with false impressions shaped by the questions. As Swann and his colleagues put it, "once respondents' answers 'let the cat out of the bag,' observers saw no reason to concern themselves with how the bag was opened."[32]

In light of these provocative findings, it is important to examine the effects of presumptuous cross-examination questions in legal proceedings in which jurors have the benefit of knowing the context of the questions (*e.g.*, the adversarial relationship between the cross-examiner and witness) and hearing the responses they evoke (*e.g.*, the witness's admission or vehement denial of the implication, or an objection from the witness's attorney).

In a recent study, 105 mock jurors were randomly assigned to one of seven groups.[33] All subjects read a transcript of a rape trial in which the defense argued that the victim was mistaken in her identification. Some subjects read a version of the case in which the cross-examiner asked a presumptuous derogatory question of the victim (*i.e.*, "Isn't it true that you have accused men of rape before?" followed by "Isn't it true that, four years ago, you called the police claiming that you had been raped?"); others read a version in which such questions were asked of an expert for the defense (*i.e.*, "Isn't it true that your work is poorly regarded by your colleagues?" followed by "Hasn't your work been sharply criticized in the past?"). Within each version, the cross-examiner's questions were met with one of three reactions: an admission ("yes," "yes it is [has]"), a flat denial ("no," "no it isn't [hasn't]"), or an objection by the witness's attorney, after which the question was withdrawn before the witness had a chance to respond. An additional group of subjects read a transcript that did not contain any presumptuous questions.

Our results provided strong but qualified support for the hypothesis that negative presumptuous questions would diminish a witness's credibility. When the recipient of the question was the victim, the question did not significantly diminish her credibility. In fact, except when the question elicited an admission, female subjects—who are generally less sympathetic to the defense in this case than males—disparaged the defense lawyer who conducted the cross-examination. When the recipient of the presumptuous question was an expert, however, the technique of cross-examination by innuendo proved highly effective. When the expert's professional reputation was called into question—even though the charge was not corroborated by other evidence—subjects lowered their ratings of his credibility as a witness (*i.e.*, he was perceived as less competent, believable, and persuasive). Indeed, among female subjects, subjective estimates of guilt were elevated in all the innuendo groups, a result that reflects the diminished impact of the defense expert. These effects were obtained regardless of whether the presumptuous question had elicited a denial, an objection, or an admission. It is particularly interesting that this effect was obtained even though many of our subjects reported that they did not actually *believe* the derogatory implications concerning the expert. In short, even when the expert denied the charge, even when his attorney objected to the question, and even though many subjects in both situations did not accept as true the cross-examiner's presumption, the witness became "damaged goods" as soon as the reputation question was raised.

Why were our mock jurors so influenced by uncorroborated presumptions? There are at least two possible explanations. First, research in communication suggests that when people hear a speaker offer a premise in conversation, they naturally assume that he or she has an evidentiary basis for that premise.[34] Within the context of a trial, it is conceivable that jurors—naive about the dirty tricks of cross-examination—adhere to a similar implicit rule. In other words, jurors may assume that a lawyer who implies something about an expert's reputation must have information to support that premise, and treat it though it were a foregone conclusion. A second possible reason for the impact of presumptuous questions is that after all the evidence in a case has been presented, jurors may be unable to separate in memory the information communicated within the questions from those contained within the answers. Studies indicate that people often remember the contents of a message but forget the source,[35] and that people often cannot discriminate among the possible sources of their current knowledge.[36] This kind of confusion is particularly likely to occur when the different sources of information are distant in time and equally plausible—as when jurors must recall after days, weeks, or months of testimony, whether a particular belief was derived from a lawyer's questions or a witness's answers.

From a practical standpoint, this study suggests that the use of presumptuous questions is a dirty trick that can be used to distort juror evaluations of witness credibility. As cross-examiners regularly employ such tactics, judges should be aware of the dangers and make a serious effort to control them. According to Rule 3.4(e) of the American Bar Association 1983 Rules of Professional Conduct, counsel "shall not allude to any matter that the lawyer does not reasonably believe is relevant or that will not be supported by admissible evidence." In practice, however, many judges demand only a "good faith belief" in the truthfulness of the assertions contained in cross-examination questions.[37]

Two approaches can be taken to the problem. Since witnesses have an opportunity to deny false assertions, and since lawyers have an opportunity to object or "set the record straight" on redirect examination, one approach is to allow cross-examiners a good deal of latitude, and trust the self-corrective mechanisms already in place. Our study suggests, however, that both a witness's denials and an attorney's objections may fall on deaf ears. In the case of our expert, subjects lowered their ratings of his credibility even when he flatly denied the charge and even when his attorney won a favorable ruling on an objection. In fact, these strategies may well backfire. People are suspicious of others who are forced to proclaim their innocence too vociferously.[38] Likewise, research indicates instructions to disregard objectionable material are often ineffective, perhaps even counterproductive.[39]

Rather than taking a hands-off policy, our results lead me to believe that judges should intervene to control presumptuous leading questions. As a matter of judicial discretion in trial management, judges may admonish counsel who insert false premises into their questions.[40] Perhaps cautionary instructions to the jury would prove effective. If jurors are moved by conjecture because they follow the implicit rule of conversational logic that speakers have an evidentiary basis for their premises, then perhaps jurors should be forewarned about the use of dirty tricks. Recall that Swann's experiment had subjects listen to an interviewer ask questions that presumed the respondent to be introverted or extroverted. Hearing the questions, subjects inferred that the interviewee possessed the implied traits. When they were told, however, that the interviewer's questions were chosen at random (*i.e.*, without a reason), subjects did not make the inference. Thus, it may be similarly effective to caution jurors that the premises contained within questions are not evidence, and alert them to possible abuses.

To summarize, psychological research indicates that suggestive examination questions can mislead a jury in two ways. First, the questions themselves can misinform others through the power of conjecture. Second, suggestive questions can actually produce support for that conjecture by shaping the witness's testimony. If counsel wants to portray a witness as greedy, lazy, neurotic, introverted, or extraverted, he or she can do so by asking a series of biasing questions. Since a witness can tell a story only in response to specific inquiries, it is not impossible to get that witness to provide the necessary evidence. Redirect examination offers a possible safety valve, and to some extent its rehabilitative potential is self-evident. It is important to note, however, that first impressions often resist change despite subsequent contradictory information,[41] and that neither denial nor judicial admonishment is likely to have fully curative effects.

D. Nonevidentiary Temptations

As part of their factfinding role, jurors are instructed to recognize and disregard nonevidentiary sources of information—much of which is revealed within the courtroom (*e.g.*, voir dire questions, inadmissible testimony, opening statements, closing arguments). Can human decisionmakers maintain separate files in memory for evidence and nonevidence? And can they delete the latter from awareness upon instruction to do so?

In a series of experiments on "reality monitoring," Marcia Johnson and her colleagues have found that people are often unable to recall the sources of their knowledge.[42] Under certain circumstances people remember the *content* of a message, while forgetting the *source*. People are especially vulnerable to confusion when the possible sources of information are equally plausible—as when jurors must recall after a trial presentation whether their beliefs are based on what was said by the lawyers or witnesses, or whether they are the product of their own self-generated inferences. In the end, it means that jurors may erroneously attribute their own versions of reality, or counsel's version, to reality itself.

Research on the effects of opening statements illustrates the possible consequences of source confusion in the courtroom. In a series of mock jury experiments, Lawrence Wrightsman and others consistently found that strong opening statements are persuasive—even when they are not subsequently borne out by the evidence.[43] In one study, for example, subjects read one of three versions of an auto theft trial. In one version, defense counsel promised in his opening statement that he would provide evidence of an alibi, evidence that was never forthcoming. In contrast to subjects to whom the claim was never made, those who received the empty promise were more likely to vote for the defendant's acquittal. The strategy failed only in the third version of the trial, where the prosecutor reminded the jury in his closing argument of the discrepancy between what was promised and what was proved.[44] Absent a reminder, jurors may simply lack the necessary awareness of the sources of their trial beliefs.

Additional problems arise when jurors are exposed to inadmissible testimony, prompted by an attorney's question and subsequently stricken from the record. It should come as no surprise that jurors are often influenced by this leakage of nonevidentiary information. In one study, for example, mock jurors read a transcript of an armed robbery and murder trial. When the only available evidence was weak and circumstantial, not a single juror voted guilty. In a second version of the case that also contained a recording of a suspicious telephone conversation between the defendant and a bookmaker, and in which the judge ruled the tape admissible, the conviction rate increased to twenty-six percent. In a third version of the case in which the judge ruled the wiretapped conversation inadmissible and admonished to disregard the tape, the conviction rate increased even further, to thirty-five percent.[45] Additional research has shown that when the judge embellishes his or her ruling by admonishing jurors at length, they become even more likely to use the forbidden information.[46]

Judicial admonishment may well backfire for a variety of reasons. First, it draws an unusual amount of attention to the information in controversy, increasing its salience relative to the evidence. Indeed, the psychology of instructions-to-disregard parallels recent studies on the paradoxical effects of thought suppression. For example, Daniel Wegner and his colleagues found that when people were told to actively suppress thoughts of a white bear, that novel image intruded upon consciousness with remarkable frequency.[47] A second problem is that instructions to disregard are a form of censorship, a restriction on the juror's decisionmaking freedom. Again, research in other contexts indicates consistently that people react against prohibitions of this sort in order to assert their right to consider all possible information.[48] A third reason why instructions-to-disregard may be counterproductive is that jurors do not share the law's "due process" model of what constitutes a fair trial, the assumption that a verdict is just if procedural fairness is achieved. Ask jurors what they seek, and most will cite outcome accuracy as the main objective (*i.e.*, "to make the *right* decision"). Thus, it is notable that jurors seem most likely to succumb to the temptation to use inadmissible evidence when that evidence exonerates the criminal defendant.[49]

Sometimes inadmissible evidence is properly introduced via the "limited admissibility rule" which permits the presentation of evidence for one purpose, but not another.[50] In such cases, the judge admits the evidence, restricts its proper scope, and instructs the jury accordingly (*e.g.*, when a defendant's criminal record is admitted for its bearing on the issue of credibility, not guilt). Can jurors compartmentalize evidence in this manner, using it to draw one inference, but not another? This rule is one of the paradoxes of evidence law, and is viewed by many as a lesson in futility. One survey revealed that ninety-eight percent of the lawyers and forty-three percent of the judges questioned believed jurors could not comply with this instruction.[51] They are probably right. Mock jurors who learn that a defendant has a criminal record and are limited in their use of that evidence are more likely to vote for conviction even though their judgments of the defendant's credibility are unaffected by that information.[52] Likewise, mock juries spend a good deal of time discussing a defendant's record—not for what it implies about credibility, but for what it suggests about criminal predispositions.[53]

E. Voices from an Empty Chair

In one trial, a defendant accused of armed robbery claims he was drinking in a bar at the time, but does not bring in alibi witnesses who were supposed to have been with him. In another trial, a party involved in a traffic accident fails to call to the witness stand a friend or relative who was a passenger during the collision. Cases such as these pose a dilemma: When a prospective favorable witness does not take the stand, should opposing counsel be permitted in closing argument to cite that witness's absence as proof of his or her adverse testimony? Should the judge invite jurors to draw negative inferences from that missing witness?

The courts are divided on how they manage this situation. Nearly a century ago, in *Graves v. United States*, the United States Supreme Court introduced what has come to be known as the missing witness rule, or empty chair doctrine. The rule states that "if a party has it peculiarly within his power to produce witnesses whose testimony would elucidate the transaction, the fact that he does not do it creates the presumption that the testimony, if produced, would be unfavorable."[54] In operational terms, this rule enables lawyers to comment on a witness's absence in closing arguments and judges to suggest possible adverse inferences to the jury. The reasons for this doctrine are straightforward.[55] The courts assume that litigants who fail to call knowledgeable witnesses are concealing evidence and should be pressured to come forward with that evidence. In addition, it is argued that jurors on their own will draw adverse inferences from the absence of an expected witness. Stephen Saltzburg, for example, suggested that once jurors are presented with a theory about a case, they naturally come to expect certain kinds of supporting proof and are likely to make adverse inferences about any party that fails to satisfy these expectations. Carrying this analysis one step further, Saltzburg argued that judges should take juror expectations and inferences into account before ruling to exclude evidence considered relevant but prejudicial.[56]

The empty chair doctrine has been criticized on at least three grounds. First, it is said to be unfair to draw adverse inferences from missing evidence because there are many other possible reasons for a witness's failure to appear in court.[57] Second, constitutional issues arise in cases where an expected witness does not testify on behalf of a criminal defendant, whose own silence is protected by the fifth amendment.[58] A third criticism of the empty chair rule is that it sends a confusing mixed signal to jurors about their role as fact finders. Although jurors are admonished time and again to base their judgments only on evidence produced in court, the missing witness instruction may encourage them to speculate on other matters not in evidence.[59]

On their own, do jurors make adverse inferences concerning absent witnesses? What are the effects of empty chair comments? Indirectly, psychological research suggests an "it depends" answer to these empirical questions. When a prospective witness is central to a case and, hence, conspicuously absent, juries are likely to speculate, even without prompting. This suggestion is based on studies indicating that people are biased against criminal defendants who remain silent, even when they are specifically admonished not to draw negative inferences.[60] In contrast, when a witness is not clearly essential to a case, juries are not likely to be influenced by his or her absence. This suggestion is based on studies on the "feature-positive effect," the finding that humans are relatively insensitive to events that do *not* occur.[61]

To examine more directly the effects of missing witnesses on legal decision-making, my students and I conducted the following mock jury study.[62] Upon arrival in a mock courtroom, fifty subjects—participating in small groups—read one of four versions of an insanity murder trial in which either a central witness (the defendant's close friend) or a peripheral witness (a co-worker of the defendant) was absent,[63] and in which the judge and opposing counsel either did or did not suggest an adverse inference.[64] Opinions of the case were assessed both before and after subjects deliberated.

The results of this experiment were generally consistent with the predictions derived from other research. Three findings in particular are noteworthy. First, all subjects were aware of the witness's absence, but when asked if they needed additional information, far more subjects in the comment than no-comment condition expressed a need for testimony from that witness. Second, there was an effect on case-related opinions: among subjects who read the missing-central transcript, empty chair comments increased the likelihood of conviction and enhanced their evaluations of the prosecuting attorney. In the missing-peripheral condition, however, the same empty chair comments decreased the likelihood of conviction and diminished subjects' evaluations of the prosecuting attorney. Third, subjects in the comment condition, after deliberating, were somewhat more likely than those in the no-comment condition to express a desire for testimony from the defendant (who did not testify). This latter result suggests the possibility that jurors who read the empty chair comments had discussed the defendant's failure to testify during their deliberations.

Is the missing witness inference "natural," an argument made by proponents of the empty chair doctrine? No, the inference is not as natural as it may seem. Subjects in the no-comment group knew that the prospective central or peripheral witness had not testified, but they did not hold the defendant responsible unless prompted to do so by the judge and opposing counsel. To be sure, all subjects recognized that the missing witness was absent, but only those in the comment condition were moved by his absence. Should empty chair comments, then, be permitted? Our study does not provide a clear answer to this second question. For trial attorneys, there are potential costs and benefits associated with empty chair comments, depending on the status of the witness in question. Lawyers who comment on a missing central witness may draw the jury's attention to a gap in the opponent's case, reap the benefits of the inferences likely to be drawn, and elicit the perception that they themselves are competent. On the other hand, attorneys who drag a missing peripheral witness into evidence risk alienating the jury by making what appears to be an implausible argument, and eliciting the perception that they themselves are desperate, if not incompetent. Our results thus support the conclusion that the empty chair doctrine cannot easily be used for unfair strategic purposes, without regard for the extent to which the jury already expects testimony from that witness.

II. THE JURY DELIBERATION PROCESS

It is often said that the distinctive power of the jury is that it functions as a group. Indeed, although the jury meets in complete privacy, the courts have articulated a clear vision of how juries should deliberate to a verdict. Basically, there are three components to this ideal.

The first component is one of independence and equality. No juror's vote counts for more than any other juror's vote. A twelve-person jury should thus consist of twelve independent and equal individuals, each contributing his or her own personal opinion to the final outcome. Unlike other task-oriented groups, the jury's role is ideally structured to promote equal participation. The cardinal rule of jury decisionmaking is that verdicts be based only on the evidence introduced in open court. By limiting the task as such, jurors are discouraged from basing their arguments on private or outside sources of knowledge. The courts try to foster this ideal in a number of ways. For example, jurors are told to refrain from discussing the trial until they deliberate, thus ensuring that each juror develops his or her own unique perspective on the case, uncontaminated by others' views. In addition, the courts often exclude from service people who are expected to exert a disproportionate amount of influence over other jurors (such as lawyers or others who have expertise in trial-relevant matters).

The second component of an ideal deliberation is an openness to informational influence. Inside the jury room, members have a duty to share information, exchange points of view, and debate the evidence. This deliberation requirement means that jurors should maintain an open mind and withhold their judgment until "an impartial consideration of the evidence with his fellow jurors."[65] It also means that consensus should be achieved through rational, persuasive argument. As the Supreme Court put it almost a century ago, "[t]he very object of the jury system is to secure unanimity by a comparison of views, and by arguments among the jurors themselves . . . . It cannot be that each juror should go to the jury-room with a blind determination that the verdict shall represent his opinion of the case at that moment; or, that he should close his ears to the arguments of men who are equally honest and intelligent as himself."[66]

The third ideal of deliberation follows from the second. Although juries should strive for a consensus of opinion, that goal should not be achieved through heavy-handed social pressure. Obviously, those who dissent from the majority should not be beaten, bullied, or harangued into surrendering their convictions for the purpose of returning a verdict. The reason is simple: if jurors comply with the majority to avoid rejection or terminate an unpleasant experience, then their final vote might not reflect their true beliefs. In the Supreme Court's words, "the verdict must be the verdict of each individual juror, and not a mere acquiescence in the conclusion of his fellows. . . ."[67]

As in other decisionmaking groups, juries reach a verdict through two processes—informational and normative.[68] Through informational social influence, individuals conform because they are genuinely persuaded by majority opinion; through normative influence, individuals comply in order to avoid the unpleasant consequences of social pressure. Indeed, groups often reject, ridicule, and punish individuals who frustrate a common goal by taking a deviant position.[69] The importance of both processes has been well documented in recent conformity research,[70] and in jury research as well.[71] As Kalven and Zeisel noted in *The American Jury*, the deliberation process "is an interesting combination of rational persuasion, sheer social pressure, and the psychological mechanism by which individual perceptions undergo change when exposed to group discussion."[72]

Although jury verdicts should follow a vigorous exchange of information and a minimum of normative pressure, the delicate balance between these competing forces can be altered by various aspects of a jury's task.[73] For example, normative influences are heightened in groups that decide on questions of values rather than facts,[74] and in groups that take frequent public ballots.[75] In addition, recent research implicates two procedural factors that may compromise the integrity of jury deliberations: (1) the dynamite charge, and (2) the acceptance of nonunanimous verdicts.

A. The Dynamite Charge

Recently, I received a phone call from a criminal lawyer whose client had been convicted on six counts of tax fraud. After two days of testimony, arguments, and instructions, the twelve-person jury spent three days deliberating. On the second day of deliberation, the jury informed the judge that it was at an impasse on some counts. The jurors were reconvened, but then on the third day said they were hopelessly deadlocked on all counts, with no verdict in sight. At that point, the judge issued a special instruction, one that is designed to prod hung juries toward a verdict. Twenty minutes later, as if a spell had been cast, the jury reached unanimous guilty verdicts on all counts.

The instruction that preceded the jury's decision was modeled after the Allen charge, first used in Massachusetts,[76] and approved by the United States Supreme Court in *Allen v. United States.*[77] Used to blast deadlocked juries into a verdict, this supplemental instruction is believed to be so effective that it is commonly known as the "dynamite charge."[78] For judges confronted with the prospect of a hung jury, this instruction can be used to avert a mistrial by imploring jurors to reexamine their own views and to seriously consider each other's arguments with a disposition to be convinced. In addition, it may state that "if much the larger number were for conviction, a dissenting juror should consider whether his doubt was a reasonable one which made no impression on the minds of so many men, equally honest, equally intelligent with himself."[79]

Trial anecdotes suggest that the dynamite charge is effective. Those who believe the effect is desirable argue that it encourages all jurors to reevaluate their positions and that, after all, those who are in the voting minority are typically obstinate holdouts who should "properly be warned against stubbornness and self-assertion."[80] Opponents, however, fear that legitimate dissenters, "struggling to maintain their position in a protracted debate in the jury room, are led into the courtroom and, before their peers, specifically requested by the judge to reconsider their position.[81] The charge places the sanction of the court behind the views of the majority, whatever they may be. . . ."[82]

The dynamite charge has its share of proponents and critics. In 1968, the American Bar Association opposed this instruction on the grounds that it coerces the deadlocked jury into reaching a verdict and places inordinate amounts of pressure on those in the minority.[83] The dynamite charge has been prohibited or restricted in certain state and federal courts.[84] In 1988, however, the United States Supreme Court ruled that the dynamite charge is not necessarily coercive, and reaffirmed its use on a routine basis.[85]

Although the dynamite charge has stirred controversy for many years, and although the Supreme Court has now upheld its use, until recently no empirical studies had examined its impact on the jury's deliberation process. Thus, my colleagues and I sought to test the hypothesis that the dynamite charge upsets the delicate balance of social influence forces, causing those in the majority to exert increasing amounts of normative rather than informational pressure, and causing those in the minority to change their votes.[86]

In order to test this hypothesis in a controlled setting, we contrived an artificial experimental situation in which lone subjects "deliberated" by voting and passing notes. Overall, seventy-two individual subjects read about a criminal tax case, thinking they would participate on a mock jury. In fact, subjects were taken to a cubicle and told they would communicate with three others in different rooms by passing notes. These so-called deliberations were structured by discrete rounds. After reading the case summary, subjects wrote down a verdict and a brief explanation. They signaled the experimenter over an intercom. The experimenter collected the subject's note, supposedly collected other subject's notes, photocopied them, and distributed the copies to each subject. After reading the other notes, subjects began a second round of deliberation—voting, writing an explanation, signaling the experimenter and receiving written feedback from three fictitious peers. Subjects were instructed that this procedure would be reiterated until the group reached unanimity. In fact, unless subjects changed their votes, the session was terminated after seven rounds. At that point, a questionnaire was administered and subjects were debriefed.

Six sets of notes—three guilty, three not guilty—were written and photocopied.[87] All subjects received three notes at a time. Those assigned to the majority received two randomly selected sets of notes that agreed with their guilty or not guilty verdicts, and one set that did not. In contrast, subjects assigned to the minority received three randomly selected sets of notes that all disagreed with their verdicts. By the end of the first round, subjects thus found themselves in either the majority or minority faction of a three-to-one split. Unless subjects changed their vote, these divisions persisted.[88] After the third round, half the subjects were reminded that since verdicts had to be unanimous, they would continue to "deliberate."[89] For the other half, the experimenter—acting as judge—delivered an instruction patterned after the *Allen* charge.

Three results were consistent with the hypothesis that the dynamite charge is effective because of normative pressure on those in the voting minority. First, among subjects caught in a deadlocked jury (*i.e.*, who remained committed to their initial votes after the third round), those in the minority changed their verdicts more often than those in the majority after receiving the dynamite charge, but not in the no-instruction control group. Second, minority subjects who heard the dynamite charge reported feeling heightened pressure from the judge—more than in the majority and minority-no-instruction groups.[90] Third, compared to all other subjects, those in the majority who received the dynamite charge exhibited in their notes diminishing amounts of informational influence strategies (*e.g.*, citing facts or laws relevant to the case), coupled with a significant increase in normative social pressure (*e.g.*, derogating those who disagreed, refusing to yield) immediately following the judge's instruction. Clearly, the dynamite charge tipped in an undesirable direction the balance of forces operating on our subjects, subjectively empowering the voting majority relative to the minority.

Taken as a whole, our results call into question the use of the dynamite charge as a means of eliciting verdicts from deadlocked juries. This study should be considered tentative, however, with regard to its generalizability to real trials. To systematically test the impact of the dynamite charge on the votes, perceptions, and behaviors of individual jurors, we contrived an artificial situation in which lone subjects "deliberated" by passing notes.[91] It remains to be seen whether the same results would emerge within live, interacting groups of jurors. It also remains to be seen whether alternative forms of instruction yield better results (i.e., verdicts from deadlocked juries through informational rather than normative influence).[92]

B. Less-Than-Unanimous-Verdicts

The problem with the dynamite charge is that it may produce verdicts in which the jury's unanimity is more apparent than real. However, even the appearance of unanimity is often not necessary. In a pair of 1972 decisions, the United States Supreme

Court ruled that states may allow juries to return verdicts without having to secure agreement from all members.[93] Finding neither a legal nor historical basis for the unanimity tradition, the Court concluded that, as a practical matter, juries function similarly under unanimous and nonunanimous decision rules. Writing for the *Johnson* majority, Justice White argued that majority jurors would maintain an open mind and continue to deliberate in good faith even after the requisite majority is reached.[94] In dissent, Justice Douglas argued that once a requisite majority is reached, majority jurors will become closed-minded, and vigorous debate would give way to "polite and academic conversation."[95]

Are unanimous and nonunanimous juries equivalent in the extent to which they achieve the ideals of deliberation? Several studies have addressed the question, and the results converge on the same answer: the differences are substantial. In one study, Charlan Nemeth had several hundred students at the University of Virginia read about a murder trial and indicate whether they believed the defendant to be guilty or not guilty.[96] Three weeks later, these students participated in six-person mock juries constructed to split four to two in their initial vote, favoring either conviction or acquittal. The groups were given two hours to reach a decision. Half were instructed to return a unanimous verdict, the other half needed only a two-thirds majority. Compared to those driven toward unanimity, majority-rule juries took less time to settle on a decision (many of these groups, in fact, concluded their deliberations without a single change in vote). When subjects were given an opportunity to evaluate the quality of their deliberations, those who had participated in majority juries were less satisfied, less certain of their verdicts, and less influenced by others' arguments.

In a more extensive study, Reid Hastie and his colleagues recruited over 800 people from jury pools in Massachusetts.[97] After a brief voir dire, these subjects were randomly assigned to participate in sixty-nine twelve-person mock juries, all of whom watched a videotape of a reenacted murder trial. An approximately equal number of juries were instructed to reach a verdict by either a twelve to zero, a ten to two, or an eight to four margin. Based on objective analyses of the deliberations as well as jurors' own subjective reports, the results were striking. Compared to unanimous juries, those that deliberated under a more relaxed rule spent less time discussing the case and more time voting. After reaching their required quorum, these groups usually rejected the holdouts, terminated discussion, and returned a verdict within just a few minutes. Needless to say, those who participated in majority juries viewed their peers as relatively closed-minded, felt less informed about the case and less confident about the final verdict. Hastie and his colleagues also observed that many of the majority jurors were quite combative during their deliberations, as "larger factions in majority rule juries adopt a more forceful, bullying, persuasive style because their members realize that it is not necessary to respond to all opposition arguments when their goal is to achieve a faction size of only eight or ten members."[98]

C. Summary: Policies that Compromise the Deliberation Process

In nineteenth century England, juries that were unable to achieve unanimity "were locked up in a cart, without meat, drink, fire, or candle, and followed the judge from town to town. Only their verdict could secure their release."[99] American juries were similarly subverted. Judges used to urge deadlocked juries to resolve their disagreements through such coercive measures as the denial of food and drink, excessive deliberation hours, and the threat of confinement. Today, the strategies may differ, but the objective is the same. The dynamite charge and the relaxation of a unanimous verdict requirement are driven by a contempt for the hung jury and the costs incurred by a mistrial. Proponents of these policies seem to base their opinions on the assumption that a jury becomes deadlocked because of one obstinate holdout, the chronic anti-conformist. Opponents, on the other hand, base their views on the belief that juries are hung as a genuine response to close, difficult cases in which the evidence allows for well-reasoned disagreement and does not compel a particular verdict. To be sure, not all deadlocked juries are created equal, and anecdotes can be found to support either position. Kalven and Zeisel's research, however, suggests that hung juries occur in only about five percent of all criminal jury trials, and do so especially in close cases in which the minority consists of a group rather than one member—a finding that lends support to the latter, more rational image.[100]

Neither the dynamite charge nor suspension of the unanimity requirement have desirable effects on the quality of the jury's decisionmaking apparatus. Used to implore the deadlocked jury to return a verdict, the dynamite charge may well encourage members of the voting majority to exert increasing amounts of normative pressure without added informational influence, thus intimidating members of a voting minority into compliance. The net result, of course, is an illusion of unanimity. Even worse is the outright acceptance of nonunanimous verdicts. This policy weakens and inhibits dissenting jurors, breeds closed-mindedness, impairs the quality of discussion, and leaves many jurors unsatisfied with the final verdict. And yet, without a potent and vocal dissent based on legitimate differences of opinion, the jury is reduced to a mere collection of individuals, losing its strength as a vital decisionmaking group.

III. CONCLUSIONS

The American trial jury is a truly unique institution. In the words of Kalven and Zeisel, "[i]t recruits a group of twelve laymen, chosen at random from the widest population; it convenes them for the purpose of the particular trial; it entrusts them with great official powers of decision; it permits them to carry on deliberations in secret and to report their final judgment without giving reasons for it; and, after their momentary service to the state has been completed, it orders them to disband and return to private life."[101]

This article rests on a conviction that juries should not be evaluated by case studies, autobiographical accounts, and news stories, but by hard empirical research designed to answer concrete, behavioral questions. With that objective in mind, trial practices that influence the decisionmaking process were examined for their effects on both individual jurors and the jury as a group.

Jurors are expected to base their opinions on an accurate appraisal of evidence to the exclusion of nonevidentiary sources of information. Thus, trials are structured by an elaborate network of rules to focus jurors on the evidence, to facilitate their search for the truth, and to insulate them from various social influences. Research on how jurors assess the credibility of witnesses, and their ability or willingness to resist the lure of certain kinds of extraneous information, gives rise to the conclusion that there is much room for improvement. To begin with, jurors are supposed to distinguish among witnesses of varying credibility, an often difficult task. Yet that task is more complicated than is necessary. To be sure, the occasional intrusion into the trial record of inadmissible testimony and objectionable arguments is an inevitable fact of life in an adversarial system. But too often, American courts compound the problem by permitting counsel to (1) use surrogates to present deposition testimony for absentee witnesses, leaving the jury to disentangle the appearance and demeanor of the messenger from the message and its original source; (2) impart information through conjecture and innuendo, leaving jurors to assume the truth of uncorroborated matters and confuse in memory the sources of their knowledge; and (3) invite jurors to draw adverse inferences from missing witnesses, leading them to create evidence from the absence of evidence, and sending a confusing mixed signal concerning speculation and the boundaries of their fact-finding role.

Turning to the jury as a group, it is perhaps the greatest asset of the jury that a group of independent citizens, strangers to one another, are placed behind closed doors and directed to reach a common decision. Bringing a diversity of perspectives to bear on the task, these jurors share information, clash in their values and argue over competing interpretations. Remarkably, out of this conflict, ninety-five percent of all juries succeed in returning a verdict. Intolerant of lengthy deliberations and the five percent of juries that declare themselves hung, however, the courts have sanctioned procedures and structural changes in the jury that widen the gap between the ideals and realities of deliberation. One example is the *Allen* instruction, otherwise known as the dynamite charge. Used to implore the deadlocked jury to return a verdict, research suggests it may tip in an undesirable direction the balance of informational and normative forces operating within the jury, further empowering the voting majority relative to the minority, and intimidating the latter into compliance. A second example is provided by the United States Supreme Court's decisions to uphold the right of states to relax the jury's unanimity requirement. Indeed, research clearly indicates that a less-than-unanimous decision rule weakens dissent, breeds closed-mindedness, impairs the quality of discussion, and leaves many jurors unsatisfied with the final verdict.

In light of recent research on human decisionmaking and behavior, consciousness should be raised in American courtrooms about common trial practices and procedures that lead individual jurors and the groups to which they belong to exhibit less-than-ideal performance. Prescriptions for how juries should function are clear. In reality, however, the American jury is too often handicapped in the pursuit of justice.

NOTES

1. McElhaney, *Dealing with Dirty Tricks*, 7 Litigation 45, 46 (1981).
2. M. Belli, Melvin Belli: My Life on Trial 107-09 (1976).
3. Allen v. United States, 164 U.S. 492, 501 (1986).

4. The mock jury paradigm involves simulating trials in the form of transcripts, audiotapes, or videotapes, and recruiting subjects to act as jurors. This method has two advantages. First, it enables researchers to secure control over events that take place in the "courtroom" and design controlled experiments that can establish causal relationships between specific trial characteristics and jury verdicts. Second, it offers a good deal of flexibility, enabling researchers to manipulate variables that cannot be touched in real cases (*e.g.*, evidence, arguments, trial procedures, judge's instructions, the composition of the jury) and obtain measures of behavior that are otherwise too intrusive (*e.g.*, mid-trial opinions; attention, comprehension, and recall; physiological arousal; videotaped deliberations). In short, trial simulations enable us to observe not only the outcome but the process of jury decision-making. A more extensive discussion of this technique appears in Bray & Kerr, *Methodological Considerations in the Study of the Psychology of the Courtroom*, The Psychology of the Courtroom 287, 296-98 (1982). For a description of practical applications, see Kassin, *Mock Jury Trials*, 7 Trial Dipl. J. 26 (1984).

As with other indirect methods of inquiry, the mock jury paradigm is not without its shortcomings. In exchange for a highly controlled environment, the approach suffers from the problem of external validity (*i.e.* generalizability to real trials). As a general rule, generalizability is enhanced by research conditions that approximate the real event. Still, legitimate empirical questions can be raised. For more detailed critiques, see Dillehay & Nietzel, *Constructing a Science of Jury Behavior*, Review of Personality and Social Psychology 246 (1980); Ebbesen & Konecni, *On the External Validity of Decision-Making Research: What do we Know about Decisions in the Real World?*, Cognitive Processes in Choice and Decision Behavior (1980).

5. For a review of arguments against notetaking, see S. Kassin & L. Wrightsman, The American Jury on Trial: Psychological Perspectives 128 (1988).

6. DePaulo & Pfeifer, *On-the-Job Experience and Skill at Detecting Deception*, 16 J. Applied Soc. Psychology 249, 261-62 (1986); Kraut & Poe, *Behavioral Roots of Person Perception: The Deception Judgments of Customs Inspectors and Laymen*, 39 J. Personality & Soc. Psychology 784, 788 (1980).

7. Zuckerman, DePaulo & Rosenthal, *Verbal and Nonverbal Communication of Deception*, 14 Advances in Experimental Soc. Psychology 1, 38-40 (1981).

8. Deceivers often wear false smiles to mask their real feelings; see Ekman, Friesen & O'Sullivan, *Smiles when Lying*, 54 J. Personality & Soc. Psychology 414, 415 (1988).

9. Deception is often accompanied by fidgety movements of the hands and feet, and restless shifts in posture. When people lie, especially when they are highly motivated to do so, there is also a rise in their voice pitch and an increased number of speech hesitations. *See* DePaulo, Lanier & Davis, *Detecting the Deceit of the Motivated Liar*, 45 J. Personality & Soc. Psychology 1096, 1096 (1983); *see also*, Streeter, Krauss, Geller, Olson & Apple, *Pitch Changes During Attempted Deception*, 35 J. Personality & Soc. Psychology 345, 348-49 (1977).

10. People sometimes become more accurate in their judgments of truth and deception when they are too busy to attend closely to what a speaker says. *See* Gilbert & Krull, *Seeing Less and Knowing More: The Benefits of Perceptual Ignorance*, 54 J. Personality & Soc. Psychology 193, 201 (1988). Although distracting jurors from the content of a witness's testimony is a ludicrous idea, it is possible that credibility judgments would be improved by a more specific demeanor instruction, one that redirects attention toward cues that are more diagnostic than facial expressions. Research suggests, for example, that when people are encouraged to pay more attention to the voice than to the face, they make more accurate judgments of truth and deception. *See* DePaulo, Lassiter & Stone, *Attentional Determinants of Success at Detecting Deception and Truth*, 8 Personality & Soc. Psychology Bull. 273, 277 (1982). Liars are also betrayed by movements of the lower body, so jurors could be instructed to consider these cues as well. Ironically, however, the witness's body is often hidden from view—by the witness stand.

11. E. Cleary, McCormick on Evidence § 5 (2d ed. 1972).

12. For a review of this literature, see Loftus & Goodman, *Questioning Witnesses*, The Psychology of Evidence and Trial Proc. 253 (1985).

13. Model Rules of Professional Conduct Rule 3.4 (1983).

14. *See generally* R. Underwood & W. Fortune, Trial Ethics (1988); Underwood, *Adversary Ethics: More Dirty Tricks*, 6 Am. J. Trial Advoc. 265 (1982).

15. McElhaney, *supra* note 1, at 45-48; Underwood, *supra* note 14, at 269-89.

16. The death of a prospective witness is an obvious problem. Those who live beyond a certain distance from the courthouse, or who are sick, handicapped, out of the country, or in prison, may also be excused. *See* Fed. R. Civ. P. 32(a)(3).

17. *See generally*, Kassin, *supra* note 4, at 27.

18. A. Morrill, Trial Diplomacy 52 (1972). Conversely, it is advisable to present the testimony of witnesses who are "singularly impressive" live rather than via deposition. *See* R. Keeton, Trial Tactics and Methods 18 (1973).

19. A. Morrill, *supra* note 18, at 52.

20. For a recent review of this literature see R. Petty & J. Cacioppo, Communication and Persuasion 204-09 (1986).

21. Kassin, *Deposition Testimony and the Surrogate Witness: Evidence for a "Messenger Effect" in Persuasion*, 9 Personality & Soc. Psychology Bull. 281, 283-84 (1983).

22. *E.g.*, Chaiken, *Communicator Physical Attractiveness and Persuasion*, 37 J. Personality & Soc. Psychology 1387, 1395 (1979); *see also* Pallak, *Salience of a Communicator's Physical Attractiveness and Persuasion: A Heuristic versus Systematic Processing Interpretation*, 2 Soc. Cognition 158, 168 (1983).

23. Kassin, Deposition Testimony and the Surrogate Witness: Further Evidence for a "Messenger Effect" in Persuasion, Unpublished data (1990).

24. Attractiveness was determined through pretesting.

25. *See, e.g.*, McCrystal, *Videotape Trials: Relief for Our Congested Courts*, 49 Den. U.L. Rev. 463, 465-66 (1973); *see also* Kornblum, *Videotape in Civil Cases*, 24 Hastings L.J. 9, 23-26 (1972).

26. *See* Conley, O'Barr & Lind, *The Power of Language: Presentational Style in the Courtroom*, 6 Duke L.J. 1375, 1386-89 (1978).

27. Danet, *'Baby' or 'fetus'?: Language and the Construction of Reality in a Manslaughter Trial*, 32 Semiotica 187, 206 (1980).

28. When other verbs were substituted for these, estimates varied considerably, *e.g.*, "collided" yielded 39 mph; "contacted" yielded 32 mph. *See* Loftus & Palmer, *Reconstruction of Automobile Destruction: An Example of the Interaction Between Language and Memory*, 13 J. Verbal Learning & Verbal Behav. 585, 586 (1974).

29. *See* Harris & Monaco, *Psychology of Pragmatic Implication: Information Processing Between the Lines*, 107 J. Experimental Psychology: General 1, 6-9 (1978); *see also* Johnson, Bransford, & Solomon, *Memory for Tacit Implications of Sentences*, 98 J. Experimental Psychology 203 (1973).

30. R. Underwood & W. Fortune, *supra* note 14, at 346.

31. Swann, Giuliano & Wegner, *Where Leading Questions Can Lead: The Power of Conjecture in Social Interaction*, 42 J. Personality & Soc. Psychology 1025, 1034 (1982); *see also* Wegner, Wenclaff, Kerker & Beattie, *Incrimination Through Innuendo: Can Media Questions Become Public Answers?*, 40 J. Personality & Soc. Psychology 822, 830-32 (1981).

32. Swann, Giuliano & Wegner, *supra* note 31, at 1033. This effect is so powerful that it even influences the self-perceptions of the respondents themselves. After being interviewed, they took personality tests in which they were asked to describe themselves on various dimensions. Those who had answered questions about introverted or extroverted behaviors later rated themselves as such on the questionnaires.

33. Kassin, Williams & Saunders, *Dirty Tricks of Cross Examination: The Influence of Conjectural Evidence on the Jury*, 14 Law and Human Behavior 373 (1990).

34. Grice, *Logic in Conversation*, 3 Syntax and Semantics 41, 44 (1975); Hopper, *The Taken-For-Granted*, 7 Human Communication Research 195, 198 (1981).

35. Kelman & Hovland, *"Reinstatement" of the Communicator in Delayed Measurement of Opinion Change*, 48 J. Abnormal & Soc. Psychology 327, 332-35 (1953); Pratkanis, Greenwald, Leippe & Baumgardner, *In Search of Reliable Persuasion Effects: III. The Sleeper Effect is Dead. Long Live the Sleeper Effect*, 54 J. Personality & Soc. Psychology 203, 205 (1988).

36. Johnson, *Discrimination the Origin of Information*, Delusional Beliefs: Interdisciplinary Perspectives (Oltmanns & Maher eds. 1987); Johnson & Raye, *Reality Monitoring*, 88 Psychological Rev. 67, 82 (1981).

37. U.S. v. Brown, 519 F.2d 1368 (6th Cir. 1975).

38. Shaffer, *The Defendant's Testimony*, The Psychology of Evidence and Trial Procedure (Kassin & Wrightman eds. 1985); Yandell, *Those Who Protest Too Much are Seen as Guilty*, 5 Personality & Soc. Psychology Bull. 44, 47 (1979).

39. Carretta & Moreland, *The Direct and Indirect Effects of Inadmissible Evidence*, 13 J. Applied Soc. Psychology 291, 291-93 (1983); Sue, Smith & Caldwell, *Effects of Inadmissible Evidence on the Decisions of Simulated Jurors: A Moral Dilemma*, 3 J. Applied Soc. Psychology 345, 351-53 (1973); Wolf & Montgomery, *Effects of Inadmissible Evidence and Level of Judical Admonishment to Disregard on the Judgments of Mock Jurors*, 7 J. Applied Soc. Psychology 205, 216-18 (1977).

40. In some cases, the courts have even sustained the right of an opposing party to call a cross-examiner to the witness stand to inquire into the "good faith basis" for a specific line of questions. *See* United States v. Cardarella, 570 F.2d 264, 268 (8th Cir. 1978); United States v. Pugliese, 153 F.2d 497, 498-99 (2d Cir. 1945).

41. *See, e.g.*, Asch, *Forming Impressions of Personality*, 41 J. Abnormal & Soc. Psychology 258, 288-90 (1946); Darley & Gross, *A Hypothesis-Confirming Bias in Labeling Effects*, 44 J. Personality & Soc. Psychology 20, 21-22 (1983); Greenwald, Pratkanis, Leippe & Baumgardner, *Under What Conditions Does Theory Obstruct Research Progress?*, 93 Psychological Rev. 216, 227 (1986); Hamilton & Zanna, *Context Effects in Impression Formation: Changes in Connotative Meaning*, 29 J. Personality & Soc. Psychology 649, 652-54 (1974); Hayden & Mischel, *Maintaining Trait Consistency in the Resolution of Behavioral Inconsistency: The Wolf in Sheep's Clothing?*, 44 J. Personality 109, 129-31 (1976); E. Jones & G. Goethals, Order Effects in Impression Formation: Attribution Context and the Nature of the Entity 42-43 (1971); Kruglanski & Freund, *The Freezing and Unfreezing of Lay Inferences: Effects on Impressional Primacy, Ethnic Stereotyping, and Numerical Anchoring*, 19 J. Experimental Soc. Psychology 448, 461-65 (1983); Lord, Ross & Lepper, *Biased Assimilation and Attitude Polarization: The Effects of Prior Theories on Subsequently Considered Evidence*, 37 J. Personality & Soc. Psychology 2098, 2108 (1979).

42. *See, e.g.*, Johnson, Bransford & Solomon, *Memory for Tacit Implications of Sentences*, 98 J. Experimental Psychology 203, 204 (1973); Johnson & Raye, *supra* note 36, at 81-82.

43. Pyszczynski & Wrightsman, *The Effects of Opening Statements on Mock Jurors' Verdicts in a Simulated Criminal Trial*, 11 J. Applied Soc. Psychology 301, 309-10 (1981); Wells, Wrightsman & Meine, *The Timing of the Defense Opening Statement: Don't Wait Until the Evidence is In*, 15 J. Applied Soc. Psychology 758, 769 (1985).

44. Pyszczynski, Greenberg, Mack & Wrightsman, *Opening Statements in a Jury Trial: The Effect of Promising More Than the Evidence Can Show*, 11 J. Applied Soc. Psychology 434, 442 (1981).

45. Sue, Smith & Caldwell, *supra* note 39, at 350-51; *see also* Caretta & Moreland, *supra* note 39, at 305-06.

46. Wolf & Montgomery, *supra* note 39, at 216.

47. Wegner, Schneider, Carter & White, *Paradoxical Effects of Thought Suppression*, 53 J. Personality & Soc. Psychology 5, 8-9 (1987).

48. This explanation is based on Brehm's 1966 theory of psychological reactance. *See* S. Brehm & J. Brehm, Psychological Reactance: A Theory of Freedom and Control 3-7 (1981); *see also* Worchel, Arnold & Baker, *The Effect of Censorship on Attitude Change: The Influence of Censor and Communicator Characteristics*, 5 J. Applied Soc. Psychology 227, 237 (1975) (for relevant empirical support).

49. Thompson, Fong & Rosenhan, *Inadmissible Evidence and Juror Verdicts*, 40 J. Personality & Soc. Psychology 453, 460 (1981).

50. Fed. R. Evid. 404(a)(3).

51. Note, *To Take the Stand or Not to Take the Stand: The Dilemma of the Defendant with a Criminal Record*, 4 Colum. J. L. & Soc. Probs. 215, 218 (1968).

52. Wissler & Saks, *On the Inefficacy of Limiting Instructions: When Jurors Use Prior Conviction Evidence to Decide on Guilt*, 9 L. & Hum. Behav. 37, 47 (1985).

53. See Shaffer, *supra* note 38, at 145. The inherent prejudice of this rule is indicated by the finding that mock jurors told of a defendant's criminal record view the remaining evidence as more damaging than those who are uninformed. *See* Hans & Doob, *Section 12 of the Canada Evidence Act and the Deliberations of Simulated Juries*, 18 Crim. L.Q. 235, 244-46 (1975).

54. Graves v. United States, 150 U.S. 118, 121 (1893).

55. E. Cleary, McCormick on Evidence § 272 (3d ed. 1984); J. Chadbourn, Wigmore's Evidence, § 286 (3d ed. 1970).

56. Saltzburg, *A Special Aspect of Relevance: Countering Negative Inferences Associated with the Absence of Evidence*, 66 Calif. L. Rev. 1011, 1012 (1978).

57. For example, a litigant may choose to protect family members and friends from the stress of cross-examination, or may fear that a witness will lack credibility. *See* Stier, *Revisiting the Missing Witness Inference: Quieting the Loud Voice from the Empty Chair*, 44 Md. L. Rev. 137, 144-45 (1985).

58. In Griffin v. California, the United States Supreme Court ruled that neither judges nor prosecuting attorneys may comment on a defendant's failure to take the witness stand. 380 U.S. 609, 615 (1965). Indeed, judges may instruct jurors *not* to draw adverse inferences from a defendant's silence. Lakeside v. Oregon, 435 U.S. 333, 340-41 (1978). Questions are thus raised about whether the fifth amendment is compromised by comments concerning absent witnesses other than the defendant. *See* McDonald, *Drawing an Inference from the Failure to Produce a Knowledgeable Witness: Evidentiary and Constitutional Considerations*, 61 Calif. L. Rev. 1422, 1423-26 (1973); *see also* Tanford, *An Introduction to Trial Law*, 51 Mo. L. Rev. 623, 680-81 (1986).

59. S. Kassin & L. Wrightsman, *supra* note 5, at 113.

60. Shaffer & Case, *On the Decision Not to Testify in One's Own Behalf: Effects of Withheld Evidence, Defendant's Sexual Preferences, and Juror Dogmatism on Juridic Decisions*, 42 J. Personality & Soc. Psychology 335, 344 (1982).

61. Fazio, Sherman & Herr, *The Feature-Positive Effect in the Self-Perception Process: Does Not Doing Matter as Much as Doing?*, 42 J. Personality & Soc. Psychology 404, 409-10 (1982); Newman, Wolff & Hearst, *The Feature-Positive Effect in Adult Human Subjects*, 6 J. Experimental Psychology: Hum. Learning & Memory 630, 647-48 (1980).

62. Webster, King & Kassin, *Voices from an Empty Chair: The Missing Witness Inference and the Jury*, Law and Human Behavior (in press).

63. *Id.* To establish juror expectations for a missing witness, defense counsel's opening statement included mention of the fact that the defendant had talked about his emotional difficulties to a close friend and to a co-worker. In the missing-central version of the case, the close friend did not testify. In the missing-peripheral version, the co-worker did not testify. All versions of the

transcript thus contained the same information, varying only in the present and absent sources of that information.

64. In the *no-comment* condition, neither the prosecutor nor the judge made reference to the missing witness. In the *comment* condition, the prosecutor argued in closing, "I put it to you, ladies and gentlemen—where is Mr. Steven Marshall (John Mills)? Is it possible that Mr. Marshall (Mills) would not have corroborated the misinformed opinion of the psychiatrists? I think it is. Members of the jury, if your best friend (co-worker) were in this kind of trouble, wouldn't you want to be here to help him? I think, in weighing the evidence, you will come to the conclusion that I have." *Id.*

Also in the comment condition, the judge's charge to the jury included the following instruction, approved for use in federal courts: "If, according to appropriate procedures, the court is shown that a witness is available to one of the parties alone, and the anticipated testimony of the witness would elucidate some material issue, and the party who fails to produce the witness offers no explanation, then the factfinder may be permitted, but is not required, to infer that the testimony would have been unfavorable to the party who failed to call the witness." *See* I. Devitt & C. Blackmar, Fed. Jury Prac. and Instructions, § 17.19 (3d ed. 1977); *see also* Fed. Judicial Ctr. Comm. to Study Crim. Jury Instructions, Pattern Crim. Jury Instructions 49 (1982) (for alternative language).

65. American Bar Association Project on Minimum Standards for Criminal Justice (1968), Standards Relating to Trial by Jury, Section 5.4. Open-mindedness is such an important aspect of deliberation that if a juror dies before a verdict is announced, the jury cannot return a verdict even if all the remaining jurors swear that the deceased had agreed with their decision. The reasoning behind this rule is that "[t]he jurors individually and collectively have the right to change their minds prior to the reception of the verdict. . . ." E. DeVitt & C. Blackmar, Fed. Jury Pract. and Instructions, § 5.23 (3d ed. 1977).

66. Allen v. United States, 164 U.S. 492, 501-02 (1896).

67. *Id.* at 501.

68. Asch, *Studies of Independence and Conformity: A Minority of One Against a Unanimous Majority*, 70 Psychological Monographs, Whole No. 416 (1956); Deutsch & Gerard, *A Study of Normative and Informational Social Influence Upon Individual Judgment*, 51 J. Abnormal & Soc. Psychology 629, 629 (1955).

69. *See, e.g.*, Schachter, *Deviation, Rejection, and Communication*, 46 J. Abnormal & Soc. Psychology 190 (1951); For a review see Levine, *Reaction to Opinion Deviance in Small Groups*, Psychology of Group Influence (P. Paulus ed. 1980).

70. *See, e.g.*, Campbell & Fairey, *Informational and Normative Routes to Conformity: The Effect of Faction Size as a Function of Norm Extremity and Attention to the Stimulus*, 57 J. Personality & Soc. Psychology 457, 458 (1989).

71. *See, e.g.*, Kaplan & Miller, *Group Discussion and Judgment*, Basic Group Processes 65 (P. Paulus ed. 1983); Kaplan & Miller, *Group Decision-Making and Normative Versus Information Influence: Effects of Type of Issue and Assigned Decision Rule*, 53 J. Personality & Soc. Psychology 306 (1987); Stasser, Kerr & Bray, *The Social Psychology of Jury Deliberations*, Psychology of the Courtroom 221 (Kerr & Bray eds. 1982).

72. H. Kalven & H. Zeisel, The American Jury 489 (1966).

73. There are important reasons to protect individual jurors from normative influences that elicit mere public compliance. First, justice is undermined when a jury renders a verdict not supported even by its membership (*e.g.*, criminal defendants should not be convicted by juries internally plagued by a reasonable doubt). Second, unanimous votes produced by normative influences may undermine perceptions of justice among those who serve on juries.

74. Kaplan & Miller, *supra* note 71, at 311.

75. Hawkins, *Interaction Rates of Jurors Aligned in Factions*, 27 Am. Soc. Rev. 689 (1962) (public vote in jury deliberation).

76. Commonwealth v. Tuey, 62 Mass. 1 (1851).
77. 164 U.S. 492 (1896).
78. It has also been called the "shotgun" instruction, the "third degree" instruction, the "nitroglycerin" charge, the "hammer" instruction, and the "hanging" instruction. *See* Marcus, *The* Allen *Instruction in Criminal Cases: Is the Dynamite Charge About to be Permanently Defused?*, 43 Mo. L. Rev. 613, 615 (1978).
79. *Allen*, 164 U.S. at 501. The full text of the charge reads as follows:

> That in a large proportion of cases absolute certainty could not be expected; that although the verdict must be the verdict of each individual juror, and not a mere acquiescence in the conclusion of his fellows, yet they should examine the question submitted with candor and with a proper regard and deference to the opinions of each other; that it was their duty to decide the case if they could conscientiously do so; that they should listen, with a disposition to be convinced, to each other's arguments; that, if much the larger number were for conviction, a dissenting juror should consider whether his doubt was a reasonable one which made no impression upon the minds of so many men, equally honest, equally intelligent with himself. If, upon the other hand, the majority was for acquittal, the minority ought to ask themselves whether they might not reasonably doubt the correctness of a judgment which was not concurred in by the majority.

Id.

80. People v. Randall, 9 N.Y.2d 413, 214 N.Y.S.2d 417, 174 N.E.2d 507 (1961) (quoting People v. Faber, 199 N.Y. 256, 260-61).
81. *Id.* at 850, 139 Cal. Rptr. at 869, 566 P.2d at 1005 (quoting United States v. Bailey, 468 F.2d 652, 662 (5th Cir. 1972)).
82. People v. Gainer, 19 Cal.3d 835, 850, 139 Cal. Rptr. 861, 869, 566 P.2d 997, 1005 (1977).
83. American Bar Association Project on Minimum Standards for Criminal Justice, Standards Relating to Trial by Jury, Standards 5.4 (1968).
84. *See* Jensen, *After* Lowenfield: *The* Allen *Charge in the Ninth Circuit*, 19 Golden Gate U.L. Rev. 75, 85 (1989); Marcus, *supra* note 78, at 617; Notes and Comments, *On Instructing Deadlocked Juries*, 78 Yale L.J. 100, 103-06 (1968).
85. Lowenfield v. Phelps, 484 U.S. 231 (1988).
86. Kassin, Smith & Tulloch, *The Dynamite Charge: Effects on the Perceptions and Deliberation Behavior of Mock Jurors.* 14 Law and Human Behavior 537 (1990).
87. Each set consisted of six notes written in the same handwriting.
88. As one might expect, several members of the minority capitulated; in these instances, the session was terminated and questionnaires administered.
89. This no-instruction control procedure was designed to resemble what often happens when jurors are dead-locked and the judge directs them to return for further discussion.
90. It is interesting that even though all subjects received the same deliberation notes, those in the minority-dynamite group imagined they were under greater pressure from the other jurors.
91. Further research is clearly needed. One approach would be to conduct field experiments on real cases in which deadlocked juries are randomly assigned to receive either the *Allen* charge or a control instruction. Because random assignment of real juries is not feasible, however, a more realistic approach is to conduct a large-scale laboratory study involving interacting mock jurors.
92. The American Bar Association, for example, offered an alternative charge, one which emphasizes jurors' duty to consult with one another without singling out those in the minority. The instruction reads:

> It is your duty, as jurors, to consult with one another and to deliberate with a view to reaching an agreement, if you can do so without violence to individual judgment. Each of you must decide the case for yourself, but do so only after an impartial consideration of the evidence with your fellow jurors. In the course of your deliberations, do not hesitate to reexamine your views and change your opinion if convinced it is erroneous. But do not surrender your honest conviction as to the weight or effect of

> evidence solely because of the opinion of your fellow jurors, or for the mere purpose of returning a verdict.

See American Bar Association Project on Minimum Standards for Criminal Justice, Standards Relating to Trial by Jury, Standard 5.4 (1968).

93. Apodaca v. Oregon, 406 U.S. 404 (1972) (the Court upheld convictions by votes of 11 to 1 and 10 to 2); Johnson v. Louisiana, 406 U.S. 356 (1972). Current practices are varied. The federal courts still require unanimous verdicts, but a handful of states permit non-unanimous verdicts in criminal trials, and over 30 states allow these verdicts in civil actions.

94.

> We have no grounds for believing that majority jurors, aware of their responsibility and power over the liberty of the defendant, would simply refuse to listen to arguments presented to them in favor of acquittal, terminate discussion, and render a verdict. On the contrary it is far more likely that a juror presenting reasoned argument in favor of acquittal would either have his arguments answered or would carry enough other jurors with him to prevent conviction.

Johnson, 406 U.S. at 361.

95.

> [N]onunanimous juries need not debate and deliberate as fully as must unanimous juries. As soon as the requisite majority is attained, further consideration is not required either by Oregon or by Louisiana even though the dissident jurors might, if given the chance, be able to convince the majority. . . . It is said that there is no evidence that majority jurors will refuse to listen to dissenters whose votes are unneeded for conviction. Yet human experience teaches that polite and academic conversation is no substitute for the earnest and robust argument necessary to reach unanimity.

Id. at 388-89.

96. Nemeth, *Interactions Between Jurors as a Function of Majority vs. Unanimity Decision Rules*, 7 J. Applied Soc. Psychology 38, 42-43 (1977).

97. R. Hastie, S. Penrod & N. Pennington, Inside the Jury 45 (1983).

98. *Id.* at 112.

99. Walker v. United States, 342 F.2d 22, 28 (5th Cir. 1965).

100. H. Kalven & H. Zeisel, *supra* note 72, at 453.

101. H. Kalven & H. Zeisel, *supra* note 72, at 3.

13

Judicial Misconduct During Jury Deliberations

Bennett L. Gershman

The relationship between judge and jury is never more intense than during the jury deliberation process. During this period, the judge exerts considerable influence over the jury, and he must use that influence prudently and sensitively. The judge ministers to the jury's personal needs, controls the deliberation schedule, facilitates review of evidence, answers jury questions about legal and factual issues, reiterates legal instructions, investigates allegations of irregularities, and determines the overall pace and extent of deliberations. In exercising these functions, the judge must strive to maintain a delicate balance between affording the jury sufficient autonomy to reach conscientiously no decision and at the same time urge the jury without improper pressure to reach a fair and an impartial verdict. This tension between the interest in conscientious disagreement and the interest in a verdict makes the jury deliberation process a fertile setting for judicial misconduct.

Two principal kinds of improper judicial behavior can occur during this process: first, judicial conduct that attempts to place undue pressure on a jury to reach a verdict, and second, judicial participation in private, ex parte communications with jurors. Each of these topics is discussed below.

COERCING A VERDICT

Verdict-Urging Instructions

"The very object of the jury system," the United States Supreme Court wrote in *Allen v. United States*, "is to secure unanimity by a comparison of views, and by arguments among the jurors themselves."[1] There is no requirement, however, that a jury agree. A hung jury is a legitimate end of a trial.[2] This inherent tension between encouraging legitimate agreement while not discouraging principled dissent has been at the root of the controversy over the degree of pressure that a judge may employ in urging a deadlocked jury to reach an agreement.[3] The so-called *Allen* charge, from the decision bearing that name, has been the subject of considerable debate since the case was decided

Reprinted by permission of West Group from the *Criminal Law Bulletin,* vol. 27 (1991), pp. 291–314.

nearly 100 years ago.[4] Known variously as the "dynamite" charge,[5] the "nitroglycerin" charge,[6] the "shotgun" instruction,[7] and the "third-degree" instruction,[8] the *Allen* charge is a supplemental instruction that, in essence, admonishes a deadlocked jury to (1) decide the case if it can conscientiously do so; (2) give deference to the views of other jurors with the objective of being convinced, and (3) urge minority jurors to reconsider the reasonableness of their convictions. The Supreme Court described the instructions as follows:

> These instructions were quite lengthy, and were, in substance, that in a large proportion of cases, absolute certainty could not be expected; that, although the verdict must be the verdict of each individual juror, and not a mere acquiescence in the conclusion of his fellows, yet they should examine the question submitted with candor, and with a proper regard and deference to the opinions of each other; that it was their duty to decide the case if they could conscientiously do so; that they should listen, with a disposition to be convinced, to each other's arguments; that, if much the larger number were for conviction, a dissenting juror should consider whether his doubt was a reasonable one which made no impression upon the minds of so many men, equally honest, equally intelligent with himself. If, upon the other hand, the majority were for acquittal, the minority ought to ask themselves whether they might not reasonably doubt the correctness of a judgment which was not concurred in by the majority.[9]

Embellishments of the *Allen* charge have elicited tolerant as well as intolerant responses by the courts. These additions have included reminding jurors of the expense and inconvenience of a retrial[10] or that the case would have to be retried by another jury, should the present jury fail to reach a verdict.[11]

The principal concern over the *Allen* charge is that it pressures minority jurors to surrender their principles by giving them the impression that the judge agrees with the majority viewpoint and by threatening continued confinement until a verdict is reached.[12] Recognition that other jurors must remain confined because of a minority juror's individual beliefs necessarily produces strong pressures to reach agreement that often have little to do with the merits of the case. Moreover, some critics ask whether the purported societal gains in fewer retrials as a result of the *Allen* charge are offset by the appellate complications in determining whether the trial judge gave a correct charge at the correct point in time during the deliberations.[13]

Although the *Allen* charge or some similar variation continues to be an accepted instruction in many jurisdictions,[14] several federal[15] and state[16] appellate courts, pursuant to their supervisory powers, have either abandoned *Allen* entirely or severely limited its use. Many of these courts favor the standard proposed by the American Bar Association (ABA), which recommends a five-part instruction upon which a deadlocked jury may properly be advised.[17] Some courts, although allowing an *Allen*-type instruction, do not permit any extensions or alterations, indicating that the instruction is the farthest limit in verdict-urging language that they will tolerate.[18]

Reviewing courts examine the totality of the circumstances surrounding the use of the charge and proceed on a case-by-case basis "to determine whether the taint of coercion was present."[19] These courts analyze the content of the instruction for particularly coercive language,[20] the failure to give an instruction balancing the interest in agreement with the interest in conscientious decision making,[21] or the speed with which the jury returned its verdict after having been given the supplemental charge.[22] Remarks emphasizing the expense and inconvenience of a retrial,[23] or suggesting that the case will have to be retried again[24] have been criticized as injecting unfair pressure on juries.

Some courts recommend that a deadlock-type instruction be given during the main charge, before the jurors take positions, at a time when there is not yet a minority to feel pressured, in order to ameliorate such pressure on minority jurors if a deadlock should occur.[25] An *Allen*-type instruction should be given only when clearly warranted,[26] although there is no absolute right for counsel to be forewarned before the *Allen* charge is given.[27] Giving such an instruction to a jury that has not indicated a deadlock may be reversible error.[28] The failure to object to a verdict-urging instruction, however, may constitute a waiver of the claim on appeal[29] or at least diminish the force of the claim by suggesting that the attorney did not at the time believe that the jury was being coerced.[30]

Threats and Intimidation

As with verdict-urging instructions, a judge must not use other techniques to pressure a jury to reach a verdict. To be sure, there is a fine line between permissible encouragement and impermissible coercion. Nevertheless, despite the judge's desire for a verdict, he must not fail to advise jurors that they should adhere to their conscience and free will in making their decision. Otherwise, legitimate dissenting jurors will feel that they are somehow responsible for undermining the cause of justice.

Judicial demands for a verdict are ordinarily found coercive because they impact most heavily upon the recalcitrant jurors, implying that these jurors are delaying the cause of justice. The Supreme Court has addressed this problem on several occasions. In *Jenkins v. United States*,[31] the Court reversed a conviction when the judge admonished a deadlocked jury: "You have got to reach a decision in this case." Although no specific prejudice was found, inherent prejudice existed based on the unacceptable risk that impermissible factors would produce a decision.[32] Similar strident warnings that, in effect, order a jury to agree on a verdict have been held legally coercive. Thus, statements such as, "I'm going to get a verdict in this case,"[33] "There has to be a verdict,"[34] "You are supposed to find guilt or innocence here—do your job,"[35] or "It is the intention of this court to keep its jury in session for as long as it may take to arrive at a verdict"[36] have been held impermissibly coercive. Also coercive is openly telling a jury that the case is a simple one since such a statement implies that the case warrants only desultory deliberation, and thereby risks putting undue pressure on legitimate dissenting jurors that the judge considers their position untenable. Thus, a judge's remarks that he "could have decided this case in ten minutes"[37] or that "there should [not] be any great difficulty in arriving at a verdict in this case"[38] are intimidating and coercive. By contrast, remarks that strongly encourage jurors to adhere to their oaths and try to reach a verdict one way or the other have been held not coercive when the judge's statements do not appear to impose on any juror the surrender of her beliefs.[39]

A judge must be careful when giving supplemental instructions to avoid singling out individual minority jurors, either directly or by implication, with intimidating remarks that convey the message that they must agree with the majority.[40] When a judge learns during deliberations of a juror problem that, if unattended, might later require the granting of a mistrial, the judge should immediately intervene to obviate the problem.[41] This intervention includes the power to investigate allegations of juror misconduct to determine whether cause exists to replace an offending juror.[42]

Any intervention must be conducted with care, however, so as to minimize pressure on legitimate minority jurors by advising them that no verdict is being demanded and that a change in vote must be a conscientious one.[43] No juror should be induced to agree to a verdict by fear that a failure to agree will be regarded as reflecting upon either his intelligence or integrity.[44] Thus, it was "egregious" for a judge, after learning that a juror was having difficulty following her oath, to direct an instruction toward that juror that intimated she was guilty of either perjury or negligence in her response to questions on voir dire, and that she was not complying with her oath as a juror.[45] If it becomes clear that a juror is incapable of fairly reaching a verdict, the declaration of a mistrial may be in order.[46]

Singling out a dissenting juror and engaging in a one-on-one discussion as to whether the juror is obstructing an agreement on a verdict is inherently coercive.[47] Threatening the jury with deliberations for an indefinite period until a lone dissenter capitulates is obviously coercive.[48] A judge acts properly, however, when he conducts a discrete and nonthreatening investigation to evaluate a report that a juror may harbor a disqualifying bias or is otherwise incapable of rendering a verdict.[49]

A judge may not place a jury under any explicit time constraints that seek to induce a verdict more swiftly than the ends of justice will allow.[50] The amount of time that a deliberating jury should be kept together and the determination of whether a mistrial should be declared if the jury cannot agree are matters within a judge's sound discretion.[51] Ordinarily, a jury must have deliberated for an extensive period, and the judge must be satisfied that agreement is unlikely within a reasonable time before a judge may discharge the jury.[52] Asking a jury to "see if you can't reach a verdict within an hour" is plainly coercive because it emphasizes speed over care and infers that the judge is anxious to conclude the case.[53] Less explicit remarks may still be found coercive if they imply a time frame within which a verdict is to be reached.[54] Even concern for the jury's well-being does not justify the judge's placing a time limit on when a verdict must be reached.[55] A judge faced with emergent circumstances must explore reasonable alternatives, including the declaration of a mistrial. Not all time-related remarks, however, are coercive. The test is whether from all the circumstances the judge's remarks conveyed the impression that it was more important for the jury to be quick than to be thoughtful.[56]

Nor may a judge threaten the jury with sequestration, express an intention to confine them indefinitely, or impose unendurable conditions upon a jury as a means of pressuring them to reach a verdict.[57] Thus, requiring a jury to deliberate for twenty-seven hours without sleep was found unduly coercive.[58] Similarly improper was requiring a jury to deliberate until 5:25 A.M., notwithstanding their impatience and fatigue.[59] Under appropriate circumstances, the availability of sequestration at a hotel for the night may be noted as a possibility, although not as a threat.[60] Threatening to keep the jury "in session" and "incommunicado" until a verdict is reached is intimidating and coercive,[61] as are threats of sequestration when the judge is aware that some of the jurors have conflicts with such an arrangement.[62]

Problems occasionally arise during the polling of a jury following the rendition of a verdict.[63] A valid verdict is not dependent on what a juror agrees to in the jury room but, rather, on what the juror agrees to when the jury gives its verdict in open court.[64] A juror has the right when polled to dissent from a verdict to which he had agreed in the jury room.[65] When this type of dissent occurs, the jury may be directed to continue their deliberations, or they may be discharged.[66] If the jury is directed to continue deliberations, no time limit should be set.[67] Moreover, it is improper for the judge to interrogate the polled juror, enter into an argument with that juror, or require an explanation of his change of position.[68]

When polling reveals the possibility of some irregularity during the deliberation process, the judge must inquire into the problem.[69] This inquiry might include questioning the juror privately about matters not within the deliberative process[70] and then taking remedial action, such as requiring further deliberations, attempting to dissipate the cause of the problem, replacing the juror, or declaring a mistrial.[71]

Inquiry Into Numerical Division

A judge's inquiry into the numerical division of the jury on the merits of the verdict may be impermissibly coercive on dissenting jurors[72] regardless of whether the judge's inquiry specifically asks the jury which side is favored. In *Burton v. United States*,[73] the Supreme Court criticized the practice of making such an inquiry, noting that such questioning serves no useful purpose, and can be harmful.[74] Later, in *Brasfield v. United States*,[75] the Court held that any judicial inquiry into a deliberating jury's numerical division is per se reversible error. *Brasfield* elaborated on the reasons for condemning the practice of inquiring into a jury's numerical division:

> We deem it essential to the fair and impartial conduct of the trial, that the inquiry itself should be regarded as ground for reversal. Such procedure serves no useful purpose that cannot be attained by questions not requiring the jury to reveal the nature or extent of its division. Its effect upon a divided jury will often depend upon circumstances which cannot properly be known to the trial judge or to the appellate courts and may vary widely in different situations, but in general its tendency is coercive. It can rarely be resorted to without bringing to bear in some degree, serious although not measurable, an improper influence upon the jury, from whose deliberations every consideration other than that of the evidence and the law as expounded in a proper charge, should be excluded. Such a practice, which is never useful and is generally harmful, is not to be sanctioned.[76]

Brasfield can be understood as a prophylactic rule designed to protect the jury from the unpredictable effects of both the inquiry itself and the jury's knowledge of the judge's awareness of its division. Both can exert subtle pressure on some jurors. The *Brasfield* decision reflects a legitimate concern that trial judges scrupulously refrain from encroaching into the jury's deliberative process to ensure that the deliberations are candid and uninhibited. Moreover, when coupled with verdict-urging instructions, the inquiry can create the impression that the court agrees with the majority, thereby reinforcing the majority's determination and melting the resistance of the minority.[77]

Although there has been some disagreement,[78] *Brasfield* clearly was not based on the constitutional dictates of due process but, rather, represented an exercise of the Supreme Court's supervisory powers over the lower federal courts.[79] Inasmuch as the decision was not constitutionally grounded, state courts need not follow it,[80] and federal courts are not required to invoke its sanction when reviewing state habeas corpus proceedings alleging a *Brasfield* violation.[81]

Those state courts that follow the underlying rationale of *Brasfield*, if not its automatic reversal policy, examine whether the inquiry was unduly coercive. These courts make this determination by analyzing the totality of the circumstances.[82] For example, repetition of the numerical inquiry aggravates the impropriety.[83] Administering verdict-urging instructions in conjunction with the numerical inquiry, as noted above, exacerbates the coercive potential by placing undue pressure on minority jurors.[84] The absence of ameliorative language is also a relevant factor.[85] Counsel's request for the numerical inquiry, however, can constitute a waiver of the claim.[86]

Even unsolicited disclosures to the judge of the jury's division can be grounds for reversal.[87] A jury note to the judge, for example, can reveal the jury's division, and even the identity of the dissenting jurors.[88] Giving a verdict-urging instruction in such circumstances could reasonably be interpreted as being directed at the dissenters and thereby be found impermissibly coercive of these jurors.[89] A judge who learns of the jury's division through an unsolicited report may in some circumstances be required to declare a mistrial.[90] Unsolicited disclosures can also result in reversal when, for example, a judge's inquiry concerning the jury's request for a review of testimony develops into an inquiry concerning the jury's division.[91] Such an occurrence can create a "coercive atmosphere," particularly when the judge singles out individual jurors for questioning.[92]

A judge's inquiry into the jury's numerical split on matters unrelated to the merits of the verdict is permissible. The Supreme Court recently addressed this issue in *Lowenfield v. Phelps.*[93] There, after being advised that the jury was deadlocked, the judge in open court asked the jurors to write on a piece of paper his or her name and whether further deliberations would be helpful in arriving at a verdict. The jurors complied. The count was eight affirmative votes and four negative votes. After some confusion, the judge again reiterated the question in slightly different form, and the jury responded, eleven-to-one, that further deliberations would be helpful. The judge then reinstructed the jury as to their duty to attempt to reach a verdict.

The Supreme Court approved the judge's inquiry. Distinguishing *Brasfield*, the Court noted that such an inquiry was clearly different from an inquiry into the merits because there was no reason to believe that a juror who was in the minority on the merits would necessarily conclude that further deliberations would not be helpful. The Court observed:

> We believe the type of question asked by the trial court in this case is exactly what the Court in *Brasfield* implicitly approved when it stated: "[An inquiry as to numerical division] serves no useful purpose that cannot be attained by questions not requiring the jury to reveal the nature of its division."[94]

Although the supplemental instruction and the return of a verdict thirty minutes later suggested the "possibility of coercion,"[95] defense counsel's failure to object indicated that "the potential for coercion now argued was not apparent to one on the spot."[96]

EX PARTE COMMUNICATIONS

A judge should not communicate with the jury on any matter pertaining to the case except after giving notice to the parties and affording them a reasonable opportunity to be present and to be heard.[97] This rule against ex parte contacts is based on concerns of orderly trial procedure and ensuring that the jury remains impartial. Proper procedure requires certain precautions.[98] The jury's inquiry should be in writing, the note should be marked as a court exhibit and read into the record in the presence of counsel and the parties, counsel should be afforded an opportunity to suggest appropriate responses, and the jury should be recalled. The judge should then read into the record the jury's note, and give the response.[99]

The Supreme Court on several occasions has delineated the permissible scope of ex parte contacts between judge and jury. In *Fillippon v. Albion Vein Slate Co.*,[100] a personal injury lawsuit, the deliberating jury sent a note to the judge asking for further instructions about the plaintiff's contributory negligence. The judge sent a written response back to the jury without notifying the parties and without recalling the jury in open court. Concluding that engaging in this ex parte communication was error, the Court observed:

> We entertain no doubt that the orderly conduct of a trial by jury, essential to the proper protection of the right to be heard, entitles the parties who attend for the purpose to be present in person or by counsel at all proceedings from the time the jury is impaneled until it is discharged after rendering the verdict. Where a jury has retired to consider its verdict, and supplementary instructions are required, either because asked for by the jury or for other reasons, they ought to be given either in the presence of counsel or after notice and an opportunity to be present; and written instructions ought not to be sent to the jury without notice to counsel and an opportunity to object. Under ordinary circumstances, and wherever practicable, the jury ought to be recalled to the court room, where counsel are entitled to anticipate, and bound to presume, in the absence of notice to the contrary, that all proceedings in the trial will be had. In this case the trial court erred in giving a supplementary instruction to the jury in the absence of the parties and without affording them an opportunity either to be present or to make timely objection to the instruction.[101]

The Court explicitly found that the supplementary instruction was harmful since it related to a substantive element in the case, was legally erroneous, and "was calculated to mislead the jury."[102]

The principle of *Fillippon* was later applied to a criminal case in *Shields v. United States.*[103] There, the judge similarly responded to a jury note indicating a partial verdict by directing the jury to continue deliberations on the remaining defendants. This communication was not made in open court, and neither the defendants nor their attorneys were present or advised of these interchanges. The Court reversed the conviction without finding any specific prejudice. It noted that "the rule of orderly conduct of jury trial entitl[es] the defendant, especially in a criminal case, to be present from the time the jury is impaneled until its discharge after rendering the verdict."[104]

The *Fillippon-Shields* principle was reaffirmed in *Rogers v. United States.*[105] There, in response to a jury note inquiring whether the judge would accept a guilty verdict with "extreme mercy of the Court," the judge instructed the bailiff "to advise the jury that the Court's answer was in the affirmative."[106] These communications were in private, without notice to defendant or an opportunity for counsel to respond. Pointing out that Rule 43 of the Federal Rules of Criminal Procedure guarantees a defendant the right to be present "at every stage of the trial including the impaneling of the jury and the return of the verdict," the Court held that the jury's message should have been answered in open court and that defendant's counsel should have been given an opportunity to be heard before the judge responded.[107]

Although the Court agreed that a violation of Rule 43 could be harmless, such a conclusion was not warranted here, since the violation was "fraught with potential prejudice."[108] The Court explained that the judge should not have indicated a willingness to accept the jury's request. Rather, the judge should have advised the jury that its request would not be binding on the court and that, in any event, the jury had no sentencing function and was required to reach its verdict without regard to sentence. Moreover, the jury returned its verdict within five minutes of receiving the judge's response, a circumstance that "strongly suggests that the trial judge's response may have induced unanimity by giving members of the jury who had previously hesitated about reaching a guilty verdict the impression that the recommendation might be an acceptable compromise."[109]

The requirement and extent of the prejudice that needs to be shown from a judge's ex parte contacts with a deliberating jury was further examined in *United States v. U.S. Gypsum Co.*[110] There, during extensive deliberations, the foreman asked to confer with the judge about the condition of the jury. Defense counsel agreed to the judge's proposed ex parte conference. At the meeting, the foreman advised the judge of the deteriorating state of health of the jurors after the lengthy trial and twice indicated that the jury was deadlocked. Near the close of the meeting, the following colloquy took place:[111]

> *The Court:* I would like to ask the jurors to continue their deliberations and I will take into consideration what you have told me. That is all I can say.
>
> *Mr. Russell (foreman):* I appreciate it. It is a situation I don't know how to help you get what you are after.
>
> *The Court:* Oh, I am not after anything.
>
> *Mr. Russell:* You are after a verdict one way or the other.
>
> *The Court:* Which way it goes doesn't make any difference to me.

The judge informed counsel of the substance of the meeting but omitted reference to the foreman's opinion that the jury was deadlocked and to the foreman's impression that the judge wanted a definite verdict.

The Supreme Court reversed the conviction, finding that the judge's ex parte communications with the jury foreman encroached on the jury's authority and foreclosed a possible "no verdict" outcome by giving the foreman the impression that the judge wanted a verdict. The event was "disturbing" for several reasons. First, just as "any ex parte meeting . . . is pregnant with possibilities for error," the instant case amply demonstrated the "pitfalls inherent in such an enterprise.[112] Moreover, "unexpected questions or comments can generate unintended and misleading impressions of the judge's subjective personal views which have no place in his instruction to the jury—all the more so when counsel are not present to challenge the statements."[113] Second, any ex parte communication to the jury through one member of the panel risks innocent misstatements of law and misinterpretations whose content cannot be determined.[114] Third, the absence of counsel from the meeting and the unavailability of a transcript aggravate the problems of having one juror serve as a conduit for communicating instructions to the whole panel.[115] The Court concluded:

> Thus, it is not simply the action of the judge in having the private meeting with the jury foreman, standing alone—undesirable as that procedure is—which constitutes the error; rather, it is the fact that the *ex parte* discussion was inadvertently allowed to drift into what amounted to a supplemental instruction to the foreman relating to the jury's obligation to return a verdict, coupled with the fact that counsel were denied any chance to correct whatever mistaken impression the foreman might have taken from this conversation, that we find most troubling.[116]

Although no actual prejudice was found, the Court, citing *Jenkins v. United States*,[117] determined that inherent prejudice was shown by the jury's swift return of a verdict following the ex parte meeting, thereby suggesting a "risk" that the foreman believed that the judge wanted a verdict and then conveyed that impression to the jury.[118]

Federal and state appellate courts ordinarily review ex parte communications according to the nature of the communication (i.e., whether it related to a substantive issue in the case or whether it concerned nonsubstantive matters).[119] Substantive communications would include communications pertaining to legal and factual issues in the case, whereas nonsubstantive communications relate to the extent of deliberations, the availability of items of evidence, and housekeeping matters, such as meal orders. The courts also examine the manner in which the communication was made and ordinarily apply waiver doctrine when counsel fails to protest the occurrence. The most decisive factor, as the Supreme Court decisions demonstrate, is the potential for prejudice, or the presence or absence of actual prejudice, from the communication.

The courts scrutinize more closely ex parte communications that relate to legal or factual matters in the case since such communications can carry a presumption of prejudice in favor of the aggrieved party.[120] Thus, ex parte responses to a jury's question about substantive matters, such as (1) the standard for contributory negligence;[121] (2) the measure of damages under a contract;[122] (3) principles of estoppel;[123] (4) construction of a contract;[124] (5) interpretation of a criminal statute;[125] (6) the need for unanimity for a verdict;[126] (7) separability of substantive offenses from conspiracy;[127] (8) the overt act requirement for conspiracy;[128] and (9) any jury polling following the verdict,[129] were found prejudicial and required reversal. Similarly, ex parte communications on nonsubstantive matters, such as responding to a jury note inquiring whether the judge would accept a particular verdict,[130] or urging a deadlocked jury to continue deliberating,[131] can also result in reversal. The courts disapprove of a per se rule of reversal[132] and analyze the ex parte communication for actual or potential prejudice.[133] Cases finding lack of prejudice look at the substance of the communication,[134] the responsiveness of the judge's communication to the jury's communication,[135] the extent of the deliberations after the ex parte communication,[136] and any curative instructions given to the jury.[137]

Apart from the substance and timing of the ex parte communication, some courts find that the error has been aggravated by the manner in which the communication was made. The absence of the judge when a jury inquiry is received and answered can be error. It is improper, for example, for a judge to communicate with the jury through court personnel.[138] Telephonic communications with the jury is also improper,[139] as is the judge's personally entering the jury room to answer the jury's questions.[140]

A claim that the judge engaged in an improper ex parte communication can be waived.[141] Counsel's voluntary absence from the courtroom may operate as a waiver,[142] as well as counsel's express consent to the judge engaging in an ex parte meeting.[143] The failure to interpose a timely objection and seek corrective action can also constitute a waiver.[144] A defendant also may waive his right to be present at a conference between judge and jury when he knowingly absents himself from the proceeding.[145] Where a statute or rule expressly commands the defendant's presence, however, counsel's consent to the defendant's absence ordinarily will not operate as a waiver.[146]

CONCLUSION

The integrity of the jury deliberation process must not be infringed by a judge's improper verdict-urging instructions, coercive remarks, or private contacts with deliberating jurors. Appellate courts carefully scrutinize deadlock instructions to determine whether the content or timing of the instructions was coercive. The courts also examine whether other coercive language might have induced a verdict that was the product not of conscientious agreement on the merits but, rather, that resulted from the pressure of time constraints and continued confinement. Although the standards are not uniform, federal and state appellate courts generally examine the judge-jury interaction on a case-by-case basis, under the totality of the circumstances, to determine whether there existed actual prejudice or a clear potential for prejudice.

NOTES

1. Allen v. United States, 164 U.S. 492, 501 (1896). There is no obligation on the part of a judge to give any special instruction when a jury reports disagreement. The judge may simply elect to declare a mistrial. United States v. See, 505 F.2d 845 (9th Cir. 1974), *cert. denied*, 420 U.S. 992 (1975). There may be double-jeopardy concerns, however, in discharging prematurely a deliberating jury. United States v. Lansdown, 460 F.2d 164 (4th Cir. 1972) (discharge of jury after it had deliberated for eleven hours without attempting to determine whether it could reach a verdict prevented retrial on double-jeopardy grounds).

2. The hung jury has been characterized as "the jury system's most interesting phenomenon. In one sense it marks a failure of the system, since it necessarily brings a declaration of a mistrial in its

wake. In another sense, it is a valued assurance of integrity, since it can serve to protect the dissent of a minority." H. Kalven & H. Zeisel, *The American Jury,* 453 (1966). See Arizona v. Washington, 434 U.S. 497, 509 (1978) (defendant's right to have trial completed by particular jury must be weighed against defendant's right to considered judgment of all jurors, rather than a judgment resulting from pressures of "protracted and exhausting" deliberations); Huffman v. United States, 297 F.2d 754, 759 (5th. Cir.) (Brown, J., dissenting) ("I think a mistrial from a hung jury is a safeguard to liberty. In many areas it is the sole means by which one or a few may stand out against an overwhelming contemporary public sentiment. Nothing should interfere with its exercise"), *cert. denied*, 370 U.S. 955 (1962); State v. Flint, 114 Idaho 806, 761 P.2d 1158, 1164 (1988) ("the hung jury is not a jurisprudential failure, but rather is a commendation on the fair and evenhanded administration of justice"). In their classic study, *The American Jury*, Professors Kalven and Zeisel found that more than 5 percent of all juries end in a mistrial. H. Kalven & H. Zeisel, *supra.*

It should be noted that many jurisdictions do not require unanimity in civil cases, and five states permit a conviction on less than a unanimous verdict. H. Kalven & H. Zeisel, *supra*, at 461 n.6. Moreover, a jury may be authorized to return a partial verdict on one or more defendants or one or more offenses. N.Y. Crim. Proc. Law § 310.70 (McKinney 1988). A judge may ask the jury to render such a partial verdict and then resume deliberations on the remaining defendants and charges. See United States v. Bascaro, 742 F.2d 1335 (11th Cir. 1984); Morgan v. United States, 380 F.2d 686 (9th Cir. 1967), *cert. denied*, 390 U.S. 962 (1968). A judge should be careful, however, not to suggest that the jury compromise its conscientiously held beliefs for the sake of expediency. United States v. Smoot, 463 F.2d 1221 (D.C. Cir. 1972).

3. Every federal appellate court, and virtually every state jurisdiction, uses some form of a supplemental jury charge. See Lowenfield v. Phelps, 484 U.S. 231, 238 n.1 (1988). Note, "Deadlocked Juries and the *Allen* Charge," 37 Me. L. Rev. 167 (1985).

4. United States v. Fioravanti, 412 F.2d 407 (3d Cir. 1969), *cert. denied*, 396 U.S. 837 (*Allen* charge an unwarranted judicial encroachment of exclusive province of the jury); United States v. Thomas, 449 F.2d 1177, 1184 n.45, 1187 (D.C. Cir. 1971) (*en banc*) (rejecting *Allen* charge as unduly coercive); United States v. Brown, 411 F.2d 930 (7th Cir. 1969), *cert. denied*, 396 U.S. 1017 (1970); Fields v. State, 487 P.2d 831, 840 (Alaska 1971) (*Allen* charge "less an object of commendation than toleration"); State v. Randall, 137 Mont. 534, 353 P.2d 1054 (1960) (rejecting *Allen* charge); State v. Thomas, 86 Ariz. 161, 342 P.2d 197 (1959) (same). See also Note, "On Instructing Deadlocked Juries," 78 Yale L.J. 100 (1968); Note, "Due Process, Judicial Economy, and the Hung Jury: A Reexamination of the *Allen* Charge," 53 Va. L. Rev. (1967); Comment, "Deadlocked Juries and Dynamite: A Critical Look at the "*Allen* Charge," 31 U. Chi. L. Rev. 386 (1964). See also Annotation, "Instructions Urging Dissenting Jurors in State Criminal Cases to Give Due Consideration to Opinion of Majority (*Allen* Charge)—Modern Cases," 97 A.L.R.3d 96 (1980); Annotation, "Verdict-Urging Instructions in Civil Case Stressing Desirability and Importance of Agreement," 38 A.L.R.3d 1281 (1971).

5. Green v. United States, 309 F.2d 852, 853 (5th Cir. 1962).

6. Huffman v. United States, 297 F.2d 754, 759 (5th Cir.) (Brown, J., concurring and dissenting), *cert. denied*, 370 U.S. 955 (1962).

7. State v. Nelson, 63 N.M. 428, 431, 321 P.2d 202, 204 (1958).

8. Leech v. People, 112 Colo. 120, 123, 146 P.2d 346, 347 (1944). *Allen* has also been described as "a sharp punch to the jury, reminding them of the nature of their duty and the time and expense of a trial, and urging them to try again to reach a verdict." United States v. Anderton, 679 F.2d 1199, 1203 (5th Cir. 1982).

9. Allen, 164 U.S. at 501.

10. United States v. Smith, 303 F.2d 341 (4th Cir. 1962); State v. Flint, 114 Idaho 806, 761 P.2d 1158 (1988); Golden v. First City Nat'l Bank, 751 S.W.2d 639 (Tex. Ct. App. 1988); Vanderbilt Univ. v. Steely, 566 S.W.2d 853 (Tenn. 1978).

11. United States v. Porter, 881 F.2d 878 (10th Cir.), *cert. denied*, 110 S. Ct. 348 (1989); United States v. Smith, 857 F.2d 682 (10th Cir. 1988); Hodges v. United States, 408 F.2d 543 (8th Cir. 1969).

12. Such an instruction can have an even more deleterious effect when the identity of the recalcitrant jurors is known and they are, in effect, singled out. See Indiana State Highway Comm'n v. Vanderbur, 432 N.E.2d 418 (Ind. Ct. App. 1982).

13. Andrews v. United States, 309 F.2d 127 (5th Cir. 1962), *cert. denied*, 372 U.S. 946 (1963) (Wisdom, J., dissenting) ("[senting) *Allen's*] time-saving merits in the district court are more than nullified by the complications it causes on appeal when the reviewing court must determine whether in the circumstances of a particular case the trial judge applied the charge properly—in substance and timing").

14. The Supreme Court recently reaffirmed the principles underlying *Allen*. Lowenfield v. Phelps, 484 U.S. 231, 237 (1988) ("[t]he continuing validity of this Court's observations in *Allen* are beyond dispute,"). See Kawakita v. United States, 343 U.S. 717 (1952) (*Allen* charge assumed to be appropriate instruction to deadlocked juries). See also Note, note 3 *supra.*

15. Several circuit courts have indicated disapproval of its use. See United States v. Thomas, 449 F.2d 1177 (D.C. Cir. 1971), United States v. Fioravanti, 412 F.2d 407 (3d Cir.), *cert. denied*, 396 U.S. 837 (1969); United States v. Brown, 411 F.2d 930 (7th Cir. 1969), *cert. denied*, 396 U.S. 1017 (1970).

16. Several states have banned the *Allen* charge. See State v. Flint, 114 Idaho 806, 761 P.2d 1158 (1988), People v. Gainer, 19 Cal. 3d 835, 566 P.2d 997, 139 Cal. Rptr. 861 (1977); State v. Thomas, 86 Ariz. 161, 342 P.2d 197 (1959); State v. Randall, 137 Mont. 534, 353 P.2d 1054 (1960); Burnette v. State, 280 Md. 88, 371 A.2d 663 (1977). It is also improper to give an *Allen* charge during the penalty phase of a capital trial. See Rush v. State, 491 A.2d 439 (Del. Super. 1985); Rose v. State, 425 So. 2d 521 (Fla. Super.), *cert. denied*, 461 U.S. 909 (1983).

17. This portion of the ABA's recommended instruction reads as follows:

> (i) [T]hat in order to return a verdict, each juror must agree thereto;
> (ii) [T]hat jurors have a duty to consult with one another and to deliberate with a view to reaching an agreement, if it can be done without violence to individual judgment;
> (iii) [T]hat each juror must decide the case for himself or herself but only after an impartial consideration of the evidence with the other jurors;
> (iv) [T]hat in the course of deliberations, a juror should not hesitate to reexamine his or her own views and change an opinion if the juror is convinced it is erroneous; and
> (v) [T]hat no juror should surrender his or her honest conviction as to the weight or effect of the evidence solely because of the opinion of the other jurors, or for the mere purpose of returning a verdict.

ABA, *Standards for Criminal Justice* § 15-4.4 (2d ed. 1986).

Several federal and state courts have adopted this standard. See Note, note 3 *supra*, at 167, 171-172 n.35 (1985) (collecting cases).

18. Potter v. United States, 691 F.2d 1275 (8th Cir. 1982) (improper "departures" impose almost impossible task of weighing prejudicial impact of variations); United States v. Harris, 391 F.2d 348, 354 (6th Cir.), *cert. denied*, 393 U.S. 874 (1968) (charge "approaches the limits beyond which a trial court should not venture in urging a jury to reach a verdict"); Vanderbilt Univ. v. Steely, 566 S.W.2d 853 (Tenn. 1978) (court requires "strict adherence" to its previously mandated charge).

19. Munroe v. United States, 424 F.2d 243, 246 (10th Cir. 1970). See United States v. Lindell, 881 F.2d 1313, 1321 (5th Cir. 1989), *cert. denied*, 110 S. Ct. 1152 (1990).

20. United States v. Porter, 881 F.2d 878, 888 (10th Cir.), *cert. denied*, 110 S. Ct. 348 (1989) (court must scrutinize language of instruction and its incorporation with other instructions); United States v. Young, 702 F.2d 133 (8th Cir. 1983) ("*Allen* charges must be utilized with great care and scrutinized carefully"); United States v. Stewart, 513 F.2d 957 (2d Cir. 1975) (improper use of "cancer" analogy but not reversible error).

21. United States v. Ronder, 639 F.2d 931 (2d Cir. 1981); People v. Ali, 65 A.D.2d 513, 514, 409 N.Y.S.2d 12 (1978), *aff'd*, 47 N.Y.2d 920, 393 N.E.2d 481, 419 N.Y.S.2d 487 (1979).

22. United States v. Webb, 816 F.2d 1263 (8th Cir. 1987) (verdict returned fifteen minutes after receiving deadlock instruction); Hodges v. United States, 408 F.2d 543, 554 (8th Cir. 1969) (jury continued deliberating for another day before reaching verdict); Williams v. United States, 338 F.2d 530 (D.C. Cir. 1964). See also United States v. U.S. Gypsum Co., 438 U.S. 422, 462 (1978).

23. Hodges v. United States, 408 F.2d 543 (8th Cir. 1969); Vanderbilt University v. Steely, 566 S.W.2d 853 (Tenn. 1978).

24. United States v. Harris, 391 F.2d 348 (6th Cir.) *cert. denied*, 393 U.S. 874 (1968); United States v. Smith, 303 F.2d 341, 343 (4th Cir. 1962).

25. United States v. McKinney, 822 F.2d 946, 951 (10th Cir. 1987); United States v. Brown, 634 F.2d 1069 (7th Cir. 1980); United States v. Silvern, 484 F.2d 879 (7th Cir. 1973). See also People v. Ali, 47 N.Y.2d 920, 393 N.E.2d 481, 419 N.Y.S.2d 487 (1979) (suggesting that supplemental instruction be given during main charge). The ABA standard also recommends that the instruction be given before the jury retires for deliberation. See ABA, note 17 *supra*, § 15-4.4(a).

26. Sullivan v. United States, 414 F.2d 714, 716 (9th Cir. 1969).

27. United States v. Rapp, 871 F.2d 957, 967 (11th Cir.), *cert. denied*, 110 S. Ct. 233 (1989).

28. Compare United States v. Contreras, 463 F.2d 773 (9th Cir. 1972) (reversible error to give *Allen* charge to jury without any indication jury deadlocked) with United States v. Martinez, 446 F.2d 118 (2d Cir.), *cert. denied*, 404 U.S. 944 (1971) (no error to give such charge sua sponte to deliberating jury) and Souza v. Ellerthorpe, 712 F.2d 1529 (1st Cir. 1983), *cert. denied*, 464 U.S. 1048 (1984) (setting deadline sua sponte held not coercive).

29. Golden v. First City Nat'l Bank, 751 S.W.2d 639 (Tex. Ct. App. 1988). But see United States v. Webb, 816 F.2d 1263 (8th Cir. 1987) (initial consent to inquiry into jury's numerical division did not waive claim as to giving of subsequent *Allen* charge).

30. Lowenfield v. Phelps, 484 U.S. 231, 240 (1988).

31. 380 U.S. 445, 446 (1965).

32. Holbrook v. Flynn, 475 U.S. 560, 570 (1976) (the test for inherent prejudice is "not whether jurors actually articulated a consciousness of some prejudicial effect, but rather whether an unacceptable risk is presented of impermissible factors coming into play").

33. Ex parte, Morris, 465 So. 2d 1180, 1182 (Ala. 1985).

34. United States v. Assi, 748 F.2d 62, 68 (2d Cir. 1984).

35. Jackson v. United States, 368 A.2d 1140, 1142 (D.C. 1977).

36. People v. Carter, 40 N.Y.2d 933, 358 N.E.2d 517, 389 N.Y.S.2d 835 (1976).

37. People v. Riley, 70 N.Y.2d 523, 532, 517 N.E.2d 520, 522 N.Y.S.2d 842 (1987).

38. Boyett v. United States, 48 F.2d 482, 483 (5th Cir. 1931).

39. United States v. Markey, 693 F.2d 594 (6th Cir. 1982) (advising jury that courthouse would be available the following morning, Christmas Eve, if jury unable to reach a consensus that afternoon not coercive); Williams v. United States, 419 F.2d 740 (D.C. Cir. 1969), *cert. denied*, 409 U.S. 872 (1972) (ordering jury back to jury room after poll produced confusion among one juror not coercive); Richardson v. State, 508 So. 2d 289 (Ala. Crim. App. 1987) (inquiring into jury's numerical division and dissuading jury from reviewing certain evidence not coercive); People v. Pagan, 45 N.Y.2d 725, 380 N.E.2d 299, 408 N.Y.S.2d 473 (1978) (admonishing jury that case was simple and that they were expected to arrive at verdict not coercive); People v. Sharff, 38 N.Y.2d 751, 343 N.E.2d 765, 381 N.Y.S.2d 48 (1975) (advising jury that it would be sequestered if it did not reach a verdict not coercive).

40. Indiana State Highway Comm'n v. Vanderbur, 432 N.E.2d 418 (Ind. Ct. App. 1982) (deadlock instruction given after identity of recalcitrant jurors known); People v. Hudson, 104 A.D.2d 157, 482 N.Y.S.2d 1009 (1984) (judge directs intimidating remarks specifically at two dissenting jurors); People v. Perfetto, 96 A.D.2d 517, 464 N.Y.S.2d 818 (1983) (singling out and confronting lone minority juror inherently coercive).

41. People v. Keenan, 46 Cal. 3d 478, 758 P.2d 1081, 250 Cal. Rptr. 550 (1988) (juror claimed to be unable to vote for death penalty).

42. People v. Burgener, 41 Cal. 3d 505, 714 P.2d 1251, 224 Cal. Rptr. 112 (1986) (reports that juror was intoxicated on marijuana); People v. McNeal, 90 Cal. App. 3d 830, 153 Cal. Rptr. 706 (1979) (juror indicates personal knowledge of disputed facts).

The broad discretionary authority of a judge to investigate allegations of juror irregularity during the trial is well settled. See United States v. Gagnon, 470 U.S. 522 (1985); Rushen v. Spain, 464 U.S. 114 (1983). The procedures adopted, however, must be protective of a defendant's right to a fair trial and an impartial jury. United States v. Yonn, 702 F.2d 1341 (11th Cir.), *cert. denied*, 464 U.S. 917 (1983); United States v. Dominguez, 615 F.2d 1093 (5th Cir. 1980). A judge also has the power to dismiss a juror who is "unable or disqualified to perform his duties." Fed. R. Crim. P. 24(c). See United States v. Rodriguez, 573 F.2d 330 (5th Cir. 1978).

43. United States v. Amaya, 509 F.2d 8, 13 (5th Cir. 1975), *cert. denied*, 429 U.S. 1101 (1977).

44. Jackson v. United States, 368 A.2d 1140, 1142 (D.C. App. 1977).

45. *Id.*

46. *Id.*

47. People v. Perfetto, 96 A.D.2d 517, 464 N.Y.S.2d 818 (1983).

48. People v. Carter, 40 N.Y.2d 933, 358 N.E.2d 517, 389 N.Y.S.2d 835 (1976).

49. People v. Keenan, 46 Cal. 3d 478, 758 P.2d 1081, 250 Cal. Rptr. 550 (1988).

50. United States v. Diharce-Estrada, 526 F.2d 637, 640 (5th Cir. 1976) ("court's opening remarks to the jurors emphasizing the dispatch he expected, coupled with the immoderate treatment accorded defense counsel for his allegedly unjustified attempts to delay the trial, can only be judged by us to have put pressure on the jury to reach a verdict more swiftly than the ends of justice will allow"): People v. Keenan, 46 Cal. 3d 478, 758 P.2d 1081, 250 Cal. Rptr. 550 (1988) (judge's remarks on Friday that he would "appreciate" a verdict on Monday not coercive due to cautionary instructions to minority jurors not to surrender conscientiously held beliefs).

51. People v. Sheldon, 136 A.D.2d 761, 523 N.Y.S.2d 220 (1988). Deliberation time allowed varies with the length of the trial. An average hung jury deliberates longer than the average jury that reaches a verdict by a ratio of about three-to-one. H. Kalven & H. Zeisel, note 2 *supra*, at 459.

52. *Id.* It should be noted that serious double jeopardy claims would arise if the judge declares a mistrial prematurely. See Arizona v. Washington, 434 U.S. 497 (1978); Logan v. United States, 144 U.S. 263 (1892).

53. Burroughs v. United States, 365 F.2d 431, 433 (10th Cir. 1966).

54. United States v. Amaya, 509 F.2d 8, 9 (5th Cir. 1975), *cert. denied*, 429 U.S. 1101 (1977) (suggesting that jury try to reach a verdict in one hour, and referring to previous jury deliberation that lasted nine days, held unduly coercive).

55. Lucas v. American Mfg. Co., 630 F.2d 291, 293 (5th Cir. 1980) (advising jury that due to impending hurricane it must reach verdict within fifteen minutes was coercive).

56. United States v. Markey, 693 F.2d 594 (6th Cir. 1982); United States v. Green, 523 F.2d 229 (2d Cir. 1975), *cert. denied*, 423 U.S. 1074 (1976); Butler v. State, 185 Tenn. 686, 207 S.W.2d 584 (1948).

57. Boyett v. United States, 48 F.2d 482, 484 (5th Cir. 1931) (judge's remarks suggested that some of jurors derelict in their duty and that judge intended to punish them by keeping them confined indefinitely until they reached a verdict). See also United States v. Chaney, 559 F.2d 1094 (7th Cir. 1977) (supplemental charge could have been understood as demanding quick verdict to avoid being locked up for night).

58. State v. Green, 254 Iowa 1379, 121 N.W.2d 89 (1963).

59. Commonwealth v. Clark, 404 Pa. 143, 170 A.2d 847 (1961).

60. Compare People v. Pagan, 45 N.Y.2d 725, 380 N.E.2d 299, 408 N.Y.S.2d 473 (1978) (appropriate reference to possible sequestration) and People v. Sharff, 38 N.Y.2d 751, 343 N.E.2d

765, 381 N.Y.S.2d 48 (1975) (same) with People v. Hudson, 104 A.D.2d 157, 482 N.Y.S.2d 1009 (1984) (threatening jurors with sequestration because of two recalcitrant jurors).

61. People v. Carter, 40 N.Y.2d 933, 358 N.E.2d 517, 389 N.Y.S.2d 835 (1976).

62. State v. Jones, 292 N.C. 513, 234 S.E.2d 555 (1977) (judge knew that some of jurors had abnormal conflicts and had promised two jurors that court would not be held over weekend, but nevertheless gratuitously threatened to confine them over weekend unless they reached verdict).

63. Section 15-4.5 of the ABA *Standards for Criminal Justice* provides:

> When a verdict has been returned and before the jury has dispersed, the jury shall be polled at the request of any party or upon the court's own motion. The poll shall be conducted by the court or clerk of court asking each juror individually whether the verdict announced is his or her verdict. If upon the poll there is not unanimous concurrence, the jury may be directed to retire for further deliberations or may be discharged.

ABA, note 17 *supra*, § 15-4.5. See United States v. Fiorilla, 850 F.2d 172 (3d Cir.) (*en banc*) (poll not impermissibly coercive), *cert. denied*, 488 U.S. 966 (1988).

64. Bruce v. Chestnut Farms-Chevy Chase Dairy, 126 F.2d 224, 225 (D.C. Cir. 1942).

65. *Id.* It should be noted, however, that there is no absolute right to have a jury polled. United States v. Shepherd, 576 F.2d 719, 724 (7th Cir.) *cert. denied*, 439 U.S. 852 (1978). If the request for a poll is not made before the verdict is recorded, it comes too late. *Id.* at 724 n.3.

66. United States v. Musto, 540 F. Supp. 318, 339 (D.N.J. 1982). Rule 31(d) of the Federal Rules of Criminal Procedure states:

> When a verdict is returned and before it is recorded the jury shall be polled at the request of any party or upon the court's own motion. If upon the poll there is not unanimous concurrence, the jury may be directed to retire for further deliberations or may be discharged.

67. State v. Sutton, 31 N.C. App. 697, 230 S.E.2d 572 (1976) (judge sends jury back to deliberate and tells them "to take no more than five minutes to ascertain whether or not the verdict which you reported yesterday was unanimous").

68. Compare Bruce v. Chestnut Farms-Chevy Chase Dairy, 126 F.2d 224 (D.C. Cir. 1942) (judge demands explanation for juror's apparent change of position) with Williams v. United States, 419 F.2d 740 (D.C. Cir. 1969) (judge acts properly to attempt to clear up confusion from poll).

69. People v. Pickett, 61 N.Y.2d 773, 461 N.E.2d 294, 473 N.Y.S.2d 157 (1984) (juror responds that verdict was arrived at "under duress").

70. The judge should be careful, however, not to inquire about matters that occurred during the deliberations themselves. *Id.*

71. *Id.*

72. See Annotation, "Propriety and Prejudicial Effect of Trial Court's Inquiry as to Numerical Division of Jury," 77 A.L.R.3d 769 (1977).

73. 196 U.S. 283 (1905).

74. The Court observed: "[W]e do not think that the proper administration of the law requires such knowledge or permits such a question on the part of the presiding judge." *Id.* at 308.

75. 272 U.S. 448 (1926).

76. *Id.* at 450. For other cases condemning the practice, see United States v. Webb, 816 F.2d 1263 (8th Cir. 1987); United States v. Sae-Chua, 725 F.2d 530 (9th Cir. 1984); United States v. Noah, 594 F.2d 1303 (9th Cir. 1979); United States v. Hayes, 446 F.2d 309 (5th Cir. 1961); United States v. Cook, 254 F.2d 871 (5th Cir. 1958). See also E. Devitt & C. Blackmar, *Federal Jury Practice and Instructions* § 5.22 (3d ed. 1977) (a "cardinal rule that the court should not ask the jury as to their numerical division").

77. Smith v. United States, 542 A.2d 823 (D.C. App. 1988) (when jury reveals its numerical division and judge then gives deadlock instruction, "potential for coercion is great"); People v. Wilson, 390 Mich. 689, 692, 213 N.W.2d 193, 195 (1973) (inquiry ordinarily "carries the improper

suggestion that the state of numerical division reflects the stage of the deliberations. It has the doubly coercive effect of melting the resistance of the minority and freezing the determination of the majority").

78. See State v. Aragon, 89 N.M. 91, 547 P.2d 574 (1976), *cert. denied*, 89 N.M. 206, 549 P.2d 284, and 455 U.S. 845 (1981); People v. Wilson, 390 Mich. 689, 213 N.W.2d 193 (1973).

79. Lowenfield v. Phelps, 484 U.S. 231, 239-240 (1988).

80. Several state courts see nothing inherently wrong in such an inquiry. See State v. Morant. 758 S.W.2d 110 (Mo. Ct. App. 1988); People v. Carter, 68 Cal. 2d 810, 69 Cal. Rptr. 297, 442 P.2d 353 (1968); Griffin v. State, 2 Ark. App. 145, 617 S.W.2d 21 (1981).

81. Lowenfield v. Phelps, 484 U.S. at 240 n.3. See Locks v. Sumner, 703 F.2d 403 (9th Cir.), *cert. denied*, 464 U.S. 933 (1983); United States *ex rel.* Kirk v. Director, Dep't of Corrections, 678 F.2d 723 (7th Cir. 1982); Cornell v. Iowa, 628 F.2d 1044 (8th Cir.), *cert. denied*, 449 U.S. 1126 (1980); Ellis v. Reed, 596 F.2d 1195 (4th Cir.), *cert. denied*, 444 U.S. 973 (1979).

82. Richardson v. State, 508 So. 2d 289 (Ala. Crim. App. 1987); State v. McEntire, 323 S.E.2d 439 (N.C. Ct. App. 1984); People v. Santiago, 108 Ill. App. 3d 787, 64 Ill. Dec. 319, 439 N.E.2d 984 (1982); State v. Roberts, 131 Ariz. 513, 642 P.2d 858 (1982).

83. Santiago, 108 Ill. App. 3d at 787.

84. United States v. Webb, 816 F.2d 1263 (8th Cir. 1987); Smith v. United States, 542 A.2d 823 (D.C. App. 1988); State v. Rickerson, 95 N.M. 666, 625 P.2d 1183, *cert. denied*, 454 U.S. 845 (1981).

85. Jackson v. United States, 368 A.2d 1140 (D.C. App. 1977).

86. Marsh v. Cupp, 536 F.2d 1287 (9th Cir.), *cert. denied*, 429 U.S. 981 (1976).

87. Williams v. United States, 338 F.2d 530 (D.C. Cir. 1964). But see United States v. Rao, 394 F.2d 354 (2d Cir.) (no error where jury volunteered its division but did not indicate which side it favored), *cert. denied*, 393 U.S. 845 (1968); People v. Sheldon, 136 A.D.2d 761, 523 N.Y.S.2d 220 (1988).

It is error for the foreman to reveal the numerical division of the jury. United States v. Jennings, 471 F.2d 1310 (2d Cir.), *cert. denied*, 411 U.S. 935 (1973); Mullin v. United States, 356 F.2d 368 (D.C. Cir. 1966); Smith v. United States, 542 A.2d 823 (D.C. App. 1988).

88. United States v. Sae-Chua, 725 F.2d 530 (9th Cir. 1984); Jackson v. United States, 368 A.2d 1140 (D.C. App. 1977).

89. Jackson, 368 A.2d 1140.

90. *Id.* at 1142.

91. United States v. Akbar, 698 F.2d 378 (9th Cir.), *cert. denied*, 461 U.S. 959 (1983).

92. *Id.* at 380.

93. 484 U.S. 231 (1988).

94. *Id.* at 240. See also Carlton v. United States, 395 F.2d 10 (8th Cir. 1968), *cert. denied*, 393 U.S. 1030 (1969).

95. Lowenfeld, 484 U.S. at 240.

96. *Id.*

97. ABA, note 17 *supra*, § 15-3.7 (judge "should not communicate with a juror or the jury on any aspect of the case itself (as distinguished from matters relating to physical comforts and the like), except after notice to all parties and reasonable opportunity for them to be present"). See also Annotation, "Propriety and Prejudicial Effect, in Federal Criminal Cases, of Communications Between Judge and Jury Members Made in the Absence of Counsel, Regarding the Ability of Jury Members to Continue Deliberations," 64 A.L.R. Fed. 874 (1983); Annotation, "Propriety and Prejudicial Effect, in Federal Civil Cases, of Communications Between Judge and Jury Made Out of Counsel's Presence and After Submission for Deliberations," 32 A.L.R. Fed. 392 (1977).

98. United States v. Ronder, 639 F.2d 931, 934 (2d Cir. 1981).

99. Occasionally, the personal nature of a note may make it appropriate to forgo reading it to the entire jury, and recalling the jury into the courtroom may be unnecessary when the inquiry concerns housekeeping details. *Id.*

100. 250 U.S. 76 (1919).
101. *Id.* at 81.
102. *Id.* at 82.
103. 273 U.S. 583 (1927).
104. *Id.* at 588-589.
105. 422 U.S. 35 (1975).
106. *Id.* at 36.
107. *Id.* at 39.
108. *Id.* at 41.
109. *Id.* at 40.
110. 438 U.S. 422 (1978).
111. *Id.* at 432.
112. *Id.* at 460.
113. *Id.* at 461.
114. *Id.*
115. *Id.*
116. *Id.* at 462.
117. 380 U.S. 445 (1965).
118. *Id.* at 462. The Supreme Court has addressed issues involving ex parte contacts between the trial judge and a juror during the trial in two recent decisions.

In Rushen v. Spain, 464 U.S. 114 (1983), the Court held in a *per curiam* opinion that the judge's private unrecorded meeting with a juror concerning her fear that certain evidence might upset her, even if a constitutional error, was harmless. This "innocuous" meeting did not include discussion of any factual or legal matters pertaining to the case, and the jury's deliberations were not found to have been biased. Although "the right to personal presence at all critical stages of the trial and the right to counsel are fundamental rights of each criminal defendant," the "day-to-day realities of courtroom life" also have to be considered. *Id.* at 117-119. "There is scarcely a lengthy trial in which one or more jurors do not have occasion to speak to the trial judge about something, whether it relates to a matter of personal comfort or to some aspect of the trial." *Id.* at 118. The Court emphasized that ex parte contacts could be of serious concern, and that convictions should be overturned when prejudice is shown.

In United States v. Gagnon, 470 U.S. 522 (1985), the judge held an ex parte meeting with a juror who was concerned about the defendant's sketching her portrait. Defendant's counsel was present at the meeting and did not object. Citing Rushen, the Court, in a per curiam opinion, held that the mere occurrence of an ex parte conversation between judge and juror in the absence of the defendant did not deprive the defendant of any constitutional right. The encounter was a "short interlude in a complex trial" and "was not the sort of event which every defendant had a right personally to attend under the Fifth Amendment." Id. at 527. The Court noted that defendants could have done nothing at the conference, and, indeed, their presence might have been counterproductive. The Court also held that counsel's failure to object to defendants' presence constituted a waiver of defendant's statutory right of presence under Federal Rule of Criminal Procedure 43. Id.

See also United States v. Madrid, 842 F.2d 1090 (9th Cir.), *cert. denied*, 488 U.S. 912 (1988); United States v. Yonn, 702 F.2d 1341 (11th Cir.) *cert. denied*, 464 U.S. 917 (1983); LaChappelle v. Moran, 699 F.2d 560 (1st Cir. 1983); People v. Mullen, 44 N.Y.2d 1, 374 N.E.2d 369, 403 N.Y.S.2d 470 (1978).
119. United States v. Rapp, 871 F.2d 957 (11th Cir.), cert. denied, 110 S. Ct. 233 (1989); People v. France, 436 Mich. 138, 461 N.W.2d 621 (1990).
120. Wallace v. Duckworth, 597 F. Supp. 1,2 (N.D. Ind. 1983); France, 436 Mich. at 139, 461 N.W.2d at 622.
121. Fillippon v. Albion Vein Slate Co., 250 U.S. 76 (1919).

122. Nations v. Sun Oil Co., 695 F.2d 933 (5th Cir.), *cert. denied*, 464 U.S. 893 (1983).
123. South Leasing v. Williams, 778 F.2d 704 (11th Cir.), *cert. denied*, 481 U.S. 1039 (1985).
124. Vogel v. American Warranty Home Serv. Corp., 695 F.2d 877 (5th Cir. 1983).
125. Collins v. State, 191 Ga. App. 289, 381 S.E.2d 430 (1989).
126. Henry v. State, 548 So.2d 570 (Ala. 1989).
127. United States v. Ronder, 639 F.2d 931 (2d Cir. 1981).
128. United States v. Burns, 683 F.2d 1056 (7th Cir.), *cert. denied*, 459 U.S. 1173 (1982).
129. Rhodes v. State, 547 So. 2d 1201 (Fla. 1989).
130. Rogers v. United States, 422 U.S. 35 (1975).
131. Shields v. United States, 273 U.S. 583 (1927); United States v. Ronder, 639 F.2d 931 (2d Cir. 1981); People v. Ciaccio, 47 N.Y.2d 431, 391 N.E.2d 1347. 418 N.Y.S.2d 371 (1979); People v. Payne, 149 A.D.2d 542, 540 N.Y.S.2d 256 (1989).
132. People v. France, 436 Mich. 138, 461 N.W.2d 621 (1990).
133. United States v. U.S. Gypsum Co., 438 U.S. 422 (1978); United States v. Widgery, 778 F.2d 325 (7th Cir. 1985); United States, *ex rel.* SEC v. Billingsley, 766 F.2d 1015 (7th Cir. 1985); Krische v. Smith, 662 F.2d 177 (2d Cir. 1981).
134. Smith v. Kelso, 863 F.2d 1564 (11th Cir.), *cert. denied*, 490 U.S. 1072 (1989); United States v. Blackmon, 839 F.2d 900 (2d Cir. 1988); United States v. Bustamante, 805 F.2d 201 (6th Cir. 1986); United States v. Widgery, 778 F.2d 325 (7th Cir. 1985); Skill v. Martinez, 677 F.2d 368 (3d Cir. 1982); People v. Aveille, 148 A.D.2d 461, 538 N.Y.S.2d 615 (1989); People v. Moran, 123 A.D.2d 646, 507 N.Y.S.2d 24 (1986).
135. United States v. Rapp, 871 F.2d 957 (11th Cir.), *cert. denied*, 110 S. Ct. 233 (1989); United States v. Breedlove, 576 F.2d 57 (5th Cir. 1978); Watson v. State, 728 S.W.2d 109 (Tex. Ct. App. 1987).
136. Compare United States v. Ronder, 639 F.2d 931 (2d Cir. 1981) (verdict reached one-half hour after improper communication) with Krische v. Smith, 662 F.2d 177 (2d Cir. 1981) (verdict reached one hour and twenty minutes after improper communication) and United States v. Rapp, 871 F.2d 957 (11th Cir.) (verdict reached twenty-seven hours after improper communication), *cert. denied*, 110 S. Ct. 233 (1989).
137. United States v. Bascaro, 742 F.2d 1335 (11th Cir. 1984); United States v. Musto, 540 F. Supp. 318 (D.N.J. 1982).
138. People v. Ciaccio, 47 N.Y.2d 431, 391 N.E.2d 1347, 418 N.Y.S.2d 371 (1979); People v. Miller, 149 A.D.2d 439, 539 N.Y.S.2d 782 (1989). See also Parker v. Gladden, 385 U.S. 363 (1966) (court bailiff's improper communication with jury deprived defendant of constitutional right to be tried by impartial jury).
139. Ortiz v. State, 543 So. 2d 377 (Fla. Dist. Ct. App. 1989).
140. State v. Estrada, 69 Haw. 204, 738 P.2d 812 (1987).
141. United States v. Gagnon, 470 U.S. 522, 527 (1985).
142. Karl v. Burlington N.R.R. Co., 880 F.2d 68 (8th Cir. 1989).
143. United States v. Musto, 540 F. Supp. 318, 335 (D.N.J. 1982).
144. United States v. Bascaro, 742 F.2d 1335 (11th Cir. 1984). *In re* Air Crash Disaster, 586 F. Supp. 711, 721 (E.D. Pa. 1984), *rev'd*, 769 F.2d 115 (1985), *cert. denied*, 488 U.S. 994 (1988); Watson v. State, 728 S.W.2d 109 (Tex. Ct. App. 1987).
145. United States v. Gagnon, 470 U.S. 529. This situation assumes that the conference involves a material part of the trial at which defendant's presence would be meaningful. People v. Mullen, 44 N.Y.2d 1, 374 N.E.2d 369, 403 N.Y.S.2d 470 (1978) (defendant's absence from informal questioning of juror in judge's chambers for possible disqualification not violative of defendant's right to be present).
146. People v. Mehmedi, 69 N.Y.2d 759, 505 N.E.2d 610, 513 N.Y.S.2d 100 (1987).

14

Time, TV, and Criminal Justice: Second Thoughts on the Simpson Trial

Samuel H. Pillsbury*

The O.J. Simpson murder trial tested many faiths. In a nation already skeptical about its criminal justice system, the case led some to question a basic legal institution—the unanimous citizen jury—and prompted others to doubt the possibility of justice in a multiracial society. But the most immediate effect of the case has been to raise questions about televising criminal proceedings.[1]

Following the Simpson verdict, judge after judge across the nation barred cameras from the trials of well-publicized cases, fearing that television would obstruct the pursuit of justice.[2] In California the legislature and the judiciary have considered a variety of restrictions on televised proceedings, including a complete ban.[3] Reviews of camera rules are underway in many other jurisdictions.[4]

Following years of laudatory studies on cameras-in-the-court experiments, in a nation with an unparalleled tradition of free press and open government, the recent surge in anti-camera sentiment represents a striking change of opinion.[5] One might ask why. What was it about the Simpson case that prompted this sudden antipathy toward the dominant media of our age? Why in a time of public skepticism about the legal system, do so many believe that restricting courtroom access will improve public confidence? Most important, is there any principled, practical way to reconcile the apparently conflicting needs of broad public access and criminal justice?

The issue of cameras in the courtroom is at bottom an issue of modernity. How much can—how much should—the legal system change to accommodate modern times? Should the legal system alter its media rules in order to restore a measure of public accessibility lost over the last century because of changes in demographics, the economy, and the legal process? How much should the legal system consider the effect of access rules on legal journalism? How much should the normally insular, deliberative processes of the legal system accommodate the public's desire for quick, open decision making? These questions have been asked

Reprinted by permission of West Group from the *Criminal Law Bulletin,* vol. 33 (1997), pp. 3–28.

for a long time, but they have taken on new urgency in the wake of the O.J. Simpson murder trial.

JOINING THE CIRCUS

On a hot July morning two years ago I drove to downtown Los Angeles to do commentary for Court TV on the Simpson preliminary hearing. As a former newspaper reporter and federal prosecutor, I had witnessed media scenes before. This was different.

The entrance to the Criminal Courts Building was mobbed with media, interested bystanders, and trial lawyers arriving for work. A long line of prospective jurors, who had been called for other cases, lined up around the block, awaiting security checks to enter the building. I pushed my way to the back of the building where the patio had been transformed into a makeshift, outdoor television studio. Lights and cameras stood pointed at anchors and commentators who perched precariously on the patio's balcony. The whole scene overlooked a parking lot filled with trailers and satellite trucks for national and international media. The Court TV trailer stood next to that of ESPN, not far from that of the E! Entertainment Network. Soon the thunder of helicopters overhead signalled the approach of O.J. Simpson's van from the jail. The helicopters belonged to the local television stations, each of which wanted to broadcast live shots of Simpson's short journey from jail to courthouse.

Later the media scene—Camp OJ as it became known—moved to the parking lot of the former state courthouse across the street. Two- and three-story structures of metal scaffolding rose above the trailers and trucks to create stages for reporters and anchors so they could be photographed with the Criminal Courts Building in the background. At street level, entrepreneurs sold buttons, t-shirts, and other trial paraphernalia. Every day the defense team entered and exited in a flurry of celebrity worship, with pictures, waves, sound bites and sometimes handshakes and autographs.

The scene at the courthouse represented but the tip of the cultural iceberg. In the media the case grew to unprecedented proportions, pushing stories of wars and international peace agreements off the air or to the back pages.[6] Journalists repeatedly referred to it as the "trial of the century"; on the eve of the trial, writer Dominick Dunne dubbed it the "Superbowl of murder trials." Meanwhile the public consumed it all and came back asking for more. Shows about O.J. earned higher ratings; magazines and newspapers that trumpeted O.J. stories sold more copies. From the preliminary hearing to the verdict, the Simpson trial dominated much casual conversion in the United States and was discussed throughout the world.[7] The case took the cult of celebrity to new heights.[8]

I started the case excited to be involved and a true believer in full television access to the courtroom. I finished with mixed feelings. On the one hand the reporters and anchors with whom I worked at Court TV were thoroughly professional: always well prepared and careful to avoid sensationalism.[9] The questions put to me were usually intelligent and insightful. On the other hand, the format of live coverage created its own limitations and emphasis. I often had to speak spontaneously about what occurred, or was going to occur in the courtroom, based on minimal information. Inevitably much of the on-camera discussion concerned strategy and inevitably much constituted second-guessing of the lawyers and judge. I was, after all, a kind of color commentator. As much as I tried to relate the case to the criminal justice system as a whole, as much as I tried to give historical perspective, the presentness of the case proved overwhelming. What counted was the issue in the courtroom, now.

I sensed a similar ambivalence in the journalists who covered the case—a pride in their professionalism, but also a disquiet about the phenomenon that was "OJ." Most of the actual trial coverage was sober-minded, careful, and informative. As a group, the reporters assigned to primary coverage were far better informed on both the facts and the law than such reporters are in most criminal cases. Nevertheless even veteran journalists were troubled by the dimensions of the coverage, by the media desperation to feed the public's hunger for information, or even speculation, about the trial. There was a sense that the case had become a cultural juggernaut, a natural force that no individual, and perhaps no institution could resist.

THE SPOTLIGHT EFFECT

In one sense, the media circus that surrounded the Simpson case is irrelevant to the question of cameras in court. Only if the circus was caused by the courtroom camera and only if it affected the in-court proceedings do we have reason to limit electronic coverage. Given Simpson's celebrity status and the sensational nature of the crime, we would certainty have had a media circus without cameras in the courtroom. Camera exclusion probably would have made the scene outside the courthouse even wilder. But the daily, up-to-the-minute, direct-from-the-courtroom coverage probably contributed to the public's mania about the case. Assuming such an effect on the public, did the broadcasts affect the chances of obtaining a just result in the Simpson case? This question remains difficult to answer, because it requires us to judge the nature and importance of a variety of interrelated factors, in a unique case. We cannot hope for a definitive answer, but we must do our analytic best, for the issues are too important to ignore.

Every case that attracts significant public attention has a dynamic that distinguishes it from the general run of criminal cases. Media interest in any case creates what may be called the spotlight effect. Media attention casts a bright public light on witnesses, jurors, lawyers, and judge, turning them into public figures at least for a while. In most cases the spotlight effect is small and probably beneficent. Like children who behave better in public than at home, those participating in a trial will generally become more conscientious when they become aware of public interest in the case. Thus a modest degree of media attention in a case may well improve the justice process.[10]

The spotlight effect in a case like Simpson is an entirely different thing. The live television camera picked out courtroom participants from their previously ordinary existence and spotlighted them for global celebrity. Live broadcasts of the Simpson case converted a small downtown courtroom into an amphitheater of unimaginable proportions, with all the participants projected to giant size, like rock stars on the screen at a concert. The lead lawyers became celebrities, commanding large lecture fees, winning television talk show appearances and million-dollar book and movie contracts. Several of the witnesses—Kato Kaelin and Rosa Lopez—even became internationally famous (or infamous) as a result of their appearance in Judge Ito's courtroom.

Most in the legal system have focused on the camera's effect on lay participants—witnesses and jurors. Many have worried that in-court cameras will make witnesses more reluctant to come forward and less candid when they do.[11] By inducing dreams of celebrity riches, it may affect the judgment and behavior of jurors. There is evidence that all these things occurred in the Simpson case, but again it is hard to link the effect to the in-court camera. The most serious instances of media-interference were probably the large-sum payments by tabloids to several potential prosecution witnesses, and the publication of a book by a potential witness.[12] However, none of these events were tied to in-court television.[13]

In general we worry less about the spotlight effect on the professional participants in a trial—the police, lawyers, and judge—but the problem may be even greater here than with nonprofessionals. Many have complained that during this highest of high-profile trials, lawyers on both sides played to the camera, making the proceedings longer and more rancorous than necessary. I'm sure this happened. How else do we explain arguments on procedural motions made outside the presence of the jury that turned into heated rhetorical exchanges between the lawyers, complete with rival slogans?[14] But this problem has a remedy. Whatever attorney dramatics the camera inspired in the Simpson case could have been curbed by a less-tolerant judge.[15] The more serious concern is that the super-bright spotlight of the in-court camera might affect the professional judgment of the lawyers involved.

We like to think that the law stands above, or at least apart from media depictions and all the vagaries of public opinion, but in real life the people who make the law, lawyers and judges, care a great deal about their public reputations. They read newspapers and watch television like everyone else, and like everyone else they care about what is said about them in print and on the screen.[16] Indeed, trial lawyers and trial judges may care more about public opinion than most; the chance to impress a public audience represents one of the biggest thrills of trial work.

We all swim in a sea of public opinion. To believe that judges, lawyers, or police involved in the legal process can stay above and apart from the vicissitudes of public opinion in a case as high-profile as Simpson is to disregard human nature. In a case like this, the spotlight effect can be enormous.[17]

None of this tells us very much about the effect of in-court television, though. The most important effects will likely remain hidden from public view. No judge, for example, will likely admit that he or she changed a ruling for fear of how the alternative would play on the evening news. No lawyer will concede that he modified an argument to please the viewing public. There is one way, however, that we can track in-court television's impact on the legal process. We can analyze its effect on legal journalism.

Judging in-court television by its impact on out-of-court journalism may seem a strange way to approach the issue. Our main concern remains safeguarding justice in the courtroom and our main threat would seem to come from journalists. Yet journalists represent both problem and solution. Legal journalism will always play a critical role in shaping public perceptions of any given case, and those perceptions will always have a great potential for influencing in-court events. Simply put, what affects legal journalism also affects criminal justice.

LIVE BROADCASTS AND THE NEWS ECONOMY

The live television broadcasts in the O.J. Simpson case simultaneously boosted public interest in the case and deprived traditional legal journalism of its main work, providing a simple, coherent narrative account of the trial. Live broadcasts fundamentally recast the news economy by making Simpson the overwhelming priority for all major media outlets and by forcing most of those outlets to go outside the courtroom to satisfy the demand for Simpson news.

News is the currency of the journalistic economy. News outlets must constantly find fresh stories to sell their audiences. When the stories concern a legal case, they usually come straight from the courtroom. Television, radio, and print reporters covering a trial normally present the important events in the courtroom since the last story or news cycle. When a significant portion of the public views the trial live on television, however, a simple report of courtroom events will not suffice. Live television thus creates competitive pressure for other kinds of stories: for stories about events outside the courtroom, and new angles on courtroom events.[18] Live broadcasts also create competition in quantity.[19] With so much material going out over the airwaves live, other media feel compelled to produce proportionately large stories of their own.

The *Los Angeles Times* coverage may illustrate this phenomenon. The paper gave the trial unprecedented space, usually playing the trial story on the front page and often including an entire page or more of coverage within. Featured prominently in the stories, sidebars and in a separate column know as "The Notepad," were the comments of a host of "legal experts" on the day's developments in the trial. The paper assigned its veteran City Hall reporter, Bill Boyarsky, to write a column entitled "The Spin," in which he covered the way the lawyers and others tried to "spin" their accounts to the jury and the public. The paper's coverage featured a large amount of strategic analysis, examining the way the prosecution and defense were trying to present their cases and how Judge Ito was trying to maintain control of the courtroom.

Perhaps the most obvious journalistic product of live broadcasts was the expert legal commentator. The academic or trial lawyer who could provide instant analysis and commentary became a staple not only of live TV coverage, but of local news hours, late night talk shows, tabloid shows and, as the *L.A. Times* coverage illustrates, print reportage as well. The legal commentator became a hot item in the new journalistic economy, supplying credibility and a new angle (or at least the appearance of a new angle) for extremely low cost, more often than not for free.[20]

The need for fresh stories in addition to straight courtroom reporting made coverage of the Simpson trial more like political or sports reporting than standard legal journalism.[21] Like political reporting, much of the coverage was cynical and strategic, reporters emphasizing who was ahead and who was behind, who was successfully manipulating the judge, the jurors, or the law.[22] As often happens in contemporary political reporting, the competitive aspects of journalism frequently overwhelmed the substantive issues. Guilt or innocence seemed less important than legal gamesmanship. As in sports reporting, journalists and their commentators often promoted the drama played out every day in the case. This was no ordinary case, this was the "trial of the century." When the case took an unexpected turn, it was always "extraordinary," "unprecedented," "incredible," or just "unbelievable."[23]

Meanwhile the tabloid enterprises, both print and electronic, pounded at the Simpson story by chasing everyone even tangentially involved, on occasion producing scoops that the rest of the media then chased. The talk shows sought guests with a relationship, close or otherwise, to the case. The frequent result of this journalistic fervor was a surrealistic Mobius strip whereby yesterday's out-of-court story—what someone said on Nightline—became today's in-court controversy. Journalists and news-makers constantly shifted places.

But how much can we blame all this on live television? The trial would have attracted sensationalized coverage anyway. Once more we cannot be certain, but the dynamics of the coverage suggest that live coverage made a real difference in the quantity, intensity, and style of case coverage. Listen to the words of a "leading network news executive" about the network's coverage of the Simpson criminal trial, which was televised, and the depositions in the Simpson civil case, which were not:

> All through our coverage of the Simpson trial, we wrestled on a daily basis with the question of whether we were doing the right thing? Was our coverage being driven by a tabloid sensibility?
>
> We never answered that question to anyone's satisfaction and I think everyone's glad to have the pressure off and get back to business as usual. . . . And without television inside the deposition on a daily basis, there's no magnetic pull to keep us focused on this event as opposed to all the others vying for our attention.[24]

THE TIME DIMENSION

Much of the legal system's resistance to cameras in the courtroom has a curmudgeonly, even reactionary, quality to it. We hear judges say, in effect: "Maybe we're old-fashioned, but the courtroom is an old-fashioned place. Television and other newfangled media have no place here." In a nation that normally views new technology as the source of salvation, this argument sounds hollow. Yet, slightly reconstituted, it expresses the central challenge presented by television coverage.

The courtroom *is* an old-fashioned place in the sense that it operates at a slower pace than most of our frenetic world. Justice requires patience, often a great deal of patience. By contrast live television is the most impatient of media, demanding constant action to satisfy a fickle audience. Television programmers live in terror of the viewer's remote control.

It's not that live television rushed the proceedings in the Simpson case. Actually the proceedings dragged on too long even according to the patient norms of the law. The important effect was indirect. Live television created a daily public fervor about the case that infected and perhaps corrupted the deliberative process in the case.

In television, the word "live" is magical. The history of television news may be told in significant measure by episodes of live reporting—from President Kennedy's assassination to the first landing on the moon, to Watergate and Iran-Contra, the Gulf War, and the Clarence Thomas confirmation hearings. Live television events of this magnitude create Marshall McLuhan's global village, where the audience experiences important events together, though physically apart.[25] In an effort to create this magical experience, news broadcasts tout the fact that a report comes "live from the scene" whenever possible. The fact that live reports are more likely to be jumbled and misleading matters little; they're exciting.

Live television reporting represents the latest example of journalism's never-ending search for the new. All journalists work in a highly perishable present. All strive to witness and then convey those electrifying moments when we feel entirely engaged. Yesterday and tomorrow count only as they affect today. Live television simply takes this drive to a new level. With live television, what counts as "new" may be a matter of minutes or seconds, not hours or days.

The law operates in a different time dimension. Justice requires deliberation; it takes time. Lawyers and judges need time to prepare for hearings and trials, time to consider the issues, time to debate, time to cool off and reconsider. The law puts no time limits on jury deliberations. We expect that appellate courts will produce opinions in a matter of months rather than days and that their holdings and reasoning will remain valid for years to come. We recognize that the wheels of justice may grind slowly in order to grind true. And while justice delayed may be justice denied, justice does not respect deadlines.

Sometimes the time differences between law and journalism are obvious. While trials produce daily news, the trials themselves often last weeks or months.[26] A frequently cited example in the Simpson case of the time gap between journalism and law was the much-hyped cross-examination of Detective Mark Fuhrman by famed defense attorney F. Lee Bailey. At the time the confrontation seemed to be won by the detective, who maintained his calm while the attorney blustered. Nevertheless Bailey pushed Fuhrman to make the surprising claim—given his personal history—that in the last ten years he had never uttered a certain racial epithet. This contention gave the defense team an opportunity at impeachment that led to the hidden treasure of the Fuhrman tapes.[27]

Live broadcasts of trials exacerbate the impatience of the media and the public, putting additional pressures on participants. How many trial lawyers, knowing their careers depend significantly on their public reputations, can put aside a day's bad reviews, knowing that the longer-term goal is more important?[28] How many judges can do the same, day after day?

But the real problem with live television in high-profile trials is simply that it works too well as drama. It *is* exciting. With its real life what's-going-to-happen-next suspense, its treatment of serious issues along with petty squabbles among the lawyers, and its many personal dramas, live coverage of criminal trials can bring entertainment-size crowds to the courthouse. At least in a case like Simpson, live television creates a mass interest that places huge and often unpredictable pressures on all participants in the legal process. The virtual presence of not hundreds or thousands, but millions and even hundreds of millions of interested spectators, constitutes an unprecedented challenge to the independence of the legal process. The time difference between live television and other media may only be a matter of degree, but it is an important matter.

VALUE OF BROAD ACCESS

The Simpson case suggests that cameras in the courtroom can create serious problems for the law. Why not just ban the camera and be done with it? Why make this odd distinction between live and other television broadcasts? The reason lies in the other half of the cameras-in-the-courtroom equation, not the problems caused by the cameras, but the benefits generated. We need to recall why public access to the courtroom has always been central to American criminal justice.

The Simpson case notwithstanding, the public probably sees less of its criminal courts today than at any time in the nation's past. In the early days of the republic, criminal courts provided entertainment for many in the community, and significant portions of the public attended high-profile trials.[29] Today's criminal courtrooms tend to be physically smaller than those of the past and are located further from the workplace.[30] Modern work patterns make court attendance more difficult. In an agricultural society, many might attend court on market day, or by rearranging their labor schedule, but in a nation where most work for others according to a fixed schedule, opportunities to view trials in person are rare. Finally, criminal trials take much longer than they once did. An observer cannot hope to see a significant trial complete in one day or two as was the norm in the early nineteenth century. Today major trials last two to four weeks, with many going on much longer.

Some will question the significance of this change in access. After all, the great majority of courtrooms remain open to the casual passerby and we have a vigorous press to report on important legal events. I think it matters a great deal.

Americans' traditional distrust of government has grown in recent years. A disturbing number believe the legal system is fundamentally corrupt. Such distrust makes it difficult to find conscientious and reliable jurors. Thus, distrust inspires extreme legislative changes that wreak havoc on the criminal justice system.[31] Perhaps most important, the power of law lies primarily in its moral authority, an authority severely diminished by public distrust.

What is the legal system to do about this crisis in public confidence? How can judges and lawyers persuade the public of the basic integrity of criminal justice? Increasing public access to the system represents one of the simplest and cheapest means of reaching a skeptical public. By itself, access will not prove sufficient, though. The public, after all, has many good reasons for believing our criminal justice system to be deeply flawed. But increased access represents a vital corrective to the belief that the legal system is an anti-public conspiracy operated by an elite group, lawyers and judges.

Public access also operates as an important corrective to the legal system's natural tendency to insularity. Lawyers speak a language and follow a set of customs that set them apart from fellow citizens. Even when lawyers and courts consciously work in the public interest, that interest tends to be defined in lawyerly ways. Courts and lawyers set their own timetables and priorities according to the values of the legal profession. Public access will permit direct critique of the legal structure. The public must see the system in action in order to challenge the basic assumptions of the legal community.[32]

Public access to the courtroom is a fundamental good. We should provide maximum access consistent with the demands of justice. Access should be limited only as needed to address the particular, demonstrated problems created by nontraditional media, that is, live television broadcasts, in very high-profile cases.

THE PROPOSAL

Criminal courtrooms should be presumptively open to all media that can be physically accommodated, with the lone exception of live television broadcasts. In the great majority of cases, live broadcasts should present no serious problem. Trial courts though should have the discretion to impose special rules on broadcasts if the danger of an extreme spotlight effect looms. Under such circumstances, live broadcasts might be barred, but cameras should still be permitted to tape proceedings for later broadcast. The broadcast delay might be as short as four to six hours or as much as twenty-four hours. Even modest delays should significantly reduce the special pressures on the system exerted by live television in high-profile trials.

The question of how much delay is a difficult one, another question of degree in this matter of degrees. The delay should be long enough to prevent the camera from dominating the public's view of the proceedings; in other words, long enough to dissipate the special power of live television. Twenty-four hours should be the maximum delay allowed, for by this time the basic story of the day in court will be widely disseminated by other media and the video broadcast would no longer dominate coverage. A longer delay would unnecessarily destroy the remaining news value of the courtroom video. The aim of the broadcast delay is not to relegate courtroom video to the historical archives, but to change its news role, from provider of suspense to provider of context.

The mechanics of the video delay should prove manageable. As with previous electronic coverage, electronic media would have to make special arrangements with the court. Media representatives would have to prove to the trial judge that no-cost, unobtrusive equipment could be installed and that the tape of proceedings would remain in the control of the court until the delay period ends. At the end of the delay period the court would release the tape for media duplication. None of this would be unprecedented in the media world.[33]

A delay order should be very much the exception. The vast majority of live broadcasts of criminal cases made to date have not generated the problems seen in the Simpson case. Only when there is a high-profile case of this dimension, when the public becomes obsessed with courtroom events, do we have the preconditions for a delay ruling.

Nor do the special problems of live television in certain high-profile cases extend to coverage by other nontraditional media. We have no experience of major problems with live radio or with still cameras. Given our commitment to broad access and lacking proof of a problem, these media should be given broad access to the courtroom. Photographers with modern cameras and film can work as quietly and unobtrusively as courtroom sketch artists. That photography may be more revealing of the participants should not argue against it.[34] And while we can imagine that live radio broadcasts might cause pressures similar to those of television, in this visually dominant age, they will be of a lesser degree.

IMPACT OF THE PROPOSAL

Although the proposed rule would give courts a new tool in regulating access, the proposal would, overall, dramatically increase public access to the courtroom. At present courts effectively bar all electronic media from all criminal trials of major public interest.[35] Horrified by the Simpson experience, and without clear authority to allow the approach advocated here, courts have chosen to close the doors to video cameras. The proposal, with its presumption of electronic access, would make the nation's criminal courts a far more familiar place to the average citizen than they are today.

In terms of audience size, however, the delay rule would reduce public access from the levels achieved during the Simpson case. We would no longer have tens or even hundreds of millions watching a single courtroom proceeding.[36] For those who believe access is a good determined according to quantity, this audience reduction will count as a strong negative. If the point of courtroom access is to foster greater understanding of the legal system, though, we should be satisfied with a procedure that, in effect, limits numbers but improves comprehension.

Make no mistake here: The broadcast delay will work largely *because* it reduces audience size. For true believers in political and marketplace democracy this is heresy. But justice depends on different principles than do partisan politics or media competition. As judges frequently remind us: The court system is not in the entertainment business.[37] When it comes to courtroom access, we should not mourn too much the loss of the Monday Night Football and "As the World Turns" audiences.[38] If the courts can improve overall public access and safeguard the deliberative process through modest limitations on nontraditional media, we all have reason to celebrate.

The broadcast delay would create a new opportunity for in-depth coverage of the legal system. The delay requirement would reduce the tension between the time dimensions of broadcasting and justice, and permit a kind of legal reporting rarely seen in television today. In the news economy the delayed broadcast would have two selling points: (1) direct visual and aural access to the courtroom and (2) context. Television would have to attempt what the print media has done to compete with electronics: concentrate on the long-term story. Television producers would have the opportunity to edit the broadcasts, not just for the ten-second clip, but for the five-minute clip. Viewers could see a witness's testimony whole, not broken up by objections and other delays. Meanwhile legal commentators could provide background and further context. Instead of incessant questioning about "Who's winning now" or,

"What happens next," television commentators might answer questions such as, "How does this all fit together?"

The proposal should not be oversold. As with any form of video, tapes of legal proceedings may be edited to give a superficial and misleading presentation of events. A heated exchange between lawyers and the court over a minor issue may be preferred to critical scientific testimony on grounds of drama. Testimony may be presented out of sequence and out of context. Arguments and rulings may be distorted. In short, the proposal does nothing to cure the standard ills of bad journalism. But then bad journalism was not the problem we set out to address.[39]

CONSTITUTIONALITY

Much of the discussion so far will strike lawyers as constitutionally suspect. Surely the First Amendment prevents the government from deliberately manipulating the media this way, prevents it from privileging one form of expression over another in order to influence the nature of coverage. The delay itself sounds like a prior restraint on publication, usually a core violation of the First Amendment.[40] Here appearances deceive. The U.S. Supreme Court has carved out a wide space for judicial and other government regulation of electronic access to the courtroom. The proposal, with its restriction closely tailored to the well-recognized problems of courtroom video broadcasts, should pass constitutional muster.

The Supreme Court has held that the press and public share a First Amendment right of access to criminal trials.[41] The press component of the right may be fulfilled by nonelectronic access, however; the First Amendment contains no mandate for cameras in the courtroom.[42] The Court's view of the camera issue has been permissive: The federal Constitution allows states to invite or to bar cameras in state courtrooms.[43] The Court's pronouncements suggest that electronic access is a matter largely committed to state courts and legislatures. Yet constitutional concerns remain.

Much rests on how the problem is categorized. Does the delay rule trigger some form of heightened scrutiny, or must it pass some lesser test? We begin with the possibility that it constitutes a prior restraint, a category of conduct subject to the most searching judicial scrutiny.[44] Although the delay acts as a temporary restraint on a form of publication, prior restraint doctrine should not apply. The rule does not restrict publication generally as does a prior restraint order.[45] Even under the delay rule all media outlets, including television, remain free to report on courtroom events without restriction. Instead the broadcast delay distinguishes one form of publication—television broadcast—from others, based on the impact that publication has on the state's critical interest in just and efficient courtroom procedures.

Under the Court's permissive approach, the delay rule may well be deemed a time, place, or manner regulation, subject to lesser scrutiny.[46] One circuit court has held that restrictions of television access to the criminal courtroom should be judged by whether they "promote significant government interests" and do not "unwarrantedly abridge . . . the opportunities for the communication of thought."[47] There can be little doubt that the government's interest in fair and efficient criminal adjudication is significant. Nor would there seem to be a serious problem with unwarranted abridgment of communication, for the proposed scheme would actually increase the amount of electronic access to the courts.[48]

The most serious constitutional questions concerning the proposal involve the potential for discrimination in implementation of the delay rule. In cases arising outside the courtroom context, the Supreme Court has struck down government restrictions on access to nontraditional speech forums when there is evidence of discrimination or excessive discretion in the restriction process.[49] The most serious discrimination problems come with viewpoint discrimination—where the government's action favors or disfavors a particular set of ideas—or discrimination between journalistic outlets. These concerns suggest some important limitations on courts ordering a broadcast delay. If a delay rule is to be constitutional, it must be uniformly applied throughout a case. All electronic outlets must have equal access to the courtroom.[50] Nor should the delay rule vary from the start of a case to its end in order to preclude a claim of advantaging one side, or one viewpoint.[51]

But what of the idea that in deciding on a delay restriction, courts rule on the anticipated content of courtroom communication, that courts are in effect given discretionary, editorial powers? After all, only cases that touch a public nerve, that arouse public interests and passions, should be subject to the delay rule. To determine the effect on the public, courts must look at least in part to the communicative content of the trial. This sounds like a violation of the separation that the First Amendment attempts to erect between media and government. To put this more concretely, we can certainly imagine a case where the court might be asked to engage in a form of communication limitation in order to further state interests. For example, a police corruption and beating trial might present testimony the government would like to soft-pedal. In this case the government might argue that the public outrage generated by the trial testimony supports a broadcast delay; thus the government's interest in avoiding embarrassment and criticism would be consonant with the reasons for electronic access restriction.[52]

We could solve the discrimination problem, of course, by eliminating all discretion. Simply make all courtroom television broadcasts subject to the same delay period. This would avoid discrimination, but at a high cost. In the vast majority of televised cases the delay would be unnecessary. The public would suffer a significant diminution in access for a limited benefit of eliminating discrimination in the implementation of the delay rule.

To gain a better perspective on the discrimination problem, and assess the proposal more broadly, we should compare the proposal with the current all-or-nothing schemes (live television or no television) that also depend on trial court discretion. In terms of access to the courtroom, the proposal represents a major improvement. More Americans would see more of the legal system under the proposal than they do under the all-or-nothing plans now in force in most jurisdictions. In terms of discrimination possibilities, the danger from the proposal is far less than with current schemes, which usually offer virtually absolute discretion to the trial court. Under the proposal, discretion is limited to whether there should be a delay and to the length of the delay, up to twenty-four hours. By contrast, current schemes usually present a sufficiently broad range of factors to consider, that trial courts have the power to bar television cameras from any case, even when the real reason is to prevent embarrassment to the judicial system. Finally, the proposal takes seriously the justice costs of electronic access to the criminal courtroom. It represents a major improvement in every way.

RETHINKING THE DEBATE: DEFINING THE PUBLIC INTEREST

Having set out the merits and legality of the proposal, I must confess a certain pessimism about its chances for adoption. Regardless of its virtues, the proposal lacks an ingredient vital to successful reform: the support of the politically powerful. In the debate over cameras in the court, we find a struggle between two political heavyweights: the courts and the media. Neither group is likely to endorse the proposal. Judges will dislike the presumption of openness; the media will dislike the idea of courts exercising control over the timing of any publication. The true public interest in courtroom access may be lost in the conflict of two powerful public institutions.

For two groups so frequently at odds, the judiciary and the media share some striking characteristics. Each enjoys a wide degree of independence within its sphere of operation based on long tradition and constitutional law. Each subscribes to a distinctive, deeply held view of the public trust in whose name the institution acts. Each wields a great deal of direct power and indirect influence over a wide variety of public and private matters. Each, when challenged, fiercely defends its independence, ideals, and influence. We see all of these traits displayed in the cameras-in-court debate.

In the months since the Simpson verdict, the discussion about in-court cameras has followed a predictable pattern, with courts and media staking rival claims to represent the public interest. The media has spoken loudest, arguing that free access is a good in and of itself, a vital part of open, democratic government.[53] Media defenders tend to dismiss the Simpson case as aberrational, and largely the fault of a too-lenient Judge Ito. The media did not lose control; the lawyers did.[54]

Meanwhile the judiciary speaks softly but carries a big gavel, closing courtrooms to cameras in the name of dignity and due process. Many judges across the nation point with horror to the Simpson case and say, "See what happens when you let in cameras." Those who favor cameras in the courtroom usually condition that support on virtually unlimited judicial discretion: Trial judges must have complete control of electronic access.

Few participants in this debate acknowledge any self-interest in the outcome, though self-interest lies just below the surface, the tidal force beneath the rhetorical white caps. For the television news media, access to the courtroom involves ratings; for the judiciary, television access involves a serious question of turf control and public prestige. Not surprisingly, both tend to see the public's interest as consistent with their own.

An example of the way the media-judiciary conflict may distort the real public interest in electronic access came in California with the post-Simpson reexamination of the issue by the state's Judicial Council.[55] After holding several hearings and collecting material from many journalists, judges, and lawyers, a subcommittee of the Council recommended that cameras be barred from all pretrial proceedings in criminal cases. From the judicial point of view the merits of this change appear substantial. Perhaps most important, prospective jurors are less likely to hear of evidence that will be excluded at trial. Meanwhile trials could be televised, subject to trial court discretion.[56]

Media reaction to the proposed pretrial ban was critical, but muted.[57] Steven Brill, founder of Court TV and vocal media proponent of broad television access, noted that the proposal would not impede his network's operations significantly because it rarely shows pretrial proceedings.[58] Nor was there any great outcry from other media outlets. Self-interest provides a ready explanation: Trials can be great television shows; by contrast, pretrial proceedings usually lack drama.

In terms of public understanding of the system, though, access to pretrial proceedings is much more important than trial access. Most criminal cases end with a guilty plea, not a trial verdict. Most critical judicial decisions in criminal cases, such as whether a motion to suppress evidence should be granted, occur pretrial. As a result, the public needs electronic access to pretrial proceedings far more than it does access to trials. Fortunately, when the Judicial Council made its final recommendation on the issue, the complete pretrial ban was eliminated, in favor of a multi-factor approach that gives trial courts a great deal of leeway in deciding whether to permit cameras at either pretrial or trial proceedings.[59]

The media-versus-judiciary conflict has also led to a certain inflexibility in the debate. Both sides tend to view the access issue in absolute terms—either cameras are allowed or not—instead of considering various intermediate positions. Accustomed to First Amendment absolutism, few in the media have seriously considered the need for restrictions on electronic access. Meanwhile the judiciary engages in turf wars, seeking protection from legislative and media interference with rules giving trial courts nearly complete discretion. We can do better than this.

CONCLUSION

The Simpson case did not go well for many different reasons. Live television was one of them. The Simpson case showed that, at least with a celebrity trial, live television has the power to seriously threaten the deliberative processes of the law. It can bring forces to bear on legal institutions and individuals that neither can reliably withstand.

But for all its problems, the camera also presents the legal system with a major opportunity to improve access to the courts and confidence in the law. Whether we realize this opportunity depends on our confidence in handling change. Does the legal system have the confidence to contemplate increasing electronic access in the face of the Simpson experience? Will the media and its advocates be willing to set aside traditional views and consider a different way of approaching the issue?

Perhaps because ours is a time of great change, we approach it with great anxiety. Fearful of losing hard-won gains, we pit tradition against innovation. But sometimes the only effective defense of the old is by the new. The best defense of traditional criminal justice values in America may be in the judicious use of electronic technology. The video camera gives us a chance to return to the time when virtually all Americans could witness the legal process in important criminal cases. To realize this opportunity, the halting efforts made by many legislatures and courts during the last two decades to open courtrooms to the viewing public should be expanded. We need only to ask television broadcasters, in a few cases, to take a little more time.

NOTES

*My thanks to colleagues David Burcham, Gary Williams and Chris May for their assistance, especially on matters constitutional, and Karen Cox, my research assistant, for her help.

I come to this issue with some personal baggage, having received my first education in law as a newspaper reporter covering criminal courts in a state, Florida, that was conducting one of the early cameras-in-the-courtroom experiments. More recently I served as an occasional television commentator during the Simpson case.

1. See Phil Kloer, "The Simpson Verdict: The Impact: Backlash Against Cameras In Court Feared," Atlanta Constitution, Oct. 4, 1995; Stephen Labaton, "Lessons of Simpson Case Are Reshaping the Law," NY Times, Oct. 6, 1995, at A1; Lyle Denniston, "Camera's Eye On Blind Justice; Simpson Trial Spells Trouble for Cause of TV Coverage in Court," Sun (Baltimore), Oct. 1, 1995. See also S.L. Alexander, "The Impact of *California v. Simpson* on Cameras in the Courtroom," 79 Judicature 169 (1996).
2. Charley Roberts, "Simpson Leads to Rethinking Of Cameras in Courtrooms," LA Daily J., Nov. 8, 1995, at 1, citing refusals to permit cameras in the trial of Richard Allen Davis for the kidnapping and murder of 12-year-old Polly Klaas, the murder retrial of Erik and Lyle Menendez (whose first trial was shown on Court-TV), the murder trial of rap star Snoop Doggy Dogg, the trial of the Texas woman charged with killing singer Selena, and the South Carolina murder trial of Susan Smith, among others.
3. See infra notes 48-51 and accompanying text.
4. For example, Massachusetts. Carolyn Ryan, "Lawmakers Propose Ban on TV Coverage of Trials," Patriot Ledger, Nov. 1, 1995. For an overview of various jurisdictional approaches and the impact of the Simpson case, see Alexander, "The Impact of *California v. Simpson*," supra note 1.

The trend toward camera restriction should not be exaggerated, however. Indeed, it may be temporary phenomenon. A legislative proposal to ban cameras in California's courts was easily defeated in the State Assembly this spring. Associated Press, "Assembly Rejects Proposed Curbs on Cameras in Court," Apr. 26, 1996. See also infra note 51. The U.S. Judicial Conference has decided to let each federal circuit decide for itself whether to permit television coverage. This represents a loosening of its previous position, which banned all television coverage. Charges Finnie, "Circuits to Set Own Rules on Camera Bans," LA Daily J., Mar. 13, 1996, at 1. The Ninth Circuit has decided to allow some television coverage of oral arguments of civil appeals, habeas corpus, and death penalty appeals but not direct criminal appeals. All television coverage at the trial level remains prohibited. Philip Carrizosa, "9th Circuit to Allow Cameras Back Into Courtroom for Oral Arguments," LA Daily J., Mar. 25, 1996, at 3. Meanwhile a variety of courts across the country have permitted television coverage of less high-profile cases. John North, "Cameras Permitted During Huskey Trial; Judge Says No to Attorney's Request," Knoxville News-Sentinel, May 8, 1996; Deborah Pines, "T.V. Cameras Allowed in U.S. Court: 'Presumptive Right' Seen in Constitution," NYLJ, May 1, 1996 at 1; Melinda Wilson, "Cable Network Puts Detroit Court in the Legal Limelight," Detroit News, Apr. 21, 1996.

5. For an overview of the studies, see Susanna Barber, News Cameras in the Courtroom (1987); Susan E. Harding, Note, "Cameras and the Need for Unrestricted Electronic Media Access to Federal Courtrooms," 69 S. Cal. L. Rev. 827, 834-850 (1996). Similar studies done internationally have been favorable as well. See David Stepniak, "Forum: Televising Court Proceedings," 18 Univ.

New S. Wales LJ 488, 490 (1995). For a recent history of the issue, see Ruth Ann Strickland & Richter H. Moore Jr., "Cameras in State Courts: A Historical Perspective," 78 Judicature 128 (1994). For a detailed overview of various jurisdictions' approaches to television coverage before the Simpson case, see Carolyn Stewart Dyer & Nancy R. Hauserman, "Electronic Coverage of the Courts: Exceptions to Exposure," 75 Geo. LJ 1633 (1987).

The turn against cameras has not been limited to the judiciary. A *Los Angeles Times* poll shortly after the Simpson trial indicated a bare majority in Los Angeles County (53 percent) believed that allowing cameras in the trial was a mistake. David Shaw, "Cameras and Circuses; The American Public Has Gotten Its Best-Ever Look At the Criminal Justice System . . . But That's A Mixed Blessing," LA Times, Oct. 9, 1995.

6. As of late September, 1995, the major networks had devoted 1,392 minutes of their nightly news broadcasts that year to the Simpson case versus 762 to the war in Bosnia and 530 to the bombing in Oklahoma. Peter Johnson, "Other News Stories Suffer During Simpson Coverage," USA Today, Sept. 27, 1995.

7. The trial became an international media event, covered extensively in Canada, Latin America, Britain, Europe, Australia, and other nations. Barry James, "Trial on the Tube Fascinated, and Appalled, Most of the World," Int'l Herald Tribune, Oct. 4, 1995; Chris Cobb, "For Canadians, Trial Was Highly Entertaining, Even Educational," Ottawa Citizen, Oct. 4, 1995; Anne Thompson, "The Simpson Verdict: The Media Trial Affects Courtrooms, Newsrooms; Worldwide Coverage Spurs Poor View of U.S.," Atlanta J., Oct. 3, 1995.

8. On the celebrity aspect of the case, see Thomas Morawetz, "Fantasy, Celebrity, and Homicide," 6 Hastings Women's LJ 209 (1995).

9. For me the network's most impressive moment came early in the trial, when the network inadvertently showed a juror's face for a moment, violating its agreement with the court. Judge Ito angrily cut off the television feed. The network quickly acknowledged its mistake, network head Stephen Brill personally apologized to the court, and the network sought to devise ways it would not recur. Based on Court TV's representations, the judge then restored the courtroom feed. For background on the network, see David A. Harris, "The Appearance of Justice: Court TV, Conventional Television, and Public Understanding of the Criminal Justice System," 35 Ariz. L. Rev. 785, 797-807 (1993); see also Paul Thaler, The Watchful Eye: American Justice in the Age of the Television Trial 55-72 (1994).

10. Reporters and trial lawyers commonly note this phenomenon in the courtroom. See Gerald Uelmen, Lessons From the Trial 96 (1996). Author Paul Thaler recounts an instance from the televised Steinberg case, in which a television report about Judge Harold Rothwax's volatility triggered a warning from his wife, and apparently caused the judge to act more temperately in the courtroom. Thaler, The Watchful Eye, supra note 8 at 170-171.

11. Prosecutors in the televised murder case of Joel Steinberg reported that a number of witnesses had expressed reluctance to testify because of the broadcasts, but all eventually did. See Thaler, The Watchful Eye, supra note 8 at 125. Even expert witnesses in the case reported added pressure from television. Id. at 126-130.

12. See Christopher A. Darden, with Jess Walter, In Contempt 235-237 (1996).

13. A ban on in-court cameras might actually increase the demand for behind-the-scenes books about the case and for the stories of would-be witnesses.

14. A fellow prosecutor has reported that Marcia Clark said the prosecution in the case was forced to make lengthy arguments against defense motions to avoid the appearance of "rolling over." Charley Roberts, "Court Cameras A Touchy Issue to Some Jurists," LA Daily J., Apr. 30, 1996, at 1. Co-prosecutor Darden makes a similar point in his recent book: "Cameras caused all the lawyers to change our approach and our style. Everyone became long-winded and abrasive. Often without meaning to, we tailored our arguments to the millions of people watching and the experts second-guessing our every move. . . . I tried to ignore the cameras; I didn't watch TV and tried to shut out what the pundits and experts were saying. But it was like walking past a funhouse mirror,

over and over, a mirror that distorts your appearance so that you look taller and fatter than you really are. It isn't long before your very identity is in doubt: 'Is that really how I am?'" In Contempt, supra note 12 at 260, 261.

For allegations that the defense played to the cameras in the televised Steinberg case, see Thaler, The Watchful Eye, supra note 9 at 132.

15. Several critics noted that defense attorneys made presentations to Judge Ito that seemed designed to generate headlines, perhaps with the intent of influencing the families of jurors and eventually the jurors themselves. David Shaw, "The Simpson Legacy: Did The Media Overfeed A Starving Public?" LA Times, Oct. 9, 1995. See Darden, supra note 12 at 357 (alleging that several jurors received news of the case from family members).

16. One judge in the courthouse I covered was reputed to hand down harsh sentences whenever a reporter was present but would then privately signal the defense attorney to come by chambers to make a motion for reduction of sentence that would be favorably received.

During the Simpson case, Judge Ito regularly received celebrity visitors to the trial in his chambers. In a small courtroom where seats were at a premium and controlled by the judge, famous authors, newscasters and celebrities seemed to have priority. The judge granted a lengthy interview to a local television station about his personal background on the eve of trial. Prosecutor Darden wrote about the judge at a pretrial, in-chambers hearing: "I sensed that Ito craved the ceremony of this trial. He seemed infatuated with the idea of being the judge in the 'trial of the century.' It was a show to him, and he was acting unlike any judge I'd ever seen." In Contempt, supra note 12 at 216. Darden also observed, "Once, after throwing a fit about the cameras, he [Judge Ito] posed for pictures with twenty-one boxes of mail, from letter writers who agreed he should turn the cameras off. It was a strange response for someone supposedly concerned about the media to then pose for the media with fan mail." Id. at 261.

Some judges are truly oblivious to the media. For example, Oliver Wendell Holmes Jr. gave up reading newspapers at an early stage in his public career, a practice that probably assisted him in avoiding the conventional assumptions of the day, and so enhanced his independence as a thinker. Holmes's insulation from popular debate may also have contributed to the worst opinion he ever authored, his notorious forced sterilization decision in Buck v. Bell, 274 US 200 (1927). See William E. Leuchtenburg, "Mr. Justice Holmes and Three Generations of Imbeciles," in The Supreme Court Reborn 3 (1995).

17. Sometimes the effect is simply to make participants feel great pressure. David Bruck, who represented Susan Smith, the South Carolina woman who drowned her two young children, reported the following reaction after hearing that the judge would not allow the proceedings to be televised. "Once the motion was granted and the cameras were unplugged, I felt like someone had pumped air back into the room. I had no idea until the cameras were gone of the effect they were having on everyone." Alexandra Marks, "O.J. Simpson Case Puts Courtroom Cameras on Trial," Christian Science Monitor, Sept. 19, 1995, at 10.

18. On the competitiveness of television journalism, see Matthew C. Ehrlich, "The Competitive Ethos in Television Newswork," 12 Critical Studies in Mass Communication 196 (1995). On the effects of in-court television on legal journalism, see Thaler, The Watchful Eye, supra note 9 at 45 (effect on print coverage of the William Kennedy Smith rape trial), 148, 197-200 (similar effects in the Steinberg case).

19. Thaler, The Watchful Eye, supra note 9 at 198.

20. Many media outlets did pay commentators, however. On the phenomenon generally, see Maura Dolan, "Simpson Case Creates TV Job Openings for Lawyers," LA Times, July 5, 1994. For an excellent overview of the benefits and problems of legal commentating, see Erwin Chemerinsky & Laurie Levenson, "The Ethics of Being a Commentator, 69 S. Cal. L. Rev. 1303 (1996).

21. For especially thoughtful critiques along these lines, see Lincoln Caplan, "Sport TV," New Republic, Oct. 23, 1995, at 18; "Why Play-By-Play Coverage Strikes Out For Lawyers," 82 ABA J. 62 (1996). Or this from the Boston Globe's ombudsman, Mark Jurkowitz:

> Let's first acknowledge that the Simpson trial was a television-driven story, with the print media relegated to a peanut gallery role. And though I'm not unalterably opposed to cameras in the courtroom, the relentless punditry generated by the live coverage trivialized and distorted the proceedings.
>
> With this trial, the obsessive TV culture of instant analysis has now moved from sports (where John Madden explains how the tackle screwed up on the previous play) to politics . . . to the criminal justice system (where commentators were picking winners and losers at every trial break).

"A Guilty Verdict for the O.J. Press," Boston Globe, Oct. 16, 1995.

22. For a critique of political reporting along similar lines, see James Fallows, Breaking the News: How the Media Undermine American Democracy (1996).

23. As two media critics put it, once television commits to live coverage of an event, "television is protective of the event. It makes clear the event's absolute priority and, in particular, its precedence over other news of all sorts." Daniel Dayan & Elihu Katz, Media Events: The Live Broadcasting of History 79 (1992).

24. Tim Rutten & Jane Hall, "Is the Public Still Hungry for Simpson News?" LA Times, Jan. 28, 1996 at A1, A27.

25. Marshall McLuhan & Bruce R. Powers, The Global Village (1989).

26. This same tension exists between journalists and legal academics who act as legal commentators. Law teachers think in terms of months and semesters. As scholars, law teachers characteristically take the long view, trying to relate the present to events distant in both past and future. But in commentating, legal academics are called upon for instant answers about the present situation.

27. See Charley Roberts, "Lawyers Split on Their Verdict Of Cameras in the Courtroom," LA Daily J., Nov. 9, 1995, at 1.

28. The defense lawyers in the Joel Steinberg case used television coverage to gauge their own efforts. "They're like film dailies, you know, the day's rushes, and we'd get a sense on the six major channels as to how they were responding, and it gave us a clue how we were coming across." Thaler, The Watchful Eye, supra note 9 at 167 (quoting Ira London, lead defense counsel).

The defense team in the Simpson case also took careful note of all coverage in the case. See Robert L. Shapiro, with Larkin Warren, The Search for Justice 23-24 (1996).

Christopher Darden notes in his book about the experience of being a prosecutor in the Simpson case, several occasions when reaction to the day's televised events had a major impact on him personally. The most prominent involved a televised pretrial hearing in which he alleged that Johnnie Cochran's characterization of his (Darden's) arguments over the admissibility of a detective's use of a racial epithet, subjected Darden to enormous personal hostility from the black community. In Contempt, supra note 12 at 201-206.

29. For example, one of the most sensational trial in early Massachusetts was the murder trial in 1850 of Harvard professor Dr. John W. Webster. So many wished to attend the trial that spectators were allowed in for only ten minutes at a time. This permitted an estimated 60,000 people to see some part of the proceedings. Leonard W. Levy, The Law of the Commonwealth and Chief Justice Shaw 218-220 (1957). In the first half of the eighteenth century, the Philadelphia criminal courts were often crowded with spectators who expected entertainment from the lawyers and witnesses. Allen Steinberg, The Transformation of Criminal Justice: Philadelphia 1800-1880, 17-24 (1989). For brief accounts of particularly sensational trials and their audiences, see Lawrence M. Friedman, Crime and Punishment in American History 252-255, 397-401 (1993).

30. This not because courthouses have moved but because workplaces have dispersed from town and city centers.

31. Here in California, the governor signed into law the broadest and least flexible version of three-strikes legislation that reached his desk. See Victor S. Sze, Note, "A Tale of Three Strikes: Slogan Triumphs Over Substance As Our Bumper-Sticker Mentality Comes Home to Roost," 28 Loy. LA L. Rev. 1047, 1051-1057 (1995). A direct result has been a great increase in criminal trials,

especially in Los Angeles County, delaying the criminal process for many, delaying or effectively precluding civil trials, and creating dangerous overcrowding in county jails and the under-prosecution and under-punishment of other felons and misdemeanants. Perhaps the most dramatic result has been that, because of three-strikes prisoners crowding the county jail in combination with a continuing budgetary crisis, misdemeanant prisoners in the county have been serving only a quarter of their sentences. Paul Feldman & Eric Lichtblau, "L.A. County Jail Inmates Serve Only 25% of Sentences," LA Times, May 20, 1996, at A1.

32. Ira Reiner, the former L.A. District Attorney and a frequent television commentator on the Simpson case made the same point this way:

> Professionals tend to have a guild mentality, and we lawyers are no different. Without being consciously aware of it, most of us have absorbed, with our law-school training, an insular, self-protective conviction that only the initiated can judge our activities. How, we think—can layfolk—lacking our expertise, training and experience—truly understand why things are the way they are and why they must be that way? . . . To put it another way, some folks feel that people should not see how sausages and laws are made. But they should. What they see, in either case, may shock or sicken them, but the end result may be better laws and healthier sausages.

"Cameras Keep Justice System In Focus," Nat'l LJ, Oct. 23, 1995, at A23.

33. Public figures and institutions sometimes release news subject to a time embargo, a promise by journalists and editors that the story not go out until a specified time. In a recent insightful essay about journalism and the U.S. Supreme Court, *New York Times* reporter Linda Greenhouse describes a process used by the Court in the release of an important decision concerning New York City's financial crisis in which reporters were allowed to read the Court's opinion an hour before its official release, but were not allowed to report it until the release time. Reporters who came to a room at the Court to read the opinion early were not allowed to leave until the official release time. "Telling the Court's Story: Justice and Journalism at the Supreme Court," 105 Yale LJ 1537, 1544 (1995).

34. This states a general presumption concerning witnesses, parties, and lawyers. Restrictions on photographing jurors and particularly vulnerable witnesses remain appropriate.

35. See supra note 2.

36. Estimates on the size of the audience for the Simpson case vary considerably. The largest audience was certainly for the verdict. Estimates of this audience range from 150 to 200 million. Steve McClellan, "All Eyes On O.J.: Verdict In Murder Trial Estimated to Have Been Seen by More than 150 Million," 125 Broadcasting & Cable, Oct. 9, 1995. Coverage of the Simpson case constituted the most successful show of the fall 1995 television season, disrupting traditional viewing patters. Joe Mandese, "O.J. Skewing New-Season Results," Electronic Media, Oct. 16, 1995, at 28.

37. For example, a judge wrote in a recent federal survey: "The basic purpose of the courts is to render justice. The basic purpose of TV is to entertain. There are many detriments to TV courtrooms and no corresponding benefits to the judiciary. Courts should not compete with soap operas, at least not in the name of promoting justice." Lyle Denniston, "Camera's Eye on Blind Justice," Sun (Baltimore), Oct. 1, 1995. Yet the criminal courts have historically provided public entertainment, see supra note 29, and the drama of crime remains an important part of criminal justice in a democratic society. See Samuel H. Pillsbury, Book Review, "The Challenge of the Dramatic: Crime Journalism," 29 Loy. LA L. Rev. 847 (1996).

38. *Washington Post* television critic Tom Shales compared the verdict in the Simpson case to "finding the one-armed man on The Fugitive, except this was real, a lot more exciting and a lot more people were fascinated by it." Steve McClellan, "All Eyes On O.J.," Broadcasting & Cable, Oct. 9, 1995.

39. The success of the delay rule also depends on the public's trust in the television media. If viewers believe that all delayed broadcasts of proceedings are distorted by media editing, then such

broadcasts will do little to improve public understanding and appreciation of the legal system. I am grateful to my research assistant Karen Cox for pointing out this problem. Perhaps I am naive but I do not see the public's distrust of the media as this severe at present. Even if it is, I believe that in the few cases like Simpson where live broadcasts cause serious problems, a delay rule remains the best compromise between access and restriction.

40. See Nebraska Press Ass'n v. Stuart, 427 US 539 (1976).

41. On the First Amendment right of access generally, see Richmond Newspapers, Inc. v. Virginia, 448 US 555 (1980); Press-Enterprise Co. v. Superior Court, 464 US 501 (1984).

42. Nixon v. Warner Communications, Inc., 435 US 589, 610 (1978): "[T]here is no constitutional right to have testimony recorded and broadcast. . . . Nor does the Sixth Amendment require that the trial—or any part of it—be broadcast live or on tape to the public. The requirement of a public trial is satisfied by the opportunity of members of the public and the press to attend the trial and to report what they have observed." See also Westmoreland v. Columbia Broadcasting Sys., Inc., 752 F2d 16, 20-23 (2d Cir. 1984); United States v. Hastings, 695 F2d 1278, 1280 (11th Cir. 1983); Combined Communications Corp. v. Finesilver, 672 F2d 818, 821 (10th Cir. 1982).

43. Chandler v. Florida, 449 US 560 (1981).

44. See Near v. Minnesota, 283 US 697 (1931).

45. C.f. Globe Newspaper Co. v. Superior Court, 457 US 596 (1982) (unconstitutional to exclude press from trial of sex offense involving minor victim).

46. See Globe Newspaper Co. v. Superior Court, 457 596, 607 n.17 (1982); United States v. Hastings, 695 F2d 1278, 1282 (11th Cir. 1983).

47. *Hastings*, 695 F2d at 1282 (quoting Young v. American Mini Theatres, Inc. 427 US 50, 63 n.18 (1976) and Richmond Newspapers Inc. v. Virginia, 448 US 555, 581, n.18 (1980).

48. The scheme might even pass strict scrutiny. For an example of a more far-reaching broadcast time-restriction that passed constitutional muster, see Action for Children's Television v. Federal Communications Comm'n, 58 F3d 654 (DC Cir. 1995) (upholding 6 a.m. to 10 p.m. broadcast ban on indecent material, finding that statutory provisions were sufficiently narrowly tailored to serve government's compelling interest in protecting the well-being of minors).

The Second Circuit has suggested a more deferential standard should apply to television access to the courtroom questions, holding that courts have general powers to regulate media coverage, including plenary power over television access. "[T]elevision coverage of federal trials is a right created by consent of the judiciary, which has always had control over the courtrooms, a consent which the federal courts . . . have not given." Westmoreland v. Columbia Broadcasting Sys., Inc., 752 F2d 16 (2d Cir. 1984).

49. Rosenberger v. Rector & Visitors of the University of Va., 115 S. Ct. 2510 (1995). See also Cornelius v. NAACP Legal Defense & Educ. Fund, Inc., 473 US 788 (1983); Legi-Tech, Inc. v. Keiper, 766 F2d 728, 734-735 (2d Cir. 1985); David W. Burcham, "High Profile Trials: Can Government Sell the "Right" to Broadcast the Proceedings?" 3 UCLA Ent. L. Rev. 169 (1996).

50. American Broadcasting Cos. Inc. v. Cuomo, 570 F2d 1080 (2d Cir. 1977) (unconstitutional to discriminate between media outlets); Quad-City Community News Serv., Inc. v. Jebens, 334 F. Supp. 8 (SD Iowa 1971) (same).

51. See generally Carey v. Brown, 447 US 445 (1980) (unconstitutional to selectively prohibit residential picketing based on content of protest); see also KFMB-TV v. Municipal Court, 221 Cal. App. 3d 1362, 271 Cal. Rptr. 109 (1990) (trial court's decision to allow taping of criminal proceedings but conditioning broadcast of the tapes on the court's approval reversed as beyond the authority granted the court under the state's rule concerning cameras in court).

52. I am grateful to Chris May for suggesting this example.

53. For example, Editorial, "Judges Should Retain TV Option; They, Not Sacramento Should Decide Camera-In-Court Issues," LA Times, Feb. 14, 1996; Cathy Young, "Don't Blame Cameras for O.J. Case," Detroit News, Oct. 3, 1995; Walter Goodman, "Television View; The Camera as

Culprit? Look Again," NY Times, July 9, 1995; Kelli L. Sager, Karen N. Frederiksen & Barbara Wartelle Wall, "The Case For Cameras in the Courtroom," 9 Cal. Litig. 11 (1996).

There were some surprising dissenters in the media, though, including Don Hewitt, long-time producer of CBS's "60 Minutes," and Max Frankel, of the *New York Times.* Hewitt, "Pencils, Yes; Camera, No," NY Times, June 20, 1995 ("'Open to the public' doesn't have to mean 'open to cameras.' . . . [L]etting cameras in can turn a courtroom into a movie set."); Frankel, "World and Image; Out of Focus," NY Times, Nov. 5, 1995 ("The camera corrupts not because it lies but because it magnifies images and issues a millionfold until they are hopelessly—and often willfully—distorted.").

54. For example: "Whatever negative impressions of the criminal justice system in general, or lawyers in particular, came out of the *Simpson* case, they were not caused by the presence of a television camera in the courtroom." Sager, et al., supra note 51 at 15.

55. The Council is a body chaired by the Chief Justice of the state's Supreme Court, and comprises primarily judges, along with four attorneys and two representatives from the state legislature. The Council acts to provide policy direction to all branches of state government on court issues.

56. Meanwhile many judges supported a complete ban on courtroom cameras. A survey of judges in the state indicated that a majority supported a ban. Task Force on Photographing, Recording and Broadcasting in the Courtroom, Report, Feb. 16, 1996 at 24. See also David Minier, "Keep Cameras Out of Court," LA Daily J., June 20, 1996.

57. The *Los Angeles Times* criticized the proposal as part of a trend to protect the legal system from public scrutiny. "Banning Cameras in Court Won't Cure What's Wrong," Feb. 26, 1996, at B4. The strongest criticism came from lawyers interested in free speech issues. William Bennett Turner, "Strict Scrutiny: Judicial Council Should Reject Proposal to Curtail Court Coverage," LA Daily J., May 9, 1996, at 6; Douglas E. Mirell, "Short-Sighted: Proposal on Cameras in the Courts Overlooks Key Judges' Views," LA Daily J. Mar. 5, 1996, at 6.

58. Maura Dolan, "Courtroom Camera Plan Called Compromise," LA Times, Feb. 24, 1996, at A22 (describing Brill as more relieved than disappointed by the proposal). Brill had earlier presented a proposal to the Judicial Council that contemplated a number of limitations, such as requiring gavel-to-gavel coverage, which would have allowed only the kind of coverage in which Court TV specializes. Other media representatives opposed Brill's plan. See Henry Weinstein, "Court TV Founder Defends Live Coverage," LA Times, Jan. 18, 1996, at B1, B6; Mike Lewis, "Broadcasters, Court TV Split Over Proposal," LA Daily J., Jan. 4, 1996, at 1.

59. See Maura Dolan, "State Panel Puts Partial Ban on Court Cameras," LA Times, May 18, 1996. The revised California Rule of Court 980 places a complete ban on televising of proceedings in chambers, jury selection, jurors, courtroom spectators, bench conferences, and lawyer conferences. 980(e)(6). Permission for other courtroom broadcasts depends on the trial court's evaluation of nineteen factors, ranging from the "[i]mportance of maintaining public trust and confidence in the judicial system" to the "privacy rights of all participants in the proceeding, including witnesses, jurors, and victims" and including "[a]ny other factor the judge deems relevant." Rule 980(e)(3)(i-xix).

15

Cameras in the Jury Room: An Unnecessary And Dangerous Precedent

Abraham Abramovsky, Jonathan I. Edelstein*

I. INTRODUCTION

On February 5, 1996, the Supreme Judicial Court of Maine decided, by a vote of five to two, to allow CBS to film a civil trial's jury deliberations in Cumberland County Superior Court for a documentary.[1] This decision, virtually without precedent in the United States, marks the first time that courts have allowed the cameras of a commercial television network inside the traditionally secret confines of the jury room.

Slightly more than a month after the Maine decision, the Arizona Supreme Court also granted CBS permission to film jury deliberations in several Arizona criminal trials. In April through June of 1996, CBS recorded jury proceedings in three criminal trials in the Maricopa County Superior Court, and will include footage from these deliberations in its documentary.[2]

Prior to these recent developments, footage of jury deliberations in the United States had aired on only one occasion, a PBS Frontline broadcast in 1986 that included footage from a Wisconsin criminal trial.[3] The broadcast caused some brief controversy, but never reached a wide audience and went largely unnoticed by legal scholars. Intended as a one-time-only experiment to educate the public about the jury process, the PBS documentary was regarded as an aberration by media commentators, legal scholars, and even the trial judge who presided over the case in which the deliberations were filmed.[4]

Maine and Arizona's actions, however, show that the PBS documentary was not a one-time incident. Now, a major commercial network with millions of viewers nationwide has been allowed inside the jury room to film juries at work. CBS's requests, which come at a time when a series of high-profile trials have reduced public confidence in the jury system,[5] again raise the question of whether televised jury deliberations will actually educate the public and raise its confidence in the jury process.

Maine and Arizona's recent actions also raise the possibility that, as some commentators have feared, a precedent has been set, which may lead to routine camera

Reprinted by permission of the *Arizona State Law Journal* from vol. 28 (1996), pp. 865–892.

access to American jury rooms.[6] Conversely, some commentators argue that routine taping of jury deliberations might promote accountability.[7] Other than the statement of the two dissenting Maine justices,[8] there has been no attempt by the courts to establish standards that govern such recordings. Thus, courts facing the issue in the future will find little guidance.

This article examines both the practical and legal implications of recording jury room deliberations. Part II outlines the historical and procedural background of cameras in the jury room, including the 1986 PBS broadcast, CBS's application to the Maine and Arizona courts, judicial and legislative actions taken on CBS's applications, and the taping by CBS of Arizona jury deliberations. Part III attempts to determine, from the 1986 broadcast and the evidence at hand from camera coverage of trials, the educational value of taping jury deliberations. Part IV examines the practical aspects of routine recording of jury deliberations, while Part V examines the doctrine of jury secrecy and constructs a framework under which courts might determine the legality of permitting cameras inside the jury room.

II. HISTORICAL AND PROCEDURAL BACKGROUND

Television cameras first entered the jury room under the eye of Stephen Herzberg, a professor of trial advocacy at the University of Wisconsin Law School.[9] Professor Herzberg, a pioneer of television trial coverage, conducted the first gavel-to-gavel coverage of a murder trial in the United States while working for a Milwaukee public television station in 1977.[10]

His research into jury selection and small-group decision-making led him to propose a documentary on the jury process designed to educate both the public and trial attorneys about the workings of the jury system.[11] Professor Herzberg believed that, in addition to strengthening public confidence in a system that was "under attack,"[12] such a documentary would provide a valuable tool for trial advocacy professors who were "teaching what we don't know."[13]

In early 1985, Professor Herzberg convinced Judge Ralph Adam Fine, then a member of the Milwaukee County Circuit Court, to allow the filming of jury deliberations in his court.[14] The chief judge of the Circuit Court, Victor Manian, also cooperated with the project, and agreed to assign an appropriate case to Judge Fine's court.[15] According to Professor Herzberg, the ideal case for a jury documentary would be simple, brief, and involve a victimless crime. He "did not want a victim on the stand to have to testify before the cameras. That would be too intrusive."[16]

In late 1985, Professor Herzberg found his "perfect case." The defendant was Leroy Reed, a 42-year-old, slow-witted predicate felon who was arrested after enrolling in a mail-order detective course and purchasing a gun in violation of Wisconsin law.[17] While loitering outside a Milwaukee courthouse attempting to learn his newfound trade by talking with police officers, Reed inadvertently produced the sales slip for his pistol when asked for identification.[18] At the police officer's request, he went home and retrieved the pistol, and was promptly arrested upon his return to the police station.[19]

The judge informed jurors that they would be filmed and gave them the opportunity to refuse to serve on the jury. Only three potential jurors of a pool of forty withdrew from the jury panel.[20] The trial itself produced few surprises. Reed's defense attorney admitted that he was technically guilty of the crime, but relied on the apparent harmlessness and sympathetic character of the slow-witted defendant to sway the jury.[21] Judge Fine himself was apparently affected by the defendant's sympathetic nature and favored the defense during the trial.[22] In fact, both the defense attorney and courtroom commentators surmised that the judge would order a new trial if the defendant were convicted.[23]

The jury took its cue from the arguments of the defense attorney and, possibly, the unspoken concurrence of Judge Fine. Although one of the jurors remarked near the beginning of deliberations that Reed was "technically . . . . guilty as sin,"[24] the consensus of the jurors was that Reed should never have been brought to trial.[25] After two and one-half hours of deliberations, the lone holdout was convinced by the other eleven jurors that there was enough "reasonable doubt" to acquit the defendant.[26] The jury's filmed deliberations aired on PBS on April 13, 1986.[27] Nothing more was heard of the concept of filming jury deliberations for another decade.

Ten years after Professor Herzberg conceived the idea of taping the deliberations of a Wisconsin criminal jury, CBS Reports decided to duplicate and surpass his efforts with a two-hour documentary that would include footage from civil and criminal juries.[28] According to CBS's production protocol, each hour of the proposed documentary would consist of three sections: trial coverage, jury deliberations, and interviews and analysis by a panel of experts.[29] The documentary would be anchored by "a major correspondent such as Dan Rather or Mike Wallace."[30] The American Bar Association's Section on Litigation agreed to sponsor the CBS project.[31]

CBS submitted its first application to film the deliberations of a civil jury in Maine.[32] Ironically, Maine is one of the most restrictive states with regard to camera coverage of trial courts.[33] Under state court rules, cameras and microphones are not allowed to record witnesses in criminal cases, although civil cases may be filmed.[34]

CBS's proposed rules of production required that all jurors, as well as the parties to the trial, receive "a full and complete description by the presiding [judge] of the nature of the project [and] their involvement in it."[35] Any juror not wishing to participate was free to decline.[36] All parties, once they agreed to be part of the project, would be asked to sign waivers agreeing not to use taped jury deliberations as a basis for appeal.[37]

The CBS production protocol also required that the cameras in the jury room be as unobtrusive as possible in order to minimize potential influence on the jurors' deliberations. Photography in the jury room would be conducted by "two hidden remote-controlled cameras," supplemented by small microphones placed strategically around the jury room.[38] CBS also requested permission to conduct a group interview with the jury following the trial.[39]

On February 5, 1996, the Supreme Judicial Court of Maine approved CBS's request without comment, issuing an administrative order indicating that Cumberland County Superior Court Justice Roland Cole would supervise the project "in accordance with the production protocol."[40] Justices Caroline Glassman and Paul Rudman, however, issued a stinging dissent, criticizing the project as lacking educational value and detrimental to justice.[41] The dissenting Justices argued that "[w]hat is represented [by CBS] to be the jury process, will not be the jury process."[42]

Shortly thereafter, the Maine legislature challenged the Supreme Judicial Court of Maine's decision. Barely a month after the decision was handed down, Maine Representative James Libby introduced emergency legislation that would make recording or viewing a recording of jury deliberations a crime punishable by a fine of $1000 or six months in prison.[43] Maine Governor Angus King, a former talk show host, expressed reservations about the bill although he stopped short of threatening to veto it if it passed.[44] On March 30, 1996, an amended version of the Libby bill[45] passed the Maine House of Representatives by a vote of 131-11, but failed narrowly in the Senate by a vote of 18-17.[46] In a second vote on April 1, the bill failed again in the Senate.[47] Adjournment of the Maine legislature on April 4 effectively precluded further consideration of the emergency bill.

All but one of the seventeen cases that Judge Cole selected as suitable for filming were ruled out by litigants or their lawyers.[48] The case finally selected was *Small v. Estate of Calder*,[49] a personal injury suit arising out of an automobile accident. Jury selection in the case was scheduled to begin on May 13, 1996; however, only days before the trial was set to begin, the case settled.[50] Because a replacement case could not be found in time, CBS abandoned plans to include a Maine jury in its documentary.[51]

However, CBS had better luck in Arizona. CBS chose to submit an application to Arizona because "the state is on the very forefront of jury reform," according to a spokesman for the Arizona Supreme Court.[52] Arizona recently enacted a number of radical jury-reform measures. These reforms allow jurors to submit questions for witnesses to trial judges,[53] take notes,[54] receive copies of jury instructions[55] and exhibits,[56] and discuss evidence among themselves before deliberation in civil cases.[57] In a unanimous decision, the Arizona Supreme Court approved CBS's application in March of 1996.[58] The decision was not accompanied by a written opinion.

In Arizona, CBS received considerably more leeway in the selection of cases for its documentary.[59] Unlike the Maine decision, which limited CBS to civil trials on a single judge's docket, the Arizona Supreme Court allowed the network freedom to select any case in which the parties gave full consent.[60] Maricopa County Superior Court Judge Ronald S. Reinstein, who supervised the CBS project in Arizona, however, set several of his own ground rules that governed the taping of jury deliberations in the Arizona courts.[61] These stipulations ruled out filming jury deliberations in murder trials, cases involving child molestation, or cases where jurors might experience retaliation.[62] According to Judge Reinstein, filming jury deliberations in a murder case might complicate the appellate process if the case were to be appealed to a federal court.[63]

CBS filmed three Arizona trials from start to finish. The first and second cases, involving possession and sale of drugs[64] and assault,[65] respectively, ended in hung juries. The third, a robbery case,[66] ended in a conviction.[67] The drug case was retried before the same judge. The second trial, in which CBS again filmed jury deliberations, resulted in a conviction.[68] At the present time, CBS plans to air its documentary in December of 1996, most likely without footage of civil jury deliberations.[69]

III. THE EDUCATIONAL VALUE OF CAMERAS IN THE JURY ROOM

One of the most pressing questions the Supreme Judicial Court of Maine considered in deciding to grant CBS permission to film jury deliberations was whether the resulting documentary would accurately represent the jury process.[70] CBS, in its production protocol, contended that the presence of cameras would not alter the deliberative process in any material manner.[71] The dissenting justices on the Maine court, however, argued that:

> [t]o film a trial and the jury deliberations that follow . . . cannot replicate a trial without the electronic intrusions. . . . By the process of measurement the object of measurement will be changed and any conclusions reached on the basis of such measurement made indefensible.[72]

Only one example, the PBS documentary, is available to evaluate whether a videotaped documentary of jury deliberations represents a true rendering of the jury process.[73] On its face, many aspects of the PBS film seem to support the proponents of filming juries. The deliberations of the Wisconsin jury depicted in the PBS documentary demonstrate a classic case of "jury nullification," or disregard of the law by the jury in the perceived interests of justice.[74] Trial Judge Fine cited this behavior, as well as the heated debate and vehement arguments between jurors recorded by PBS, as evidence that the experiment worked. He concluded that "the contents of the deliberations persuades [sic] me [that the jurors] were oblivious of the cameras."[75]

Other observers disagreed. Television commentator George V. Higgins argued that the recorded deliberations in the Reed trial showed the "Hawthorne effect."[76] According to Higgins, the "Hawthorne effect" occurs when "[p]eople aware that they are being observed alter their behavior (in this case, adopting vast eloquence and extreme circumspection) to meet what they imagine to be the expectations of the observers."[77]

The results of the filmed Arizona jury deliberations arguably support Higgins' conclusion. Two of three trials selected for the CBS documentary ended in hung juries, a rate significantly higher than the national average of five percent in criminal cases.[78] This might indicate that the presence of cameras in the jury room caused jurors to harden their positions and be more reluctant to compromise, possibly for fear of appearing weak-willed if they changed their minds. Arizona State University law professor Gary Lowenthal, however, commented before the trials that the presence of cameras in the jury room "might increase the pressure on holdouts. . . . [and] [k]nowing that they were being scrutinized by millions of other people might increase that pressure."[79]

Notably, the Maine defense attorney in *Small v. Estate of Calder* agreed to allow the filming of jury deliberations in that case precisely because he believed that jurors would alter their behavior to his client's benefit.[80] He reasoned that jurors, "knowing they were being filmed, would pay closer attention to his defense," presumably so that they would not appear ignorant when debating its merits on television.[81]

It is also significant that the publicity surrounding the CBS program, both before and during the trials, was likely much greater than that surrounding the 1986 PBS Frontline report. The Wisconsin courts handled the approval and case selection process for the 1986 documentary with great circumspection; there was practically no pretrial publicity surrounding the groundbreaking media event. Conversely, the CBS documentary has already received a significant amount of comment and legislative action following from the Supreme Judicial Court of Maine's ruling. Furthermore, CBS is a commercial network with an audience of millions, as compared to the small, primarily urban and educated audience reached by PBS.[82] It is reasonable to conclude that media consciousness among the jurors who will be featured in CBS's proposed program was much higher than that of the jurors whose deliberations PBS recorded.

The Arizona jurors whose deliberations CBS recorded likely knew well before their trials began that they would be national media figures. Their media consciousness, in fact, may mirror that displayed by recent participants in televised high-profile trials. For example, the courtroom participants' media awareness reached a disturbing apex in the recent murder trial of O.J. Simpson. During the Simpson trial, the public was treated to the spectacle of attorneys, witnesses, and even the trial judge, playing to the cameras despite the extreme seriousness of the business at hand. The unobtrusiveness of CBS's recording process may have prevented camera consciousness from reaching such a high level. However, the simple knowledge that their deliberations would become a national media event raises at least the possibility that the deliberation process was altered to a disquieting degree.[83]

As noted by the dissenting justices on the Maine court, there are other troubling aspects of filming jury deliberations.[84] The inclusion of only those who consent to being filmed might compromise the selection of the jury pool. These jury pools will contain only those "who do not mind thinking out loud before millions of observers, or those who will serve but in silence."[85] This alteration of the jury pool even prior to jury selection, contended Justices Glassman and Rudman, "by its nature will distort the deliberative process" by ensuring the empanelment of a non-representative jury.[86]

Other factors also call into question the efficacy of CBS's documentary as an educational tool. The CBS and PBS documentaries both involve carefully chosen cases. The 1986 Frontline broadcast involved a trial chosen for simplicity and lack of a victim.[87] The deliberations shown were arguably not representative of the work that takes place in jury rooms because they did not involve the more complicated questions of evidence, law, and character that cases generally present. Additionally, the requirement that all parties involved consent to the filming will likely influence CBS's documentary. By definition, the cases shown by CBS are not representative because they involve the atypical situation where all jurors give prior consent to publicly air their deliberations.

In addition, CBS's production protocol calls for each hour of the two-hour documentary to be divided into three segments, only one of which will consist of footage of jury deliberations.[88] In other words, assuming that CBS accords equal time to each segment, the deliberation process in each trial will be condensed to approximately twenty minutes of film. Twenty minutes of carefully edited footage may not adequately represent hours or even days of painstaking deliberation. Even in the PBS documentary, in which two and one-half hours of deliberations were condensed into forty-five minutes of footage, one commentator worried that key aspects of the deliberative process may have "ended up on the cutting-room floor."[89] In addition, Maine Rep. Libby distinguished commercial coverage from public television coverage by pointing out that the editing process would be different for a CBS documentary. Rep. Libby noted that commercial networks, unlike public television stations, would be concerned with maximizing their ratings as well as depicting the truth.[90] Thus, a danger exists that networks may selectively edit in a way that maximizes sensationalism but compromises authenticity.

Finally, Rep. Libby also articulated a common-sense objection to CBS's documentary: the videotape of the 1986 Frontline broadcast is still available to those who regard videotaped jury deliberations as a valid educational measure.[91] With the secrecy of the jury room already breached once by television cameras, it is not necessary to do so again for educational purposes. As Justices Glassman and Rudman noted, "[t]he public would be better served by a documentary that emphasized, rather than intruded upon, the confidentiality of juror deliberations and the protection afforded the public from any abuses of that process."[92]

IV. SHOULD JURY DELIBERATIONS ROUTINELY BE RECORDED?

When jury deliberations were filmed by PBS in 1986, many regarded the project as a one-time-only media experiment. Although CBS has no immediate plans to repeat its entry into the jury room, the continuing public interest in the jury process[93] suggests that the CBS documentary will not be the last time that camera coverage of jury deliberations is attempted. Video coverage of trials followed a similar path from its beginnings more than two decades ago. The history of cameras in the courtroom began with experimental coverage by public television stations and continued through coverage by commercial stations into demands for routine access.[94] Now, a majority of states, including some of those that initially opposed camera coverage of trials, allow television stations to film the trial process.[95]

Arguably, allowing cameras access into trial courts only expands the publicity of a process that is already public, whereas jury coverage is an intrusion into a process that has been traditionally private.[96] Similar processes have breached equally long-standing traditions in the American jury system. Empaneling anonymous juries, for instance, was regarded as unthinkable in an American court for centuries, until dicta in an obscure 1964 federal case indicated that such juries might be acceptable under certain circumstances.[97] Thirteen years passed between that statement and the empaneling of the first anonymous jury in the New York City federal trial of drug kingpin Leroy Barnes and his associates.[98] Some regarded this event as an extraordinary measure in a trial of a particularly dangerous defendant.[99] However, matters have since progressed to the point where two California judges were empaneling anonymous juries in all criminal cases, until recently ordered to stop by a California appellate court.[100] It is a long way from an experimental CBS documentary to routine camera coverage of jury deliberations, but the triple precedent set by the courts of Wisconsin, Maine, and Arizona demonstrates that such coverage is no longer unthinkable.

Certainly, arguments could be made in favor of routine recording of jury deliberations. Juries are, traditionally, one of the least accountable elements of the American judicial system, deliberating in secret and basing their judgments on factors beyond the control of trial judges and attorneys.

Moreover, a recent string of high-profile trials in which jury deliberations have achieved bizarre results focused public attention on the jury system and caused some to wonder whether juries should be made more accountable.[101] Race, in particular, has been cited as a possible deciding factor in the trials of O.J. Simpson, Lemrick Nelson, Jr., and the police officers who beat Rodney King.[102] In more routine criminal matters, recent statistics indicate that criminal juries in predominately black and Hispanic Bronx County, New York, acquit 47.6 percent of black defendants and 37.6 percent of Hispanic defendants in serious felony cases, as opposed to a seventeen percent acquittal rate nationwide.[103]

The O.J. Simpson trial, especially, visibly affected American confidence in the jury system. Many Americans were bewildered by the jury's not guilty verdict, with the majority of white Americans believing Simpson guilty and the majority of black Americans believing him innocent.[104] In the aftermath of the Simpson case, national polls showed diminished confidence in the justice system.[105] Much of this doubt focused on the racially divided jury, which took only hours to acquit Simpson, despite a nine-month trial.[106] The jurors figured prominently in angry letters to the editor throughout the country, and even Los Angeles District Attorney Gil Garcetti expressed his difficulty in understanding the jury's decision.[107]

Similarly, the 1992 New York jury acquittal of Lemrick Nelson, Jr., for the murder of Hasidic scholar Yankel Rosenbaum during the Crown Heights riots, also focused public attention on the jury system. After the trial, the public witnessed the spectacle of jurors attending a party at defense attorney Arthur Lewis' home with the defendant and his family.[108] Likewise, in the Illinois trial of Davon Neverdon, a jury of eleven blacks and one Asian-American acquitted the black defendant despite overwhelming evidence.[109] The sole Asian-American juror passed a note to the judge during deliberations suggesting that "race may be playing some part" in the decision process.[110]

During the public debate following the Simpson trial, defense attorney William Kunstler revealed in a televised interview that when representing a minority defendant "as an attorney, you would want as many blacks, as many third world people, as you can get on [the jury]."[111] Law professor Paul D. Butler has gone so far as to suggest that black jurors should routinely acquit black defendants accused of non-violent crimes.[112]

In the aftermath of these high-profile trials and controversial statements, commentators have suggested a number of measures to rein in maverick juries and make the jury system more accountable to the judicial system, litigants, and the American public at large. These suggestions include reducing or eliminating peremptory challenges, outlawing jury consultants, and allowing non-unanimous verdicts.[113] Some commentators even suggest discarding the jury system entirely and, instead, conducting trials before professional jurors or judges alone to improve the system's accountability.[114]

Routine taping of jury deliberations may provide the ultimate method of insuring jury accountability and restoring public confidence in the jury system. If jury deliberations were recorded, the content would be available to the public and, more importantly, to the trial judge, appellate judges, and attorneys. Judges and attorneys could determine, with a certainty never before possible, whether extraneous factors such as race, ethnicity, religion, or political alignment entered the jury's discussion of the case. Furthermore, other common examples of jury misconduct, such as discussion of testimony that the trial judge had ordered stricken from the record, would be apparent at once to the attorneys or jurists examining the record of the deliberations.[115]

The presence of cameras also could inhibit discussion of outside factors and serve as a hedge against "jury nullification." Certainly, if interested parties and the public could determine instantly whether the jury has done its job correctly, public confidence in juries would likely increase, and it would be possible to remedy the few instances of misconduct. Finally, taping jury deliberations, which are an important factor in most trials, could serve the interests of an open judicial system by exposing the most secret aspect of the trial process.

Equally compelling arguments exist for excluding cameras from the jury room. To begin with, any system of recording jury deliberations will have the vices of its virtues—taped deliberations may indeed reveal jury misconduct or discussion of extraneous factors, but they also open the door to a stream of potential litigation arising from either party's interpretation of the recorded discussions as evidence of misconduct.

While jurors are allowed, and in fact encouraged, to consider factors such as the character of the litigants and witnesses in their fact-finding,[116] the line between permissible discussion of character and impermissible discussion of factors extraneous to the case is a fine one. Interested parties may call upon the already overburdened American court system to draw this line over and over again if jury deliberations are recorded for later examination.[117] Attorneys for criminal defendants[118] or civil litigants will no doubt find grounds for appeals based on odd and often tangential juror statements.[119]

Furthermore, appeals based on alleged misconduct in the jury room might require deposition or trial testimony from the juror or jurors who made the disputed statements to determine his or her state of mind. Thus, jury service could expand into an extended series of examinations before appellate courts. Members of jury pools, many of whom already consider jury service an onerous duty,[120] would become even more reluctant to serve.

Even more important, however, is the effect of recording jury deliberations on free debate in the jury room. Despite CBS's contention that jurors quickly forget the presence of cameras once deliberations begin, it seems inevitable that camera consciousness will seep into the jury deliberation process. This may be especially true in high-profile trials where the cameras are a constant and obtrusive presence during the trial itself. Under such conditions, some jurors may feel inhibited not just from discussing matters extraneous to the case, but also from considering vital questions of guilt and innocence. Jurors may censor themselves to avoid appearing soft on crime, to avoid perceived alignment with unpopular social or political opinion, or simply because they fear appearing foolish on television. In small-town environments where police, prosecutors, plaintiffs, and defendants may be neighbors of the jurors, the presence of cameras might also inhibit jurors from probing deeply when such questioning might compromise their relationship with their neighbors.[121] Recorded jury deliberations may make jurors wonder whether "they are being 'politically correct' instead of . . . being just" in their deliberations.[122] In other words, jurors might tailor their deliberations to public opinion rather than the substance of the case. Certainly, with the recent spate of opportunistic attacks by politicians on the judiciary,[123] it is also possible to imagine attacks by political figures on juries or even individual jurors whose decisions are seen as, for example, soft on crime. It bears noting that, unlike judges or prosecutors, jurors have not voluntarily entered the public arena and should not have to withstand criticism from elected officials.

Recording jury deliberations may also compromise juror safety. When deliberations remain private, it is impossible to determine which jurors may have argued vehemently for conviction and which argued for acquittal. With recorded deliberations, however, jurors who argue for conviction are identifiable and potentially at risk of retaliation by criminal defendants. In trials involving dangerous defendants such as prominent organized crime figures, this threat against jurors or their families is very real and might inhibit jurors from arguing and voting for conviction. In fact, the effect of this situation on deliberations might reach beyond criminal cases; jurors might feel threatened to speak their minds in acrimonious civil cases.[124] This could heighten the often-noted syndrome of juror trauma,[125] contributing further to citizens' reluctance to serve on juries.

Ultimately, the routine presence of cameras in jury rooms could compromise the right of litigants "to a verdict based on the independent judgment of twelve jurors."[126] Impartiality is compromised when verdicts are "affected by outside influences."[127] The amount of outside influence that would result from recording jury deliberations and opening them to routine scrutiny is impossible to calculate. Any gains resulting from routine recording of jury deliberations are outweighed by the losses to impartiality and free debate. Judge Fine himself, despite his satisfaction with the results of the PBS documentary, recognized this problem when he warned that he was "not in favor of televising jury deliberations again. . . . If it would ever become routine, there would be slippage, [and a] loss of anonymity."[128] Thus, Judge Fine strongly opposed taping the jury deliberations.[129]

V. IS RECORDING JURY DELIBERATIONS LEGAL?

By centuries-old tradition, jury deliberations in the American legal system are secret. This doctrine, which maintains that the confidentiality of jury deliberations insures impartiality and freedom from outside influence, has been acknowledged repeatedly by federal and state courts.[130] The United States Supreme Court, while acknowledging that courts might pierce the confidentiality of jury deliberations to investigate alleged corrupt conduct on the part of a juror,[131] stated that "[f]reedom of debate might be stifled and independence of thought checked if jurors were made to feel that their arguments and ballots were to be freely published to the world."[132]

Federal law and the laws of seven states prohibit recording jury deliberations.[133] However, in the majority of states, the secrecy of trial jury deliberations is a matter of common law.[134] Until the decision of the Supreme Judicial Court of Maine, no appellate court had ruled on the application of the jury secrecy doctrine to the presence of cameras in the jury room. An analogous line of cases concerning the presence of outsiders during jury deliberations suggests that the standard for piercing jury confidentiality is high.[135]

Cases involving the presence of outsiders in the jury room during deliberations are rare, and almost always result in a finding of reversible error on appeal.[136] In several cases, federal courts have considered the propriety of allowing alternate jurors to remain present in the jury room during deliberations.[137] Rule 24(c) of the Federal Rules of Criminal Procedure requires that courts dismiss alternate jurors at the beginning of deliberations.[138] However, in cases where alternate jurors were not dismissed, courts commonly look beyond the letter of Rule 24(c) to determine whether the error that resulted from the presence of alternate jurors was harmless.[139] The Fourth Circuit in *United States v. Virginia Erection Corp.*[140] found reversible error in one such case, stating that even if the alternate

> heeded the letter of the court's instructions and remained orally mute throughout, it is entirely possible that his attitude, conveyed by facial expressions, gestures or the like, may have had some effect upon the decision of one or more jurors. In any event, the presence of the alternate in the jury room violated the cardinal principle that the deliberations of the jury shall remain private and secret in every case. The presence of any person other than the jurors to which the case has been submitted for decision impinges upon that privacy and secrecy. It is possible that [the alternate juror's] presence may have operated to some extent as a restraint upon the jurors and their freedom of action and expression.[141]

More recently, the Ninth Circuit in *United States v. Olano*[142] concurred with the *Virginia Erection Corp.* decision, concluding that the presence of an alternate juror during deliberations is "inherently prejudicial."[143] The Supreme Court reversed on narrowly technical grounds,[144] holding that, because *Olano* was a plain error rather than a harmless error case,[145] the respondents were required to make a specific showing that the alternate jurors prejudiced their trial.[146] Although the Supreme Court rejected the Ninth Circuit's characterization of the presence of alternate jurors as inherently prejudicial, it specifically noted that it was not considering the issue of whether the Government could have met the burden of proving lack of prejudice had the issue been one of harmless error under Rule 52(a).[147]

In *Johnson v. Duckworth*,[148] the Seventh Circuit attempted to set a standard by which such prejudice or lack thereof might be evaluated. In *Johnson*, the court also declined to hold that the mere presence of alternate jurors during deliberations was prejudicial; however, the court "agree[d] that to stifle free debate in the jury room would hinder significantly the jury's ability to reach a 'commonsense judgment.'"[149] The *Johnson* court concluded that "if an intrusion into the jury's privacy has, or is likely to have, the effect of stifling such debate, the defendant's right to trial by jury may well have been violated."[150] In ruling that the mere presence of alternate jurors would not rise to this standard, the Seventh Circuit emphasized that alternate jurors are selected by the same process through which jurors are selected.[151] The selection process subjects alternate jurors to peremptory challenge by the prosecutor and defense attorney, exposing them to the evidence in exactly the same manner as regular jurors.[152] Cameras, unlike alternate jurors, are not subject to voir dire; neither are the millions of viewers whose presence camera coverage would constructively bring into the jury room. Thus, the presence of cameras could be as influential—or more so—as the presence of an alternate juror.

The Seventh Circuit in *Johnson*, while upholding a verdict reached in the presence of an alternate juror, acknowledged that "[o]ther 'strangers' to the regular jury stand in stark contrast to the alternate."[153] In those rare cases where outsiders other than sworn alternate jurors intrude into the privacy of the jury room, courts nearly always find reversible error.[154] In *Little v. United States*,[155] the Tenth Circuit vacated a verdict reached after a court stenographer entered the jury room during deliberations to read instructions to the jury.[156] The Tenth Circuit held that:

> no one should be with a jury while it is engaged in its deliberations. The jury system is founded upon the proposition that interested jurors will hear the evidence in open court, and upon that evidence and that alone, deliberate among themselves until a verdict is reached. To permit various persons . . . to be with the jury in its deliberations is to open the door to grave abuse and strike directly at the heart of the system.[157]

New York State's highest court also noted recently that "certain outsiders, such as a bailiff or other court official, may inhibit or influence the jury by their mere presence."[158] In *People v. Knapp*, an early case involving the presence of a bailiff in a jury room during deliberations, the Michigan Supreme Court ordered a new trial.[159] The court stated that the bailiff, having "no business in the room,"[160] may have entered

> because of his bias, and in order that he may report to a friendly party what may have been said to his prejudice, or that he may protect him against unfavorable comment through the unwillingness of jurors to criticise freely the conduct and motives of one person in the presence of another who is his known friend. Or the officer may be present with a similar purpose to protect a witness whose testimony was likely to be criticised and condemned by some jurors.[161]

In other words, the court concluded that the presence of an outsider who might report the contents of the discussion to interested parties could inhibit jurors from candid discussion of the testimony of witnesses or the statements of the prosecuting attorney.[162] Although a bailiff is not identified with the prosecution or the defense and is thus a neutral party at a criminal trial, she or he might nonetheless have personal ties to one or more interested parties, especially in a rural or small-town setting; thus, there is a significant chance that a bailiff's presence could inhibit juror discussions. Notably, commentators criticize the presence of cameras in the jury room for having exactly this chilling effect upon deliberations.[163]

Courts have found that entry of jury verdicts despite the presence of other outsiders in the jury room, such as police officers, constitutes reversible error. In *People v. Bacon*,[164] a New York court held that allowing a village police officer to enter a jury room was reversible error even in the absence of a statute prohibiting his presence.[165] The *Bacon* court held that:

> Because the law does not say the officer cannot be present is no reason to say that he should be there. . . . The necessity for [confidentiality of deliberations] is assumed in every case and the jury sent out as of course. The presence of a single other person in the

jury room is an intrusion upon this privacy and tends to defeat the purpose for which they are sent out.[166]

The *Bacon* court further stated that "[it] is the duty [of the court] to insure and enforce that practice which avoids cause for suspicion and makes certain such rights."[167] Even if the arguments made by proponents of cameras in the jury room are correct, they are not probable, at least under our current state of knowledge. Thus, the presence of recording devices during deliberations inevitably creates the "cause for suspicion" which *Bacon* tells us courts must avoid.[168]

In the few cases where courts have permitted the presence of outsiders in the jury room, courts have taken pains to acknowledge safeguards that allow jury confidentiality to be preserved.[169] In *People v. Guzman*,[170] the New York Court of Appeals allowed a sign language interpreter to assist a hearing-impaired juror during deliberations.[171] In allowing the presence of an outsider under these extraordinary circumstances, the *Guzman* court directed that the interpreter be sworn to keep the confidence of the jury room, which, "together with ethical constraints . . . should provide sufficient assurance that the signer will not make public the proceedings in the jury room."[172]

These decisions offer analogies to camera coverage of jury deliberations. Cameras in the jury room will make not one, but millions, of outsiders constructively present during deliberations. Such presence will, without doubt, rise to the *Johnson* standard of reversible error because of the likelihood that it would stifle free debate in the jury room.[173] Significantly, the *Johnson* court required a showing of only a likelihood that free debate would be stifled, not an actual showing.[174]

Even if the distribution of taped jury deliberations is limited to attorneys and appellate judges, the presence of recording devices nonetheless creates a law enforcement presence similar to that of a bailiff or other officer of the court, which has been overwhelmingly found to be inherently prejudicial.[175] The existence of a jury deliberation recording, which could be examined later for evidence of misconduct, could cause jurors to censor themselves much as if an officer of the court were actually present in the jury room.

In addition, safeguards such as those described in *Guzman* are impossible to apply to camera coverage.[176] Given these factors, routine recording of jury deliberations would clearly violate the law.

Even a case where all parties waive their objections to camera coverage of jury deliberations rests on questionable legal ground. Some authority supports the proposition that parties might consent to certain intrusions upon the jury process.[177] Conversely, however, the *Johnson* court noted that "when strangers are permitted to intrude upon such privacy [of the jury], an error of constitutional dimensions may well have been committed."[178] If the presence of cameras in the jury room impinges upon the defendant's right to trial by jury,[179] it is highly questionable whether courts should allow a defendant to waive a right as fundamental as the right to a fair trial. Thus, regularly recorded jury deliberations may be, as at least one court has held when considering the presence of alternate jurors during deliberations, "an error so far destructive to the invaded right, that the error could not by mere consent be rendered harmless."[180]

VI. CONCLUSION

While compelling arguments favor recording jury deliberations, both as a one-time-only educational project and as a routine means of ensuring jury accountability, the arguments against such a procedure outweigh those in favor of it. As an educational tool, recorded jury deliberations are of dubious value because the influence of taping on the jury pool and jury deliberations renders the actions of the recorded jury unlike those of a "typical" American jury. Additionally, because of the careful selection of the case and the editing of the deliberation footage to fit documentary length, the trial process is not accurately represented.

If jury deliberations are routinely recorded, any gain in accountability is offset by the damage to free debate in the jury room, jury privacy, and the centuries-old tradition of jury deliberation secrecy. The PBS recording of a Wisconsin jury's deliberations is available to those who feel that taped deliberations are a valid means of studying and analyzing the jury process; repeating the experiment serves no further educational purpose and sets a potentially dangerous precedent. Despite the gains that might result from CBS's documentary, courts and lawmakers should not allow cameras to enter any further into the American justice system. The potential negative impact is too great.

NOTES

*I would like to thank my parents, my sisters, and Elizabeth Gordon for their fortitude in enduring my endless conversations on this topic whenever I came to visit.

1. *See* Administrative Order, No. SJC-228, 1996 Me. LEXIS 32, at *1 (Me. Feb. 5, 1996); *see also* Jason Wolfe, *CBS to Film Jurors at Work in Maine Court*, Portland Press Herald, Feb. 7, 1996, at 1A.

2. Telephone Interview with George Logan, Administrative Office of the Court, Arizona Supreme Court (Aug. 17, 1996). The trials in which CBS filmed jury deliberations were State v. York, No. CR-93/09611 (Ariz. Sup. Ct. Maricopa Co., Doherty, J.), State v. Lopez, No. CR-95/10855 (Ariz. Sup. Ct., Maricopa Co., Gerst, J.), and State v. Solano, No. CR-95/06739 (Ariz. Sup. Ct., Maricopa Co., Ryan, J.). *Id.*

3. *See* Trustman Senger, *TV Preview: Trial by Jury on Frontline*, Wash. Post, Apr. 8, 1986, at C2.

4. Margaret E. Guthrie, *Film Takes an Inside Look at Deliberations of Jurors*, Nat'l L.J., Apr. 14, 1986, at 8.

5. Ray Archer, *Soundness of Jury System Challenged*, State J.-Reg. (Springfield, Ill.), June 23, 1996, at 15; Mark Curriden, *Bitterness Is Growing Against Jury System*, Chattanooga Times, Jan. 31, 1986, at A1; Cathleen Decker, *The Simpson Legacy*, L.A. Times, Oct. 8, 1995, at S2.

6. *See* Guthrie, *supra* note 4, at 8.

7. *See* Alan Calnan, *The Insurance Exclusionary Rule Revisited: Are Reports of Its Demise Exaggerated?*, 52 Ohio St. L.J. 1177, 1234 (1991).

8. Administrative Order, Statement in Nonconcurrence, No. SJC-228, 1996 Me. LEXIS 32, at *3-6 (Feb. 5, 1996) (Glassman and Rudman, JJ., dissenting) [hereinafter Statement in Nonconcurrence].

9. Catherine Foster, *Popular Law Professor Combines '60s with '80s*, L.A. Times, Dec. 10, 1989, at N9.

10. *Id.*
11. Guthrie, *supra* note 4, at 8.
12. *Id.*
13. *Id.*
14. *Id.* Judge Fine now sits on the Wisconsin Court of Appeals.
15. *Id.*
16. *Id.*
17. Senger, *supra* note 3, at C2. Reed had served a seven-year prison term for armed robbery, but had complied strictly with the rules of his probation for nine years after his release. Guthrie, *supra* note 4, at 8.
18. Senger, *supra* note 3, at C2; Guthrie, *supra* note 4, at 8.
19. *Id.*
20. Guthrie, *supra* note 4, at 8.
21. George V. Higgins, *Television: Truth, but Not the Whole Truth*, Wall St. J., Apr. 14, 1986, at 26.
22. *Id.*
23. *Id.* A motion for mistrial had been offered by the defense early in the trial, and Judge Fine had held it under advisement throughout the proceedings. *Id.*
24. Guthrie, *supra* note 4, at 8.
25. *Id.*
26. *Id.*
27. *Id.*
28. *CBS Reports: Inside the Jury Room*, Production Protocol, 1996 Me. LEXIS 32, at *6 (Feb. 5, 1996) [hereinafter Production Protocol]. This is the application made to the Supreme Judicial Court of Maine by CBS, and is available on LEXIS as an addendum to the Supreme Judicial Court of Maine's Administrative Order, *supra* note 1.
29. Production Protocol, *supra* note 28, at *6. The analysis would include interviews with the trial judge, nationally prominent attorneys, and "academicians who have studied how juries decide cases." *Id.* at *10. CBS's proposed analysis would not include "body language experts, handwriting analysts or other such pop psychologists." *Id.*
30. *Id.* at *6.
31. Administrative Order, *supra* note 1, at *1.
32. *Maine Court Rules CBS Can Film Jury Deliberation*, Reuters Fin. Rep., Feb. 6, 1996, *available in* LEXIS, News Library, Curnws File.
33. *Id.* Coverage of Maine trials is governed by the Rules Governing Photographic and Electronic Coverage of Trial Courts, adopted by the Supreme Judicial Court of Maine on July 11, 1995. Order-Cameras in the Courtroom, Maine Rules of Court 307 (West 1996).
34. *Maine Court Rules*, *supra* note 32.
35. Administrative Order, *supra* note 1, at *2.
36. Production Protocol, *supra* note 28, at *10.
37. *Id.* at *9.
38. *Id.* at *11-12. The Production Protocol also discussed the possibility of constructing "blinds," such as one-way mirrors, to mask the presence of cameras in the jury room. *Id.* at *12.
39. *Id.* at *13.
40. Administrative Order, *supra* note 1, at *1. In addition, the Cumberland County Superior Court proposed to select the jury panel for the CBS case from a "seasoned pool," that is, from a pool of citizens who were in their third week of jury service and had previously served as jurors on one or more trials. Telephone Interview with Lucille Lepitre, Clerk, Cumberland County Superior Court (Mar. 1 1996). Maine residents called for jury duty must serve a full three weeks, and are not released from service after sitting as jurors on a trial. *Id.* It was hoped that the use of such an

experienced pool would minimize the potential inhibitory effect of camera coverage by selecting jurors who would be more familiar with and confident in the deliberation process. *Id.*

41. Statement in Nonconcurrence, *supra* note 8, at *3-6; *see infra* text accompanying notes 84-86.

42. Statement in Nonconcurrence, *supra* note 8, at *6.

43. H.P. 1360, 117th Leg., 2d Reg. Sess. (Me. 1996). The full text of the Libby bill, introduced as a measure to protect jury secrecy, is as follows:

> **An Act to Prohibit the Photographing or Videotaping of Jury Deliberations Emergency preamble.**
>
> Whereas, Acts of the Legislature do not become effective for 90 days after adjournment unless enacted as emergencies; and
>
> Whereas, there is no public right of access to jury deliberations; and
>
> Whereas, it is uniformly recognized that juries function best when there is a free, open and candid debate; and
>
> Whereas, the presence of cameras or other electronic recording devices in jury deliberation rooms could adversely affect the free, open and candid debate of juries being filmed; and
>
> Whereas, this adverse effect would deprive litigants of justice; and
>
> Whereas, the Supreme Judicial Court recently decided to allow CBS News to film jury deliberations in civil trials occurring in Cumberland County by placing cameras in jury deliberation rooms; and
>
> Whereas, filming is planned to begin in May, prior to the expiration of the 90-day period for nonemergency legislation; and
>
> Whereas, in the judgment of the Legislature, these facts constitute an emergency within the meaning of the Constitution of Maine and require the following legislation as immediately necessary for the preservation of the public peace, health and safety; now, therefore,
>
> Be it enacted by the People of the State of Maine as follows:
> Sec. 1. 4 M.R.S.A. Section 122 is enacted to read:
> **Section 122.** Electronic recording of jury deliberations
>
> The recording or viewing of jury meetings or deliberations by electronic means is prohibited. As used in this section, "electronic means" includes, but is not limited to, still photography, videotaping or audiotaping and direct live video or audio feeds. A person who violates this section is guilty of a Class E crime.
>
> **Emergency clause.** In view of the emergency cited in the preamble, this Act takes effect when approved.

Id. Cf. 18 U.S.C. § 1508 (1996) (prohibiting recording or eavesdropping); Va. Code Ann. § 18.2-468 (Michie 1996) (prohibiting sound recording only); S.D. Codified Laws Ann. § 23A-35A-20 (1996) (making recording of jury deliberations a felony); Cal. Penal Code § 167 (Deering 1996) (prohibiting the recording of jury deliberations but containing a provision allowing jurors to consent to such recording); N.C. Gen. Stat. § 14-227.2 (1995) (prohibiting recording or listening without consent of the jury).

44. *See* Peter Jackson, *CBS Taping Prompts Bill; Plan Opposes Cameras in Maine Jury Room*, Bangor Daily News, Mar. 22, 1996, *available in* WESTLAW, 1996 WL 2188522 (quoting King spokesman Dennis Bailey as stating that "[w]e could learn some valuable lessons from [the CBS tape]").

45. *See* H.P. 1360, *supra* note 43, Judiciary Comm. Amendment A (March 30, 1996). The amended version of the bill replaced the word "viewing" with "transmittal" and struck out the provision making violation of the proposed legislation a criminal offense. *Id.*

46. A. Jay Higgins, *Supplemental Budget Gets $52 Million Legislative Nod*, Bangor Daily News, Apr. 1, 1996, *available in* LEXIS, News Library, Curnws File.

47. *See* H.P. 1360, *supra* note 43.

48. Jason Wolfe, *TV Justice Documentary Won't Include Maine Jurors*, Portland Press Herald, May 18, 1996, at 1A.

49. Me. CV 95-518 (1996). This suit was filed after Donaldson Calder drove his car into the rear end of John Small's vehicle, causing injuries to Small. Donaldson died after suffering a stroke near the time of the accident, leaving an issue of fact as to whether Donaldson's stroke precipitated the accident or whether the accident caused the stroke. *Id.* Determination of this fact would impact on Donaldson's negligence and possible liability to Small. *Id.; see also* Wolfe, *supra* note 48, at 1A.

50. Wolfe, *supra* note 48, at 1A.

51. *Id.*

52. *CBS Seeks Jury Room Cameras: Wants to Record Process in Arizona Criminal Trial*, Ariz. Daily Star, Feb. 7, 1996, at 1A (quoting Arizona Supreme Court spokesman Bill Norman).

53. Ariz. R. Civ. P. 39(b)(10).

54. Ariz. R. Civ. P. 39(p).

55. Ariz. R. Civ. P. 51(b)(3).

56. Ariz. R. Civ. P. 18.6(d).

57. Ariz. R. Civ. P. 39(f); *see also* William H. Carlile, *Arizona Jury Reforms Buck Legal Traditions*, Christian Science Mon., Feb. 22, 1996, at 1.

58. Wolfe, *supra* note 48, at 1A.

59. Telephone Interview with John O'Leary, Chair, A.B.A. Litig. Sec. (Mar. 8, 1996).

60. *Id.*

61. *CBS News Will Show Jury System at Work in Four Ariz. Cases*, Ariz. Daily Star, July 20, 1996, at 2B.

62. *Id.*

63. *CBS Seeks Jury Room Cameras*, *supra* note 52, at 1A.

64. State v. Solano, No. CR-95/06739 (Ariz. Sup. Ct., Maricopa Co., Ryan, J.). The charges against the defendant, Modesta Solano, included possession of marijuana with intent to sell, trafficking in marijuana, possession of cocaine, and trafficking in controlled substances. *Id.*

65. State v. York, No. CR-93/09611 (Ariz. Sup. Ct., Maricopa Co., Doherty, J.). The defendant, Troy York, was charged with aggravated assault. *Id.*

66. State v. Lopez, No. CR-95/10855 (Ariz. Sup. Ct., Maricopa Co., Gerst, J.). The defendant, Arturo Lopez, was accused of robbing a convenience store. *Id.*

67. *Id.*

68. State v. Solano, No. CR-95/06739 (Ariz. Sup. Ct., Maricopa Co., Ryan, J.). The defendant was sentenced on July 11, 1996, to five years in Arizona state prison. Interview with George Logan, *supra* note 2.

69. Interview with George Logan, *supra* note 2.

70. *See* Statement in Nonconcurrence, *supra* note 8, at *5-6.

71. Production Protocol, *supra* note 28, at *7. CBS contended that

> [w]hile the knowledge that cameras are rolling—even though they are unseen—may initially influence the jurors' dress, manner of speech, or other superficial characteristics, it is not likely to change the verdict itself. In our experience, self-consciousness tends to disappear quickly when there is serious business at hand (e.g., a heart transplant to perform, to name one life-or-death situation that we have recently been permitted to videotape)."

Id.

72. Statement in Nonconcurrence, *supra* note 8, at *5-6.

73. Several behavioral studies have, however, been made of mock juries. One of the most comprehensive of these was conducted by Reid Hastie, Steven Penrod, and Nancy Pennington, who published their results. Reid Hastie et al., Inside the Jury (1983). Subjects in this study were selected from jury pools in three Massachusetts counties, subjected to a brief voir dire, and shown a videotape of an actual homicide trial. *Id.* at 45-47. The subjects, who had been divided into several groups, were then taken to adjoining deliberation rooms and informed that their deliberations would be recorded. *Id.* at 51. The authors concluded, based on comparison of the discussions of each

mock jury, that the presence of recording devices had little measurable impact on their deliberations. *Id.* at 231. The authors were quick to warn, however, that "it would be unwise to generalize from these observations to actual jury behavior." *Id.* The degree to which the added responsibility of service on a trial jury would alter this behavior pattern, if any, remains unknown and unknowable.

74. *See* Andrew D. Leipold, *Rethinking Jury Nullification*, 82 Va. L. Rev. 253 (1996); *see also* Jack B. Weinstein, *Considering Jury "Nullification": When May and Should a Jury Reject the Law to Do Justice*, 30 Am. Crim. L. Rev. 239 (1993). Professor Leipold states that "[jury] [n]ullification occurs when the defendant's guilt is clear beyond a reasonable doubt, but the jury, based on its own sense of justice or fairness, decides to acquit." Leipold, *supra*, at 253.

75. Guthrie, *supra* note 4, at 8.

76. Higgins, *supra* note 21, at 26.

77. *Id.*

78. *Jury System Judged Outdated by Many*, State J.-Reg. (Springfield, Ill.), May 14, 1995, at 9 (citing a study completed by the Center for Jury Studies). This conclusion is echoed by Harry Kalvin and Hans Zeisel in their 1966 study, *The American Jury.* Harry Kalven & Hans Zeisel, The American Jury (1966). It is noteworthy that no state averages more than 15 percent hung juries in serious criminal trials. *See* Simpson Trial Monitored for Insight into Jury System, Dallas Morning News, Sept. 24, 1995, at 10A.

79. *CBS Seeks Jury Room Cameras*, *supra* note 52, at 1A. *But see CBS News Will Show Jury System at Work in Four Ariz. Cases*, *supra* note 61, at 2B (quoting Judge Reinstein as saying that "deliberations remained pure").

80. Wolfe, *supra* note 48, at 1A.

81. *Id.*

82. *See* Mercedes M. Cardona, *Show to Feature Leading Experts*, Pensions & Inv., June 26, 1995, at 43 (quoting B. Thomas Willison, the executive producer of a PBS investment program, as saying that PBS viewers are better educated and "more financially solvent" than the public at large).

83. Notably, even some supporters of CBS's proposed documentary have acknowledged the possibility that media consciousness might affect the deliberations of the jurors. A Bangor Daily News editorial, written soon after the Supreme Judicial Court of Maine's decision, lauded the educational possibilities of CBS's proposal but added that "the architects of the experiment are forewarned. The hidden presence of a camera lens might magnify human nature . . . . [t]he burden here is on the judge to monitor behavior and pull the plug on taping if there are signs it is overwhelming the process." *Jury on Camera*, Bangor Daily News, Feb. 8, 1996, *available in* LEXIS, News Library, Curnws File.

84. *See* Statement in Nonconcurrence, *supra* note 8, at *3-6.

85. *Id.* at *5.

86. *See id.*

87. *See supra* text accompanying notes 15-17.

88. Production Protocol, *supra* note 28, at *6.

89. Higgins, *supra* note 21, at 26.

90. Jackson, *supra* note 44.

91. *Maine Moves to Block CBS Documentary on Jury Process*, Reuters, Mar. 20, 1996, *available in* LEXIS, News Library, Curnws File.

92. Statement in Nonconcurrence, *supra* note 8, at *5.

93. *See* Barbara Bradley, *Juries and Justice: Is the System Obsolete*, Wash. Times, Apr. 24, 1995, at 6.

94. *See, e.g.*, Christopher Stern, *Cameras OK'd in Federal Appeals Courts*, Broadcasting and Cable, Mar. 18, 1996, at 22 (quoting Radio-Television News Directors' Association President David Bartlett in support of opening all American courts, including the United States Supreme Court, to camera coverage).

95. New York, for instance, which is currently the headquarters of Court TV and one of the primary sources of trials broadcast on that network, was the forty-third state to allow trial broadcasts. New York did not allow camera coverage of trials until June 16, 1987, six years after the Supreme Court had validated trial broadcasts in Chandler v. Florida, 449 U.S. 560 (1981), and nine years after the Conference of State Chief Justices had voted 44-1 to endorse limited trial coverage. *See* Mark Uhlig, *Governor Signs a Bill Allowing Court Cameras*, N.Y. Times, June 17, 1987, at B2. Even the federal courts, which have long been hostile to camera coverage, have become more open in recent times. The Judicial Conference of the United States voted on March 12, 1996, to reverse its 1994 ban on camera coverage of federal appellate courts. *See* Stern, *supra* note 94, at 22. It is noteworthy that the experimental Florida rules governing trial coverage described in *Chandler*, adopted by the Florida Supreme Court in 1977. *See also* Petition of Post-Newsweek Stations, Florida, Inc., 347 So. 2d 404 (1977), bear a striking resemblance to the rules contained in CBS's Production Protocol to insure unobtrusiveness in its experimental jury coverage, *see* Production Protocol, *supra* note 28, at *6-15; *Chandler*, 449 U.S. at 566; *Petition of Post-Newsweek*, 347 So. 2d at 405-06.

96. *See* cases cited *infra* note 130.

97. *See* United States v. Borelli, 336 F.2d 376, 392 (2d Cir. 1964).

98. United States v. Barnes, 604 F.2d 121 (2d Cir. 1979), *cert. denied*, 446 U.S. 907 (1980).

99. *See* Eric Wertheirn, *Anonymous Juries*, 54 Fordham L. Rev. 981, 984 (1986).

100. *See* Catherine Gewertz, *Judge Halts His Blanket Use of Jury Anonymity in Bellflower*, L.A. Times, Jan. 10, 1995, at 3; *see also* Nancy J. King, *Nameless Justice: The Case for the Routine Use of Anonymous Juries in Criminal Trials*, 49 Vand. L. Rev. 123 (1996) (advocating routine empanelment of anonymous juries as a means of alleviating "juror stress").

101. *See A Conversation with Gil Garcetti*, L.A. Daily News, Oct. 29, 1995, at V1.

102. *See* Tanya E. Coke, *Lady Justice May Be Blind, But Is She a Soul Sister? Race-Neutrality and the Ideal of Representative Juries*, 69 N.Y.U. L. Rev. 327 (1994).

103. Benjamin A. Holden et al., *Does Race Affect Juries? Injustice with Verdicts*, Chi. Sun-Times, Oct. 8, 1995, at 28. Other statistics cited in this article include an acquittal rate of 28.7 percent in predominantly black Washington, D.C., and an acquittal rate of 30 percent for 1993 in Wayne County, Mich., which includes Detroit. *Id.*

104. *See* Clarence Page, *Deep Racial Split Is Ever Apparent After O.J. Verdict*, Fresno Bee, Oct. 12, 1995, at B5 (comparing the reactions of white Americans to the Simpson verdict with the reactions of black Americans to the verdict in the trial of the police officers accused of beating Rodney King); Tony Knight, *Debating Simpson Verdict*, L.A. Daily News, Oct. 16, 1995, at N1.

105. Betsy Streisand, *And Justice for All?*, U.S. News & World Rep., Oct. 9, 1995, at 46. Among the results of a U.S. News & World Report poll of 1000 registered voters cited in this article are as follows: 25 percent of Americans believe that the Simpson trial shows that there is no justice in America, 85 percent believe the trial shows that there is different justice for those who have money and those who do not; more than 60 percent of black Americans (as opposed to 30 percent of whites) believe that there is different justice for black and white Americans. *Id.*

106. *See* Knight, *supra* note 104, at N1.

107. *A Conversation with Gil Garcetti*, *supra* note 101, at V1.

108. *See* Patricia Hurtado & Curtis Rist, *Nelson Jurors Angry at Judge and Critics*, Newsday, Oct. 31, 1992, at 4.

109. Holden et al., *supra* note 103, at 28.

110. *Id.*

111. *CNN & Company* (CNN television broadcast, July 14, 1994).

112. Brigitte Greenberg, *Professor Urges Black Jurors to Defy Law in Non-Violent Cases*, Star-Ledger (Newark, N.J.), Dec. 25, 1995, *available in* WESTLAW, 1996 WL 11809012. Professor

Paul Butler, who has espoused this position for several years, recently explained his reasoning in *Racially Based Jury Nullification: Black Power in the Criminal Justice System*, 105 Yale L.J. 677 (1996).

113. *Dissatisfaction with the Jury System Is Growing, and More Reform Is Expected*, Nat'l L.J., Dec. 25, 1995, at C12.

114. Beth Taylor, *What Makes a Jury Tick? 12 Varied People: There's No Foolproof Formula for Picking and Persuading Jurors—or Predicting Their Verdicts*, Orlando Sentinel, Mar. 17, 1996, at G1.

115. At least one author has suggested that jury deliberations might be recorded in order to ensure that juries follow the "insurance exclusionary rule," which holds that evidence that a party is or is not insured may not be admitted to prove negligence. *See* Calnan, *supra* note 7, at 1234-44. Professor Calnan suggests that recording jury deliberations might be useful in determining whether juries take into account insurance coverage which provides parties with a "deeper pocket" with which to pay damages. *Id.* He suggests placing a recording device in plain view in the jury room during deliberations and limiting the distribution of the record thus produced to the parties' attorneys and appellate judges. *Id.* at 1235.

116. *See, e.g.*, Debates in the Convention of the Commonwealth of Massachusetts (1788), *reprinted in* 2 The Debates on the Adoption of the Federal Constitution 109-14 (Jonathon Elliott ed., 2d ed. 1836). This doctrine has been a part of American jurisprudence from the early days of the United States. *See id.* (including comment from Mr. Holmes that defendant should be tried in the vicinity where his alleged offense was committed so local jurors could judge his character and the credibility of witnesses).

117. *See* Note, *Public Disclosures of Jury Deliberations*, 96 Harv. L. Rev. 886, 896 (1983) ("Many of the decisions that jury critics call 'errors' are not errors at all: instead, they are instances of proper and necessary compromise or of 'nullification' of a law that does not square with some collective sense of justice."). This Note is concerned with post-trial interviews of jurors rather than jury-room recordings, and reaches the conclusion that radical measures to prevent such disclosures are unnecessary in part because post-trial interviews are highly unlikely to affect appellate proceedings. *Id.* Such an effect would be far more likely to occur if actual records of deliberations were available.

118. It is important to note that, in criminal cases, appeals based on jury misconduct can only be made by the defense. The doctrine of double jeopardy protects an acquitted defendant from retrial even when the verdict is achieved by means of jury tampering or other fraud on the justice system. David S. Rudstein, *Double Jeopardy and the Fraudulently-Obtained Acquittal*, 60 Mo. L. Rev. 607, 620-31 (1995). Routine recording of jury deliberations would thus tip the balance of the appellate process in favor of the defense.

119. But see Calnan, *supra* note 7, at 1242, arguing that "the fear that too much scrutiny of jury behavior will result in an avalanche of motions, appeals, and retrials is founded on a mistrust of counsel, jurors or the system itself." Professor Calnan, however, admits that the system has had "varying degrees of success" in attempting to curb abuse of process with sanctions or disciplinary action. *Id.*

120. See, for example, Jan Hoffman, *Jury Duty Dodgers Tell It to the Judge*, N.Y. Times, Apr. 8, 1996, at B1, indicating that 30,000 residents of New York County (Manhattan) who have been called for jury service have failed to appear. *Id.* The article quotes New York County Clerk Norman Goodman as stating that "it's a miracle" that 30 percent of jurors called for service during March 1996 had appeared. *Id.* In January, only 15 percent of those called had appeared for jury service. *Id.*

121. *See* Note, *supra* note 117, at 890.

Conscientious jury service will always call for courage; especially in small, close-knit communities, the office requires its holders to take a public stand. But jurors' willingness to depart from community

> expectations becomes even less probable if a wide audience may discover precisely how much each individual contributed to an unpopular verdict or which jurors delayed or thwarted a popular one.

Id.

122. David Sharpe, *Maine High Court Says CBS Can Tape Jury Deliberations*, Phoenix Gazette, Feb. 7, 1996, at A11 (quoting Boston defense attorney Tom Hoopes).

123. Among the most egregious examples of this problem are the recent attacks on Federal District Judge Harold Baer for suppressing evidence gained from search of suspected drug courier Carol Bayless. Don Van Natta, Jr., *Judge Finds Wit Tested by Criticism*, N.Y. Times, Feb. 7, 1996, at B2, and on New York Criminal Court Judge Lorin Duckman by Governor George Pataki and Mayor Rudolph Giuliani; Michael Slackman, *Top Judge Says Attacks Will Influence Rulings*, Newsday, Mar. 2, 1996, at A11. In both of these examples, criticism was out of proportion to the facts. *See* Jim Dwyer, *Making Dumb Remarks Is Judge's Only Blunder*, Daily News (N.Y.), Apr. 23, 1996, at 5.

124. *See, e.g.*, United States v. Real Property Known as 77 East 3rd Street, 849 F. Supp. 876 (S.D.N.Y. 1994) (holding that potential threat to jurors' safety in a civil forfeiture action, involving the notorious Hell's Angels motorcycle gang, was sufficient to warrant the empanelment of an anonymous jury even though there was no precedent for doing so in a civil case).

125. *See* Daniel W. Shuman et al., *The Health Effects of Jury Service*, 18 Law & Psychol. Rev. 267, 268-72 (1994) (surveying relevant research and suggesting that "jurors may experience stress . . . from the trial process itself"; a survey of hundreds of former jurors indicated that up to 47 percent showed symptoms of depression at some point during the trial process); James E. Kelley, *Addressing Juror Stress: A Trial Judge's Perspective*, 43 Drake L. Rev. 97 (1994) (reporting an Iowa study of more than 500 jurors showing that post-traumatic stress symptoms often continue long after trial).

126. United States v. Watson, 669 F.2d 1374, 1391 (11th Cir. 1982).

127. *Id.*

128. Guthrie, *supra* note 4, at 8.

129. *Id.*

130. *See, e.g.*, *Watson*, 669 F.2d at 1391 ("Jury deliberations are kept private and secret to ensure that the verdict . . . is not affected by outside influences or matters extrinsic to evidence presented at trial."); *In re* Globe Newspaper Co., 920 F.2d 88, 94 (1st Cir. 1990) ("a special historical and essential value applies to the secrecy of jury deliberations which is not applicable to other trial and pre-trial proceedings"); Babson v. United States, 330 F.2d 662, 665-66 (9th Cir. 1964) ("A juror must be insulated against influences and protected against pressures that would tend to fetter him in the free exercise of his own judgment. To this end the law requires that all deliberations by a jury must be conducted in the utmost privacy."); People v. Bouton, 405 N.E.2d 699, 703 (N.Y. 1980) ("The strong public policy favoring the absolute confidentiality of jury deliberations is not lightly to be disregarded."); People v. Oliver, 241 Cal. Rptr. 804, 806 (Ct. App. 1987) ("Equally implicit in this constitutional guaranty is the right to have the jury's deliberations conducted privately and in secret, free from all outside intrusions, and extraneous influences or intimidations."). Also worthy of note is the letter sent to the Senate Judiciary Committee in 1956 by then-Deputy Attorney General William P. Rogers in support of the enactment of 18 U.S.C. § 1508, stating that "such practices [as the recording of jury deliberations], however well intentioned, obviously and inevitably stifle the discussion and free exchange of ideas among jurors . . . and are inconsistent with the principles of the Seventh Amendment to the Constitution of the United States, which requires that the right to trial by jury be preserved." *See* H.R. Rep. No. 2807, 84th Cong. (1956), *reprinted in* 1956 U.S.C.C.A.N. 4151.

131. *See* Clark v. United States, 289 U.S. 1, 13-14 (1933).

132. *Id.* at 13.

133. *See* 18 U.S.C. § 1508 (1996); Ala. Code § 13A-10-130 (1996); Cal. Penal Code § 167 (Deering 1996); Haw. Rev. Stat. § 710-1077 (1995); Mich. Comp. Laws § 750.120b (1996); N.C.

Gen. Stat. § 14-227.2 (1995); S.D. Codified Laws Ann. § 23A-35A-20 (1996); Va. Code Ann. § 18.2-468 (Michie 1996). Under California law, recording trial jury deliberations without the consent of the jury is a misdemeanor. Cal. Penal Code § 167. This would tend to prohibit routine taping of jury deliberations in California, but would allow a CBS-style experiment. North Carolina is the only other state which specifically allows recording of deliberations with the consent of the jury. *See* N.C. Gen. Stat. § 14-227.2.

134. *See* State v. Lehnherr, 569 P.2d 54, 55 (Or. Ct. App. 1977); People v. Bacon, 136 N.Y.S.2d 431, 432 (Tioga County Ct. 1954), *aff'd*, 127 N.E.2d 81 (N.Y. 1955).

135. *See infra* note 136 and accompanying text.

136. *See, e.g.*, United States v. Virginia Erection Corp., 335 F.2d 868 (4th Cir. 1964) (alternate juror); People v. Knapp, 3 N.W. 927 (Mich. 1879) (bailiff); Little v. United States, 73 F.2d 861 (10th Cir. 1934) (court stenographer); People v. Bacon, 136 N.Y.S.2d 431 (Tioga County Ct. 1954) (police officer), *aff'd*, 127 N.E.2d 81 (N.Y. 1955).

137. *See infra* notes 140-153 and accompanying text.

138. Fed. R. Crim. P. 24(c).

139. *See* Fed. R. Crim. P. 52(a). Rule 52 provides as follows: "(a) Harmless Error. Any error, defect, irregularity or variance which does not affect substantial rights shall be disregarded." The burden of proof is on the prosecution in determining that error is harmless. *See, e.g.*, United States v. Olano, 507 U.S. 725, 741 (1993), *rev'g* 934 F.2d 1425 (9th Cir. 1991).

140. 335 F.2d 868 (4th Cir. 1964).

141. United States v. Virginia Erection Corp., 335 F.2d 868, 872 (4th Cir. 1964) (citation omitted).

142. 934 F.2d 1425 (9th Cir. 1991), *rev'd*, 507 U.S. 725 (1993).

143. *Olano*, 934 F.2d at 1438-39.

144. *See Olano*, 507 U.S. at 741.

145. *See* Fed. R. Crim. P. 52(b).

146. *Olano*, 507 U.S. at 739 ("Respondents have made no specific showing that the alternate jurors in this case either participated in the jury's deliberations or 'chilled' deliberation by the regular jurors.").

147. *Id.* at 740.

148. 650 F.2d 122 (7th Cir. 1981).

149. *Johnson*, 650 F.2d at 125.

150. *Id.; see also* Little v. United States, 73 F.2d 861, 866-67 (10th Cir. 1934).

> We conclude that where the entire record affirmatively discloses that an error has not affected the substantial rights of an appellant, it will be disregarded. But where error occurs which, within the range of a reasonable possibility, may have affected the verdict of a jury, appellant is not required to explore the minds of the jurors in an effort to prove that it did in fact influence their verdict.

Id.

151. *Johnson*, 650 F.2d at 125.

152. *Id.; see also* Comment, *Criminal Law: Alternate Jurors: Substitution After Submission of Case: Presence During Deliberations of Jury*, 24 Cal. L. Rev. 735, 738 (1936).

> But this reasoning [that the presence of non-jurors might prejudice the jury], though it may be valid when the intruder is a total stranger, loses its force when the intruder is an alternate juror chosen in the same way as a regular juror, subjected to the same test of impartiality, and required to possess all the qualifications of a regular juror.

Id.

153. *Johnson*, 650 F.2d at 125.

154. *See, e.g.*, Mattox v. United States, 146 U.S. 140, 151 (1892); Rickard v. State, 74 Ind. 275, 277-78 (1881) (reversing convictions reached where bailiff had communicated with jurors during deliberations).

155. 73 F.2d 861 (10th Cir. 1934).

156. *Id.* at 864.
157. *Id.* (citations omitted). The court noted that sending a stenographer into the jury room in the absence of the defendant and defense counsel might lead to "a mistake in the reading of a shorthand symbol . . . an unconscious or deliberate emphasis or lack of it, an innocent attempt to explain the meaning of a word or a phrase, and many other events which might readily occur, would result in irremediable prejudice to the defendant." *Id.*
158. People v. Guzman, 555 N.E.2d 259, 263 (N.Y. 1990); *see also* Kokas v. Commonwealth, 237 S.W. 1090, 1093 (Ky. 1922) ("In the face of so grave an error as that committed by the trial court in this case [by allowing a stenographer into the jury room during deliberations], the appellate court . . . must assume that the error amounted to such an invasion of the appellant's constitutional rights as to deprive him of a fair and impartial trial."). *But see* People v. Oliver, 241 Cal. Rptr. 804, 808 (Ct. App. 1987) (holding that although "[t]he presence of the court reporter in the jury room during deliberations . . . violated both the statute [Cal. Penal Code § 167] and the Constitution," her presence was not per se reversible error because "alone among court officers, the reporter can be perceived as absolutely neutral with no interest in the outcome nor involvement with the substance of the proceedings"). Note that cameras in the jury room will inevitably be placed by someone with "an interest in the outcome" of the proceedings, whether the cameras are placed there by television stations interested in maximum ratings and sensational coverage or by jurists interested in compiling a record for possible use on appeal.
159. 3 N.W. 927 (Mich. 1879).
160. *Id.* at 929-30.
161. *Id.*
162. *See id.*
163. *See* Sharpe, *supra* note 122, at A11.
164. 136 N.Y.S.2d 431 (Tioga County Ct., 1954), *aff'd*, 127 N.E.2d 81 (N.Y. 1955).
165. *Bacon*, 136 N.Y.S.2d at 432.
166. *Id.*
167. *Id.*
168. *Id.*
169. *See, e.g.*, People v. Guzman, 555 N.E.2d 259, 262-63 (N.Y. 1990).
170. 555 N.E.2d 259 (N.Y. 1990).
171. *Id.* at 262-63.
172. *Id.* at 263. The court acknowledged that "the general rule is that nonjurors are not allowed in the jury room during deliberations. This rule protects the jury from outside influence, promotes uninhibited discussion and maintains secrecy." *Id.* at 262.
173. *See* Johnson v. Duckworth, 650 F.2d 122, 125 (7th Cir. 1981).
174. *Id.*
175. *See supra* notes 154-63 and accompanying text.
176. *See Guzman*, 555 N.E.2d at 263. The court directed that sign language interpreters be sworn to keep the confidence of the jury room. *Id.* This would, naturally, be antithetical to the purpose of camera coverage of jury deliberations.
177. *See, e.g.*, People v. Valles, 593 P.2d 240 (Cal. 1979) (holding that a criminal defendant could stipulate to the presence of an alternate juror in the jury room during deliberations); Miller v. State, 79 S.E. 232 (Ga. Ct. App. 1913).
178. *Johnson*, 650 F.2d at 124.
179. *See id.* at 125.
180. People v. Bruneman, 40 P.2d 891, 894 (Cal. Ct. App. 1935), cited in dissenting opinion in *Valles*, 24 Cal. 3d at 128 (Mosk, J., dissenting).

PART FOUR

Punishment and Sentencing

"Killing humans is an act so awesome, so destructive, so irremediable that no killer can be looked upon with anything but horror, even when that killer is the state."

—Henry Schwarzschild,
American Civil Liberties Union, 1981

INTRODUCTION

Once a defendant has been adjudicated guilty of a crime by a jury, a judge, or by his or her own admission of guilt, the state has the constitutional right to impose a punitive sanction. Most sentencing decisions are made by judges. However, in a few jurisdictions, the determination of punishment for certain types of crimes, such as capital murder, is the responsibility of the jury. For most offenses, offenders are sentenced on the day of conviction or on the following day. Although judges are generally limited in their discretion regarding the severity of sentence, either by statutory provisions or by sentencing guidelines, they still have a considerable amount of latitude in selecting the type of punishment. For example, potential sentencing options include fines, community sentences such as probation or house arrest, confinement in jail or prison, and capital punishment. Determining the most appropriate punishment for a particular offender is difficult because the criminal court system is influenced by a number of competing rationales for sentencing:

- "The punishment should fit the crime."
- "The sentence should act as a warning to others."
- "Lock 'em up and throw away the keys."

- "An eye for an eye, a tooth for a tooth."
- "Rehabilitate offenders so they can be safely returned to society."

It is the responsibility of the judge to choose among these competing rationales when determining the appropriate sentence. A judge's decision may be influenced by his or her personal characteristics, by organizational factors such as prison overcrowding, or by community considerations.

This section examines a number of the current debates regarding punishment. For example, is there racial discrimination in the application of the death penalty? Should victims be allowed to actively participate in the sentencing process? Does 'three strikes and you're out' laws reduce serious crime? Should capital punishment be imposed on juvenile murderers? Should corporal punishment serve as an appropriate alternative to prison for noncapital offenders? These are a few of the intriguing and controversial questions addressed in this section.

In the first article in this section, "Themes of Injustice: Wrongful Convictions, Racial Prejudice, and Lawyer Incompetence," Bennett L. Gershman discusses some of the problems that manifest themselves in the criminal justice system. These problems include the conviction of innocent defendants, racial prejudice, and lawyer incompetence. Gershman argues that the greatest injustice that a society could perpetrate against its citizenry is to convict and possibly execute an innocent person. Even so, he cites several instances where innocent defendants have been erroneously convicted, sentenced to death, and eventually executed. Gershman also believes that racial discrimination still persists in the application of the death penalty. One half of the persons on death row in the United States are African American or Hispanic. Even more revealing is that research on discrimination and the death penalty shows that black defendants convicted of killing white victims have a much high probability of being sentenced to death than similarly situated white offenders who kill black victims. Finally, Gershman believes that the ability of public defenders and appointed counsel to provide quality defense services to indigent defendants is being threatened by their excessive case loads, insufficient funding, and inadequate training and supervision.

A number of measures have been introduced over the last several years to improve victim satisfaction with the criminal justice system. Victim participation in the sentencing of criminal offenders is one such popular measure. In "Victim Participation at Sentencing," Valerie Finn-DeLuca argues that victim impact evidence should be permitted only within carefully constructed guidelines. Because the United States Supreme Court decision in *Payne* appears to allow unlimited testimony of questionable value and relevance, Finn-DeLuca believes that the constitutional rights of defendants may be in jeopardy. She suggests that it would have been far more helpful and reasonable for the Court to require states to develop specific criteria for the admission of victim impact evidence. For example, the process that evolved form the *Furman* decision, which required the states to develop explicit criteria for the imposition of the death penalty so as to preclude its arbitrary imposition, could have been employed. The Court in *Payne* could have also required states to identify the specific types of victim impact evidence that would be admissible in a court of law. In concluding her article, Finn-Deluca recommends that the Supreme Court should review the constitutionality of these criteria individually based on jurisdictional considerations and on the rights of defendants.

In the third article, "'Three Strikes and You're Out': The Impact of California's New Mandatory Sentencing Law on Serious Crime Rates," Lisa Stolzenberg and Stewart J. D'Alessio analyzed time-series data drawn from 10 California cities to determine the effect of California's three-strikes law on serious crime levels. They found that the three-strikes law did not decrease serious crime rates below the level expected on the basis of preexisting trends. The authors offered a few plausible reasons for why California's three-strikes law had little affect on serious crime. One possibility was that because current sentencing practices already confined a substantial proportion of high-risk offenders behind bars, a diminishing marginal return could be expected from further increases in levels of incarceration. A second explanation for their findings concerned the relationship between age and crime. The effectiveness of three-strikes legislation as a crime control strategy depends on the duration of criminal careers. By the time offenders are confined for their third strike, their criminal careers usually are on the decline, if not concluded. A final plausible explanation pertained to juvenile crime. Although juveniles currently account for a large percentage of the serious crime committed in the United States, juvenile offenders were not affected by the three-strikes law in California. Consequently, the implementation of the three-strike law probably had little impact on juvenile crime levels.

In *Thompson* and *Stanford*, the United States Supreme Court addressed the question of whether juvenile offenders should be subjected to capital punishment. On the surface, the Court's promulgation of a bright line rule defining those age 16 or above as "adults" for the purpose of execution seemed to be a forthright disposition of the issue. Yet, as Kenneth E. Gewerth and Clifford Dorne point out in "Imposing the Death Penalty on Juvenile Murderers: A Constitutional Assessment," the Court's bright line rule obscures some deep divisions within the Court and some faulty, illogical reasoning. First, the Court seems to have no clear method for determining the extent (or even the existence) of a national consensus regarding the execution of juveniles. Second, both supporters and opponents of the juvenile death penalty are guilty of selective perception. Finally, after *Stanford*, there seems to be a more fundamental disagreement about how the constitutionality of a punishment—any punishment—is to be judged.

In the final article, "Don't Spare the Rod: A Proposed Return to Public, Corporal Punishment of Convicts," Whitney S. Wiederman proposes an innovative strategy for dealing with crime and criminals. Her model has two basic components. First, Wiederman argues that retribution should be used as the primary rationale for punishing criminals. Second, after society's need for vengeance has been satisfied, any residual stigma should be directed at the crime rather than at the offender. This practice allows an offender who has been punished for his or her crime to reenter society as a productive citizen. To implement her model, Wiederman advocates the use of corporal punishment in public rather than imprisonment for all noncapital crimes. Although corporal punishment may seem to be a rather barbaric means to address the crime problem, Wiederman believes that it is a reasonable and viable alternative to current methods of punishment.

16

Themes of Injustice: Wrongful Convictions, Racial Prejudice, and Lawyer Incompetence

Bennett L. Gershman*

There has always existed a tension between justice and law.[1] Contrary to popular belief, justice and law are not coextensive. They may coincide, for example, when law is used to end racial or other invidious discriminatory practices. On the other hand, justice and law may be strikingly at odds, as in the Los Angeles jury's verdict last year acquitting four police officers in the brutal beating of Rodney King. There are just laws. And there are unjust laws. There are judges who believe they should dispense justice. And there are judges who believe they should mechanically apply the law, regardless of the equities.

Notwithstanding the election of a new president, and a potentially new make-up of the Supreme Court, there is much cause for concern over justice in the United States. To borrow from Shakespeare, "the times are out of joint."[2] The Bill of Rights, whose two-hundredth anniversary we celebrated recently, has been sapped of much of its vitality over the past twenty years by a determined Supreme Court, two conservative presidents, and a law-and-order Congress. Virtually every key protection of the Bill of Rights has been diluted, eviscerated, or interpreted out of existence.[3] A recent polls shows that few 1990s Americans can identify the Bill of Rights or are aware of its guarantees.[4] Two of its greatest defenders—Justices William J. Brennan and Thurgood Marshall—are gone. And the highest court mirrors the public's insensitivity and apathy by continuing a steady retreat from its long-recognized function "to be watchful for the constitutional rights of the citizen, and against any steady encroachments thereon."[5]

This erosion of judicial protection for individual rights is also reflected in the agonizing death of Habeas Corpus, the Great Writ of liberty second only to the Magna Carta. We have witnessed over the past decade a frantic legal foot-race between a majority of the Supreme Court and some members of Congress to abolish habeas corpus, thereby preventing state inmates from seeking federal judicial redress for constitutional violations. To be sure, as with any legal remedy, habeas corpus can be abused. But statistics show that writs from state prisoners on death row have been found meritorious in one third to one half of all cases.[6] Not long ago, we watched anxiously as a few federal judges in California stayed an execution so that they could decide whether using cyanide gas for executions—the kind used in the concentration camps of World War II—violated evolving constitutional standards of decency.[7] In a

Reprinted by permission of West Group from the *Criminal Law Bulletin*, vol. 29 (1993), pp. 502–515.

tense, early morning battle of judicial power, a majority of the Supreme Court firmly directed the execution to proceed, reminding us of Chief Justice Rehnquist's view about delays in executions: "Let's get on with it."[8]

Diminished protection for individual liberties parallels diminished protection for civil rights. Blatant prejudice and racial discrimination continue to infect the criminal justice system. There was a time when northerners in this country would deride the southern judicial system for operating a racist justice. Between 1930 and 1974, of the 455 men executed in the south for rape, 405, or 89 percent were black. Virtually all of the complainants were white.[9] But we delude ourselves if we think that racial prejudice is confined to the South. A recent report by the New York State Judicial Commission on Minorities states that minority users of the New York State court system "face many of the same travesties as did their southern counterparts—unequal access, disparate treatment, and frustrated opportunity."[10]

Further, our nation's appetite for executing people, even arguably innocent people, seems to be increasing. There are presently 2,729 inmates on death row.[11] We will execute more men and women this year than in any year since the Supreme Court allowed executions to resume in 1976. At a time in our history when the highest court in the land makes life and death decisions based on technical procedural grounds, rather than justice, and begins an opinion that will decide whether a condemned man will live or die with the words, "This is a case about federalism,"[12] it is important to talk about justice.

However, defining the idea of justice, and the quintessential "just result," often proves a frustrating and elusive task. The term itself is so indefinite and subjective. Is justice done when a condemned prisoner is put to death for murder without an opportunity to present new evidence of his innocence?[13] Is it justice when a court's interpretation of the Civil Rights Act prevents judges from hearing claims against persons charged with obstructing access to an abortion clinic?[14] These examples may appear to some to be the antithesis of justice. Others, however, may see them as perfectly neutral applications of law.

Rather than talk about the concept of justice in the abstract, it might be more realistic to talk about the other side of justice, the concept of injustice. For if the meaning of justice eludes us, the meaning of injustice might be easier to grasp. Perhaps participants in the criminal justice system can arrive at greater understanding and sensitivity about their professional obligations, and confront justice issues more effectively and even compassionately, by focusing on the subject of injustice: what broad categories provide the grist for miscarriages of justice; who is responsible for perpetrating those injustices; how they can be corrected, if it is not too late.[15] Three overriding themes of injustice come to mind: convicting the innocent, racial prejudice, and lawyer incompetence.

CONVICTING THE INNOCENT

Our society, as expressed by the Supreme Court in the landmark case of *In re Winship*,[16] has made a fundamental value judgment that it is far worse to convict an innocent person than to let a guilty person go free. Indeed, we probably could reach a consensus that the greatest injustice any society can perpetrate is to convict, and possibly even put to death, an innocent person. We read recently of two men released from a California state penitentiary after spending seventeen years in jail for what the judge described as a "concocted murder conviction."[17] Of the 2,729 men and women on death row in the United States, there are several persons who, based on reports of newly discovered evidence, probably are innocent. We prefer not to think about such matters. We prefer to trust prosecutors, judges, and juries to do the right thing.

Prosecutors, however, often do not do the right thing, as several recently highly publicized murder cases have documented.[18] Judges also shirk their responsibility to prevent miscarriages of justice, as demonstrated by the Supreme Court's anti-habeas crusade.[19] Juries also make mistakes, terrible mistakes, particularly when the prosecution's proof is mistaken or fabricated.[20] Persons who carefully examined the evidence have made a persuasive case that Roger Coleman in Virginia, and Leonel Herrera in Texas, had strong claims to innocence.[21] Indeed, virtually every law-enforcement official in the state of Texas was convinced that Randall Dale Adams was guilty of murdering a police officer, until a courageous film-maker—not a lawyer, prosecutor, or judge—produced a documentary entitled "The Thin Blue Line," which exposed the Texas judicial system at its most vicious and corrupt, and which led to Adam's exoneration.[22]

According to a well-known study published in 1987, more than 350 people in this century have been erroneously convicted in the United States of crimes punishable by death; 116 of those were sentenced to death and 23 actually were executed.[23] This same study found that there have been twenty-nine mistaken convictions in capital cases in New York State, sixteen of which resulted in death verdicts.[24] New York State leads all states in executing the innocent; eight New Yorkers have been executed in error.[25] And a recent study prepared by the New York State Defenders Association concludes that fifty-nine wrongful homicide convictions have occurred in New York between 1965 and 1988.[26]

Judges, lawyers, and the general public trust the legal system to make reliable determinations of guilt. The right to counsel, confrontation, compulsory process, trial by jury, and heightened standards of proof manifest our society's commitment to truth. We also trust that claims of innocence will be heard before it is too late. Consider in this context the case of Roger Coleman. He was found guilty of raping and murdering Wanda McCoy in 1981, and sentenced to death. A lengthy article in the *New Republic* makes a powerful case for Coleman's innocence.[27] He was represented at trial by court-appointed lawyers who had never before defended a murder case. Proof of his innocence was presented and rejected by a Virginia trial court. Coleman sought to appeal to the state court of appeals, but Coleman's lawyers filed their notice of appeal two days late. Because of this procedural error, the Virginia court rejected his appeal. Coleman then unsuccessfully sought federal habeas corpus review, seeking to have his claim of innocence examined on the merits. The Supreme Court, in upholding the refusal of the federal courts to entertain Coleman's petition on the merits, never discussed whether Coleman might have been innocent.[28] The majority opinion discussed whether a decision of a state court finding procedural default because a lawyer's filing delay is entitled to respect under principles of federalism. The Court said that it was. Coleman was executed on May 22, 1992.

Consider also the case of Leonel Herrera. Herrera was sentenced to death for the murder of a police officer in Texas in 1981.[29] Herrera maintained from the beginning that he was innocent. His conviction was based largely on his own statements, which he claimed were fabricated by the police. Herrera offered several affidavits and eyewitness accounts to prove his innocence, including an eyewitness affidavit from the real murderer's own son. Last February, a federal district judge stayed the execution to allow Herrera to prove his innocence at an evidentiary hearing. The Texas director of criminal justice appealed, and the Court of Appeals for the Fifth Circuit reversed, ordering Herrera's execution for the following day.[30] In dispensing its swift justice, the court wrote the following chilling words: "Herrera's claim of 'actual innocence' presents no substantial claim for relief. The rule is well established that claims of newly discovered evidence, casting doubt on petitioner's guilt, are not cognizable in federal habeas corpus."[31] The court of appeals held, in essence, that the Constitution does not forbid the execution of an innocent man.

Herrera filed a petition in the Supreme Court hours before his scheduled execution. He sought an appeal and a stay of his execution. The Supreme Court responded in a manner that reflects the nightmarish, Kafkaesque quality that so much of current death penalty jurisprudence was acquired. The Court allowed Herrera the opportunity to bring his appeal. Four justices—Justices Blackmun, Stevens, O'Connor, and Souter—granted certiorari, because that number is required under Supreme Court rules for a case to be heard.[32] The question on which these justices granted certiorari was whether it violates the Eighth and Fourteenth Amendments to execute a person who has been convicted of murder, but who is innocent. However, the Supreme Court rules require a majority of five justices to stay an execution. And a majority of the justices—Chief Justice Rehnquist, and Justices White, Kennedy, Scalia, and Thomas—believed that the execution should proceed on schedule, notwithstanding that the Court had decided to hear the condemned man's case.[33] Herrera's execution was set for April 15. Two days before the execution, the Texas court of criminal appeals, by a five to three vote, stayed Herrera's execution to allow the Supreme Court to consider the merits of the claim.[34]

The Court heard arguments last October, and decided the case in January.[35] Speaking for a five-judge majority, Chief Justice Rehnquist wrote that, although Herrera's proof of innocence had some probative value, it came too late. Moreover, he did not present a sufficient showing to entitle him to a hearing to prove his innocence. His only recourse would be to seek executive clemency. Herrera was executed on May 12, 1993.

Under the U.S. criminal justice system, any death case—indeed, virtually every sort of criminal case—from beginning to end is exclusively an exercise of the prosecutor's use, and abuse, of power.[36] Ethically the prosecutor is obligated "to seek justice, not merely to convict."[37] In pursuit of "justice," the prosecutor alone decides what criminal charges to bring, and whether to charge a murder case as a capital case. The prosecutor alone decides whether to allow a defendant to plead guilty, to grant immunity to accomplices, to rely on the testimony of jailhouse informants, or to disclose to the defense exculpatory evidence. All of these decisions are largely unreviewable, and, therefore, subject to abuse. The prosecutor literally decides who goes to jail, and who goes free; who lives, and who dies. The recent prosecutions of John

Gotti and Manual Noriega demonstrated astonishingly broad grants of immunity to murderers and drug traffickers so that they would become government witnesses; these people had criminal records far more extensive and serious than the defendants on trial.[38] Public exposés increasingly describe how purchased, and frequently perjurious, testimony by government informants is used to convict defendants, often with a wink and a nod from the prosecutor.[39] Many prosecutors, if they are candid, would admit that testimony of jailhouse stoolpigeons is often utterly unreliable, but unbelievably effective before a jury. Some prosecutors have even been heard to boast that "Any prosecutor can convict a guilty man; it takes a great prosecutor to convict an innocent man."[40]

Concealment by prosecutors of favorable evidence that would assist a defendant in proving his innocence is pervasive and probably accounts for as many miscarriages of justice as any other single factor.[41] Prosecutors, because of their superior resources and early involvement with police in criminal investigations, invariably accumulate evidence that may cast doubt on a defendant's guilt. A prosecutor is legally and ethically obligated to turn over this evidence to the defense.[42] Many prosecutors obey these rules. Many other prosecutors, however, violate these rules, sometimes inadvertently, sometimes willfully. The published decisions describing such misconduct are merely the tip of the iceberg; most of this misconduct occurs beyond public or judicial scrutiny, in the twilight zone of criminal justice of which only prosecutors and police are aware. Moreover, the absence of meaningful professional discipline of prosecutors for such misconduct makes these tactics almost routine, and a cause for deep concern.[43]

Courts, bar associations, and legislatures should be much more alert to this quagmire in criminal justice. Reversals of convictions should be required automatically for the deliberate suppression of evidence. Disciplinary sanctions against prosecutors should be the norm rather than the exception. Legislation should be enacted making it a crime for prosecutors to willfully suppress evidence resulting in a defendant's wrongful conviction, the degree of the prosecutor's culpability related to the gravity of the conviction.

It should come as no surprise that the Supreme Court and the federal courts have abdicated much of their responsibility to ensure high standards for prosecutors.[44] However, state courts occasionally have filled this breach. Some state courts, notably the New York State Court of Appeals, have affirmatively used their own state constitutions to protect individual rights when the federal Constitution, as interpreted by the Supreme Court, fails to provide adequate protection.[45] This "new federalism" is a healthy and welcome legal development, particularly at a time when fair play for persons charged with crime is not a popular view.

RACIAL PREJUDICE

Racial prejudice continues to haunt U.S. criminal justice. In its recent report, the New York State Judicial Commission on Minorities decried what it saw as the many similarities between apartheid and the travesties of justice found to exist in the U.S. South. The commission's findings include the frequency of all-white juries in counties of substantial minority populations; minorities clustered in the worst courthouses in the state; blacks receiving sentences of incarceration where whites do not, and longer sentences than similarly situated whites; underrepresentation of minorities as administrators, despite their availability in the labor pool; and judges taking twice as long to explain to whites certain of their rights as they do to blacks. In short, the commission concluded, "there is in New York State in the 1990's the reality of a biased court system."[46]

Racial discrimination in the application of the death penalty is a window to racial discrimination generally. One half of the persons on death row in the United States are black or hispanic. But that is not the real story. Perhaps the most shocking statistic reveals that defendants charged with killing white victims are at least four times, and as much as eight times, more likely to receive a death sentence as those charged with killing black victims in otherwise similar cases. The most carefully documented study, the Baldus study, examined over 2,000 murder cases in Georgia, and isolated 230 nonracial variables.[47] The study concluded that a defendant's odds of receiving a death sentence were 4.3 times greater if the victim was white than if the victim was black. In some states, disparities are even higher.[48] In Maryland, killers of whites are eight times more likely to be sentenced to death than killers of blacks; in Arkansas, they are six times more likely; and in Texas, they are five times more likely.[49] The race of the victim also operates as a "silent aggravating circumstance" in the jury's decision to impose the death penalty.[50]

In *McCleskey v. Kemp*,[51] the Supreme Court, although accepting the validity of the Baldus study, declined to find the practice unconstitutionally discriminatory. McCleskey has been called the "Dred Scott" decision of this century.[52] Justice Brennan, in one of his greatest dissents, recalled that 130 years ago the Supreme Court denied U.S. citizenship to blacks, and a mere 3 generations ago sanctioned racial segregation. Warren McCleskey's evidence, Justice Brennan wrote, confronts us with "disturbing proof" that "we remain imprisoned by the past as long as we deny its influence in the present."[53] "It is tempting to pretend," he said, "that minorities on death row share a fate in no way connected to our own." This is "an illusion . . . for the reverberations of injustice are not so easily confined. . . . [T]he way in which we choose those who will die reveals the depth of moral commitment among the living." Justice Brennan concluded:

> The court's decision today will not change what attorneys in Georgia tell other Warren McCleskeys about their chances of execution. Nothing will soften the harsh message they must convey, nor alter the prospect that race undoubtedly will continue to be a topic of discussion. McCleskey's evidence will not have obtained judicial acceptance, but that will not affect what is said on death row. However many criticisms of today's decision may be rendered, these painful conversations will serve as the most eloquent dissents of all.[54]

Warren McCleskey was executed on September 25, 1991.

Racial injustice in jury selection also continues unabated. *Batson v. Kentucky*[55] sought to eliminate such discrimination. But blacks and other minorities continue to be excluded from juries, and both prosecutors and defense lawyers continue to provide spurious reasons for the strikes.[56] The California jury that acquitted the four police officers of beating Rodney King did not include any blacks. The blatant circumvention of *Batson* in New York State recently prompted Judge Bellacosa, in an opinion joined by Chief Judge Wachtler and Judge Titone, to urge the total elimination of peremptory challenges.[57] Judge Bellacosa wrote that "peremptories have outlived their usefulness and, ironically, appear to be disguising discrimination—not minimizing it, and clearly not eliminating it."[58]

INCOMPETENCE OF COUNSEL

Finally, the inadequacy of representation, which all members of the legal profession should take very seriously, needs to be addressed. The ability of public defenders and appointed counsel to deliver quality defense services is being threatened by lack of funds, huge volume, and often inept training and supervision.[59] The vast majority of criminal defendants in New York State and nationwide are too poor to afford private counsel and therefore must rely for their constitutionally guaranteed defense on legal aid and counsel assigned by the court. There are many talented, although grossly underpaid, attorneys representing indigent defendants. The quality of representation in New York State is probably much higher than the quality of representation nationwide. The dismal level of indigent representation nationwide is particularly noticeable in those jurisdictions that allow capital punishment. An American Bar Association task force recently concluded that "the inadequacy and inadequate compensation of counsel at trial" was one of the "principal failings" of the capital punishment system.[60] All too often defense lawyers are ill-trained and unprepared. Consider the following examples.[61]

1. Larry Heath was executed last year. His court-appointed lawyer's appellate brief contained only a single page of argument, raised only a single issue, and cited only a single legal precedent.
2. Herbert Richardson was executed in 1989. His appellate brief failed to mention that at his sentencing hearing the prosecutor argued, without any basis in the record, but with no objection by defense counsel, that Richardson should be sentenced to death because he belonged to a black muslim organization in New York, had killed a woman in New Jersey, and had been dishonorably discharged from the military. Richardson's lawyer was later disbarred for other reasons.
3. Arthur Jones was executed in 1986. He was represented at trial by a court-appointed lawyer who made no opening or closing statement and offered no evidence at the penalty phase. During the postconviction phase he was represented by a sole practitioner just two years out of law school who had never handled a capital case.
4. Horace Dunkins, a mentally retarded black man who was executed in 1989, was represented by a lawyer so incompetent that the jury was never told that Dunkins was mentally retarded. Dunkins had an IQ of sixty-five and the mental age of a ten-year-old.
5. The capital trial of a battered woman was interrupted for a day when her defense lawyer appeared in court so intoxicated that he was held in contempt and sent to jail for the day and night.

6. A defense lawyer requested an adjournment between the guilt phase and penalty phase of a murder trial so that he could read the state's death penalty statute.
7. A lawyer's brief was sent back to him by the appellate court because it did not cite a single case.
8. A capital defendant was visited only once by his lawyer in eight years. In another case, the lawyer never visited his client in eight years.

One confronts these examples with shock and dismay. Are they merely aberrations? Or do they reflect a much more prevalent condition? Clearly, incompetent lawyering and injustice go hand in hand.

While persons of means are able to obtain "the best counsel money can buy,"[62] these lawyers are also finding their role increasingly more difficult to perform effectively. More and more privately retained lawyers are being subpoenaed to testify against their clients, particularly in connection with their receipt of legal fees, and have been jailed for refusing to testify before grand juries.[63] Prosecutors are increasingly using the statutory summonsing power of the Internal Revenue Service to force criminal defense lawyers to disclose the identities of clients who pay cash.[64] There has been rising incidence of law office searches, disqualification of attorneys, forfeiture of attorney fees, and prosecution of attorneys under obstruction of justice statutes for giving legal advise to clients.[65] The future of our adversary system is at risk by these tactics.

CONCLUSION

The law can be a vital force for justice, as well as for injustice. We look to it to find rational solutions to problems and disputes, and we hope that these solutions achieve justice. When that happens, the law has a meaning beyond its often arid and sterile language. When that does not happen, when innocent persons are convicted, when racism continues to infect our courts, and when lawyers fail in their obligations, we confront injustice. It is at that time that those who participate in the criminal justice system can more fully appreciate their own responsibility to dispense justice, and to eliminate injustice.

NOTES

*This essay is based on remarks delivered on Law Day 1992 before the Rockland County Bar Association, New City, N. Y.

1. For an excellent coursebook addressing this fascinating subject, see A. D'Amato & A. Jacobson, *Justice and the Legal System* (1992).
2. W. Shakespeare, *Hamlet*, Act I, scene v.
3. W. Kunstler, *"The Bill of Rights—Can It Survive?,"* 26 Gonz. L. Rev. 1 (1991).
4. *"Poll Finds Only 33% Can Identify Bill of Rights,"* N.Y. Times, Dec. 15, 1991, at 33.
5. Boyd v. United States, 116 U.S. 616, 636 (1886).
6. J. Liebman, *Federal Habeas Corpus Practice and Procedure* § 2.2, 23-24 n. 97 (1988) (49 percent success rate); Godbold, "Pro Bono Representation of Death Sentenced Inmates," 42

Rec. N.Y. City B. Ass'n 859, 873 (1987) (one third success rate). See also Barefoot v. Estelle, 463 U.S. 880, 915 (1983) (Marshall, J., dissenting) (over 70 percent of cases decided in favor of death sentenced petitioners).

7. Vasquez v. Harris, 112 S. Ct. 1713, 1714 (1992) ("No further stays of Robert Alton Harris' execution shall be entered by the federal courts except upon order of this Court."). See also Bishop, "After Night of Court Battles, a California Execution," N.Y. Times, Apr. 22, 1992, at 1.

8. *Id.*

9. United States v. Wiley, 492 F.2d 547, 555 (D.C. Cir. 1974) (Bazelon, J., concurring).

10. *New York State Judicial Commission on Minorities* vii (1990) (letter dated May 16, 1990, from Franklin H. Williams, Esq., Chairman of the Commission, to Chief Justice Sol Wachtler).

11. Death Row U.S.A. 1 (Spring 1993).

12. Coleman v. Thompson, 111 S. Ct. 2546, 2552 (1991).

13. Herrera v. Collins, 113 S. Ct. 853 (1993).

14. Bray v. Alexandria Women's Health Clinic, 113 S. Ct. 753 (1993).

15. The catalyst for the discussion of the subject of justice in terms of injustice came from the late Edmund Cahn's outstanding work, *Confronting Injustice* (1967).

16. 397 U.S. 358 (1970).

17. Mydans, "After 17 Years, Sunshine and Freedom," N.Y. Times, Mar. 27, 1992, at A14.

18. The cases are those of Randall Dale Adams in Texas, James Richardson and Joseph Brown in Florida, and Eric Jackson in New York. See B. Gershman, *Abuse of Power in the Prosecutor's Office*, *The World & I* 477, 480 (June 1991).

19. Greenhouse, "A Window on the Court—Limits on Inmates' Habeas Corpus Petitions Illuminate Mood and Agenda of the Justices," N.Y. Times, May 6, 1992, at A1.

20. The recent scandal in upstate New York involving fake evidence may be merely an indication of a much more pervasive phenomenon. See "Former State Trooper Explains Ways He Fabricated Evidence," N.Y. Times, Apr. 16, 1993, at B5; "Trooper's Fall Shakes Both Police and Public," N.Y. Times, Nov. 15, 1992, at 41; Suro, "Ripples of a Pathologist's Misconduct in Graves and Courts of West Texas," N.Y. Times, Nov. 22, 1992, at 22; Holloway, "False Changes by Woman Culminate in Her Arrest," N.Y. Times, Oct. 18, 1992, at 47.

21. *Killing Justice—Government Misconduct and the Death Penalty*, Death Penalty Information Center (1992).

22. Gershman, "The Thin Blue Line: Art or Trial in the Fact-Finding Process?" 9 Pace L. Rev. 275 (1989).

23. Bedau & Radelet, "Miscarriages of Justice in Potentially Capital Cases," 40 Stan. L. Rev. 21, 36 (1987).

24. *Id.* at 37.

25. Rosenbaum, "Inevitable Error: Wrongful New York State Convictions, 1965–1988," 18 N.Y.U. Rev. L. & Soc. Change 807, 809 (1990–1991).

26. *Id.* at 808.

27. Tucker, "Dead End," New Republic 21 (May 4, 1992).

28. Coleman v. Thompson, 111 S. Ct. 2546 (1991).

29. Herrera v. Collins, 954 F.2d 1029 (5th Cir. 1992).

30. *Id.*

31. *Id.* at 1033.

32. Herrera v. Collins, 112 S. Ct. 1074 (1992).

33. *Id.*

34. Suro, "Inmate Given Stay to Argue That Execution Would Violate Rights," N.Y. Times, Apr. 14, 1992, at A21.

35. Herrera v. Collins, 113 S. Ct. at 853.

36. B. Gershman, *Prosecutorial Misconduct* (1985).

37. ABA *Standards for Criminal Justice* § 3-1.2(c) (3d ed. 1992).

38. Johnston, *"No Victory for Panama,"* N.Y. Times, Apr. 11, 1992, at 1 (prosecution called forty witnesses who were convicted drug traffickers, fifteen of whom were granted immunity for crimes more serious than those for which Noriega stood trial).
39. "Use of Jailhouse Informers Reviewed in Los Angeles," N.Y. Times, Jan. 3, 1989, at A14.
40. Note 22, *supra* at 275.
41. The cases of prosecutorial suppression of evidence are legion. See B. Gershman, *Prosecutorial Misconduct*, Ch. 5. Very recently, in People v. Alfred Davis, 81 N.Y.2d 281 (1993), the New York Court of Appeals unanimously reversed a conviction obtained by the Manhattan district attorney for suppressing exculpatory evidence. See also "The 'Brady' Rule: Is It Working?" Nat'l L.J. 1 (May 17, 1993).
42. Brady v. Maryland, 373 U.S. 83 (1963). See also *ABA Standards for Criminal Justice* § 3-3.11(a) (3d ed. 1992).
43. Rosen, "Disciplinary Sanctions Against Prosecutors for 'Brady' Violations: A Paper Tiger," 65 N.C.L. Rev. 693 (1987).
44. See United States v. Williams, 112 S. Ct. 1735 (1992) (federal courts have no supervisory authority over prosecutorial suppression of exculpatory evidence before grand juries); United States v. Hasting, 461 U.S. 499 (1983) (federal courts may not use supervisory power to deter prosecutorial misconduct without first determining whether misconduct was harmless error).
45. See, e.g., People v. Vilardi, 76 N.Y.2d 67, 556 N.Y.S.2d 518, 555 N.E.2d 915 (1990) (refusing to apply Supreme Court decision limiting prosecutor's disclosure obligations). See also Kaye, "Dual Constitutionalism in Practice and Principle," 61 St. John's L. Rev. 399 (1987); Brennan, "State Constitutions and the Protection of Individual Rights," 90 Harv. L. Rev. 489 (1977).
46. See note 10, *supra.*
47. D. Baldus, G. Woodworth & C. Pulaski, Jr., *Equal Justice and the Death Penalty: An Empirical Analysis* (1990).
48. *"Killers of Blacks Escape the Death Penalty,"* Dallas Times Herald, Nov. 17, 1985, at 1.
49. *Id.*
50. Tabak & Lane, "The Execution of Injustice: A Cost and Lack-of-Benefit Analysis of the Death Penalty," 23 Loy. L.A. L. Rev. 59, 90 (1989).
51. 481 U.S. 279 (1987).
52. Kennedy, "McCleskey v. Kemp: Race, Capital Punishment, and the Supreme Court," 101 Harv. L. Rev. 1388, 1389 (1988).
53. 481 U.S. at 344.
54. *Id.* at 344-345.
55. 476 U.S. 79 (1986).
56. See, e.g., Hernandez v. New York, 111 S. Ct. 1859 (1991); People v. Kern, 75 N.Y.2d 638, 554 N.E.2d 1235, 555 N.Y.S.2d 647 (1990).
57. People v. Bolling, 79 N.Y.2d 317, 591 N.E.2d 1136, 582 N.Y.S.2d 950 (1992) (concurring opinion).
58. 79 N.Y.2d at 326.
59. Gershman, "Defending the Poor," 29 Trial 47 (March 1993).
60. ABA Task Force Report, *Toward a More Just and Effective System of Review in State Death Penalty Cases* 7 (Aug. 1990).
61. The following examples were provided by Stephen B. Bright, Esq., Director, Southern Center for Human Rights, in a Statement to the Committee on the Judiciary, U.S. Senate, regarding the nomination of Ed Carnes to the U.S. Court of Appeals for the Eleventh Circuit (Apr. 1, 1992).
62. Morris v. Slappy, 461 U.S. 1, 23 (1983) (Brennan, J., concurring).
63. Stern & Hoffman, "Privileged Informers: The Attorney-Subpoena Problem and a Proposal for Reform," 136 U. Pa. L. Rev. 1783 (1988).
64. United States v. Goldberger & Dubin, 935 F.2d 501 (2d Cir. 1991).
65. Gershman, "The New Prosecutors," 53 U. Pitt. L. Rev. 393 (1992).

17 Victim Participation at Sentencing

Valerie Finn-DeLuca

BACKGROUND OF THE VICTIMS' RIGHTS MOVEMENT

In colonial times, the American criminal justice system functioned without effective police forces or prosecutors;[1] victims relied on self-help or the help of their families for law enforcement.[2] They did their own investigation, paid for arrest warrants, and then paid an attorney to prosecute the case. Thus, the victim made the important decisions, with a focus on restitution.[3]

In the nineteenth century, public prosecutors took over the victims' responsibilities, became society's advocates, and shifted the focus of criminal justice from restitution to deterrence and punishment. Victims lost control and their role in the justice system was often limited to testifying for the prosecution.[4] This shift has continued, and today the victim's role is a shadow of what it was in earlier times. The concerns of the modern criminal justice system bear little relation to the victim; rather, they center on assuring the fairness and lawfulness with which penalties are imposed, devising means for rehabilitating criminals, and increasing the effectiveness and efficiency with which criminals are apprehended and prosecuted.[5]

This change often leaves victims feeling dissatisfied with, and resentful of, the criminal justice system. Victims are frequently unable to rid themselves of feelings of guilt and shame associated with criminal victimization, and thus transfer a sense of disorder, powerlessness, and fear to other spheres of their lives.[6] The presumption that the prosecutor represents the victim's interests is contradicted by many of their experiences;[7] many describe a feeling of revictimization by the criminal justice process, and studies show that their grievances pertain largely to the procedures of the system rather than unjust outcomes.[8]

Several decades ago, the victims' rights movement was born out of this dissatisfaction and a desire to empower victims of crime. One of its motivating theories was that victims needed to be given a voice and listened to if they were to experience the restoration of personal power necessary for psychological healing. Other goals included helping the victim regain a sense of control and satisfying a desire for retribution.[9]

Reprinted by permission of West Group from the *Criminal Law Bulletin*, vol. 30 (1994), pp. 403–428.

In the 1960s, the movement's efforts centered on state compensation programs and the use of restitution in sentencing. During the 1970s, large scale reform in victim-oriented services and legislation addressed other needs.[10] In recent years, public interest in victims' rights has been fueled by high crime rates and frustration with law enforcement efforts to reduce crime. The emergence and growth of victims' groups, especially among women, has heightened political attention toward certain types of crime, and spurred research on the psychological impact of victimization as well.[11] These dynamics, combined with continued victim dissatisfaction, led to calls for additional legislative reform[12] and policies that promote more victim involvement in the criminal justice system.[13] As a result, extensive federal and state legislation was passed in the 1980s concerning victims' rights, and a President's Task Force was commissioned. These developments have significantly changed the complexion of the issue in this country.

VICTIMS' RIGHTS AT THE NATIONAL LEVEL

In 1982, Congress passed the first legislation dealing specifically with victims' rights. The Victim and Witness Protection Act of 1982 (VWPA)[14] was intended to elevate the role of the victim, the "forgotten person" in the criminal process. The VWPA's stated purpose was to "enhance and protect the necessary role of crime victims and witnesses in the criminal justice process."[15] It was aimed at protecting victims and witnesses from intimidation, providing social and medical services, and encouraging notification of and consultation with victims.[16] The VWPA amended Rule 32 of the Federal Rules of Criminal Procedure to require a victim impact statement (VIS) as part of presentencing reports,[17] and specified that the VIS be used in all crimes with a human victim.[18] The VWPA was drafted primarily as a model for states because most federal crimes do not have conventional victims.[19]

Also in 1982, President Ronald Reagan established the President's Task Force on Victims of Crime, which recommended over 100 victim-oriented reforms of state and federal government, the judiciary and criminal justice professionals.[20] It concluded that

> victims, no less than defendants, are entitled to their day in court. Victims, no less than defendants, are entitled to have their views considered. A judge cannot evaluate the seriousness of a defendant's conduct without knowing how the crime has burdened the victim. A judge cannot reach an informed determination of the danger posed by a defendant without hearing from the person he has victimized.[21]

The Task Force reasoned that when the court hears from the defendant's lawyer, family, friends, minister, and others, simple fairness dictates that the one who has suffered the harm of the defendant's crime be given a role during sentencing.[22] Its recommendations included abandoning the exclusionary rule; minimal, if any, cross examination of the victim by the defense counsel; elimination of plea bargaining; and preventive detention of the accused.[23] The asserted purpose of these changes was to make the system more victim-friendly and to equalize the rights of the victim with the rights of the accused. By 1986, a follow-up report on the President's Task Force issued by the Justice Department indicated that 75 percent of its initial recommendations had been implemented.[24]

An amendment to the U.S. constitution to incorporate victims' rights has been proposed unsuccessfully.[25] However, this tactic has met with greater success on the state level.[26]

VICTIMS' RIGHTS ON THE STATE LEVEL

States have employed a wide range of devices for assuring victims' rights. State legislation frequently provides for victim notification of hearing dates and important decisions regarding their cases, victim participation in court proceedings, use of victim impact statements at sentencing, victim restitution and compensation, protection from intimidation, and "Son of Sam" laws.[27] Some states also give the victim a right to a speedy trial.[28] Ninety-eight percent of jurisdictions allow impact commentary from family, friends, or legal representatives if the actual victim is unable to participate due to death, age, or incapacitation.[29]

Specific provisions vary greatly. California was the first state to expressly guarantee victim's rights through a state constitutional amendment in 1982.[30] The initiative included provisions for restitution,[31] consideration of public safety in setting bail,[32] unrestricted admission of prior felony convictions,[33] and an absolute right for the victim to appear at sentencing and parole hearings.[34]

In Rhode Island, "a victim of a crime shall, as a matter of right, be treated by agents of the State with dignity, respect and sensitivity during all phases of the criminal justice process."[35] The state also provides for victim compensation and a right to address the court regarding the impact of the crime on the victim.[36]

The Michigan model requires the prosecutor to confer with the prosecuting witness before jury selection and trial, if requested, and allows the victim to give his or her opinion regarding plea bargaining negotiations.[37] A *Miranda*-like notice of the statutory rights of the victim is also required.[38]

Despite these provisions, enforcement of victims' rights is often problematic. No cause of action against the state is provided if the procedures are not followed, so their effect is more akin to guidelines for the courts and other criminal justice agencies than enforceable rights.[39] In no state may failure to provide for the victim's rights be grounds to overturn a defendant's conviction or sentence.[40]

VICTIM PARTICIPATION AT SENTENCING

Victim involvement at sentencing is one of the most visible and popular provisions in victims' rights legislation. By July 1987, forty-eight states allowed victim participation at sentencing in some form,[41] and two general models have emerged. Under the first model, a written victim impact statement is introduced at sentencing, often in a presentence report; the statement may include an objective assessment of the effects of the crime on the victim or the victim's family, subjective commentary about their feelings and opinions regarding the crime and sentence, or both. The second model expands on the first by allowing the victim or victim's family to present oral testimony at the sentencing hearing.[42] However, this type of testimony has provoked numerous constitutional challenges, especially where oral statements are offered. Not surprisingly, the issue has been hotly contested in capital punishment cases in particular.

Booth v. Maryland

The first case challenging the admissibility of victim impact statements, *Booth v. Maryland*,[43] reached the U.S. Supreme Court in 1987. John Booth was convicted of murdering an elderly couple, Irvin and Rose Bronstein, in their home during an apparent robbery. The prosecutor requested the death penalty, and under the applicable Maryland law, Booth elected to have his sentence determined by the jury rather than the judge.[44] State law required the compilation of a presentence report by the State Division of Parole and Probation (DPP) describing Booth's background, employment history, criminal record, and education. The state also mandated the inclusion of a victim impact statement in this report.[45] Specifically, the report was to:

(i) Identify the victim of the offense;
(ii) Itemize any economic loss suffered by the victim as a result of the offense;
(iii) Identify any physical injury suffered by the victim as a result of the offense along with its seriousness and permanence;
(iv) Describe any change in the victim's personal welfare or familial relationships as a result of the offense;
(v) Identify any request for psychological services initiated by the victim or the victim's family as a result of the offense; and
(vi) Contain any other information related to the impact of the offense upon the victim or the victim's family that the trial court requires.[46]

Obviously, much of the information in the report was to be provided to the DPP by the victim or the victim's family.

The victim impact statement was given to the jury in written form; it emphasized the victims' outstanding characteristics, the close relationship which the couple shared, the large number of their friends, the size of the funeral, and the emotional and personal problems of family members since the murders. Several family members also expressed opinions that the murderer could never be rehabilitated or forgiven. Defense counsel objected to all of this information on the grounds that it was both irrelevant and unduly inflammatory, in violation of the Eighth Amendment.[47]

Booth was sentenced to death in the murder of Irvin Bronstein, and to life imprisonment for Rose Bronstein's murder.[48] The Maryland Court of Appeals found no error in the admission of the victim impact evidence because it was a "relatively straightforward and factual description of the effects of these murders on the members of the Bronstein family," and upheld the sentences.[49]

A closely divided U.S. Supreme Court reversed. Justice Powell, writing his valedictory opinion for the majority,[50] held that the information provided to the jury in the victim impact statement was irrelevant to the capital sentencing decision, and therefore introduced an unacceptable risk that the jury might impose the death penalty in an arbitrary and capricious manner.[51] Powell's reasoning was rooted deeply in the Court's earlier capital punishment jurisprudence:

> [W]e have said that a jury must make an "*individualized* determination" whether the defendant in question should be executed, based on "the character of the individual and the circumstances of the crime. . . ." [A] state statute that requires consideration of other factors must be scrutinized to ensure that the evidence has some bearing on the defendant's "personal responsibility and moral guilt." To do otherwise would create a risk that a death sentence will be based on considerations that are "constitutionally impermissible or totally irrelevant to the sentencing process." (citations omitted)[52]

The Court viewed victim impact evidence as unrelated to the defendant's blameworthiness[53] and likely to distract the jury from consideration of appropriate factors regarding the defendant. The Court also held that the ability of the family to articulate its grief, or even the very existence or nonexistence of a family, would inject an additional arbitrary and unacceptable factor into the sentencing decision.[54]

The *Booth* Court "reject[ed] the contention that the presence or absence of emotional distress of the victim's family, or the victim's personal characteristics, are proper considerations in a capital case."[55] It determined that family members' opinions and characterizations of the crime could serve no purpose but to inflame the jurors, who are no doubt aware of the anger and grief that a murder victim's family endures, saying that "the admission of these emotionally charged opinions as to what conclusions the jury should draw from the evidence clearly is inconsistent with the reasoned decision making [required] in capital cases."[56]

Finally, the Court recognized that it would be almost impossible for a defendant to rebut victim impact evidence; even if he were willing to run the strategic risk of attacking the victim's family in front of the jury, such a move would further deflect their appropriate focus from the convicted defendant.[57] Thus, the Court concluded that the introduction of a victim impact statement at the sentencing phase of a capital murder trial violated the Eighth Amendment and remanded the case for a new sentencing determination.[58]

A spirited group of four dissenters in *Booth* would have allowed the jury to consider the victim impact evidence. In their opinion, the majority's conclusion that a defendant could not be held accountable for the full extent of the harm he caused, including impact on the victim's family, was completely unfounded. They also argued for the right of the victim to be treated as an individual whose death represents a unique loss to society and, in particular, to his family.[59] If, as a matter of legislative policy, a state decides that the jury should have testimony of the victim's family to weigh the degree of harm and corresponding degree of punishment, the dissenters would find no constitutional defect.[60]

South Carolina v. Gathers

In 1989, the Supreme Court expanded its decision in *Booth* to include situations in which the prosecutor, rather than the victim's family, introduced evidence regarding the victim's personal characteristics. In *South Carolina v. Gathers*,[61] the prosecutor was permitted at sentencing to read from a religious tract and prayer cards that the murder victim was carrying at the time of his attack, and drew inferences to the jury from the fact that the victim carried a voter registration card.[62] In an opinion by Justice Brennan, the Court held that "the content of the various papers the victim happened to be carrying when he was attacked was purely fortuitous, and cannot provide any information relevant to the defendant's moral culpability."[63] They affirmed the Supreme Court of South Carolina, which concluded that the prosecutor's remarks "conveyed the suggestion that appellant deserved a death sentence because the victim was a religious man and a registered voter."[64] This case was found to be indistinguishable from *Booth* and the irrelevance of victim characteristics was reaffirmed.[65]

Again, strong dissenting opinions were voiced in *Gathers*. The minority members would have distinguished *Gathers* from *Booth* and allowed the evidence to be admitted on the grounds that the comments in question related to the victim himself, not the victim's family.[66] However, they clearly stated their desire to overrule *Booth* outright if they could muster one additional vote.[67]

Payne v. Tennessee

The opportunity to overrule *Booth* and *Gathers* presented itself rather quickly. By 1991, when *Payne v. Tennessee*[68] reached the Supreme Court, there had been two significant changes in the Court. Justices Powell and Brennan had been replaced by Justices Kennedy and Souter. The delicate balance had shifted to give the proponents of victim impact evidence a majority.

Payne involved a particularly gruesome multiple homicide. Twenty-eight-year-old Charisse Christopher and her two children, Nicholas and Lacie, three and two years old respectively, were each stabbed numerous times with a butcher knife. The defendant, Pervis Tyrone Payne, whose girlfriend lived across the hall from the Christophers, entered their apartment uninvited after several hours of drinking, using cocaine and reading pornography. He became violent when Charisse refused his sexual advances; all three were stabbed numerous times. When the police arrived, blood covered the walls and floors throughout the apartment; Charisse and Lacie were dead, but miraculously Nicholas was still alive, and survived the knife wounds that completely penetrated his body from front to back.[69]

Although he denied his involvement throughout the trial, the physical evidence against Payne was overwhelming. Payne was convicted of two counts of first degree murder and one count of assault with intent to commit murder.[70] At sentencing, the defendant presented four witnesses to testify on his behalf. His parents and girlfriend testified as to Payne's good character and his lack of any prior record. They also stated that he did not drink or use drugs, and that it would be inconsistent with his character for him to commit these crimes. A clinical psychologist testified that Payne was mentally handicapped, as evidenced by a low score on an IQ test, and told the jury that the defendant was the most polite prisoner with whom he had ever worked.[71]

Victim impact evidence was also admitted, in clear violation of both *Booth* and *Gathers*. This evidence formed the basis of Payne's appeal. The testimony was presented by Charisse Christopher's mother, grandmother of the other victims, who testified as to Nicholas' reaction to the crime. She stated that he missed his mother and sister, worried about them, and did not understand why they did not come home. The prosecutor incorporated testimony about the effects on Nicholas into her closing argument as well, focusing on the boy's presence and consciousness during the crime, and the fact that he knew what had happened to his loved ones. The prosecutor encouraged the jury to fashion its verdict so that Nicholas would feel that justice was done when he grew up. She repeatedly asked the jurors to focus on the victims, rather than the alleged good reputation of the defendant. The jury subsequently imposed the death penalty.[72]

The Supreme Court of Tennessee affirmed the conviction and death sentences over Payne's objection to the use of victim impact evidence as violative of his Eighth Amendment rights, citing *Booth.* The Tennessee Supreme Court characterized the grandmother's testimony as "technically irrelevant" and found that it did not create an unconstitutional risk of arbitrary imposition of the death penalty.[73] Regarding the prosecutor's closing argument, the court found the statements therein "relevant to [Payne's] personal responsibility and moral guilt," and that under the circumstances of the case, the physical and mental condition of the child left for dead were relevant to the defendant's blameworthiness.[74]

The U.S. Supreme Court also affirmed, and thereby overturned *Booth* and *Gathers.* The Court's new majority, led by Chief Justice Rehnquist, held that the Eighth Amendment created no per se bar to a state's decision to permit the admission of victim impact evidence.[75] Rehnquist cited the dissenting opinions in *Booth* and *Gathers* extensively:

> We are now of the view that a State may properly conclude that for the jury to assess meaningfully the defendant's moral culpability and blameworthiness, it should have before it at the sentencing phase evidence of the specific harm caused by the defendant. "The State has a legitimate interest in counteracting the mitigating evidence which the defendant is entitled to put in, by reminding the sentencer that just as the murderer should be considered as an individual, so too the victim is an individual whose death represents a unique loss to society and in particular to his family." *Booth,* 482 U.S. at 517, 107 S. Ct. at 2540 (White, J., dissenting). By turning the victim into a "faceless stranger at the penalty phase of a capital trial," *Gathers,* 490 U.S. at 821, 109 S. Ct. at 2216 (O'Connor, J., dissenting), *Booth* deprives the State of the full moral force of its evidence and may prevent the jury from having before it all the information necessary to determine the proper punishment for a first-degree murder.[76]

The Court deferred to state legislatures as the appropriate measure of societal consensus as to when the death penalty can be justly imposed, subject only to Eighth Amendment limitations, including the consideration of mitigating factors. States were given latitude in developing sentencing procedures, including the use of victim impact evidence, for the entirely legitimate purpose of informing the sentencing authority about the specific harm caused in each case. If evidence introduced would be unduly prejudicial, resulting in an unfair trial, the defendant would have recourse through the due process clause of the Fourteenth Amendment.[77]

Rehnquist buttressed his argument by referring to numerous previous cases and the Federal Sentencing Guidelines of 1987, which favor admitting a wide range of relevant information. The Federal Sentencing Guidelines calibrate sentences, depending on a number of factors relating to the subjective guilt of the defendant and the harm caused by his acts.[78] In *Eddings v. Oklahoma*,[79] the Court held that consideration of all relevant information presented by the defendant must be allowed in capital cases; likewise, in *Gregg v. Georgia*,[80] the Court favored open and far-reaching argument at presentencing hearings and praised the state legislature for not imposing unnecessary restrictions on evidence that can be offered.[81]

The Court also faulted *Booth* for misreading its *Woodson v. North Carolina* precedent.[82] *Woodson*, Rehnquist said, was not intended to eliminate the introduction of any category of evidence, only to mandate consideration of relevant mitigating evidence.[83] By concluding otherwise, the *Booth* Court

> unfairly weighted the scales in a capital trial; while virtually no limits are placed on the relevant mitigating evidence a capital defendant may introduce concerning his own circumstances, the State is barred from either offering "a glimpse of the life" which the defendant "chose to extinguish," *Mills v. Maryland,* 486 U.S. 367, 397, 108 S. Ct. 1860, 1876, 100 L. Ed. 2d 384 (1988) (Rehnquist, C.J., dissenting), or demonstrating the loss to the victim's family and to society which [has] resulted from the defendant's homicide.[84]

In response to the difficulty of rebutting victim impact statements that was a concern in *Booth*, the Court observed that much of the evidence in question would have already been presented during the guilt phase of the trial. Also, the fact that tactical considerations might preclude the defendant from challenging victim impact evidence was held to merely reflect the adversarial nature of the process, leaving the fact finder to weigh the merits of the information.[85]

Finally, the *Payne* Court dismissed the concern that some victims would be viewed as more valuable to society than others if victim characteristics were considered. The Court noted that victim impact evidence is not offered to encourage comparative judgments of this kind, and juries are not faced with the worth of various victims. In support of this contention, Rehnquist cited *Gathers*, where the fact that the victim was unemployed and mentally handicapped did not lead the jury to impose a lighter sentence on his murderer.[86]

In conclusion, *Payne* held that individualized consideration of the defendant did not require consideration wholly apart from the crime committed, and that the harm caused to the victim and the victim's characteristics were legitimate elements of the sentencing determination. The Court did not rule, however, on the second type of evidence used in *Booth*, the admission of victims' opinions regarding the crime, because that issue did not arise in *Payne.*[87]

CRITICISM OF *PAYNE* AND VICTIM PARTICIPATION

The *Payne* decision has been widely criticized, as was *Booth* before it. Much of the criticism relates to the Justices' conclusions, issues that are not addressed, and protection of defendants' rights. The wisdom of victim impact evidence in general has also been the focus of much negative commentary.

Irrelevance of the Victim's Character

The fundamental split on the U.S. Supreme Court in the victim impact cases hinged on the kinds of specific harm that bear on a reasoned moral response to crime and punishment.[88] The disagreement can be explained by the differing implications of the moral retribution model and the social retribution model of criminal justice. The moral retribution model of the *Booth* majority does not justify victim participation because the model focuses only on the moral blameworthiness of the defendant.[89] This focus on moral guilt, not the full range of foreseeable consequences of the defendant's act, precludes direct victim involvement and a relative blameworthiness calculation.[90] The social retribution model of the *Payne* majority does justify the introduction of evidence relating to the victim's character and harm.[91] It focuses on personal responsibility and is based on the premise that accountability should turn on outcome more than intent.[92] However, this latter route is fraught with problems.

Traditionally, the focus at sentencing hearings has always been on the defendant. *Payne* calls this tradition into serious question; it poses a serious risk of crossing the line between social retribution and vengeance by allowing the victim to freely wield his or her anger, frustration, and moral superiority before the jury. Vengeance conflicts with two fundamental principles of retributive sentencing: proportionality to the crime and equality among similarly situated defendants.[93] The Court "ventures into uncharted seas of irrelevance"[94] by concluding "that the prosecutor may introduce evidence that sheds no light on the defendant's guilt or moral culpability, and thus serves no purpose other than to encourage jurors to decide in favor of death rather than life on the basis of their emotions rather than reason."[95]

The *Payne* majority also misconstrues the *Booth* Court's concern with a minitrial on the victim's character; the concern is not one of tactical difficulty for the defendant in rebutting the evidence, but rather that the jury will be distracted into basing its decision on prejudicial and irrelevant considerations.[96] *Payne* fosters the use of constitutionally forbidden criteria, such as race, social standing, religion, and sexual orientation, by sanctioning the introduction of impertinent factors; this type of evidence cannot be defined as just.[97] When the focus of a sentencing hearing shifts toward the victim, the justice system's traditional concern for the defendant's constitutional rights can be forgotten too easily.[98]

Justice Rehnquist supports introducing the victim's character as evidence of his uniqueness, and claims that it is not meant to result in comparative judgments among victims or between the victim and the defendant.[99] But this explanation is implausible because such information encourages the sentencing authority to weigh the blameworthiness of the defendant and the victim.[100] Furthermore, the uniqueness argument fails in light of the fact that prosecutors only dwell on the victim's merits; one's vices would also show uniqueness, but are never called upon for this purpose. Whatever the stated goal, relying on such proof clearly enhances certain victims by identifying them as more worthy of concern than others.[101]

Payne also concludes that victim impact is a proper consideration at sentencing because the law is riddled with examples of charges or sentences that are determined by the harm caused. The examples cited by the majority—the reckless driver who kills a pedestrian versus the one who does not—are, indeed, cases in which the harm was not intended, yet is relevant at sentencing. However, legislatures have identified these classes of crimes in advance as crimes that should be charged and punished more severely.[102] This is very different from the use of such a criteria by a judge or jury in the sentencing determination of a particular case, where policy considerations are not at issue and individual prejudices are difficult to extricate.

The *Payne* decision holds the potential for abuse of the other side of the coin as well; if the victim's character can be used as an aggravating factor, it can also be used in mitigation.[103] *Payne* encourages the sentencing authority to pay attention to differences among victims rather than their common humanity, which, in turn, encourages the defendant to place the character of the victim on trial at the sentencing phase.[104] Decisions based on the relative worth of the victim are offensive to a sense of justice and cannot be reconciled with the Eighth Amendment.[105] Of course, few defense attorneys are likely to attack victims of impeccable character like the ones in *Booth*, but in other cases where the victim is a drunk, drug user, insane, unorthodox, or without friends, the defense may be unable to resist the door opened by *Payne.*[106]

Finally, *Payne* "abandons rules of relevance that are older than the Nation itself."[107] Since the victim's character is irrelevant to the defendant's moral culpability, the fact that a wide range of relevant factors have traditionally been considered at sentencing does not support *Payne's* result.[108]

Mitigating Evidence

In *Payne*, the Court challenged the propriety of allowing the defendant to present unlimited mitigating evidence but not allowing the prosecutor to present similar evidence about the victim.[109] This reasoning is fundamentally flawed. As Justice Stevens points out in his dissent, the victim is not on trial, so his character can be neither an aggravating nor a mitigating factor.[110] The fear that the unlimited opportunity to present mitigating evidence "unfairly weigh[s] the scales"[111] of justice toward the defendant in this case is highly implausible; the testimony offered by the four witnesses on Payne's behalf was conclusory and only supported the contention that he had no prior record.[112] Given the weight of the evidence and the fact that the jury found four aggravating factors,[113] the victims' rights certainly do not seem to have been jeopardized.[114]

Furthermore, the prosecutor can counteract mitigating evidence with specific rebuttal and proof of aggravating factors. The debate occurs, then, not with one side muted, as Justice Scalia argued in his *Booth* dissent, but with both sides arguing about one individual whose future hinges on the outcome.[115] It may be acceptable and even desirable for the jury to become inflamed when considering aggravating evidence about the defendant or the crime, but not about the victim or the victim's family.[116]

Procedural safeguards in the Bill of Rights are intended to protect defendants from the disproportionately powerful state; no balance between the individual and the state was intended. Nor should evidence about the defendant be balanced with evidence about the victim; the victim is not on trial.[117] *Payne* engenders support for witnesses to the victim's life being permitted to share a podium with witnesses to the defendant's life; this produces a superficial symmetry that is pleasing to the public eye but inappropriate in the construct of the sentencing trial.[118]

Victim Participation Inconsistent With Sentencing Goals

The traditional goals of sentencing are retribution, deterrence, incapacitation, and rehabilitation.[119] However, capital punishment is fundamentally different in kind from other types of punishment,[120] so the goals of capital sentencing differ as well. Because the general deterrent effect of the death penalty is hotly debated, capital punishment may not be justified on general deterrence grounds alone; specific deterrence and rehabilitation clearly are not considerations. Life imprisonment would serve to incapacitate a criminal as well as capital punishment, so this cannot be an overriding goal of capital sentencing either. Thus, retribution is arguably the only goal of capital punishment, the ultimate tool to regain the societal balance of benefits and burdens that the defendant's crime upset. The narrowness of capital sentencing goals lends itself to fewer rational justifications for victim participation. It raises awareness of the harm caused, but victim harm is difficult to measure objectively and tends to inflame the sentencer.[121]

Some commentators advocate the recognition of a fifth goal of sentencing: maintaining social order. Under this theory, society punishes the wrongdoer as an alternative to vigilante or self-help justice by the victim. In this way, expectations of both society and the victim that the law will be enforced are fulfilled. The victim's role would be quite broad in accomplishing this goal, and a wide range of information would be admitted, including the victim's opinions regarding the accused and the appropriate sentence. Extensive victim participation would be justified if social order were a recognized goal of criminal punishment. However, courts or legislatures would have to recognize such a goal explicitly to justify such victim involvement, and this has not yet occurred.[122]

Encouraging Prosecutorial Misconduct

By adding victim impact evidence to the prosecutor's arsenal, the state may actually discourage the proper presentation of evidence.[123] The prosecutor in *Payne*, for example, employed the theatrics of stabbing a cardboard diagram of the victim with the murder weapon and making comments that constituted ethics violations, but did not even try to rebut the mitigating evidence that the defendant introduced.[124] Such a rebuttal could have been accomplished rather easily. Where victim impact evidence is allowed, prosecutors may be tempted to rely on evidence that appeals solely to the sympathies and emotions of the jurors, without serving any legitimate purpose. The defendant then bears the heavy burden, after the fact, of proving that the evidence inflamed the jury and was prejudicial. In *Payne* and other cases like it,[125] the court has been very lenient in finding error to be harmless beyond a reasonable doubt. It is likely that prosecutors will take full advantage of the opportunities created here, when the questionable evidence benefits the prosecutor's case greatly, and courts turn a blind eye to prosecutorial misconduct and improper admission of evidence.

Due Process Clause as a Safety Net

The *Payne* decision asserts that the defendant's right to a fair trial is protected under the due process clause of the Fourteenth Amendment, so no prohibition on victim impact evidence is needed. Presumably, if evidence is admitted that is overly prejudicial or inflammatory to the defendant, the due process clause affords an adequate remedy.[126] However, this conclusion is questionable in light of some of the Court's decisions. As previously discussed, the prosecutorial misconduct in *Payne* was well documented and widely criticized throughout the appeal process.[127] Yet, it was not found to be prejudicial.[128] In an even more shocking case, *United States v. Serhant*,[129] the defendant was convicted of mail fraud; the prosecution included a suicide note from one of the investors in the presentence report, and contended that the victim committed suicide as a result of his involvement in the defendant's scheme. The Court found that this evidence was not overly inflammatory or emotional, and sustained the sentence; the Court of Appeals for the Seventh Circuit upheld the decision. It is difficult to imagine how much more prejudicial a victim impact statement would have to be to raise due process concerns.[130] Given the nature of these decisions, there seems to be little chance for success in challenging victim impact evidence on due process grounds, no matter how extreme the facts. The latitude given to states in setting criminal justice policy and the reluctance to find prejudice create a heavy burden for the defendant in alleging any constitutional violation.[131]

REALITIES OF VICTIM INVOLVEMENT

The crimes for which victims or victim's families are most likely to participate at sentencing are violent crimes and sexual assaults.[132] Yet, despite the fact that victim participation is available in most jurisdictions, the vast majority of victims do not exercise that option. Less than 18 percent of victims or families attend sentencing, only 15 percent submit written statements, and only 9 percent present oral statements where permitted.[133] Some victims fail to participate because they are unaware of that option; others are discouraged from participating by actors in the criminal justice system. Other victims lack interest or accept current sentencing procedures. Finally, some victims simply are not convinced of the importance of their role or want to put the crime behind them.[134] For these reasons, unless victims are formally solicited and asked to participate, they rarely exercise their rights.[135]

In addition to the problem of low participation rates, victim impact evidence has not lived up to its promise of empowering victims because it is only admissible after the accused has been convicted at trial. Since over 90 percent of criminal cases end in a negotiated guilty plea and no trial is held, most victims never get the opportunity to present such evidence.[136] This situation has led some commentators to advocate victim involvement in plea negotiations as well as sentencing to give the victim a more effective voice, and some jurisdictions do allow this now.[137] This proposition may give the victim a veto power in the plea bargaining context. If the victim, prosecutor, and defendant cannot come to an agreement, the prosecutor must fulfill his obligation to take the case to trial, just as in any other unsuccessful plea negotiation.[138] Therefore, this alternative arguably empowers the victim without jeopardizing the rights of the defendant, intruding on the judicial sentencing authority, or excessively hampering prosecutorial discretion.[139]

Surprisingly, inclusion of the victim in the sentencing or plea bargain stage has not created delays or harsher sentences as critics feared.[140] There is no evidence that victims uniformly seek harsh sentences, and there is even some evidence to the contrary. In one study of 100 cases, when victims were given the opportunity to choose from several viable sentencing alternatives, all but one was willing to accept an alternative to incarceration.[141] However, there is no conclusive evidence that participation increases victims' level of satisfaction with the process either.[142] Proponents of victim participation may be dismayed to learn that court attendance, in and of itself, seems to improve victim evaluation of sentencing decisions as much as direct involvement with the prosecutor, police, and defense counsel, if not more so.[143]

CAUTION: POLITICAL AGENDA

The term "victims' rights" represents an appealing concept, seemingly free from controversy and acceptable to all; no one wants to be considered antivictim.[144] However, most of the victims' rights activity in the United States has a decidedly conservative bent.[145] Conservatives focus on retribution and incapacitation to punish criminals and control crime, unlike the liberal approach centered on rehabilitation and social reform. Conservatives have been hostile to the "handcuffing" of law enforcement by the development of rights of the accused, and have used the symbolic strength of "victims' rights" to counteract these developments.[146]

Although victims' rights are commonly viewed as responding to perceived injustices in the criminal process, genuine concern about victims and victimization has increasingly been replaced by the concerns of advocates of the crime control model.[147] Conservatives have latched on to the symbolic value of the victim and used it as a substitute for the state on the side of the scale opposite the accused.[148] However, this tactic has many perils. The victim is portrayed as a pure, blameless stranger preyed upon by the criminal, which exploits the public's fear of future victimization. "Rights" are used as a powerful rhetorical device that suggests freedom and independence and trumps the rights of criminal defendants. The changes advocated under this oversimplified definition of "victim" and vague concept of "rights" are geared toward the implementation of a conservative agenda.[149]

For example, the President's Task Force on Victims of Crime recommended abolishing the exclusionary rule because victims should not have to pay for the government's mistakes. The Task Force argued that innocent people have no use for and cannot benefit from the rule, only the guilty could take advantage of it.[150] This position is not supported by any empirical data, only incomprehensible claims that the exclusionary rule leads to police inaction, unending continuances, delays, and retrials.[151] Efforts to identify any victim's right that outweighs the constitutional right to be free from unreasonable search and seizure are strained at best. There is far more evidence that Task Force members were simply hostile to the rule itself, aside from any concern for the victim.[152]

Other substantive changes recommended by the President's Task Force and conservative groups also veil attempts to impose stricter punishments on defendants in line with the crime control model. These include, but are not limited to, a victim's right to a speedy trial, the abolition of plea bargaining, and preventive detention.[153] The rhetoric in support of these proposals turns on alleged concern for victims, but, in reality, it has little to do with the victim's needs or desires. For example, in attempting to abolish plea bargaining, proponents claim that testifying against the accused is cathartic for victims. However, little concern is given to the fact that the courtroom may not be an appropriate setting for such an emotional experience. Nor is a victim's willingness or ability to testify taken into account. In fact, an absolute ban on plea bargaining eliminates consideration of the individual victim altogether. Thus, the real goal is revealed: to convict the defendant on the highest charge possible, regardless of the psychological state or preference of the victim. The rhetoric in support of a victim's right to a speedy trial and preventive detention are equally transparent and insensitive to the victim's real needs.[154]

The changes proposed in the name of victims' rights often have little to do with the narrow category of past victims who give the symbol meaning.[155] They have much more to do with fanning the fears of future victimization and stripping defendants of procedural safeguards. This agenda seriously endangers individual rights because the enormous political appeal of victims' rights frequently precludes any thoughtful critique.[156] A line exists beyond which expanding victim rights means infringing on the rights of others. The U.S. Constitution and the values that form the foundation of a free society require that society resist crossing that line despite short-term political appeal.[157]

CONCLUSION

If victim impact evidence is to be allowed at all, it must be allowed only within carefully constructed guidelines. The Court provides no guidelines in *Payne*, and would seem to permit unlimited testimony of questionable value and relevance that could seriously jeopardize defendants' constitutional rights. It would have been far more helpful and reasonable for the court to require states to develop a thoughtful criteria for the admission of such evidence. The process that evolved from the *Furman*[158] decision could have been employed: there, the Court required the states to develop reasoned criteria for the imposition of the death penalty that precluded its arbitrary imposition. In *Payne*, the Court could likewise have required the states to determine specific categories of victim impact evidence that would or would not be admissible and to explain why. Then, the Court could review the constitutionality of these criteria individually, based on the justification given and the defendant's rights implicated. This would still have represented a retreat from *Booth*, but at least it would have provided a more reasoned and fair basis for determining what information could be admitted.

Legislatures are better positioned to create guidelines of this sort; they should strive to eliminate inappropriate use of victim impact statements that may violate the rights of the accused, yet remain sensitive to the original goals of the victims' rights movement. Carefully drafted statutes could also deter prosecutorial violations of due process.[159] However, legislatures apparently cannot be counted upon because of the tremendous political appeal of victims' rights.

The Supreme Court's decision in *Payne v. Tennessee* and much of the federal and state legislation in this area ill-serve the needs of victims by creating the illusion that victims play a primary role in case disposition, when, in fact, the complex psychological and emotional effects of crime have not been carefully considered. More sensitive, commonsense concern for the victim, such as providing information and explaining the decisions made in the course of a criminal prosecution, could go a long way to reduce feelings of alienation and frustration without jeopardizing the rights of the accused.

The criminal justice system is not equipped to nurture the victims of crime or their families, nor should it be. The forum is not suited to respond to grief and has little therapeutic value. Recognizing this fact does not amount to complacency toward the victim.[160] Other venues are more appropriate for dealing with victims' issues and should be pursued with more fervor than solutions of the victim participation variety.

NOTES

1. Davis, Kunreuther & Connick, "Expanding the Victim's Role in the Criminal Court Dispositional Process: The Results of an Experiment," 75 J. Crim. L. 491, 491-492 (1984).
2. Henderson, "The Wrongs of Victim's Rights," 37 Stan. L. Rev. 937, 938 (1985).
3. Davis, Kunreuther & Connick, note 1 *supra*, at 491-492.
4. *Id.*
5. McDonald, "Toward a Bicentennial Revolution in Criminal Justice: The Return of the Victim," 13 Am. Crim. L. Rev. 649, 649 (1976).
6. McLeod, "An Examination of the Victim's Role at Sentencing: Results of a Survey of Probation Administrators," 71 Judicature 162, 162 (1987) (citing Kelly, "Victims' Perceptions of Criminal Justice," 11 Pepp. L. Rev. 15 (1984)).
7. Erez, "Victim Participation in Sentencing: Rhetoric and Reality," 18 J. Crim. Just. 19, 21 (1990).
8. *Id.* at 19.
9. McLeod, "Victim Participation at Sentencing," 22 Crim. L. Bull. 501, 504 (1986) (citing Zehr & Umbreit, "Victim-Offender Reconciliation: An Incarceration Substitute?" 46 Fed. Prob. 63 (1982)).
10. *Id.* at 501.
11. Erez, note 7 *supra*, at 19.
12. McLeod, note 9 *supra*, at 502.
13. McLeod, note 6 *supra*, at 162.
14. VWPA, Pub. L. No. 97-291, 96 Stat. 1248 (codified at 18 U.S.C. 3579-3580 (1982)).
15. VWPA § 2(b)(1).
16. Hellerstein, "The Victim Impact Statement: Reform or Reprisal?" 27 Am. Crim. L. Rev. 391, 393-394 (1989).
17. Fed. R. Crim. P. 32(c)(2)(C).

18. Hellerstein, note 16 *supra*, at 395 (citing S. Rep. No. 97-532, 97th Cong., 2d Sess. 10, reprinted in 1982 U.S.C.C.A.N. 2515, 2516.
19. VWPA § 2(b)(3).
20. Kennard, "The Victim's Veto: A Way to Increase Victim Impact on Criminal Case Dispositions," 77 Cal. L. Rev. 417, 423 (1989).
21. Erez, note 7 *supra*, at 22 (citing President's Task Force on Victims of Crime 76-77 (1982)).
22. Gilmore, "*Payne v. Tennessee:* Rejection of Precedent, Recognition of Victim Impact Worth," 41 Cath. U.L. Rev. 469, 479 n.79 (1982).
23. Henderson, note 2 *supra*, at 967-969.
24. Gilmore, note 22 *supra*, at 480 n. 80.
25. The President's Task Force suggested adding the following language to the Sixth Amendment: "Likewise, the victim in every criminal prosecution shall have the right to be present and to be heard at all critical stages of judicial proceedings." Hellerstein, note 16 *supra*, at 396-397 (citing President's Task Force on Victims of Crime 114 (1982)).
26. Roland, "Progress in the Victim Reform Movement: No Longer the "Forgotten Victim," 17 Pepp. L. Rev. 35, 38 (1989).
27. "Son of Sam" laws generally require that any money that the defendant receives by selling the rights to his story be set aside pending the disposition of the case; then, if the defendant is convicted, the funds must be used to satisfy any award of restitution and court costs, with the remainder contributed to state victim compensation programs. *Id.* at 57.
28. *Id.* at 40-41 (citing National Organization for Victim Assistance, *Victim Rights and Services: A Legislative Directory* 6-7 (1987)).
29. McLeod, note 6 *supra*, at 167.
30. Case Note, "Eighth Amendment No Longer Bars Victim Impact Statement Admission in Capital Sentencing Proceedings: *Payne v. Tennessee*," 61 U. Cinn. L. Rev. 261, 275 (1992) (authored by Matthew v. Brammer) (citing Cal. Const. art. I, § 28).
31. Cal. Const. art. I, § 28(b).
32. Cal. Const. art. I, § 28(d).
33. Cal. Const. art. I, § 28(f).
34. Roland, note 26 *supra*, at 39.
35. R.I. Const. art. I, § 23.
36. Roland, note 26 *supra*, at 39.
37. Van Rogenmorter, "Crime Victims—A Legislative Perspective," 17 Pepp. L. Rev. 59, 65 (1989) (citing Mich. Comp. Laws § 780.756(3)).
38. *Id.* at 62 (citing Mich. Comp. Laws § 780.753).
39. Roland, note 26 *supra*, at 41.
40. Van Regenmorter, note 37 *supra*, at 69.
41. McLeod, note 6 *supra*, at 162.
42. McLeod, note 9 *supra*, at 503-504.
43. Booth v. Maryland, 482 U.S. 496, 107 S. Ct. 2529, 96 L. Ed. 2d 440 (1987).
44. See Md. Ann. Code art. 27, § 413(b) (1982).
45. Md. Ann. Code art. 41, § 4-609(c) (1986).
46. *Id.*, § 4-609(c)(3).
47. U.S. Const. amend. VIII. The Eighth Amendment states: "Excessive bail shall not be required, nor excessive fines imposed, nor cruel and unusual punishment inflicted."
48. *Booth*, 482 U.S. at 500-501.
49. Booth v. State, 306 Md. 120, 223, 507 A.2d 1098, 1124 (1986).
50. Berger, "*Payne* and Suffering—A Personal Reflection and a Victim-Centered Critique," 20 Fla. St. U.L. Rev. 21, 33 (1992).
51. Booth v. Maryland, 482 U.S. at 501-502.

52. *Id.* at 502.
53. *Id.* at 503-504.
54. *Id.* at 505.
55. *Id.* at 507.
56. *Id.* at 508-509.
57. *Id.* at 506-507.
58. *Id.* at 509.
59. *Id.* at 517 (White, J., dissenting).
60. *Id.* at 517-518.
61. South Carolina v. Gathers, 490 U.S. 805, 109 S. Ct. 2207, 104 L. Ed. 2d 876 (1989).
62. *Gathers*, 109 S. Ct. at 2208.
63. *Id.* at 2211.
64. State v. Gathers, 295 S.C. 476, 484, 369 S.E.2d 140, 144 (1988).
65. *Gathers*, 109 S. Ct. at 2210.
66. *Id.* at 2212 (O'Connor, J., dissenting).
67. *Id.*
68. Payne v. Tennessee, 501 U.S. 808, 111 S. Ct. 2597 (1991).
69. 111 S. Ct. at 2601-2602.
70. *Id.* at 2603.
71. *Id.* at 2602-2603.
72. *Id.* at 2603.
73. State v. Payne, 791 S.W.2d 10, 18 (Tenn. 1990).
74. *Id.* at 19.
75. Payne v. Tennessee, 111 S. Ct. at 2609.
76. *Id.* at 2608.
77. *Id.*
78. *Id.* at 2605-2606.
79. 455 U.S. 104, 114, 102 S. Ct. 869, 877, 71 L. Ed. 2d 1 (1982).
80. 428 U.S. 153, 203-204, 96 S. Ct. 2909, 2939, 49 L. Ed. 2d 859 (1976).
81. Payne v. Tennessee, 111 S. Ct. at 2606.
82. Woodson v. North Carolina, 428 U.S. 280 (1976).
83. *Id.* at 2607.
84. *Id.*
85. *Id.*
86. *Id.* However, note that the prosecutor in *Gathers* did not focus on these characteristics, as Rehnquist seems to imply. The prosecutor's comments emphasized the victim's religious proclivities and participation in the political process.
87. *Id.* at 2611 n.2.
88. Berger, note 50 *supra*, at 30.
89. Talbert, "The Relevance of Victim Impact Statements to the Criminal Sentencing Decision," 36 U.C.L.A. L. Rev. 199, 266 (1988–1989).
90. Berger, note 50 *supra*, at 29.
91. Talbert, note 89 *supra*, at 226-227.
92. Berger, note 50 *supra*, at 29.
93. Henderson, note 2 *supra*, at 995.
94. Payne v. Tennessee, 111 S. Ct. at 2627 (Stevens, J., dissenting).
95. *Id.* at 2625.
96. *Id.* at 2630.
97. Berger, note 50 *supra*, at 48.
98. Hellerstein, note 16 *supra*, at 395.

99. *Payne*, 111 S. Ct. at 2607.
100. Hellerstein, note 16 *supra*, at 398.
101. Berger, note 50 *supra*, at 45-47.
102. *Payne*, 111 S. Ct. at 2629 (Stevens, J., dissenting).
103. Berger, note 50 *supra*, at 52-54.
104. This tactic has received a great deal of attention in rape trials in particular, and has led to outcries for restrictions on the types of information that the defendant can present regarding the victim's past sexual history and so forth.
105. Jump, "*Booth v. Maryland:* Admissibility of Victim Impact Statements During the Sentencing Phase of Capital Murder Trials," 21 Ga. L. Rev. 1191, 1210 (1987).
106. Berger, note 50 *supra*, at 50.
107. Payne v. Tennessee, 111 S. Ct. at 2629 (Stevens, J., dissenting).
108. *Id.* at 2627.
109. Lockett v. Ohio, 438 U.S. 586, 98 S. Ct. 2954, 57 L. Ed. 2d 973 (1978), required individualized sentencing determinations in virtually all cases involving a death sentence. To this end, the sentencer must be allowed to consider all mitigating evidence presented by the defendant to eliminate "the risk that the death penalty will be imposed in spite of factors which may call for a less severe penalty." *Lockett*, 98 S. Ct. at 2965.
110. *Payne*, 111 S. Ct. at 2627 (Stevens, J., dissenting).
111. *Id.* at 2607.
112. Brammer, note 30 *supra*, at 290.
113. The jury only needed to find one aggravating factor to impose capital punishment. Tenn. Code Ann. 39-13-204(g)(1).
114. Brammer, note 30 *supra*, at 289.
115. Berger, note 50 *supra*, at 47.
116. Jump, note 105 *supra*, at 1212.
117. Payne v. Tennessee, 111 S. Ct. at 2627 (Stevens, J., dissenting).
118. Berger, note 50 *supra*, at 48.
119. Talbert, note 89 *supra*, at 199.
120. Furman v. Georgia, 408 U.S. 238, 286-287 (1972).
121. Talbert, note 89 *supra*, at 221-222.
122. *Id.* at 227-231.
123. Brammer, note 30 *supra*, at 291.
124. State. v. Payne, 791 S.W.2d 10, 20 (Tenn. 1990). The prosecutor commented that if ever a case called for the death penalty, this was it. This was found to be a violation of the Code of Professional Responsibility, DR 7-106(c)(4), which states: "[A] lawyer shall not . . . assert his professional opinion as to the justness of a cause. . . ."
125. Darden v. Wainwright, 477 U.S. 168, 106 S. Ct. 2464 (1986). In *Darden*, the prosecutors, in their closing argument, implied that the death penalty would be the only guarantee against similar acts in the future and referred to the defendant as an animal. One prosecutor also made several offensive comments reflecting an extremely emotional reaction to the case. The Court commented that these remarks were improper but did not affect the fairness of the result. Four Justices dissented.
126. Payne v. Tennessee, 111 S. Ct. at 2608.
127. See note 124 *supra.*
128. State v. Payne, 791 S.W.2d at 20.
129. 740 F.2d 548 (7th Cir. 1984), cited in Hellerstein, note 16 *supra*, at 418 n.160.
130. Hellerstein, note 16 *supra*, at 418 n. 160.
131. Brammer, note 30 *supra*, at 287 n.223.
132. McLeod, note 6 *supra*, at 165.

133. *Id.*
134. *Id.*
135. Hellerstein, note 16 *supra*, at 398.
136. Kennard, note 20 *supra*, at 430.
137. *Id.* at 434.
138. *Id.* at 452.
139. *Id.* at 444.
140. Erez, note 7 *supra*, at 25 (citing Hough & Maxon, "Dealing With Offenders: Popular Opinion and the Views of Victims—Finding From the British Crime Survey," 24 How. J. Crim. Just. 160, 160-175 (1985)).
141. Kennard, note 20 *supra*, at 446-447.
142. *Id.* at 434.
143. Hagan, "Victims Before the Law: A Study of Victim Involvement in the Criminal Justice Process," 73 J. Crim. L. 317 (1984).
144. Hellerstein, note 16 *supra*, at 395.
145. Henderson, note 2 *supra*, at 951.
146. *Id.* at 947.
147. *Id.* at 951.
148. *Id.* at 948.
149. *Id.* at 950-952.
150. Hellerstein, note 16 *supra*, at 396-397 (citing President's Task Force on Victims of Crime 27-28 (1982)).
151. Henderson, note 2 *supra*, at 985.
152. *Id.* at 983.
153. *Id.* at 968, 976-977.
154. *Id.* at 977-982.
155. *Id.* at 965.
156. Brammer, note 30 *supra*, at 287.
157. *Id.* at 287-288.
158. Furman v. Georgia, 408 U.S. 238 (1972).
159. Brammer, note 30 *supra*, at 282.
160. Berger, note 50 *supra*, at 59.

18

"Three Strikes and You're Out": The Impact of California's New Mandatory Sentencing Law on Serious Crime Rates

Lisa Stolzenberg, Stewart J. D'Alessio

INTRODUCTION

Mandatory sentencing laws have become extremely popular in recent years. According to the Bureau of Justice Assistance (1996), virtually every state and the federal government have enacted some type of mandatory sentencing law. The primary purpose of these laws is to increase the severity of criminal sanctions by requiring that offenders convicted of certain crimes serve fixed minimum prison terms. Chronic or habitual offenders usually have been the targets of this type of legislation. In the past, habitual offender statutes could be found in the criminal codes of nearly every state. These statutes enabled prosecutors to seek enhanced penalties when a defendant had one or more prior felony convictions. If an individual was arrested for a crime, charged as a habitual offender, and found guilty of the crime, then he or she would receive a long prison sentence, frequently life in prison without the possibility of parole.

More recently, several states and the federal government have augmented their habitual offender statutes by enacting new, highly publicized "three strikes and you're out" laws that severely limit the discretion of prosecutors and judges. For example, if a three-strikes law applies in a particular case, the prosecutor is required to pursue the case under the statute. The prosecutor has no discretion in the matter unless, of course, he or she allows a plea to a lesser offense to circumvent the law. In addition, if the defendant is convicted, the judge is expected to impose the mandated sentence. Mitigating factors such as offender remorse or rehabilitation considerations are not deemed relevant in determining severity of sanction. Three-strikes laws vary considerably in terms of the number and type of offenders they affect. In some states (e.g., California, Colorado, Louisiana), the statutes are broadly defined, allowing the third "strike" to accrue even for a minor felony conviction such as motor vehicle theft. In a recent highly publicized case, for example, a defendant received a mandatory prison

Reprinted by permission of Sage Publications from *Crime & Delinquency*, vol. 43 (1997), pp. 457–469.

sentence of 25 years to life under California's three-strikes law after being convicted of stealing a slice of pizza from a group of children. In this case, the sentence is as onerous as the one that would have resulted had the defendant raped a woman or molested a child because the statute does not distinguish between crime types. In several other states (e.g., New Mexico, North Carolina, Washington) and the federal government, three-strikes laws are drawn more narrowly to specifically target repeat violent offenders. The new federal law, for example, affects only defendants in federal courts who have accumulated three convictions for crimes involving serious injuries to their victims.

The primary rationale for three-strikes legislation emanated from the research on career criminals. In their landmark study, *Delinquency in a Birth Cohort*, Wolfgang, Figlio, and Sellin (1972) traced a cohort of 9,945 boys born in Philadelphia in 1945 through their 18th birthday in 1963. The major finding of their study was that a small group of juvenile offenders, those who were arrested five or more times by age 18, made up only 6% of the Philadelphia cohort but accounted for 52% of all arrests of cohort members. Wolfgang et al. also found that these juveniles were arrested for the majority of the serious crimes committed by the cohort. For example, they were arrested for 71% of the homicides, 73% of the rapes, 82% of the robberies, and 69% of the aggravated assaults. The findings generated from the study undertaken by Wolfgang et al. have been replicated by a number of other important empirical works (Shannon, McKim, Curry, and Haffner 1988; West and Farrington 1977). The policy implications of this research are obvious; if society can incapacitate the relatively small number of potential habitual offenders early in their criminal careers, then a substantial reduction in crime levels can be realized.

However, although three-strikes laws have proliferated across the country, a question remains as to whether they have reduced crime. To our knowledge, there have been no empirical studies conducted to assess their effectiveness in reducing crime levels. The only study to touch on this issue was a projection analysis of the incapacitative effect of California's three-strikes law undertaken by Greenwood, Rydell, Abrahamse, Caulkins, Chiesa, Model, and Klein (1996) at the RAND Corporation. They estimated that a fully implemented three-strikes law would reduce serious felonies between 22% and 34% and that about one third of this reduction would be for violent crimes such as murder, rape, or aggravated assault. The other two thirds reduction would be for less violent felonies including less injurious assaults, most robberies, and residential burglaries. Greenwood et al. also noted that their study probably understated the impact of California's three-strikes law on crime levels because it did not consider the possibility of a deterrent effect of the law. Because the application of the three-strikes law is mandatory, the severity of punishment for violating it is considerably higher than that for violating other types of criminal statutes. Consequently, the deterrent effect associated with three-strikes legislation probably is greater than that associated with other types of habitual offender sentencing laws.

Using data calibrated in monthly intervals and an interrupted time-series design with nonequivalent dependent variables, we analyzed the effect of California's three-strikes law on serious crime rates in the 10 largest cities in the state: Anaheim, Fresno, Long Beach, Los Angeles, Oakland, Sacramento, San Diego, San Francisco, San Jose, and Santa Ana. We focused on these major cities because of their higher concentrations of serious offenders. California provided an important context for this study for several reasons. First, because it was one of the first states to implement a mandatory three-strikes law (having done so in March 1994), many states have modeled their legislation on the California law. Second, California implemented one of the toughest laws in the nation. Specifically, the law provides for a mandatory prison sentence of 25 years to life for an offender convicted of any felony following two prior convictions for serious crimes. It also doubles the prison sentence for second-strike offenders, requires consecutive prison sentences for multiple-count convictions, and limits good time credits to 20% after the first strike.[1] Third, a greater number of defendants (more than 3,000) have been charged under California's three-strikes law than in any other state. We believed that because of these factors, California provided an excellent context for analyzing the effect of three-strikes legislation on crime rates.

The data and analytic strategy used in this study also were well suited for the task at hand. First, although no research design guarantees correct inferences, the interrupted time-series design with nonequivalent dependent variables we employed is considered among the strongest of the nonexperimental designs for drawing causal inferences (Cook and Campbell 1979). This design, which is depicted as follows, involves comparisons of series of observations (O) over time expected to be affected by an intervention (×) with a control series not expected to be influenced by the same intervention:

$$O_{A1}\ O_{A2}\ O_{A3}\ O_{A4}\ O_{A5} \times O_{A6}\ O_{A7}\ O_{A8}\ O_{A9}\ O_{A10}$$

$$O_{B1}\ O_{B2}\ O_{B3}\ O_{B4}\ O_{B5}\quad O_{B6}\ O_{B7}\ O_{B8}\ O_{B9}\ O_{B10}$$

This design rules out the largest number of plausible alternative explanations for a hypothesized causal relationship because the comparison series helps to reduce the possibility of history effects. In addition, although the simple diagram shown depicts only one experimental and one comparison series, multiple experimental and comparison series were examined in this study. Specifically, we analyzed one experimental and one comparison series for each of the 10 California cities.[2]

Second, we used month rather than year as our unit of analysis because monthly data are considered superior for interpreting change and for reducing the confounding of history effects (McCleary and Hay 1980). Analyzing monthly data also permits greater flexibility in applying more sophisticated and efficient statistical procedures because of the increased number of observations.

Third, because this analysis compared changes in serious crime rates within several cities over time and did not predict changes across jurisdictions, we reduced potential biases resulting from differences in city crime-reporting practices.

DATA AND VARIABLES

For each city, time-series data for the 1985–95 period were obtained from the California Department of Justice, Uniform Crime Reporting (UCR) Program.[3] These data include monthly tabulations of offenses known to police.

Two dependent variables were used in this analysis. The first, the serious crime rate, was measured as the number of reported index crimes (willful homicide, forcible rape, robbery, aggravated assault, burglary, and motor vehicle theft) divided by the city population and multiplied by 100,000. This measure is referred to as the California Crime Index (CCI), which is used by the California Department of Justice.

The second dependent variable, the petty theft rate, was measured as the number of reported misdemeanor larcenies (i.e., thefts less than $50) divided by the city population and multiplied by 100,000. Because the third strike committed in California must be a felony offense, we expected the rate of reported misdemeanor crime to be unaffected by the new law. We examined the petty theft rate because it is the only misdemeanor crime category for which reported crime data were available in the UCR Program.

We analyzed the effect of California's three-strikes law with a dummy variable coded 0 before March 1994 and 1 otherwise. Based on previous research (Greenwood et al. 1996), we expected the actuation of the three-strikes law to have a strong and negative effect on serious crime levels.

DESCRIPTIVE ANALYSIS AND FINDINGS

Figure 1 depicts mean changes between the preintervention (January 1985 to February 1994) and postintervention (March 1994 to December 1995) periods for the CCI and petty theft rates for the 10 California cities. Even a cursory glance at this fig-

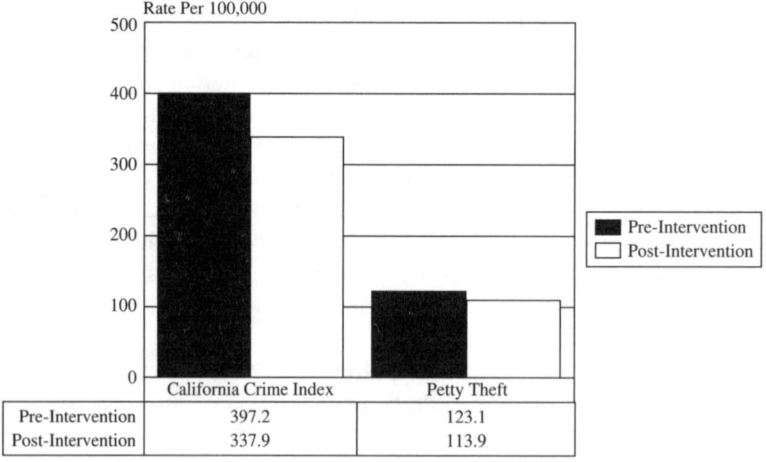

	California Crime Index	Petty Theft
Pre-Intervention	397.2	123.1
Post-Intervention	337.9	113.9

FIGURE 1: Means for Pre- and Postintervention California Crime Index and Petty Theft Rates (10 largest cities in California)

Note: Cities are Anaheim, Fresno, Long Beach, Los Angeles, Oakland, Sacramento, San Diego, San Francisco, San Jose, and Santa Ana. Data for Los Angeles for August 1986 and for Oakland for all of 1995 were estimated. The mean difference between the pre- and postintervention series was significant at the .01 level (one-tailed *t* test) for both the California Crime Index and petty theft rates.

ure reveals a reduction for both series following the implementation of the three-strikes law. The overall means for the CCI and petty theft rates during the preintervention period are 397.2 and 123.1, respectively. After the enactment of the law, the CCI rate dropped by 15% and the petty theft rate declined by 7%. These reductions are statistically significant at the .01 level of analysis.

However, although these results appear to support the position that the three-strikes law reduced both serious and petty theft crime in California, it is important to recognize that simple comparisons of pre- and postintervention means are only suggestive. Further evidence is needed before accepting these findings as definitive because it is not possible to say whether the observed decrease in crime levels was due to the three-strikes law or whether it was the result of a preexisting downward trend. To illustrate this point, we constructed a diagram that depicted both the CCI and petty theft rates over time (see Figure 2). The vertical line in Figure 2 represents the implementation of the three-strikes law. A visual examination of this figure suggests that both the CCI and petty theft rates already were declining prior to the establishment of the three-strikes law. Consequently, a question remains as to whether the observed reduction in crime during the postintervention period, as depicted in Figures 1 and 2, resulted from the three-strikes law or from a preexisting downward trend in crime levels. To answer this question, we undertook the intervention analysis.

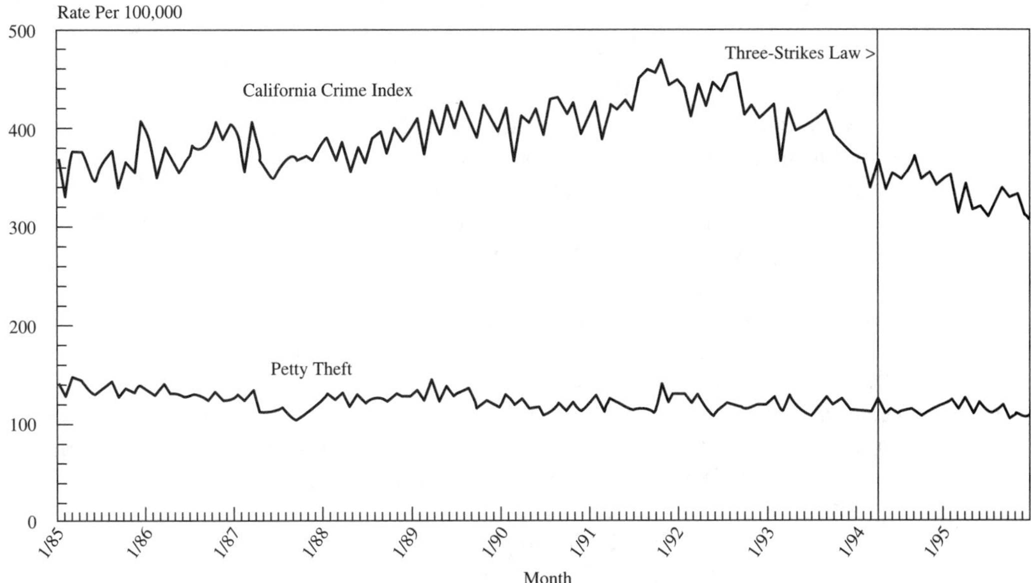

FIGURE 2: California Crime Index and Petty Theft Rates Over Time (10 largest cities in California)

Note: Cities are Anaheim, Fresno, Long Beach, Los Angeles, Oakland, Sacramento, San Diego, San Francisco, San Jose, and Santa Ana. Data for Los Angeles for August 1986 and for Oakland for all of 1995 were estimated. California's three-strikes law was implemented in March 1994.

INTERVENTION ANALYSIS AND FINDINGS

Although the mechanical and mathematical details of the intervention analysis used here are rather complex, the underlying principle is appealingly simple. Basically, the trend in the CCI rate before the three-strikes law went into effect was compared to the trend after the onset of the law. If the difference between the two is negative and greater than one would expect from chance, then a significant effect of the three-strikes law on the CCI rate can be inferred. Of course, because the three-strikes law pertains only to felony crimes, one would expect a greater effect of the law on the CCI rate than on the petty theft rate control series.

We began the time-series analyses by constructing univariate autoregressive integrative moving average (ARIMA) models for the CCI rates and the petty theft rate series for each of the California cities.[4] The time period from January 1985 to February 1994 was used for this purpose. After constructing the univariate ARIMA models, the intervention variable was added to represent the effect of the three-strikes law. We considered three intervention models. First, we considered the possibility that the serious crime rate declined sharply after the three-strikes law went into effect and then remained at this lower level over time. We also considered the possibility that the three-strikes law had a small initial impact on the serious crime rate that grew larger over time. Finally, we tested whether crime initially was reduced by the three-strikes law but then returned to preexisting levels as time passed.

Preliminary analyses indicated that for each of the cities, the abrupt permanent change model provided the best fit to the data.[5] The results for this intervention model are presented in Table 1. The results generally indicate that the three-strikes law did not decrease the CCI rate below that expected on the basis of preexisting trends. Although 6 of the 10 intervention coefficients were negative, only the coefficient for Anaheim was statistically significant. The intervention parameter (ω), which can be interpreted as the change in the level of the series that was due to the intervention, indicates that the CCI rate decreased in Anaheim by 16% following the onset of the three-strikes law.[6] Preexisting trends in the CCI rate cannot account for this decline.

Table 1 also shows, as predicted, little evidence that the three-strikes law had an effect on the petty theft rate. Again, only Anaheim showed a significant effect of the law, but the intervention coefficient was in the positive direction. That is, the petty theft rate *increased* by 65% following the implementation of the law, which suggests the possibility of a displacement effect. That is, some offenders may have committed misdemeanor instead of felony offenses to circumvent the three-strikes law. It also is possible that some of the increase in the petty theft rate might be due to changes in arrest and charging practices. For example, some police officers and prosecutors may have circumvented the three-strikes law by charging defendants with misdemeanor rather than felony offenses. Although these interpretations seem plausible, it is important to point out that none of the coefficients for the other nine cities were significant. Thus, it is possible that this is an aberrant finding. In sum, our results indicate that preexisting trends, rather than the three-strikes law, accounted for the reduction in crime levels initially observed in Figures 1 and 2.

TABLE 1 Intervention Estimates for Effect of Three-Strikes Law on California Crime Index and Petty Theft Rates, 1985–95

	California Crime Index		*Petty Theft*	
	ω_o	*SE*	ω_o	*SE*
Anaheim	−.170*	.070	.500*	.116
Fresno	.066	.071	−.141	.108
Los Angeles[a]	−.014	.039	.012	.058
Long Beach	.017	.061	−.165	.077
Oakland[b]	−.045	.062	.009	.108
Sacramento	.002	.053	−.114	.074
San Diego	−.036	.058	−.001	.077
San Francisco	−.113	.057	.116	.129
San Jose	.026	.050	.050	.076
Santa Ana	−.031	.068	−.056	.072

a. The California Crime Index and petty theft rates for Los Angeles for August 1986 were estimated with a Kalman filter because of coding errors in the data for that month.
b. The analysis for Oakland covers only the 1985–94 time period because data were unavailable for 1995.
$^*p < .01$ (one-tailed test).

DISCUSSION AND CONCLUSION

We began by noting that although California and several other states have implemented controversial three-strikes laws, few studies, if any, have been undertaken to evaluate their effectiveness in reducing crime. Against this backdrop, we analyzed time-series data drawn from 10 California cities to determine the effect of California's three-strikes law on crime levels. The results indicate that California's three-strikes law, whether one looks at Fresno, Long Beach, Los Angeles, Oakland, Sacramento, San Diego, San Francisco, San Jose, or Santa Ana, had little observable influence on either the CCI rate or the petty theft rate. The absence of an effect is rather surprising considering the data presented in Figures 1 and 2. Based on the maximum-likelihood results, it appears that the observed drop in the CCI and petty theft rates following the onset of the three-strikes law resulted from a preexisting downward trend in crime levels. It is important to point out, however, that not all of our findings are entirely consistent with this conclusion. For example, we noted that Anaheim did experience a substantial reduction in the CCI rate and an increase in the petty theft rate during the postintervention time period. These changes cannot be explained by a preexisting trend.

The question that begs answering is why California's three-strikes law has had little effect on serious crime. We offer a few conjectures that warrant discussion. One possibility is that because current sentencing practices already confine a substantial proportion of high-risk offenders behind bars, a diminishing marginal return can be expected by further increases in levels of incarceration (Canela-Cacho, Blumstein, and Cohen 1997; Zimring and Hawkins 1995). In California, for example, convicted felony offenders with serious prior criminal records already were receiving enhanced penalties prior to the implementation of the three-strikes law (Greenwood et al. 1996). California's determinate sentencing law, which was implemented in 1981, provided that a person convicted of a serious felony could be sentenced to an additional five years in prison for each previous serious felony conviction. Additional enhanced penalties for repeat offenders included third- and fourth-strike provisions for crimes involving great bodily injuries or the use of force likely to produce such injuries. These provisions stipulated that anyone convicted for crimes such as murder or forcible rape after serving two previous prison terms for violent felonies could receive a prison term of 20 years to life. A convicted felony offender with three prior prison terms could get a life sentence without the possibility of parole. In sum, because habitual offenders in California already were receiving enhanced penalties, it seems unlikely that the three-strikes law would have any discernible effect on crime levels simply because it raised the severity of punishment slightly further.

A second explanation for our findings concerns the relationship between age and crime. The effectiveness of three-strikes legislation as a crime control strategy depends on the duration of criminal careers.[7] By the time we confine offenders for their third strike, their criminal careers usually are on the decline, if not concluded. Research on the relationship between age and criminal activity shows that crime typically is a young person's game (Farrington 1986). For example, the peak age for property offenses is 16, whereas the peak age for violent offenses is 18. The frequency of offending among individuals typically continues unabated until age 30, when both violent and property offending rates begin to decline (Nagin, Farrington, and Moffitt 1995). Because habitual offenders are unlikely to pose a serious crime threat beyond the age of 30, and because the average age of offenders admitted to prison is 31 (Austin 1996), it seems unlikely that California's three-strikes law, by incapacitating offenders already at the tail ends of their criminal careers, would have any substantive impact on reducing the overall crime rate.

A third, related explanation pertains to juvenile crime. Juveniles currently account for a large percentage of the serious crime committed in the United States. For example, although juveniles between the ages of 10 and 17 years constituted about 25.0% of the population in 1994, they accounted for 19.4% of the arrests for violent crimes and 35.1% of the arrests for property crimes (Federal Bureau of Investigation 1995). For some crimes such as homicide, the situation is worsening. Over the past decade, the rate of homicide committed by teenagers between the ages of 14 and 17 years has more than doubled. It increased more than 170%, from 7.0 per 100,000 in 1985 to 19.1 per 100,000 in 1994 (Fox 1996). In California, juvenile offenders were not affected by the three-strikes law.[8] Consequently, it seems unlikely that juvenile crime was affected in any substantial way by the three-strikes law.

Although our results have important policy implications, it would be premature to accept them as definitive and final. Certain questions need to be addressed. Our data were drawn from several large cities in one state. Would our failure to find a strong negative effect of the three-strikes law hold for cities in other states? Does city size play a role in determining the effectiveness of three-strikes legislation? Other researchers should consider replicating this study in other jurisdictions. The more frequently such research is conducted, the greater the confidence we can place in the generalizability of our findings.

A second limitation is that we are unable to argue convincingly in this article that the three-strikes law did not reduce crime levels among those individuals eligible to be sanctioned under the law. It is entirely possible that the three-strikes law did actually deter persons with one or more prior felony convictions from participating in illegal activities. To discern such an effect, a comparison would need to be made between the number of crimes committed by individuals with one or more felony convictions prior to the implementation of the three-strikes law and the number of crimes committed by these same individuals after the law went into effect. Such data were not available to us, but this issue should be investigated in future research.

Notwithstanding these problems, the implications of our findings for policy are rather clear. The notion that California's three-strikes law significantly reduced crime has been implicitly assumed by policy makers and academicians alike, but such a belief has not been supported by this study. When preexisting trends were taken into account, California's three-strikes law had little observable effect on either the CCI rate or the petty theft rate. It would seem particularly fruitful for other researchers to identify more precisely the specific mechanisms responsible for our findings. Such a specification would allow us to better understand why the three-strikes law was not really that effective in reducing serious crime. It also seems clear that those who share our interest in curtailing crime might be prudent to consider shifting their attention away from three-strikes legislation as a means of crime control to other, more cost-effective measures. Because our findings show that California's three-strikes law did not achieve its objective of reducing crime, through either deterrence or incapacitation, we conclude that policy makers probably should consider revising, repealing, or justifying the use of the three-strikes law on purely retributive grounds.[9]

Despite our findings, the effect of three-strikes legislation and other types of selective incapacitation measures on crime levels is likely to remain of interest to policy makers around the country. This is an important question that is raised frequently with little empirical evidence on which to base definitive answers. The purpose of this article was to shed additional light on this issue. We fully expect that our findings and conclusions will be elaborated and challenged in future empirical work.

NOTES

1. See Greenwood et al. (1996) for a detailed discussion of California's three-strikes law.
2. One potential threat to internal validity was encountered by our calculation of multiple tests of statistical significance. By conducting multiple tests, we increased the probability of making a Type I error. That is, we increased the likelihood of falsely concluding that a relationship existed between the onset of the three-strikes law and the serious crime rate. We attempted to minimize this error by choosing the more conservative significance level of .01 rather than the conventional level of .05 and by concluding that a relationship exists only on the basis of a pattern of significant results rather than on the basis of one or two substantive coefficients.

3. See McCleary and Hay (1980) for a more detailed discussion of ARIMA modeling procedures.
4. Data for Oakland were unavailable for 1995.
5. Results from analyses using the gradual permanent model and the abrupt temporary model showed that the three-strikes law had little impact on either the CCI rate or the petty theft rate for any of the California cities.
6. We transformed the intervention coefficient, which is stated in the natural logarithm, into a percentage change score by using the following formula: Percentage Change = $[(e^{(\omega O)} - 1)100]$.
7. In addition, the effectiveness of three-strikes laws is contingent on our ability to recognize and apprehend offenders for the third actual felony in which they engage.
8. Prior juvenile adjudications for serious crimes count as strikes if the juvenile was 16 years of age.
9. Revisions of California's three-strikes law currently are underway. On June 20, 1996, the California Supreme Court decided that judges should be given discretionary latitude in determining whether or not to invoke the three-strikes statute in particular cases.

REFERENCES

Austin, James. 1996. "The Effect of 'Three Strikes and You're Out' on Corrections." Pp. 155–74 in *Three Strikes and You're Out*, edited by D. Shichor and D. K. Sechrest. Thousand Oaks, CA: Sage.

Bureau of Justice Assistance. 1996. *National Assessment of Structured Sentencing*. Washington, DC: U.S. Department of Justice.

Canela-Cacho, Jose A., Alfred Blumstein, and Jacqueline Cohen. 1997. "Relationship Between the Offending Frequency (λ) of Imprisoned and Free Offenders." *Criminology* 35:133–71.

Cook, Thomas D. and Donald T. Campbell. 1979. *Quasi-Experimentation: Design and Analysis Issues for Field Settings*. Boston: Houghton Mifflin.

Farrington, David. 1986. "Age and Crime." Pp. 189–250 in *Crime and Justice: An Annual Review of Research*, vol. 7, edited by M. Tonry and N. Morris. Chicago: University of Chicago Press.

Federal Bureau of Investigation. 1995. *Crime in the United States, 1994*. Washington, DC: Government Printing Office.

Fox, James Alan. 1996. *Trends in Juvenile Violence: A Report to the United States Attorney General on Current and Future Rates of Juvenile Offending*. Washington, DC: U.S. Department of Justice, Bureau of Justice Statistics.

Greenwood, Peter W., C. Peter Rydell, Allan F. Abrahamse, Jonathan P. Caulkins, James Chiesa, Karyn E. Model, and Stephen P. Klein. 1996. "Estimated Benefits and Costs of California's New Mandatory-Sentencing Law." Pp. 53–89 in *Three Strikes and You're Out*, edited by D. Shichor and D. K. Sechrest. Thousand Oaks, CA: Sage.

McCleary, Richard and Richard A. Hay, Jr. 1980. *Applied Time Series Analysis for the Social Sciences*. Beverly Hills, CA: Sage.

Nagin, Daniel, David Farrington, and Terrie Moffitt. 1995. "Life-Course Trajectories of Different Types of Offenders." *Criminology* 33:111–39.

Shannon, Lyle, Judith L. McKim, James P. Curry, and Lawrence J. Haffner. 1988. *Criminal Career Continuity: Its Social Context*. New York: Human Sciences Press.

West, Donald J. and David P. Farrington. 1977. *The Delinquent Way of Life*. London: Heinemann.

Wolfgang, Marvin E., Robert M. Figlio, and Thorsten Sellin. 1972. *Delinquency in a Birth Cohort*. Chicago: University of Chicago Press.

Zimring, Franklin E. and Gordon Hawkins. 1995. *Incapacitation: Penal Confinement and the Restraint of Crime*. New York: Oxford University Press.

19

Imposing the Death Penalty on Juvenile Murderers: A Constitutional Assessment

Kenneth E. Gewerth, Clifford K. Dorne

For nearly a century, the juvenile court has existed to shield the majority of youthful offenders from the full weight of the criminal law. As Justice Abe Fortas noted in *Kent v. United States*, a juvenile placed under the court's protection is entitled to a variety of "special rights and immunities." For example:

> He is . . . shielded from publicity. He may be confined, but with rare exceptions, he may not be jailed along with adults. He may be detained, but only until he is 21 years of age. The court is admonished by the statute to give preference to retaining the child in the custody of his parents "unless his welfare and the safety and protection of the public cannot be adequately safeguarded without . . . removal." The child is protected against the consequences of adult conviction such as the loss of civil rights, the use of adjudication against him in subsequent proceedings and disqualification for public employment.[1]

In theory at least, the special procedures of the juvenile court "provide measures of guidance and rehabilitation for the child and protection for society. . . ."[2] And, despite intense criticism, confidence in the juvenile court's rehabilitative orientation remains strong. For example, the National Coalition of State Juvenile Justice Advisory Groups has recently taken the position that "the vast majority of juvenile offenders can be successfully rehabilitated when provided with a treatment program that has a specific plan of care. . . ."[3]

Policymakers recognize, however, that there are some youths who are extremely dangerous, or not amenable to the treatment offered by the juvenile court. As a result, all the states and the District of Columbia have established mechanisms for transferring or waiving juvenile court jurisdiction in these exceptional cases so that young offenders can be tried in a criminal court and punished as adults.[4] Once a case is waived to adult court for trial, an accused youth loses the "special rights and immunities" offered by the juvenile court. In addition, the accused youth is subject to the full range of penalties for criminal behavior, including, at least in some jurisdictions, execution.[5]

Reprinted by permission of the authors from *Judicature*, vol. 75 (1991), pp. 6–15.

While the number of juvenile offenders on death row is extremely small,[6] recent U.S. Supreme Court decisions,[7] and the publicity generated in another case involving an Indiana juvenile named Paula Cooper,[8] have prompted many to examine this difficult problem in some detail. The purpose of this article is to review the constitutional issues surrounding the capital punishment of offenders whose crimes were committed as juveniles. To facilitate the analysis of this complex topic, we will begin with a brief review of the standards and methods judges must employ to determine if a punishment violates the constitutional ban on cruel and unusual punishment. Then, we will consider the judicial interpretation and application of such standards to juvenile executions. The issue of "youth as a mitigating factor" is emphasized, but other concerns are addressed as well, such as public opinion, laws of other nations, the juvenile offender's psychological responsibility, and whether or not executing juveniles satisfies the so-called social "objectives" of capital punishment. The conclusion brings these issues back to bear on the Eighth Amendment as they may guide future high court reviews of juvenile death penalty cases.

THE CONSTITUTION AND THE DEATH PENALTY

General Limits Imposed by the Eighth Amendment

The general limits on the states' power to punish are set out in four U.S. Supreme Court cases. Under the rulings in *Wilkerson v. Utah*[9] and *In re Kemmler*,[10] the cruel and unusual punishment clause prohibits the physical torture of offenders and barbaric forms of execution, such as crucifixion or burning at the stake, while *Weems v. United States* bars "all punishments which, by their excessive length or severity, are greatly disproportionate to the offense charged."[11] In addition, the Court has recognized that the scope of the Eighth Amendment is dynamic. As Chief Justice Earl Warren noted in *Trop v. Dulles*, "[t]he Amendment must draw its meaning from the evolving standards of decency that mark the progress of a maturing society."[12] Later in the same opinion, he went on to note that the critical question for determining the constitutionality of a sanction was "whether [the] penalty subjects the individual to a fate forbidden by the principle of civilized treatment . . . [or violates] the dignity of man."[13]

Standards for Assessing the Constitutionality of Punishments

Taken together, *Wilkerson*, *Kemmler*, *Weems*, and *Trop* set out the general constitutional standards that must be met before the death penalty can be imposed; such standards are important because they tell us, in general, what can and cannot be done to other human beings who have broken the law. However, merely establishing the standards for the constitutional use of the death penalty is not enough; judges are also required to apply these standards in particular cases, and through application, give them meaning. Thus, a number of other decisions are important because they elaborate on the general standards outlined above. For example, *Solem v. Helm*,[14] addresses the requirement of proportionality. Tracing the concept as far back as the Magna Carta, the Court found proportionality to be a "deeply rooted and frequently repeated" principle in common law, a longstanding feature of Supreme Court jurisprudence, and a basic requirement of each criminal sentence.[15]

To determine if a sentence is proportional, courts first must weigh the harshness of the penalty in relation to: (1) the gravity of the offense, as measured by factors such as the harm to the victim, the harm to society, the absolute magnitude of the offense, the offender's role in the crime and whether the crime was attempted or completed; and (2) the offender's culpability, taking into account such factors as the offender's intent and motive. Second, proportionality may be judged by comparing the challenged punishment to the punishments imposed on other offenders in the same jurisdiction. If those convicted of more serious offenses are punished less harshly, then it is likely that the challenged punishment is disproportionate. Finally, the court must compare the challenged punishment to the sanctions for similar crimes in other jurisdictions. Here, disproportionality is likely if many other jurisdictions punish a similar offense less harshly.[16]

In *Furman v. Georgia*,[17] Justice William Brennan discusses the "human dignity" standard set out in *Trop.* First, to be acceptable, a punishment must not be so severe that it reduces "members of the human race [to the level of] nonhumans, as objects to be toyed with and discarded."[18] Second, the punishment must not be arbitrarily inflicted; it must be carried out in the "great majority of cases in which it is legally available";[19] otherwise the penalty becomes so rare that its imposition is, in the words of Justice Potter Stewart, "wanton and freakish."[20] Third, there must be some "objective" evidence that the punishment is acceptable to contemporary society.[21] Finally, the punishment must not be "excessive" in that it involves

> the pointless infliction of suffering. If there is a significantly less severe punishment adequate to achieve the purposes for which the punishment is inflicted, the punishment inflicted is unnecessary and therefore excessive [citation omitted].[22]

Furman also makes clear that "objective" criteria are to be used to determine if a sanction is consistent with, or contrary to, contemporary societal values. The sources of information for this judgment include: (1) the history of the punishment; (2) the extent to which its use is authorized by legislatures in other jurisdictions; (3) the extent to which it is actually imposed and carried out in other jurisdictions; and (4) the extent to which the punishment is supported in public opinion.[23]

Finally, in his discussion of excessive punishments, Justice Brennan also pointed out that the excessiveness of a penalty was to be judged, in part, in relation to its purpose and its effectiveness: any quantum of punishment above the amount necessary to achieve a valid penological goal was cruel and unusual.[24]

In this section we have briefly described the various factors that must be considered in order to determine whether a sanction such as the death penalty is permissible under the Eighth Amendment. To make this decision, a judge must weigh a complex constellation of factors about the offender, the offense, the victim, and the society. Using the framework developed so far, we will now turn our attention to the U.S. Supreme Court decisions focusing on the use of capital punishment in cases involving juvenile offenders.

THE COURT AND JUVENILE EXECUTIONS

As Joseph L. Hoffman[25] notes, the imposition of death sentences against juvenile offenders has been challenged by petitioners on several occasions. In the past, the Court chose to avoid the question by declining to hear some cases,[26] or deciding others without reaching the death penalty issue.[27]

Recently, however, the question of juvenile executions was squarely presented to the Court in three cases: *Thompson v. Oklahoma,*[28] *Stanford v. Kentucky,*[29] and *Wilkins v. Missouri.*[30] Factually, the cases were similar: 15-year-old William Wayne Thompson and three older accomplices had been sentenced to death for the murder of Charles Keene, Thompson's brother-in-law; 17-year-old Kevin Stanford was convicted and sentenced to die for the robbery, rape, and murder of a young woman, while 16-year-old Heath Wilkins was convicted and sentenced for the murder of a convenience store clerk. On appeal, all three petitioners claimed that the imposition of a death sentence against those who were juveniles at the time of their crimes constituted cruel and unusual punishment.[31] The petitioners differed, however, on where the line separating adults from juveniles should be drawn for the purposes of execution: Thompson urged the Court to prohibit the execution of those who were 18 and under at the time of their crimes; Stanford wanted to draw the line at 17 or under, while Wilkins would have drawn the line at 16 years of age or below.

The Court reversed Thompson's sentence by a 5-3 vote, but affirmed the punishments of Stanford and Wilkins. Taken together, the three cases fix the line between juveniles and adults for the purposes of execution at the age of 16 or above. This "bright line" rule, however, masks deep divisions among the justices on several issues. Close examination of *Thompson* and *Stanford* reveals fundamental disagreements over: (1) the existence of a national consensus forbidding the execution of juveniles; (2) the extent to which the laws of other Western European nations and the opinions of "respected professional organizations"[32] should be taken into consideration when deciding on the constitutionality of juvenile executions in the United States; (3) the degree to which juveniles could be held responsible for their actions; (4) whether the execution of juveniles contributed to the retributive or deterrent goals of punishment; and (5) whether the small number of juveniles executed represents the "wanton and freakish" application of the death penalty condemned by Justice Stewart in *Furman.*[33]

A NATIONAL CONSENSUS?

In *Thompson*, and again in *Stanford*, the Court reaffirmed that the "evolving standards of decency" was the proper test for judging the constitutionality of juvenile executions; there was also agreement that these evolving standards of decency could be accurately measured by state legislative action.[34] However, both cases are marked by sharp disagreements about how this review of state legislation is to be conducted, resulting in opposite conclusions about the acceptability of sentencing young people to death.

Voting to overturn the sentence against Thompson, a plurality (composed of Justices John Paul Stevens, Thurgood Marshall, Harry Blackmun, and Brennan) first divided the states (including the District of Columbia) into three categories: those that abolished the death penalty for any offender (14);[35] those that authorized the death penalty and established a minimum age for its imposition (18);[36] (noting that all 18 jurisdictions in this category set the minimum age for execution at 16 or older at the time of the crime); and those that authorized the death penalty but did not establish a minimum age for its use (19);[37] They then eliminated from consideration the 19 states in the latter category, "because they do not focus on the question of where the chronological age line should be drawn."[38] Thus, for those in the *Thompson* plurality, nearly two-thirds of the total jurisdictions in the U.S. (32 of 51) have acted to restrict the death penalty in such a way that it cannot be imposed on someone below the age of 16, if at all. To the plurality, this represented an adequate consensus against the practice of executing juveniles.

Writing separately in *Thompson*, Justice Sandra Day O'Connor also voted to overturn Thompson's sentence. Her analysis of state legislation was similar to the plurality's: she combined the number of states that had abolished capital punishment altogether with those that established a minimum age for execution, and concluded that "strong counterevidence would be required to persuade me that a national consensus against this practice does not exist."[39]

Writing for the dissent, Justice Antonin Scalia (joined by Justices William Rehnquist, and Byron White) began his discussion of the evolving standards of contemporary society by noting a trend ignored by the plurality: the fact that several jurisdictions have recently *lowered* the age at which jurisdiction in juvenile cases can be waived to adult court.[40] He then objected to the plurality's resort to creative accounting in its review of state legislation.

> It is beyond me why an accurate analysis would not include within the computation the larger number of states (19) that have determined that no minimum age for capital punishment is appropriate, leaving that to be governed by their general rules for the age at which juveniles can be held criminally responsible.[41]

To the dissenting justices, the assessment of contemporary standards regarding capital punishment should focus only on the jurisdictions that have it. When the analysis is restricted to this group,

> . . . the Federal Government and almost 40% of the States, including a majority of the States that include capital punishment as a permissible sanction allow for the imposition of the death penalty on any juvenile who has been tried as an adult, which category can include juveniles under 16 at the time of the offense[. I]t is obviously impossible for the plurality to rely upon any evolved societal consensus discernible in legislation.[42]

Upon reflection, however, it is clear that the dissent has resorted to some creative accounting of its own in the analysis of state legislation. Their statement to the effect that ". . . almost 40% of the states . . . include capital punishment as a permissible sanction [against juveniles tried as adults]" is true as far as it goes: if the 19 jurisdictions that authorize execution without setting a minimum age are considered relative to all jurisdictions in the U.S., then ". . . almost 40%" of the jurisdictions (i.e. 19 of 51) apparently do authorize juvenile executions. Reported as a proportion (40 per cent), there does seem to be something of a consensus favoring the capital punishment of juveniles. But, looking only at the raw frequencies used to compute the proportion of ". . . almost 40%," the dissent's consensus evaporates: of the 37 jurisdictions with capital punishment, about half (18) do set a minimum age of at least 16, while about half (19) do not.

The following year, the Court once again considered the question of juvenile executions in *Stanford v. Kentucky.*[43] Not unexpectedly, the justices on each side of the issue reiterated many of the arguments raised earlier in *Thompson*, including a review of state legislation in search of consensus. This time, however, a plurality (composed of Justices Scalia, Rehnquist, White, and Anthony Kennedy) affirmed the death sentences against the petitioners, Stanford and Wilkins. Writing for the plurality in *Stanford*, Justice Scalia noted that of the 37 states that had capital punishment, only 15 would have prohibited the death of Stanford while only 12 would have barred the execution of Wilkins.[44] Thus, in a majority of states with capital punishment, both offenders could be executed. As a result:

> [T]his does not establish the degree of national consensus this Court has previously thought sufficient to label a particular punishment cruel and unusual. In invalidating the death penalty for rape [sic] of an adult woman, we stressed that Georgia was the *sole* jurisdiction that authorized such a punishment [citation omitted; emphasis in original]. In striking down capital punishment for participation in a robbery in which an accomplice takes a life, we emphasized that only eight jurisdictions authorized similar punishment [citation omitted]. In finding that the Eighth Amendment precludes the execution of the insane . . . we relied upon . . . the fact that "no State in the Union" permitted such punishment [citation omitted]. And, in striking down a life sentence without the possibility of parole under a recidivist statute, we stressed that "i[t] appears that [petitioner] was treated more severely than he would have been in any other state [citation omitted].[45]

Notice, however, a pronounced shift in Justice Scalia and the plurality's definition of "consensus" in this review of legislation: where previously (in *Thompson*) they suggested that a consensus in favor of juvenile executions could be discerned since ". . . almost 40%" (i.e. 19 of 51) of the jurisdictions authorized the practice, they now seem to be suggesting (in *Stanford*) that a consensus *against* juvenile executions could only exist if the vast majority of states prohibited them. Apparently, consensus is more easily seen when writing in dissent.

In *Stanford*, Justice O'Connor once again filed separately. This time, however, she joined Justices Scalia, Rehnquist, White, and Kennedy in affirming the sentences against Stanford and Wilkins. To Justice O'Connor, the fact that "every single American legislature that has expressly set a minimum age for capital punishment has set that age at 16 or above"[46] was sufficient to distinguish *Thompson* from *Stanford.*

In their dissent in *Stanford*, Justices Stevens, Marshall, Blackmun, and Brennan relied once more on an analysis of state legislation to support their conclusion that the sentences of Stanford and Wilkins ought to be struck down. This time, they counted 15 jurisdictions that prohibited capital punishment for any offender,[47] 15 that authorized the death penalty, but set a minimum age of 17 or 18 for its use, and 18 authorizing execution without specifying a minimum age for its use. As in *Thompson*, the jurisdictions in the latter category were eliminated from consideration on the grounds the one could "not assume . . . that a legislature that has never specifically considered the issue has made a conscious moral choice to permit the execution of juveniles."[48] Since the remaining 30 jurisdictions would not have permitted the execution of Stanford or Wilkins, Justices Stevens, Marshall, Blackmun, and Brennan once again perceived a consensus against the execution of juveniles.

Looking at the treatment of the consensus issue in both *Thompson* and *Stanford*, it would seem that the position of Stevens, Marshall, Blackmun, Brennan, and O'Connor, which maintains that there is a strong consensus against the practice of executing juvenile offenders, is the most consistent and reasonable one.

THE VIEWS OF OTHER COUNTRIES

Are the Views of Other Countries Relevant to U.S. Policy on Juvenile Executions?

To further support the assertion that the execution of offenders below the age of 16 was contrary to evolving standards of decency, the *Thompson* plurality of Stevens, Marshall, Blackmun, and Brennan also pointed out that the American Bar Association and the American Law Institute opposed the practice and that it had been outlawed in many other countries, including the Soviet Union.[49]

The *Thompson* dissent questioned the relevance of this evidence in a footnote, suggesting that the laws and practices of other nations "cannot be imposed upon Americans through the Constitution." According to the dissent, "the practices of other nations,"

> particularly other democracies, can be relevant to determining whether a practice uniform among our people is not merely an historical accident, but rather so "implicit in the concept of ordered liberty" that it occupies a place not merely in our mores but, text permitting, in our Constitution as well [citation omitted]. But where there is not first a settled consensus among our own people, the views of other nations, however enlightened the Justices of this Court may think them to be, cannot be imposed on Americans through the Constitution.[50]

Unfortunately, this argument is flawed in two respects. First, Justice Scalia seems to be suggesting that other nations rejection of juvenile executions is irrelevant to the present case because there is a lack of consensus on the issue in the United States. This appears inconsistent with his previous argument that there is a consensus favoring juvenile executions in the United States, since "almost 40%" of the jurisdictions allow them. Assuming *arguendo* that Justice Scalia's previous statement in *Thompson* is correct, and there is a consensus in America on this issue, then the views of the international community become relevant by the terms of his own argument. Once the relevance of other nations' laws have been accepted, it becomes impossible to ignore the fact that these views weigh heavily against the practice of sentencing juveniles to death.

Second, under Justice Scalia's reasoning, it would be necessary to acknowledge the laws and practices of other countries only after a "settled consensus" is discerned in American society. Presumably, the views of other countries would then be used to reinforce this "settled consensus." However, if the fundamental task of the U.S. Supreme Court is the resolution of legal conflict, it seems reasonable to expect that this task would be most effectively carried out when the Court's decisions take into account as much information as possible, including, when necessary, the legislation of other countries. To restrict the Court's view of international legislation to only those laws that are consistent with accepted policies in this country would force a selective perception of reality that would hamper the development of American constitutional law. The Court's subsequent decision in *Stanford* fails to resolve the debate over this issue. Each side merely reiterates the positions adopted in *Thompson.*[51]

HOLDING JUVENILES RESPONSIBLE

As discussed above, the Eighth Amendment requires a rough proportionality between the magnitude of the punishment and the culpability of the offender. Thus, in *Thompson*, it was necessary for the Court to decide "whether the juvenile's culpability should be measured by the same standard as that of an adult."[52] In consideration of this issue, the *Thompson* plurality, Justice O'Connor, and the dissent all start from a similar premise, but reason to very different conclusions. All discussions of the responsibility issue begin by acknowledging that the punishment for offenders should be directly related to their personal culpability.[53] Stevens, Marshall, Blackmun and Brennan follow this with the observation that minors cannot vote or exercise other rights, since "the normal 15-year-old is not prepared to assume the full responsibilities of an adult."[54] This line of reasoning is then used as partial support for the holding that those below the age of 16 at the time of their crimes cannot be put to death. For the *Thompson* plurality, 16 years of age is a significant "bright line" separating childhood from adulthood, since this is the age (in most states) when minors begin to take on at least some adult responsibilities. Moreover, in all those states that have expressly considered the issue, it represents the minimum age for execution.[55]

Justice O'Connor was less comfortable with such sweeping generalizations about the maturity of minors:

> I agree that "proportionality requires a nexus between the punishment imposed and the defendant's blameworthiness" [citation omitted]. Granting the plurality's other premise—that adolescents are generally less blameworthy than adults who commit similar crimes—it does not necessarily follow that all 15-year-olds are incapable of the moral culpability that would justify the imposition of capital punishment.[56]

Similarly, the dissenting justices in *Thompson* (Scalia, Rehnquist, and White) could find ". . . no rational basis for discerning . . . a societal judgment that no one so much as one day under 16 can *ever* be mature and morally responsible enough to deserve that penalty."[57]

The Court's struggle over the issues of juvenile responsibility and maturity arise because these ideas are *loose concepts*—that is, notions with no fixed boundaries. As

Max Black has pointed out, reasoning with loose concepts is problematic, since the customary rules of logic provide no specific method for distinguishing loose concepts from their opposites (in this case maturity from immaturity or responsibility from irresponsibility), yet nontheless presume that some *ad hoc* line of separation exists.[58] According to Black, loose concepts are meaningful *provided* we recognize that, at some point, someone will have to decide where to draw the line between a loose concept and its opposite, "just because there are not and cannot be any *rules* for [doing so]."[59]

Clearly then, logic alone cannot separate those juveniles who should be held responsible and executed from those who should not. But what of social science research or legislative practice? Can either of these support the bright line rule laid down in *Thompson?* The answer, it seems, is no. Unfortunately, while empirical research based on studies of large numbers or juveniles may demonstrate that many are indeed "less mature and less responsible than adults," "susceptible to influence and to psychological damage," "lack[ing in] experience, perspective, and judgment," "more impulsive and less self-disciplined,"[60] such evidence will not support the hasty generalization that these qualities are characteristics of *all* juveniles. Nor would the findings of these studies support the conclusion that any *particular* juvenile is immature, irresponsible, easily influenced, impulsive, or lacking in self-discipline; any such inference would be an example of what social scientists call the "ecological fallacy."[61]

As for legislation, it is probable that state laws preventing those below a certain age from voting, marrying, driving, or purchasing alcohol more possibly spring from the need for administrative convenience rather than a blanket presumption that all minors are too immature to vote, marry, drive, or drink. While there may be some persons below the age of 16 who are responsible enough to vote, marry, drive, or drink, it would be impractical to screen the juvenile population in order to find them; a much more plausible solution is to deny these rights to all below a certain age. Therefore, to the extent that these age-based restrictions do flow from the need for administrative convenience, they provide little justification for adopting a similar "bright line" rule governing juvenile executions. Since the number of juvenile offenders sentenced to death is vastly smaller than the number who may be potentially responsible enough to vote, marry, drive, or drink, the state can afford to conduct a much more detailed examination of each offender to determine if they can, in fact, be held responsible for their crimes.[62]

Finally, the *Thompson* plurality's assumption that all juvenile offenders are irresponsible is problematic because it overlooks the fact that:

> [the] constitutional rules relating to the maturity of minors must be drawn with an eye to the decision for which the maturity is relevant [citation omitted] It is surely constitutional for a state to believe that the degree of maturity that is necessary to fully appreciate the pros and cons of smoking cigarettes or even of marrying may be somewhat greater than the degree necessary to fully appreciate the pros and cons of brutally killing a human being.[63]

From the passage above, it seems that those in the dissent are distinguishing between: (1) complex situations, in which people must weigh a complicated set of factors before deciding what behavior is appropriate; and (2) simple situations, where the appropriate behavior can be readily determined. According to Justice Scalia, a global presumption that all juveniles are immature is most appropriate in complex situations, since they may not be capable of the sophisticated reasoning the circumstances demand. These situations may also require the imposition of bright line rules applicable to all youths.

On the other hand, a global presumption of immaturity and bright line rules would be inappropriate in simple situations where the choice of correct behavior is clear cut. For the dissent, juvenile killers face a simple decision, since the laws against killing are well known. Thus, no global presumption of immaturity is required, and the plurality's bright line rule preventing their execution is unnecessary. The issue of juvenile responsibility was also addressed in *Stanford;* it represents what is probably the most significant aspect of the case. Writing for the *Stanford* plurality, Justice Scalia disposes of the responsibility issue by flatly rejecting the idea that "no 16-year-old is 'adequately responsible' or significantly deterred"[64] enough to be subject to the death penalty. However, for Justice O'Connor and those in the *Stanford* dissent, merely acknowledging that *some* juveniles may be responsible enough to be executed is not enough to validate the execution of juveniles. According to O'Connor and the dissent,[65] the Court must conduct an additional analysis to "judge whether the 'nexus between the punishment imposed and the defendant's blameworthiness is proportional."[66]

At the very least, it appears that Justice Scalia's avoidance of a proportionality analysis represents a significant break with past death penalty cases. After *Stanford*, it is not clear what role disproportionality analysis has in evaluating the constitutionality of a punishment: it may be relegated to a secondary consideration, or perhaps it is no longer necessary at all.

THE GOALS OF PUNISHMENT

As indicated above, punishments that serve no valid purpose are "excessive" under the Eighth Amendment, and cannot be imposed.[67] Later, in *Gregg v. Georgia*,[68] the Court considered the death penalty in relation to the accepted goals of punishment. The Court decided that execution served the ends of retribution and deterrence.[69] Thus, in *Thompson*, the Court had to determine if the execution of juveniles was consistent with these goals as well. In deciding the issue, the plurality took note of "the teenager's capacity for growth, and society's fiduciary obligations to its children" as well as "the lesser culpability of the juvenile offender"[70] and concluded that the execution of those who were less than 16 years of age at the time of their crimes could not be justified on retributive grounds. They also concluded that deterrence was an inappropriate justification, since: (1) juveniles, being impulsive, were unlikely to indulge in the cost-benefit analysis of actions that the doctrine presupposes; and (2) the small number of juveniles executed during the 20th century had reduced the threat of punishment to the point of insignificance.[71]

Given their previous reluctance to make presumptions about the culpability of all those who committed crimes prior to the age of 16, both Justice O'Connor and the

Thompson dissent were similarly unwilling to conclude that the execution of such offenders could never further the goals of retribution or deterrence. As a result, neither Justice O'Connor nor the faction composed of Scalia, Rehnquist, and White were willing to invalidate Thompson's sentence on the grounds that it served no valid penological purpose.[72]

Thompson's bright line rule and the plurality's contention that juvenile executions cannot be justified on retributive grounds are criticized in a recent article by Hoffmann.[73] According to Hoffmann,[74] retributive justice requires *two* types of proportionality: (1) cardinal proportionality, which dictates that punishment be proportional to the harm caused by the crime and the offender's culpability; and (2) ordinal proportionality, which requires that equally culpable offenders guilty of similar crimes receive similar punishments. So far, in Hoffmann's[75] view, the debate about the juvenile death penalty has focused on its cardinal proportionality. Arguably, for a juvenile convicted of homicide, a life sentence would just as easily satisfy the cardinal proportionality requirement as would death. Thus, those opposed to the execution of juveniles have a much stronger argument "if the debate is cast solely in terms of cardinal proportionality."[76] In *Thompson*, the discussion of juvenile executions in relation to the principles of retributive justice does focus on cardinal proportionality. Consequently, its justification on retributive grounds becomes difficult, and a bright line rule prohibiting the execution of those under 16 at the time of the crime seems appropriate.

However, if *Thompson's* bright line rule is considered in light of the concept of ordinal proportionality, a serious flaw becomes apparent. Because juveniles under the age of 16 at the time of their offense cannot be executed, they receive more lenient treatment compared to nonjuvenile offenders who may be just as blameworthy, but who are eligible for the death penalty.[77] From the perspective of retributive theory, injustice flows from *Thompson* because:

> age itself is not the factor that renders the imposition of the death penalty against most juveniles arguably unjust. Rather, age is simply a "proxy," and an imperfect one at that, for a combination of factors that determines the relative culpability of a juvenile murderer. These factors include maturity, judgment, responsibility, and the capability to assess the possible consequences of one's conduct. Because age only imperfectly reflects this complex combination of factors, the adoption of a "bright line" ban on the death penalty for juveniles, fashioned in terms of age, necessarily violates the concept of ordinal proportionality.[78]

Hoffmann[79] suggests that guided discretion statutes applied across the board to all offenders, or a set of rebuttable presumptions about culpability based on age, are more consistent with the principles of retributive theory than the bright line rule laid down in *Thompson.* Since the *Stanford* plurality centered its opinion almost exclusively on the analysis of state legislation to decide the issues presented in the case, they apparently saw little need to explore once more the relationship between juvenile executions and the valid goals of punishment.

The *Stanford* dissent does address the issue once again, however. And again Brennan, Marshall, Blackmun, and Stevens argue that the various age-based restrictions on juvenile activities as well as social science evidence supports the following conclusion: As a class, juveniles are immature, unable to fully appreciate the consequences of their actions, and more impulsive, and therefore are not fit subjects for retribution or deterrence.[80]

WANTON AND FREAKISH?

By one estimate, no more than 20 individuals who were under 16 at the time of their crimes have been executed during this century. Bureau of Justice Statistics figures also show that only five of the 1,393 persons sentenced to death from 1982 to 1986 were under 16 at the time of the crime.[81] The plurality interpreted these data as objective indicators of jury behavior, demonstrating that juvenile executions had little public support, were "cruel and unusual in the way that being struck by lightning is cruel and unusual," and, therefore, contrary to contemporary standards of decency.[82]

Justice O'Connor's view of the data was slightly more cautious. While acknowledging that the plurality may be correct, she pointed out that an accurate interpretation could only be obtained by comparing the actual number of executions and death sentences imposed with the number of times prosecutors actually decided to seek the death penalty in juvenile cases. Because an actual execution results from a joint decision of the prosecutor and the jury (and perhaps the judge and others), it is impossible to determine the meaning of sentencing or execution data without first examining the behavior of all those who contributed to the decision.[83]

To the dissent, the fact "that no fewer than five murderers who committed their crimes under the age of 16 were sentenced to death in five different states between the years 1984 and 1986"[84] represented strong public support *for* juvenile executions. Moreover, to the dissent the small number of juvenile executions resulted from (1) a decline in overall public support for capital punishment; and (2) the movement away from mandatory, automatic death penalty schemes in favor of guided discretion systems that require individualized consideration of each death sentence. Both of these forces, however, were considered irrelevant to the question of whether the execution of juvenile offenders should *ever* be permitted.

The dissent then presented additional statistical data showing that the execution of female offenders was just as rare an occurrence as the execution of juveniles, and pointed out the inconsistency in banning the execution of the latter but not the former.

The debate over the meaning of the data on juvenile executions illustrates the difficulties judges encounter when, in the course of interpreting statistical data, they try to crossbreed a precise numerical quantity (5 death sentences or 20 actual executions) with an inexact verbal standard ("cruel and unusual," or "wanton and freakish"). Despite the effort to rely on "objective indicators" to determine the meaning of contemporary standards of decency, and the meaning of "cruel and unusual" punishment, the fact is that these judgments are ultimately subjective. The number of times a punishment is imposed or carried out is a poor way to judge its acceptability: how certainly can anyone say that the imposition of five death sentences in a period of time is wanton and freakish but more than five is not? It is similarly absurd to intimate that the execution of juveniles would become more acceptable by increasing the rate at which females are executed.

The dilemma judges face is complicated by the distribution of juvenile crime in the population. Whether crime is counted by official statistics (arrest, prosecution, or conviction records) or by various "unofficial" measures (self reports), "persistent and grave violations of the law are the experience of a minority."[85] Given that the number of serious juvenile offenders is small to begin with, we would not expect the number of young people to be sentenced to death to be very large under any circumstances.

WEIGHING MITIGATING FACTORS

In juvenile death penalty cases, judges and juries are presented with other possible mitigating factors in addition to youth. In three highly publicized cases, an array of mitigating factors were presented by defense attorneys to no avail. The judge and/or juries decided that the aggravating factors outweighed the various mitigating circumstances. The three respective states represented here are South Carolina, Indiana, and Louisiana. These cases sparked national and international debate. Of course, such debates centered on whether an "enlightened society" should resort to the use of the death penalty for juvenile murderers. The debates also addressed the more common mitigating factors raised in juvenile death penalty cases such as backgrounds of severe child maltreatment, mental retardation, the role of peer pressure (or the presence of an adult who encourages the juvenile to murder), and extreme drug and/or alcohol abuse.[86]

For example, the case of *Roach v. Martin*, involved the following facts:

> . . . [I]n Fort Jackson, South Carolina, a 17-year-old mentally retarded youth and a 16-year-old companion were living with a 22-year-old soldier in a rented, run-down house . . . Alcohol, THC, PCP, marijuana, and other drugs were readily available. . . . [A]fter heavy drinking and consuming drugs, the three decided to look for a girl to rape. They drove to a baseball park in nearby Columbia. They parked next to a young couple, a 17-year-old boy and his 14-year-old girl friend. On orders from the soldier, they shot the boy three times with a high powered rifle, killing him instantly. Then they drove off with the girl to a secluded area where each raped her repeatedly. Finally, they finished her off by shooting her and mutilating her body.
>
> The three were soon arrested by police. The youngest youth agreed to testify against the soldier and the 17-year-old in exchange for a lighter sentence. Both the soldier and the 17-year-old eventually entered guilty pleas and were sentenced to death. After lengthy appeals, the soldier was executed. . . . James Terry Roach, the 17-year-old who killed the boy and the girl and mutilated the girl's body was executed. . . . A crowd cheered outside the prison walls as the execution of Roach occurred.[87]

The second case involves 15-year-old Paula Cooper who was convicted of stabbing to death a 78-year-old Bible teacher in Gary, Indiana. This occurred while Cooper and three other teenage girls were attempting to rob the woman in her own home. The prosecutor successfully argued that Cooper was the "ring leader," as she actually brought the knife into the teacher's home. The girls took $10 and the victim's car. "There was a public outcry. . . . People in Gary wanted Paula Cooper to get the electric chair. There was that element of betrayal, of the girls being a traitor in killing someone who tried to help kids."[88] Cooper was reared in a violent home. Her father routinely required her and her sister to strip so he could whip their bare skin. Cooper also watched her mother get raped, and when she was 9, had joined her mother and sister in a suicide attempt.

While Paula Cooper was on death row, her case took some unusual turns. First, the grandson of the victim became one of her staunchest supporters. He travelled Europe, attempting to gain support through a petition drive to have Cooper's sentence commuted to life in prison.[89]

The third case occurred in Louisiana and involved Dalton Prejean. As a 14-year-old, Prejean killed a Lafayette taxi cab driver during a robbery and was adjudicated in juvenile court. He was sent to a training school and was released early, as the judge felt that he was responding well to treatment programs. At age 17, Prejean and three companions left a night club, and after driving a short distance, were pulled over by Louisiana State Trooper Donald Cleveland. When trooper Cleveland began to frisk Dalton's brother, Joseph, Dalton shot the trooper at close range killing him. Dalton Prejean was convicted of first degree murder and sentenced to death.[90]

A series of events served to prolong the execution for 13 years (list is not exhaustive):

- The trooper's wife sued the juvenile court judge responsible for releasing Prejean from the training school in a wrongful death action. The judge was found not to be liable under the "judicial immunity doctrine."
- Prejean appealed his conviction to U.S. district court on four grounds: the judge allowed the jury to see grisly photographs of the body; racial composition of the jury (Prejean was black); racial discrimination on the part of the jury in handing down the death penalty instead of life in prison; and youthful age at the time of the homicide—17. Prejean lost all four issues.
- Prejean's age remained an issue through appeals to the U.S. circuit court of appeals and to the U.S. Supreme Court. Again, Prejean's death sentence was not commuted.
- Prejean then applied to the Louisiana Pardon Board for a commutation. "By this time, he had 8 previous 'stays of execution,' 11 lawyers, 20 different legal issues presented to 6 different courts and a total of 35 judges."[91] At the pardon hearing, defense attorneys emphasized Prejean's mental retardation and the fact that he was an abused child. The board voted to commute the death sentence, shortly thereafter, Governor Buddy Roemer reversed this decision (the board's role is to make recommendations to the governor, but this does not bind the governor in making the final decision). Prejean was executed in May, 1990.

Like the cases of *Eddings* and *Bell*, the cases of *Roach*, *Cooper*, and *Prejean* involved some mitigating factors in addition to youthful age. Why then were Eddings and Bell spared, but Roach and Prejean executed?

A few observations can be made here. The extent and quality of legal representation for the defense is relevant. Many of these attorneys are indigent defenders who earn only a few thousand dollars per year for a single death penalty case while they have a "human life placed in their hands." Still, some anti-death penalty activist groups have adopted the defense's case, providing extensive resources and funding; this occurred in the Prejean case, among others. Naturally, the particular values of the decisionmaker (judge or jury) are germane, as is the intensity of public outcry for a death sentence.

Ultimately, however, the aggravating aspects of the *Roach* and *Prejean* cases outweighed the mitigating factors as perceived by the decisionmakers (judge or jury). While all murders committed by juveniles are shocking due to the youth of perpetrator, the facts in the Roach case were unusually grisly and horrible. The facts in the Prejean case involved the killing of a police officer by a youth who had killed before. Nonetheless, all current death penalty statutes require a judge or jury to weigh aggravation against mitigation; this punctuates the individuality of each case. It is not the legislative intent for such laws to standardize definitions of aggravation and mitigation. Rather, such standards are supposed to reflect the ideological climate and social values of the particular state; that is, "evolving standards of decency."

CONCLUSION

In *Thompson* and *Stanford*, the Court struggled to find an objective and logical answer to the question of whether juvenile offenders should be subject to capital punishment. On the surface, the promulgation of a bright line rule defining those age 16 or above as "adults" for the purpose of execution seems to be a forthright disposition of the issue.

Yet, as we have tried to show, the Court's bright line rule obscures some deep divisions within the Court and some faulty, illogical reasoning in both of these critical decisions. First, the Court seems to have no clear method for determining the extent (or even the existence) of a national consensus regarding the execution of juveniles; both supporters and opponents are capable of slanting an analysis of state legislation to suit their own arguments.

Second, both supporters and opponents of the juvenile death penalty are guilty of selective perception. For example, supporters of juvenile executions have, with little justification, decided to ignore the great weight of international opposition to the juvenile death penalty, while those opposed to execution have steadfastly held to the shaky conclusion that all juveniles under the age of 16 are too immature to be held responsible for their actions.

Finally, after *Stanford*, there seems to be a more fundamental disagreement about how the constitutionality of a punishment—any punishment—is to be judged. The sole focus of the plurality's analysis in *Stanford* was whether petitioner's death sentences were consistent with the standards of contemporary societies. Having decided that the sentences were acceptable, the plurality saw no need to go any further and consider, as a separate issue, whether death sentences were disproportionate to the offense. If this interpretation is correct, than the plurality has radically altered the way in which death penalty cases will be reviewed. After *Stanford*, it may no longer be true that "the Eighth Amendment demands more than that a challenged punishment be acceptable to contemporary society"[92] This may well become the primary test of the constitutionality of a punishment in the future.

NOTES

1. Kent v. United States, 86 S.Ct. 1045, 1055 (1966).
2. *Id.* at 1054.
3. Whitehead and Lab, Juvenile Justice: An Introduction 399 (Cincinnati, Ohio: Anderson Publishing Company, 1990).
4. For an overview of waiver provisions in the U.S., see generally, Jamison and Flannagan, Sourcebook of Criminal Justice Statistics—1989 159-161 [Table 1.105] (Washington D.C.: Bureau of Justice Statistics, 1989).
5. *E.g.* Thompson v. State, 724 P.2d 780, 784 (Okla. Crim. App. 1986).
6. In 1986, there were 1,772 on U.S. death rows, 37 of whom committed their capital crimes when they were 15, 16, or 17 years of age. See Streib, Death Penalty For Juveniles xi (Indiana: Indiana University Press, 1987). More recently, the total U.S. death row inmate population rose to over 2250. Thirty-seven states currently have death penalty statutes on their books.
7. *See generally*, Eddings v. Oklahoma, 102 S.Ct. 869 (1982); Thompson v. Oklahoma, 108 S.Ct. 2687 (1988); Stanford v. Kentucky, 109 S.Ct. 2969 (1989).
8. Hackett, King, and Stanger, *Indiana Killer, Italian Martyr: A Death Row Cause*, Newsweek, September 21, 1987, at 37.
9. Wilkerson v. Utah, 99 S.Ct. 345 (1879).
10. In re Kemmler, 136 S.Ct. 930 (1890).
11. O'Neil v. Vermont, cited in Weems v. United States, 30 S.Ct. 544, 551 (1910).
12. Trop v. Dulles, 78 S.Ct. 590, 598 (1958).
13. *Id.* at 597-98.
14. Solem v. Helm, 103 S.Ct. 3001 (1983).
15. *Id.* at 3006.
16. *Id.* at 3010.
17. Furman v. Georgia, 92 S.Ct. 2726 (1972).
18. *Id.* at 2743.
19. *Id.* at 2745, quoting Wilkerson v. Utah, *supra* n. 9.
20. Furman v. Georgia, *supra* n. 17, at 2763 (Stewart, concurring).
21. *Id.* at 2746-47.
22. *Id.* at 2747.
23. *Id.* at 2746-47, 2756-57, 2774-75, 2778-93.
24. *Id.* at 2747.
25. Hoffman, *On the Perils of Line Drawing: Juveniles and the Death Penalty*, 40 Hastings L.J. 229-30 (1989).
26. *E.g.*, Roach v. Martin, 757 F.2d 1463 (4th Cir. 1985), *cert denied*, 474 U.S. 1039 (1986); Trimble v. State, 478 A.2d 1143 (1983) *cert denied*, 469 U.S. 1230 (1985); Canaday v. State, 455 So.2d 713 (Miss. 1984), *cert denied*, 469 U.S. 1221 (1985); Tokman v. State, 435 So.2d 664 (Miss. 1984), *cert denied*, 467 U.S. 1256 (1984).
27. *E.g.* Bell v. Ohio, 98 S.Ct. 2977 (1978); Eddings v. Oklahoma, 102 S.Ct. 869 (1982).
28. Thompson v. Oklahoma, *supra* n. 7.
29. Stanford v. Kentucky, *supra* n. 7.
30. *Wilkins* was consolidated with *Stanford.*
31. Thompson v. Oklahoma, *supra* n. 7, at 2691; Stanford v. Kentucky, *supra* n. 7, at 2974.
32. Thompson, *id.* at 2696.
33. Furman v. Georgia, *supra* n. 17, at 2763.
34. Thompson v. Oklahoma, *supra* n. 7, at 2692, 2706, 2714-15; Stanford v. Kentucky, *supra* n. 7, at 2794-95, 2982. For a critique of the Supreme Court's reliance on legislation as an indicator of contemporary standards of decency, see Note [Ricotta], *Eighth Amendment—The Death Penalty for*

Juveniles: A State's Right or a Child's Injustice?, 79 J. Crim. L. and Criminology 921, 939-42 (1988).

35. The jurisdictions in this category are: Alaska, District of Columbia, Hawaii, Iowa, Kansas, Maine, Massachusetts, Michigan, Minnesota, New York, North Dakota, Rhode Island, West Virginia, and Wisconsin. Thompson v. Oklahoma, *supra* n. 7, at 2694-95 n.25.

36. The jurisdictions in this category include: California, Colorado, Connecticut, Georgia, Illinois, Indiana, Kentucky, Maryland, Nebraska, Nevada, New Hampshire, New Jersey, New Mexico, North Carolina, Ohio, Oregon, Tennessee, Texas. Thompson v. Oklahoma, *supra* n. 7, at 2696 n.30.

37. The jurisdictions included in this category are: Alabama, Arizona, Arkansas, Delaware, Florida, Idaho, Louisiana, Mississippi, Missouri, Montana, Oklahoma, Pennsylvania, South Carolina, South Dakota, Utah, Vermont, Virginia, Washington, Wyoming. Thompson v. Oklahoma, *supra* n. 7, at 2695, n.26.

38. Thompson v. Oklahoma, *supra* n. 7, at 2695.

39. *Id.* at 2706-7.

40. *Id.* at 2716.

41. *Id.*

42. *Id.*

43. Stanford v. Kentucky, supra n. 7.

44. *Id.* at 2975.

45. *Id.* at 2975-76.

46. *Id.* at 2981.

47. Apparently, in the period between *Thompson* and *Stanford*, Vermont repealed a statute punishing some murders with death. The remaining portion of the law, which authorized death as punishment for some types of kidnapping, was voided by *Furman.* See *Stanford*, *supra* n. 7, at 2983 n. 1.

48. *Id.* at 2983.

49. Thompson v. Oklahoma, *supra* n. 7, at 2696.

50. *Id.* at 2716, n. 4.

51. Stanford v. Kentucky, *supra* n. 7, at 2975, n. 1 and 2984-6.

52. Thompson v. Oklahoma, *supra* n. 7, at 2698.

53. Stevens, Marshall, Blackmun, and Brennan explicitly acknowledge this premise in *Thompson* at 2698, while Justice O'Connor's recognition of this premise occurs in *Thompson* at 2708.

In the *Thompson* dissent, Justice Scalia's recognition of this idea is less clearly stated. However, at one point in the opinion he writes: "I might even agree with the plurality's conclusion if the question were whether a person under 16 when he commits a crime can be deprived of the benefit of a rebuttable presumption that he is not mature and responsible enough to be punished as an adult."

Later, he quotes Justice Powell's statement in Fare v. Michael C. 99 S.Ct. 2560 (1979) at 2576 n.4. "Some of the older minors become fully 'streetwise', hardened criminals, deserving no greater consideration than that properly accorded all persons suspected of crime."

Taken together, these two statements seem to reflect a belief by Justice Scalia that criminal responsibility can vary between individuals.

54. Thompson v. Oklahoma, *supra* n. 7, at 2693.

55. *Id.* at 2692-96; Appendices A–F.

56. *Id.* at 2708-09.

57. *Id.* at 2718 (emphasis in original).

58. For a complete discussion of the problems of reasoning with loose concepts, see Black, Margins of Precision 1-13 (New York: Cornell University Press, 1970).

59. *Id.* at 11-12 (emphasis in original).

60. Thompson v. Oklahoma, *supra* n. 7, at 2698.
61. Nettler, Explaining Crime (3rd ed.) 100-101 (New York: McGraw Hill, Inc., 1984).
62. Hoffmann, *supra* n. 25, at 281-82; Stanford v. Kentucky, *supra* n. 7, at 2977.
63. Thompson v. Oklahoma, *supra* n. 7, at 2718 n. 5 (dissenting opinion).
64. Stanford v. Kentucky, *supra* n. 7, at 2979.
65. *Id.* at 2986-2994.
66. *Id.* at 2981.
67. Furman v. Georgia, *supra* n. 17, at 2747; Gregg v. Georgia, 96 S.Ct. 2909, 2929 (1976).
68. Gregg v. Georgia, *id.* at 2929-30.
69. *Id.* at 2930-31.
70. Thompson v. Oklahoma, *supra* n. 7, at 2699.
71. *Id.* at 2700.
72. *Id.* at 2708-09, 2718-19.
73. Hoffmann, *supra* n. 25.
74. *Id.* at 248-50.
75. *Id.* at 257.
76. *Id.* at 258.
77. *Id.* at 233.
78. *Id.* at 234-35.
79. *Id.* at 283-84.
80. Stanford, *supra* n. 7, at 2993-94.
81. Thompson v. Oklahoma, *supra* n. 7, at 2697.
82. *Id.* at 2697.
83. *Id.* at 2798.
84. *Id.* at 2717.
85. Nettler, *supra* n. 61, at 82.
86. For a general discussion of the role of aggravating and mitigating circumstances in capital cases, see Shapiro, *First Degree Murder Statutes and Capital Sentencing Procedures: An Analysis and Comparison of Statutory Systems for the Imposition of Statutory Systems for the Imposition of the Death Penalty in Georgia, Florida, Texas and Louisiana*, 24 Loyola L. Rev. 709 (1978); Lemon, *Constitutional Criminal Law—The Role of Mitigating Circumstances in Considering the Death Penalty.* 53 Tulane L. Rev. 608 (1979); Amnesty International, The Death Penalty: An Amnesty International Report (London: Amnesty International, 1979); Streib, *supra* n. 6; Wikberg and Rideau, *Death Watch*, Angolite, January–February (1990).
87. Champion, Corrections in the United States: A Contemporary Perspective 437 (Englewood Cliffs, NJ: Prentice-Hall, 1990).
88. *Id.* at 439.
89. Knoxville News-Sentinel, January 3, 1988, at 12.
90. Prejean v. Blackburn, 743 F.2d 1093 (1984).
91. *Id.*
92. Gregg v. Georgia, *supra* n. 67, at 2929.

20

Don't Spare the Rod: A Proposed Return to Public, Corporal Punishment of Convicts

Whitney S. Wiedeman

I. INTRODUCTION

It does not require much reflection to realize that the current system of criminal punishment is failing miserably. The modern penal system cannot achieve its declared goals of general deterrence or rehabilitation, and it is only successful as a specific deterrent during periods in which convicts are actually imprisoned. America needs to take an entirely new approach to dealing with crime, and with criminals. The model I suggest has two parts. First, make retribution the fundamental reason for inflicting punishment. Second, once society has satisfied its need for vengeance, focus the stigma on the crime rather than on the criminal and allow convicts who have suffered the penalty for their actions to reenter society as productive members. To follow this model, and for the other benefits it may provide, I suggest we use public corporal punishment other than imprisonment for all noncapital crimes.

The first elements of this idea are appearing all over the country. The Mississippi House of Representatives passed a bill allowing judges to order paddling instead of jail time for minor crimes.[1] A state senator in New York proposed a similar bill for the punishment of graffiti artists,[2] as did two state legislators from Tennessee who followed the same model I propose with their recommendation of public caning for those convicted of property crimes.[3] Louisiana and New Mexico have seen corporal punishment bills proposed and defeated.[4] This recent renewed interest can be at least partially credited to the 1994 caning of Michael Fay in Singapore for vandalism. His case has made people willing to reexamine why corporal punishment fell into such disfavor.

Corporal punishment may appear to be a barbaric solution to the problems of a civilized society, but it is in fact a reasonable, rational alternative to the systemic prison overcrowding and rampant recidivism that are part of our current approach to crime and criminals. I hope that this Comment will stimulate debate about punishment alternatives to imprisonment generally and corporal punishment specifically.

† Reprinted by permission of the *American Journal of Criminal Law*, from vol. 23 (1996), pp. 651–673.

Further, I hope it will lead to a renewed interest in the public application of punishment in order to provide a better opportunity for deterrence in addition to the retribution achieved by the punishment itself.

II. A "PROFESSIONAL" APPROACH TO CRIMINAL JUSTICE

Neither corporal punishment nor public punishment is a particularly original idea. Both have been used in some cultures for centuries.[5] But both types of punishment are uncommon in the Western world, especially the United States. These punishments have been replaced by the "professional" model of crime control, which began its popular rise in the early nineteenth century.[6]

The professional model is based on the premise that criminal punishment is best placed in the hands of individuals who are specially trained in criminal justice administration of some type—police, lawyers, judges, prison guards, and probation officers. The belief is that these people are trained to deal with criminals, that they know how to administer punishment (most frequently imprisonment under this model) and when or if a convict should be allowed to resume his place in normal society.

The problems with this approach are not immediately obvious. After all, during the Renaissance and the Industrial Revolution, we came to believe that we could look at everything from a scientific perspective. Economics helps us understand patterns of financial activity; sociology, explains why people interact as they do; psychology helps us to interpret and predict human behavior and beliefs; so surely criminology would help us to understand and deal with crime. With that thought, all the various parts of today's criminal justice system began to develop. We began to rely on police to apprehend wrongdoers. We depended on the courts to make determinations of guilt or innocence. And we left punishment in the hands of professionals who made prisons their preferred choice of punishment, perhaps in an effort to shift the focus of their actions toward the mind of the prisoner and away from the infliction of bodily pain.[7] By this effort, they sought to end the abusive extremes of corporal punishment responsible for people dying under the lash or being maimed by some device. They also followed the whole professional model to impose better control over determinations of guilt or innocence by developing a system with bias toward avoiding wrongful prosecution even at the expense of letting the guilty go unpunished. By monopolizing crime control, they sought to avoid vigilante approaches that might even lead to punishment of death for innocent people who had been wrongly accused.

The problem with the professional model is not so much in the parts as in the premise. The model was at least partially developed in response to notorious acts and atrocities committed against individuals who had been charged with crimes. Particularly good examples of this can be found in the literature regarding punishment of criminal slander in England, which punishment often resulted in terrible mutilation of the offender.[8] But the professionals blamed corporal punishment for allowing that abuse rather than looking at the nature of society to determine why those sorts of things happened. This reaction was almost certainly in part because changing a punishment system was easier than altering society's view of crime and criminals.

III. PRISONS ARE OUR CHOICE, AND OUR CHOICE IS WRONG

Cesare Beccaria is one of the more notable eighteenth-century proponents of corporal punishment, especially imprisonment as one type of corporal punishment. Beccaria believed that the mind of a criminal needed to be changed and could be changed by punishing it rather than the body.[9] Unfortunately, systematic imposition of psychic punishments is impossible; mental punishment is possible only indirectly by the professional approach, so prison became the chosen alternative.

However what form were our newly developing prisons to take? In the United States, we developed two totally distinct systems of imprisonment. On one hand, we had the Pennsylvania system, which was the closest we could get to punishment of mind instead of body. Under this system, each prisoner was kept in solitary confinement, was never allowed to associate with other prisoners, and, when enjoying the minimal exposure to society in the form of a guard, was not allowed to speak. Nor was he spoken to by the guard if at all avoidable.[10]

Elsewhere in the north, the development of the Auburn system in Auburn, New York was a response to both the perceived need for prisons and the economic realities which limited the ability to maintain prisons operating under the Pennsylvania system. Prisoners here were kept in larger prisons, and allowed to work with each other in the daytime, although communication with other prisoners and guards was still largely prohibited. This system was far less expensive to society and quickly became the primary model for prisons in the United States.[11]

Though prisons were intended to take other forms of corporal punishment out of the criminal justice system, in fact the first aspect of past punishments to disappear was their public application. By privatizing punishment, professionals hoped to prevent the hardening of society to an escalating pattern of abusive punishments; what they achieved was a weakening of one of the most frequently articulated reasons for imposing criminal punishments at all: general deterrence of the populous from committing a similar crime.

Proponents make several arguments in support of prisons. They suggest that prisons allow the opportunity to rehabilitate criminals and that prisons are designed to keep prisoners out of society until they show that they can be a part of it. Another argument is that prisons are the most humane way to punish wrongdoers. Ironically, another faction of prison supporters believe that prisons should be wretched, miserable places where the inmates should suffer every indignity. Those making that argument do seem to give retribution due regard as a reason for punishment, but we do not keep convicts in prison forever. Although making prisons unlivable might make criminals eager to stay out of them, it might also condition prisoners to violence and depravity to such a degree as to make it impossible for them to rejoin society as contributing members.

The problems with these latter arguments in favor of prisons follow the pattern set by the flaws in the former arguments. Prisons simply do not achieve the goals that their proponents desire. The high rate of recidivism shows that prisons are not suitable as houses of rehabilitation.[12] Of special note is the fact that the juvenile crime rate is growing, or at least the media and politicians perceive it to be growing as measured by all the attention the topic has drawn in recent years. If true, it would show that the whole idea of criminal punishment by imprisonment cannot serve as a general deterrent.

As to the issue of the relative humanity of prison versus corporal punishment, consider this: prisoners can reasonably be expected to face assault, sodomy, or murder on a daily basis through the entire term of their imprisonment. How can this be the most humane way to punish them? Prisons were intended to prevent the excesses of punishment meted out in times past and to end the torturous extremes to which corporal punishment had been taken on criminals for even the most petty offenses. But there is an irreconcilable difference between the goal and the reality of prison life. With this in mind, reconsider the humanity of a painful, but brief and controlled application of corporal punishment, conducted in a public setting, thus delivering retribution, deterrence, and the opportunity for rehabilitation into society.

IV. THE FIRST CHALLENGE: IS CORPORAL PUNISHMENT UNCONSTITUTIONAL?

Without question, the first attack on a proposed system of public, corporal punishment will be that it violates the Eighth Amendment. However, the founders clearly accepted corporal punishment as a viable alternative to other forms of criminal punishment. As mentioned above, the prison system did not truly begin to develop in this country until the 1800s. Before that, towns had stocks, pillories, and whipping posts to deal with criminals, as well as the occasional jail to hold a few people when the need arose.[13]

Looking at the applicable terms of the Eighth Amendment may provide further enlightenment. "Cruel" is defined as brutal, savage, or barbarous.[14] "Unusual" means scarce, peculiar, or abnormal.[15] The courts have defined "cruel and unusual punishment" to mean "an unnecessary and wanton infliction of pain." "Wanton" means unconscionable, unbridled, or unrestrained.[16] "Unnecessary" is defined as needless or gratuitous.[17] Corporal punishment, as I recommend it, is certainly scarce in our penal system, at least as punishment is controlled and applied by the state rather than by prison inmates. There are certainly people who feel corporal punishment would be savage and barbarous. But, if applied correctly, it would, by the fact that a specific penalty is imposed for a specific crime, be neither wanton nor unnecessary. This holds true in the same way that imprisonment is considered to be necessary and restrained if the sentence applied is proportionate to the crime.

Another set of cases holds that the Eighth Amendment must be applied with an eye toward an evolving standard of justice.[18] What exactly this means is in question. Whatever the courts intended when they set that standard, it is as easily interpreted as a strengthening of the standard with more direct penalties for crimes as it is to see it as a liberalization of punishment policies.

There is one significant body of law relating specifically to the use of corporal punishment—*Ingraham v. Wright*[19] and the line of cases that follow it. *Ingraham* does not discuss physical punishments for criminals, however, but deals instead with how they may be used against schoolchildren who misbehave in the classroom. The decision remains significant, though, because of the freedom it gives teachers and schools to maintain discipline. Under the Supreme Court guidelines established in this case, no hearing is required to determine the necessity of corporal punishment.[20] The only relevant factor is the judgment of the teacher or principal. Later cases have focused not on whether the teacher had a right to punish, but only on whether a certain amount of punishment was excessive. If a teacher can discipline a child with corporal punishment for relatively minor infractions, surely society can punish duly convicted criminals in a similar way. What I am proposing is a scaled-up version of spanking, just as stealing a car is a scaled-up version of stealing little Johnny's glue.

There is frequently some confusion between the ideas of corporal punishment of children and abuse, just as commentators have confused corporal punishment of criminals with torture. Beating a child severely is abusive. But sending a child to bed without dinner or locking a child in his room can also be abuse. The problem is not with the punishment, but with its application. The same holds true for a penal use of corporal punishment. If applied properly, it could be made no more torturous or barbaric than any other method of criminal punishment.

Courts have failed to directly attack any possible harm corporal punishment may cause. For example, Delaware used the lash to maintain discipline in its prisons until the 1950s.[21] The practice was discontinued and removed from the list of available punishments twenty years later, but not because of any ruling by the Supreme Court. Additionally, no federal court has ever found corporal punishment of criminals unconstitutional, even when certain punishments were found to be inappropriate.

V. PROCEDURAL CHALLENGES

One of the benefits of this proposed system would be that the punishment could be applied in its entirety immediately after sentencing. This is also likely to be one of the grounds on which this idea is challenged. Undoubtedly, a challenge will be raised that an immediate application of corporal punishment would violate due process by depriving a convict of the right to appeal. However, only in rare cases are criminals allowed to remain out on bail pending appeal. Thus, they are being punished before they can pursue an appeal, even an ultimately successful one.

The same sort of cases that allow bail to be extended past conviction today would allow it under a system of corporal punishment. However, where bail is not continued, a person would still be on the street having already received the full measure of his punishment while he pursued an appeal, rather than behind bars. This would probably lead to a reduction in criminal appeals, but it might also lead to more situations in which bail would be continued so as to maintain the incentive to appeal on real questions of law and procedure. This immediate infliction of the punishment could not be extended to capital punishment under the present holdings of the Supreme Court.[22] Convicts would be allowed the full range of appeals for capital crimes, but they could still be imprisoned while they pursued those appeals.

VI. SHAMING AS AN ASPECT OF PUNISHMENT

Retribution is the reason for punishment, but corporal punishment is primarily aimed at punishing the body. Just as the courts have recognized that there is a mental aspect to criminal behavior, so too should the court realize that there be mental punishment imposed on the criminal. Shaming might be the best means of accomplishing that mental punishment.

The difficulties in making shaming a part of criminal punishment are that it must come from all of society rather than simply from the members of the criminal justice system, and it must be designed so as to not stigmatize an offender permanently. Instead, it should merely encourage remorse on the part of the criminal. If it stigmatizes him, he is likely to rebel against a society in which he cannot find a place, and he will continue to break the law.

If society can create an atmosphere in which an offender feels the weight of the public's disapproval of his bad actions, he will be discouraged from committing those actions. This sort of pressure, even though applied informally, can be stronger and more effective than anything the formal, "professional" approach can provide. Japan is an excellent example of this philosophy in action.[23]

In Japan, the culture holds that the actions of individuals reflect on their family, their friends, and their superiors in the workplace. Compare that to the United States where people are hardly willing to take responsibility for their own actions, much less those of others. Although the Japanese may sometimes take this belief to irrational extremes, as when parents commit suicide because their child is convicted of a crime,[24] they are still better able to control individual behavior through this informal, cultural pressure than the American system is with all of its police, courts, and prisons. This is proven by the fact that Japan is the only industrial society to have a net decrease in the crime rate since World War II.[25]

The United States does make some use of shaming, but it is almost completely negative, stigmatizing convicts so that they may never again feel like true citizens. By labeling them as convicts, we force them to the fringes of society. They become part of a subculture where criminal behavior is the norm rather than the exception. By telling individuals they are worthless, they come to believe it; by telling someone he is a thug and a hooligan, he begins to act like it. This is shaming, but it is disintegrative, driving a wedge between the individual and society. This type of shaming fails because it creates too much identification between the criminal and the crime.

Instead, society needs to distance act from actor to make criminals understand that their behavior has earned them disapproval, and to give them a manageable route by which they can regain society's good graces. This will provide the benefits of specific deterrence and a true opportunity for rehabilitation because the criminal has a real chance to return as a productive citizen. This would in turn reduce recidivism and possibly provide some general deterrence as well.

VII. PUBLIC, CORPORAL PUNISHMENT ALLOWS FOR REINTEGRATIVE SHAMING

Corporal punishment applied in a public setting creates an excellent situation for shaming that does not stigmatize but reintegrates. The punishment is quickly applied and quickly finished, allowing the offender to immediately reenter society. Contrast this with imprisonment, which takes criminals out of the mainstream culture and puts them in a close, continued association with a group of people who have proved their willingness to break the law, where a convict is almost inevitably socialized to other criminals' ways of thinking. When people who have served their time do return to the outside world, they find that it has changed, and their roles in it have changed even more.

By keeping people convicted of crimes out of prison, we eliminate the negative socialization they receive there and, we hope, replace it with a positive socialization of everyday life. By making the punishment public, we try to add a sense of guilt and embarrassment to the proceeding. To make sure that the shame is not disintegrative, perhaps we could give the option of anonymity to the offender.[26] This might let the person feel the full weight of societal disapproval while still allowing them to avoid any long-term stigmatization that would inhibit a smooth return to society.

VIII. HOW WOULD THIS SYSTEM WORK?

A system of public, corporal punishment would require a great deal of work to implement. The people and government of this country would have to undergo a radical change in the way they think about crime, criminals, and criminal punishment. The first steps would be to design a plan that could gain legislative support at the state level and to craft it so that it could withstand challenges at every judicial level, up to and including the Supreme Court. Of course, like capital punishment, it would probably not survive in every state jurisdiction, but the states that adopt it would quickly see its advantages.

My preferred method of administering the punishment would be by flogging for violent, noncapital crimes and also for the more serious property crimes. A less physically painful punishment such as the pillory could be used for other less serious crimes and the majority of "victimless" crimes. An alternative to the lash could be to use electric shock, which is perhaps more easily quantified and qualified as to the degree of punishment, but less visible and visceral. For the whip, however, I would recommend the use of some sort of whipping machine to assure greater uniformity in application.[27] A machine would also help avoid administrative variations in leniency and oppressiveness that might arise if a person were to administer the punishment manually.

I would establish a maximum amount of penalty, perhaps the Biblical, Mosaic proscription against giving more than forty lashes. Then there would be lesser gradations for every varied degree of harm, of course leaving some flexibility for judicial determination based on particular circumstances. Additionally, the probation system could remain intact, allowing suspension of all or part of the penalty pending the fulfillment of court ordered requirements. Recidivism would receive short shrift, however. Repeat offenders would be subject to increasingly harsh penalties, and incorrigible criminals, who nevertheless do not seem to merit capital punishment, would be the only class of convicts still receiving imprisonment for a term of years.

IX. THE REDUCED SOCIAL COST OF CORPORAL PUNISHMENT

All punishment has a social cost. And any system of criminal justice has an even greater social cost. It requires time and money to maintain police forces, prosecutor's offices, and prisons. We have to pay judges and take people out of their work to serve on juries. Utilitarianism, as presented by Bentham, and the modern economic analyses of the law by Judge Richard Posner and Steven Shavell are powerful arguments that espouse the deterrent motive for criminal punishment to reduce costs to society by reducing total crime levels.[28] These scholars' arguments are worth mentioning here, though, because the ideas can be extended to support the use of corporal punishment instead of imprisonment.

It does involve less social cost to prevent a harm than to correct one by punishing someone for committing that harm. It is also best to streamline any system that is designed to prevent, correct, or punish wrongdoing. By using corporal punishment as our primary method of dealing with criminals instead of prisons, we could dramatically reduce the burden in dollars and time that our current criminal justice system imposes on society. It costs as much per year to keep a person in a maximum security prison as it does to send a person to a private university. If there were a viable alternative available, who would argue that the money is better spent on the convict than on the student? As I propose it, a properly administered system of corporal punishment would keep most of the people charged with noncapital crimes out of prison altogether because punishment could be administered immediately after sentencing in many cases.

In keeping with the utilitarians and economic theorists, the public display of punishment should provide further reductions in cost by a general deterrent effect on the populous. They could see the punishment applied and understand it in a way that many people might not understand imprisonment. The concept of imprisonment is somewhat difficult to understand, and may not be properly appreciated by many people who contemplate committing a criminal action, especially because the punishment is administered, quite literally, behind closed doors. Corporal punishment, on the other hand, is relatively easy to understand because we have all suffered pain at one time or another. The concept is easier to absorb, but the application would surely be better appreciated if it were made public, and people could get at least a secondhand understanding of the penalty.

Additionally, research has consistently shown that swift and sure punishment, whatever the nature, is the best form of deterrence. While a convict could begin a prison sentence immediately, the entire sentence could not be applied at once as with corporal punishment. Because the social costs of corporal punishment's application are lower, the punishment would probably be applied often, even if partially probated—for example, being sentenced to ten lashes and receiving five, with the other five to be given for any future criminal acts, even if less serious than the initial crime.

This corporal punishment, administered publicly, should serve as an admirable deterrent even to those people who are willing to risk the penalties for commission of a crime under the existing penal system. It may also lower the recidivism rate because the escalating penalties function as a strong specific deterrent. Add in the simple fact that it costs less to whip someone than it does to imprison them, and the virtues of this idea become more pronounced. Economic savings alone should make this an attractive solution to our escalating costs of criminal justice even if it does not end up to be a greater general deterrent than the present system.

Judge Posner does not share my belief that, in addition to its value as a retributive measure, public corporal punishment could provide a deterrent effect if applied in my overall system. While his work does not seem to be a response to any previous work espousing corporal punishment, he does address the economic value of "afflictive punishments."[29] With specific regard to flogging, Posner believes that the pain suffered is so brief that it would lack a deterrent effect, as compared to a prison sentence, and that, for very minor crimes, a simple fine could be as effective as any physical punishment.[30] Obviously I disagree, but his point is well taken. Flogging is a short-term pain that perhaps needs public administration to gain the long-term deterrent effect provided by shaming and embarrassing the offender.

X. WHY WILL THIS SYSTEM WORK?

There are several things about crime that are fairly consistent across cultural lines. Offenders are more frequently male than female, especially for violent crimes.[31] Young people (under thirty, and even under twenty-five) commit far more crimes than older people.[32] Urban areas have higher crime rates than rural areas.[33] Even people with strong ties to society, whether through economic advantage, good job opportunities, good education opportunities, positive relationships with family and friends, or simply a strong sense of community, are less likely to commit crimes than people with poor education, bad jobs, negative personal relationships, and a general feeling of disadvantage.[34] In other words, the better socialized a person is and the more he feels that he plays a part in society and can benefit by participating, the less likely he is to act out against the beliefs and ideals of society, including our general respect for life, liberty, and private property.

By increasing the positive socialization of a target group of young, disadvantaged males and strengthening their ties to mainstream culture, we should be able to dramatically reduce the crime rate. The money saved by reducing the number and population of prisons can be spent to these ends. The money can go to schools and community centers, or be used as an incentive to people starting small businesses, or as an incentive to businesses willing to train and hire disadvantaged youth.

Furthermore, by making punishment for actions rather than actors we can work to achieve the desired goal of retribution without the negative impact of stigmatization. Also, along with general deterrence, we also gain an opportunity for specific deterrence by showing the transgressor his error, giving him his just punishment, allowing him his freedom, and telling him to go forth and sin no more. Finally, by reducing the prison population, especially the itinerant portion charged with lesser crimes, we reduce the impact of forces that might drive individuals to join the criminal subculture that might further separate them from society by continued conflict.

The corporal punishment under this system would go toward all who break the law. The shaming would be a societal weight against those who break the law and a psychological obstacle to those who are considering breaking the law. The benefits, however, would be most felt by those who are most likely to feel the punishments, which we hope would produce the long-term result of an overall reduction in the crime rate by the group statistically most likely to commit crimes in the first place.

XI. CONCLUSION

This proposal should have enough merit to appeal to both those who believe that we should give criminals a second chance and those who feel criminals should suffer harsh penalties for their bad actions. Of course, knowing the pattern of American behavior, it is more likely that neither side will appreciate the benefits of this plan and will attack any perceived shortcomings.

The law and order extremists will most likely say that corporal punishment lets convicted criminals off too easily and puts them back on the streets too quickly, giving them the opportunity to repeat their crimes. To an extent, they would be right, but that is exactly the point. Convicts should be put back into society as rapidly and smoothly as possible after they receive due punishment for their actions. Convicts should consider themselves to be an integrated and integral part of mainstream society so they will be disinclined from committing future bad acts. The offenders can be reminded of the harsh penalties for recidivism, so that while incorrigible offenders may be relatively free to perpetrate new crimes against the community, they will not be able to do it for very long.

The "everybody deserves a second chance" group will no doubt be upset by the perceived severity of the punishments I propose and will use the Eighth Amendment as the first rallying point of their attack. I would remind them of two things. First, the cruel and unusual punishment standard is flexible, which makes it open to relatively wider interpretation than other constitutional provisions,[35] and at no time has corporal punishment been ruled unconstitutional. Second, if the state can impose corporal punishment on our children, through teachers, without a hearing,[36] surely the state can impose a substantially similar penalty on criminals after they have been duly convicted in a court of law.

Another challenge might be the previously mentioned claim that immediate punishment after sentencing would violate due process by reducing the opportunity to appeal convictions. But because convicts are imprisoned while they pursue appeals, they are punished, or "telished"[37] even if their appeals are ultimately successful. Despite the physical and mental suffering caused by corporal punishment and shaming, they cause far less of a social or economic burden on a recipient than imprisonment does. Post-punishment offenders are at liberty to seek jobs and continue personal relationships at a time when they would be incarcerated in today's penal system.

Because of all this, what I have proposed might be the best means of dealing with the criminal justice system problems we have in the United States. However, it will take a dramatic change in public attitudes and government views to advance such a program. First, the public must be made to understand that stigmatization of criminals is counterproductive if we are trying to lower the crime rate. Instead we should seek to express distaste for criminal behavior in a more associative way so as to strengthen an offender's bonds with society. The criminal must be made to accept corporal punishment as a valid and viable substitute for imprisonment as it is used in our modern, professional system.

A state legislative body would then have to amend its penal code to virtually eliminate prisons as a penalty. This would not need to be immediate but could be imposed gradually to a few offenses at a time, as long as the long term goal is kept in mind. Furthermore, the courts must be convinced that this is not a step back towards barbarism, but is instead a return to a more efficient, logical method of dealing with criminal behavior.

Corporal punishment has been used successfully for centuries in many countries as an aid to, or a replacement for imprisonment. By using it here, we could save money that is spent on prisons to achieve other social goals. By making the punishment public, we can add general and specific deterrent effects to the retributive effects already established. And by coupling the corporal punishment and shaming to successfully reintegrate the offender into society, we can separate the criminal from the crime and give a person a chance to redeem himself. This will strengthen the long term specific deterrent effect on the individual and, eventually, the general deterrent effect on society as a whole.

Corporal punishment would return the criminal justice system to its proper place as a small part of the system to promote the general welfare. And, not only could we begin to combat the crime problem of today, we could see more a profound reduction in youthful offenders and a greater impact on the generations to follow.

XII. APPENDIX A

MISSISSIPPI LEGISLATURE **REGULAR SESSION 1995**
By: Representative Cameron **To: Judiciary B**

HOUSE BILL NO. 106[38]

AN ACT TO PRESCRIBE THE SENTENCE OF CANING FOR CRIMINAL OFFENSES AND TO PROVIDE CERTAIN DEFINITIONS; TO PRESCRIBE CANING AS AN ADDITIONAL PENALTY FOR CERTAIN VIOLATIONS OF CRIMINAL LAWS; AND FOR RELATED PURPOSES.

BE IT ENACTED BY THE LEGISLATURE OF THE STATE OF MISSISSIPPI:

SECTION 1. (1) In addition to any other punishment provided by law, any person who is found guilty of any criminal act in a court of this state may, in the discretion of the court, be punished as provided by this act. Caning shall be administered by the Department of Corrections as ordered by the court.

(2) For the purposes of this section, "caning" means not less than two (2) nor more than ten (10) strikes with a cane on the buttocks of an offender administered as determined by the sentencing court.

SECTION 2. This act shall take effect and be in force from and after July 1, 1995.

MISSISSIPPI LEGISLATURE **REGULAR SESSION 1995**
By: Representative Stevens **To: Judiciary B**

HOUSE BILL NO. 365

AN ACT TO AMEND SECTION 47-7-33 AND 99-19-25, MISSISSIPPI CODE OF 1972, TO AUTHORIZE CIRCUIT AND COUNTY COURTS TO REQUIRE THE PERFORMANCE OF LABOR AS A SENTENCING ALTERNATIVE; AND FOR RELATED PURPOSES.

BE IT ENACTED BY THE LEGISLATURE OF THE STATE OF MISSISSIPPI:

SECTION 1. Section 47-7-33, Mississippi Code of 1972, is amended as follows:

47-7-33. When it appears to the satisfaction of any circuit court or county court in the State of Mississippi, having original jurisdiction over criminal actions, or to the judge thereof, that the ends of justice and the best interest of the public, as well as the defendant, will be served thereby, such court, in termtime or in vacation, shall have the power, after conviction or a plea of guilty, except in a case where a death sentence or life imprisonment is the maximum penalty which may be imposed or where the defendant has been convicted of a felony on a previous occasion in any court or courts of the United States and of any state or territories thereof, to suspend the imposition or execution of sentence, and place the defendant on probation as herein provided <u>or require the defendant to perform labor as determined by the court for the county where the defendant resides or was convicted,</u> except that the court shall not suspend the execution of a sentence of imprisonment after the defendant shall have begun to serve such sentence. In placing any defendant on probation, the court, or judge, shall direct that such defendant be under the supervision of the Department of Corrections <u>and the court may require the defendant to perform labor as determined by the court for the county where the defendant was convicted.</u>

When any circuit court or county court places a person on probation in accordance with the provisions of this section and that person is ordered to make any payments to his family, if any member of his family whom he is ordered to support is receiving public assistance through the State Department of Public Welfare, the court shall order him to make such payments to the county welfare officer of the county rendering public assistance to his family, for the sole use and benefit of said family.

SECTION 2. Section 99-19-25, Mississippi Code of 1972, is amended as follows:

99-19-25. The circuit courts and the county courts, in misdemeanor cases, are hereby authorized to suspend a sentence and to suspend the execution of a sentence, or any part thereof, on such terms as may be imposed by the judge of the court. Such terms may include the performance of labor as determined by the court to be performed in the county where the defendant resides or was convicted. Provided, the suspension of imposition or execution of a sentence hereunder may not be revoked after a period of five (5) years.

The justice courts, in misdemeanor cases, are hereby authorized to suspend a sentence and to suspend the execution of a sentence, or any part thereof, on such terms as may be imposed by the judge of the court. Provided, the suspension of imposition or execution of a sentence hereunder may not be revoked after a period of two (2) years. Provided, however, the justice courts in cases arising under the Implied Consent Law shall not suspend any fine.

SECTION 3. This act shall take effect and be in force from and after July 1, 1995.

Amendment to HB 365
By: Representatives Blackmon, Smith(27th), Bailey, Flaggs

Amend after the period of the last sentence in Amendment Number One [to Amendment Number Two] to House Bill #365 by adding the following:

Exempt from the coverage of this Act are individuals who proclaim their ancestry to be from the Valley of the Nile, the Tigris-Euphrates area, Kush, Axum, Red Sea area, Ethiopia, Sudan, Niger Timbuktu, Senegal, Tekrur, Morocco, Mali, Gao, the Upper Volta region, Songhay, Zimbabwe, the Western or Eastern Hemisphere.

Further that individuals who proclaim their belief in a Supreme Being are exempted from the coverage of this Act.

Further that individuals who can trace their ancestry to have begun beyond the continental borders of the United States are exempted from this Act.

Further that individuals who can trace their ancestry to those who were delivered into bondage under the license granted to Gomes Reynals, the work of John Hawkins, The Company of Royal Adventures, The Guinea Company or any ships controlled by Portugal, Spain, the Dutch, England, France, Belgium or Holland are exempted from this Act.

Finally, individuals who are pregnant, of unsound mind, suffering from any illness, below the age of 17, or who just plain object, verbally or in writing to being dealt any blows to their person at the hands of anyone proclaiming to do so in the name of the State of Mississippi are exempted from this Act.

Amend further the Title to conform.

XIII. APPENDIX B

Senate Bill 153
42nd Legislature—State of New Mexico—First Session, 1995

AN ACT

RELATING TO CRIMINAL LAW; PRESCRIBING PENALTIES FOR GRAFFITI THAT CAUSES DAMAGE TO REAL OR PERSONAL PROPERTY; AMENDING A SECTION OF THE NMSA 1978.

BE IT ENACTED BY THE LEGISLATURE OF THE STATE OF NEW MEXICO:

Section 1. Section 30-15-1.1 NMSA 1978 (being Laws 1990, Chapter 36, Section 1) is amended to read:

"30-15-1.1 UNAUTHORIZED GRAFFITI ON PERSONAL OR REAL PROPERTY.—

A. Graffiti consists of intentionally and maliciously defacing any real or personal property of another with graffiti or other inscribed material inscribed with ink, paint, spray paint, crayon, charcoal or the use of any object without the consent or reasonable ground to believe there is consent of the owner of the property.

B. Whoever commits graffiti to real or personal property when the damage to the property is one thousand dollars ($1,000) or less is guilty of a petty misdemeanor and [~~may be required~~] shall be sentenced to placement for a period of two days in stocks, which shall be located in a public place, or shall be required to perform a mandatory sixty hours of community service within a continuous four-month period immediately following his conviction. [~~and~~] The offender also may be required to make restitution to the property owner for the cost of damages and restoration. [~~If the damage to the property is greater than one thousand dollars ($1,000) he is guilty of a fourth degree felony and may be required to perform a mandatory one hundred twenty hours of community service within a six month period immediately following his conviction and may be required to provide restitution to the property owner for the cost of damages and restoration as a condition of probation or following any term of incarceration as a condition of parole.~~]

C. Whoever commits graffiti to real or personal property when the damage to the property is greater than one thousand dollars ($1,000) is guilty of a third degree felony and shall be sentenced to:

(1) serve a period of incarceration of not less than three years;

(2) placement for a period of seven days in stocks, which shall be located in a public place; or

(3) five strokes on the buttocks with a bamboo cane, which shall be administered by a martial arts expert.

D. In addition to the penalties set forth in Subsection C of this section, whoever commits graffiti to real or personal property when the damage to the property is greater than one thousand dollars ($1,000) may be required to:

(1) perform a mandatory one hundred twenty hours of community service within a continuous six-month period immediately following his conviction; and

(2) make restitution to the property owner for the cost of damages and restoration as a condition of probation or following any term of incarceration as a condition of parole."

Section 2. EFFECTIVE DATE.—The effective date of the provision of this act is July 1, 1995.

XIV. APPENDIX C

STATE OF NEW York
505—A
1995–1996 Regular Sessions
IN SENATE
January 11, 1995

Introduced by Sens. MALTESE, VELELLA—read twice and ordered printed, and when printed to be committed to the Committee on Children and Families—committee discharged, bill amended, ordered reprinted as amended and recommitted to said committee

AN ACT to amend the family court act and the penal law, in relation to authorizing the use of paddling as punishment for juvenile delinquents and youthful offenders found to have committed an act of graffiti

The People of the State of New York, represented in Senate and Assembly, do enact as follows:

Section 1. Section 352.2 of the family court act is amended by adding a new subdivision 1-a to read as follows:

1-a. (a) In addition to any other disposition authorized pursuant to this section, the court may order the paddling of any respondent thirteen years of age or older found to have committed act which would constitute the offense of making graffiti, as defined in section 145.60 of the penal law. The court, in ordering such paddling shall consider the age, condition and disposition of the respondent and all attending and surrounding circumstances in determining whether and to what extent paddling shall be ordered. Paddling, if ordered, shall be administered in either the courtroom or such other suitable location as determined by the court at a time set by the court no less than seventy-two hours nor more than fourteen days after the dispositional hearing. Paddling shall be administered by a parent or guardian of the respondent. However, if a parent or guardian refuses to administer the paddling, or if the court determines the parent or guardian failed to administer a satisfactory paddling, the court may order an appropriate court officer to administer the paddling.

(b) For the purpose of this subdivision:

(i) A "paddle" shall be made of hardwood that is three-quarters of an inch thick. The handle of such paddle shall be six inches long and one and one-quarter inches wide. The paddle area shall be eighteen inches long and six inches wide;

(ii) "Paddling" shall mean not more than ten strikes with a paddle on the buttocks of a respondent administered on the outside of normal apparel, as determined by the court.

§ 2. The penal law is amended by adding a new section 60.12 to read as follows"

§60.12 Authorized disposition; making graffiti.

1. In addition to any of the dispositions authorized by this article, the court may order the paddling of any youth convicted of the crime of making graffiti who is adjudicated as a youthful offender pursuant to article seven hundred twenty of the criminal procedure law.

2. Paddling, if ordered, shall be administered in either the courtroom or such other suitable location as determined by the court at a time set by the court no less than seventy-hours nor more than fourteen days after sentencing of such youthful offender. Paddling shall be administered by a parent or guardian of such youthful offender. However, if a parent or guardian refuses to administer the paddling, or if the court determines the parent or guardian failed to administer a satisfactory paddling, the court may order an appropriate court officer to administer the paddling.

3. For the purpose of this section:

(a) A "paddle" shall be made of hardwood that is three-quarters of an inch thick. The handle of such paddle shall be six inches long and one and one-quarter inches wide. The paddle area shall be eighteen inches long and six inches wide;

(b) "Paddling" shall mean not more than ten strikes with a paddle on the buttocks of a respondent administered on the outside of normal apparel, as determined by the court.

§ 3. This act shall take effect on the first day of November next succeeding the date on which it shall become a law, and shall apply to offenses committed on or after such effective date.

THE STATE OF NEW YORK
3804
1995–1996 Regular Sessions

IN ASSEMBLY
February 15, 1995

Introduced by M. of A. SEMINERIO—read once and referred to the Committee on Codes

AN ACT to amend the family court act and the penal law, in relation to authorizing the use of paddling as punishment for juvenile delinquents and youthful offenders found to have committed an act of graffiti

The People of the State of New York, represented in Senate and Assembly, do enact as follows:

Section 1. Section 352.2 of the family court act is amended by adding a new subdivision 1-a to read as follows:

1-a.(a) In addition to any other disposition authorized pursuant to this section, the court may order the paddling of any respondent thirteen years of age or older found to have committed act which would constitute the offense of making graffiti, as defined in section 145.60 of the penal law. The court, in ordering such paddling shall consider the age, condition and disposition of the respondent and all attending and surrounding circumstances in determining whether and to what extent paddling shall be ordered. Paddling, if ordered, shall be administered in either the courtroom or such other suitable location as determined by the court at a time set by the court no less than seventy-two hours nor more than fourteen days after the dispositional hearing. Paddling shall be administered by a parent or guardian of the respondent. However, if a parent or guardian refuses to administer the paddling, or if the court determines the parent or guardian failed to administer a satisfactory paddling, the court may order an appropriate court officer to administer the paddling.

(b) For the purpose of this subdivision:

(i) A "paddle" shall be made of hardwood that is three-quarters of an inch thick. The handle of such paddle shall be six inches long and one and one-quarter inches wide. The paddle area shall be eighteen inches long and six inches wide;

(ii) "Paddling" shall mean not more than ten strikes with a paddle on the buttocks of a respondent administered on the outside of normal apparel, as determined by the court.

§ 2. The penal law is amended by adding a new section 60.12 to read as follows"

§60.12 Authorized disposition; making graffiti.

1. In addition to any of the dispositions authorized by this article, the court may order the paddling of any youth convicted of the crime of making graffiti who is adjudicated as a youthful offender pursuant to article seven hundred twenty of the criminal procedure law.

2. Paddling, if ordered, shall be administered in either the courtroom or such other suitable location as determined by the court at a time set by the court no less than seventy-hours nor more than fourteen days after sentencing of such youthful offender. Paddling shall be administered by a parent or guardian of such youthful offender. However, if a parent or guardian refuses to administer the paddling, or if the court determines the parent or guardian failed to administer a satisfactory paddling, the court may order an appropriate court officer to administer the paddling.

3. For the purpose of this section:

(a) A "paddle" shall be made of hardwood that is three-quarters of an inch thick. The handle of such paddle shall be six inches long and one and one-quarter inches wide. The paddle area shall be eighteen inches long and six inches wide;

(b) "Paddling" shall mean not more than ten strikes with a paddle on the buttocks of a respondent administered on the outside of normal apparel, as determined by the court.

§ 3. This act shall take effect on the first day of November next succeeding the date on which it shall become a law, and shall apply to offenses committed on or after such effective date.

NOTES

1. Miss. H. R. 106 &365. *Interest Grows in Spanking as Way to Punish Criminals*, Austin Am-Statesman, Feb. 8, 1995, at A1.
2. See Appendix C.
3. *Id.*
4. *Id.* See Appendix C.
5. The most modern example of this is, of course, the caning of Michael Fay in Singapore, but the lash was used in virtually every European country until at least the eighteenth century, and flogging still occurs in some Islamic and Asian countries.
6. Lawrence M. Friedman, *Crime and Punishment in American History* 186, 312 & 407 (1993). *See generally* John Braithwaite, *Crime, Shame, and Reintegration* 5-8 (1989) (discussing the professional approach generally without a timetable of development).
7. See Cesare Beccaria, *On Crimes and Punishments*, for a look at what is perhaps the first published opinion regarding the use of mental rather than physical punishment in a modernizing society. Note that Beccaria did arguably support corporal punishment at an early point in his career, but he shifted to a belief that imprisonment for life, with hard labor, was the best punishment available to civilized man.
8. *See* George R. Scott, *The History of Corporal Punishment.* The work is little more than a catalogue of the worst atrocities committed while corporal punishment was still in wide use, but, although it may or may not be representative of the average use of such punishments, it does help to show what stirred up opposition to corporal punishment in the name of a civilized society. *See also* William Andrews, *Old Time Punishments* (1991) (listing types and uses of physical punishments in Britain from about the fifteenth century until the early nineteenth century).
9. *See generally* Beccaria, *supra* note 7.
10. Joseph Senna & Larry Siegel, *An Introduction to Criminal Justice* 564 (1978); Lawrence M. Friedman, *Crime and Punishment in American History* 78 (1993).
11. Senna & Siegel *supra* note 10, at 565; Friedman, *supra* note 10, at 79.
12. Almost 70% of all convicted felons will be back in prison within six years of their initial release on probation or parole. Senna & Siegel, *supra* note 10, at 527 (citing Allen Beck & Bernard Shipley, *Recidivism of Young Parolees* 1 (1987)).
13. Friedman, *supra* note 10.
14. Oxford Unabridged Dictionary.
15. *Id.*
16. *Id.*
17. *Id.*
18. Trop v. Dulles, 356 U.S. 86, 101 (1958).
19. 97 S.Ct. 1401 (1977).
20. *Id.*
21. Robert G. Caldwell, *Red Hannah* (1947).
22. *Furman v. Georgia*, 408 U.S. 238 (1972); later cases all require procedural and substantive due process to ensure justice and fairness in the criminal system.
23. Braithwaite, *supra* note 6, at 61-65.
24. *Id.* at 63 (citing D.H. Bayley, *Accountability and Control of the Police: Some Lessons for Britain*, in The Future of Policing (1983).
25. Braithwaite, *supra* note 6, at 61.
26. Possible ways to achieve this range from simply not publicizing the name of one being punished to giving the person a hood to wear so that their face is not revealed. Quite possibly, some people might feel that they have gotten away with something if their identity is not revealed during the punishment. For that reason, recidivists might be denied the opportunity for anonymity.

27. Jeremy Bentham proposed a machine of this sort to be an ideal administer of punishment. He believed punishment should be doled out primarily for its deterrent effects. I only support deterrence as a secondary reason for punishment, but I agree that it would be worthwhile to use this machine.
28. Richard A. Posner, *An Economic Theory of the Criminal Law*, 85 Colum. L. Rev. 1193 (1985); Steven Shavell, *Criminal Law and the Optimal Use of Nonmonetary Sanctions as a Deterrent*, 85 Colum. L. Rev. 1232 (1985); Jeremy Bentham, *Principles of Penal Law*, 1 Works of Jeremy Bentham 365 (ed. 1843).
29. Posner, *supra* note 28, at 1209.
30. *Id.* at 1212.
31. Braithwaite, *supra* note 6, at 44.
32. *Id.* at 45.
33. *Id.* at 47.
34. *Id.* at 47-49.
35. See *supra* note 18.
36. See *supra* note 19.
37. "Telishment" is a term coined by John Rawls to give a name to punishments put upon an innocent person, since, by definition, punishment is only done to guilty people. Thus, if an innocent person is imprisoned for a crime he did not commit, he is telished.
38. This bill died in committee on 1 February 1995.